Toolkit for Working with
JUVENILE SEX OFFENDERS

Toolkit for Working with
JUVENILE SEX OFFENDERS

Edited by

DANIEL S. BROMBERG
Special Psychological Services, LLC, Bloomfield, NJ, USA

WILLIAM T. O'DONOHUE
University of Nevada, Department of Psychology, Reno, NV, USA

ELSEVIER

AMSTERDAM • BOSTON • HEIDELBERG • LONDON
NEW YORK • OXFORD • PARIS • SAN DIEGO
SAN FRANCISCO • SINGAPORE • SYDNEY • TOKYO
Academic Press is an imprint of Elsevier

Academic Press is an imprint of Elsevier
32 Jamestown Road, London NW1 7BY, UK
225 Wyman Street, Waltham, MA 02451, USA
525 B Street, Suite 1800, San Diego, CA 92101-4495, USA

British Library Cataloguing-in-Publication Data
A catalogue record for this book is available from the British Library

Library of Congress Cataloging-in-Publication Data
A catalog record for this book is available from the Library of Congress

ISBN: 978-0-12-405948-1

For information on all Academic Press publications
visit our website at elsevierdirect.com

Typeset by MPS Limited, Chennai, India
www.adi-mps.com

CONTENTS

LIST OF CONTRIBUTORS

Natalie Bennett
Department of Psychology, University of Nevada, Reno, NV, USA

Lorraine T. Benuto
Administrative Faculty Department of Psychology, University of Nevada, Reno and Northcentral University, The Graduate School, CA, USA

Kenneth E. Blackstone
Blackstone Polygraph, Inc., Atlanta, GA, USA

Gerry D. Blasingame
Training, Program Development, and Consultation, Redding, CA, USA

Jackson Tay Bosley
University Behavioral Health Care, Rutgers University, Piscataway, NJ, USA

Daniel S. Bromberg
Special Psychological Services, LLC, Bloomfield, NJ, USA

Olga Cirlugea
Department of Psychology, University of Nevada, Reno, NV, USA

Edward J. Daly III
Department of Educational Psychology, University of Nebraska-Lincoln, NE, USA

Polly M. Daro
Department of Educational Psychology, University of Nebraska-Lincoln, NE, USA

Clare-Ann Fortune
School of Psychology, Victoria University of Wellington, New Zealand

Ashley Haidle
Marriage and Family Therapist Intern

Sean Hiscox
Associates in Psychological Services, Somerville, NJ, USA

Robert Kinscherff
Massachusetts School of Professional Psychology, Newton, MA, USA

Raymond A. Knight
Department of Psychology, Brandeis University, Waltham, MA, USA

Craig Latham
Latham Consulting Group, LLC, Northampton MA, USA

Alexandros Maragakis
University of Nevada, Reno, NV, USA

Joshua Medjuck
Department of Psychology, University of Nevada, Reno, NV, USA

Diane G. Mercier
Private Practice, Reno, NV, USA

Kirk A. B. Newring
Forensic Behavioral Health, Papillion Nebraska and Nebraska Wesleyan University, Lincoln, Nebraska, NE, USA

Maureen A. O'Connor
Department of Educational Psychology, University of Nebraska-Lincoln, NE, USA

William T. O'Donohue
University of Nevada, Reno, NV, USA

Gary O'Reilly
School of Psychology, University College Dublin, Republic of Ireland

James M. Ogilvie
Griffith Youth Forensic Service, Griffith University, Mt Gravatt, Queensland, Australia

Joseph J. Plaud
Applied Behavioral Consultants, LLC, Whitinsville, MA, USA

Bobbie Print
G-MAP Services Limited, Sale, Cheshire, UK

Stephanie E. Scott
Special Psychological Services, LLC, Bloomfield, NJ, USA

Ken D. Schafer
Griffin Home Friends of Youth, Renton, and Private Practice, Burien, Washington, WA, and Department of Educational Psychology, University of Nebraska-Lincoln, Lincoln, NE, USA

Susan R. Schmidt
Center on Child Abuse and Neglect, University of Oklahoma Health Sciences Center, Oklahoma City, OK, USA

Danielle C. Shumack
Griffith Youth Forensic Service, Griffith University, Mt Gravatt, Queensland, Australia

Judith E. Sims-Knight
Department of Psychology, University of Massachusetts Dartmouth, MA, USA

Stephen Smallbone
School of Criminology and Criminal Justice, Australian Research Council, and Griffith Youth Forensic Service, Griffith University, Mt Gravatt, Queensland, Australia

Mackenzie Sommerhalder
Department of Educational Psychology, University of Nebraska-Lincoln, NE, USA

Charlene Steen
Private Practice (Retired), Napa, CA, USA

Whitney Strong
Department of Educational Psychology, University of Nebraska-Lincoln, NE, USA

Robert Stuyvesant
Private Practice, Reno, NV, USA

Tony Ward
School of Psychology, Victoria University of Wellington, New Zealand

Jennifer G. Wheeler
Pacific Evaluation, Consultation, & Treatment Services, PLLC, Seattle Washington, WA, USA

Eleanor L. Woodford
Griffith Youth Forensic Service, Griffith University, Mt Gravatt, Queensland, Australia

PREFACE

The Handbook of Child and Adolescent Sexuality: Developmental and Forensic Psychology (Bromberg & O'Donohue, 2013) was our first joint project. Although of potential utility to a wide audience, it was our assumption that a high percentage of the readership would be clinical, forensic, and developmental psychologists, as well as graduate and post-doctoral students in these disciplines. In the Handbook, we noted that little is known about the base rate and types of sexual behaviors that are normative in children and adolescents. We wrote the following: "Knowing the base rates of phenomena is important, because one cannot know how typical or uncommon a phenomenon is without first knowing its base rate in the population. The dearth of knowledge regarding base rates of normative sexual behaviors in young persons is problematic because such lack of knowledge reduces the ability of clinical scientists to understand and produce effective interventions for statistically non-normative and/or problematic sexual behaviors" (Bromberg & O'Donohue, 2013, p. 21).

The focus of this Toolkit is quite different from the focus of our first joint project. Here, our intended audience is practitioners engaged in the assessment and treatment of juveniles whose sexual interests and/or behaviors are statistically non-normative and/or problematic. There is a compelling rationale for intervening with this population. It is generally thought to be easier and preferable to address problematic thoughts, feelings, and behaviors early in the lifespan rather than later, after well-entrenched problems have derailed an individual from a "normative" developmental trajectory. Intervening during adolescence may reduce a given adolescent's number of incidents of sexual perpetration or number of victims. This reduces the emotional cost to potential victims and their loved ones, and the financial cost of treating potential victims. Moreover, the financial burden to society of paying for the incarceration of adult sex offenders may be reduced if sexual offending behaviors can be eliminated while such perpetrators are still minors.

Although there is a dearth of "gold-standard," evidence-based assessment and intervention strategies for use with this population, we attempted to cull the best strategies currently available. We begin with a chapter on legal and ethical issues pertaining to assessment and treatment. Sample consent forms are provided. This chapter is followed by others on paper-and-pencil assessment instruments, penile plethysmography, and polygraphy. The final chapter regarding assessment provides readers with information about, and sample reports of, dispositional evaluations.

The Toolkit continues with chapters on intervention strategies. We begin with a chapter on relapse prevention (RP) containing a case vignette and forms useful for conducting RP. Because the Good Lives Model (GLM) shows promise as a treatment approach with adult offenders, we elected also to include a chapter on use of the GLM with adolescents. Chapters are included on other treatment foci, as well. Topics include the following: remediation of academic skill and performance deficits; strategies for modifying problematic sexual interests; treatment of offenders who are also sexual abuse victims; increasing social skills; integrating families into treatment; working with juveniles who have developmental disabilities; and documenting treatment for ethical and legal purposes. Finally, readers will find chapters regarding outpatient treatment models, giving courtroom testimony, and developing a practice around juvenile sex offending.

Because of the far-reaching consequences of juveniles' problematic sexual behaviors, we hope that clinical researchers will continue working to expand the technology available to clinicians who work with this population. It will be our pleasure and privilege to update and expand the Toolkit to incorporate advances in the field.

Daniel S. Bromberg, Ph.D., ABPP
William T. O'Donohue, Ph.D.

REFERENCE

Bromberg, D. S., & O'Donohue, W. T. (2013). Research methods: Current strategies, obstacles to research, and future directions. In D. S. Bromberg & W. T. O'Donohue (Eds.), *Handbook of child and adolescent sexuality: Developmental and forensic psychology* (pp. 21–40). San Diego, CA: Elsevier.

ACKNOWLEDGMENTS

I (DSB) gratefully acknowledge those who taught me, including the adolescents with whom I have worked. Certainly, they have taught me as much as I have taught them.

I thank Shelley, Lauren, and Sarah for their patience while I worked on this book. Several individuals with direct involvement in the *Toolkit* deserve special thanks. I am most grateful to Bill O'Donohue for collaborating on this project. We are grateful to our publisher, Nikki Levy of Elsevier, for her confidence that we would produce a quality product. Barbara Makinster, also of Elsevier, worked with us to ensure that the *Toolkit* came together in a timely manner. Stephanie Scott, my assistant, kept the project moving and engaged in troubleshooting.

I (WTO) thank my family, Jane, Katie, and Anna, for all their support and kindness. I thank Daniel Bromberg for his excellent scholarship, unflagging good humor, and all his hard work.

CHAPTER 1

Informed Consent or Assent for Assessment, Treatment and Releases of Information

Robert Kinscherff* and Craig Latham**
*Massachusetts School of Professional Psychology, Newton, MA, USA
**Latham Consulting Group, LLC, Northampton, MA, USA

INFORMED CONSENT AS AN ETHICAL AND LEGAL OBLIGATION

Informed consent for professional services is an ethical and legal obligation in all North American jurisdictions. Informed consent for professional services is a fundamental right that is protected under international law, frameworks of ethical codes, as well as federal law (such as HIPAA) and state law (such as statutes and regulations). The elements of an adequate informed consent are described below, but it is critical to appreciate that genuine informed consent is a process rather than a moment. That is, while an informed consent form might be signed prior to initiating assessment or treatment, it may be necessary to revisit informed consent should the patient/client later become confused or unclear about the elements of informed consent. Revisiting informed consent is required should there be a substantive change in circumstances or the methods or goals of the professional services offered.

There is nothing ethically or legally magic about a signature on a consent form. Courts have found that signatures on forms alone are insufficient to document an adequate informed consent. An adequate informed consent requires that: (1) the individual who is offering informed consent has been provided sufficient information to allow a reasonable person to make a considered decision about the professional services involved; (2) the individual demonstrates that they have a sufficient understanding of the information offered so that they can actually make considered decisions; and (3) the individual has been afforded a meaningful opportunity to ask questions or expressed concerns. Simply informing individuals about limits of confidentiality or testimonial privilege, the nature of professional services to be rendered, or other aspects of providing professional

Toolkit for Working with Juvenile Sex Offenders.
DOI: http://dx.doi.org/10.1016/B978-0-12-405948-1.00001-3

services is a necessary but insufficient step in obtaining adequate informed consent. In addition to providing information about the professional services to be rendered, the professional provider has an obligation to determine that the legal client offering informed consent has a sufficient understanding of the information to be able to make reasoned decisions when authorizing (or declining to authorize) professional services.

The obligation to secure adequate and meaningful informed consent and "assent" (which we define below) is a particularly solemn professional duty since there is often at least some degree of implicit or explicit coercion involved in the provision of professional services to alleged or adjudicated juvenile sexual offenders or youth with problematic sexual behaviors. For example, being placed on probation by a juvenile court that is conditioned on participating in community-based assessment or treatment is a "voluntary" alternative to commitment to a juvenile justice authority. Discharge conditioned upon effective engagement in specialized juvenile sexual offender services in a residential treatment or a juvenile "secure treatment" or incarceration facility is "voluntary" in the sense that a youth can simply refuse to participate and accept the consequences of being "stuck" in institutional care for some period of time. A juvenile referred for a court-ordered evaluation can refuse to participate and accept whatever consequences may be imposed by the court which, in sexual offenses, may include longer-term confinement within the juvenile justice system.

In addition to varying degrees of coercion involved in providing professional services to this population, assessments and treatment commonly involve intrusive inquiries regarding sexual perpetration and victimization, sexual behaviors and arousal, sexual interests, and masturbation practices. Effectiveness of assessment and treatment over time may be judged, at least in part, upon self-disclosures in these domains and others that are commonly outside of routine clinical inquiry or expectation when providing services to other clinical populations. As a result, it is particularly important to assure the adequacy of informed consent and assent and to appreciate that the process of obtaining them may be subject to particularly strict scrutiny if it is later challenged.

KEY ELEMENTS OF INFORMED CONSENT

The basic elements of an adequate informed consent include:

1. *Identification of the legal client.* The legal client is the individual or entity who has the legal authority to engage in the process of informed

consent and then to authorize or decline to authorize professional services. An adequate informed consent can never be obtained from an individual who lacks the legal authority to offer it. Once the legal client has been identified, the practitioner should determine what other "ethical clients" (such as the youthful minor, third parties, others) are involved in the case.

2. *Identification of the ethical client(s).* Provision of professional services with adjudicated juvenile sexual offenders or youth with problematic sexual behaviors commonly involves ethical clients (and must always involve a legal client). The most obvious ethical client is the youth receiving assessment, treatment or other professional services. A youth under age 18 ordinarily cannot provide informed consent or authorize professional services, but the professional clearly has ethical obligations that include securing adequate informed consent from the appropriate legal client, clarifying one's professional role and maintaining professional boundaries, provision of competent services, efforts to secure the youth's "assent," (discussed below), and termination of services that are ineffective or no longer necessary. There are commonly "third party" ethical clients as well. For example, a clinical professional working in a juvenile justice setting or residential treatment setting will have ethical obligations to the organization. Some professionals working with youth who have sexually victimized others consider "society" or "potential future victims" also to be ethical clients. This is understandable but cannot be used to justify deviating from the duties owed to the legal client or from research-based "best practices" with the youth receiving services. For example, identifying "society" or "potential future victims" as ethical clients cannot be used to justify professional practices that are punitive or shaming, overly restrictive, fall below accepted standards of care or practice, or are inattentive to legitimate boundaries of confidentiality or testimonial privilege.
3. *Obtaining informed consent and "assent".* Informed consent can only be obtained from the legal client who has the capacity to authorize professional services following a sufficient informed consent process. Nonetheless, efforts are made to secure the "assent," or willingness to participate, of the youth or other interested parties (such as the parent(s) or legal guardian) when it is a court-ordered evaluation. In that situation, the court is essentially authorizing the evaluation but steps are taken to secure the "assent" of the youth and parent(s) or legal guardian by describing the role of the professional, the nature

and purpose of the evaluation process, any relevant limitations on confidentiality or testimonial privilege and the like in terms that are understandable and developmentally appropriate for the youth and sufficiently detailed to inform the parent(s)/legal guardian. Court-ordered evaluation may proceed without the assent of the youth or parent(s)/legal guardian, although a parent/legal guardian or attorney for the youth may advise the youth not to participate directly in the evaluation process. The goal of seeking assent is to communicate respect and regard for the position of the youth and others – and, ideally, to secure their engaged involvement with full appreciation of the circumstances in which they find themselves – but offering assent is not required to proceed with professional services.

4. *The role of the professional(s) in providing professional services.* The professionals providing services should identify their *professional background* at a level of detail sufficient to inform the legal client (and others) about their relevant training and experience. This is particularly important if the youth has *special characteristics* (such as an intellectual or developmental disability, unusual or complex clinical presentation, or is identified as posing particularly challenging cultural or linguistic competency issues). The *scope and nature of services* to be provided (such as assessment, treatment, other) should be described. If the identified legal client is not the parent or legal guardian of the youth, then the identified legal client and the role of the professional must be disclosed. For example, if the evaluation is court ordered, provided for an attorney, or arranged by a governmental agency or a contracted services provider, then the parent(s) or legal guardian of the youth must be informed that the professional is actually providing services to a legal client other than them. The *goal(s) of the services to be provided* (discussed below) for the legal client must also be disclosed as well as any *reasonably foreseeable outcomes* of providing those services to the youth. For example, when providing a court-ordered assessment to aid the court in making a disposition decision following adjudication, the potential outcomes might be a community-based probation or commitment to a juvenile justice authority. Additionally:
   - Consideration must be given to the *context* in which the professional services are to be provided and relevant information provided in obtaining informed consent and assent. As examples, the following contexts all may raise potentially complex issues in one or more areas, such as confidentiality and testimonial privilege

(discussed below), that require disclosure and discussion when obtaining adequate informed consent or assent

- *community-based assessment or treatment for sexual misconduct that has not resulted in sexual offense charges* (confidentiality and privilege issues including mandated reporting, identification of the legal client, consequences should the youth fail to engage in professional services authorized by the legal client)
- *community-based assessment or treatment as a condition of probation* or other conditional liberty (identification of the legal client, confidentiality and privilege issues regarding information exchanges, consequences of failure to engage in the required professional services)
- *treatment following adjudication provided in an out-of-home placement* providing specialized juvenile sexual offender programming (confidentiality and privilege, consequences of failure to engage in treatment, clarity about who is the legal client; clarity regarding third-party access to the treatment records)
- *pre-adjudication evaluation retained by defense counsel* (attorney–client privilege, proactive clarity regarding expectations about mandated reporting, attorney as the identified client who controls the work product)
- *court-ordered pre-adjudication evaluation* of sexual offense or sexual recidivism risk when the youth denies the alleged misconduct (right against self-incrimination, proper waiver of any psychotherapist-patient privilege,[1] significant problems with the scientific reliability of assessment or clinical capacity to distinguish reliably among actual innocence, lying when denying the alleged misconduct, or clinical "denial" when assessment occurs before court adjudication of the alleged misconduct).[2]

[1] See discussion of "testimonial privilege" below. Communications with licensed mental health professions in many jurisdictions are presumed to be protected by "testimonial privilege" that protects them from introduction into legal proceedings unless (a) the communications are subject to a legally recognized exception, and (b) the individual is informed that their expectation of privacy or protection of communications does not apply. Adequate informed consent involves letting the individual know that the assessment is court ordered, the identified client is the court, and that statements made during the course of assessment may be communicated to the court.

[2] Court-ordered assessment of a youth charged with a sexual offense is particularly problematic when it is requested prior to adjudication or admission before the court of the alleged sexual misconduct. This referral context raises significant legal issues implicating Fifth Amendment rights against self-incrimination, Sixth Amendment guarantees of effective assistance of counsel, waiver of any

- *Forensic and clinical roles* must be carefully distinguished and communicated for purposes of assent and informed consent, and practitioners are cautioned against mixing or confusing those roles. If the clinician is a trainee or a professional acting under a clinical supervisor, then this must be disclosed to the identified legal client and a reliable means provided through which the identified legal client can reach the supervising professional.
- *Supervisors, supervisees, and trainees.* A *"supervision"* relationship means that the supervised professional or trainee is acting on behalf of the supervisor. Legally and ethically, the supervised case is the supervisor's case for which the supervisor has ultimate responsibility. A supervised professional or trainee must follow the direction of the supervisor even if the supervised professional holds an independent license. This contrasts with *"consultation"* in which the consultant does not hold ultimate responsibility for the case and the professional receiving consultation is free to accept, modify or reject the guidance offered by the consultant. Sometimes professional providers call their relationship a "supervision" relationship when, in fact, it is a consultation relationship. For example, persons engaging in "peer supervision" are rarely agreeing to accept full legal and ethical responsibility for the cases brought for discussion, or have "supervisors" when, in fact, they are free to make independent professional decisions in the "supervised" cases. Providers are advised

psychotherapist–patient privilege, and the presumption of innocence prior to formal adjudication or admission. This referral context also raises substantive issues regarding the scientific reliability of evaluations conducted in this context. It raises serious professional practice and ethical issues such as: (a) whether the evaluator should or should not assume the misconduct occurred at all or that all of the details of the alleged misconduct are accurate; (b) whether the evaluator should – or even scientifically can – assign any meaning to the juvenile defendant's denial of the alleged misconduct; and (c) the scientific basis of rendering an opinion regarding the need for specialized juvenile sexual offender treatment or sexual recidivism risk prior to adjudication – especially if the alleged sexual misconduct is the first instance of charged sexual offense. The potential legal pitfalls and the serious professional practice and ethical issues led Massachusetts to essentially bar Juvenile Court referrals for "sexual offender evaluations" to its statewide system of juvenile court clinics in this context. There are some very narrow exceptions to this ban but they are procedurally complex and very rarely used. Professionals should be mindful of the complex legal and clinical issues involved in this referral context and proceed with extreme caution – if at all – in providing court-ordered "sexual offender evaluations" prior to adjudication or legally-binding admission by the youth when the youth is denying the alleged sexual misconduct. Consideration must also be given to the consequences should a youth later rescind any admission to sexual offense charges given under these circumstances. For example, youth will sometimes admit to charged sexual misconduct but later insist during subsequent assessment or treatment that "I only did it because my lawyer told me to" or "I only admitted to that to get a plea deal but it didn't really happen (at all or as alleged)".

to distinguish clearly between "supervision" and "consultation" relationships. This is because adequate informed consent requires that a supervisee or trainee under supervision disclose that fact and provide the name and contact information for the supervising professional. Additionally, trainees must disclose the fact that they are trainees operating under supervision.

5. *The goals and purposes of the professional services and the methods to be relied upon.* Informed consent requires adequate appreciation of the goals and purposes of the professional services. For assessments, this means clarity regarding the questions prompting referral, the assessment methods to be relied upon, and any relevant limitations or significant controversies regarding those methods. For treatment, this means clarity regarding the goals of treatment, the treatment methods to be used and their anticipated impact upon achieving the goals of treatment, the method by which progress in treatment will be determined, and the process by which treatment will be adjusted to match needs and relative degrees of progress. Where treatment will require specific activities by the youth (such as group participation, self-disclosures, or "homework", such as journaling or completing assigned activities), these should also be disclosed. Any consequences for failure to engage adequately in expected activities (such as termination of services, lowering of privilege levels, revocation of probation) also need to be disclosed.
6. *Relevant limits on confidentiality and testimonial privilege.* Practitioners providing services to youth with problematic sexual behaviors or adjudicated sexual offenses must be thoroughly familiar with professional ethics, relevant laws and regulations in their jurisdiction, and local practices regarding professional privacy. Adequate informed consent requires full transparency regarding confidentiality and testimonial privilege and any relevant limitations on these dimensions of privacy in professional services.
   - *Confidentiality* is a legal and ethical duty to maintain privacy regarding information from and about the recipients of professional services that is obtained when acting in a professional capacity. The parent(s) or legal guardian(s) of minors ordinarily are the gatekeepers of confidentiality (such as when they sign releases of information), although there may be mandated exceptions to confidentiality (such as mandated reporting of child maltreatment or duties to warn/protect potential victims).
   - *Testimonial privilege* is an exception to a citizen's obligation to testify that is granted by legislators, such as attorney–client privilege,

spousal privilege, psychotherapist–patient privilege, and other testimonial privileges. Testimonial privilege creates a "firewall" between the person receiving professional services and introduction of their "professional communications" into legal proceedings, such as depositions or court hearings. Recipients of professional services are ordinarily entitled to testimonial privilege unless there are specific exceptions (such as a therapist testifying at a patient's civil commitment proceeding). If testimonial privilege is not going to "attach" in the professional relationship, then a specific warning to the person receiving the services, and the parent(s)/legal guardian if that person is a minor, is required. Practitioners are strongly advised to familiarize themselves with law in their jurisdiction regarding testimonial privilege. In some jurisdictions, parent(s)/legal guardians can assert or waive testimonial privilege for their minor child while in others, courts have held that the testimonial privilege literally belongs to the person receiving the professional services, even if that person is a minor who can neither assert nor waive testimonial privilege. In those jurisdictions, such as Massachusetts, parents/legal guardians cannot authorize their minor child's therapist to be deposed or testify in court hearings – courts appoint a Guardian ad Litem to recommend whether the minor's interests are best served by preserving the privacy of the professional relationship or by having the information provided by the child revealed during legal proceedings.

- *Special considerations with youth with problematic sexual behaviors or adjudicated sexual offenses.* Assessment and treatment with these youth can pose challenges in legal and ethical management of the dimensions of privacy of professional services.
  - For example, youth undergoing *court-ordered assessment* must be specifically cautioned that there is no expectation of privacy (testimonial privilege) and that the results of assessment will be provided to the court
  - Practitioners providing *assessments retained by defense counsel* will need to inform youth that the results of the assessment will be revealed to defense counsel. And, practitioners will need to know whether working under retainer by defense counsel protects what they learn during assessment under attorney–client privilege (which may trump mandated reporting), inform defense counsel prior to beginning the assessment that they

believe mandated reporting requirements trump attorney–client privilege, or whether statutes or case law in their jurisdiction are entirely clear about whether or not they are governed by attorney–client privilege or the mandated reporting requirement

- Informed consent would also require proactively notifying the identified legal client and those from whom assent is sought (the youth, others) if assessment or *treatment should include an expectation that disclosures of previously unknown episodes of sexual misconduct will be shared* with District Attorneys, courts or probation officers, or others.

7. *Discussion of the basis in behavioral science for the proposed assessment(s) or course of treatment.* Sufficient informed consent and assent requires discussion of the basis in behavioral science for the proposed assessment or course of treatment.[3] The basis may range from evidence-based practice, to "best practices" approaches, to familiar and common practices without much basis in research but at least some anecdotal support, to innovative (if possibly idiosyncratic) practices, to experimental approaches with little or no research basis. The legally identified client can offer adequate informed consent even for experimental approaches as long as the experimental nature has been disclosed and if more conventional alternatives to experimental approaches are revealed. For assessments, informed consent requires discussion of the assessment methods and their scientific reliability in responding to the referral questions to be addressed by the assessment. For treatment, informed consent requires discussion of the treatment modalities to be implemented, their basis in behavioral science, and any significant controversies and reasonable alternatives to the treatment proposed. These forms are comparable in style to forms used in outpatient psychotherapy practices where standard assessment and treatment techniques are employed, and they typically range from one to two pages in length. The key issue for professional judgment is: what level of detail in describing the assessment or treatment modalities is sufficient for the person offering informed consent to be able to offer a meaningful, reasonably informed consent in light of factors such as the legal or clinical stakes involved, the intrusiveness of the methods used, the respective risks and benefits, or the level of empirical support for the assessment

[3] For a thorough review and discussion of assessment and treatment approaches based in behavioral science and "best practices" see: Rich (2011).

tool or treatment method? Special considerations for youth with problematic sexual behaviors or adjudicated sexual offenses include: controversies in the use of assessment approaches and tools, particularly those focused upon *prediction of sexual recidivism risk*[4]; controversies in the use of *plethysmograph and other measures of sexual arousal* with adolescents in pre-adjudication and post-adjudication contexts; controversies regarding *use of polygraphy*[5] in pre-adjudication and post-adjudication contexts; and, controversies about use of *"relapse prevention" treatment approaches* with youth with limited histories of sexual misconduct. Both proponents and critics often have strong views about these issues but, for purposes of obtaining informed consent, the goal is to present a brief but balanced and prudent account of these controversies and practices sufficient to allow reasoned decision making in the informed consent process. See, for example, the sample "Consent for use of Polygraph Examination" form from the Stetson School on page 22 of the Appendix and the discussion above in this section regarding factors to be considered in making a professional judgment as to the level of detail called for in an adequate informed consent.

8. *Disclosures of reasonably foreseeable risks, benefits and alternatives to the proposed assessment and/or treatment.* Informed consent requires disclosure of reasonably foreseeable risks and benefits of assessment or treatment, reasonable alternatives to the proposed assessment or treatment, and the risks or benefits of no assessment or treatment. This can pose challenges for professional work with youth with problematic sexual behaviors or adjudicated juvenile sexual offenders. For example, there are important controversies regarding: the basis in behavioral science to assess reliably the likelihood of sexual recidivism given the low base rate of sexual re-offense by youth following detection; special complications arising when assessing females since most of the relevant research has been conducted on male adolescents; research regarding the general desistance of non-sexual and sexual misconduct as youth mature into young adulthood; and concerns regarding the criminogenic effects of congregating youth with histories of misconduct in

[4] For a review of controversies and scientific limitations of reliable sexual recidivism risk assessments among adolescent sexual offenders, see: Vitacco, Caldwell, Ryba, Malesky, and Kurus (2009).

[5] Polygraphy is used by approximately half of surveyed juvenile sexual treatment programs in the USA. Polygraphy is rarely used with other kinds of juvenile offenders and, in other countries, its use with juvenile sexual offenders is rare or banned. For a review of clinical and ethical issues see: Chaffin (2011).

residential treatment or juvenile incarceration settings. On the other hand, there is research indicating that specialized juvenile sexual offender treatment substantially reduces recidivism rates. The overarching obligation is for practitioners to provide a balanced and research-informed disclosure of risks, benefits and alternatives to proposed courses of assessment and treatment for purposes of informed consent and assent.

9. *Discussions of fees and other obligations.* Adequate informed consent requires discussion of any fees or other obligations (such as participation in the assessment or treatment proposed) with the identified legal client and/or with parents/legal guardians or others.

The basic obligation is to secure an adequate informed consent (and assent) prior to the provision of professional services and to revisit it as necessary. There are ordinarily ethical and legal exceptions to the obligation to obtain informed consent prior to providing professional services, such as responding to genuine emergency circumstances where exigent circumstances authorize providing required care to prevent imminent and very serious (often limited to physical) harm to the individual or to others. However, these exceptions tend to be very narrow and the usual expectation is that informed consent will be obtained prior to providing professional clinical services or revisited as circumstances, methods or goals change over time.

There are some differences among the ethics codes of professional associations and among state laws and regulations regarding informed consent. Practitioners are advised to be familiar with the ethics codes of their professions, applicable statutes and regulations in their states, and local practices. That being said, practitioners are also cautioned to be wary when local practices – although seemingly familiar and well settled – conflict with applicable law or regulations, or with the provisions of professional ethics codes or professional practice guidelines. Additionally, organizations often have policies and procedures about obtaining informed consent (and assent). Professionals working within organizations should be familiar with relevant policies and practice expectations, but alert to potential conflicts between organizational expectations and relevant law, regulations, and professional ethics codes and practice guidelines.

WHO CAN GIVE INFORMED CONSENT FOR A MINOR?

The general rule is that informed consent for professional clinical services must be given by the parent or legal guardian of a minor under age 18.

Practitioners should be familiar with relevant state law and regulations in the jurisdictions in which they practice. However, we offer the following general rules:

- *Legal custody* of a minor means that the parent, legal guardian or legal custodian of the minor has the authority to authorize, direct or terminate treatment, sign or decline to sign releases of information, and to provide informed consent for the minor. Particularly in post-divorce situations, legal custody may be permitted for some decisions but not for others. For example, one parent may have legal custody for all purposes while the other parent may have legal custody only for purposes of educational decisions but not for making decisions about religious practice, medical and behavioral health care, recreational activities, or contact with extended family members.
- *Physical custody* of a minor means that the parent or other individual provides some degree of caretaking for the minor and the minor resides with them for periods of time. Persons with physical custody but without legal custody cannot make decisions on behalf of a minor, authorize care or provide informed consent, or bar a professional service authorized by a parent or other individual who does have legal custody of the child. Practitioners are advised to be familiar with relevant laws and regulations in their own jurisdiction since parents who have only physical custody may still have residual rights to inspect medical or educational records unless specifically prohibited by a court from doing so.
- *Married parents have joint legal custody* for the child and practitioners are ordinarily permitted to presume that parents with joint legal custody are acting cooperatively in agreement about what constitutes the "best interests" of their child. This permits married parents to provide informed consent on behalf of both parents unless a practitioner has a reasonable basis to suspect that the two parents may not be in agreement about the provision of professional services. Because clinical "best practices" with children and adolescents involves communicating with both parents, practitioners are strongly advised to inquire specifically of a parent seeking services if the other parent agrees with the decision to do so and to secure authorization to communicate with the other parent. If one parent seeking services reports that the other parent opposes involvement of the minor in services or declines specifically to authorize the practitioner to communicate with the other parent, the practitioner is strongly cautioned to view this as a "red flag" and to decline

to offer professional services until and unless both parents with joint legal custody agree to professional services.

- *Legally separated or divorced parents* often have *joint legal custody* on a "temporary" basis while the divorce process is underway or "permanent" post-divorce joint legal custody after the case is concluded and a final judgment issued covering child custody arrangements. Separated, divorcing or divorced parents with joint legal custody each have equal authority to authorize professional services. However, just as with married parents, practitioners are advised to inquire specifically about whether both parents agree to the professional services being sought and whether the parent seeking the services will agree to communication with the other parent to discuss that parent's perception of the child and the child's needs, the nature and goals of treatment, and other important aspects of providing professional services. As with married parents, an indication by a separated or divorced parent that the other parent (with joint legal custody) is unaware of, or opposed to, the professional services is a major "red flag," as is a refusal by the parent to approve of the practitioner directly communicating with the other parent.
- Sometimes one separated or divorced parent has *sole legal custody* of the child. If so, only that parent can authorize professional services and provide informed consent. This is true even if the other parent has some degree of *physical custody or visitation* since a court may allow a child to spend time in the residence of a divorced parent or otherwise visit but not allow that parent to make legal decisions about matters such as religious upbringing, education, medical and mental health care, and the like.
- Separated or divorced parents may not always accurately know or report whether they have joint legal custody or some arrangement of sole legal custody and shared physical custody. Practitioners should consider asking to review a copy of any temporary or final divorce decree prior to providing professional services or relying upon a sole parent's informed consent, particularly when getting a "red flag" response from a parent. *If parents with joint legal custody disagree* about authorizing professional clinical services the practitioner is well advised to require that they come to an agreement (documented in writing) or secure a court order authorizing services before proceeding to provide any non-emergency services.
- *Step-parents* will ordinarily not have legal custody of a step-child unless they have adopted the minor or have been made a legal guardian of

a child through a court proceeding. Practitioners should assure themselves that a step-parent seeking services can provide an ethically and legally sufficient informed consent on behalf of a child or adolescent.

- *Relatives* of a minor will ordinarily not be able to offer an ethically and legally sufficient informed consent on behalf of a child or adolescent unless they have been appointed by a court as the guardian of the child or otherwise specifically been granted the legal authority to authorize professional clinical services.
- *Employees of governmental child protection services and their contracted providers* cannot ordinarily offer an ethically and legally sufficient informed consent on behalf of a minor unless that minor has been placed by a court into the legal custody of the child protection authority. If an employee of a governmental child protection authority does have "temporary" or "permanent" legal custody of a child, then the employee can ordinarily stand in the place of a parent to make the same kinds of decisions a parent would on behalf of a child. For example, case workers or case supervisors for youth in the legal custody of state child protection agencies can typically provide informed consent for assessment or treatment.
- Youth who *are receiving services by state or county mental health authorities, public health authorities, or developmental disability authorities* cannot be presumed to be in the legal custody of those governmental bodies. Services provided by or through these governmental bodies will not necessary or even routinely mean that a youth is in their legal custody even if that youth is "placed" in a program or a facility which they operate directly or for which they contract. Practitioners should be familiar with law in their jurisdiction to avoid confusion.
- Jurisdictions vary regarding the capacity of *state or county juvenile justice authorities* to authorize clinical professional services. In some jurisdictions, parents who are legal custodians of a youth committed to a juvenile justice authority still retain parental authority to decide what kinds of non-emergency clinical professional services their child may receive. This is the case even though the juvenile justice authority has the authority to control the physical placement of the youth (community, residential treatment facility, incarceration). In other jurisdictions, juvenile justice authorities may be presumed to have the authority to assign youth "committed" to them by courts to treatment programs that include specialized assessment and treatment with the expectation that youth will participate. Practitioners are advised to be

sufficiently familiar with the relevant laws, policies and practices in the jurisdiction(s) in which they engage in professional services.

- *Courts may issue orders for assessment or treatment* of a youth. These Court orders are ordinarily viewed as authorizing the clinical provider to provide specific professional services. The parent or legal guardian may nonetheless decline to consent to the participation of the child even if the court has authorized the provider to provide them. Similarly, attorneys representing youth may advise the youth to decline participation or to avoid discussing alleged or adjudicated sexual misconduct during interactions with the professional services provider. Failure to participate may have negative consequences for the youth (such as violation of probation, revocation of a conditional liberty, or transfer to a more secure level of facility-based care), but it is rare that a Court can absolutely compel an individual actively to engage in behavioral health services. The best practice for the clinician is to inform the Court that the parent or legal guardian has refused to provide consent for the services or that the attorney has advised the child not to participate, and ask for instructions about how to proceed.
- Some states provide for the *status of an "emancipated minor"* that permits a minor to authorize their own care and treatment as if they were an adult. The circumstances that may result in a youth being recognized as an "emancipated minor" will vary by state but can include a minor who is or has been legally married, is pregnant (or believes she is), is a member of the Armed Forces, has been living substantially separately from their parents/caregivers and providing solely for themselves or, is the primary caretaker for their own child. Practitioners should be aware of circumstances recognized in the jurisdictions where they practice that might make a youth an "emancipated minor" and whether or not a specific court declaration of being an "emancipated minor" is required before the youth can authorize (or decline to authorize) their own clinical care after an adequate informed consent.
- *Emergency services* can ordinarily be provided without informed consent if the services are required to manage imminent risk of significant injury to a minor. Practitioners should be familiar with the provisions of law relevant to providing emergency services in their jurisdiction and with the tenets of their professional ethics code bearing upon providing emergency care. In the first instance, it is important to be able to demonstrate that the practitioner is operating in genuinely emergency circumstances and that proceeding without informed consent is

not simply a convenience for the practitioner or an effort to be helpful. It will also be important to be able to articulate concretely the specific imminent risks of significant harm to the minor and how the professional's responses would manage these specific risks.

INFORMED CONSENT AS RECOGNITION OF FUNDAMENTAL FAIRNESS AND DIGNITY

The modern legal and ethical doctrines of informed consent and assent emerged in the mid-20th century as the first international human rights doctrine in an effort to protect vulnerable and marginalized persons from medical experimentation or treatment without consent. The need to obtain a legally and ethically adequate informed consent or assent reflects values of fundamental fairness (providing sufficient information for reasonable decision making) and dignity (reflected in meaningful engagement in informed consent or assent). These values are particularly important when working with highly stigmatized and often very vulnerable youth such as those adjudicated formally as sexual offenders, labeled inaccurately and usually pejoratively as "sex offenders" although never charged or adjudicated for a sexual offense, or otherwise labeled in ways that tend to reduce their identities solely to their sexual misconduct.

Practitioners must be familiar with relevant professional ethics codes and practice guidelines for their own profession and should be familiar with those of related professions and professional organizations. They should also be familiar with law, regulation and practices involving informed consent and assent for the jurisdiction(s) in which they practice professionally. In "gray area" situations, practitioners might also carefully consider what information they personally would need or want to know or understand if in the position of authorizing professional assessment or treatment for themselves, their own children, or others with whom they have close relationships.

APPENDIX

SAMPLE INFORMED CONSENT DOCUMENTS

Sample documents in the Appendix include those provided with the permission of the Stevens Treatment Programs (Swansea, MA) and the

Stetson School (Barre, MA). They are offered as templates for consideration as practitioners and programs devise, revise or implement their own informed consent procedures and documentation. The authors gratefully acknowledge and thank these programs for their willingness to provide these documents. Our thanks also to Steven Bengis and Phil Rich for their assistance and support in accessing sample documents and their deeply thoughtful and professional work with youth with problematic sexual behaviors.

SUMMARY OF INFORMED CONSENT/LIMITS OF CONFIDENTIALITY FORM FOR RECORDS (STEVENS TREATMENT PROGRAMS, SWANSEA MA)

NAME was informed about the purpose and process of assessment and treatment at **PROVIDER AGENCY NAME**. He was told that the information he provided during the course of the assessment period would be used in a written assessment report that would be given to **AGENCY/PARENT**. He was also told that if, at any time during the assessment process or during treatment, he made any statements indicating that he was going to harm himself or another person, that information would be disclosed to the outside agency and/or authorities in order to protect him or others. **NAME** was also told that if he disclosed any information not previously known and reported regarding any past abusive behaviors committed by another person directed toward himself, or, any past abusive behaviors he had committed toward another person, including a child, or toward an animal, this information would also be disclosed to the outside agency and/or authorities in order to assure everyone's safety. The clinician made certain that **NAME** understood these limitations of confidentiality by asking him if he understood and by having him repeat the information and explain the information in his own words. **NAME** was told that his participation in this assessment process was voluntary and that he did not have to participate if he did not want to. **NAME** indicated that he understood and he agreed to participate. Furthermore, **NAME'S** parent/s and/or legal guardian/s have given permission for **NAME** to participate in this assessment, as well as to participate in treatment, at **PROVIDER AGENCY NAME**.

STETSON SCHOOL, INC.
455 South Street
P. O. Box 309
Barre, Massachusetts 01005-0309

Telephone: (978) 355-4541
FAX: (978) 355-2706

"100 Years of Caring for Children"

Residential Treatment
& Special Education

Authorization and Consent for Release of Information

Student: ______________________ DOB: ____________ Admission Date: ____________

I, ______________________________, am the __legal guardian of this student, or __the student and am aged 18 or older, and hereby authorize Stetson School to obtain information from and/or release information to:

Name: ______________________________ **Relationship:** ____________________

And/or: **Agency/School/School District:** ______________________________________

Address: ____

Phone: (____) ____________________ **Fax:** (____) ________________

Consent to Obtain and/or Release the Following Information/Records

****No treatment-related information may be released to a school/school district without the additional completion of Stetson School form CN12, *Release of Treatment Information to School System***

	Obtain	Release
Treatment Reports, Treatment Summaries, Treatment Plans, and/or Individual Service Plans (ISP)	___	___**
Educational Records, Reports, Data, Summaries, and/or Individual Education Plans (IEP)	___	___
Educational/psychoeducational Testing/Evaluation	___	___
Grades, Reports Cards	___	___**
Psychological Test Results and Evaluations	___	___**
Psychiatric Evaluations	___	___**
Records of School-based Social, Behavioral, and Emotional Functioning and/or Difficulties/Problems	___	___
School Guidance Counseling and/or Therapeutic Counseling Records	___	___**
Substance Abuse Records, Including Evaluations and Treatment Records	___	___**
Medical Reports and Information that May Contain Information Pertaining to HIV	___	___**
Psychiatric Records, Including Records of Psychiatric Treatment	___	___**
Medical Reports and Medical Information	___	___**
Medical Lab Reports	___	___**
Legal Information	___	___**
Polygraph Records	___	___**

__Other: ____

__Other: ____

The information is to be released for:
__Assessment __Treatment Planning __ Educational Planning __Discharge Planning
__ Other: ____

I understand that my consent to release information is voluntary and that these records are protected under Federal Confidentiality regulations (47 CFR, Part 2) and cannot be disclosed without written consent unless otherwise provided for in the regulations.

I understand that this consent to release information is in effect until thirty (30) days past the discharge date from Stetson School for the above named student, or until ______________(date), but I may revoke this consent at any time either in writing or verbally, except to the extent that action has been taken in reliance on it (e.g., probation, parole, etc.).

______________________________________ ____________________
Signature of parent, legal guardian, or student if aged 18 or older Date

______________________________________ ____________________
Name and Signature of Witness Date

This authorization for and consent to release confidential information is in compliance with the Health Care Health Insurance Portability and Accountability Act (HIPAA) of 1996

Form CN2.V6 (S5)

STETSON SCHOOL, INC.

455 South Street
P. O. Box 309
Barre, Massachusetts 01005-0309

Telephone: (978) 355-4541
FAX: (978) 355-2706

"100 Years of Caring for Children"

Residential Treatment
& Special Education

Child/Adolescent Consent to Pre-Admission Interview and Assessment: Problem Sexual Behavior Track

Child/Adolescent Name: ______________________________ Date of Birth: ____________

I understand that I am being asked to participate in an interview specifically to evaluate my appropriateness for placement and treatment at the Stetson School, and to assess my history of sexual behavior. The purpose of this interview and assessment is for treatment planning. I understand I will be asked specific questions about my sexual interests and behaviors. I will also be asked general background information which will include questions about other behaviors and my history, as well as family, friends, and personal interests. I understand that during the course of the interview(s), I may feel uncomfortable as a result of the interviewer learning about my sexual behaviors and my history, and I may ask to end the interview at any time.

I understand that Stetson School treats children and adolescents with problematic sexual behavior, and that the purpose of this interview is to help identify whether Stetson School is an appropriate treatment placement for me.

Any information I give during the interview(s) will be recorded in my record. However, all such information will be kept completely confidential by Stetson School. This means that information will not be shared with anyone outside of Stetson School without my permission, except:

1. If a court orders a review of or subpoenas my records.
2. If during the interview process I identify a planned crime or victim.
3. If during the interview process I reveal a previously unreported case of child abuse or neglect.

Under these situations, I understand that Stetson School may be required to reveal information about me to the proper authorities without my consent.

My signature means that I understand the purpose of the interview/assessment, I understand the limits of confidentiality, and I agree to be interviewed. I understand also that, if I am aged 17 or younger, my parent, legal guardian, or a social service agency representative must also agree to this interview.

______________________________ ____________
Signature of Child/Adolescent *Date*

______________________________ ____________
Signature of Legal Guardian or Agency Representative *Date*

Relationship/Role: __ *Parent* __ *Legal Guardian* __ *Agency Representative*

______________________________ ____________
Signature of Stetson Staff *Date*

Form CN33-PSB.V1 (S4)

STETSON SCHOOL, INC.
455 South Street
P. O. Box 309
Barre, Massachusetts 01005-0309

Telephone: (978) 355-4541
FAX: (978) 355-2706

"100 Years of Caring for Children"

Residential Treatment
& Special Education

Agreement of Limited Confidentiality:
Problem Sexual Behavior Track

Student: ______________________________ DOB: ____________ Admission Date: __________

I, ______________________________, have been informed and acknowledge that I have limited rights of confidentiality regarding my treatment at Stetson School.

I understand that I am in treatment at Stetson School in order to deal with my sexual behavior problems and any harm my sexual behavior has caused to others, to work on my own sexual behavior problems, and to learn healthy ways to think, feel and behave. It is important to be fully accountable for my own actions, and that means accepting the consequences for my past, current and future behavior.

Therefore:

a. I understand, consent, and agree to unrestricted communication between and among members of my treatment team. The members of my treatment team while I am at Stetson School may include:
   - Stetson School staff from all departments,
   - my case worker,
   - my school department from my home town and educational advocate,
   - my probation or parole officer,
   - my parent and/or legal guardian, and
   - other individuals who may be responsible for my custody, care, supervision, treatment, and maintenance while I reside at Stetson.

   Members of my treatment team will talk with each other, both on the phone and in writing, about issues related to my progress in treatment, such as my participation in groups, my behaviors in the past, and my behavior and attitude at Stetson School.

   Stetson School staff who work closely with me will read my file and know my past behaviors and treatment issues. This is important, so that staff can work together to maintain a safe place for me and to help me in my treatment.

   During my treatment at Stetson School, when I talk about how I have harmed others in a sexual way, this information will be shared with the staff at Stetson School who work closely with me and with my treatment team.

b. I also understand, consent, and agree to unrestricted communication between and among Stetson School treatment team members and any other individual or agency with whom Stetson School treatment team members judge communication is necessary when:
   - I have communicated something that reveals that I am contemplating or have committed a crime or a harmful act or
   - Because, in their professional opinion, my behavior presents a clear and imminent danger to either myself or others.

   I understand that whatever I tell an interviewer, counselor, therapist, or other Stetson School staff member concerning such circumstances is not privileged or private, and may not be held confidential. In these circumstances the individuals or agencies Stetson School may communicate with include, but are not limited to, the court, the victim, and social and human service agencies.

c. I also understand that sexual assault is a criminal offense with serious consequences to the victim and the community. I allow Stetson School to report to the appropriate authorities any consequences or possible occurrence of sexual offense on my part, regardless of how Stetson School gains knowledge of such behavior or potential behavior.

   I understand that such authorities may include the district attorney's office, state police, local police, probation or parole officers, social service agencies or youth authorities.

d. I further understand that all Stetson School staff and members of my treatment team are obligated under state law to report to the appropriate authorities any and all cases of known or suspected neglect or abuse toward children, the disabled, and/or the elderly, or the planned commission of a significant crime or act of violence. There is also a general obligation for my treatment team to inform the authorities and others if, in their professional opinion, my behavior presents a clear and imminent danger to either myself or others.

I acknowledge that this waiver is signed without threat, promise, or coercion and is a voluntary act on my part.

Student Signature	*Date*

Print: *Legal Guardian Name* *If student is age 17 or younger*	*Legal Guardian Signature*	*Date*
Print: *Witness Name*	*Witness Signature*	*Date*

STETSON SCHOOL, INC.

455 South Street
P. O. Box 309
Barre, Massachusetts 01005-0309

Telephone: (978) 355-4541
FAX: (978) 355-2706

"100 Years of Caring for Children"

Residential Treatment & Special Education

Consent for Use of Polygraph Examination

Student: ______________________ Date of Birth: __________ Date of Consent: ____________

I understand that Stetson School requests the use of polygraph testing at times in the treatment of its students. The polygraph is used to assess truthfulness in the individual being tested, and is sometimes referred to a "lie detector." The polygraph is an instrument that records physiological changes in a person undergoing questioning in an effort to ascertain truth or deception. A polygraph records respiratory activity, galvanic skin resistance or conductivity, and cardiovascular activity, in an effort to distinguish between truthfulness and deception.

The polygraph examination is a valuable investigative aid when used in conjunction with, but not as a substitute for, a thorough investigation, and the polygraph may be used to verify, corroborate or refute statements or obtain additional information

Stetson School employs the polygraph as an aid to treatment, and especially to establish responsibility for illegal or other inappropriate actions, to better understand the motivations and behaviors of students, and/or to make determinations about the appropriateness or effect of treatment. In some cases, a polygraph test may be the only way to establish whether a student is being honest or dishonest about a current or past behavior. In general, Stetson School will only request the use of a polygraph when there is no other clear means for establishing truthfulness. *At Stetson School, polygraph information is not used to determine guilt or innocence, and is not attached to a criminal proceeding.*

The polygraph test at Stetson School will only be given by persons fully trained in the use of the polygraph. The polygraph test will only be given with the express and signed consent of the parent/legal guardian and the student. Permission may be revoked at any time, and the student may refuse to take the polygraph test at any time.

By signing this consent form you hereby grant permission to Stetson School to administer one or more polygraph tests, and release Stetson School from any future liability that may arise as a result of the polygraph examination. In addition, you hereby grant permission to Stetson School to release any information necessary for the polygraph examination and to include polygraph results in the student's treatment record.

Videotaping Polygraph Tests

We may request that polygraph tests be videotaped or otherwise recorded in order to ensure that the rights of the student are maintained during the polygraph test and/or to later verify answers given by students during the test. Your signature gives consent to video tape or otherwise record polygraph testing sessions, as part of the session.

I __**do** __**do not** consent to polygraph testing
I __**do** __**do not** consent to the videotaping/recording of polygraph sessions

______________________________ ______________
Student Signature *Date*

______________________________ ______________________________ ______________
Parent or Legal Guardian Name (Print) *Parent or Legal Guardian Signature* *Date*

______________________________ ______________________________ ______________
Witness Name (Print) *Witness Signature* *Date*

Form CN5.V4 (S5)

STETSON SCHOOL, INC.

455 South Street
P. O. Box 309
Barre, Massachusetts 01005-0309

Telephone: (978) 355-4541
FAX: (978) 355-2706

"100 Years of Caring for Children"

Residential Treatment
& Special Education

Release of Treatment Information to School System:
Problem Sexual Behavior

Student: ________________________________ DOB: ______________ Admission Date: __________

It is important for the parent or legal guardian of students to understand that highly sensitive information may be released through records of Stetson School's treatment and attendance at Stetson School treatment planning meetings.

Stetson School maintains separate educational and treatment records. Educational records at Stetson School contain details of academic participation, progress, and performance. Treatment records contain details of the student's history that include history of sexually abusive or other sexually troubled behavior, as well as treatment interventions, participation, and progress, and assessed risk for sexually re-offending. For this reason, treatment records contain highly sensitive information not usually released to a school system.

Accordingly, Stetson School will only release clinical and treatment information to the student's home school or other school with the clear and informed consent of the parent or legal guardian that such information can be shared with a sending school. In the event that such records become part of the student's permanent educational record, highly confidential information regarding placement at Stetson School and treatment plans, treatment progress, and details of treatment will be available to anyone having access and the right to read the student's school records in his home school.

Similarly, highly confidential and sensitive treatment material is discussed during Individual Service Plan meetings, other treatment plan meetings, and case conferences at Stetson School. Accordingly, representatives from the student's home school system may only attend such meetings with the clear and informed consent of the parent or legal guardian in full knowledge that sensitive and confidential treatment issues are discussed during such meetings.

I, ____, am the __ legal guardian of this student, or __ the student and am aged 18 or older.

_ I authorize Stetson School to **release** identified treatment records, **as shown below**, to the school system named below

__Treatment Reports/Summaries, and/or Individual Service Plans (ISP)
__Psychological Test Results and Evaluations
__Substance Abuse Treatment Records, including Evaluations
__Non-HIV Medical Reports/Information
__Medical Lab Reports
__Discharge Summaries
__Psychiatric Evaluations/Records
__Polygraph Records
__HIV Medical Reports/Information
__Legal Information
__Other: ____

_ I authorize Stetson School to allow representatives of the school system named below to **attend** treatment meetings at Stetson School

_ I do not authorize Stetson School to release identified treatment records to the school system

_ I do not authorize Stetson School to allow representatives of the school system named below to attend treatment meetings at Stetson School

I understand that my consent to release information is voluntary and that these records are protected under Federal Confidentiality regulations (47 CFR, Part 2) and cannot be disclosed without written consent unless otherwise provided for in the regulations. I understand that this consent to release information is in effect until thirty (30) days past the discharge date from Stetson School for the above named student, or until ______________(date), but I may revoke this consent at any time either in writing or verbally, except to the extent that action has been taken in reliance on it (e.g., probation, parole, etc.).

School System: ____

Address: ____

______________________________________ ____________
Signature of Parent/Legal Guardian, or Student if Aged 18 or Older *Date*

______________________________ ______________________________ __________
Print: Witness Name *Witness Signature* *Date*

This authorization for and consent to release confidential information is in compliance with the Health Care Health Insurance Portability and Accountability Act (HIPAA) of 1996

Form CN12-PSB.V6 (S5)

STETSON SCHOOL, INC.
455 South Street
P. O. Box 309
Barre, Massachusetts 01005-0309

Telephone: (978) 355-4541
FAX: (978) 355-2706

"100 Years of Caring for Children"

Residential Treatment
& Special Education

Consent for Use of Plethysmograph Examination

Student: ______________________________ Date of Birth: ____________ Date of Consent: __________

I understand that Stetson School requests the use of plethysmograph (PPG) testing at times in the treatment of its students in order to better understand the sexual interests of an individual student. The PPG is used to recognize and assess sexual thoughts, interests, and preferences. Stetson School uses the PPG assessment in conjunction with, but not as a substitute for, therapy and other forms of treatment, and can help us to explore and better understand sexual interests in our students. The use of the PPG is also used to help monitor changes in sexual interest during the course of treatment, and can also promote self disclosure in students.

The PPG assessment is not administered at Stetson School or by Stetson School staff. It is administered by clinical staff trained in the use of the PPG and occurs off -campus. The PPG assessment is only given with the express and signed consent of the parent/legal guardian and the student. Permission may be revoked at any time, and the student may decide not to take the PPG test at any time. The PPG is a small flexible gauge which the student places on his penis, while sitting alone in a monitored room. There are no cameras or observation windows. He communicates with the PPG technician through an intercom and is shown or listens to descriptions of sexual activities. The student is asked to describe his interest and response to each sexual activity and the PPG measures any changes in penile tumescence (erection).

Student

I understand that I am giving my consent to participate in an assessment designed to evaluate my sexual interests. I will be asked to answer questionnaires and tests that explore my history and my sexual behavior and interests. My sexual interests will also be measured by recording my erection responses while I look at or listen to sexual material. This sexual material may be very explicit and will include sexual activities relating to my sexual interests. While I observe or listen to these sexual materials, my erection will be measured by a small gauge that I place around my penis in the privacy of a private room. This gauge is cleaned with an antiseptic prior to my use of it. To ensure that the readings obtained are accurate I understand that the PPG technician may need to check that the gauge is properly attached prior to my beginning the PPG assessment session. However, I will always be alone in a private room when my responses are actually being measured.

I understand that the PPG assessment is only used to measure my sexual interests, and that I will discuss my sexual thoughts and interests with my Stetson School clinician as part of my on-going treatment at Stetson School. This may include any emotional discomfort I feel about the PPG process and the thoughts or emotions I have before, during, and after use of the PPG. I understand that any information I give during the PPG assessment will be added to my treatment record at Stetson School.

By signing this consent form I agree to participate in PPG assessment and give permission to Stetson School to release any information necessary to the PPG examiner. The use of the PPG has been explained to me fully and I have had any questions answered to my satisfaction. The use of the consent form has also been explained to me fully and I understand what I am giving consent for. I also understand that I may withdraw my consent for PPG assessment at any time.

______________________________________ ____________
Student Signature *Date*

______________________________ ____________________________ __________
Print: Witness Name *Witness Signature* *Date*

– Legal guardian consent continued on next page –

Form CN16.V2 (S5) Plethysmograph Examination Consent Form: Double-Sided Form/Page 1 of 2

STETSON SCHOOL, INC.
455 South Street
P. O. Box 309
Barre, Massachusetts 01005-0309

Telephone: (978) 355-4541
FAX: (978) 355-2706

"100 Years of Caring for Children"

Residential Treatment
& Special Education

Consent for Use of Abel Assessment of Sexual Interest

Student: ______________________ Date of Birth: __________ Date of Consent: __________

I understand that Stetson School at times requests the use of the Abel Assessment of Sexual Interest (AASI) in the treatment of its students in order to better understand the sexual interests of an individual student.

The AASI is a two-part computerized test used to identify sexual thoughts and interests. The first part of the test uses a questionnaire to ask students about their sexual behaviors and interests and is designed to better understand sexual thoughts, attitudes, and truthfulness. The second part of the test explores sexual interests by showing the student slide photographs of clothed adults, adolescents and children.

Stetson School uses the AASI as an aid to treatment. The AASI test is helpful when used in conjunction with, but not as a substitute for, therapy and other forms of treatment, and can help us to explore and better understand sexual interests in our students.

In general, Stetson School will only request the use of the AASI when there is no other clear means for establishing patterns of sexual interest, other than by self-report. *At Stetson School, the AASI is not used to determine whether a student will or will not re-engage in sexually abusive or sexually inappropriate behavior, and is not attached to a criminal proceeding nor intended to be used in a court of law.*

The AASI test is administered by clinical staff trained in the use of the AASI. The AASI is only given with the express and signed consent of the parent/legal guardian <u>and</u> the student. Permission may be revoked at any time, and the student may decide not to take the AASI test at any time.

By signing this consent form you hereby grant permission to Stetson School to administer the AASI to the student, to release any information necessary to the AASI examiner, and to include AASI results in the student's treatment record.

______________________________ ______________
Student Signature *Date*

If student is age 17 or younger

______________________________ ______________________________ __________
Print: Parent or Legal Guardian Name) *Parent or Legal Guardian Signature* *Date*

______________________________ ______________________________ __________
Print: Witness Name) *Witness Signature* *Date*

Form CN17.V4 (S5)

SAMPLE INFORMED CONSENT FOR TREATMENT OF PROBLEMATIC SEXUAL BEHAVIOR

GENERIC ASSOCIATES, INC.

____

Child's name

____

Date of birth

____

Medical record number

My child has been referred to Generic Associates, Inc. for treatment. The primary goal of the treatment is to reduce my child's problematic sexual behavior. The type and extent of services that he/she will receive were determined following an initial assessment and discussion of the results with me during which I had an opportunity to ask questions regarding the goals of treatment, the techniques to be used during treatment, assessment measures to be used to track treatment progress, confidentiality and any reasonably foreseeable limitations on confidentiality for this treatment, financial and insurance arrangements, and expectations of my child, myself, and others during the course of treatment.

I understand that while the mental health services listed below may provide significant benefits, such as reducing problematic sexual behavior, increasing impulse control, increasing social skills, and decreasing symptoms of trauma, they may also pose risks. Services may elicit uncomfortable thoughts and feelings or may intensify thoughts or feelings related to troubling memories.

I give my consent to the following services:

_____ Social skills training

_____ Anger management

_____ Decision making and problem solving

_____ Healthy sexuality education

_____ Dialectical behavior therapy (DBT)

_____ Trauma-focused Cognitive-Behavioral Therapy (TF-CBT)

_____ Family therapy

_____ Multisystemic therapy (MST)

_____ Individual psychotherapy

_____ Other (please specify) ___________________________________

I understand that a separate discussion and informed consent process will occur should recommendations be made that my child undergo additional diagnostic procedures (such as psychological testing) or laboratory procedures (such as a polygraph or plethysmograph).

I understand that all information shared with the clinicians at Generic Associates, Inc. is confidential and that no information will be released without my consent. If this treatment is the result of a legal requirement such as a condition of probation or other conditional liberty, a court order, a referral by a state child protection agency, or as a result of expectations by another third party, I acknowledge that any limitations upon the expectation of confidentiality or testimonial privilege have been discussed with me. Additionally, I also understand that there are specific and limited exceptions to this confidentiality which include the following:

A. when there is risk of imminent danger to____(child)______ or to another person from______(child)___or another person involved directly in this treatment (such as a family member when providing family therapy), the clinician is required by law to take necessary steps to prevent such danger;

B. when there is suspicion that a child, disabled person, or elder is being sexually or physically abused or is at risk of such abuse, the clinician is legally required to inform the proper authorities;

C. when, in the opinion of the treating clinician, steps must be taken to access voluntary or involuntary psychiatric evaluation or hospitalization in urgent circumstances, and the clinician may have to communicate the basis of urgent concern to health care providers, a court, or others;

D. when a valid court order is issued for medical records, the clinician and the agency are bound by law to comply with such requests;

E. when information may otherwise be legally disclosed such as in the event a formal complaint is filed about the treatment or related professional services, or there are disputes regarding reimbursement for services. Should these unusual circumstances arise, I understand that I would be informed in advance regarding the potential need to disclose information and given an opportunity to address the circumstances giving rise to concern, consent to the disclosure of the information, and/or to voice my concerns regarding a potential disclosure of information.

If I have any questions or concerns regarding this consent form or about the services offered at Generic Associates, Inc., I may discuss them with my child's clinician. If my questions or concerns are not adequately addressed with my child's clinician, I may address them with the Director of Clinical Services. I hereby consent to the services checked above, and I understand that I may revoke my consent for Generic Associates, Inc. to treat my child at any time.

______________________________ ____________
Parent or Guardian Date

______________________________ ____________
Clinician Date

BIBLIOGRAPHY AND RESOURCES

American Academy of Child and Adolescent Psychiatry. (2010). *Principles of practice of child and adolescent psychiatry*. Washington, DC. Retrieved from http://www.aacap.org/AACAP/About_Us/Principles_of_Practice_of_CAP.aspx.

American Academy of Psychiatry and Law. (2005). *Ethics guidelines for the practice of forensic psychiatry:* Retrieved from http://www.aapl.org/ethics.htm.

American Mental Health Counselors Association. (2010). *Code of ethics*. Alexandria: Retrieved from http://ww.amhca.org/about/codetoc.aspx.

American Psychological Association. (2010) *Ethical principles of psychologists and code of conduct*. Washington, DC: Retrieved from http://www.apa.org/ethics/code/index.aspx.

American Psychological Association, Division 41 Psychology-Law Society. (2011). *Specialty guidelines for forensic psychologists*. Washington, DC: Retrieved from http://www.ap-ls.org/aboutpsychlaw/SpecialtyGuidelines. php.

Association for the Treatment of Sexual Abusers. (2001). *Professional code of ethics*. Retrieved from http://www.atsa.com/pdfs/COE.pdf.

Butters, R. P., & Vaughan-Eden, V. (2011). The ethics of practicing forensic social work. *Journal of Forensic Social Work, 1*, 61–72.

Chaffin, M. (2011). The case of juvenile polygraphy as a clinical ethics dilemma. *Sexual Abuse: A Journal of Research and Treatment, 23*, 314–328.

National Association of Social Workers.(2008). *Code of ethics*. Washington, DC: Retrieved from http://www.socialworkers.org/pubs/code/default.asp.

National Organization of Forensic Social Work. (1987). *Code of ethics*. Middletown: Retrieved from http://ww.sofsw.org.

Rich, P. (2011). *Understanding, assessing and rehabilitating juvenile sexual offenders*. Hoboken: Wiley.

Vitacco, M. J., Caldwell, M., Ryba, N. L., Malesky, A., & Kurus, S. J. (2009). Assessing risk in adolescent sexual offenders: Recommendations for clinical practice. *Behavioral Sciences & the Law, 27*, 929–940.

CHAPTER 2

Assessment of Dynamic Treatment Targets for Juveniles Who Sexually Offend

Raymond A. Knight* and Judith E. Sims-Knight**

*Department of Psychology, Brandeis University, Waltham, MA, USA
**Department of Psychology, University of Massachusetts Dartmouth, MA, USA

INTRODUCTION

Assessment of juveniles who have sexually offended (JSOs) is essential to inform placement decisions (e.g., inpatient or outpatient treatment, reunification when sibling incest is involved, foster or residential placement), to guide legal dispositions, and to provide the basis for treatment planning (Prescott, 2007). This chapter focuses on identifying the critical domains that should be targeted in evaluating JSOs and on recommending appropriate tools for assessing these domains.

Andrews and Bonta (2006) have articulated three primary principles that their extensive research has found essential for effective treatment of correctional populations. These have been labeled the risk, needs, and responsivity (RNR) principles. The *risk* principle maintains that treatment services should be differentially allocated according to offenders' risk levels, with higher risk levels receiving greater intensity. The *need* principle argues that treatment and management should target factors that are closely related to recidivism, and thus that are labeled criminogenic needs. Only non-criminogenic features that facilitate therapeutic engagement should be addressed. The *responsivity* principle urges that treatment uses methods that are appropriate to the individual learning capacities and styles, cultural and socioeconomic characteristics, and personality traits of the clients. The RNR principles have an excellent empirical treatment efficacy record among generic criminal samples (Andrews & Bonta, 2006) and, recently, they have also been shown equally efficacious for both JSOs and adults who have sexually offended or abused (ASOs) (Hanson, Bourgon, Helmus, & Hodgson, 2009). These results led Hanson et al. (2009) to

Toolkit for Working with Juvenile Sex Offenders.
DOI: http://dx.doi.org/10.1016/B978-0-12-405948-1.00002-5

recommend that RNR principles are essential for all sexual offender treatment programs.

Assessment is an integral part of any RNR program. In addition to its dependence on risk evaluation to guide treatment resource allocation (the risk principle), its demand for individualized treatment (the need and responsivity principles) requires an evaluation of each person's problems and proclivities. Andrews and Bonta take it a step further, however (Andrews, Bonta, & Wormith, 2011). As a central part of their RNR program, they propose not only the reliable and valid assessment of offender risk traits, but also the description of an offender's standing on such traits relative both to a normative sample and to an appropriate offender subgroup. Moreover, their program requires that therapists share feedback with their clients about the results of these assessments and that such feedback be used to help monitor improvement. Thus, the RNR model recommends assessment-based treatment, a strategy that has been found effective in other intervention domains (Poston & Hanson, 2010).

The RNR model, therefore, provides an empirical justification for the significance of assessment in the treatment of JSOs and an overarching theoretical guidance for determining the domains that should be part of this assessment. Overall risk needs to be assessed to determine the allocation of treatment resources, and the targets of treatment should include both those traits that are contributing directly to recidivism and are essential to maximize the learning and involvement of particular JSOs. Our goal in this chapter is to focus on treatment planning, but we will first describe the current state of risk assessment, because those who treat JSOs must also assess and manage risk.

CRITICAL PERSPECTIVE ON RISK ASSESSMENT OF JSOs

Although the assessment of risk is an essential cornerstone of any RNR program, how such an assessment should be understood and used in managing JSOs remains controversial. An important distinction must be made between risk management, which is the identification of where youth are relative to other youth on domains that have been found important for risk and the allocation of appropriate treatment resources, and risk prediction, which is the claim that the risk metric can predict with adequate accuracy which youth will recidivate in various ways. There is an important debate right now about whether the current state of our knowledge and the accuracy of our measures are sufficient to establish *predictive* risk levels for juveniles. It has been argued that for determining many legal consequences, risk prediction per se is not sufficiently accurate for JSOs to identify youth at high risk (e.g., Caldwell, 2013; Cauffman, Kimonis, Dmitrieva, & Monahan, 2009; Hempel, Buck, Cima, & van Marle, 2013). Rather, we should be in the business of risk management. If we believe that we must "do no harm" with our measurements, we should not be providing numerical estimates of re-offense risk for juveniles that will be used to put those youth in harm's way. In contrast, instruments of sufficient reliability and validity exist to help us manage risk.

The Estimate of Risk of Adolescent Sexual Offense Recidivism (ERASOR; Worling & Curwen, 2001) and the Juvenile Sex Offender Assessment Protocol-II (J-SOAP-II; Prentky & Righthand, 2003), which are the most widely used risk assessment instruments for juveniles, yield at best mixed results for predicting sexual recidivism when they have been assessed by independent investigators (e.g., Caldwell, Ziemke, & Vitacco, 2008; Martinez, Flores, & Rosenfeld, 2007; Parks & Bard, 2006; Spice, Viljoen, Latzman, Scalora, & Ullman, 2013; Voljoen et al., 2008). Although the Youth Level of Service/Case Management Inventory (YLS/CMI) has shown some ability to predict general criminal recidivism (AUC = 0.62; Onifade et al., 2008), it has not fared as well in predicting sexual recidivism (Viljoen, Elkovitch, Scalora, & Ullman, 2009). The AUC of 0.62 found in predicting general criminal recidivism with the YLS/CMI would be useful to determine whether greater treatment resources should be allocated to a youth with purportedly higher risk, but would likely yield an unacceptably high level of false positives or false negatives (depending on the cut-off chosen) for labeling a youth as "dangerous," and jeopardizing his future by providing community notification on the Internet.

Multiple factors make prediction problematic in adolescents: (1) the plasticity of developing traits in adolescence; (2) the low base rates of sexual recidivism among children and adolescents (e.g., Caldwell, 2007; Waite et al., 2005); and (3) the lack of consensus on how to define predictors for adolescents (Miccio-Fonseca & Rasmussen, 2009b). These problems, along with the inconsistency of risk prediction in extant follow-up studies, argue that use of the current risk instruments should be limited to what they do best – providing important guides to the allocation of treatment resources and helping to individualize and prioritize the critical domains related to recidivism that should be the focus of treatment and management.

TYPES OF ASSESSMENTS

A variety of assessment strategies are available for different treatment domains. Clinical ratings based on interview or clinical file review and self-report assessments exist for all domains. For some domains there are behavioral or physiological assessments, including penile plethysmography (PPG), galvanic skin response, and response times. Observational measures (by residential staff, parents, teachers, etc.) are also available for some domains. In this section, we will discuss general issues in the most widely used assessment strategies.

There are several risk instruments available that use interviews and clinical file reviews to assess overall risk and to help guide the evaluation of potential treatment targets. Among these, the ERASOR and the J-SOAP-II are the most widely used risk assessment instruments for JSOs. These have the advantage of including many of the domains identified as important in risk assessment in a single instrument and each has accrued reasonable empirical support, which we will describe in our discussion of each assessment domain. Although the Juvenile Sexual Offense Recidivism Risk Assessment Tool (the JSORRAT-II) has some support as a purely empirically-based actuarial of overall risk, it is predominantly based on static (historical) factors and less focused on the assessment of dynamic (changeable) traits.

Although self-report has acquired a bad reputation among sexual offender researchers (e.g., Kalmus & Beech, 2005), nonetheless, the empirical studies that compare self-report to other assessment strategies have shown that it often yields equally or more valid responses than interviewer-obtained information. Self-report has been compared to clinical interviews, risk assessments, PPG, Psychopathy Checklist-Revised (PCL-R), and observational measures. When self-report inventories have been developed specifically for antisocial or offender populations, these measures have yielded equivalent predictive accuracy to risk-appraisal procedures, and they contribute incremental validity to file and interview generated risk-appraisals in predicting criminal justice outcomes (Walters, 2006). When compared to PPG, self-report has often been found to provide greater group differentiation (Day, Miner, Sturgeon, & Murphy, 1989; Laws, Hanson, Osborn, & Greenbaum, 2000; Seto, Lalumière, Harris, & Chivers 2012; Stinson & Becker, 2008). A self-report inventory of psychopathy, Psychopathic Personality Inventory (PPI), has been found to add incremental validity to the PCL-R (Camp, Skeem, Barchard, & Lilienfeld, 2013).

The results of comparing self-report to observer ratings are complex, but still supportive of the use of self-report. When compared to ratings of knowledgeable observers, self-report agrees moderately well with observations, and the correlations are higher when the trait is more observable (Kenrick & Funder, 1988). Furthermore, even when correlations between observer ratings and self-report are small, both techniques yield comparable results when correlated with outcome variables (Dishion, Nelson, & Yasui, 2005). Several studies have identified situations in which self-report is superior to other techniques. Self-report of early abuse experiences by youth may provide superior evidence for predicting outcomes than either caseworker or parental reports (Eckenrode, Izzo, & Smith, 2007). When measuring *affective* dispositions, self-report explains variance that is not accounted for by observer measures (Grove & Tellegen, 1991; Meehl, 1959). Finally, respondents often are willing to reveal sensitive information, such as male–male sex or abortions in computerized self-report inventories than they are in either human-conducted interviews or in paper-and-pencil interviews, in which people tend to skip questions they do not want to answer (Gribble, Miller, Rogers, & Turner, 1999).

Based on currently available research, clinical interviews, risk assessment instruments, observational ratings, and self-report all have a role in assessment. Self-report may be preferred when asking about sensitive information, such as early abuse or current sexual practices, and when assessing respondents' affective attitudes. In contrast, when offenders are asked to self-report on their criminal or unsavory behaviors, they are likely to lie and such information needs to be corroborated by other assessment strategies. Self-report is counterindicated in clients who have trouble understanding what they read, although they may be able to cope if questions are read to them (Gribble et al., 1999). Both self-report and clinical interview may also suffer from lying and defensive minimization. Self-report measures typically provide scales that measure social desirability, denial, and faking, and their use has been recently shown to be effective in a meta-analysis of research using psychopathy self-report measures (Ray, Hall, Rivera-Hudson, Poythress, & Lilienfeld, 2013). Furthermore, it is likely that all measures (other than observations by others) will be problematic under adversarial conditions (Hindman & Peters, 2001). Thus it is important to establish a therapeutic alliance when assessing treatment needs and to include measures of response biases in all instruments.

For each domain we will describe the assessment tools that have the most validity and most widespread use.

TREATMENT DOMAINS RELATED TO RISK

The need principle of RNR requires that treatment targets should be chosen based on their empirically demonstrated risk. Several domains have emerged in the JSO follow-up literature that have sufficient relation to recidivism that they should both be evaluated as part of a comprehensive assessment for JSOs and be targeted for treatment. For each critical domain we will first briefly consider the empirical justification for the importance of assessing that domain. Although priority will be given for evidence that a particular domain predicts sexual recidivism, prediction of general criminal and violent recidivism will also be considered, because such evidence identifies criminogenic needs that must be addressed in those who sexually offend. Moreover, for those domains that appear more important in generic offending, we will consider some evidence gathered on non-sex offending juvenile samples. Finally, we will give weight to evidence that a particular domain differentiates JSOs from generic delinquents, because such data indicate that the difference might represent a particular need for JSOs. The major assessment domains we will consider include hypersexuality and sexual deviance, sexual preferences, antisociality and impulsivity, the callous-unemotional components of psychopathy, aggressive and violent fantasies and behavior, intimacy and friendships, and victimization.

After justifying each domain, we will suggest potential appropriate assessment tools for the domain, weighing each measure's differential utility, which includes not only consideration of its reliability and validity for measuring the particular target domain, but also determination of whether there is any empirical evidence for its use specifically with JSOs. Consistent with the principles for assessment in the Association for the Treatment of Sexual Abusers (ATSA) Practice Standards and Guidelines (2005), we recommend that any comprehensive evaluation include both multiple sources of information (e.g., the JSO, family members, criminal justice resources) and multiple types of assessment modes (e.g., interview, psychometric testing, archival record sources, performance-based measures). This chapter is intended only to provide a broad overview of assessment. Each domain and its assessment could generate its own chapter.

Hypersexuality and Sexual Deviance

Sexualization is a heterogeneous domain comprising multiple facets. Deviation can occur in the frequency or intensity of fantasies or behaviors, in the age preference of the partner or victim (e.g., pedophilia), or in the arousal target or preferential arousal behavior (e.g., the paraphilias). Although there is evidence for substantial covariations among the sexual drive, sexual preoccupation, and sexual appetitive behavioral components of sexual behavior including some sexually deviant behavior (e.g., drive, preoccupation, pornography use, and some paraphilias; Knight & Cerce, 1999), little support has been found for the covariation of the appetitive components and sexual age preference (e.g., Knight & King, 2012). Nonetheless, risk instruments for both juveniles (e.g., J-SOAP-II, ERASOR) and adults (e.g., SRA-FV; ASOAP-II) have oftentimes categorized these two separate sexual domains together. We will consider them separately, referring to the first complex as sexualization and the second as sexual preference. We turn first to sexualization.

Supporting Research

In Hanson and Bussiere's (1998) meta-analysis, sexual deviance emerged as an important predictor of recidivism for adults. In more recent meta-analyses of predictive factors that included JSOs (Hanson & Morton-Bourgon, 2004; McCann & Lussier, 2008) and reviews of sexual recidivism (e.g., Worling & Långström, 2006), sexualization, as indexed by previous sexual charges/convictions, deviant/paraphilic sexual interests, or sexual preoccupation, has been shown to have moderate predictive potency. The ability of this component to predict the persistence of sexually coercive behavior from adolescence into adulthood has, however, had only mixed support (e.g., Parks & Bard, 2006; Rubinstein, Yeager, Goodstein, & Lewis, 1993; Sample & Bray, 2003; Zimring, Jennings, Piquero, & Hays, 2009; Zimring, Piquero, & Jennings, 2007). For the simple prediction of sexual recidivism within adolescence, the risk instruments have not fared much better. The J-SOAP II has yielded inconsistent results (e.g., Prentky, 2006; Viljoen et al., 2008) and only obsessive sexual interests/preoccupation with sexual thoughts on the ERASOR has been found to correlate significantly with short-term sexual recidivism in a recent prospective study (Worling, Bookalam, & Litteljohn, 2012). In an exploratory analysis of potential risk factors, Knight, Ronis, and Zakireh (2009) found that the sexual scales of Sexual Preoccupation, Sexual Compulsivity, and Sexual Drive; Atypical Paraphilias, Exhibitionism, Voyeurism; scales measuring offense planning; and scales capturing various aspects of pornography use emerged as potential predictors. The variety of sexual behavior and fantasy assessed by these scales suggests multiple avenues of assessment that might ultimately increase the predictive potency of existing risk instruments, which have tended to be limited to sexual offending and deviant interests.

In addition to its role in predicting recidivism, the components of sexualization have consistently been found to differentiate JSOs and ASOs from control samples. A number of investigations have found that sexually coercive males have consensual sex at an earlier age and have more consensual sex partners than do non-coercive males (e.g., Abbey, McAuslan, Zawacki, Clinton, & Buck, 2001; Kjellgren, Priebe, Svedin, & Långström, 2010; Koss & Dinero, 1988; Malamuth, Sockloskie, Koss, & Tanaka, 1991). Consistent with Kjellgren et al. (2010), Ronis and Knight (2013) found that sexual drive and preoccupation discriminated sexually coercive males from non-coercives in both community and general criminal samples. Regardless of criminal status or age (juvenile or adult), sexually coercive males reported higher levels of sexual drive, frequency of sexual behavior, and sexual deviance. Both ASOs and JSOs have been found to report more sexual compulsivity, more sexual preoccupation, and a higher sex drive than community control males on the Multidimensional Inventory of Development, Sex, and Aggression (the MIDSA), a contingency-based, computerized inventory created to assess multiple components of sexually aggressive behavior (see MIDSA, 2011).

As would be expected, individuals high on sexualization have been found to have a higher number of sex partners (Kalichman & Rompa, 1995, 2001), to have an increased risk for HIV and other sexually transmitted diseases (Kalichman & Cain, 2004; Parsons, Kelly, & Bimbi, 2008), and to be high in sexual risk taking, including a greater propensity to engage in unprotected sex (Dodge et al., 2008; Janssen, Goodrich, Petrocelli, & Bancroft, 2009; Kalichman & Cain, 2004). High sexualization covaries with compulsive masturbation, number of affairs, frequency of both prostitution itself and sex with prostitutes, pornography use, cybersex, voyeurism, exhibitionism, and sexual harassment (Carnes & Wilson, 2002). These components of sexual fantasies and behavior appear to be at least as important in juvenile samples as in adult samples (Knight, 2004). In clinical samples of individuals with paraphilic and hypersexual disorders, the onset of unconventional or intensive sexual arousal has been found to occur in adolescence (e.g., Abel, Becker, Cunningham-Rathner, Mittelman, and Rouleau, 1988; Kafka, 1997). Hypersexuality is also related to variables beyond pure sexuality. It has been found to correlate with factors measuring expressive aggression toward women, pervasive anger, sadism, and offense planning for both adults who sexually offend (ASOs) and JSOs (Knight & Cerce, 1999). Moreover, individuals high in sexualization are also at increased risk for substance abuse and impulse-related problems, as well as being more vulnerable to negative affect disorder, such as mood and anxiety disorders (e.g., Långström & Hansen, 2006).

It is not clear what aspects of sexual behavior constitute the core of the construct underlying these predictive sexual variables. Analyses indicate that all of these "sexualization" scales are highly correlated in both adult and juvenile samples (Knight, 1999; Knight & Cerce, 1999). Kafka (1997, 2003) has hypothesized that hypersexuality, which he defined as excessive sexual drive and preoccupation or sexual appetitive behavior, constitutes the core, underlying construct of other types of dyscontrolled sexual behavior, including the paraphilias and sexual coercion. Consistent with this hypothesis, Ronis and Knight (2013) found that sexual behavior and fantasies were important discriminators between sexually coercive and non-coercive males. Moreover, Knight and Sims-Knight (2003, 2004) found that hypersexuality predicted sexually coercive behavior against women and age appropriate females in both adult and juvenile samples, both criminal and non-criminal. Regardless of the potential underlying processes, extant data suggest that a more differentiated and extensive evaluation of the components of sexualization might be useful both to improve the predictive validity of risk instruments and for identifying those with a higher probability to continue their sexually coercive behavior into adulthood.

Assessment Tools

In contrast to sexual preference assessment, which we discuss in the next section, the tools for assessing hypersexuality and most forms of sexual deviance are limited to self-report measures, interviews, and official clinical/criminal file review. Among the inventories and scales available to measure this domain are the Sexual Addiction Screening Test (Carnes, 1991); the Sexual Compulsivity Scale (Kalichman & Rompa, 1995); the Compulsive Sexual Behavior Inventory (Coleman, Miner, Ohlerking, & Raymond, 2001; Miner, Coleman, Center, Ross, & Rosser, 2007); the Hypersexual Behavior Inventory (HBI; Reid et al., 2012); the Clarke Sexual History Questionnaire (CSHQ; Paitich, Langevin, Freeman, Mann, & Handy, 1977), the Thorne Sex Inventory (TSI; Thorne, 1966), the Multiphasic Sex Inventory (MSI-II; Nichols & Molinder, 1989); the Multidimensional Inventory of Development, Sex, and Aggression (MIDSA, 2011); and the Egodystonic Hypersexuality scale that van Outsem et al. (2006) added to the Adolescent Sexual Abuse Project (ASAP) assessment pack, developed by Beckett, Brown, and Gerhold (1997). Only the last three have scales that have been empirically tested on JSOs, and only the MSI-II and the MIDSA scales have easily available standardized scores that allow the evaluator to establish the respondent's location on specific domains relative to controls. In RNR, such placement is essential for identifying relative treatment needs.

The MSI-II for adolescent males is a 559-item questionnaire designed to assess the various sexual characteristics, and is available at http://www.nicholsandmolinder.com. It has six validity scales and 20 sexual content scales, including measures of four primary paraphilias and several secondary paraphilias. Although the juvenile offender standardization sample for the MSI-II is reasonable, and several studies of ASOs have been done (e.g., Clark & Grier, 1995; Kalichman, Henderson, Shealy, & Dwyer, 1992; Kalmus & Beech, 2005; Mackaronis, Strassberg, & Marcus, 2011; Schlank, 1995; Simkins, Ward, Bowman, & Rinck, 1989; Stinson & Becker, 2008), few studies have been done with JSOs (e.g., Butz & Spaccarelli, 1999). Nevertheless, it provides a viable assessment of sexual deviance for both adults and juveniles and assessments of denial and duplicity (Kalmus & Beech, 2005; Stinson & Becker, 2008).

The MIDSA is a computerized self-report inventory that provides a clinical report to support therapeutic interventions with both JSOs and ASOs. It was designed as a treatment-planning assessment to measure most of the domains that have been found important in predicting recidivism risk for juveniles and adults (e.g., Hanson & Morton-Bourgon, 2005; Knight & Thornton, 2007; Worling & Långström, 2006). In keeping with Andrews and Bonta's principles, it provides standardized scores or percentiles for respondents both relative to a community sample and to a compatible age and offense-type criminal control. Of the 25 empirical studies published using the MIDSA, ten have focused on JSOs. The MIDSA Clinical Manual (MIDSA, 2011) and the software for installing and administrating the inventory are available at http://www.midsa.us/learnmore.php. In addition to scales directly assessing aspects of sexual excitation (Sexual Compulsivity, Sexual Preoccupation, and Hypersexuality), the MIDSA provides five paraphilia scales (Voyeurism, Exhibitionism, Transvestism, Scatologica, Fetishism – excluding its two Sadism scales, which we will consider in our discussion of the aggression domain) and five pornography use scales (Conventional Heterosexual Pornography, Child Pornography, Violent Pornography, Homosexual

Pornography, and Early Exposure to Pornography) giving a comprehensive assessment of high sexualization and its major correlates. Although the inclusion of the paraphilias (except pedophilia) and pornography use broaden sexualization to encompass the targets of arousal, they are highly correlated with arousal (Knight & Cerce, 1999), so we include them with this domain. Like the MSI-II, the MIDSA also provides several scales to assess denial and impression management (MIDSA, 2011).

Other than self-report questionnaires, the only available way to evaluate sexualization is to use interview and chart review data to rate clinical scales. Both the J-SOAP-II (available from www.csom.org/pubs/jsoap.pdf) and the ERASOR (available from www.erasor.org) have items that relate to high sexualization. On the J-SOAP-II, Sexual Drive and Preoccupation is an item on its Scale 1, Sexual Drive/Preoccupation, which is a heterogeneous scale that amalgamates sexual preference, sexual aggression, sexual victimization, offense planning, sexual offense frequency and duration, number of victims, and sexual victimization. The ERASOR has three related items, Obsessive sexual interests/Preoccupation with sexual thoughts, Attitudes supportive of sexual offending, and Unwillingness to alter deviant sexual interests/attitudes. One could argue that presence of the J-SOAP-II item or any of the three ERASOR items could be considered reason to target this domain, but it would be difficult to determine what proportion of JSOs such a strategy would target. As we indicated earlier, the sexual items/domains in the J-SOAP II and ERASOR have been inconsistent in predicting recidivism, possibly because of their limited range, non-optimal and inadequately differentiated cutoffs for identifying deviance, and narrowness of coverage of sexualization.

Sexual Age and Gender Preference

Sexual age and gender preferences assess non-normative person targets of sexual arousal.

Supporting Research

Substantial empirical data support the differentiation between rapists and child molesters. Distinct structural equation models account for their etiology (e.g., Daversa & Knight, 2007; Knight & Sims-Knight, 2003, 2004). Specific neurodevelopmental antecedents and their correlates discriminate offenders who focus on children from those who assault women (e.g., Blanchard et al., 2002, 2003; Bogaert, 2001; Cantor et al., 2004; Cantor, Blanchard, et al., 2005; Cantor, Klassen, et al., 2005). In addition to their unique erotic preferences (Blanchard, Klassen, Dickey, Kuban, & Blak, 2001), rapists and child molesters can also be differentiated on a number of criminological and behavioral characteristics that are relevant to their treatment and dispositions (Bard et al., 1987; Christie, Marshall, & Lanthier, 1979; Harris, Knight, Smallbone, & Dennison, 2011; Prentky & Knight, 1991; Sitnikov, Goldberg, Daversa, & Knight, 2007). Finally, data suggest that actuarials developed to capture the unique attributes of rapists and child molesters may yield more accurate predictions of each group's sexual recidivism (Knight & Thornton, 2007; Parent, Guay, & Knight, 2011). It is not surprising that different typological models are required for each (Knight, 2010; Knight & King, 2012).

Sexual preference is also an important risk for sexual recidivism. Meta-analyses that focused primarily on ASOs, but also included JSO samples, have supported the hypothesis that deviant sexual age preferences significantly predict the risk of sexual recidivism (Hanson & Bussière, 1998; Hanson & Morton-Bourgon, 2004). Although for juveniles the discrimination between sexual preferences for children and age-appropriate peers is difficult because of the young age of the perpetrator, nonetheless, several studies have found an association between deviant age sexual arousal or fantasies and sex offense recidivism among JSOs (Kahn & Chambers, 1991; Kenny, Keogh, & Seidler, 2001; Schram, Milloy, & Rowe, 1991; Weinrott, 1996; Worling & Curwen, 2000), and Miner (2002) found that preoccupation with children was related to non-sexual and any recidivism. Worling and Curwen (2000) reported that sexual interest in children was significantly associated with sex offense recidivism in a sample of 58 adolescent males followed between 2 and 10 years. Moreover, both a meta-analysis specifically targeting JSOs (McCann & Lussier, 2008) and a review of the literature (Worling & Långström, 2006) reached a similar conclusion. In contrast, the predictive validity of having a male victim has been less consistent. Sexual interest in boys has sometimes covaried with recidivism (e.g., Hanson & Bussière, 1998), but other times it has not (e.g., Hanson & Morton-Bourgon, 2004). There is, nonetheless, an overall consensus about the importance of assessing sexual age and gender preference, but there is controversy about the optimal strategy for such assessment, especially among juveniles.

Assessment Tools

The evaluation of sexual preferences/interests offers the clinician a great variety of different types of assessment types, including physiological assessments like plethysmography (PPG; Lalumière, Quinsey, Harris, Rice, & Trautrimas, 2003; Quinsey & Chaplin, 1982), card sort (Holland, Zolondek, Abel, Jordan, & Becker, 2000; Laws et al., 2000), viewing time (Abel, Huffman, Warberg, & Holland, 1998; Glasgow, Osbourne, & Croxen, 2003), experimental physiological or perceptual/cognitive tasks (e.g., galvanic skin response, pupillometry, electroencephalographic measures, the attentional blink task, the Emotional Stroop, and the Implicit Association task), clinical rating scales (e.g., the J-SOAP-II and the ERASOR), and self-report questionnaires (CSHQ, MIDSA, and MSI-II).

In research studies, plethysmography remains the gold standard for discriminating among sexual preferences (Kalmus & Beech, 2005; Lalumière et al., 2003). Nonetheless, because of its difficulties dealing with faking, the high incidence of low-responding participants, low retest reliabilities, lack of standardized procedures, and the costs, difficulties of administration, and perceived invasiveness of the procedure (Kalmus & Beech, 2005; Looman, Abracen, Maillet, & DiFazio, 1998; Marshall & Fernandez, 2000; Serin, Mailloux, & Malcolm, 2001), PPG has often been seen as providing suboptimal clinical utility even for adult assessment (Kalmus & Beech, 2005; Marshall & Fernandez, 2003). For adolescents, the validity data for PPG are more problematic and less consistent (for a review see Worling, 2012). When both the concern about the questionable exposure of adolescents to visual and/or auditory stimuli depicting deviant sexual activities (Worling, 1998) and the worry about re-traumatizing youth who have been sexually abused (Worling, 2012) are added to these methodological concerns, the downsides of the use of such measurement make a compelling argument against its use.

Viewing time solves the ethical dilemmas posed by PPG for adolescents, and it has a sufficient track record in discriminating child molesters from rapists to earn a "high" rating on discriminative efficacy among adult samples from Beech and Kalmus (2005). It is, however, not without its critics for adolescents (Fischer & Smith, 1999; Smith & Fischer, 1999). Abel et al. (2004) found that viewing time of children on the Abel Assessment for Sexual Interest (AASI; www.abelscreening.com) was longer for JSOs who molested children than non-molesters (AUC = 0.64), and that viewing time was correlated with the number of victims and of child offenses for adolescents. Unfortunately, despite some evidence of discriminative validity, the research with adolescents has been limited and many unanswered issues must be addressed before use with adolescents can be recommended (Worling, 2012).

Attentional blink measures, which show some promise with adults (Beech et al., 2008), have not been successful with adolescents (Crooks, Rostill-Brookes, Beech, & Bickley, 2009). The other potential physiological or perceptual cognitive measures we cited above have not been tested on adolescents, and so do not represent assessment options at the present time.

Both the ERASOR and the J-SOAP-II have items that assess aspects of sexual preference. The ERASOR has deviant sexual interest, ever sexually assaulted a child, indiscriminate choice of victims, and ever sexually assaulted a male victim. The Sexual Drive/Sexual Preoccupation scale of the J-SOAP-II includes male child victim as an item.

Despite, as we discussed earlier, the bad reputation of self-report, especially in the area of reporting about sexual crimes (Kalmus & Beech, 2005), the self-report of sexual preference has fared well among juveniles (Seto, Lalumière, & Blanchard, 2000; Worling, 2006). No standardized instrument has, however, been directly validated for preference identification for adolescents. The MSI-II and the MIDSA provide similar packages of sexual history questions and child molester scales (MSI-II Child Molestation and MIDSA Child Sexual Arousal and Child Molester Cognitive Distortions scales, respectively), and the scales on both have shown some ability to differentiate between rapists and child molesters in adult samples (Knight, 2010; Stinson & Becker, 2008). Given the current available evidence, a reasonable and prudent strategy, consistent with Worling (2012) recommendation to do no harm and warning about the lability of juveniles' sexual preferences, would be to approach the evaluation of sexual preferences using multiple assessments, including self-report (MSI-II or MIDSA), a viewing procedure (e.g., AASI-2 or Affinity; Glasgow [2009], www.pacific-assmt.com/products/affinity-2-5), and interviews of adult caregivers.

Antisocial Behavior and Impulsivity

Supporting Research

Antisocial behavior in its many guises has been shown to covary consistently with sexually coercive behavior, especially against women (Knight & Guay, 2006; Prentky & Knight, 1991) and is a predictor of multiple other forms of risky sexual behavior (Ramrakha et al., 2007). Both juveniles and adults who sexually offend have been characterized as high in impulsivity and antisociality (Hunter, Figueredo, Malamuth, & Becker, 2004; Knight & Guay, 2006; Knight & Prentky, 1993; Prentky, Knight, Lee, & Cerce, 1995;

Seto & Lalumière, 2006; Worling, 2001). Antisociality is not only an important predictor of generic recidivism among ASOs (e.g., Walters, Knight, Grann, & Dahle, 2008) and JSOs (e.g., Långström, 2002; Långström & Grann, 2000), but it also emerges as a consistent predictor of subsequent sexual offending for adults (e.g., Hanson & Morton-Bourgon, 2005; Knight & Thornton, 2007). The findings for juveniles are less consistent (e.g., Caldwell et al., 2008; Gretton, McBride, Hare, O'Shaughnessy, & Kumka, 2001; Worling, 2001, but in contrast see Långström, 2002; Rasmussen, 1999; Sipe, Jensen, & Everett, 1998; Worling & Curwen, 2000 for no relation with subsequent sexual offending). Nonetheless, McCann and Lussier (2008) found in their meta-analytic study that a cluster of variables measuring antisociality significantly predicted sexual recidivism in juveniles. Non-sexual recidivism is consistently found to be a more likely outcome than sexual recidivism in both juveniles and adults who sexually offend (Caldwell, 2002; Knight & Thornton, 2007; Zimring, 2004). Because of its inconsistent role in predicting *sexual* recidivism in juveniles, Worling and Långström (2006) listed antisocial interpersonal orientation and impulsivity as only *possible* risk factors for sexual recidivism.

Assessment Tools

Although there are a large number of scales that measure some aspects of antisociality (see Prentky & Edmunds, 1997 for a partial sampling), only a handful have empirical track records with JSOs in peer-reviewed journals. Included in this group are two method types: (1) rating scales (e.g., the Youth Level of Service/Case Management Inventory [YLS/CMI; Hoge & Andrews, 2011], the Multiplex Empirically Guided Inventory of Ecological Aggregates for Assessing Sexually Abusive Adolescents and Children [MEGA♪; Miccio-Fonseca, 2008, 2009; Miccio-Fonseca & Rasmussen, 2009a,b], the Psychopathy Checklist: Youth Version [PCL-YV; Forth, Kosson, & Hare, 2003], and items on the three major juvenile risk instruments – the J-SOAP-II, the ERASOR, and the J-SORRAT-II [Epperson, Ralston, Fowers, DeWitt, & Gore, 2006; http://www.defenseforsvp.com/Resources/SARATSO/JSORRAT-II_ScoringManual_05Jun3.pdf]), and (2) self-report inventories (e.g., the Jesness Inventory–Revised [JI-R; Jesness, 1986, 1988]; the Millon Adolescent Clinical Inventory [MACI; Millon, 1993]; the Minnesota Multiphasic Personality Inventory [MMPI-2, MMPI-A; Butcher et al., 1992]; and the MIDSA [MIDSA, 2011]). We will focus on this subset of measures that have garnered at least some evidence on JSOs.

Rating Scales

The YLS/CMI (https://ecom.mhs.com/(S(4qpkewvmjkmwtaehlxmwvh55)/; Hoge & Andrews, 2011) comprises 42 risk/need items that are clustered into eight subdomains: Prior and Current Offenses, Family Circumstances/Parenting, Education/Employment, Peer Associations, Substance Abuse, Leisure/Recreation, Personality/Behavior, and Attitudes/Organization. The items are rated as present or absent and summed to generate both the subdomain scores and a total risk/needs score, which indicate low, moderate, high, or very high risk in each domain and overall. The Substance Abuse, Personality/Behavior, and Attitudes/Organization domains assess various aspects of antisociality. The instrument is based on a semistructured interview with a juvenile offender intended to aid in the development of a case management plan. The interrater reliability and predictive validity of the YLS/CMI for generic samples of juvenile offenders have been supported by a number of studies (see Hoge, 2005, for a review), and it has been standardized on a large sample of juveniles. Although the YLS/CMI has shown some ability to predict general criminal recidivism among juveniles (Olver, Stockdale, & Wormith, 2009), it has mixed results predicting sexual recidivism (Olver et al., 2009; Viljoen et al., 2009). Nonetheless, its scores are useful for determining whether aspects of antisociality should be targeted for a youth who scores at high risk for the appropriate domains.

The MEGA♪ (lcmf@cox.net, psmith@alliant.edu; Miccio-Fonseca, 2013) is a clinician-rated 75-item risk, treatment planning, and intervention improvement instrument for male and female youth through age 19, that assesses seven "ecological aggregates": Neuropsychological, Family Lovemap, Antisocial, Sexual Incident, Stratagem, and Relationship. Although not currently available for general use, its release is imminent (Miccio-Fonseca, 2013). Its ratings are based on clinician interviews and chart review, and its implementation requires instrument-specific training. It provides the advantages of being sensitive to developmental stages, appropriate for females as well as males, and developed exclusively from conceptualization to implementation on and for juveniles on a large and diverse sample of youths. Its aggregates have been shown to have reasonable internal consistency, and it correlates significantly with the J-SORRAT-II, suggesting some potential for predictive validity (Miccio-Fonseca, 2008). The Antisocial Aggregate assesses prior non-sexual offending and antisocial behavior in the home, school, and community.

The PCL:YV (https://ecom.mhs.com/(S(egwzhe4542ucbb55dloa4pjc))/product.aspx?gr=saf&prod=pclyv&id=overviewis; Forth et al., 2003) is the downward extension to adolescence of the gold standard for measuring psychopathy, the Psychopathy Checklist–Revised (PCL-R; Hare, 2003). It is a 20-item scale, with each item rated on a 0, 1, 2 metric and summed for total and facet scores. It has been found to have good to excellent interrater reliability (see Forth et al., 2003, for a review) and to correlate significantly both with other measures of disruptive, antisocial behavior, as well as with deficits in executive cognitive functioning and with difficulties negotiating interpersonal relationships (e.g., Kosson, Cyterski, Steuerwald, Neumann, & Walker-Matthews, 2002; Rogers, Johansen, Chang, & Salekin, 1997). Although it does not appear to predict generic recidivism for females (Vincent, Odgers, McCormick, & Corrado, 2008), it consistently predicts general criminal recidivism for male adolescents (Olver et al., 2009; Vincent et al., 2008), but it is less consistent at specifically predicting violent recidivism (Vincent et al., 2008). Like its adult PCL-R counterpart (Walters et al., 2008), the behavioral, Antisocial Facet 4 appears to be the most consistent predictor of both non-violent and violent recidivism for adolescent males (Vincent et al., 2008). Unlike the PCL-R, there appears to be little evidence that PCL-YV alone predicts sexual recidivism (Gretton et al., 2001; Hempel et al., 2013; Olver et al., 2009; Viljoen et al., 2009), except for Caldwell et al. (2008), which might be a function of the extremely high PCL:YV scores in their study. In general, however, the weight of the data on the PCL:YV suggests that it, and especially its Impulsivity and Antisociality facets, are a sensitive measure of this risk factor.

Despite its inconsistent role in predicting sexual recidivism, the J-SOAP-II devotes an entire domain to Impulsive/Antisocial Behavior that includes items like school behavior problems, juvenile antisocial behavior, and multiple types of offenses. The ERASOR includes in its Psychosocial Functioning domain the items antisocial interpersonal functioning and poor self-regulation of affect and behavior (impulsivity). Consistent with the J-SOAP-II and ERASOR, the JSORRAT-II includes an assessment of impulsivity/antisociality through two items measuring disruptive school behavior and the frequency of adjudicated non-sexual offenses.

Self-report Inventories

The JI-R (Jesness, 1983, 1986, 1988, 1996; www.mhs.com/product.aspx?gr=saf&id=overview&prod=ji-r) is a 160-item inventory that yields scores on 11 trait scales intended to provide a simple, hand-scored procedure for classifying delinquents and non-delinquents into one of nine personality subtypes according to a manual (Jesness & Wedge, 1985).

Computer scoring and computer-generated profile and interpretive reports are also available. The JI–R scales were standardized on a normative sample of 3421 non-delinquents and 959 delinquents; its scales show good reliability and validity; and it includes scales to assess response biases. The Social Maladjustment scale assesses the respondent's endorsement of the acceptability of behavior that is generally regarded as antisocial, and the Alienation scale measures the respondent's distrust of others, especially of authority figures. The most recent revision also has Conduct Disorder and Oppositional Defiant Disorder scales. Two of the Jesness types, the Unsocialized active and the Unsocialized passive, are socially non-conforming adolescents, with the active subtype being more delinquent and aggressive. The Autonomy-Oriented type also shows high self-reported delinquency (Harris & Jones, 1999; Jesness, 1988). Although there is substantial research using the JI-R to assess delinquents, only a couple of studies have examined JSOs specifically. Oliver, Hall, and Neuhaus (1993) found that JSOs exhibited *less* deviant personalities on the JI-R than non-sex offending violent controls, and Butz and Spaccarelli (1999) found that JSOs who used force exhibited no differences on the JI-R from those who did not. Despite its lack of data on JSOs, the inventory provides useful data about various aspects of antisociality. It has been argued in the delinquency/criminological literature that differentiating among the various types of antisocial motivation is critical both to treatment specificity (Harris & Jones, 1999) and to outcome (Listwan, Van Voorhis, & Ritchey, 2007; Underwood, Barretti, Storms, & Safonte-Strumolo, 2004).

The MACI (Millon, 1993; http://psychcorp.pearsonassessments.com/HAIWEB/Cultures/en-us/Productdetail.htm?Pid=PAg501) is a 160 true-false item questionnaire that yields four types of scales – 4 validity/reliability scales, 12 personality patterns scales, 8 expressed concerns, and 7 clinical syndromes. The items and norms for the MACI were generated using samples of 13- to 19-year-old adolescents from a variety of clinical settings, and its scales show good reliability and validity (Salekin, Leistico, Schrum, & Mullins, 2005).

The MACI provides the clinician with information on a wide variety of psychological problems, including aspects of impulsivity and antisociality, and the instrument has substantial validation in juvenile justice settings (Baum, Archer, Forbey, & Handel, 2009). The Unruly, Forceful, and Oppositional scales capture aspects of impulsivity and antisociality (e.g., Murrie & Cornell, 2000), with the Unruly most directly assessing antisocial acting out. Two Clinical Syndromes – Delinquent Predisposition and Impulsive Propensity – assess behavioral dyscontrol and poor impulse control aspects of youths' adaptations. Clinicians should consider base rate scores of greater than 74 on these scales as indicative of problems with antisociality that require intervention (Salekin et al., 2005).

Several studies have used the MACI to assess JSOs. Zakireh, Ronis, and Knight (2008) found that, with the exception of Sexual Discomfort and Child Abuse Scales, generic JSOs tended to score lower on MACI scales than non-sexual delinquent controls. Zakireh et al. (2008) and Burton (2008) found mixed results on the Forceful scale, but in neither study did the JSOs score at or above the clinically significant level. In other research on JSOs, the scales of the MACI have not been found to predict general or sexual recidivism (Kennedy, Licht, & Caminez, 2004). In contrast, in research on delinquent youth, the antisocial components of two psychopathy scales developed from MACI items predicted general and violent recidivism in a 2-year follow-up (Salekin, Ziegler, Larrea, Anthony, & Bennett, 2003). In cluster analytic studies, similar subtypes have emerged for JSOs (Oxnam & Vess, 2008; Richardson, Kelly, Graham, & Bhate, 2004) and ASOs (Bard & Knight, 1987), with each study identifying a predominantly antisocial/aggressive subtype.

The MMPI has a long history of use with sexual offenders and is one of the most frequently used psychometric assessments for ASOs (Schwartz & Cellini, 1995). A recent review (Baum et al., 2009) of the MMPI-A (http://psychcorp.pearsonassessments.com/HAIWEB/Cultures/en-us/Productdetail.htm?Pid=PAg522) indicates the usefulness of this adolescent version in juvenile justice settings. An early review of the ASO literature (Knight, Rosenberg, & Schneider, 1985), however, pointed out that a major weakness of the MMPI in the area of sexual aggression was its failure to sample adequately the domains most relevant to sexual offending. Even in the area of antisociality, where its Psychopathic Deviant scale (Pd, #4) has shown a small effect for predicting sexual recidivism (Hanson & Bussière, 1998), the MMPI's sampling of impulsive and antisocial items is suboptimal. A recent study comparing high and low risk ASOs did not find differences on this scale and, indeed, found only that the Infrequency (F) scale differentiated these groups (Coxe & Holmes, 2009). Although the test might be used to assess general psychopathology, its ability to delineate the specific treatment targets for ASOs and JSOs appears somewhat limited, and there is a paucity of research done using the MMPI-A on JSOs. What has been done (e.g., Freeman, Dexter-Mazza, & Hoffman, 2005a; Losada-Paisey, 1998) has yielded mixed results in differentiating JSOs from generic delinquents, even on the Psychopathic Deviant scale.

The MIDSA (http://www.midsa.us) has multiple scales that measure antisociality and impulsivity. Its three factor-analytically derived juvenile antisocial scales measure Delinquency, Alcohol and Drug Abuse, and Behavioral and Aggressive Problems. The latter two scales discriminate JSOs from community controls (MIDSA, 2011), paralleling or exceeding the same discrimination demonstrated for ASOs on these three scales (Knight, 2004; MIDSA, 2011). These three scales are the cornerstones of the antisocial latent trait in both JSO and ASO etiological models of sexually coercive behavior against women and age-appropriate peers (Knight & Sims-Knight, 2004, 2011). The same etiological model and antisocial latent trait predict sexually coercive behavior in a community sample (Knight & Sims-Knight, 2003). These juvenile antisocial scales correlate significantly with archival ratings of PCL:YV Facet 4 on a JSO sample (Graham & Knight, 2013). The MIDSA also has an Impulsivity Scale that discriminates residential JSOs from outpatient JSOs, but not from delinquent samples (Zakireh et al., 2008). In contrast to the JI-R, the MACI, and the MMPI-A, the MIDSA Juvenile Antisocial and Impulsivity scales provide T and percentile scores that locate the respondent relative to community controls and a sample of JSOs in residential treatment, respectively.

Callous-Unemotional Trait

Supporting Research

There is evidence that the presence among youth of callous-unemotional (CU) traits, which is Frick's (1998) term for the Affective-Interpersonal features of psychopathy, identifies a subgroup of antisocial youth who are deficient in conscience development (Frick, O'Brien, Wootton, & McBurnett, 1994; Frick, Bodin, & Barry, 2000). These youth have been found to manifest more severe aggressive behavior in mental health, forensic, and community samples (Frick & Marsee, 2006). CU traits appear to contribute most to proactive aggression (Kimonis et al., 2006). When CU traits are accompanied by conduct disorder, these youths have been found to show characteristics that parallel those found in adult psychopaths (Barry et al., 2000; Blair, 1999; Frick, Lilienfeld, Ellis, Loney, & Silverthorn, 1999; Loney, Frick, Clements, Ellis, & Kerlin, 2003).

Both juveniles and adults who sexually coerce age-appropriate peers and adult women have consistently been found to have higher scores on scales measuring the CU component of psychopathy than non-criminal community males (MIDSA, 2011). Caputo, Frick, and Brodsky (1999) compared a group of juveniles who had sexually offended to a group of violent juvenile non-sexual offenders and a group of juvenile offenders with only "non-contact" property and drug offenses on the Psychopathy Screening Device (PSD), a youth version of the PCL-R. The JSOs had higher scores than both non-sexual offender groups on the factor that corresponded to the PCL-R CU factor. Lawing, Frick, and Cruise (2010) found that JSOs with CU traits were significantly higher than low CU JSOs in the number of their sexual offense victims, the use of violence with their victims, and engagement in sexual offense planning. In the Knight and Sims-Knight etiological model for rape, the CU construct constitutes one of the three etiological paths for both juveniles and adults (Knight & Sims-Knight, 2004, 2011).

CU traits appear to be consistent over time, even in juveniles (Fontaine, Rijsdijk, McCrory, & Viding, 2010; Lynam, Caspi, Moffitt, Loeber, & Stouthamer-Loeber, 2007). They have been particularly useful in identifying a subgroup of delinquent youth who manifest severe and stable antisocial behavior (Frick & White, 2008; Kimonis & Frick, 2010; Viding & McCrory, 2012). High CU youth have been found to exhibit dysfunctions in multiple areas including social/emotional, cognitive, and biological (Frick & Viding, 2009). CU predicts later delinquency and a persistent antisocial history (Byrd, Loeber, & Pardini, 2012; Pardini, Obradovic, & Loeber, 2006). In other community samples, youth high on CU traits have been found on follow-up to exhibit the greatest number of conduct problems and psychopathology (Dadds, Fraser, Frost, & Hawes, 2005; Frick, Stickle, Dandreaux, Farrell, & Kimonis, 2005; Moran et al., 2009).

Among sex offenders, the affective facet and, particularly, assessments of lack of empathy have had a spotted history (cf. MIDSA, 2011 for a review). They neither appear to predict sexual nor general recidivism for ASOs (Hanson & Bussière, 1998) or JSOs (Långström & Grann, 2000; Worling & Långström, 2006). Whereas lack of empathy was not identified as a potential covariate of persistence into adulthood, the arrogant and deceitful personality characteristics including the Conning/Superficial Charm and Grandiosity scales did show promise of covarying with persistence of adolescent sexual offending into adulthood (Knight et al., 2009). The most effective assessment of lack of empathy in JSOs appears to be when it is assessed in reaction to the youth's own victims and not in general, but even here evidence for prediction of recidivism is lacking and current assessment tools do not sufficiently assess the multiple interacting systems that are required for an understanding and differentiation of the empathy defificiencies of JSOs (Varker, Devilly, Ward, & Beech, 2008). Consequently, for now, assessment emphasis should be placed on the interpersonal aspects of CU in assessing JSOs.

Assessment Tools

Many of the measures cited in the section on antisociality and impulsivity have scales that measure aspects of callous unemotionality. Among the clinical rating instruments that have been used with JSOs, the YLS/CMI has inflated self-esteem and inadequate guilt feelings in the Personality/Behavior domain and callous, little concern for others in the Attitudes/Orientation domain (Hoge & Andrews, 2011). In the MEGA♪, the assessment of callousness is woven into the Antisocial Aggregate (Miccio-Fonseca, 2008), with several items in the Antisocial Aggregate assessing whether the youth disregards others. The PCL:YV, like its adult counterpart, yields scores on Interpersonal and Affective facets (Forth et al., 2003). In the self-report measures, the Egotistic, Forceful, and Social Insensitivity scales of the MACI assess aspects of this construct, as do the Conning/Superficial Charm, Lack of Perspective Taking, and Lack of Empathy scales on the MIDSA. The Inventory of Callous-Unemotional Traits (ICU; Frick, 2004) has yielded reasonable reliability and concurrent, predictive, and incremental validity, and has been widely used in research, but it has not been widely used in clinical assessment, and recent factor analyses indicate that it requires scale refinement (Byrd, Kahn, & Pardini, 2013). The emergence of specific treatment strategies that appear to be differentially effective with high CU youth (Viding & McCrory, 2012; Waller, Gardner, & Hyde, 2013) make this an important trait to assess.

Aggressive and Violent Fantasies and Behavior

Supporting Research

In the risk literature with both adults and juveniles scant attention has been paid to the seriousness of violence which has been operationalized, unfortunately, in a multiplicity of ways from simply the use of physical force to the infliction of serious damage. Although Hanson and Bussière (1998) did not find in their predominantly adult meta-analysis of recidivism that physical victim injury and the use of force predicted sexual recidivism, Hanson and Morton-Bourgon (2004) found a small effect size for the degree of force used in a sexual offense. In the Massachusetts Treatment Center follow-up of ASOs, sadism and pervasive anger emerged as significant predictors for adult rapists, but not for child molesters (Knight & Thornton, 2007). Hanson and Morton-Bourgon's (2005) meta-analysis, which primarily included adult samples, found that problems with emotional regulation of mood states, of which anger is a part, were associated with sexual recidivism. Studies of adolescents using retrospective self-report have also suggested that negative emotions such as anger, frustration, sadness, and boredom may serve as immediate precursors to sex offending (Worling & Långström, 2003). Some evidence suggests that the use of threats, force or weapons may increase recidivism risk for JSOs (e.g., Epps, 1997; Kahn & Chambers, 1991; Rich, 2009), and somewhat higher recidivism rates may be found in "violent" as compared to "non-violent" juvenile samples (e.g., Rubinstein et al., 1993; Sipe et al., 1998).

Violence remains, however, a poorly defined construct in the risk literature (e.g., Knight & Prentky, 1990; Marshall & Hucker, 2006), and inconsistent results for JSOs led Worling and Långström (2006) to classify it only as a "possible" risk factor in their review of risk factors. Despite these problems, items for sexualized violence or excessive violence in sexual offenses are found in both the J-SOAP and ERASOR, and exploratory analyses suggest that if more differentiated measures are assessed, aspects of coercive and sadistic fantasies and behavior may have potential predictive potency for the persistence of juvenile sexual offending into adulthood (Knight et al., 2009). Recent work on paraphilic coercive fantasies and sadism on adult samples supports the hypothesis that there is a single dimension anchored by a lack of coercive fantasies on the lower end, running through fantasies of control and coercion, to fantasies of humiliating and frightening during sex, to purposely hurting, and ending in extreme sadism at the upper end (Knight, Sims-Knight, & Guay, 2013). This important construct has been labeled the Agonistic dimension.

Assessment Tools

As we indicated above, the J-SOAP-II has a Sexualized Aggression item in the Sexual Drive/Preoccupation Domain that attempts to rate the expressive or gratuitous violence in sexual offenses, and the ERASOR has the item: threats of, or use of, excessive violence/weapons during sexual offense. High scores on these items may indicate that this domain should be a treatment focus. Recently, there have been attempts to fashion more reliable clinical rating sadism scales (Mokros, Neumann, Schilling, & Eher, 2012), but these scales have only been applied to adults, and their clinical utility has not been established. In self-report instruments, the MSI-II has a Bondage and Discipline scale, and the MIDSA has Sadistic Fantasy and Sadistic Behavior scales and a separate Child Sexual Sadism scale. In addition, the MIDSA has pervasive anger scales that include Constantly Angry, Physically Fighting, and Fantasies of Hurting People, and also expressive aggression scales measuring non-sexual aggressive behavior and fantasies against women. Thus, the MIDSA provides a more comprehensive assessment of both sexual and non-sexual aggressive behavior and fantasies, and norms for JSOs that provide a relative placement of the youth. The fantasy and behavior sadism scales of the MIDSA have been found to predict the amount of damage done during sexual crimes for ASOs (Robertson & Knight, 2014), and the fantasy scale plays the same role in the JSO rape etiology model as it does in the ASO model (Knight & Sims-Knight, 2003). Correlative analyses of both the sexual and non-sexual aggression scales have yielded consistent results across both juvenile and adult samples (Knight & Cerce, 1999; MIDSA, 2011).

Intimacy and Friendships

Supporting Research

JSOs have been found to have fewer appropriate peer relationships (Bagley & Shewchuk-Dann, 1991; Milloy, 1994), to be more likely to be characterized as isolated and/or low in social competence (Awad & Saunders, 1991; Hunter, Figueredo, Malamuth, & Becker, 2003), and to be significantly higher than community controls in emotional loneliness (van Outsem et al., 2006). In general, JSOs who are socially isolated or who are deficient in forming emotionally intimate peer relationships are at higher risk for sexual recidivism (Worling & Långström, 2006). Inadequate social relationships have been found to contribute to recidivism for both adults and adolescents (Hanson & Bussière, 1998; Långström & Grann, 2000; Worling et al., 2012).

Assessment Tools

Although there is a general consensus among clinicians and researchers that deficits in social and interpersonal relationships are characteristic of a subset of sex offenders, particularly child molesters, there is surprisingly little evidence for the utility of any one specific metric for assessing social competence and intimacy deficits. Fortunately, there are both risk assessment and self-report measures available to meet the need of employing assessments tapping multiple sources, and these instruments have shown some validity with JSOs. The ERASOR's lack of intimate peer relationships/social isolation item has been found to correlate with sexual recidivism (Worling et al., 2012). The J-SOAP-II has a similar item, quality of peer relationships, but no comparable validity data are available for this item. Among the self-report measures, the MIDSA provides the most comprehensive assessment of peer relationships and their quality. It includes reliable measures of both friendship and romantic intimacy that locate a respondent relative to other JSOs and controls, as well as detailed descriptions of the nature of adolescents' friendships. Although the evidence supporting the validity of the intimacy scales is limited, preliminary analyses of adult social competence and intimacy data indicate reasonable reliability and concurrent validity (Martin, Sims-Knight, & Knight, 2013).

Victimization

Supporting Research

The issue of a JSO experiencing trauma and abuse occupies a unique place among the cluster of assessment domains. The presence of abuse in juveniles requires immediate clinical attention. The identification of an abusive relationship could affect dispositional decisions as well as decisions about the kind of treatment to implement. Failure to recognize trauma in a youth's life could raise barriers to the establishment of a therapeutic alliance. Consequently, victimization would need to be evaluated, even if it did not predict recidivism. Victimization and its measurement are complex, controversial issues that exceed the space that we have to justify its adequate and comprehensive assessment. Issues of the severity, the developmental timing, the duration, the relationship with the perpetrator, the number of perpetrators, and the nature of the abuse are all potentially relevant factors (Knight & Sims-Knight, 2011). Yet, most recidivism studies employ simple dichotomous or trichotomous indicators of the presence or absence of victimization. Some data support the hypothesis that more differentiated assessment of abuse variables show greater promise of predicting recidivism (Knight et al., 2009). Numerous issues require more extensive investigation, like whether particular forms of abuse covary differentially with specific outcomes, and whether the cumulative, allostatic load imposed by various types of abuse may capture predictive variance better than the individual types of abuse it comprises.

There is little dispute that sexual victimization is more prevalent among JSOs than other delinquent adolescents, and that the amount of physical abuse they experience is equivalent to other disturbed youth

(Seto & Lalumière, 2010), but data on the predictive potency of both sexual and physical abuse have been inconsistent (Worling & Långström, 2006). Among adult rapists, the level of physical abuse appears to be more related to recidivism than having experienced sexual abuse (Knight, 1999). Both sexual and physical/emotional abuse play important predictive roles in the etiological models of both juvenile offending against appropriate aged females (Knight & Sims-Knight, 2004) and their offending against children (Daversa & Knight, 2007). A growing body of research demonstrates that the age at which sexual abuse occurs (Andersen, Tomada, Vincow, Polcari, & Teicher, 2008; Grabell & Knight, 2009), the youth's relationship to the perpetrator of such abuse (Berman & Knight, 2013), and the severity of the abuse (Burton, Miller, & Shill, 2002) affect the consequences of that abuse.

Assessment Tools

Although Worling and Långström (2006) dismissed sexual victimization as a likely predictor of recidivism among JSOs, nonetheless, they listed problematic parent–adolescent relationships as a promising risk factor, and the ERASOR has items for parental rejection or poor parent offender relationships, a high stress family environment, and parents not supporting treatment. The J-SOAP has items for a sexual victimization history, caregiver inconsistency, and either a history of being physically assaulted or exposed to family violence. The J-SORRAT has items both for physical and sexual abuse of the youth. Consequently, among the major risk assessment instruments, there is a consensus that abuse, especially within the context of the family, constitutes an important risk factor, and a "2" on any of the items on the ERASOR or J-SOAP-II or a "1" or "2" on the J-SORRAT-II Items 8 or 9 should elicit therapeutic attention to that area. The MEGA♪ evaluates victimization within the youth's overall family history in its Family Lovemap aggregate, assessing multiple aspects of the youth's relationships with significant caregivers (Miccio-Fonseca, 2008).

A number of self-report and interview instruments have been generated to assess trauma. Among these are the Trauma Symptom Checklist for Children (TSCC; Briere [1996]; www.parinc.com), the Childhood Trauma Questionnaire (CTQ; Bernstein et al., 1994]; http://www.pearsonassessments.com/HAIWEB/Cultures/en-us/Productdetail.htm?Pid=015-8102-339&Mode=summary); and the Traumatic Life Events Questionnaire (TLEQ; Kubany et al., [2000]; http://www.ptsd.va.gov/professional/pages/assessments/tleq.asp). Many of the available trauma scales and questionnaires have been reviewed with examples and sources in Strand, Pasquale, and Sarmiento (2011) (http://www.ncswtraumaed.org/wp-content/uploads/2011/07/Child-and-Adolescent-Trauma-Measures_A-Review-with-Measures.pdf).

The TSCC has been widely used in child trauma research (Nader, 2004; Ohan, Myers, & Collett, 2002), and the CTQ has also been used in exploring the developmental antecedents of sexually aggressive behavior in JSOs (e.g., Brown & Burton, 2010; Burton, 2008). These instruments provide scales that are reliable and allow comparisons to community controls on generic domains of abuse. The MIDSA, in contrast, not only provides comparison to community controls and to JSOs on caregiver scales of Emotional Abuse and Acceptance-Neglect, but also because of its computerized, contingency-based questioning, it yields detailed and individualized information about the respondent's experience of sexual abuse, physical abuse, caregiver instability, and vicarious violence, providing data about the severity, duration, frequency, age of experiencing, and relationship to the perpetrator of the abuse. The report communicates these results in narrative, tables, figures, and scales. The chaotic family lives of many JSOs (Daversa & Knight, 2007; Knight & Sims-Knight, 2004) require the detailed assessment of multiple forms of abuse.

SUMMARY AND CONCLUSIONS

In our selective consideration of the assessment of treatment domains for JSOs, we have been guided by RNR principles and have focused on the criminogenic need domains that have most consistently been found to covary with recidivism – hypersexuality and sexual deviance, age and gender sexual preferences, antisocial behavior, callous-unemotionality trait, aggressive fantasies and behavior, intimacy and friendships, and victimization. In identifying assessment tools, we have concentrated on instruments that have some empirical track record with JSOs. We have attempted to evaluate each instrument's reliability and validity and its ability to locate the youth on relevant dimensions relative both to community and offender comparative groups, so as to provide the clinician with a metric for the determination of treatment needs and the prioritization of such needs. We have also attempted to include multiple methods and sources. Although there are no overall standardized clinical interviews that have been designed to assess all domains, guidelines for interviewing JSOs have been provided elsewhere (e.g., Prescott, 2007).

Our strategy of presenting for each needs domain all the instruments that have some evidence for validity for JSOs led us to identify multiple measures from which the clinical evaluator could choose. To establish a comprehensive assessment that covered all domains, a clinician could cherry-pick among various instruments in each domain to create his/her own individualized battery. In contrast, a potentially more practical strategy would be to choose a smaller number of more comprehensive instruments that assess from different perspectives all or most of the multiple domains that must be considered. Clinically assessed risk instruments like the J-SOAP-II and the ERASOR provide items for many of the domains, but they are limited in their differentiation among juveniles on each potential domain and do not provide either comparisons to controls or relative statuses among JSOs. On several of the domains, the MEGA♪ attempts to provide this greater differentiation among JSOs. The MIDSA is the only self-report inventory that measures all domains and provides both differentiation among JSOs and the relative placement of the respondent compared to community controls.

We recommend that the clinical evaluator employ both a clinical rating scheme and a self-report measure. For both it is essential that the evaluator first establish at least rapport and preferably a therapeutic alliance to maximize client cooperation. Administering the self-report assessment first, after some basic trust relationship is established, allows the results of the self-report to be used subsequently to inform the clinical interview. The results of the self-report can also be shared with the client in the development of treatment goals. Instruments like the MIDSA can be readministered to monitor therapeutic change.

REFERENCES

Abbey, A., McAuslan, P., Zawacki, T., Clinton, A., & Buck, P. (2001). Attitudinal, experiential, and situational predictors of sexual assault perpetration. *Journal of Interpersonal Violence*, *16*, 784–806.

Abel, G. G., Becker, J. V., Cunningham-Rathner, J., Mittelman, M., & Rouleau, J. -L. (1988). Multiple paraphilic diagnoses among sex offenders. *Bulletin of the American Academy of Psychiatry and the Law*, *16*, 153–168.

Abel, G. G., Huffman, J., Warberg, B., & Holland, C. L. (1998). Visual reaction time and plethysmography as measures of sexual interest in child molesters. *Sexual Abuse: A Journal of Research and Treatment*, *10*, 81–95.

Abel, G. G., Jordan, A., Rouleau, J. L., Emerick, R., Barboza-Whitehead, S., & Osborn, C. (2004). Use of visual reaction time to assess male adolescents who molest children. *Sexual Abuse: A Journal of Research and Treatment*, *16*, 255–265.

Andersen, S. L., Tomada, A., Vincow, E. S., Polcari, A., & Teicher, M. H. (2008). Preliminary evidence for sensitive periods in the effects of childhood sexual abuse on regional brain development. *Journal of Neuropsychiatry and Clinical Neuroscience*, *203*, 292–301.

Andrews, D. A., & Bonta, J. L. (2006). *The psychology of criminal conduct* (4th ed.). Cincinnati: Anderson.
Andrews, D. A., Bonta, J., & Wormith, J. S. (2011). The risk-need-responsivity (RNR) model: Does adding the good lives model contribute to effective crime prevention? *Criminal Justice and Behavior, 38*, 735–755.
Association for the Treatment of Sexual Abusers (2005). Practice Standards and guidelines for the evaluation, treatment, and management of adult male sexual abusers. Retrieved from <http://www.atsa.com/professional-issues>.
Awad, G. A., & Saunders, E. B. (1991). Male adolescent sexual assaulters: Clinical assessment of dynamic treatment targets for juveniles who sexually offend 57 observations. *Journal of Interpersonal Violence, 6*, 446–460.
Bagley, C., & Shewchuk-Dann, D. (1991). Characteristics of 60 children and adolescents who have a history of sexual assault against others: Evidence from a controlled study. *Journal of Child and Youth Care, 6*, 43–52.
Bard, L. A., Carter, D. L., Cerce, D. D., Knight, R. A., Rosenberg, R., & Schneider, B. (1987). A descriptive study of rapists and child molesters: Developmental, clinical, and criminal characteristics. *Behavioral Sciences and the Law, 5*, 203–220.
Bard, L. A., & Knight, R. A. (1987). Sex offender subtypes and the MCMI. In C. Green (Ed.), *Conference on the millon inventories (MCMI, MBHI, MAPI)*. Minneapolis: National Computer Systems, pp. 133-137.
Barry, C. T., Frick, P. J., DeShazo, T. M., McCoy, M. G., Ellis, M., & Loney, B. R. (2000). The importance of callous-unemotional traits for extending the concept of psychopathy to children. *Journal of Abnormal Psychology, 109*, 335–340.
Baum, L. J., Archer, R. P., Forbey, J. D., & Handel, R. W. (2009). A review of the Minnesota multiphasic personality inventory–adolescent (MMPI-A) and the Millon adolescent clinical inventory (MACI) with an emphasis on juvenile justice samples. *Assessment, 16*, 384–400.
Beckett, R., Brown, S., & Gerhold, D. (1997). *The adolescent sex offender assessment pack*. Oxford: Oxford Forensic Psychology Service.
Beech, A. R., Kalmus, E., Tipper, S. P., Baudouin, J., Flak, V., & Humphreys, G. W. (2008). Children induce an enhanced attentional blink in child molesters. *Psychological Assessment, 20*, 397–402.
Berman, A. K., & Knight, R. A. (2013). *The relation of familiarity with sexual abusers to subsequent adaptation in youth who have sexually offended*. Manuscript submitted for publication.
Bernstein, D. P., Fink, L., Handelsman, L., et al. (1994). Initial reliability and validity of a new retrospective measure of child abuse and neglect. *American Journal of Psychiatry, 151*, 1132–1136.
Blair, R. J. R. (1999). Responsiveness to distress cues in the child with psychopathic tendencies. *Personality and Individual Differences, 27*, 135–145.
Blanchard, R., Christensen, B. K., Strong, S. M., Cantor, J. M., Kuban, M. E., & Klassen, P., (2002). Retrospective self-reports of childhood accidents causing unconsciousness in phallometrically diagnosed pedophiles. *Archives of Sexual Behavior, 31*, 511–526.
Blanchard, R., Klassen, P., Dickey, R., Kuban, M. E., & Blak, T. (2001). Sensitivity and specificity of the phallometric test for pedophilia nonadmitting sex offenders. *Psychological Assessment, 13*, 118–126.
Blanchard, R., Kuban, M. E., Klassen, P., Dickey, R., Christensen, B. K., & Cantor, J. M., (2003). Self-reported head injuries before and after age 13 in pedophilic and nonpedophilic men referred for clinical assessment. *Archives of Sexual Behavior, 32*, 573–581.
Bogaert, A. F. (2001). Handedness, criminality, and sexual offending. *Neuropsychologia, 39*, 465–469.
Briere, J. (1996). Trauma symptom checklist for children (TSCC): *Professional Manual*. Florida: Psychological Assessment Resources.

Brown, A., & Burton, D. L. (2010). Exploring the overlap in male juvenile sexual offending and general delinquency: Trauma, alcohol use, and masculine beliefs. *Journal of Child Sexual Abuse*, *19*, 450–468.

Burton, D. L. (2008). An exploratory evaluation of the contribution of personality and childhood sexual. *Sexual Abuse: A Journal of Research and Treatment*, *20*, 102–115.

Burton, D. L., Miller, D. L., & Shill, C. T. (2002). A social learning theory comparison of the sexual victimization of adolescent sexual offenders and nonsexual offending male delinquents. *Child Abuse & Neglect*, *26*, 893–907.

Butcher, J. N., Williams, C. L., Graham, J. R., Archer, R. P., Tellegen, A., Ben-Porath, Y. S. et al. (1992). *Minnesota multiphasic personality inventory-adolescent (MMPI-A): Manual*. San Antonio: Pearson.

Butz, C., & Spaccarelli, S. (1999). Use of physical force as an offense characteristic in subtyping juvenile sexual offenders. *Sexual Abuse: A Journal of Research and Treatment*, *11*, 212–232.

Byrd, A. L., Kahn, R. E., & Pardini, D. A. (2013). A validation of the Inventory of Callous-Unemotional Traits in a community sample of young adult males. *Journal of Psychopathology and Behavioral Assessment*, *35*, 20–34.

Byrd, A. L., Loeber, R., & Pardini, D. A. (2012). Understanding desisting and persisting forms of delinquency: The unique contributions of disruptive behavior disorders and interpersonal callousness. *Journal of Child Psychology and Psychiatry*, *53*, 371–380.

Caldwell, M. F. (2002). What we do not know about juvenile sexual reoffense risk. *Child Maltreatment*, 7, 291–302.

Caldwell, M. F. (2007). Sexual offense adjudication and sexual recidivism among juvenile offenders. *Sexual Abuse: A Journal of Research and Treatment*, *19*, 107–113.

Caldwell, M. F. (2013). Accuracy of sexually violent person assessments of juveniles adjudicated for sexual offenses. *Sexual Abuse: A Journal of Research and Treatment*, *25*, 516–526.

Caldwell, M. F., Ziemke, M. H., & Vitacco, M. J. (2008). An examination of the Sex Offender Registration and Notification Act as applied to juveniles: Evaluating the ability to predict sexual recidivism. *Psychology, Public Policy, and Law*, *14*, 89–114.

Camp, J. P., Skeem, J. L., Barchard, K., & Lilienfeld, S. O. (2013). Psychopathic predators? Getting specific about the relation between psychopathy and violence. *Journal of Consulting and Clinical Psychology*, *81*, 467–480.

Cantor, J. M., Blanchard, R., Christensen, B. K., Dickey, R., Klassen, P. E., & Beckstead, A. L., (2004). Intelligence, memory, and handedness in pedophilia. *Neuropsychology*, *18*, 3–14.

Cantor, J. M., Blanchard, R., Robichaud, L. K., & Christensen, B. K. (2005). Quantitative reanalysis of aggregate data on IQ in sexual offenders. *Psychological Bulletin*, *131*, 555–568.

Cantor, J. M., Klassen, P. E., Dickey, R., Christensen, B. K., Kuban, M. E., & Blak, T., (2005). Handedness in pedophilia and hebephilia. *Archives of Sexual Behavior*, *34*, 447–459.

Caputo, A. A., Frick, P. J., & Brodsky, S. L. (1999). Family violence and juvenile sex offending: The potential mediating role of psychopathic traits and negative attitudes toward women. *Criminal Justice and Behavior*, *26*, 338–356.

Carnes, P. J. (1991). Sexual addiction screening test. *Tennessee Nurse*, *54*, 29.

Carnes, P. J., & Wilson, M. (2002). The sexual addiction assessment process. In P. J. Carnes & K. M. Adams (Eds.), *Clinical management of sex addiction* (pp. 3–20). New York: Brunner-Routledge.

Cauffman, E., Kimonis, E. R., Dmitrieva, J., & Monahan, K. C. (2009). A multimethod assessment of juvenile psychopathy: Comparing the predictive utility of the PCL:YV, YPI, and NEO PRI. *Psychological Assessment*, *21*, 528–542.

Christie, M. M., Marshall, W. L., & Lanthier, R. D. (1979). *A descriptive study of incarcerated rapists and pedophiles*. Report to the Solicitor General of Canada.

Clark, M., & Grier, P. E. (1995). Using the Multiphasic Sex Inventory with child molesters. *Psychological Reports*, 77, 623–625.

Coleman, E., Miner, M., Ohlerking, F., & Raymond, N. (2001). Compulsive Sexual Behavior Inventory: A preliminary study of reliability and validity. *Journal of Sex and Marital Therapy*, *27*, 325–332.

Coxe, R., & Holmes, W. (2009). A comparative study of two groups of sex offenders identified as high and low risk on the Static-99. *Journal of Child Sexual Abuse*, *18*, 137–153.

Crooks, V. L., Rostill-Brookes, H., Beech, A. R., & Bickley, J. A. (2009). Applying rapid serial visual presentation to adolescent sexual offenders: Attentional bias as a measure of deviant sexual interest? *Sexual Abuse: A Journal of Research and Treatment*, *21*, 135–148.

Dadds, M. R., Fraser, J., Frost, A., & Hawes, D. J. (2005). Disentangling the underlying dimensions of psychopathy and conduct problems in childhood: A community study. *Journal of Consulting and Clinical Psychology*, *73*, 400–410.

Daversa, M. T., & Knight, R. A. (2007). Generating a model for sexual coercion against children in adolescent sexual offenders. *Criminal Justice and Behavior*, *34*, 1313–1333.

Day, D. M., Miner, M. H., Sturgeon, V. H., & Murphy, J. (1989). Assessment of sexual arousal by means of physiological and self-report measures. In D. R. Laws (Ed.), *Relapse prevention with sex offenders* (pp. 115–123). New York: Guilford Press.

Dishion, T. J., Nelson, S. E., & Yasui, M. (2005). Predicting early adolescent gang involvement from middle school adaptation. *Journal of Clinical Child and Adolescent Psychology*, *34*, 62–73.

Dodge, B., Reece, M., Hebernick, D., Fisher, C., Satinsky, S., & Stupiansky, N. (2008). Relations between sexually transmitted infection diagnosis and sexual compulsivity in a community-based sample of men who have sex with men. *Sexually Transmitted Infections*, *84*, 324–327.

Eckenrode, J., Izzo, C. V., & Smith, E. G. (2007). Physical abuse and adolescent development. In R. Haskins, F. Wulczyn, & M. B. Webb (Eds.), *Practical knowledge for child welfare practitioners: Findings from the National Survey of Child and Adolescent Well-being* (pp. 226–242). Washington, DC: Brookings Institute.

Epperson, D. L., Ralston, C. A., Fowers, D., DeWitt, J., & Gore, K. S. (2006). Actuarial risk assessment with juveniles. In D. Prescott (Ed.), *Risk assessment of youth who have sexually abused: theory, controversy, and emerging strategies* (pp. 118–169). Oklahoma City, OK: Wood & Barnes.

Epps, K. J. (1997). Managing risk. In M. S. Hoghughi, S. R. Bhate, & F. Graham (Eds.), *Working with sexually abusive adolescents* (pp. 35–51). London: Sage.

Fischer, L., & Smith, G. (1999). Statistical adequacy of the Abel Assessment for Interest in Paraphilias. *Sexual Abuse: A Journal of Research and Treatment*, *11*, 195–205.

Fontaine, N. M. G., Rijsdijk, F. V., McCrory, E. J. P., & Viding, E. (2010). Etiology of different developmental trajectories of callous-unemotional traits. *Journal of the American Academy of Child and Adolescent Psychiatry*, *49*, 656–664.

Forth, A. E., Kosson, D. S., & Hare, R. D. (2003). *The psychopathy checklist: Youth version.* Toronto, Ontario, Canada: Multi-Health Systems.

Freeman, K. A., Dexter-Mazza, E. T., & Hoffman, K. C. (2005a). Comparing personality characteristics of juvenile sex offenders and non-sex offending delinquent peers: A preliminary investigation. *Sexual Abuse: A Journal of Research and Treatment*, *17*, 3–12.

Freeman, K. A., Dexter-Mazza, E. T., & Hoffman, K. C. (2005b). Erratum. *Sexual abuse: A Journal of Research and Treatment*, *17*, 353–354.

Frick, P. J. (1998). Callous-unemotional traits and conduct problems: A two-factor model of psychopathy in children. In D. J. Cooke, R. D. Hare, & A. Forth (Eds.), *Psychopathy: Theory, research, and implications for society* (pp. 47–51). Cordresch, The Netherlands: Kluwer Press.

Frick, P. J. (2004). The inventory of callous-unemotional traits. Unpublished rating scale: University of New Orleans.

Frick, P. J., Bodin, S. D., & Barry, C. T. (2000). Psychopathic traits and conduct problems in a community sample and clinic-referred samples of children: Further development of the psychopathy screening device. *Psychological Assessment, 12*, 382–393.

Frick, P. J., Lilienfeld, S. O., Ellis, M., Loney, B. R., & Silverthorn, P. (1999). The association between anxiety and psychopathy dimensions in children. *Journal of Abnormal Child Psychology, 27*, 383–392.

Frick, P. J., & Marsee, M. A. (2006). Psychopathy and developmental pathways to antisocial behavior in youth. In C. J. Patrick (Ed.), *Handbook of psychopathy* (pp. 353–374). New York: Guilford Press.

Frick, P. J., O'Brien, B. S., Wootton, J. M., & McBurnett, K. (1994). Psychopathy and conduct problems in children. *Journal of Abnormal Psychology, 103*, 700–707.

Frick, P. J., Stickle, T. R., Dandreaux, D. M., Farrell, J. M., & Kimonis, E. R. (2005). Callous-unemotional traits in predicting the severity and stability of conduct problems and delinquency. *Journal of Abnormal Child Psychology, 33*, 471–487.

Frick, P. J., & Viding, E. (2009). Antisocial behavior from a developmental psychopathology perspective. *Development and Psychopathology, 21*, 1111–1131.

Frick, P. J., & White, S. F. (2008). Research review: The importance of callous-unemotional traits for developmental models of aggressive and antisocial behavior. *Journal of Child Psychology and Psychiatry, 49*, 359–375.

Glasgow, D. V. (2009). Affinity: The development of a self-report assessment of paedophile sexual interest incorporating a viewing time validity measure. In D. Thornton & D. R. Laws (Eds.), *Cognitive approaches to the assessment of sexual interest in sexual offenders*. New York: John Wiley & Sons, Ltd.

Glasgow, D. V., Osbourne, A., & Croxen, J. (2003). An assessment tool for investigating paedophile sexual interest using viewing time: An application of single case research methodology. *British Journal of Learning Disabilities, 31*, 96–102.

Grabell, A., & Knight, R. A. (2009). Examining childhood abuse patterns and critical periods in juvenile sexual offenders. *Sexual Abuse: Journal of Research and Treatment, 21*, 208–222.

Graham, F. J., & Knight, R. A. (2013). *The Role of Psychopathy and Intelligence in Mediating the Relation Between Early Abuse and Subsequent Violence in Adolescence*. Poster presented at the fifth biennial meeting of the Society for the Scientific Study of Psychopathy, Washington, DC.

Gretton, H. M., McBride, M., Hare, R. D., O'Shaughnessy, R., & Kumka, G. (2001). Psychopathy and recidivism in adolescent sex offenders. *Criminal Justice and Behavior, 28*, 427–449.

Gribble, J. N., Miller, H. G., Rogers, S. M., & Turner, C. F. (1999). Interview mode and measurement of sexual behaviors: Methodological issues. *Journal of Sex Research, 36*, 16–24.

Grove, W. M., & Tellegen, A. (1991). Problems in the classification of personality disorders. *Journal of Personality Disorders, 5*, 31–42.

Hanson, R. K., Bourgon, G., Helmus, L., & Hodgson, S. (2009). The principles of effective correctional treatment also apply to sexual offenders: A meta-analysis. *Criminal Justice and Behavior, 36*, 865–891.

Hanson, R. K., & Bussière, M. T. (1998). Predicting relapse: A meta-analysis of sexual offender recidivism studies. *Journal of Consulting and Clinical Psychology, 66*, 348–362.

Hanson, R. K., & Morton-Bourgon, K. E. (2004). *Predictors of sexual recidivism: An updated meta-analysis*. User report 2004-02. Ottawa: Public Safety and Emergency Preparedness Canada.

Hanson, R. K., & Morton-Bourgon, K. E. (2005). The characteristics of persistent sexual offenders: A meta-analysis of recidivism studies. *Journal of Consulting and Clinical Psychology, 73*, 1154–1163.

Hare, R. D. (2003). *The psychopathy checklist-revised technical manual* (2nd ed.). Toronto, Canada: Multi-Health Systems.

Harris, D. A., Knight, R. A., Smallbone, S., & Dennison, S. (2011). Post-release specialization and versatility in sexual offenders referred for civil commitment. *Sexual Abuse: Journal of Research and Treatment, 23*, 243–259.

Harris, P. W., & Jones, P. R. (1999). Differentiating delinquent youths for program planning and evaluation. *Criminal Justice and Behavior, 26*, 403–434.

Hempel, I., Buck, N., Cima, M., & van Marle, H. (2013). Review of risk assessment instruments for juvenile sex offenders: What is next? *International Journal of Offender Therapy and Comparative Criminology, 57*, 208–228.

Hindman, J., & Peters, J. M. (2001). Polygraph testing leads to better understanding adult and juvenile sex offenders. *Federal Probation, 65*, 8–15.

Hoge, R. D. (2005). Youth level of services/case management inventory. In T. Grisso, G. Vincent, & D. Seagrave (Eds.), *Mental health screening and assessment in juvenile justice* (pp. 283–294). New York: Guilford Press.

Hoge, R. D., & Andrews, D. A. (2011). *Youth level of service/case management inventory 2.0 (YLS/CMI 2.0): User's manual.* Toronto: Multi-Health Systems.

Holland, L. A., Zolondek, S. C., Abel, G. G., Jordan, A. D., & Becker, J. V. (2000). Psychometric analysis of the sexual interest cardsort questionnaire. *Sexual Abuse: A Journal of Research and Treatment, 12*, 107–122.

Hunter, J. A., Figueredo, A. J., Malamuth, N. M., & Becker, J. V. (2004). Developmental pathways in youth sexual aggression and delinquency: Risk factors and mediators. *Journal of Family Violence, 19*, 233–242.

Hunter, J. A., Figueredo, A. J., Malamuth, N. M., & Becker, J. V. (2003). Juvenile sex offenders: Toward the development of a typology. *Sexual Abuse: A Journal of Research and Treatment, 15*, 27–48.

Janssen, E., Goodrich, D., Petrocelli, J. V., & Bancroft, J. (2009). Psychophysiological response patterns and risky sexual behaviour in heterosexual and homosexual men. *Archives of Sexual Behavior, 38*, 538–550.

Jesness, C. F. (1983). *The jesness inventory (Rev. ed.).* Palo Alto: Consulting Psychologists Press.

Jesness, C. F. (1986). Validity of jesness inventory classification with nondelinquents. *Educational and Psychological Measurement, 46*, 947–961.

Jesness, C. F. (1988). The jesness inventory classification system. *Criminal Justice and Behavior, 15*, 78–91.

Jesness, C. F. (1996). *The jesness inventory manual.* North Tonawanda: Multi-Health Systems.

Jesness, C. F., & Wedge, R. F. (1985). *Jesness inventory classification system: Supplementary manual.* Palo Alto: Consulting Psychologists Press.

Kafka, M. P. (1997). Hypersexual desire in males: An operational definition and clinical implications for males with paraphilias and paraphilia-related disorders. *Archives of Sexual Behavior, 26*, 505–526.

Kafka, M. P. (2003). Sex offending and sexual appetite: The clinical and theoretical relevance of hypersexual desire. *International Journal of Offender Therapy & Comparative Criminology, 47*, 439–451.

Kahn, T. J., & Chambers, H. J. (1991). Assessing reoffense risk with juvenile sexual offenders. *Child Welfare, 70*, 333–345.

Kalichman, S. C., & Cain, D. (2004). The relationship between indicators of sexual compulsivity and high-risk sexual practices among men and women receiving services from a sexually transmitted infection clinic. *Journal of Sex Research, 41*, 235–241.

Kalichman, S. C., Henderson, M. C., Shealy, L. S., & Dwyer, M. (1992). Psychometric properties of the multiphasic sex inventory in assessing sex offenders. *Criminal Justice and Behavior, 19*, 384–396.

Kalichman, S. C., & Rompa, D. (1995). Sexual sensation seeking and sexual compulsivity scales: Reliability, validity, and HIV prevention services. *Health Psychology, 16*, 369–373.

Kalichman, S. C., & Rompa, D. (2001). The sexual compulsivity scale: Further development and use with HIV positive persons. *Journal of Personality Assessment, 76*, 379–395.

Kalmus, E., & Beech, A. R. (2005). Forensic assessment of sexual interest: A review. *Aggression and Violent Behavior, 10*, 193–217.

Kennedy, W. A., Licht, M. H., & Caminez, M. (2004). False positives among adolescent sex offenders: Concurrent and predictive validity of the Millon Adolescent Clinical Inventory. *Journal of Offender Rehabilitation, 39*, 1–13.

Kenny, D. T., Keogh, T., & Seidler, K. (2001). Predictors of recidivism in Australian juvenile sex offenders: Implications for treatment. *Sexual Abuse: A Journal of Research and Treatment, 13*, 131–148.

Kenrick, D.T., & Funder, D. C. (1988). Profiting from controversy: Lessons from the person-situation debate. *American Psychologist, 43*, 23–24.

Kimonis, E. R., & Frick, P. J. (2010). Oppositional defiant disorder and conduct disorder grown-up. *Journal of Developmental and Behavioral Pediatrics, 31*, 244–254.

Kimonis, E. R., Frick, P. J., Boris, N. W., et al. (2006). Callous-unemotional features, behavioral inhibition, and parenting: Independent predictors of aggression in a high-risk preschool sample. *Journal of Child and Family Studies, 15*, 745–756.

Kjellgren, C., Priebe, G., Svedin, C. G., & Långström, N. (2010). Sexually coercive behavior in male youth: Population survey of general and specific risk factors. *Archives of Sexual Behavior, 39*, 1161–1169.

Knight, R. A. (1999). Validation of a typology for rapists. *Journal of Interpersonal Violence, 14*, 297–323.

Knight, R. A. (2004). Comparisons between juvenile and adult sexual offenders on the multidimensional assessment of sex and aggression. In G. O. Reilly, W. L. Marshall, R. Beckett, & A. Carr (Eds.), *Handbook of clinical interventions with young people who sexually abuse* (pp. 203–233). London: Routledge.

Knight, R.A. (2010). Typologies for rapists: The generation of a new structural model. In A. (2010). Schlank (Ed.), *The sexual predator* (Vol 4, pp. 17-1–17-28). NY: Civic Research Institute.

Knight, R. A., & Cerce, D. D. (1999). Validation and revision of the multidimensional assessment of sex and aggression. *Psychologica Belgica, 39-2/3*, 187–213.

Knight, R. A., & Guay, J. P. (2006). The role of psychopathy in sexual offenders against women. In C. J. Patrick (Ed.), *Handbook of psychopathy* (pp. 512–532). New York: The Guilford Press.

Knight, R. A., & King, M. W. (2012). Typologies for child molesters: The generation of a new structural model. In B. K. (2012). Schwartz (Ed.), *The sexual offender* (Vol. 7). Kingston: Civic Research Institute, Inc.

Knight, R. A., & Prentky, R. A. (1990). Classifying sexual offenders: The development and corroboration of taxonomic models. In W. L. Marshall, D. R. Laws, & H. E. Barbaree (Eds.), *The handbook of sexual assault: Issues, theories, and treatment of the offender* (pp. 23–52). New York: Plenum Press.

Knight, R. A., & Prentky, R. A. (1993). Exploring the characteristics for classifying juvenile sexual offenders. In H. E. Barbaree, W. L. Marshall, & S. M. Hudson (Eds.), *The juvenile sex offender* (pp. 45–83). New York: Guilford Press.

Knight, R.A., Ronis, S.T., & Zakireh, B. (2009). Bootstrapping persistence risk indicators for juveniles who sexually offend. *Behavioral Sciences and the Law, 27*, 878–909.

Knight, R. A., Rosenberg, R., & Schneider, B. (1985). Classification of sexual offenders: Perspectives, methods, and validation. In A. W. Burgess (Ed.), *Research handbook on rape and sexual assault* (pp. 222–293). New York: Garland Publishing Inc.

Knight, R. A., & Sims-Knight, J. E. (2003). Developmental antecedents of sexual coercion against women: Testing of alternative hypotheses with structural equation modeling. In R. A. Prentky, E. S. Janus, & M. C. Seto (Eds.), *Sexually coercive behavior: Understanding and management* (Vol. 989, pp. 72–85). New York: Annals of the New York Academy of Sciences.

Knight, R. A., & Sims-Knight, J. E. (2004). Testing an etiological model for male juvenile sexual offending against females. *Journal of Child Sexual Abuse, 13*, 33–55.

Knight, R. A., & Sims-Knight, J. E. (2011). Risk factors for sexual violence. In J. W. White, M. P. Koss, & A. E. Kazdin (Eds.), *Violence against women and children, Volume 1: Mapping the terrain* (pp. 125–172). Washington, DC: American Psychological Association.

Knight, R. A., Sims-Knight, J. E., & Guay, J. -P. (2013). Is a separate disorder category defensible for paraphilic coercion? *Journal of Criminal Justice, 41*, 90–99.

Knight, R. A., & Thornton, D. (2007). *Evaluating and improving risk assessment schemes for sexual recidivism: A long-term follow-up of convicted sexual offenders.* Final report, NCJ 217618, http://nij.ncjrs.gov/publications.

Koss, M. P., & Dinero, T. E. (1988). Predictors of sexual aggression among a national sample of male college students. In R. A. Prentky & V. L. Quinsey (Eds.), *Human sexual aggression: Current perspectives* (pp. 133–147). New York: The New York Academy of Sciences.

Kosson, D. S., Cyterski, T. D., Steuerwald, B. L., Neumann, C. S., & Walker-Matthews, S. (2002). Reliability and validity of the PCL:YV in non-incarcerated adolescent males. *Psychological Assessment, 14*, 97–109.

Kubany, E. S., Leisen, M. B., Kaplan, A. S., Watson, S. B., Haynes, S. N., Owens, J. A., et al. (2000). Development and preliminary validation of a brief broad-sprectrum measure of traumaexposure: The traumatic life events questionnaire. *Psychological Assessment, 12*, 210–224.

Lalumière, M. L., Quinsey, V. L., Harris, G. T., Rice, M. E., & Trautrimas, C. (2003). Are rapists differentially aroused by coercive sex in phallometric assessments?. In R. A. Prentky, E. Janus, & M. Seto (Eds.), *Sexual coercion: Understanding and management* (pp. 211–224). New York: New York Academy of Sciences.

Långström, N. (2002). Long-term follow-up of criminal recidivism in young sex offenders: Temporal patterns and risk factors. *Psychology, Crime & Law, 8*, 41–58.

Långström, N., & Grann, M. (2000). Risk for criminal recidivism among young sex offenders. *Journal of Interpersonal Violence, 15*, 855–871.

Långström, N., & Hanson, R. K. (2006). High rates of sexual behavior in the general population: Correlates and predictors. *Archives of Sexual Behavior, 35*, 37–52.

Lawing, K., Frick, P. J., & Cruise, K. R. (2010). Differences in offending patterns between adolescent sex offenders high or low in callous–unemotional traits. *Psychological Assessment, 22*, 298–305.

Laws, D. R., Hanson, R. K., Osborn, C. A., & Greenbaum, P. E. (2000). Classification of child molesters by plethysmographic assessment of sexual arousal and a self-report measure of sexual preference. *Journal of Interpersonal Violence, 15*, 1297–1312.

Listwan, S. J., Van Voorhis, P., & Ritchey, P. N. (2007). Personality, criminal behavior, and risk assessment: Implications for theory and practice. *Criminal Justice and Behavior, 34*, 60–75.

Loney, B. R., Frick, P. J., Clements, C. B., Ellis, M. L., & Kerlin, K. (2003). Callous-unemotional traits, impulsivity, and emotional processing in antisocial adolescents. *Journal of Clinical Child and Adolescent Psychology, 32*, 66–80.

Looman, J., Abracen, J., Maillet, G., & DiFazio, R. (1998). Phallometric nonresponding in sexual offenders. *Sexual Abuse: A Journal of Research and Treatment, 10*, 325–336.

Losada-Paisey, G. (1998). Use of the MMPI-A to assess personality of juvenile male delinquents who are sex offenders and nonsex offenders. *Psychological Reports, 83*, 115–122.

Lynam, D. R., Caspi, A., Moffitt, T. E., Loeber, R., & Stouthamer-Loeber, M. (2007). Longitudinal evidence that psychopathy scores in early adolescence predict adult psychopathy. *Journal of Abnormal Psychology, 116*, 155–165.

Mackaronis, J. E., Strassberg, D. S., & Marcus, D. K. (2011). The latent structure of multiphasic sex inventory-assessed pedophilic interest. *Psychological Assessment, 23*, 1017–1022.

Malamuth, N. M., Sockloskie, R. J., Koss, M. P., & Tanaka, J. S. (1991). Characteristics of aggressors against women: Testing a model using a national sample of college students. *Journal of Consulting and Clinical Psychology*, *59*, 670–681.

Marshall, W. L., & Fernandez, Y. M. (2000). Phallometric testing with sexual offenders: Limits to its value. *Clinical Psychology Review*, *20*, 807–822.

Marshall, W. L., & Fernandez, Y. M. (2003). Sexual preferences are they useful in the assessment and treatment of sexual offenders? *Aggression and Violent behavior*, *8*, 131–143.

Marshall, W. L., & Hucker, S. J. (2006). Issues in the diagnosis of sexual sadism. *Sexual Offender Treatment*, *1*, 1–4.

Martin, G., Sims-Knight, J. E., & Knight, R.A. (2013). *Sex offenders' interpersonal functioning: Intimacy dispositions and social competence*. Manuscript submitted for publication.

Martinez, R., Flores, J., & Rosenfeld, B. (2007). Validity of the juvenile sex offender assessment protocol-II (J-Soap-II) in a sample of urban minority youth. *Criminal Justice and Behavior*, *34*, 1284–1295.

McCann, K., & Lussier, P. (2008). Antisociality, sexual deviance, and sexual reoffending in juvenile sex offenders: A meta-analytical investigation. *Youth Violence and Juvenile Justice*, *6*, 363–385.

Meehl, P. E. (1959). Some ruminations on the validation of clinical procedures. *Canadian Journal of Psychology*, *13*, 102–128.

Miccio-Fonseca, L. C. (2008). *MEGA♪: Multiples empirically guided inventory of ecological aggregates for assessing sexually abusive adolescents and children (ages 19 and under)*, manual and rating booklet. Available from the author (lcmf@cox.net).

Miccio-Fonseca, L. C. (2009). MEGA♪: A new paradigm in protocol assessing sexually abusive children and adolescents. *Journal of Child & Adolescent Trauma*, *2*, 124–141.

Miccio-Fonseca, L. C. (2013). MEGA♪-An ecological risk assessment tool for sexually abusive adolescents and children (ages 4 to 19). Paper presented at the 28th national adolescent perpetration network conference, Portland, OR.

Miccio-Fonseca, L. C., & Rasmussen, L. A. (2009a). Advancement in risk assessment of sexually abusive youth: Applicability of MEGA♪ to low intellectual functioning youth. *Journal of Child & Adolescent Trauma*, *2*, 161–178.

Miccio-Fonseca, L. C., & Rasmussen, L. A. (2009b). New nomenclature for sexually abusive youth: Naming and assessing sexually violent and predatory offenders. *Journal of Aggression, Maltreatment & Trauma*, *18*, 106–128.

MIDSA clinical manual. (2011). *Bend: Augur Enterprises, Inc.* Available at http://www.midsa.us.

Millon, T. (1993). *Millon adolescent clinical inventory: Manual*. Minneapolis, MN: National Computer Systems.

Milloy, C. D. (1994). *A comparative study of juvenile sex offenders and non-sex offenders*. Washington State Institute for Public Policy.

Miner, M. H. (2002). Factors associated with recidivism of juveniles: An analysis of serious juvenile sex offenders. *Journal of Research on Crime and Delinquency*, *39*, 421–436.

Miner, M. H., Coleman, E., Center, B. A., Ross, M., & Rosser, B. R. S. (2007). The compulsive sexual behavior inventory: Psychometric properties. *Archives of Sexual Behavior*, *36*, 579–587.

Mokros, A., Schilling, F., Eher, R., & Nitschke, J. (2012). The severe sexual sadism scale: Cross-validation and scale properties. *Psychological Assessment*, *24*, 764–769.

Moran, P., Rowe, R., Flach, C., Briskman, J., Ford, T., Maughan, B., et al. (2009). Predictive value of callous-unemotional traits in a large community sample. *Journal of the American Academy of Child and Adolescent Psychiatry*, *48*, 1079–1085.

Murrie, D. C., & Cornell, D. G. (2000). The Millon adolescent clinical inventory and psychopathy. *Journal of Personality Assessment*, *75*, 110–125.

Nader, K. O. (2004). Assessing traumatic experiences in children and adolescents: Self-reports of DSM PTSD criteria B-D symptoms. In J. Wilson & T. Keane (Eds.), *Assessing psychological trauma and PTSD* (pp. 513–537) (2nd ed.). New York: Guilford Press.

Nichols, H. & Molinder, I. (1989). *Multiphasic sex inventory-II manual*. Available from Nichols and Molinder at http://www.nicholsandmolinder.com.
Ohan, J. L., Myers, K., & Collett, B. R. (2002). Ten-year review of rating scales. IV: Scales assessing trauma and its effects. *Journal of the American Academy of Child & Adolescent Psychiatry*, *41*, 1401–1422.
Oliver, L. L., Hall, G. C. N., & Neuhaus, S. M. (1993). A comparison of the personality and background characteristics of adolescent sex offenders and other adolescent offenders. *Criminal Justice and Behavior*, *20*, 359–370.
Olver, M. E., Stockdale, K. C., & Wormith, J. S. (2009). Risk assessment with young offenders: A meta-analysis of three assessment measures. *Criminal Justice and Behavior*, *36*(4), 329–353.
Onifade, E., Davidson, W., Campbell, C., Turke, G., Malinowski, J., & Turner, K. (2008). Predicting recidivism in probationers with the Youth Level of Service Case Management Inventory (YLS/CMI). *Criminal Justice and Behavior*, *35*, 474–483.
Oxnam, P., & Vess, J. (2008). A typology of adolescent sexual offenders: Millon adolescent clinical inventory profiles, developmental factors, and offence characteristics. *Journal of Forensic Psychiatry & Psychology*, *19*, 228–242.
Paitich, D., Langevin, R., Freeman, R., Mann, K., & Handy, L. (1977). The clarke SHQ: A clinical sex history questionnaire for males. *Archives of Sexual Behavior*, *6*, 421–435.
Pardini, D., Obradovic, J., & Loeber, R. (2006). Interpersonal callousness, hyperactivity/impulsivity, inattention, and conduct problems as precursors to delinquency persistence in boys: A comparison of three grade-based cohorts. *Journal of Clinical Child and Adolescent Psychology*, *35*, 46–59.
Parent, G., Guay, J. P., & Knight, R. A. (2011). An assessment of long-term risk of recidivism by adult sex offenders: One size doesn't fit all. *Criminal Justice and Behavior*, *38*, 188–209.
Parks, G. A., & Bard, D. E. (2006). Risk factors for adolescent sex offender recidivism: Evaluation of predictive factors and comparison of three groups based upon victim type. *Sexual Abuse: A Journal of Research and Treatment*, *18*, 319–342.
Parsons, J. T., Kelly, B. C., & Bimbi, D. S. (2008). Explanations for the origin of sexual compulsivity among gay and bisexual men. *Archives of Sexual Behavior*, *37*, 817–826.
Poston, J. M., & Hanson, W. E. (2010). Meta-analysis of psychological assessment as a therapeutic intervention. *Psychological Assessment*, *22*, 203–212.
Prentky, R., & Edmunds, S. B. (1997). *Assessing sexual abuse: A resource guide for practitioners*. Brandon, VT: The Safer Society Press.
Prentky, R. A. (2006). *Risk management of sexually abusive youth: A follow-up study*. Final report, 2002-IJ-Cx 0029, http://nij.ncjrs.gov/publications.
Prentky, R. A., & Knight, R. A. (1991). Identifying critical dimensions for discriminating among rapists. *Journal of Consulting and Clinical Psychology*, *59*, 643–661.
Prentky, R. A., Knight, R. A., Lee, A. F. S., & Cerce, D. D. (1995). Predictive validity of lifestyle impulsivity for rapists. *Criminal Justice and Behavior*, *22*, 106–128.
Prentky, R. A. & Righthand, S. (2003). *Juvenile sex offender assessment protocol – II manual (JSOAP–II)*. Available from Center for Sex Offender Management at http://ww.csom.org.
Prescott, D. S. (2007). *Assessing youth who have sexually abused: A primer*. Holyoke: NEARI Press.
Quinsey, V. L., & Chaplin, T. C. (1982). Penile responses to nonsexual violence among rapists. *Criminal Justice and Behavior*, *9*, 372–384.
Ramrakha, S., Bell, M. L., Paul, C., Dickson, N., Moffitt, T. E., & Caspi, A. (2007). Childhood behavior problems linked to sexual risk taking in young adulthood: A birth cohort study. *Journal of the American Academy of Child & Adolescent Psychiatry*, *46*, 1272–1279.
Rasmussen, L. A. (1999). Factors related to recidivism among juvenile sexual offenders. *Sexual Abuse: A Journal of Research and Treatment*, *11*, 69–85.
Ray, J.V., Hall, J., Rivera-Hudson, N., Poythress, N. G., & Lilienfeld, S. O. (2013). The relation between self-reported psychopathic traits and distorted response styles: A meta-analytic review. *Personality Disorders: Theory, Research, and Treatment*, *4*, 1–14.

Reid, R. C., Carpenter, B. N., Hook, J. N., et al. (2012). Report of findings in a DSM-5 field trial for hypersexual disorder. *Journal of Sexual Medicine, 9*, 2868–2877.

Rich, P. (2009). *Juvenile sexual offenders: A comprehensive guide to risk evaluation.* New York: Wiley.

Richardson, G., Kelly, T. P., Graham, F., & Bhate, S. R. (2004).). A personality-based taxonomy of sexually abusive adolescents derived from the Millon adolescent clinical inventory (MACI). *British Journal of Clinical Psychology, 43*, 285–298.

Robertson, C. A., & Knight, R. A. (2014). Relating sexual sadism and psychopathy to one-another, non-sexual violence, and sexual crime behaviors. *Aggressive Behavior, 40*(1), 12–23.

Rogers, R., Johansen, J., Chang, J. J., & Salekin, R. T. (1997). Predictors of adolescent psychopathy: Oppositional and conduct-disordered symptoms. *Journal of the American Academy of Psychiatry and Law, 25*, 261–271.

Ronis, S. T., & Knight, R. A. (2013). *The role of sexual motivation in sexual offending behavior.* Manuscript submitted for publication.

Rubinstein, M., Yeager, C. A., Goodstein, C., & Lewis, D. O. (1993). Sexually assaultive male juveniles: A follow-up. *American Journal of Psychiatry, 150*, 262–265.

Salekin, R. T., Leistico, A. -M. R., Schrum, C. L., & Mullins, J. (2005). Millon adolescent clinical inventory. In T. Grisso, G. Vincent, & D. Seagrave (Eds.), *Mental health screening and assessment in juvenile justice.* New York: Guilford Publications, Inc.

Salekin, R. T., Ziegler, T. A., Larrea, M. A., Anthony, V. L., & Bennett, A. D. (2003). Predicting dangerousness with two Millon adolescent clinical inventory psychopathy scales: The importance of egocentric and callous traits. *Journal of Personality Assessment, 80*, 154–163.

Sample, L. L., & Bray, T. M. (2003). Are sex offenders dangerous? *Criminology and Public Policy, 3*, 59–82.

Schlank, A. M. (1995). The utility of the MMPI and the MSI for identifying a sexual offender typology. *Sexual Abuse: A Journal of Research and Treatment*, 7, 185–194.

Schram, D. D., Milloy, C. D., & Rowe, W. E. (1991). *Juvenile sex offenders: A follow-up study of reoffense behavior.* Olympia, WA: Washington State Institute for Public Policy, Urban Policy Research and Cambie Group International.

Schwartz, B. K., & Cellini, H. R. (1995). *The sex offender: Corrections, treatment, and legal practice.* Kingston: Civic Research Press.

Serin, R. C., Mailloux, D. L., & Malcolm, P. B. (2001). Psychopathy, deviant sexual arousal, and recidivism among sexual offenders. *Journal of Interpersonal Violence, 16*, 234–246.

Seto, M. C., & Lalumière, M. L. (2006). Conduct problems and juvenile sexual offending. In H. E. Barbaree & W. L. Marshall (Eds.), *The juvenile sex offender* (pp. 166–188) (2nd ed.). New York: Guilford Press.

Seto, M. C., & Lalumière, M. L. (2010). What is so special about male adolescent sexual offending? A review and test of explanations through meta-analysis. *Psychological Bulletin, 136*, 526–575.

Seto, M. C., Lalumière, M. L., & Blanchard, R. (2000). The discriminative validity of a phallometric test for pedophilic interests among adolescent sex offenders against children. *Psychological Assessment, 12*, 319–327.

Seto, M. C., Lalumière, M. L., Harris, G. T., & Chivers, M. L. (2012). The sexual responses of sexual sadists. *Journal of Abnormal Psychology. 121*, 739–752, http://dx.doi.org/10.1037/a0028714

Simkins, L., Ward, W., Bowman, S., & Rinck, C. M. (1989). The multiphasic sex inventory: Diagnosis and prediction of treatment response in child sexual abusers. *Annals of Sex Research, 2*, 205–226.

Sipe, R., Jensen, E. L., & Everett, R. S. (1998). Adolescent sexual offenders grown up: Recidivism in young adulthood. *Criminal Justice and Behavior, 25*, 109–124.

Sitnikov, L., Goldberg, J., Daversa, M. T., & Knight, R. A. (2007). The interplay of the factors of psychopathy and borderline personality disorder in predicting violence in sexual

offenders. *Poster presented at the 2nd Biannual Meeting of the Society for the Scientific Study of Psychopathy*, St Petersberg, Florida.
Smith, G., & Fischer, L. (1999). Assessment of juvenile sexual offenders: Reliability and validity of the abel assessment for interest in Paraphilias. *Sexual Abuse: Journal of Research and Treatment, 11*, 207–216.
Spice, A., Viljoen, J. L., Latzman, N. E., Scalora, M. J., & Ullman, D. (2013). Risk and protective factors for recidivism among juveniles who have offended sexually. *Sexual Abuse: A Journal of Research and Treatment, 25*, 347–369.
Stinson, J. D., & Becker, J.V. (2008). Assessing sexual deviance: A comparison of physiological, historical, and self-report measures. *Journal of Psychiatric Practice, 14*, 379–388.
Strand, V.C., Pasquale, L.E., Sarmiento, T.L. (2011). *Child and adolescent trauma measures: A review*. Children and Families Institute for Research, Support and Training Fordham University Graduate School of Social Service. Available at http://ww.ncswtraumaed.org/wp-content/uploads/2011/07/Child-and-Adolescent-Trauma-Measures_A-Review-with-Measures.pdf.
Thorne, F. C. (1966). The sex inventory. *Journal of Clinical Psychology, 22*, 367–374.
Underwood, L. A., Barretti, L., Storms, T. L., & Safonte-Strumolo, N. (2004). A review of clinical characteristics and residential treatments for adolescent delinquents with mental health disorders: A promising residential program. *Trauma Violence Abuse, 5*, 199–242.
van Outsem, R., Beckett, R., Bullens, R., Vermeiren, R., van Horn, J., & Doreleijers, T. (2006). The adolescent sexual abuser project (ASAP) assessment measures – Dutch revised version: A comparison of personality characteristics between juvenile sex offenders, juvenile perpetrators of non-sexual violent offences and non-delinquent youth in the Netherlands. *Journal of Sexual Aggression, 12*, 127–141.
Varker, T., Devilly, G. J., Ward, T., & Beech, A. R. (2008). Empathy and adolescent sexual offenders: A review of the literature. *Aggression and Violent Behavior, 13*, 251–260.
Viding, E., & McCrory, E. J. (2012). Genetic and neurocognitive contributions to the development of psychopathy. *Development and Psychopathology, 24*, 969–983.
Viljoen, J. L., Elkovitch, N., Scalora, M. J., & Ullman, D. (2009). Assessment of reoffense risk in adolescents who have committed sexual offenses. *Criminal Justice and Behavior, 36*, 981–1000.
Viljoen, J. L., Scalora, M., Cuadra, L., Bader, S., Chavez, V., Ullman, D., et al. (2008). Assessing risk for violence in adolescents who have sexually offended: Predictive validity of the ERASOR, PCL:YV, YLS/CMI, and Static-99. *Criminal Justice and Behavior, 35*, 5–23.
Vincent, G. M., Odgers, C. L., McCormick, A. V., & Corrado, R. R. (2008). The PCL: YV and recidivism in male and female juveniles: A follow-up into young adulthood. *International Journal of Law and Psychiatry, 31*, 287–296.
Waite, D., Keller, A., McGarvey, E. L., Wieckowski, E., Pinkerton, R., & Brown, G. L. (2005). Juvenile sex offender re-arrest rates for sexual, violent nonsexual and property crimes: A 10-year follow-up. *Sexual Abuse: A Journal of Research and Treatment, 17*, 313–331.
Waller, R., Gardner, F., & Hyde, L. W. (2013). What are the associations between parenting, callous–unemotional traits, and antisocial behavior in youth? A systematic review of evidence. *Clinical Psychology Review, 33*, 593–608.
Walters, G. D. (2006). Risk-appraisal versus self-report in the prediction of criminal justice outcomes: A meta-analysis. *Criminal Justice and Behavior, 33*, 279–304.
Walters, G. D., Knight, R. A., Grann, M., & Dahle, K. -P. (2008). Incremental validity of the psychopathy checklist facet scores: Predicting release outcome in six samples. *Journal of Abnormal Psychology, 117*, 396–405.
Weinrott, M. R. (1996). *Juvenile sexual aggression: A critical review*. Boulder: University of Colorado, Institute for Behavioral Sciences, Center for the Study and Prevention of Violence.
Worling, J. (2012). The assessment and treatment of deviant sexual arousal with adolescents who have offended sexually. *Journal of Sexual Aggression, 18*, 36–63.

Worling, J. R. (1998). Adolescent sexual offender treatment at the SAFE-T program. In W. L. Marshall, Y. M. Fernandez, S. M. Hudson, & T. Ward (Eds.), *Sourcebook of treatment programs for sexual offenders* (pp. 353–365). New York: Plenum Press.

Worling, J. R. (2001). Personality based typology of adolescent male sexual offenders: Difference in recidivism rates, victim selection characteristics, and personal victimization histories. *Sexual Abuse: A Journal of Research and Treatment*, *13*, 149–166.

Worling, J. R. (2006). Assessing sexual arousal with adolescent males who have offended sexually: Self-report and unobtrusively measured viewing time. *Sexual Abuse: A Journal of Research and Treatment*, *18*, 383–400.

Worling, J. R., Bookalam, D., & Litteljohn, A. (2012). Prospective validity of the estimate of risk of adolescent sexual offense recidivism (ERASOR). *Sexual Abuse: A Journal of Research and Treatment*, *24*, 203–223.

Worling, J. R., & Curwen, T. (2000). Adolescent sexual offender recidivism: Success of specialised treatment and implications for risk prediction. *Child Abuse and Neglect*, *24*, 965–982.

Worling, J. R., & Curwen, T. (2001). The "ERASOR" estimate of risk of adolescent sexual offense recidivism, Version 2.0. Ontario: SAFE-R Program, Thistletown Regional Centre.

Worling, J. R., & Långström, N. (2003). Assessment of criminal recidivism risk with adolescents who have offended sexually: A review. *Trauma, Violence, & Abuse*, *4*, 341–362.

Worling, J. R., & Långström, N. (2006). Assessing risk of sexual reoffending. In H. E. Barbaree & W. L. Marshall (Eds.), *The juvenile sex offender* (pp. 219–247) (2nd ed.). New York: Plenum Press.

Zakireh, B., Ronis, S. T., & Knight, R. A. (2008). Individual beliefs, attitudes, and victimization histories of male juvenile sexual offenders. *Sexual Abuse: Journal of Research and Treatment*, *20*, 323–351.

Zimring, F. (2004). *An American travesty: Legal responses to adolescent sexual offending*. Chicago: University of Chicago Press.

Zimring, F. E., Jennings, W. G., Piquero, A. R., & Hays, S. (2009). Investigating the continuity of sex offending: Evidence from the second Philadelphia birth cohort. *Justice Quarterly*, *26*, 58–76.

Zimring, F. E., Piquero, A. R., & Jennings, W. G. (2007). Sexual delinquency in racine: Does early sex offending predict later sex offending in youth and young adulthood. *Criminology and Public Policy*, *6*, 507–534.

CHAPTER 3

Penile Plethysmography

Joseph J. Plaud* and Kenneth E. Blackstone**
*Applied Behavioral Consultants, LLC, Whitinsville, MA, USA
**Blackstone Polygraph, Inc., Atlanta, GA, USA

WHAT IS PENILE PLETHYSMOGRAPHY (PPG)?

PPG is both a procedure and a technology designed to measure sexual arousal in the human male. The "procedural" elements of PPG involve the presentation of sexual stimuli to a person and the concomitant measurement of changes in the circumference, length, or volume of the penis as a result of being exposed to the stimuli from a beginning point to an end point. The "technological" elements of PPG refer to the apparatus itself which records, translates and transmits these changes in penile responses during the procedure. A basic PPG apparatus is shown in Figure 3.1.

However, both procedural and technological elements of the PPG continue to evoke controversy in both research and applied clinical settings. In this chapter, we will review both elements of PPG evaluations, with special consideration given to adolescent sexual offenders.

WHY USE PPG?

PPG has been a major evaluation tool primarily used with adult sexual offenders for over half a century because it is the most direct (i.e., physiological) way to measure a male's relative patterns of sexual arousal (Rosen & Beck, 1988). Why is this important? The significance of PPG is primarily a result of the relationship of a person's sexual arousal to their overt sexual behavior (most notably sexually offending behavior), a phenomenon generally termed the sexual preference hypothesis (Gaither & Plaud, 1998; Leitenberg & Henning, 1995). The implication here is that those who engage in sexual offending behavior generally are more sexually aroused by stimuli which are associated with the sexual offense than by mutually consenting sexual activity with a peer or an adult. An implication of this hypothesis is that underlying patterns of sexual arousal also are related to sexual fantasies concerning the areas of sexual interest. Support for the

Toolkit for Working with Juvenile Sex Offenders.
DOI: http://dx.doi.org/10.1016/B978-0-12-405948-1.00003-7

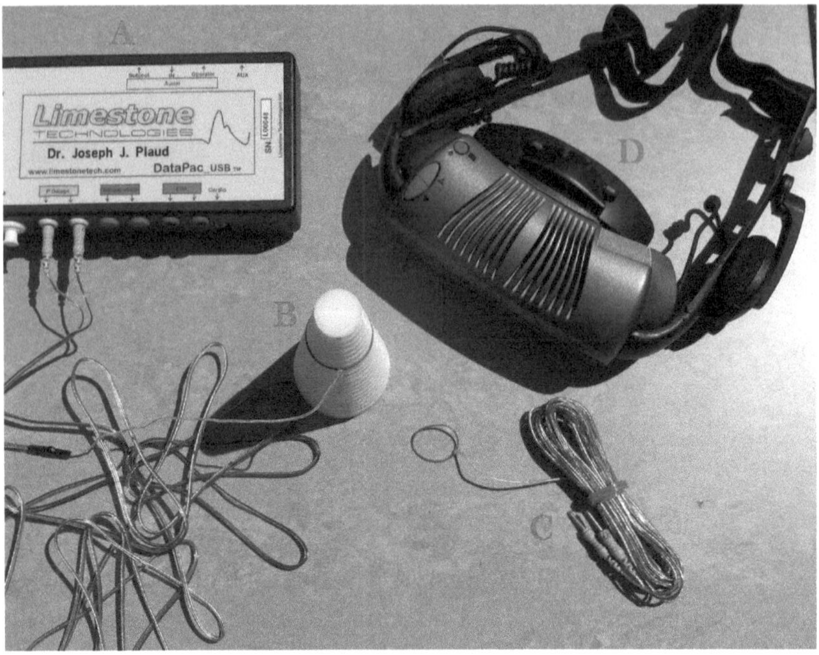

Figure 3.1 The basic PPG. (A) Analog-to-digital converter (also known as A/D or A to D) which converts the voltage changes as a function of changes in penile tumescence to millimeters or centimeters of circumference around the penis. (B) Cone used to calibrate the specific strain gauge used in the procedure. (C) Penile strain gauge (also known as mercury-in-rubber gauge) which is most frequently utilized in PPG evaluations. (D) Stimulus presentation device, in this case goggles worn like glasses which project visual sexual stimuli accompanied by ear pieces which project auditory sexual stimuli.

validity of the sexual preference hypothesis comes from several studies spanning the last several decades, and usually with extra-familial child molesters (e.g., Barbaree & Marshall, 1989). There is less support from studies concerning rapists (Barbaree, 1990; Barbaree & Marshall, 1991; Blader & Marshall, 1989), or sexual violence in general (Plaud & Bigwood, 1998).

WHAT ABOUT FEMALES?

As elaborated above, the physiological measurement of male sexual arousal is straightforward and involves measuring changes in the circumference, length, or volume of the penis. As the penis is an external sexual organ (among other functions), it is not difficult to design devices to measure changes in the penis, as will be detailed below. The female sexual response, although involving many similarities in terms of basic physiology, involves more internal processes that are more difficult to measure and interpret. As such, PPG has not been a major approach to the measurement of female sexual arousal. However, devices have been invented to accomplish this goal, usually termed photoplethysmography (e.g., Rosen & Beck, 1988).

A photoplethysmograph device generally involves an optical device (technology) coupled with a procedural technique that is designed to measure changes in female blood volume in a specific area of a female's bed of tissue. If the bed of tissue in question involves sexual responding, a female would insert a device into her vagina which emits light waves designed to measure changes in vaginal pulse amplitude (flow of blood in the vaginal wall). This response is due to the basic physiological phenomenon of female sexual arousal, like its male counterpart, involving the flow of blood within the major sexual organs.

Given the intrusiveness of photoplethysmography, the advent of newer technologies has advanced procedures designed to be non-invasive. Measurement of peripheral, rather than vaginal, pulse via photoplethsmography is one example of less invasive methodology (Allen, 2007). Although there is debate concerning the psychometric properties of male PPG, there is no professional or scientific consensus as to either the reliability or validity of photoplethysmography (Jago & Murray, 1988). Beyond the more difficult and invasive mechanics of measuring female sexual arousal lies the more complex statistical interpretations of the photoplethysmography waveforms generated from the procedure. Add to that the fact that the vast majority of known sexual offenders, whether adolescent or adult, are male (upwards of 80%; Douard & Schultz, 2011), the conclusion is that photoplethysmography remains an experimental procedure.

USING PPG WITH ADOLESCENTS VERSUS ADULTS

PPG should be used cautiously with adolescents. Given the nature of PPG evaluations, in which the subject attaches a strain gauge to his penis and then listens to and/or views a wide variety of sexually explicit stimuli, consideration of the adolescent's level of cognitive development, his emotional maturity, understanding of the procedure, and his assent to undergoing the evaluation all merit special consideration. The adolescent subject of a PPG evaluation should understand that he will be in a completely private room.

He should understand that there are certain risks or discomforts during the examination process, which may include the following: a level of discomfort when viewing or listening to sexually explicit or erotic stimuli; the fact that some subjects may become psychologically uncomfortable placing an object (the strain gauge) on his penis; and that some adolescents may become uncomfortable by listening to or viewing this kind of material.

After the PPG procedure is completed, it is imperative to have a discussion with the subject to make sure that he was not unduly uncomfortable during the procedure. It should also be explained to him that he may withdraw his participation in PPG evaluation at any point during the procedure. Further, the administration of a PPG to an adolescent can only be initiated by paying close attention to not only the assent of the adolescent subject, but also the consent of the adolescent's parent or legal guardian, as well as any government or legal authority involved in a particular case.

It is also important to point out that the vast majority of research on the validity of PPG has been with adults who are either sexual offenders or volunteer subjects, usually college students over the age of 18 years. Generalizing the findings of PPG research from these populations may not be valid (Plaud, Gaither, Hegstad, Rowan, & Devitt, 1999). PPG may be used with adolescents as well as adults because the underlying process of sexual arousal in post-pubescents remains the same: sexual arousal is most directly evidenced in both adolescents and adults by the engorgement of blood in the penis.

One of the major reasons to employ PPG evaluations as part of an adolescent risk assessment is that the more information we have about the underlying patterns of sexual arousal the better. Seto & Lalumiere (2010) found that among other factors, atypical sexual interest patterns may be linked to repeat sexual offending in adolescents. As such, data generated from a PPG evaluation may also allow for the clinician to provide feedback so that the adolescent sexual offender himself may become more aware of his present patterns of sexual arousal, and more open to participation in psychological treatment. Researchers have estimated that at least 30% of perpetration of child sexual abuse, and approximately 20% of rapes, are committed by adolescents (Davis & Leitenberg, 1987). As with adult sexual offenders, we can rely upon self-report, objective personality testing, collateral information from others, official records, such as police reports and court transcripts, or other indirect or subjective sources of information in making decisions about current risk of sexual acting out. Given the direct relationship between sexual arousal and sexual behavior, and the implications of having insufficient or incorrect information sources, a best practice is always to have as much high-quality information as possible in reaching conclusions about risk. Although PPG can be an important element in adolescent risk assessment, there are caveats.

Younger adolescents tend to evidence more generalized and stronger penile responding to sexual stimuli compared with older adolescents and adults (Kaemlngk, Koselka, Becker, & Kaplan, 1995). These findings support the conclusion that as adolescents age, their sexual arousal patterns become more fixed; therefore PPG results, especially in young adolescents, probably do not reflect later patterns of sexual arousal in contrast to PPG results with adults.

Additionally, Worling (2012) detailed several other important issues relevant to adolescent PPG evaluation, which include the following:

1. Due to the fact that sexual arousal is not fixed in adolescence, sexual deviance itself may not be the central issue; rather impulse control issues related to their inappropriate or abusive sexual behaviors may be more significant. Further, sexual arousal patterns may change over the course of an individual's sexual development
2. There are no fixed baselines of normative sexual arousal for adolescents
3. Research on PPG validity has been conducted on adults, and more research is needed in adolescent populations.

Worling advises that a combination of approaches, which includes self-report and other measures, including behavioral measures, be relied upon in the evaluation process.

THE DEVELOPMENT AND USE OF PPG

As discussed above, an important issue in understanding both sexual offending and re-offending concerns the measurement of sexual deviance (Gray & Plaud, 2005; Hanson & Bussiere, 1998; Hildebrand, de Ruiter, & de Vogel, 2004; Olver & Wong, 2006). Not only is the detection of underlying sexual arousal patterns critical in the evaluation and treatment of paraphilias (Abel & Blanchard, 1976; Alford, Morin, Atkins, & Schoen, 1987; Gray & Plaud, 2005; Laws & Marshall, 1991; Marshall, 1973, 1979), but also for the ability to predict who may re-offend in the future (Hawes, Boccaccini, & Murrie, 2013). The penile plethysmograph was developed specifically to measure relative patterns of sexual arousal in the human male (Freund, 1963). The reason for the development of the PPG is quite straightforward; the implications of using this technology are not. PPG was developed to measure sexual arousal in the most direct manner: by recording changes in the erectile tissue surrounding the penis as it becomes filled with blood. This is the most basic overt physiological manifestation of sexual arousal in the human male. Despite this basic physiology, it remains the case that controversy surrounds the use of PPG as a tool of basic sexual research as well as clinical applications with sexual offenders (Gaither & Plaud, 1998; O'Donohue & Plaud, 1994). This is not to say that basic behavioral research on patterns of sexual arousal has not been conducted; it has, especially in the principles of basic conditioning and habituation of sexual arousal in respondent or classical conditioning (Plaud & Martini, 1996; Rachman, 1966; Rachman & Hodgson, 1968), operant conditioning (Cliffe & Parry, 1980; Rosen, Shapiro, & Schwartz, 1975), and habituation and spontaneous recovery (Koukounas & Over, 1993; Meuwissen & Over, 1990; O'Donohue & Plaud, 1991; Plaud, Gaither, Amato-Henderson, & Devitt, 1997). In most of the scientific studies of the conditioning, habituation and predictive utility of sexual arousal research, the PPG has been the essential tool of measurement. And yet the apparatus and the procedure are seemingly plagued by controversy. We now turn to an understanding of why this has been the case during the past 60 years.

THE EVOLUTION OF PPG

The scientific assessment of male sexual arousal patterns was first conducted by Freund (1963), using an instrument which recorded changes in volumetric pressure, or penile volume, which was termed phallometry. In an early and important study, Freund was able correctly to classify subjects according to their stated sexual preferences by measuring changes in penile volume in response to stimuli depicting male and female adults and children. Subsequent to this research, there arose a number of different types of penile circumference gauges in the study of human sexual arousal (Bancroft, Jones, & Pullan, 1966; Fisher, Gross, & Zuch, 1965). In the early days of phallometry, there was debate over which type of measure of male arousal (or penile tumescence) was the most sensitive indicator (Abel & Blanchard, 1976; McConaghy, 1989, 1992; Wheeler & Rubin, 1987). At the present time, it is the case that circumferential measures are the most commonly used procedure in penile plethysmography (Howes, 1995), and will be referred to in what follows as the standard strain gauge of PPG assessment. Examples of data graphs (oftentimes referred to as "strip charts") generated for PPG evaluations are presented in Figure 3.2.

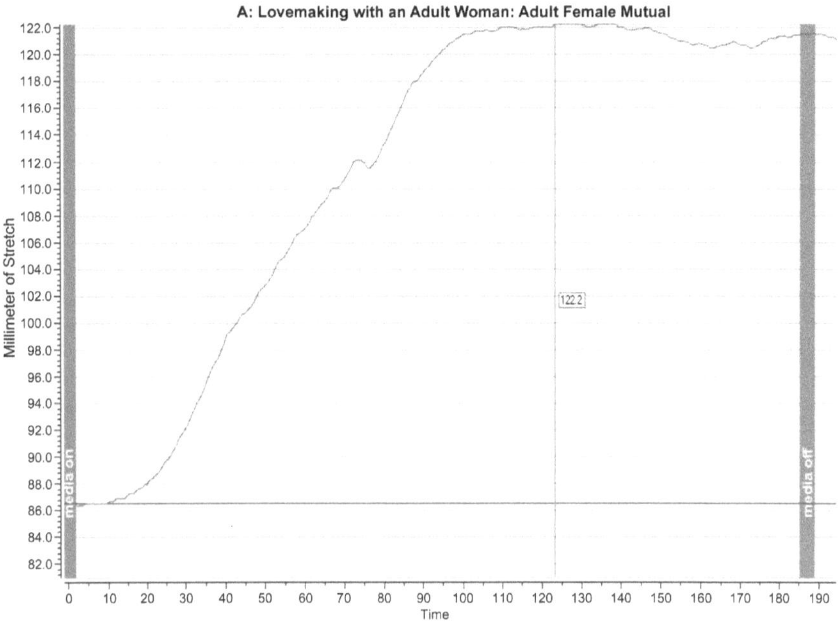

Figure 3.2 Examples of data reports ("strip charts") generated from PPG evaluations. (A) Significant sexual responding by a self-identified male heterosexual to consensual heterosexual behavior. Peak penile tumescence reached over 30 millimeters. Please note: on all PPG "strip charts" depicted in Figure 3.2 (A to E), the x-axis shows the time in seconds since the stimulus period began; the y-axis shows millimeters of penile tumescence, with baseline penile tumescence represented by the horizontal purple line. The red line is therefore a compilation of penile circumference changes throughout the sexual stimulus period in question. For all figures in this series it is important to follow the red line from the onset of the sexual stimulus in question, to its offset. For example, in (A), a stimulus is presented to the subject describing consensual sexual behavior, including sexual intercourse, with a female adult. When the stimulus commences, the baseline penile circumference of the subject is measured at slightly over 86 millimeters. As the stimulus continues from left to right (time being measured on the x-axis), the subject's penis continues to engorge with blood, reflected in continued penile tumescence up to a maximum of 122 millimeters, or approximately 36 millimeters in penile circumference change from baseline tumescence when the stimulus period commenced. This high level of penile responding was maintained until the end of the stimulus period, shown (A) by the blue vertical bar entitled "media off". (B) Significant sexual responding by a self-identified male homosexual to consensual heterosexual behavior. Peak penile tumescence reached almost 30 millimeters. (C) Significant sexual responding by a male denying pedophilic sexual interests demonstrating sexual arousal towards a female child. (D) Significant sexual responding by a self-identified male pedophile to the rape of a male child. (E) Insignificant sexual responding during a stimulus presentation depicting sexual interactions with a female adult. This type of response pattern is sometimes referred to as a "flatline" response.

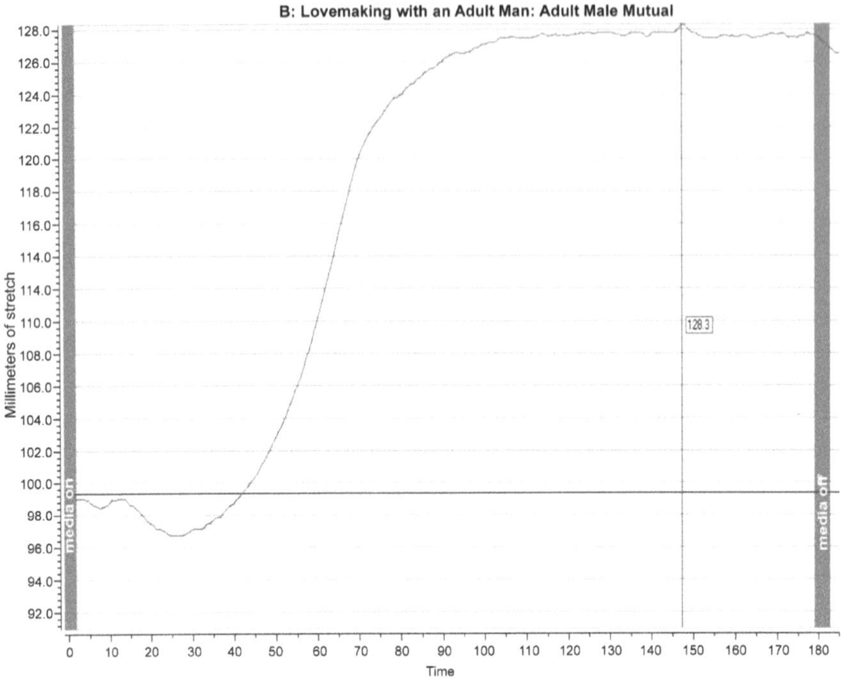

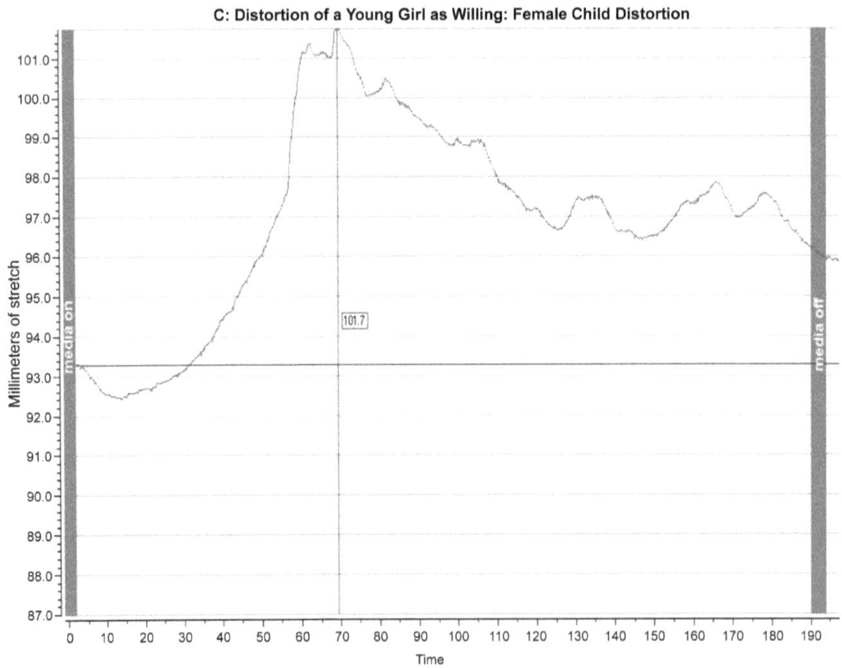

Figure 3.2 (Continued)

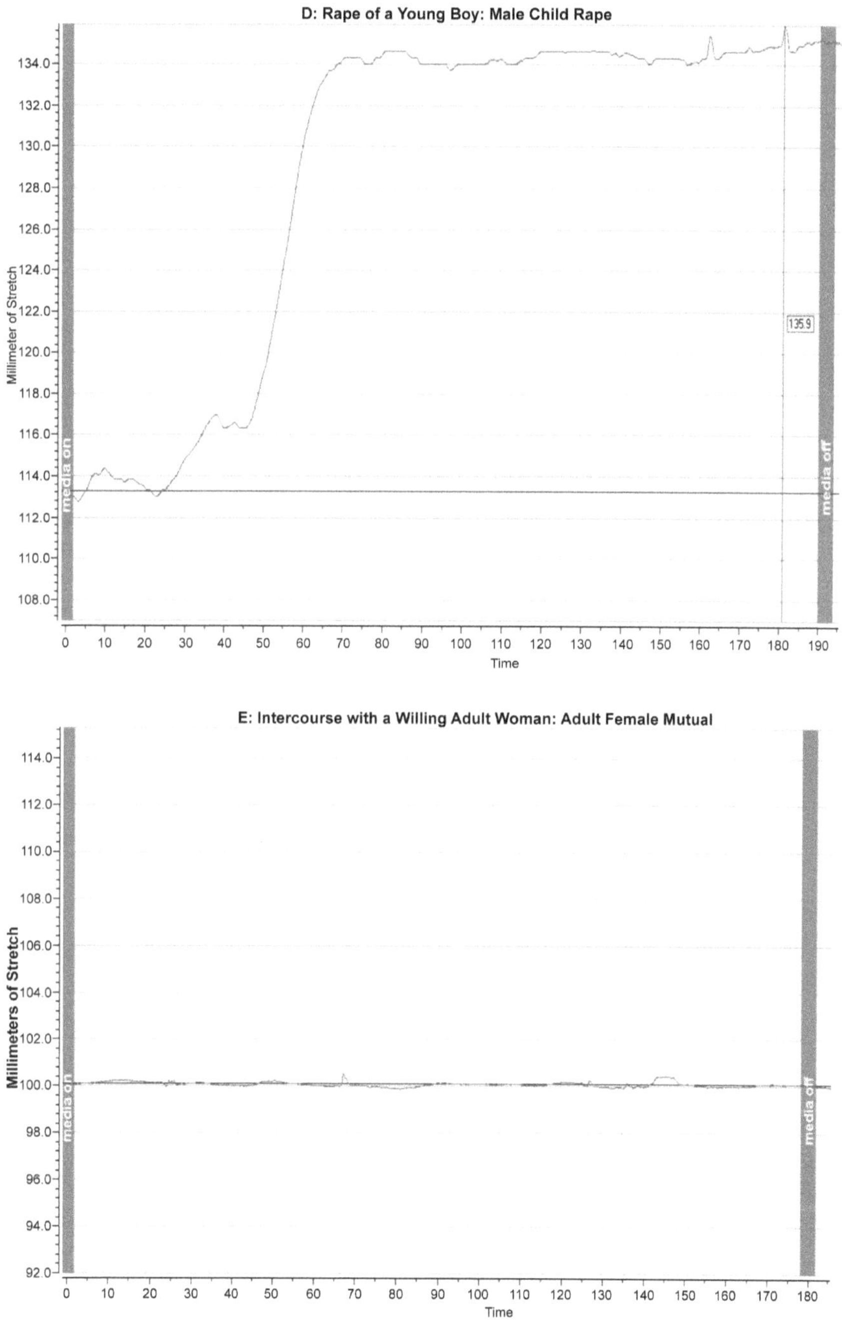

Figure 3.2 (Continued)

Insofar as the prediction of sexual offense recidivism is concerned, a meta-analysis conducted by Hanson and Bussiere (1998) found that deviant sexual arousal measured via PPG was the single greatest predictor of sexual offense recidivism. As a general statement given the state of the research on PPG, there is empirical support for the finding that an individual is more likely to act in a sexual manner when that person is sexually aroused to the person or type of sexual activity upon which the sexual arousal is based, as described in detail below. The most used circumferential PPG device (called a strain gauge) is a small rubber-like ring (also called a mercury in rubber strain gauge) which the subject of a PPG evaluation places on his penis in privacy, after the device is first calibrated according to a standard procedure in which changes in voltage are converted to millimeter or centimeter benchmarks. The PPG procedure is designed to be private and non-intrusive.

As a general summary concerning the research basis of PPG as valid measure of sexual arousal: (1) PPG has been in use in both research laboratories and clinical settings for over 60 years, much longer than other physiological measures such as positron emission tomography (PET) and magnetic resonance imaging (MRI) scans, for example; (2) the PPG is a widely used instrument in most of the world, and has been for quite a long period of time; and (3) the PPG is an objective measure of sexual arousal based upon the principles of male physiology. As a matter of fact, the majority of research on sexual arousal patterns (O'Donohue & Plaud, 1994) has been conducted with sexual offenders. Behavioral researchers have used PPG to examine such issues as the classical conditioning (Gaither, Rosenkranz, & Plaud, 1998; Plaud & Martini, 1996; Rachman, 1966; Rachman & Hodgson, 1968), operant conditioning (Cliffe & Parry, 1980; Kantorowitz, 1978; Rosen, 1973; Rosen et al., 1975), and habituation and spontaneous recovery (Koukounas & Over, 1993; Meuwissen & Over, 1990; O'Donohue & Geer, 1985; O'Donohue & Plaud, 1991; Plaud et al., 1997) of sexual arousal with human males.

In a review of all of the physiological measures in use over 30 years ago (e.g., skin conductance, heart rate, blood pressure, pupillary responses, and temperature), Zuckerman (1971) concluded that penile erection measures were the most sensitive measures of sexual arousal available. Proulx (1989) asserted that penile responses are the only physiological responses which are specific to sexual arousal in men and can differentiate between sexual arousal and other arousal states, such as anger and fear. Thus, many researchers agree that the penile plethysmograph is a reliable and valid means of assessing a male's sexual arousal patterns (Gaither et al., 1998; Howes, 1995; Maletzky, 1995). Frenzel and Lang (1989), for example, found that in terms of reliability, PPG achieved a coefficient alpha of 0.93 for 27 sexual stimuli.

Despite the thousands of research studies published to date using penile plethysmography, its validity has been questioned (e.g., Laws, 2003; McConaghy, 1989, 1992). A major reason for this concerns the fact that different types of stimuli are used by different researchers (and clinicians), thereby making comparisons of different studies difficult at best (Howes, 1995; Maletzky, 1995). Also, several researchers have questioned the external validity of plethysmographic research using "normal" samples because of a possible volunteer bias which may exist (e.g., Farkas, Sine, & Evans, 1978; Gaither & Plaud, 1998; Morokoff, 1986; Nirenberg, Wincze, Bansal, Liepman, Engle-Friedman et al., 1991; Plaud et al., 1999; Wolchik, Spencer, & Lisi, 1983; Wolchik, Braver, & Jensen, 1985). Table 3.1 summarizes the major areas of variability in conducting PPG evaluations.

Table 3.1 Potential Sources of Variability in Penile Plethysmograph Evaluations

1. The type of strain gauge used and the proper placement of the strain gauge
2. The type of sexual stimuli used (audio, video, both)
3. Specific sexual scenes depicted by the sexual stimuli used
4. Duration of both stimulus and detumescence (quiet) periods
5. The instructions given to the client
6. The type of specific PPG technology employed, including type of recording instrumentation
7. The data sampling rate and type of data interpretation used of PPG results
8. Whether or not probes for dissumulation (faking) were employed during the procedure
9. The setting of the assessment facility (e.g., prison vs outpatient setting)

PPG: STIMULUS CHARACTERISTICS

A key element in plethysmographic research is the stimuli which are presented to elicit sexual arousal. It is important to state from the beginning of this analysis that both the reliability as well as the validity of PPG as an assessment technique are affected by the stimulus characteristics used in the procedure (Gaither & Plaud, 1998; Howes, 1995; Plaud et al., 1999). As elucidated by Gaither and Plaud (1998), sexual stimuli used in PPG evaluations can be divided into primary and secondary characteristics. Primary characteristics of sexual stimuli are those stimulus characteristics that vary between categories (e.g., deviant vs normal which generally refers to adult or peer consensual sexual activities vs prepubescent or non-consensual types of sexual interactions) and are thought to be most salient in distinguishing between subjects according to their stated sexual preferences (e.g., age or sex of stimulus). Secondary characteristics, meanwhile, are those which may vary both within and between categories but are not typically considered to be salient: they may even be considered idiosyncratic. Examples of secondary characteristics include mode of stimulus presentation (audio, visual, or both visual and audio), type of sexual activities depicted, the order of stimulus presentations, and so forth. The results of PPG assessments are normally considered to be due to the manipulation of primary characteristics; yet, if they are not controlled, some secondary characteristics may confound those results (Plaud et al., 1999).

One finding from the laboratory, for example, is that the mode of stimulus presentation can have differential impact on PPG results. For males, films or videos tend to elicit greater physiological arousal than slides or still photographs, or audiotaped descriptions (Abel & Blanchard, 1976; Abel, Blanchard, Barlow, & Mavissakalian, 1975; Abel, Blanchard, & Barlow, 1981; Freund, Langevin, & Zajac, 1974; Kolarsky & Madlafousek, 1972; McConaghy, 1974; Sandford, 1974). Some of these studies have been criticized due to the fact that the content of the stimuli were not matched between modes. One study that did address this issue was conducted by Julien and Over (1988). The researchers examined differences in male sexual arousal across five modes of stimulus presentation: film, slides, audiotaped descriptions (spoken text), written text, and fantasy. For this study, the researchers produced a film which was divided into eight 2-minute segments. Each segment consisted of the same male and female engaging in a different sexual activity. Photographs were taken simultaneously from the same angle as the movie camera for the slides. The spoken text and written text consisted of factual descriptions of the activities taking place in each segment. In the fantasy condition, the subject was given a factual description of the activities he was to imagine which also corresponded to each segment of the video. They found that the film elicited significantly greater arousal than slides, spoken text, and written text which did not differ significantly from one another. Fantasy elicited significantly less arousal than the other four modes. Julien and Over suggested that film may be the most arousing because it: (1) contains a dynamic aspect, a "transformation of information over space and time" which is lacking in slides; and (2) "possibly the dynamic aspects of visual stimulation cannot be conveyed with the same saliency through words" (pp. 140–141). These same issues apply to adolescents undergoing PPG evaluations, and the effects may be even more pronounced (Kaemlngk et al., 1995).

Perhaps the single greatest issue that requires attention in the administration of the PPG concerns the specific type of sexual activities that are depicted. Some researchers who have used slides or videos, use stimuli which present only a nude or seminude person in a non-sexual pose (e.g., McConaghy, 1974; Sandford, 1974). The problem, of course, is that this type of stimulus does not elicit high levels of arousal. High, Rubin, and Henson (1979) found that a video presented in color did not elicit greater physiological sexual arousal than the same film in black and white for eight males. Another secondary stimulus characteristic inherent in videos is the presentation of the accompanying sound. Many of the studies reported in the literature do not state whether the accompanying sound was presented (e.g., High et al., 1979; Julien & Over, 1988; McConaghy, 1974).

THE IMPACT OF SEXUAL EXPERIENCE ON PPG EVALUATIONS

While PPG represents a major tool into laboratory research on the parameters of sexual arousal and behavior, the main utility of plethysmographic assessments concerns its clinical applications, most notably with sexual offenders (e.g., those suspected or convicted of child molestation, rape, or exhibitionism) or who seek treatment for a sexual disorder (e.g., a fetish). During the assessment, the subject's penile tumescence is continuously recorded while he is presented a number of different stimuli representing several categories of sexual interest. The subject's maximum change in penile circumference during each stimulus category is then converted into a standardized score or percentage of full erection (Barbaree & Mewhort, 1994; Earls, Quinsey, & Castonguay, 1987; Laws, 2003). Comparisons of relative patterns of sexual arousal for the person being evaluated (so-called ipastive comparisons) are then made in order to quantify within each subject his relative patterns of sexual arousal. The PPG analysis rests on the central assumption that the category or categories which elicited the greatest arousal during stimulus presentations are that person's sexual preferences. So, then, what implication does the quantification of relative patterns of sexual arousal via PPG administration have for sexual behavior, including sexually offensive behavior in adolescents and adults?

RESOURCES FOR LEARNING MORE ABOUT PENILE PLETHYSMOGRAPHY

As discussed at length in this chapter, there is no one set of equipment, no one procedure involved in PPG evaluations. Nothing substitutes for academic-based training in both the basic science and clinical application of PPG. This is usually done in advanced training in a graduate program in clinical or forensic psychology under the supervision of a trained academician who has studied and published research using PPG. Alternatively, there are post-doctoral settings in clinics and medical centers which have sexual offender treatment programs. A clinician with graduate or undergraduate training in psychology or allied professional fields should perform PPG evaluations only after adequate training under supervision is completed This recommendation is consistent with the ethical principles of most of the major mental health professional organizations.

With regard to purchasing the necessary equipment to conduct PPG evaluations, there are two major resources: (1) Limestone Technologies (http://www.limestonetech.com/index.cfm/product-lines/sex-offender-management/); and (2) Behavioral Technology (http://www.btimonarch.com/). Both companies offer the hardware and software needed to equip a complete PPG laboratory. They also provide resources for proper training in the administration and interpretation of PPG.

The best way to find a qualified professional to administer PPG evaluations is to make contact with a licensed mental health professional in your local area whose clinical expertise involves evaluating and treating sexual offenders. Such professionals typically have information about PPG evaluation resources in a particular geographic location. Alternatively, local universities or medical centers with academic programs involving sexual offender evaluation and treatment services would also be a resource. On the web, the Safer Society Foundation (http://www.safersociety.org/) maintains a database on professionals and organizations which provide clinical services in assessing and treating sexual offenders. Regardless of the referral source, it is always important to ensure that any professional who offers PPG services has the proper clinical training and experience, as detailed above.

SUMMING IT UP: SEXUAL OFFENDER RISK ASSESSMENTS AND PPG

Despite ongoing debate and criticism of the PPG as an assessment tool of relative patterns of sexual arousal, when properly utilized, PPG can add significantly to risk assessments for both adolescent and adult sexual offenders. However, with adolescents, direct physiological measurement using PPG should be interpreted more cautiously, in line with the analysis earlier in this chapter concerning PPG evaluation issues specific to adolescents. It is also important to remember that PPG evaluation results should never be used in isolation in any sexual offender evaluation. Data on patterns of sexual arousal do not independently predict whether or not a sexual offender will re-offend. Many factors go into the prediction of who will or will not recidivate sexually (Hanson & Morton-Bourgon, 2005). In other words, there is no one profile of sexual offenders that will differentiate recidivists from non-recidivists (Laws, 2003). However, given the fact that adolescent sexual arousal patterns may change as youth sexually mature into adulthood (Kaemlngk et al., 1995), it may be critical to have data on a sexual offender's present pattern of sexual arousal. Too often, current diagnostic conclusions are made without any evidence of current sexual deviance. This situation sometimes leads to clinical diagnostic imprecision (O'Donohue, Regev, & Hagstrom, 2000), and to errors in professional judgment of future risk.

When the relevant factors concerning PPG evaluations in sexual offender risk assessments are examined, the main strengths of PPG evaluations include the following:

1. Identification of those who have excessive arousal to what variety of stimuli. It is documented that there is a relationship between a person's patterns of sexual arousal and the probability that he may act upon that arousal, as described above in the sexual preference hypothesis. An important first step in risk evaluations is to have an adequate assessment of the person's unique sexual arousal patterns, which is precisely what the PPG has been developed to assess.
2. Discernment of a lack of arousal to stimuli of consenting appropriate sexual interactions. It has also been shown that a lack of sexual arousal to sexually appropriate stimuli (e.g., individuals engaged in consensual sexual activities) is sometimes associated with sexually abusive behavior. PPG can not only assess for this possibility, but behavioral treatment regimens can then be developed to address problematic sexual arousal patters that might go unnoticed if a PPG assessment were not performed (see Chapter 10).

One of the most pressing issues facing researchers and practitioners is providing for a more standardized process of administration that addresses many of the issues discussed in this chapter: stimulus modality and type;

the type of strain gauge employed; software and hardware standards; and agreed upon strategies for data analysis and interpretation. Many of these issues were raised more than two decades ago (e.g., O'Donohue & Letourneau, 1992). Laws (2003) observed that: "Whether empirical evidence supports its continued use or not, whether its procedural faults are remedied or not, PPG will survive" (p. 21). As PPG now reaches into its seventh decade of use as a research and assessment tool, Laws' prediction has the ring of truth to it. But that does not mean that we should cease to strive for such standardization across continents. Such standardization ultimately will serve both the research community and those who employ the PPG in the interest of public safety.

REFERENCES

Abel, G. G., & Blanchard, E. B. (1976). The measurement and generation of sexual arousal in male sexual deviates. In M. Hersen, R. M. Eisler, & P. M. Miller (Eds.), *Progress in behavior modification* (Vol. 2, pp. 99–136). New York: Academic Press.

Abel, G. G., Blanchard, E. B., Barlow, D. H., & Mavissakalian, M. (1975). Identifying specific erotic cues in sexual deviation by audiotaped descriptions. *Journal of Applied Behavior Analysis*, *8*, 247–260.

Abel, G. G., Blanchard, E. B., & Barlow, D. H. (1981). Measurement of sexual arousal in several paraphilias: The effects of stimulus modality, instructional set and stimulus content on the objective. *Behavior Research and Therapy*, *19*, 25–33.

Alford, G. S., Morin, C., Atkins, M., & Schoen, L. (1987). Masturbatory extinction of deviant sexual arousal: A case study. *Behavior Therapy*, *18*, 265–271.

Allen, J. (2007). Photoplethysmography and its application in clinical physiological measurement. *Physiological Measurement*, *28*, R1–R39.

Bancroft, J. H., Jones, H. G., & Pullan, B. P. (1966). A simple transducer for measuring penile erection with comment on its use in the treatment of sexual disorders. *Behavior Research and Therapy*, *4*, 239–241.

Barbaree, H. E. (1990). Stimulus control of sexual arousal: Its role in sexual assault. In W. L. Marshall, D. R. Laws, & H. E. Barbaree (Eds.), *Handbook of sexual assault* (pp. 115–142). New York: Plenum.

Barbaree, H. E., & Marshall, W. L. (1989). Erectile responses among heterosexual child molesters, father-daughter incest offenders, and matched nonoffenders: Five distinct age preference profiles. *Canadian Journal of Behavioral Sciences*, *21*, 70–82.

Barbaree, H. E., & Marshall, W. L. (1991). The role of male sexual arousal in rape: Six models. *Journal of Consulting and Clinical Psychology*, *59*, 621–630.

Barbaree, H. E., & Mewhort, D. J. K. (1994). The effects of the z-score transformation on measures of relative erectile response strength: A re-appraisal. *Behavior Research and Therapy*, *32*, 547–558.

Blader, J. C., & Marshall, W. L. (1989). Is assessment of sexual arousal in rapists worthwhile? A critique of current methods and the development of a response compatibility approach. *Clinical Psychology Review*, *9*, 569–587.

Cliffe, M. J., & Parry, S. J. (1980). Matching to reinforcer value: Human concurrent variable-interval performance. *Quarterly Journal of Experimental Psychology*, *32*, 557–570.

Davis, G. E., & Leitenberg., H. E. (1987). Adolescent sex offenders. *Psychological Bulletin*, *101*, 417–427.

Douard, J. D., & Schultz, P. D. (2011). Scapegoating the sex offender – The monstrous other. In B. Schwartz (Ed.), *Handbook of sex offender treatment* (pp. 18-1–18-22). Kingston: Civic Research Institute.

Earls, C. M., Quinsey, V. L., & Castonguay, L. G. (1987). A comparison of three methods of scoring penile circumference changes. *Archives of Sexual Behavior, 16*, 493–500.

Farkas, G. M., Sine, L. F., & Evans, I. M. (1978). Personality, sexuality, and demographic differences between volunteers and nonvolunteers for a laboratory study of male sexual behavior. *Archives of Sexual Behavior, 7*, 513–520.

Fisher, C., Gross, J., & Zuch, J. (1965). Cycle of penile erection synchronous with dreaming (REM) sleep. *Archives of General Psychiatry, 12*, 23–45.

Frenzel, R. R., & Lang, R. (1989). Identifying sexual preferences in intrafamilial and extrafamilial child sexual abusers. *Sexual Abuse: A Journal of Research and Treatment, 2*, 255–275.

Freund, K. (1963). A laboratory method of diagnosing predominance of homo- or hetero-erotic interest in the male. *Behavior Research and Therapy, 12*, 355–359.

Freund, K., Langevin, R., & Zajac, Y. (1974). A note on the erotic arousal value of moving and stationary human forms. *Behavior Research and Therapy, 12*, 117–119.

Gaither, G. A., & Plaud, J. J. (1998). The effects of secondary stimulus characteristics on male sexual arousal. *Journal of Sex Research, 34*, 231–236.

Gaither, G. A., Rosenkranz, R. R., & Plaud, J. J. (1998). Sexual disorders. In J. J. Plaud & G. H. Eifert (Eds.), *From Behavior Theory to Behavior Therapy* (pp. 152–171). Boston: Allyn & Bacon.

Gray, S. R., & Plaud, J. J. (2005). A comparison of the Abel Assessment for Sexual Interest and penile plethysmography in an outpatient sample of sexual offenders. *Journal of Sexual Offender Civil Commitment: Science and the Law, 1*, 1–10.

Hanson, R. K., & Bussiere, M. T. (1998). Predicting relapse: A meta-analysis of sexual offender recidivism. *Journal of Consulting and Clinical Psychology, 66*, 348–362.

Hanson, R. K., & Morton-Bourgon, K. (2005). The characteristics of persistent sexual offenders: A meta-analysis of recidivism studies. *Journal of Consulting and Clinical Psychology, 73*, 1154–1163.

Hawes, S. W., Boccaccini, M. T., & Murrie, D. C. (2013). Psychopathy and the combination of psychopathy and sexual deviance as predictors of sexual recidivism: Meta-analytic findings using the Psychopathy Checklist -Revised. *Psychological Assessment, 25*, 233–243.

High, R. W., Rubin, H. B., & Henson, D. (1979). Color as a variable in making an erotic film more arousing. *Archives of Sexual Behavior, 8*, 263–267.

Hildebrand, M., de Ruiter, C., & de Vogel, V. (2004). Psychopathy and sexual deviance in treated rapists: Association with sexual and nonsexual recidivism. *Sexual Abuse: A Journal of Research and Treatment, 16*, 1–24.

Howes, R. J. (1995). A survey of plethysmographic assessment in North America. *Sexual Abuse: A Journal of Research and Treatment, 7*, 9–24.

Jago, J. R., & Murray, A. (1988). Repeatability of peripheral pulse measurements on ears, fingers and toes using photoelectric plethysmography. *Clinical Physics and Physiological Measurement, 9*, 319–330.

Julien, E., & Over, R. (1988). Male sexual arousal across five modes of erotic stimulation. *Archives of Sexual Behavior, 17*, 131–143.

Kaemlngk, K. L., Koselka, M., Becker, J. V., & Kaplan, M. S. (1995). Age and adolescent sexual offender arousal. *Sexual Abuse: A Joumal of Research and Treatment, 7*, 249–257.

Kantorowitz, D. A. (1978). Personality and conditioning of tumescence and detumescence. *Behavior Research and Therapy, 16*, 117–123.

Kelly, R. J. (1982). Behavioral reorientation of pedophiliacs: Can it be done? *Clinical Psychology Review, 2*, 387–408.

Kolarsky, A., & Madlafousek, J. (1972). Female behavior and sexual arousal in heterosexual male deviant offenders. *Journal of Nervous Mental Disorders, 155*, 110–118.

Koukounas, E., & Over, R. (1993). Habituation and dishabituation of male sexual arousal. *Behavior Research and Therapy, 31*, 575–585.

Laws, D. L. (2003). Penile plethysmography: Strengths, limitations, innovations. In D. Thornton & D. R. Laws (Eds.), *Cognitive Approaches to the Assessment of Sexual Interest in Sexual Offenders* (pp. 7–29). London: Sage.

Laws, D. R., & Marshall, W. L. (1991). A conditioning theory of the etiology and maintenance of deviant sexual preference and behavior. In W. L. Marshall, D. R. Laws, & H. E. Barabaree (Eds.), *Handbook of sexual assault*. New York: Plenum.

Leitenberg, H., & Henning, K. (1995). Sexual fantasy. *Psychological Bulletin, 117*, 469–496.

Maletzky, B. M. (1995). Editorial: Standardization and the penile plethysmograph. *Sexual Abuse: A Journal of Research and Treatment, 7*, 5–7.

Marshall, W. L. (1973). The modification of sexual fantasies: A combined treatment approach to the reduction of deviant sexual behavior. *Behaviour Research and Therapy, 11*, 557–564.

Marshall, W. L. (1979). Satiation therapy: A procedure for reducing deviant sexual arousal. *Journal of Applied Behavior Analysis, 12*, 377–389.

McConaghy, N. (1974). Penile volume responses to moving and still pictures of male and female nudes. *Archives of Sexual Behavior, 3*, 565–570.

McConaghy, N. (1989). Validity and ethics of penile circumference measures of sexual arousal: A critical review. *Archives of Sexual Behavior, 18*, 357–369.

McConaghy, N. (1992). Validity and ethics of penile circumference measures of sexual arousal: A response to McAnulty and Adams. *Archives of Sexual Behavior, 21*, 187–195.

Meuwissen, I., & Over, R. (1990). Habituation and dishabituation of female sexual arousal. *Behavior Research and Therapy, 28*, 217–226.

Morokoff, P. J. (1986). Volunteer bias in the psychophysiological study of female sexuality. *The Journal of Sex Research, 22*, 35–51.

Nirenberg, T. D., Wincze, J. P., Bansal, S., Liepman, M. R., Engle-Friedman, M., & Begin, A. (1991). Volunteer bias in a study of male alcoholics' sexual behavior. *Archives of Sexual Behavior, 20*, 371–379.

Olver, M. E., & Wong, S. C. (2006). Psychopathy, sexual deviance, and recidivism among sex offenders. *Sexual Abuse: Journal of Research and Treatment, 18*, 65–82.

O'Donohue, W., & Letourneau, E. (1992). The psychometric properties of the penile tumescence assessment of child molesters. *Journal of Psychopathology and Behavioral Assessment, 14*, 123–174.

O'Donohue, W., & Plaud, J. J. (1991). The long-term habituation of human sexual arousal. *Journal of Behavior Therapy and Experimental Psychiatry, 22*, 87–96.

O'Donohue, W., & Plaud, J. J. (1994). The conditioning of human sexual arousal. *Archives of Sexual Behavior, 23*, 321–344.

O'Donohue, W., Regev, L., & Hagstrom, A. (2000). Problems with the DSM-IV diagnosis of pedophilia. *Sexual Abuse: A Journal of Research and Treatment, 12*, 95–105.

O'Donohue, W. T., & Geer, J. H. (1985). The habituation of sexual arousal. *Archives of Sexual Behavior, 14*, 233–246.

Plaud, J. J., & Bigwood, S. J. (1998). The relationship of male self-report of rape supportive attitudes, sexual fantasy, social desirability and physiological arousal to sexually coercive stimuli. *Journal of Clinical Psychology, 53*, 935–942.

Plaud, J. J., & Martini, J. R. (1996). The respondent conditioning of male sexual arousal. *Behavior Modification, 23*, 254–268.

Plaud, J. J., Gaither, G. A., Amato-Henderson, S., & Devitt, M. K. (1997). The long-term habituation of sexual arousal in human males: A crossover design. *The Psychological Record, 47*, 385–398.

Plaud, J. J., Gaither, G. A., Hegstad, H. J., Rowan, L., & Devitt, M. K. (1999). External validity of psychophysiological sexual arousal research: To whom do our research results apply? *Journal of Sex Research, 36*, 171–179.

Proulx, J. (1989). Sexual preference assessment of sexual aggressors. *International Journal of Law and Psychiatry, 6*, 431–441.

Rachman, S. (1966). Sexual fetishism: An experimental analogue. *Psychological Record, 16*, 293–296.

Rachman, S., & Hodgson, R. J. (1968). Experimentally-induced "sexual fetishism": Replication and development. *Psychological Record, 18*, 25–27.

Rosen, C. R., & Beck, J. G. (1988). *Patterns of sexual arousal: Psychophysiological processes and clinical applications*. New York: Guilford.

Rosen, R. C. (1973). Suppression of penile tumescence by instrumental conditioning. *Psychosomatic Medicine, 35*, 509–514.

Rosen, R. C., Shapiro, D., & Schwartz, G. (1975). Voluntary control of penile tumescence. *Psychosomatic Medicine, 37*, 479–483.

Sandford, D. A. (1974). Patterns of sexual arousal in heterosexual males. *The Journal of Sex Research, 10*, 150–155.

Seto, M. C., & Lalumiere, M. L. (2010). What is so special about male adolescent sexual offending? A review and test of explanations through meta-analysis. *Psychological Bulletin, 136*, 526–575.

Wheeler, D., & Rubin, H. B. (1987). A comparison of volumetric and circumferential measures of penile erection. *Archives of Sexual Behavior, 16*, 289–299.

Wolchik, S. A., Spencer, S. L., & Lisi, I. S. (1983). Volunteer bias in research employing vaginal measures of sexual arousal: Demographic, sexual and personality characteristics. *Archives of Sexual Behavior, 12*, 399–408.

Wolchik, S. A., Braver, S. L., & Jensen, K. (1985). Volunteer bias in erotica research: Effects of intrusiveness of measure and sexual background. *Archives of Sexual Behavior, 14*, 93–106.

Worling, J. (2012). The assessment and treatment of deviant sexual arousal with adolescents who have offended sexually. *Journal of Sexual Aggression, 18*, 36–63.

Zuckerman, M. (1971). Physiological measures of sexual arousal in the human. *Psychological Bulletin, 75*, 297–329.

CHAPTER 4

The Polygraph

Kenneth E. Blackstone* and Joseph J. Plaud**
*Blackstone Polygraph, Inc. Atlanta, GA, USA
**Applied Behavioral Consultants, LLC, Whitinsville, MA, USA

INTRODUCTION

There is considerable debate on the use of psychophysiological tools and techniques in many areas of psychological inquiry, including sexual behavior (O'Donohue & Plaud, 1994). This debate extends to the "pros and cons" of using polygraph in cases involving sexual behavior, including juvenile sexual behavior. More generally, the polygraph has been used with juveniles since 1923, with one of the earliest juvenile sex offender treatment programs requiring polygraph starting in 1984 (Lundell, 2013, private communication). The polygraph is used today with juveniles: before adjudication to assess deception (Adang, 1995; Craig & Molder, 2003); and post-adjudication in the monitoring of juvenile sex offenders on probation and parole (Adang, 1995; Blackstone, 2008; Craig & Molder, 2003; Emerick & Dutton, 1993). Some would question whether juveniles are viable candidates for polygraph, while others realize that fitness is determined per individual, not per group. While there is a dearth of empirical research specific to the use of the polygraph with a juvenile population, there are studies showing mixed results: some suggesting that age has no direct effect on the detection of deception with physiological measures (Bradley, Russell, & Li, 1996; Craig, Raskin, & Kirscher, 2011); some indicating that juveniles under 11 were less detectable on a guilty knowledge task than older juveniles and adults (Abrams, 1975). Some would question whether a polygraph examination can be given to an adult or juvenile against their will, while others realize that while the polygraph may be "mandated", the polygraph examiner cannot administer an examination if a person is unwilling. In addition and adding to the confusion, there are studies which equate accuracy with utility and reports which mistake the polygraph for magic and voodoo (Blackstone, 2011; Hindman & Peters, 1988, 2001; Marston, 1938).

Toolkit for Working with Juvenile Sex Offenders.
DOI: http://dx.doi.org/10.1016/B978-0-12-405948-1.00004-9

PART 1: HISTORY

Though the history of the polygraph instrument has no definite starting point, the first mechanical medical device, the pulsilogium, was invented by Italian physiologist and physician Sanctorius (1561–1636). In 1875, three centuries and hundreds of experiments later, both Wilhelm Wundt (1832–1920) and William James (1842–1910) founded a psychological laboratory at their respective universities, one at the University of Leipzig and one at Harvard University. The German psychologist-psychiatrist Hugo Munsterberg (1863–1916) started his studies as Wundt's student and research assistant, obtained a PhD in physiological psychology in 1885, an MD in 1887 and opened his own psychological laboratory at the University of Freiburg. In 1892, William James hired Munsterberg to run the Harvard laboratory. Best known for controversial books like "On the Witness Stand" and "Suggestive articles on the relation of modern psychology to the ascertainment of truth in courts of law" (Munsterberg, 1907) his research focused on the use of word-association testing for credibility assessment and he is known as the "first scientist to lay out the rationale for a science of lie detection" (Adler, Herman, & Larson, 1928). In 1915, "after approximately two years of research" one of Munsterberg's students, William Marston (1893–1947), had seen little success with word-association testing and reported to Munsterberg that he had "discovered that systolic blood pressure changes reveal deception". Dr Munsterberg died on the lecture platform the next year but Marston's experiments continued; his report "Systolic Blood Pressure Symptoms of Deception" was published in the *Journal of Experimental Psychology* in April of 1917 (Marston, 1917). He continued at Harvard where he earned a law degree in 1918 and a PhD in psychology in 1921. In 1921, Dr Marston published "The Physiological Possibilities of the Deception Test" in the *Journal of Criminal Law and Criminology* (Marston, 1921) and one of the readers was John A. Larson, PhD.

Larson

Dr Larson was a Berkeley police officer with a Masters degree in fingerprint identification and a PhD in physiology and was a medical student at the University of California-Berkeley (UCB). With the cooperation of the UCB psychology department, he designed a multichannel instrument that recorded both cardiovascular activity and respiration. As a Berkeley investigator, Dr Larson tested 861 persons in 328 criminal cases – 182 suspects confessed – 310 persons were cleared of suspicion (Marston, 1938). In 1923,

Larson moved to Chicago to complete medical school and work as a criminologist with the Illinois Department of Public Welfare. He also conducted deception testing of "some 600 men in the penitentiaries" (McCormick, 1927), for the courts, and for various police agencies in Illinois.

Institute for Juvenile Research

A large number of Larson's tests were of juveniles at the Institute for Juvenile Research in Chicago. After getting his MD, he was hired as Chief Psychiatrist for the Illinois Prison Department and also worked at the Institute for Juvenile Research as a psychiatrist. At the Institute, he worked with Herman M. Adler, MD in the evaluation of delinquency cases and he tested hundreds of juveniles using an updated Cardio-Pneumo Psychogram (aka Berkeley Polygraph). "Deception and Self-Deception", authored by Larson and Adler, referred to 120 uses of the polygraph with juveniles on issues such as cheating, rape, sexual promiscuity, and malingering. The use of the polygraph at the Institute continued, "Deception Tests with Juvenile Delinquents" was authored by Vern W. Lyon of the Institute for Juvenile Justice Research and published by the American Psychological Association in 1935. Read at the forty-third annual meeting of the American Psychological Association, Ann Arbor, MI, September 4–7, 1935, this paper described a study involving 100 randomly selected individuals, all under 18, with an average IQ of 85. The participants, 81% male, had all been investigated by authorities and then referred by the Juvenile Court of Chicago for evaluation. In Lyon's study, "physiological evaluations were made only with a cardiosphygmograph and pneumograph, and without the electrodermal we use today, but were effective regardless of the age of the examinee" (Adang, 1995). Lyon reported that over 50% of the results had bearing on the Court's decisions and 100% were consistent with investigations and court findings (Lyon, 1935; Matte, 1998).

While Larson's efforts in Chicago could be seen as a starting point, the use of polygraph with juveniles did not stop there: in the *American Bar Journal* in 1964, Judge Pfaff wrote: "Since March 1962 … Los Angeles Superior Court has been utilizing the polygraph in domestic relations cases, first in child custody, and later in paternity cases. Attorneys were so satisfied with the results that they, not the judge, suggest the use of polygraph" (Ferguson & Miller, 1974). Along the same lines, the California Youth Authority reported that: "Since the polygraph began in the Youth Authority, examiners have been instrumental in discovering the perpetrators of literally hundreds of crimes, some extremely serious, and many innocent wards have been cleared of false allegations by polygraph use" (Lewis, 1979).

Polygraph in Criminal Court

The first criminal case where the polygraph was used as stipulated evidence in a jury trial was in 1935 in Columbia County, Wisconsin (Loniello and Grignano, 1935). While attitudes differ per jurisdiction and per courtroom, the polygraph is admissible as evidence in federal and military courts per Daubert and Scheffer and in 21 states. This author (Blackstone) has testified on polygraph tests introduced in civil, juvenile, and family courts, both with and without stipulation. At present, New Mexico, after approving the examiner and the examination, allows the polygraph without stipulation and courts in the remaining 20 (Alabama, Arizona, Arkansas, California, Delaware, Florida, Georgia, Idaho, Indiana, Iowa, Kansas, Nevada, New Jersey, North Dakota, Ohio, South Carolina, South Dakota, Utah, and Washington, Wyoming) admit polygraph results only by stipulation. There are, however, exceptions: it is possible for the polygraph to be admitted by judge's ruling, usually over-objection or due to an open-door and they have applied to cases of alleged perpetrators and alleged victims in all age groups. For example: in *Chambers v. State*, the polygraph results of both a 10-year-old girl's examination and the examination of the defendant were stipulated and admitted in trial. Chambers, the victim's mother's boyfriend, was deceptive on his examination, convicted of statutory rape and sentenced to 20 years. He appealed on the grounds that the polygraph test was insufficient evidence to corroborate the victim's claim and the appeals court agreed and reversed the conviction, alluding to the polygraph examiner's failure to comply with agreement of counsel. The Georgia Supreme Court reversed that decision. Chambers is important in that it treated the results of both examinations equally; corroborating the complaint and impeaching the denial of the perpetrator. In another case, *Commonwealth v. Butler*, the polygraph examination of an 11-year-old girl was admitted as evidence. At a church-based school in Pittsburg, Pennsylvania, the girl complained that Butler, who was pastor of that church, had reached under her skirt and fondled her buttocks, as well as rubbed his clothed genital area against her. Butler was convicted in 1991 and his motions for a New Trial and Arrest of Judgment were denied.

Post-Adjudication Polygraph

The post-adjudication treatment and monitoring of adults and juveniles has added another dimension to the polygraph field. In 1966, in the Wabash County Circuit of Illinois, Judge Clarence E. Partee employed the polygraph while deciding on probation applications and, 4 years later, began to require that probationers take annual polygraphs. In 1969, Judge John C. Tuttle in the Walla Walla District Court of Washington, developed a similar plan to monitor probationers. In 1973, in the Multnomah County Circuit of Oregon, Judge John C. Beatty, Jr added a polygraph stipulation to probation agreements made in his Court. These initiatives included testing of adults and juveniles.

The earliest program specific to juveniles started in 1984, in Jackson County, Oregon. In this program, adjudicated juveniles, both in semi-secure facilities and on probation, were referred by their respective treatment agency for polygraph testing. Jackson County was later designated a National Resource Site by the Center for Sexual Offender Management (CSOM), US Department of Justice (Lundell, 2013, private communication). In Jefferson County, Colorado, in 1989, a similar program began. Polygraph examiners would conduct examinations of juvenile probationers and detainees for treatment programs, semi-secure facilities, and state-funded juvenile detention centers (Jenks, 2013, private communication). In 2000, for example, The Colorado General Assembly amended and passed legislation (section 16-11.7-103, C.R.S.) that required the Sex Offender Management Board to develop and prescribe a standardized set of procedures for the evaluation and identification of juvenile sex offenders. The Board, which had originated in 1992, then prescribed procedural and qualifying standards for polygraph examiners as well as quality control standards. These and other programs were sometimes mandatory, such as in Florida 948.30 (a) "As part of a treatment program, participation at least annually in polygraph examinations to obtain information necessary for risk management and treatment and to reduce the sex offender's denial mechanisms". As a result of these and many other initiatives, the post-adjudication polygraph is common today during the management of adult and juvenile sex offenders and is used federally and in all states to some degree, with frequencies ranging from one to six times a year per sex offender.

According to the US Department of Justice (DOJ), there were an estimated 125 910 rapes and sexual assaults in 2009 (the most recent year for which data are available) and the National Juvenile Justice Network reports that juveniles were responsible for 12% of rape incidents and 19% of other sex crime incidents (Zimring, 2004). As of April 19, 2013, there are 747 408 registered sex offenders in the USA and its territories and about 35 states have juveniles on public sex offender registries – with some subjecting children younger than 14 to registration from 25 years to life; 265 000 of these registered offenders are currently under the supervision of correctional agencies (National Center for Missing and Exploited Children, 2013; Pittman, 2013b).

Note: Today's per annum rate of post-adjudication sex offender testing is unknown. However, by using the known data an estimate of 927 000 is not unreasonable ($3.5 \times 265\,000 = 927\,500$).

The polygraph is used with sex offender specific treatment in prison and during probation and parole, and in 19 of the 20 states with civil commitment laws. Federally, the polygraph is used during probation, during sex offender specific treatment in prison, and during civil commitment. Some are adults, some are juveniles, and some are now adults whose last offense was committed when a juvenile. There is also a comparatively small fraction of voluntary participants in periodic polygraph testing who are non-adjudicated.

PART 2: FAQ AND SPECIAL CONSIDERATIONS

The polygraph is used today with juveniles, before adjudication to assess deception (Adang, 1995; Craig & Molder, 2003) and post-adjudication in the monitoring of juvenile sex offenders on probation and parole (Adang, 1995; Blackstone, 2008; Craig & Molder, 2003; Emerick & Dutton, 1993). The applications found in juvenile testing will be limited to specific issue testing, disclosure testing, and maintenance testing. Another application seen with juveniles is confirmatory testing, which is the testing of an alleged victim/witness to confirm an allegation.

Professionals who are responsible for the evaluation and/or treatment of juveniles and who wish to augment their work with any of these applications will often have concerns.

How Can You Test a Young Person About Sexual Behavior When They are Still Developing Their Values, Their Beliefs About What is Right and What is Wrong?

Subsequent to an assortment of values and consequences, many are concerned that the polygraph, especially with juveniles, is unreasonable – what is *normal* in one culture is *perverted* in another. What is *healthy* in one culture is *illegal* in another. Teachers in Norway, for example, describe preschool children exploring their genitals and the genitals of their playmates as "coitus training", while preschool and school-aged children engaging in the exact same behavior in the USA are described as "perpetrators of inappropriate sexual behavior" (Vizard, Monck, & Misch, 1995). From Sweden come "stories about children acting out sexually, including undressing and simulating intercourse or even simulating threesomes etc. The teachers approach was that as long as the children are not physically hurting each other or anyone is coerced to participate, they would step back. They would of course not allow actual penetration… but sexual curiosity was otherwise not shunned. …teachers were more worried of the consequences of shaming a child's sexual development by indicating that sex was 'wrong'" (Karlsson, 2013, private communication). In seeming contrast, in the USA, "Jacob C. was 11 years old and living in Michigan when he was convicted of criminal sexual conduct for touching his younger sister's genitals. After serving a three-year sentence, he was placed on the state's sex offender registry and forced to live separately from his mother and sister, in a foster home" (Pittman, 2013a).

While it is quite true that cultural norms play a large role in how sexual behavior among juveniles is viewed, it is also true that the polygraph should not address the view. Polygraph should address the physical behavior and it should never address perspective or interpretation.

What is the Youngest Age for Testing With the Polygraph?

The American Polygraph Association, in the current model policy for post-conviction testing, includes in 9.2.2. *Age*: Persons whose chronological age is 12 years or greater should be considered suitable for polygraph testing unless they are substantially impaired. Polygraph testing should not be attempted with persons whose Mean Age Equivalency (MAE) or Standard Age Score (SAS) is below 12 years as determined by standardized psychometric testing (e.g., IQ testing, and adaptive functioning). How the above parameters were established is unknown.

While there is a dearth of empirical research specific to the use of the polygraph with a juvenile population, there are studies showing mixed results; some suggesting that age has no direct effect on the detection of deception with physiological measures (Bradley et al., 1996; Craig et al., 2011) and some indicating that juveniles under 11 were less detectable on a guilty knowledge task than older juveniles and adults (Abrams, 1975).

Some would question whether juveniles are viable candidates for polygraph, while others realize that fitness is determined per individual, not per group. SCOTUS, in Wheeler v. United States identified four factors to be considered in determining competency: (1) the child's ability to distinguish between truth and falsehood and to understand his ability to speak the truth; (2) the child's capacity at the time of the occurrence to perceive the events accurately; (3) the child's ability to retain an independent recollection of the occurrence; and (4) the child's capacity to translate the memory into words and to answer simple questions about it. These four prongs serve as an excellent baseline for determining competency for polygraph testing.

The Body and Mind of a Juvenile are Different than Adults, aren't They?

Whether the respondent is an adult or an adolescent; a male or a female; a "normal" person or a person with a personality disorder, all respondents have an autonomic nervous system with the same checks and balances. Whether the juvenile has a clear memory of the issue at hand is the concern. One might argue that executive functioning is not established until about the age of 21, but executive functioning is about decision making and the questions asked are simple and dichotomous – if not understood during the interview the physiological measures are not conducted.

Based on experience, this author (Blackstone) would suggest that juveniles tend to show fatigue, restlessness, and lack of attention after lengthy interviews. To avoid negative impact, the examiner should expect a two-phase examination. For example: 13-year-old Jason is interviewed for one hour and the session ends with a review of claims/disclosures. The second session is then scheduled within a 48-hour period to confirm those claims/disclosures (physiological measures).

The Juvenile I Am Seeing has Conduct Disorder and No Conscience. He Doesn't Care That He Raped His Sister. Will a Polygraph Work on Such a Personality?

There are no studies specific to the use of the polygraph with juveniles with specific personality disorders or traits. However, there are other studies that should be considered. Many feel that psychopathic habitual liars can easily "beat" the polygraph (Barland & Raskin, 1973; Ferguson & Miller, 1974; Floch, 1950; Levitt, 1955) because they are without conscience and are very adept at manipulating and deceiving others (Clancy, Noyes, & Travis, 1974; Cleckley, 1964). However, the term *pseudologia fantastica* suggests habitual or compulsive lying – not an absence of an autonomic nervous system (ANS). Moreover, several studies have addressed this issue and the result is consistent – psychopaths are as easy to detect as non-psychopaths. For example, in 1975, as part of his University of Utah doctoral dissertation, Gordon Barland conducted a study of 77 polygraph examinations he had conducted between 1973 and 1974. These were private examinations referred to him by law enforcement, and both prosecuting and defense attorneys. In that sample, the criminal suspects had been psychologically evaluated with an MMPI by Barland as part of the pre-test interview and their respective Pd (psychopathic defiance) scores were later weighed against a complex criterion: polygraph outcome, a five legal expert panel, and subsequent judicial reviews. A comparison of the 15 highest (top 2%) and 15 lowest (bottom 76%) Pd score and the outcomes of the polygraph and the criterion reviews showed no statistical differences in the two groups. This was later presented at the Society for Psychophysiological Research, Salt Lake City, Utah (Barland, 1975, 2011, private communication).

In 1978, Dr David Raskin and Dr Robert Hare found that "psychopaths were as easily detected as non-psychopaths, and psychopaths showed evidence of stronger electrodermal responses and heart rate decelerations". In this particular study, Dr Hare led a research team that conducted a mock-crime study using a group of 48 prisoners who were incarcerated in Lower Mainland Regional Correctional Centre in Bumaby, British Columbia. They were then evaluated by Dr Hare and half were diagnosed as psychopaths. They were then put into subgroups, half of each subgroup was "guilty" of taking $20 in a mock crime and the other half was "innocent". All of the participant inmates (psychopath and non-psychopath) were then examined by Dr David Raskin (then University of Utah Department of Psychology). Raskin tested the participants with a polygraph instrument using the Utah Zone of Comparison test format. The significant outcomes, after excluding inconclusive tests, were that the overall accuracy rate for all participants was 95%, there were no false-negative results in the study, and the psychopaths (guilty and innocent) were tested at a slightly higher rate of accuracy than was the entire group. The psychopaths were tested with an accuracy rate of 95.8% (Raskin & Hare, 1978).

Can the Court Really Force My Juvenile Client to Take a Polygraph?

No. While the polygraph may be "mandated", a polygraph examiner cannot administer an examination if a person is unwilling. Court rulings on the polygraph with juvenile sex offenders include In RE: DS, which comes from Warren County, Ohio. In that case, a learning disabled

11-year-old was adjudicated as a juvenile for rape and was ordered to take and pass polygraph examinations at the discretion of his therapist and probation officer. The Appeals Court affirmed the conviction and the Ohio Supreme Court reversed it in 2006, stating:

> *before a polygraph can be considered to be a reasonable probationary condition for a juvenile, there must be a showing that a polygraph is needed for therapeutic reasons in a particular case, that is, for the treatment and monitoring of the juvenile's behavior, and condition of probation for juvenile that he submit to and pass polygraph tests as may be directed by his probation officer or therapists was not reasonable; and condition of probation did not eliminate juvenile's rights against self-incrimination, and thus juvenile could assert them before giving answers that might incriminate him.*

PART 3: METHODOLOGY

The purpose of the polygraph, like any test, is to record and measure responses to an identifiable stimulus. In the polygraph test, that stimulus is intended to be a question but, because the test is 90% psychology, the possibility of contamination is significant. Part 3 will describe the polygraph instrument and the polygraph procedure, with an emphasis on parameters designed to discourage those contaminating factors. The discussion of methodology will be limited to the Comparison Question Technique (CQT) because, "In the field, the comparison question test (CQT) is the most commonly used technique for the detection of deception with the polygraph with adults" (Horowitz et al., 1997) and juveniles (Craig & Molder, 2003).

Physiology

The polygraph instrument simply records respiration, electrodermal activity, and cardiovascular activity to give the examiner a continuous monitor of the autonomic nervous system (ANS). Sometimes referred to as the visceral nervous system, the ANS is the part of the peripheral nervous system that acts as a control system. Its main purpose is maintaining homeostasis by regulating the body's visceral organs (heart rate, respiration rate, and perspiration, digestion and salivation, urination, sexual arousal and diameter of the pupils). These controls are generally automatic, performed without conscious effort or sensation, but some, such as breathing, work both involuntarily and in tandem with the conscious mind.

The main components of the ANS are the parasympathetic nervous system (PNS) and sympathetic nervous system (SNS) and these branches, while complementary, typically function in opposition to each other. For a loose analogy, one may think of the sympathetic branch as the *accelerator* and the parasympathetic branch as the *brake*.

The modern polygraph chart will include thoracic respiration, abdominal respiration, electrodermal activity, blood volume and pulse, and vasomotor activity.

Emergency Situations

The PNS serves as a means of conserving energy – another loose analogy would be the cruise control on a car. The PNS is usually dominant and the SNS, while it is always active at a basal level (sympathetic tone), becomes more active, or dominant, in stressful circumstances requiring quick responses. Also known as *emergency situations*, these will be either physical novelties (distraction, pain) or psychological novelties (emotion, cognitive arousal, or behavioral). In an *emergency situation*, a person's sympathetic branch is aroused automatically (sympathetic arousal) and then, to regain homeostasis, the parasympathetic branch counterbalances this arousal (allostasis).

At times, when the initial arousal is extreme, the parasympathetic compensation will be excessive (parasympathetic overcompensation).

Psychology

R.C. Davis, then professor of psychology at Indiana University, offered three possible explanations for physiological reactions during a polygraph examination: "the conditioned response theory, the conflict theory, and the punishment theory" (Davis, 1961) and the exact cause of physiological change during deception will probably never be identified. "It is not, however, imperative that we define the cause to prove that there is an effect. It is quite possible, and acceptable, to have a test validated as accurate for its specified purpose without having a complete theoretical understanding of the underlying theoretical constructs" (construct validity, Cook and Campbell, 1979).

Today, it is agreed that the psychological factors at play during deception can be identified as emotional arousal, cognitive arousal, and behavioral conditioning (Barland, 2011, private communication; Blackstone 2008, 2011) and there is an abundance of related theories (Table 4.1).

Table 4.1 Theories of Psychological Factors

The fear of detection theory (emotion)	Larson (1932)
Guilt and shame (emotion)	Munsterberg (1908)
Success and defeat (emotion)	Marston (1938)
Cognitive/intellectual awareness (cognitive)	Piaget (source unknown)
Conflict (cognitive)	Munsterberg (1908), Davis (1961)
Psychological set (cognitive)	Barland (1975)
Dichotomization (cognitive)	Ben-Shakhar (1990)
Arousal/attention (cognitive)	Raskin (1978)
Amount of information (cognitive)	Heslegrave (1981)
Novelty (cognitive)	Heslegrave (1981)
Retrieval difficulty (cognitive)	Heslegrave (1981)
Deception (lie) theory (cognitive)	
Psychophysiology (behavioral)	Raskin (1979)
Behavioral inhibition (behavioral)	Gray (1976) source unknown
Classical conditioning {crime} (behavioral)	Davis (1961)
Classical conditioning {punishment} (behavioral)	Lindsey (1955) source unknown

To determine which of the psychological factors caused or will cause sympathetic arousal at a certain time is, at least for now, a feat that is beyond science. The notion that physiological reactions occur for a reason limited to one theory is "incompatible with the psychophysiological literature" (Senter, Weatherman, Krapohl & Horvath 2010). The Fear of Detection theory is probably the favorite of polygraph schools and may be the most common explanation given by polygraph examiners: described as a fight or flight response (Cannon, 1915) (also called the fight-or-flight-or-freeze response, hyperarousal, or the acute stress response) the emotion of fear is the most common explanation given by polygraph examiners and, as a result, some are concerned that a polygraph examiner must somehow instill fear. While the fear response is easy to explain and is always a possible factor, fear is not a requirement. If fear (or any other emotion) were a requirement, low emotion situations, such as the 9 high quality laboratory studies of the Utah Zone shown in Table 4.2, would not have an average accuracy rate of 91%.

Differential Salience

Today, the term "differential salience" "provides a defensible and comprehendible theoretical framework through which a variety of explanations can be explained". Using salience we can "account for physiological responses that occur for a variety of reasons" (Senter et al., 2010). When

Table 4.2 Laboratory studies of the Utah Zone

	Guilty (Positive)				Innocent (Negative)			
Study	**n**	**% Correct**	**% Incorrect**	**% Inc.**	**n**	**% Correct**	**% Incorrect**	**% Inc.**
Driscoll et al. (1987)	20	90	0	10	20	90	0	10
Ginton et al. (1982)	2	100	0	0	13	85	15	0
Honts et al. (1994)	20	70	20	10	20	75	10	15
Horowitz et al. (1997)	15	53	20	27	15	80	13	7
Kircher & Raskin (1988)	50	88	6	6	50	86	6	8
Podlesny & Raskin (1978)	20	70	15	15	20	90	5	5
Podlesny & Truslow (1993)	72	69	13	18	24	75	4	21
Raskin and Hare (1978)	24	88	0	12	24	88	8	4
Rovner et al. (1979)	24	88	0	12	24	88	8	4
Means	247	80	8	12	210	84	8	8
Percent decisions		90	10			92	8	

From Raskin, D. C., & Honts, C. R. (2001). The comparison question test. In M. Kleiner (ed.). *Handbook of Polygraph Testing*, London: Academic Press, Chapter 1.

considering the underlying cause of arousal during polygraph testing, it is useful to think of a "continuum of causes, rather than one simple explanation" (Handler and Honts, 2007).

Effect (Deception Criteria)

The first modern paper on deception criteria was written in 1942 by Paul Trovillo, then a forensic psychologist at the Chicago Police Scientific Crime Detection Laboratory. In his paper "Deception Test Criteria", Dr Trovillo identified a total of 23 physiological response patterns as indicative of deception. For the cardiograph, he listed 11 responses, for the respiration tracing, he listed six responses and, for the electrodermal (GSR), he listed six. He also noted what he called ambiguities in all three channels (Ansley, 2008; Trovillo, 1942). Today, per research published between 1914

Table 4.3 Phasic response patterns considered for manual scoring

Channel	Response Pattern	Researchers
Cardiograph	Amplitude (primary)	Barland and Raskin (1973), Harris et al. (2000), Kircher & Raskin (1988), Podlesny & Truslow (1993)
Cardiograph	Duration	Harris et al. (2000), Kircher & Raskin (1988)
Pneumograph	Suppression (primary) (includes apnea)	Barland and Raskin (1973), Cutrow et al. (1972), Harris et al. (2000), Nakayama (1984), Patrick & Iaconno (1991), Wakamatsu & Yoshizumi (1968)
Pneumograph	Baseline (primary)	Harris et al. (2000), Kircher & Raskin (1988)
Pneumograph	I + E ratio	Benussi (1914), Burtt (1921a,b), Landis & Gullette (1925)
Pneumograph	Bradypnea (primary)	Barland and Raskin (1973), Cutrow et al. (1972), Patrick & Iaconno (1991)
Photoplethysmograph	Vasoconstriction	Kircher & Raskin (1988)
GSR – EDA	Amplitude (primary)	Harris et al. (2000), Kircher & Raskin (1988), Kugelmass et al. (1968), Patrick & Iacono (1991), Podlesny & Truslow (1993)
GSR – EDA	Duration	Kircher & Raskin (1988), Podlesny & Truslow (1993)
GSR – EDA	Complexity	Harris et al. (2000), Kircher & Raskin (1988)

Source: Blackstone, K. E. (2011). The polygraph, sex offenders, and the court; What professionals should know about polygraph … and a lot more. Concord: Emerson Books.

and 2000, there are 10 phasic response patterns (Table 4.3) which are considered for manual scoring.

Idiosyncratic Responses

Idiosyncratic responses are phasic responses that are exceptional to an individual and are repeated during physiological measures. They may be unique in their timing, or be an unusual pattern, or both. There is argument as to whether an idiosyncratic response should or should not be included as a response indicative of deception because it is "non-scientific" (Honts, 2009; Krapohl, 2009). Should an examiner use idiosyncratic responses that examiner should detail their reason for including them in test data analysis.

Test Data Analysis

Cleve Backster (1924–2013) was director of the CIA polygraph school until 1960, after which he opened a private school where he developed the first manual/numerical scoring system to assign value to deception criteria. His initial purpose was to assist his students in chart interpretation but, today, manual scoring is the only defensible means of scoring a Comparison Question Test (CQT).

Today there are four manual scoring systems for CQT formats (Weaver, 2009):

- The Backster method
- The Utah method
- The Federal or USAMPS (United States Army Military Police School) method
- The Empirical Scoring System (ESS).

These systems have their differences, some subtle and some not so subtle. The ESS, for example, recognizes only the five primary response patterns while other scoring systems include both primary and secondary patterns. Also the ESS has different cut-off scores for decisions and a different response window than other systems. Some CQT techniques require the use of a specific scoring system while other techniques are more flexible and allow an examiner to choose his methodology, however, the method used should always be consistent with literature and with the training the examiner has received.

Test Data Analysis – Digital

In 1974, John Reid and his staff met with Matthew Petrovic of the Northwestern University Biomedical Laboratories and Petrovic proposed the development of a method utilizing artificial intelligence for analyzing polygraph tracings. As the computer was foreign and the possibilities were unrealized, Reid declined. In 1990, the first commercially viable computerized polygraph system, both software and devices, came from the Axciton Corporation in Houston, Texas. About 2 years earlier, David Raskin and John Kircher at the University of Utah developed a system consisting of a device that measured charts coming from an analog instrument. Today, as a result of battle between manufacturers and operating systems, digital polygraph instruments are manufactured by Lafayette, Axciton, Stoelting, and Limestone and some digital algorithms unique to the instrument (Axciton + Whitestar) and some algorithms are more universal (PolyScore. QuESt, OSS-2 and OSS-3, and Identifi).

Garbage in – Garbage out

A computer scoring read-out such as "Deception Indicated – likelihood of deception is greater than 0.99" is quite impressive. Also, computerized algorithms are faster and thereby more convenient, but they:

- assume that the questions are written properly
- assume that the respondent fully understands the question
- ignore phasic responses that are outside of a fixed response interval.

Improvements in digital test data analysis, especially in measurement, continue but, for now, the outcome of an examination should not be based solely on a computerized scoring system. Impressive and convenient do not equal accurate.

Caution – Identifiable Stimulus

The test data analysis methodology described above assumes that only one stimulus (relevant issue) is causing a response. When examinations are extended to cover a broader scope, the reliability will decrease. A loose analogy would be using a blender (polygraph) to make fresh orange juice (reliable outcome). If only fresh oranges are used, then you have fresh orange juice. If rotten apples (improperly formed questions) and fresh oranges (properly formed questions) are blended you have bad fruit juice. If you blend apples, oranges and other fruit you may have a tasty drink, but it is not orange juice (your initial purpose).

Interview

At the onset of a pre-test interview, the person being interviewed (respondent) is a candidate for polygraph testing. The purpose of that portion of the interview is first to confirm the willingness of a candidate and then to analyze that candidate's competency and fitness for further testing.

Willingness

To establish willingness, this author requires that (1) the parent or legal guardian of that individual is in agreement with polygraph testing; (2) the court or legal representative is in agreement with the examination; (3) any medical doctor involved is in agreement with polygraph testing; and (4) any mental health professional involved is in agreement with the examination. Then, after obtaining signed permission, the examiner interviews the candidate to (5) determine their personal willingness to take the polygraph examination. The candidate, if willing, is then asked to sign a waiver agreeing to the examination and agreeing to the release of the results to designated parties such as the parent, the treatment provider, and the corrections supervisor.

Of the above, all steps are required for juveniles and 2–5 are required for adults.

Competency

The courts accept child witnesses and the Supreme Court of the United States (Wheeler v. United States) identified four factors to be considered in determining competency:

1. a child's ability to distinguish between truth and falsehood and to understand his ability to speak the truth
2. the child's capacity at the time of the occurrence to perceive the events accurately
3. the child's ability to retain an independent recollection of the occurrence
4. the child's capacity to translate the memory into words and to answer simple questions about it.

This author, based on the polygraph examination of about ten thousand individuals, about a thousand under the age of 18, incorporates the Wheeler guidelines when considering the competency of a candidate, adult or juvenile. Other factors to consider include physical and psychological fitness for testing.

Physical Fitness

Polygraph examiners are not medical doctors and interviews are best delayed if medical fitness is in question. While a cursory review of systems is required, opinions about physical fitness are based on observation, self-report, and opinions of qualified professionals. If the candidate sees a medical doctor and that medical doctor has approved polygraph testing, the examiner will be concerned about physical issues, such as recent trauma, changes in medication, and fatigue.

Psychological Fitness

Examiners must inquire about previous psychiatric or psychological consultation and treatment. This inquiry is not for the purpose of diagnosis, but to determine if a condition is in existence and if that condition may be a contaminating factor. Psychological contamination can be brought to the polygraph examination (distractions, outside issues) and this is when the examiner uses the interview to sort through possible distractions. Some distractions, such as general anxiety due to unfamiliarity, can be removed at the onset of the interview and some distractions, such as a wife in labor at the hospital or winning the lottery, require a delay of testing. The latter type of distraction can often be avoided by communication prior to the examination.

Target Issue

Once willingness, competency, and fitness have been confirmed, the specific purpose of the upcoming test (aka target issue) must be agreed upon. This is sometimes referred to as case review. Although an examiner will already know the expected target and the respondent's stance, this must be addressed at the onset of the interview to clarify the issue and confirm the respondent's stance. If the examination is event-specific and the issue at hand is the validity of a statement or denial, then that allegation is specified. In that situation, if the target issue is an act that occurred during a designated time or at a certain location and if that respondent denies the act, then the time and general location becomes the target issue. If the examination is for screening behavior, a limited timeframe must be agreed upon and that is the target issue. The target issue (event or period) is then discussed and generic questions written during preparation are posed. The goals of this period are to establish objectivity, allow a narrative, and to establish the respondent's stance on that issue (denial, description). The outcome of the examination can be questionable if the pre-test interview is exploratory and is used to generate disclosures. The examiner can seem accusatory and the topic is unclear.

Question Construction

The questions asked during the physiological measures in a polygraph examination will be limited to five types of questions: Irrelevant/neutral, Symptomatic, Sacrifice Relevant, Comparative, and Relevant questions. With the greatest concerns being uncertainty and unnecessary novelty, there are standards for the construction of each type of question. Variance from these standards makes the outcome questionable.

Relevant Questions

As the outcome of the examination is based on a collective score of all relevant questions, a polygraph examination report will always include the relevant questions. When a polygraph report lands on your desk and you are curious about the reliability of the outcome, see if these rules were followed:

Rule 1: The relevant questions must be questions the respondent can be absolutely certain about.

Rule 2: Relevant questions must not cause any unnecessary mental activity. They must be simple, direct and unemotional.

Rule 3: Relevant questions must address a physical behavior that has only one interpretation.

Note: In confirmatory testing, the action verb can be a possibly ambiguous term, such as rape.

Rule 4: Relevant questions must deal with a direct physical act, not an interpretation of an act.

Rule 5: Relevant questions must have only one action verb, dealing with only one physical act.

Rule 6: Relevant questions must have a well-defined timeframe.

Rule 7: Relevant questions must have only one dimension.

Rule 8: Relevant questions must have only one physical target.

Rule 9: Relevant questions must not address intention or purpose.

Rule 10: Relevant questions deal with the act, not the result of an act.

Rule 11: Qualifiers are placed as a prefix, not a suffix.

Question Review

At the end of the pre-test interview, the questions are revised and then in their new form they are reviewed with the respondent. As part of this review, the respondent is asked for their interpretation and the examiner must be attentive to uncertainty. If the examiner fails to establish rapport and does not encourage a narrative, "an examinee will not readily admit he does not understand a question" (Ansley, 1998). While this review is an opportunity for the respondent to point out any errors or lack of certainty in the meaning of the questions, it is also an opportunity for the examiner to avoid post-test concerns such as these:

- "My son said he didn't understand the questions you asked him – is that why he was deceptive?"
- "My son said you asked him questions he didn't understand – aren't you supposed to explain them?"
- "Are you sure my client understood the questions?"

Relevant Question Grouping

The final decision (outcome) of a polygraph test is limited to the scope of the relevant question group and "(it) is generally recognized that decision accuracy is degraded when multiple issues are presented in the same test" (Krapohl, 2006). If, as discussed earlier, the pre-test interview focuses on the target or relevant issue and not on peripherals that are possibly contaminating and if the relevant question group addresses a single physical act, then the stimulus can be identified as that relevant issue. If the stimulus can be identified then you have a diagnostic or "forensic" test. If, however, the relevant issues are independent issues, either occurring in the same incident (multifaceted) or in the same time period (multi-issue), the stimulus cannot be identified and you have a utility test. In the book "Polygraph, Sex Offenders and the Court", Blackstone addressed the differences between forensic and utility testing and pointed out that "forensic polygraph has safeguards which keep its error rate below 10 per cent, while utility tests ... actually invite errors" and " a positive outcome (deception indicated) cannot be reached when using a utility test" (Blackstone, 2011).

What if There are Multiple Issues?

The notion of measuring the response to an identifiable stimulus demands that the stimulus can actually be identified. If there are multiple issues at hand, and the examiner is concerned with accuracy, the examiner must prioritize and use a single-issue test to address each issue. But, *what if the examiner uses the utility approach where the relevant questions are independent? Does that mean the test is unreliable?* No, it does not.

A positive outcome (deception indicated) cannot be reached when using a utility test. If a utility test has been given and significant reactions (significant reactions is not deception indicated) are noticeable, the examiner must follow up with a single-issue test about that issue. This is called the Successive Hurdles Approach. Failure to conduct a follow-up examination on a multiple-issue examination is an error unique to utility testing. Other possible errors to consider are:

Mixing Known with Unknown

It is an error to mix questions about a specific incident with a question about possible behavior outside of that incident. "Did you touch your sister's bare vagina", "On July 10, 2007, did you touch your sister's bare vagina", and "Did you touch your sister's friend Deb between the legs?" The first two questions are fine, but by adding the third one and asking about a second target (sister's friend Deb) when there has been no allegation of that makes it a mixture of known and unknown. If there is a known issue, the examiner should first resolve that issue. By adding an unknown issue/target, the examiner has turned a reliable examination into a 50-50 utility test and has lost any claim to objectivity.

Mixing Timeframes

Another error in the grouping of relevant questions is to mix timeframes; the relevant questions address more than one period of time. *Since your last test, have you had physical sexual contact with an underage person? Since your last test have you had physical sexual contact with anyone younger than 18? Before your conviction, did you have physical sexual contact with anyone under the age of 18?* This type of error is fairly common in the screening tests of convicted sex offenders. In a group of relevant questions, the timeframe must be constant – the target may change, especially in a screening test, but the timeframe must be constant.

Novelty

Novelty – deviation from what seems normal – is a factor that can cause sympathetic arousal. Novelty could be an outside interference, noticeable change in the examiner's voice, a difference in the period of time between questions, and it could be a difference in the structure of the different questions. Imagine that all questions, with one exception, are simple: *Did you shoot that man? Did you shoot that man in that parking lot?* Are you lying to me when you say you did not shoot that man in that parking lot? The physiological reactions associated with differential salience could result from "guilt, fear, excitement, content complexity or even delight" (Vrij, 2008).

Comparative Questions

Relevant questions are measured by comparing them to Comparison questions. The rules for construction of comparative questions and relevant questions are quite different. Some formats are designed for certain types of comparative questions and some are flexible. The different forms of comparative questions are:

- Probable lie crime controls that address the same form of behavior in a different time period
- Non-specific lie control (with or without a time bar) that address honesty, or overall truth
- Directed lie controls where the respondent is instructed to lie to a certain question.

Note: "With and without a time bar" can also be identified as "exclusive and inclusive".

There is no research that shows that a certain form is more or less effective. For example, Dr Charles Honts, a primary developer and researcher on the Utah technique, states that although the Utah was designed for probable lies, the directed lie works just as well. "My opinion is that the research shows no consistent differences in the validity of properly conducted DL and PL polygraphs" (Honts, private communication 2008).

While relevant questions are simple and direct, and cover a limited time period, comparatives are complex, vague, and broad in scope. Negative or NDI calls are not based on a "lack of response" but on a constantly greater response to the comparative than to the relevant. With comparative questions, the examiner is encouraging mental activity due to vagueness or complexity and the greatest errors in formulation of a comparative question include making it too definite (the opposite of broad, complex, vague) or too strong (causing it to overshadow the relevant) or there is little if any distinction between the comparative and the relevant.

Rules to follow:

Rule 1: Comparison questions must not be detailed or specific.

Rule 2: Comparison questions must not be more salient than relevant questions.

Rule 3: When testing about sexual behavior, the comparison questions must not address sexual behavior.

Validated Techniques

Techniques are set formats with specific protocols as to structure, content, sequence, and test data analysis. These techniques are designed for different issues and venues, but the purpose of any technique is to eliminate possibly contaminating factors. As of 2012, the American Polygraph Association (APA) standards require that:

> *A member polygraph examiner shall use a validated testing technique. For purposes of these standards a testing technique shall be considered valid if supported by research conducted in accordance with the APA's research standards. Upon request for a minimum of five years from publication, researchers of polygraph techniques shall provide reasonable access to validation data for critical review. Where examinations deviate from the protocols of a validated testing technique the deviations should be noted and justified in writing (3.9.1).*

As of 2012, the APA recognizes a total of 19 techniques (Table 4.4) as validated when "… there exists at least two published empirical studies, original and replicated, demonstrating an unweighted average accuracy rate of …" and also requires different levels of overall accuracy for different forms of testing. These forms with their respective levels are:

- Evidentiary: 0.90 and above
- Paired (testing of an alleged perpetrator and the accuser): 0.86 and above
- Investigative: 0.80 and above.

Note: Coming from four different families (Utah Zone, Federal Zone, Backster Zone, and MGQT), some of the techniques are virtually the same examination, but used in a different study and given a different name.

The only multi-issue screening test, the Directed Lie Screening Test (DLST) or Test for Espionage and Sabotage (TES) is designed for counter-intelligence screening and, of the remaining techniques, all but one is designed for single issue testing. That technique, the Air Force Modified General Question Test (AFMGQT) is designed for multifaceted testing, which is testing about possibly independent parts of the same incident.

If examiners are concerned with optimal testing and following the standards of the APA, any positive test (Deception Indicated) of a sex offender (adult or juvenile) must be the result of a single-issue examination. When using a multi-issue or multifaceted technique, that examiner must use the Successive Hurdles Approach, which is following the screening test with a single-issue test, to reach a positive conclusion.

PART 4: POST-ADJUDICATION POLYGRAPH OF JUVENILES – PRACTICAL APPLICATIONS

The parameters described earlier are the same in all venues and in all applications of the polygraph instrument. The post-adjudication testing of juvenile sex offenders is no exception. The applications found in juvenile post-adjudication testing will be limited to specific issue testing, disclosure testing, and maintenance testing. Another application, known as confirmatory testing, seen with juveniles is the testing of an alleged victim/witness to confirm an allegation. The scenarios described below come from actual situations the author was involved in as an examiner.

Confirmatory Testing

An alleged victim of a sexual offense is asked to take a polygraph. This often appears when there is a lack of corroborating evidence, but often these tests take place in pairs (alleged victim and alleged perpetrator).

Scenario 1: 12-year-old Sarah has told her friend, who told her mother, who told Sarah's mother Betty that the day she stayed home from school; "a man with green eyes raped me". Betty immediately takes Sarah to the hospital to be examined and when they reach the hospital Betty remembers that she owes money to the same hospital – they turn

Table 4.4 Recognized APA techniques

Technique	Scoring System	Correct Decisions*	Standard Deviation	0.95 Confidence Intervals	INC	Standard Deviation	0.95 Confidence Intervals
Evidentiary (0.90 and above)							
Utah ZCT RCMP	Utah	0.939	0.038	0.864 to 0.999	0.185	0041	0.104 to 0.266
Utah ZCT PLC	Utah	0.931	0.026	0.879 to 0.983	0.077	0.028	0.022 to 0.133
Utah ZCT combined	Utah	0.930	0.026	0.875 to 0.984	0.107	0.028	0.048 to 0.165
Federal or Utah ZCT	ESS	0.921	0.028	0.866 to 0.977	0.098	0.030	0.039 to 0.157
Federal You-Phase[1]	ESS	0.904	0.032	0.841 to 0.966	0.192	0.033	0127 to 0.256
Utah ZCT DLC	Utah	0.902	0.31	0.841 to 0.962	0.073	0.25	0.023 to 0.122
Paired (0.86 and above)							
Federal You-Phase	7-position	0.883	0.035	0.813 to 0.952	0.168	0.037	0.096 to 0.241
Federal ZCT	7-position evidentiary	0.880	0.034	0.813 to 0.948	0.085	0.029	0.028 to 0.141
AFMGQT[1]	ESS	0.875	0.039	0.798 to 0.953	0.170	0.036	0.100 to 0.241
Backster You-Phase[1]	Backster	0.862	0.037	0.787 to 0.932	0.196	0.040	0.117 to 0.275
Federal ZCT	7-position	0.860	0.037	0.801 to 0.945	0.171	0.040	0.113 to 0.269
Investigative (0.80 and above)							
DLST (TES)[1]	ESS	0.858	0.037	0.786 to 0.930	0.090	0.026	0.039 to 0.142
DLST (TES)[1]	7 Position	0.844	0.039	0.768 to 0.920	0.088	0.028	0.034 to 0.142
CIT	Lykken	0.823	0.041	0.744 to 0.903	NA	NA	NA
AFMGQT[1]	7-position	0.817	0.042	0.734 to 0.900	0.197	0.030	0.138 to 0.255

Outliers – questionable							
MQTZCT[2]	Matte	0.994	0.013	0.968 to 0.999	0.029	0.015	0.001 to 0.058
IZCT[3]	Horizontal	0.989	0.10	0.969 to 0.999	0.066	0.026	0.015 to 0.116

*Not including inconclusive findings.

ESS = Empirical scoring system.

Thirty-seven studies satisfied the qualitative and quantitative requirements for inclusion in the meta-analysis. These studies described the results of 52 different experimental or survey results, involving 289 different scorers who provided 12665 scored results of 4283 examinations, including 6597 scores of 2300 confirmed deceptive examinations, 6068 scores of 1983 confirmed truthful exams. Some of the cases were scored by multiple scorers and using multiple TDA methods (APA executive summary, 2011).

Excluding outlier results, diagnostic techniques produced a combined unweighted decision accuracy rate of 0.921, with a combined inconclusive rate of 0.088. PDD techniques suitable for multi-issue screening exams produced a combined decision accuracy rate of 0.850 with a combined inconclusive rate of 0.125. The unweighted aggregation of all validated PDD techniques, excluding outlier results, produced a decision accuracy level of 0.871 with an inconclusive rate of 0.127.

Scoring System refers to the required scoring system for the technique. The same technique can have different CD with different scoring systems.

APA executive summary, 2011

[1]Executive summary report indicates that publications are pending.

[2]Generalizability of this outlier result is limited by the fact that the authors and investigators have advised the necessity of intensive training available only from the technique developer, and have suggested that the complexity of the technique exceeds that which other professionals can learn from the published resources (APA executive summary, 2011).

[3]Generalizability of this outlier result is limited by the fact that no measures of test reliability have been published for this technique (APA executive summary, 2011).

around at the door of the hospital and go back home. Sarah repeats the story at school the next day and the police are called. A medical examination is never done and the only evidence is a forensic interviewer who has reported to the police "Sarah seems to be telling the truth". Ten months into the investigation, a police polygraph examiner is contacted. There is no defense attorney involved and the district attorney's office gets an agreement signed by the parent. After preparation and talking with Betty and Sarah, the examiner decides to continue with the examination. An agreement has been made that the outcome might lead to a post-test interview. Sarah is given the most accurate examination available and the relevant questions were: *Did the man with green eyes rape you? Did the man with green eyes rape you at your house? Did the man with green eyes rape you at your house on … ?* The outcome, based on manual scoring was "Deception Indicated". In the post-test interview, the outcome is discussed and Sarah admits that "I made it up … I was talking to my girlfriend, she told me about having sex with her boyfriend and I told her about being raped. She called her mother and her mother called my Mom. It just got out of hand … it seems like you are the first person I have told who was really listening".

Specific Issue Testing

Offenders are denying the instant offense or a significant part of that offense.

Scenario 2: 13-year-old Johnny is accused of performing oral sex on his 9-year-old half-brother. He was arrested and given a stipulated release by the Juvenile Court. As part of the agreement, he saw a psychologist and was to see a polygraph examiner. His mother was first interviewed by both examiners and she was in agreement. When interviewed by the psychologist he denied the incident. While discussing the target issue with the polygraph examiner, he gave details as to how he and his brother watched an orgy scene in a movie "John Carpenter's Vampires" and then mimicked that scene. There was no test given and Johnny was referred back to the psychologist for further discussion.

Disclosure Testing

Offenders are tested to see if they are fully disclosing about the instant offense or the instant offense behavior or, more generally, about deviant behavior prior to a certain point (usually point of conviction). A rule to remember: the broader the scope, the lower the specificity.

Scenario 3: Johnny from Scenario 2 has stated that he and his brother had consensual sex, but the police report suggests the use of force. The psychologist asks the examiner to continue with the examination and focus on the claim of force. A week after the initial interview, Johnny was re-interviewed and was asked these relevant questions: *Did you physically force your brother to perform oral sex on you? Did you physically force your brother to perform oral sex on you that night in your bedroom?* Johnny was deceptive and admitted that his brother had resisted and eventually ran from the bedroom. Johnny later revealed to the psychologist that he had also molested his younger sister and a younger cousin.

Maintenance testing

Offenders are tested to see if they are following the guidelines of their treatment.

Scenario 4: David was adjudicated at the age of 16 for voyeurism – watching his older sister shower. Stipulations include psychological evaluation, but he avoids and refuses for 2 years. At the age of 18, he finally sees a psychologist where, in his evaluation (testing and clinical interview), he admits to the charge and denies any history of voyeurism. Then referred to a polygrapher, disclosure testing revealed an extensive history of peeping and public masturbation. He denied going the "next step" and "having physical sexual contact" with anyone he secretly watched. During the next 2-year period, David becomes a registered sex offender on adult probation and he is tested quarterly. Because of his background, his tests are broken into two segments, one about peeping and one about "masturbation to fantasies about forcible sex". He is deceptive each time he is tested. While the psychologist assumes that the deception is general or that David is withholding information about his own victimization, the polygraph examiner remembers a rapist with a similar MO who he had seen earlier in his career. In subsequent meetings with David's probation officer and psychologist, the polygraph examiner compares David's MO and the rapist from the past. Less than a month later, during an ATSA convention, the examiner gets a phone call from David's probation officer. David's probation had been revoked because he was arrested for rape and three more charges of rape were pending. They all included peeping, masturbation, and rape.

CONCLUSION

From a Clinician's Perspective

When Dr Adler and Dr Larson presented at the American Neurological Society meeting in Atlantic City, NJ in May of 1927, they referred to:

> *Case 5: A girl, referred to the Institute for Juvenile Research for sex delinquency, lied to the psychiatrist regarding her sex life. The psychiatrist frequently refers such cases for a deception test either because of apparent discrepancies, or suspected ones. The record shows rather marked changes in the blood pressure curve following her denial, as contrasted with the curve with answers to other questions were given. She confessed. The resistance to the discussion of sex having been removed, the psychiatrist was then able to begin psychotherapy.*

The polygraph procedure has changed greatly since that time, but the purpose remains the same. The "resistance" is removed.

From an Attorney's Perspective

In his controversial 1908 book "On the Witness Stand", Munsterberg wrote about the "rapid progress of experimental crimino-psychology" and about the physiological assessment of witness credibility, to which John Wigmore rejoined a year later in the Illinois Law Review and in his famous book Wigmore on Evidence "if there is ever a psychological test for the valuation of witnesses the law will run to meet it". Contrary to Dean Wigmore's prophesy, the law has instead been running in the opposite direction, at least until the installment of the polygraph in the post-adjudication monitoring and evaluation of sexual offenders.

From the Authors' Perspective

The Court's unwillingness to accept an under-explored method in 1923 and behaviorist John Watson's subsequent recommendation of "laboratory for another 25 years" were both well founded, however, the opinions which currently blockade the polygraph are no more than adherence to custom. Today, opinions and methods which could have been challenged in the courtroom and subsequently improved are instead coalesced with myths and misconceptions broadcast on television and reiterated during coffee breaks. Instead of arguments about the polygraph, the Court hears arguments about tradition and fears that the polygraph will somehow replace the jury system.

From the Perspective of Truth-telling Victims and Truth-telling Deniers

In *Chambers v. State*, the polygraph results of both a 10-year-old girl's examination and the examination of the defendant were stipulated and admitted in trial. Chambers, the victim's mother's boyfriend, was deceptive on his examination, convicted of statutory rape and sentenced to 20 years. He appealed on the grounds that the polygraph test was insufficient evidence to corroborate the victim's claim and the appeals court agreed and reversed the conviction, alluding to the polygraph examiner's failure to comply with agreement of counsel. The Georgia Supreme Court reversed that decision. Chambers is important in that it treated the results of both examinations equally; corroborating the complaint and impeaching the denial of the perpetrator. In another case, Commonwealth v. Butler, the polygraph examination of an 11-year-old girl was admitted as evidence. At a church-based school in Pittsburg, Pennsylvania, the girl complained that Butler, who was pastor of that church, had reached under her skirt and fondled her buttocks, as well as rubbed his clothed genital area against her. Butler was convicted in 1991 and his motions for a New Trial and Arrest of Judgment were denied. Both Butler and Chambers wish the Courts had stuck to tradition.

REFERENCES

Abrams, S. (1975). The validity of the polygraph technique with children. *Journal of Police Science and Administration, 3*, 310–311.

Adang, S. R. (1995). The use of the polygraph with children. *Polygraph, 24*, 259–274.

Adler, Herman, M., & Larson, J. A. (1928). Deception and self-deception. *Journal of Abnormal Psychology and Social Psychology, 22*, 364–371.

Ansley, N. (1998). Question formulation. *Polygraph, 27*, 181–183.

Ansley, N. (2008). Development of deception criteria prior to 1950. *Polygraph, 37*, 17–25.

Barland, G. H. (1975). *Detection of deception in criminal suspects: A field validation study.* Dissertation University of Utah.

Barland, G. H., & Raskin, D. C. (1973). Detection of deception. In W. F. Prokasy & D. C. Raskin (Eds.), *Electrodermal activity in psychological research* (pp. 417–477). New York: Academic Press.

Blackstone, K. E. (2008). Post conviction polygraph in the community and court: Raising the bar on PCSOT examiners. *The Forensic Examiner, 17*, 72–79.

Blackstone, K. E. (2011). *The polygraph, sex offenders, and the court; What professionals should know about polygraph ... and a lot more.* Concord: Emerson Books.

Bradley, M. T., Russell, E. C., & Li, K. (1996). Differentiating levels of moral development using the guilty knowledge test. Unpublished manuscript.

Cannon, W. B. (1915). *Bodily changes in pain, hunger, fear and rage: An account of recent researches into the function of emotional excitement.* New York: Appleton.

Clancy, J., Noyes, R., & Travis, T. A. (1974). The psychopathic personality. *Postgraduate Medicine, 55*, 175–180.

Cleckley, H. (1964). *The mask of sanity*. St Louis: Mosby.
Cook, T. D., & Campbell, D. T. (1979). *Quasi-experimentation: Design and analysis issues for field settings*. Boston: Houghton Mifflin.
Craig, R. A., & Molder, C. (2003). The use of law enforcement polygraph tests with juveniles. *Journal of Credibility Assessment and Witness Psychology*, *4*, 63–74. Reprinted (2004) Polygraph, 33, 190–200.
Craig, R. A., Raskin, D. C., & Kirscher, J. C. (2011). The use of physiological measures to detect deception in juveniles. *Polygraph*, *40*, 86–99.
Davis, R. C. (1961). Physiological responses as a means of evaluating information. In A. D. Biderman & H. Zimmer (Eds.), *The manipulation of human behaviour*. New York: Wiley.
Emerick, R. L., & Dutton, W. A. (1993). The effects of polygraph on the self report of adolescent sex offenders: Implications for risk assessment. *Annals of Sex Research*, *6*, 83–103.
Ferguson, M., & Miller, A. L. (1974). *Polygraph for the defense*. Springfield, IL: Charles C Thomas.
Handler, M., & Honts, C. R. (2007). Psychophysiological mechanisms in deception detection. *Polygraph*, *36*, 221–232.
Hindman, J., & Peters, J. M. (1988). Research disputes assumptions about child molesters, 7. *National District Attorneys Association Bulletin*, *1*, 3.
Hindman, J., & Peters, J. M. (2001). Polygraph testing leads to better understanding adult and juvenile sex offenders. *Federal Probation Newsletter*, *65*, 3.
Honts, C. R. (2009). Presentation to the Florida Polygraph Association, November.
Krapohl, C. (2006). Comparison of evidentiary and investigative decision rules. *Polygraph*, *35*, 55–62.
Krapohl, D. J. (2009). Numerical evaluation and wise decisions. *Polygraph*, *38*, 57–71.
Larson, J. A. (1932). *Lying and its detection; A study of deception and deception tests*. Chicago: University of Chicago Press.
Lewis, W. B. (1979). Polygraph today in court and CYA. *California Youth Authority Quarterly*, *32*, 25–29.
Lyon, V. (1935). Deception tests with juvenile delinquents. *Psychological Bulletin*, *32*, 685–686.
Marston, W. (1917). Systolic blood pressure symptoms of deception. *The Journal of Experimental Psychology*, *2*, 117–163.
Marston, W. (1921). The physiological possibilities of the deception test. *The Journal of Criminal Law and Criminology*, *11*, 551–570.
Marston, W. (1938). *The lie detector test*. New York: Richard R. Smith. (reprinted 1989 by American Polygraph Association) pp. 1–179.
Matte, J. A. (1998). *Forensic psychophysiology using the polygraph*. J.A.M. Publications.
McCormick, C. T. (1927). Deception-tests and the law of evidence. *California Law Review*, *15*, 484.
Munsterberg, H. (1907). Psychology and the "Third Degree". *McClure's Magazine*, *29*, 614–621.
Munsterberg, H. (1908). *On the witness stand; Essays on psychology and crime*. Doubleday, Page and Company.
National Center for Missing and Exploited Children. 2013 http://www.missingkids.com.
O'Donohue, W. T., & Plaud, J. J. (1994). The conditioning of human sexual arousal. *Archives of Sexual Behavior*, *23*, 321–344.
Pittman, N. (2013a). Sex offenders aren't all monsters. *The Daily Beast*, May.
Pittman, N. (2013b). *Raised on the registry: The irreparable harm of placing children on the sex offender registries in the US*. Human Rights Watch.
Raskin, D. C., & Hare, R. D. (1978). Psychopathy and detection of deception in a prison population. *Psychophysiology*, *15*, 126–136.
Ben-Shakhar, G., & Furedy, J. J. (1990). *Theories and Applications in the Detection of Deception: A Psychophysiological and International Perspective*. New York: Springer-Verlag.

Senter, S., Weatherman, D., Krapohl, D., & Horvath, F. (2010). Psychological set or differential salience: a proposal for reconciling theory and terminology in polygraph testing. *Polygraph, 39*, 109–117.
Trovillo, P. V. (1942). Deception test criteria. *Journal of Criminal Law and Criminology, 33*, 338–358.
Vizard, E., Monck, E., & Misch, P. (1995). Child and adolescent sex abuse perpetrators: A review of the research literature. *Journal of Child Psychology and Psychiatry, 56*, 731–756.
Vrij, A. (2008). *Detecting lies and deceit: Pitfalls and opportunities* (2nd ed). Chichester: Wiley.
Weaver, R. S. (2009). The numerical evaluation of polygraph charts: evolution and comparison of three major systems. *Polygraph, 38*, 2–12.
Zimring, F. E. (2004). *An American travesty*. Chicago: University of Chicago Press.

CASES CITED

Chambers v. State, 245 S.E.2d 467 (Ga 178), 22CrL 2139.
Commonwealth v. Butler, 621 A.2d 630 (Pa.Super. 1993).
Frye v. United States, 293 F. 1013 (D.C. Cir. 1923).
In re D.S., 111 Ohio St.3d 361 (2006).
Ohio v. Sharma (Case No. CR 06-09-3248).
State v. Loniello and Grignano (Circuit Court of Columbia County, Wisconsin 1935).
Wheeler v. United States, Tex, 16 S.Ct. 93, 159 U.S. 523. 40 L.Ed. 244 (1895).

CHAPTER 5

Writing Dispositional Evaluations of Juveniles Adjudicated for Sexual Offenses and Juveniles with Sexual Behavioral Problems

Daniel S. Bromberg
Special Psychological Services, LLC, Bloomfield, NJ, USA

INTRODUCTION

Numerous authoritative texts regarding report writing exist (e.g., Heilbrun, Grisso, & Goldstein, 2009; Grisso, 2013). The purpose of this chapter is to synthesize the theoretical underpinnings underlying forensic mental health assessments for juveniles adjudicated for sexual offenses and juveniles with sexual behavior problems and to guide clinicians in communicating the findings of their evaluations in an effective manner. Sample reports are provided that integrate generally accepted principles of forensic report writing.

At the outset, it is important for readers to understand particular terms used in this chapter. An adolescent adjudicated for a sexual offense is an adolescent (generally ages 13–17, inclusive) whose alleged problematic sexual behaviors have been brought to a court to determine if those problematic behaviors have, in fact, been displayed and if those behaviors constituted a criminal offense.[1] Sexual offenses for which an adolescent can be arrested and criminally charged will vary by jurisdiction. In contrast, there are many adolescents who, despite having engaged in some form of illegal sexual behavior for which they could have been arrested, were not arrested and processed through the justice system.

A forensic mental health assessment (FMHA) is "an evaluation that is performed as part of the legal decision-making process, for the purpose of assisting the legal decision-maker or one of the litigants in using relevant

[1] This "ultimate (legal) issue" is determined by the trier of fact. The trier of fact is likely to be a judge, rather than a jury, in a juvenile matter. Although the topic of considerable professional controversy, it is generally accepted that forensic evaluators should *not* offer opinions on the probable innocence or guilt of the examinee (e.g., Tillbrook, Mumley, & Grisso, 2003).

Toolkit for Working with Juvenile Sex Offenders.
DOI: http://dx.doi.org/10.1016/B978-0-12-405948-1.00005-0

clinical and scientific data (Heilbrun, 2001, p. 3, as cited in Heilbrun, Grisso & Goldstein, 2009, pp. 11–12)." These authors noted that FMHA's are undertaken specifically to produce evidence that will be used in court. Such assessments are guided by a specific legal question facing a legal decision-maker. The forensic mental health examiner determines the type of data needed to answer specific legal questions and develops an assessment procedure designed to obtain this information. In such an evaluation, an examiner's primary allegiance is to the legal process and its decision-makers, not to the examinee. An adolescent adjudicated for a sexual offense would undergo an FMHA.

Grisso (2010) made the following points:

> *… Forensic reports are written to meet the demands of legal forums, non-clinical readers and decision-makers, and due process constraints. Some reports for use by courts are indeed clinical reports in terms of their content, when the examiner is asked simply to address clinical issues rather than apply them to a forensic question. Even in those cases, however, the information must be conveyed in different ways than in general clinical reports because of the demands of a non-clinical audience and legal use.*

According to Grisso (2010), there is a professional consensus regarding the general organization of forensic reports. Reports should begin with an introductory section containing the reason for referral, the sources of data upon which the evaluator relied, and the manner in which the examinee was informed of the limits of confidentiality. A second section containing data relevant to the referral question(s) should follow the introductory section. The third section should provide the examiner's interpretations of the data that are relevant to addressing the forensic referral question(s). Such a general outline allows for considerable variation in subheadings within each section. Subheadings will vary based upon the demands of jurisdictions, different types of forensic and/or clinical questions, and the examiner's preferences for organizing the content for a particular case.

Although FMHA's of juveniles with problematic sexual behaviors can be written for an assortment of purposes, this chapter will be limited to dispositional evaluations. Dispositional evaluations focus on the needs of the adolescent and provide the court with recommendations regarding a rehabilitation plan. Dispositional evaluations provide information useful in determining the degree of security and types of services that are needed.

Adolescents with sexual behavior problems who are not adjudicated may undergo mental health assessments that are non-forensic in nature. Such evaluations may be needed to address a youth's need for services, as well as to address some of the questions that would ordinarily be addressed in an FMHA. Such issues commonly include the level of structure and supervision the youth needs (e.g., at home receiving outpatient services, residential treatment setting, or secure care setting). Although these two adolescents are distinct from a legal perspective, in practice, these populations overlap substantially in their needs. Therefore, for purposes of this chapter, these two populations will be treated as one. Certain components of the FMHA may not apply to evaluations conducted for clinical, rather than forensic purposes.

GENERAL GUIDING PRINCIPLES

Issues of informed consent and assent are complicated in work with minors. These issues are further complicated when psycholegal matters are being addressed. Kinscherff and Latham (this volume) provide an excellent discussion of issues regarding consent and assent for evaluations of alleged juvenile sex offenders.

Although there is no professional consensus regarding the "proper" or "best" way to write and organize a dispositional evaluation, there are some general guidelines to which practitioners are advised to adhere. These general guidelines were culled from DeMier (2010), Grisso (2010, 2013), and Tillbrook, Mumley, and Grisso (2003).

- Report what is necessary and do not report what is not necessary. (Decide what is relevant to the psycholegal or referral question(s), and be able to justify inclusion and exclusion of information on the basis of relevance.)
- Sequence and describe information in a way that will make sense to a reader. (Arrange information in a way that is easy to follow, adjust the structure of the report as needed to accomplish this, and use language that your audience will understand.)
- Separate facts from inferences and opinions. (Facts can be verified. Inferences and opinions are what is suggested by the facts.)
- Explanations involve showing *why* you think what you think. (A significant component of forensic work is education, the natural role of the expert.)

- Regarding testing, it is sometimes helpful to include a one or two sentence explanation of each test used. Detail any non-standard procedures used and the potential impact of these procedures on test results. Report all test results, not just those that support your hypotheses.
- Explain your rejection of other possible opinions and conclusions. (Demonstrate that you were alert to, and actively considered, alternative hypotheses. Explain why your data best supports your conclusion. Explaining rejected ideas should be an important part of the process of arriving at your opinions.)
- Do *not* offer an opinion regarding the ultimate legal issue (e.g., Guilty or Not Guilty of a given offense). Ultimate legal issues are for the trier(s) of fact (i.e., judge or jury) to decide.

Missing Information

Although I have identified several important components of reports, it is common for practitioners to have to produce a dispositional evaluation before all information has been received. From a strictly scientific perspective, it makes little sense to draw conclusions and make recommendations from incomplete data. Therefore, responsible practitioners may be tempted to withhold their reports until they have received all relevant information.[2] However, in the often-messy, day-to-day practice of forensic psychology, withholding a report under such conditions is often impractical and may be viewed as obstructing the needs of the referring agency.

The need for producing a report in the absence of all information desired is driven by several factors. Judges often do not like to keep juveniles in custody for more than a few days without having an assessment of the level of risk the juvenile poses to others, recommendations regarding necessary services, and an assessment of the least restrictive environment in which the juvenile should be placed. Similarly, in cases referred by state child protective service agencies, such information is needed because a safety plan may have been implemented wherein the juvenile cannot live at home with siblings and/or attend school until recommendations are received. In plain English, the juvenile will probably remain in limbo (out-of-home and/or in juvenile detention, receiving minimal or no schooling, and minimal or no mental health services) until a report is produced with an estimate of the level of risk the juvenile poses to public

[2] Although information that is critical to include will vary from case to case, a clinician will usually need some combination of all arrests and the outcome of those arrests (e.g., charges dismissed, sentenced to probation, sentenced to a juvenile detention facility) and victim statements.

safety and recommendations regarding necessary services and appropriate placement (i.e., in the community receiving outpatient services, in a residential treatment setting, within a locked psychiatric unit, or in a "secure care setting"—a euphemism for a juvenile detention facility).

In matters where information is missing and a report must be produced nonetheless, professional ethics dictates that the examiner be clear what information is missing and why such information is not included in the report. It is also important to request that the referring agency provides the information when it becomes available and to note that one's recommendations must be viewed as being tentative and are subject to modification after all relevant information has been received (American Psychological Association, 2002, 2013). It is also reasonable to state that one's recommendations are tentative and cannot be made within a reasonable degree of psychological certainty.

Making Statements Within a Reasonable Degree of Psychological Certainty

In forensic reports, there is generally an expectation that psychologists will present findings "within a reasonable degree of psychological certainty." Faigman (2006, p. 1224) as cited in Heilbrun, Grisso, and Goldstein (2009, p. 53) pointed out that this concept "has no empirical meaning and is simply a mantra repeated by experts for purposes of legal decision-makers who similarly have no idea what it means." For practical purposes, asserting that conclusions have been made "within a reasonable degree of psychological certainty" means that the psychologist has employed generally accepted assessment methods, is confident in his or her findings, and is not merely guessing.

Least Restrictive Alternative (or Environment)

There are a finite number of options regarding the placement of youth. Although the options will vary by jurisdiction, they are often as follows: return home (with or without supervision by juvenile probation and with or without services on an outpatient basis); another community-based placement (e.g., placement with a relative or in a foster home or therapeutic foster home, with or without supervision by juvenile probation, and with or without services provided on an outpatient basis); placement (often far from the youth's home) in a residential treatment facility (often while under supervision of a probation officer); and incarceration in a juvenile detention facility (in which mental health services and all other rehabilitative services may be quite limited).

When making recommendations about the setting in which a youth should be placed, evaluators should recommend the least restrictive alternative. Grisso (2013, pp. 184–185) explained the concept of least restrictive alternative as follows:

> *Most states acknowledge (by statute or case law) that juvenile courts are allowed to deprive delinquent adolescents of liberty only to the extent necessary to promote their rehabilitation and to protect the public. This concept, called "least restrictive alternative," is intended to discourage routine commitments to secure juvenile facilities. Where applicable, it requires that a youth must be placed in community-based programs or nonsecure facilities whenever possible, unless it is shown that greater security is needed.... As a general rule, the concepts of least restrictive alternative... should influence clinicians' reasoning and recommendations in rehabilitation evaluations. They should recommend the least restrictive alternative that will provide necessary rehabilitation services and adequate public protection.*

SAMPLE REPORTS

In the remainder of this chapter, I will present sample reports that illustrate the general principles discussed heretofore. Multiple reports are displayed to illustrate the assortment of ways in which evaluation results can be organized and displayed. Reports are annotated to draw readers' attention to salient components of each report and provide insight into the factors I considered when drawing conclusions and making recommendations. Readers are encouraged to read all the sample reports, as some issues annotated in the first report (and in some subsequent reports) will not be repeated in other reports. Of course, identifying information pertaining to each examinee, his family, and victim(s) has all been disguised to protect confidentiality.

COURT-ORDERED EVALUATION OF A 14-YEAR-OLD MALE WHO VICTIMIZED A 7-YEAR-OLD FEMALE RELATIVE

Forensic Psychological Evaluation

Name	Date of Birth	Date of Evaluation	Date of Report
Miguel Rivera	x/xx/95	08/20/10	08/31/10

Reason for Referral

Miguel Rivera was referred for evaluation by the Division of Youth and Family Services (DYFS), Big Urban Local Office. He is a 14-year-old male who has been incarcerated at the Essex County Juvenile Detention Center (ECJDC) in Newark, New Jersey, for having sexually abused his 7-year-old female cousin. Miguel had previously been sexually abused by his uncle, the victim's father. On August 12, 2010, the Hon. John Judge, Jr., JSC, ordered that Miguel undergo a juvenile-sex-offender-specific evaluation.

Sources of Information

Every source of information available to me is displayed here. The utility of my conclusions and recommendations depends on the information upon which I relied.

Records reviewed at the Essex County Juvenile Detention Center
- Intake information contained in Social Services file
- Juvenile Order of Disposition; Superior Court of New Jersey, Chancery Division-Family Part, County of Urban; No docket number displayed; signed by Hon. John Judge, Jr., JSC; signed 08/12/10
- Juvenile Order of Disposition; Superior Court of New Jersey, Chancery Division-Family Part, County of Urban; No docket number displayed; signed by Hon. Paul Judicious, JSC; signed 07/28/10
- Complaint—Juvenile Delinquency; Superior Court of New Jersey, Chancery Division-Family Part, County of Urban; No docket number displayed; signed by Det. Angel Wings, #100, Urban County Prosecutor's Office; signed 07/20/10
- Arrest Report, Big City (NJ) Police Department; File number unclear, but appeared to be xx-C-xxx-xx; signed 07/20/10
- Officer's Report, Essex County Juvenile Detention Center; signed by Ofc. Jones, #202 on 07/26/10 at 6:02 PM

Records received from DYFS
- Assorted medical records from St. Joseph's Hospital and Medical Center, Big City, NJ, and from St. Michael's Hospital Behavioral Health Services, Another City, NJ
- Clinical interview
- Psychological testing
- Collateral information provided verbally by Sasha Worker, DYFS Case Manager, on 08/20/10

Background Information

On July 20, 2010, Miguel was arrested for the sexual abuse of his 7-year-old female cousin, M.P.

> **Victims' names should never be displayed. Initials are used instead to protect confidentiality.**

On that same date, Miguel provided a statement to police that was videotaped in which he confessed to having anally penetrated M.P. Two days prior, M.P. gave a video-recorded statement to police that Miguel had put his penis in her buttocks. Records from the Social Services file at ECJDC revealed that Miguel is gang-affiliated (BP, also recorded as MS). These records also indicated that he has not previously been arrested.

In a court order dated July 28, 2010, the following was ordered: Miguel was to continue to be remanded to ECJDC; he was to be placed on suicide supervision; St. Michael's Hospital and St. Joseph's Medical Center were to turn Miguel's medical records over to his defense attorney; Miguel was to have a medical assessment; and he was to have no contact with his biological father until such contact is approved by the Division.

On July 26, 2010, while in custody at the ECJDC, Miguel complained that he was having difficulty breathing. Although it was noted that medical staff responded, the records available to me gave no information about the outcome of the medical evaluation.

Review of medical records revealed the following: Miguel had previously been hospitalized for engaging in self-injurious behaviors (i.e., cutting) and had been experiencing auditory hallucinations; he has been medicated to address symptoms of depression; and in February of 2010, Miguel was non-compliant with taking medication and assaulted his mother, resulting in police involvement and evaluation at a local hospital.

Miguel's DYFS Case Manager informed me that when interviewed, Miguel's cousin-victim disclosed that she had witnessed her father engaging in sexual behaviors with Miguel and one of his younger brothers.

As of the writing of this report, the Division had not yet received records from Miguel's school. Therefore, information about his level of cognitive functioning (i.e., IQ scores) is not currently known to me.

Clinical Interview

The present evaluation was conducted at the Essex County Juvenile Detention Center in Newark, New Jersey. After his mother signed the consent form for forensic evaluation, Miguel read the consent form and provided written assent to proceed with the evaluation. The nature and purpose of the evaluation had been explained verbally, as well, as were the limits of confidentiality. He attended to these explanations as they were provided to him and demonstrated his understanding by summarizing the foregoing information in his own words.

Miguel's affect was flat on presentation and varied little throughout the course of the evaluation. He was quite reserved and generally spoke only when spoken to. Even then, his responses were brief. His level of personal grooming appeared to be appropriate for an adolescent his age. There was no evidence of psychotic symptoms at the time of evaluation.

Presumably, readers do not need to be concerned that this adolescent was psychotic at the time of the evaluation. This is one indicator that the results of this evaluation may be relied upon as an accurate assessment of the examinee's psychological experiences.

Miguel's fund of knowledge and ability to express himself appeared to be below-average for an adolescent his age. For example, although he was able to count to 100 by fives, he made several mistakes while doing so. In addition, when asked, he said that he would not have been able to continue counting above 100. He made mistakes when asked to recite the alphabet. When asked to start over, other than omission of the letter "r," he recited the alphabet correctly. He provided a "don't know" response when asked to provide definitions of "the truth" and "a lie." After I provided him with definitions, I provided sample truthful and untruthful statements and asked him to tell me if each statement was "the truth' or "a lie."

Information in this paragraph suggests that his intellectual functioning may be below average. In the Recommendations section of this report (#4), I suggested that I be provided with IQ scores.

He quickly demonstrated that he was able to differentiate between "the truth" and "a lie" and agreed to be truthful during his assessment.

Prior to his arrest, he had been living at home with his mother, his brothers, ages 13, 10, and 6, and his sister, who is 3 years old. His aunt, her husband, and their newborn infants also live in the home.

Miguel has a problematic relationship with his mother and has historically had minimal contact with his father. Although he characterized his mother as being "good" and said that "she takes care of us," he provided no other information about her and displayed no change in affect (e.g., smiling) when discussing her. His relationship with her began to deteriorate when he wanted to spend time with his 16-year-old girlfriend, Jocelyn. At that time, he started "flippin' out" and defying his mother. His mother disciplined him by not permitting him to leave their residence.

Miguel's father left the family before Miguel's third birthday. Although his father lives in the area, Miguel does not know exactly where his father lives "'cause he moved." When asked if he would like to have more frequent contact with his father, Miguel said, "I been lookin' for him, but he never wanted to see me since I was young."

I asked Miguel if there are any adults in his life with whom he has a close relationship. He described having such a relationship with his mother's brother who lives in South Big City, New Jersey. Miguel said, "I usually be with him more than my Mom, so I usually tell him everything that happens to me."

Miguel was asked about an assortment of symptoms that individuals sometimes experience. Although he denied experiencing sleep-related problems, he acknowledged that he periodically has nightmares about the fetus that his 16-year-old girlfriend miscarried. He acknowledged that he sometimes daydreams, but gave a "don't know" response when asked about the content. He denied having somatic complaints and experiencing both soiling and nighttime wetting. Miguel acknowledged having previously engaged in self-injurious behavior (i.e., cutting) and showed me scars from self-inflicted wounds on his left bicep and on the side of his left wrist. He also showed me a wound that resulted from having poked himself on the abdomen with a knife while intoxicated. Approximately two years ago (at or about the time his uncle had sodomized him), Miguel had thought about killing himself by throwing himself over waterfalls close to where he had lived. He did not act on this ideation because he thought about the likely impact his suicide would have on his sister. He denied having experienced suicidal ideation since that time. Miguel denied ever having harmed animals but acknowledged that he would like to stab or shoot one particular individual who lives in Big City, New Jersey. He did not disclose the identity of that individual. Although Miguel periodically experienced auditory hallucinations, he denied having had any such experiences in the recent past. He was unable to recall when the auditory hallucinations stopped. Beginning at the age of 13, he heard a woman's voice telling him to kill one of his brothers.

Although there were no indications of psychosis at the time of his evaluation, this information suggests that he previously experienced psychotic symptoms.

When considering the least restrictive environment (LRE) that is appropriate, I was mindful that he may pose a risk to the physical safety of others.

He recalled having gotten headaches during those episodes. He denied ever having had visual hallucinations.

I asked Miguel about a possible history of aggressive behavior and substance abuse. He is a member of the "MS" street gang. In response to inquiry, he denied ever having injured or killed anyone, but acknowledged having witnessed individuals being stabbed to death. He described a problematic pattern of alcohol consumption. On Friday nights, he shares two $100 bottles of liquor with three other individuals. That quantity of alcohol is consumed between 9 PM and 6 AM. He consumes greater quantities of alcohol on Saturday nights. (Readers will note not only the quantity of alcohol consumed, but also the price of the alcohol and that it is consumed throughout the nighttime and early morning hours.)

Again, when considering LRE, this suggests the need for an environment that provides structure and supervision, as well as the need for a substance abuse evaluation.

Miguel began using marijuana when he was 13 years old. He uses two "bags" per day, seven days a week. He denied experimentation with, and use of, all other illicit substances and abuse of prescription medications.

Findings from Psychological Testing

Miguel completed the Personality Assessment Inventory—Adolescent (PAI-A). The PAI-A contains several validity scales. These scales suggest that while results are valid, the PAI-A should be interpreted with some caution. It appeared that Miguel had some problems understanding or attending to test items. He also responded so as to indicate some bizarre and unlikely symptoms. There are several possible explanations for such a response pattern: he may have purposefully exaggerated symptoms and/or; the response pattern may have resulted from confusion or careless responding and/or; his responses may be indicative of a plea for help.

His clinical profile had significant elevations across several different scales. Overall, the profile is one of an individual with a pattern of substance abuse problems

This is consistent with what he told me about his alcohol and marijuana use during the interview.

who is experiencing an anxiety disorder. He has been experiencing physical symptoms of anxiety such as sweaty palms, trembling hands, feelings of irregular heartbeats, and shortness of breath.

This is consistent with the incident noted in Background Information.

He did *not* report experiencing cognitive symptoms of anxiety such as excessive worry, negative expectations, diminished attention span, and difficulties with concentration. There were also indications of moods that are variable and sometimes elevated.

Three problematic personality traits became apparent. First, impulsivity appears to be a significant problem for Miguel. This impulsivity makes him prone to engage in behaviors that are detrimental to his own well-being. Second, his impulsivity appears to be accompanied by a marked need for stimulation and excitement. It is probable that he often exhibits reckless behaviors that are dangerous to others as well as to himself. Third, Miguel apparently has difficulties with anger management. He described himself as being prone to extreme displays of anger, including proneness to damage property and make threats to injure others. It is probable that individuals who interact with him are intimidated by his temper and his potential for violence.

On the PAI-A, Miguel reported periodically experiencing thoughts of self-harm.

His responses suggest that he has a greater interest in, and motivation for, mental health treatment than is typical of adolescents. The foregoing suggests an awareness of important problems in his life requiring professional assistance to remedy.

Finally, based upon an individual's responses to test items, the PAI-A yields DSM-IV diagnostic possibilities that the evaluator might wish to consider. Based upon Miguel's responses, the following diagnostic possibilities were suggested: Intermittent Explosive Disorder and substance abuse-related issues. It was suggested that an emerging Borderline Personality Disorder be ruled out.

Miguel completed the Trauma Symptom Checklist for Children (TSCC). Scores on validity scales embedded within this instrument revealed a valid test protocol. Scores on the following scales revealed trauma-related symptoms of clinically significant severity: Anxiety (T = 74); Anger (T = 74); Posttraumatic Stress (T = 66); and distress regarding sexual matters (SC-D scale, T = 77). Scores obtained on the Dissociation (T = 60) and Dissociation-Fantasy scales (T = 60) suggest subclinical, yet significant symptoms of dissociation.

These trauma-related symptoms are consistent with his self-reported history of exposure to potentially traumatic events.

Follow-up inquiry regarding his TSCC responses revealed the following: periodically, he has intrusive recollections of his own sexual abuse and of having witnessed individuals die as a result of having been stabbed to death; he was involved in a motor vehicle accident approximately one month prior to his incarceration, lost consciousness for a period of time, had severe memory problems for the following two to three days, and refused to allow his mother to seek follow-up medical care for him; and he is almost always fearful of getting shot on the streets. Finally, his current level of sexual motivation and ability to perform is far below what is typical for boys his age. Although he had strong sexual urges prior to having been sodomized at age 12, his sexual urges have been diminishing since that time. Moreover, when he does engage in sexual behavior, although his erection is maintained, he is sometimes unable to ejaculate after having had sufficient sexual stimulation. Although unable to provide an estimate of how often he is unable to ejaculate, his posture at that time (i.e., gazing at the floor rather than making eye contact with me, and slowed, tentative speech) led me to conclude that this occurs with considerable frequency and that Miguel experiences considerable embarrassment about this sexual performance problem.

Inquiry About and Measures Used to Assess Miguel's Sexual History

I asked Miguel to complete Friedrich's Adolescent Sexual Behavior Inventory (ASBI) to facilitate discussion about his sexual history. Although Miguel recalled first having sexual feelings at the age of 13, he was unable to recall the content of the sexual thoughts. He was unable to recall when he first had an erection. Although he denied ever having masturbated himself, he said that his girlfriend "does it for me (that is, masturbates me)." Similarly, he denied having wet dreams. His first consensual sexual experience occurred at the age of 14 with a 16-year-old girl (the girl whom he impregnated). He indicated that he had had one additional female sexual partner. Also on the ASBI, Miguel revealed that he is afraid of men

This seems generally consistent with his having been sexually abused by an uncle.

and that he is unhappy with his looks and uncomfortable with his own body.

Miguel was asked to provide me with details about his sexual abuse of his seven-year-old cousin, M.P. He began by saying that he was under the influence of alcohol and marijuana at the time "I did that."

This, too, suggests the need for a substance abuse evaluation. Although he may or may not have been under the influence at the time, he might have offered this as a circumstance to justify/excuse his inappropriate behavior.

When asked to provide details, Miguel said that his cousin pulled her skirt up, he pulled her panties down, and rubbed his penis against her anal opening twice before discontinuing the sexual contact. (He provided no information as to how he persuaded and/or forced her to pull her skirt up.) When asked if he had an erection at the time, Miguel said, "I was a little hard, not much." He denied having had sufficient time or sexual arousal to ejaculate. When asked why he discontinued the sexual contact prior to ejaculating, he said, "Because it was my cousin, that's why I stopped." Miguel gave a "don't know" response when asked why he initiated sexual contact with his seven-year-old cousin. When asked if he had been experiencing sexual arousal prior to having acted out against his cousin, Miguel said, "Not that much." He denied having experienced sexual fantasies about his cousin and other prepubescent girls. When asked how his sexual abuse of his cousin had been discovered, Miguel said, "I think her Dad snitched." Miguel explained that his uncle, Jose Rivera, had also sexually abused M.P. and that his uncle is incarcerated for the offense. When I asked what led Miguel to believe that his uncle had sexually abused M.P., Miguel explained that he had been in their residence and, unbeknownst to his uncle, he saw his uncle on top of M.P. and both of them had their clothes off.

I asked Miguel to tell me about his experiences as a sexual abuse victim. He was sexually abused by his uncle, Jose Rivera, on two separate occasions when he was 12 years old. Miguel said, "He forced me and hit me the first time. The second time, I was high. I fell asleep and woke up in his room." When asked to elaborate, Miguel explained that his uncle had hit him "tied my hands up and he did what he did." When asked to specify what his uncle had done, Miguel said that his uncle had attempted to kiss him on the mouth and then inserted his penis into Miguel's buttocks. He denied that his uncle had attempted to engage him in oral sex. He also denied that his uncle ejaculated. The incident of sexual abuse was interrupted by a knock on the door. His uncle quickly dressed himself, but it was unclear from Miguel's explanation whether Miguel or his uncle had put Miguel's clothes back on him. His uncle responded to the knock at the door by explaining that he was cleaning his room. In response to inquiry, Miguel denied having experienced any form of sexual arousal or emotional excitement at any time during the incident. He described the incident as having been "scary" and he found the nature of the sexual contact to have been quite aversive.

The second incident occurred on Miguel's 13th birthday. He had gone to his uncle's residence under the influence of marijuana and fell asleep in the living room. I asked what led Miguel to believe that he had been sexually abused. He explained that upon awakening, he found himself in his uncle's bed next to his uncle, who was asleep. Miguel's underwear was missing and his arms were bruised.

I asked Miguel to describe the impact that these incidents of sexual abuse had had on him. He provided a "don't know" response.

Miguel completed the Adolescent Sexual Interest Cardsort and provided implausible responses. He denied finding almost all of scenarios depicted to be even mildly sexually arousing. He reported a scenario involving consensual intercourse with an 18-year-old female to be slightly sexually arousing.

Assessment of Risk for Engaging in Sexual Offending Behaviors

At the present time, there are no empirically validated, actuarial instruments that can be used to accurately estimate the risk of adolescent sexual re-offending. However, based on the best available research data and consensus in professional clinical opinion, a number of high-risk factors have been identified in the literature. The Estimate of Risk of Adolescent Sexual Offense Recidivism (The ERASOR: Worling & Curwen, 2001) summarizes the available research and expert clinical opinion, and this instrument can be used to estimate an adolescent's risk of sexual re-offense.

Miguel should be considered to pose a **high** level of risk for COMMITTING CONTACT SEXUAL OFFENSES against pre- and peri-pubescent females. (This estimate is offered because of the combination of factors known *and* unknown at the time of the writing of this report.) Although his level of risk for committing sexual offenses against adult females and males of any age is unknown at the present time, it appears to be low.

Risk would be best managed by implementing the recommendations displayed later in this report.

It is important to note that rapid developmental changes occur during the adolescent years. Because of these changes, and because much of the supporting research on adolescent re-offending is based on follow-up data of less than three years, the foregoing estimate of risk should be reassessed after no more than two years. Reassessment is also warranted after significant changes in any of the following domains have occurred: social; environmental; familial; sexual; physical; or psychological.

Summary

Although I call this section "Summary" and I summarize major findings, I go beyond summarizing findings to provide interpretations and hypotheses about the meaning of the data.

Miguel Rivera was referred for evaluation by the Division of Youth and Family Services (DYFS), Big Urban Local Office. He is a 14-year-old male who has been incarcerated at the Essex County Juvenile Detention Center (ECJDC) in Newark, New Jersey, for having sexually abused his 7-year-old female cousin. Miguel had previously been sexually abused by his uncle, the victim's father. On August 12, 2010, the Hon. John Judge, Jr., JSC, ordered that Miguel undergo a juvenile-sex-offender-specific evaluation.

Miguel acknowledged having sexually abused his 7-year-old female cousin on a single occasion. He claimed to have been under the influence of alcohol and marijuana at the time. He said that his cousin pulled her skirt up, he pulled her panties down, and rubbed his penis against her anus twice before discontinuing the sexual contact. He claimed to have experienced a minimal degree of sexual arousal at the time of the offense and provided a "don't know" response when asked why he initiated sexual contact with her. He denied having experienced sexual fantasies about his cousin and other prepubescent girls. Miguel was himself sexually abused by his victim's father when he was 12 years old and then again on his 13th birthday. It is unclear what connection, if any, there is between his uncle having sodomized him and his having engaged in penile-anal rubbing with his uncle's daughter. Although my knowledge of the details of Miguel's offense against M.P. is based upon collateral information provided by his DYFS Case Manager via telephone (in contrast to having personally reviewed DVDs or transcripts of Prosecutor's Office interviews of Miguel, his victim, and other relevant individuals), his description of his offense was generally consistent with information provided by the Division.

Miguel appeared to be an inaccurate historian regarding his own sexual experiences. He was unable (or unwilling) to recall important elements of his sexual history and provided an implausible description of his recent sexual behaviors. For example, he said that his girlfriend sometimes masturbates him but denied that he has ever masturbated himself and denied ever having had a nocturnal emission (i.e., a "wet dream"). He was also unable/unwilling to provide any clear description of stimuli and situations that he finds sexually arousing.

Findings from the present evaluation strongly suggest that Miguel poses a (non-sexual) threat to the physical well-being of other individuals, including adults. He is affiliated with a street gang. Although he denied having injured or killed others, he acknowledged having witnessed murders. Assessment results revealed several risk factors for engaging in community violence

This conclusion is based upon information from the interview as well as hypotheses generated based on his pattern of responding to test items.

including a propensity for extreme displays of anger, a need for stimulation and excitement, and an impulsive response style.

Results of the present assessment, in combination with historical events, reveal that Miguel may also continue to pose a threat to his own physical safety. He has a serious substance abuse problem (i.e., alcohol and marijuana) and was previously psychiatrically hospitalized for engaging in self-injurious behaviors and because he experienced auditory hallucinations. He previously experienced suicidal ideation and had generated a plan for self-destruction. It is important to note that these experiences occurred after he had been physically restrained, then sodomized, by his uncle. It is likely that the extreme behaviors displayed resulted from the trauma endured as a sexual abuse victim. The foregoing is an hypothesis that should be tested within a therapeutic context and cannot be offered within a reasonable degree of psychological certainty (due, in part, to my not having access to a familial history of possible mental health problems).

Despite the assortment of severe mental health problems identified in this report, there is cause for cautious optimism. Scales embedded with one psychological test (i.e., the PAI-A) suggested that he perceives the need for mental health treatment to address the assortment of issues with which he presented. This is cause for cautious optimism because many adolescents with a history of engaging in antisocial behaviors do not perceive any need for a change in their behaviors.

The following recommendations are offered within a reasonable degree of psychological certainty based upon the information currently available to me. If additional information becomes available that is substantially inconsistent with information currently available to me, modifications to the psychological recommendations may be warranted.

Recommendations

1. Miguel should be placed in a residential treatment facility that

> I considered options I might recommend (e.g., supervision by Probation while living at home, supervision by Probation while living in a foster home, a residential treatment facility, or a secure-care setting such as a juvenile detention facility). I eliminated less restrictive, community-based options because of the probable danger to self and others. My opinion is that a residential treatment facility is the LRE in which his need for structure, supervision, and services can be met.

offers a very high level of structure and supervision. At a minimum, the following services would need to be available: juvenile-sex-offender-specific therapy (both individual and group); psychiatric monitoring and counseling to address problems that might arise on a daily basis. It is probable that Miguel will need additional services as discussed in recommendations #3 and below. If such services are not regularly available on-site, arrangements should be made for such services to be delivered at the earliest time possible.

2. If Miguel displays significant rule-breaking behaviors in a residential treatment program that provides a high level of structure and supervision, the Court should consider remanding him to a Juvenile Justice Commission (JJC) secure care facility.
3. Miguel should undergo a substance abuse evaluation and comply with resulting recommendations.
4. Because Miguel's school records were unavailable as of the writing of this report, I encourage the Division to provide me with his most recent IQ scores when this information becomes available. Information about his level of cognitive functioning may warrant minor changes to the recommendations offered in this report.

If his IQ is quite low and/or if he has severe skill deficits in reading or writing, modifications may need to be made for him to benefit from treatment.

5. Miguel's academic programming should be reviewed and he should be provided with remediation in basic academic skill domains as needed. He would also benefit from job sampling, supervision by a job coach, and referral to the New Jersey Division of Vocational Rehabilitation Services (DVR). These recommendations are offered so as to assist Miguel in acquiring the skills necessary to becoming a productive member of society.

Although I have incomplete data, I believe it probable that he will meet criteria for having one or more disabilities that would qualify him for services through this agency. If I am wrong, he will not be accepted. However, I want readers to plan for instruction in "what TO do (i.e., acquire skills needed to be a law-abiding, productive member of society)," not simply "what NOT to do (i.e., engage in antisocial behaviors, including committing sexual offenses)." Daly et al. (this volume) provides a more detailed discussion of modifying contingencies to bring about behavioral changes.

6. Miguel should undergo a thorough medical evaluation by a pediatrician with fellowship-level training in child maltreatment. Specific medical issues to be addressed are as follows: he should undergo examination to address the possibility of sexually transmitted disease and/or physical trauma that might have resulted from having been sodomized approximately two years ago; explore a possible medical explanation for his periodic inability to ejaculate after sufficient sexual stimulation; and to explore possible sequelae from the motor vehicle accident he was in approximately one month prior to the time of evaluation (he lost consciousness for an unspecified length of time and had some memory loss for two to three days after the accident).
7. Once Miguel is psychiatrically stable, he would benefit from participating in trauma-focused cognitive-behavioral therapy (TF-CBT; Deblinger & Heflin, 1996) to address his sexual abuse and the murder(s) that he has witnessed. It is likely that he would benefit from TF-CBT more so than from other forms of psychotherapy to address his trauma-related symptoms.

There are many types of trauma-specific therapies, however, TF-CBT is an evidenced-based treatment that has demonstrated efficacy with children and adolescents who have experienced trauma and traumatic loss.

8. It is a reasonable hypothesis that his substance abuse and/or self-injurious behaviors (i.e., cutting) serve to self-regulate his moods and that his gang affiliation is, in part, an attempt to regain power and control he did not have during his incidents of sexual abuse. Therefore, he may need assistance in acquiring normative and adaptive strategies to regulate his own mood by way of dialectical behavior therapy, DBT, before he is able to tolerate TF-CBT. Therefore, DBT may serve as an important component in achieving psychiatric stability.
9. Prior to re-integration into the Big City, NJ, community setting, at least one of the mental health professionals with whom Miguel is working should reassess the possibility of his injuring or killing an individual in Big City whose identity was not disclosed during the present evaluation.

Daniel Bromberg, Ph.D., ABPP
Licensed Psychologist, NJ Lic. #SI004033
Board Certified in Cognitive & Behavioral Psychology
American Board of Professional Psychology

COURT-ORDERED EVALUATION OF A 15-YEAR-OLD MALE ALLEGED TO HAVE ASSAULTED A 16-YEAR-OLD FEMALE PEER

Forensic Psychological Evaluation

Name	Date of Birth	Date of Evaluation	Date of Report
Quantez Brown	xx/xx/96	10/26/11 & 10/29/11	10/31/11

Reason for Referral

Quantez Brown was referred for evaluation by the Division of Youth and Family Services (DYFS), Big Urban Local Office. He is a 15-year-old male who has been incarcerated at the Essex County Juvenile Detention Center (ECJDC) in Newark, New Jersey, for allegedly sexually assaulting a 16-year-old female peer. The Division requested a juvenile-sex-offender-specific evaluation to assist in determining Quantez's placement and service needs.

Sources of Information

Records received from the Division of Youth and Family Services

- Juvenile Order of Disposition—Superior Court of New Jersey—Chancery Division, Family Part—County of Urban; State in the Interest of Quantez Brown; signed by Juan Jues, J.S.C.
- Complaint—Juvenile Delinquency; Chancery Division-Family Part, County of Big Urban 11-12345; Docket #FJ-xx-xxx-xx; signature of Complainant illegible on my copy, but badge # appears to be 1234, signed on 10/13/11; Ofc. E. Policia's name of the Big Urban Police was also displayed on the document
- Big Urban (NJ) Police Department; File Control #11-12345; Two pages listing individuals involved in the incident and two pages of Narrative; completed by P.O. E. Policia #1234
- School records (Including, but not limited to, the following: attendance records from Sept and Oct 2011; Big Urban High School Student Suspension Request Form, dated 02/07/11 and 12/16/10; Big Urban High School Class Attendance/Loss of Credit Verification Form dated 10/07/10; Report Card dated 6/15/10 from Dr. Peter Piper, Jr. School (sic.); Printout of NJASK scores from Grades 6 and 4; Notice of ineligibility for Special Education and Related Services, dated 7/26/05)
- Court Report (DCF 26-80), Report date of 10/21/11; Case ID #56789

Letter addressed to "Dear Ms. Smith," written by Jane Doe, MS, Reunity House Big Urban Clinician, Family Connections, regarding Sarah Brown, dated 10/19/11
Family Intervention Services Case Plan for Quantez Brown, signed by meeting participants on 10/07/11
Letter addressed to "Dear Ms. Smith," written by Michael Ortiz, MA, and Sarah Rivera, LCSW, of Family Intervention Services, signed on 09/28/11
Clinical interview
Psychological testing
Collateral information provided via e-mail from DYFS Case Manager

Background Information

On or about October 13, 2011, Quantez was arrested and charged with one count of Aggravated Sexual Assault and one count of Criminal Restraint. The alleged victim's account of what occurred is as follows: S.N., a 16-year-old girl, claimed to have gone for a walk with Quantez and his cousin, Y.J. (age not displayed in records available), during school hours. S.N. claimed that she felt safe with Quantez and Y.J., as Quantez is her second cousin and she had previously dated Y.J. The three stopped at a store, got chips and soft drinks, then went for a walk in a nearby abandoned stadium. Quantez pulled her sweatpants off her body, but discovered that she was wearing beige school uniform pants underneath her sweatpants. Each of the boys removed one of S.N.'s sneakers and S.N. told them to stop and attempted to stop them. Quantez held both of S.N.'s arms behind her using one hand while he covered her mouth with his other hand. Y.J. removed S.N.'s pants and attempted to have vaginal intercourse with her. However, he was unable to achieve full intromission. The boys switched positions and Quantez achieved full intromission. While Quantez was having intercourse with S.N., Y.J. straddled her chest and attempted to put his penis in her mouth. Y.J. then had intercourse with her while Quantez watched. All the while, S.N. was attempting to close her legs and push the boys off. The sexual assault stopped when both boys thought they heard others entering the stadium.

Information provided by the Division indicated that Quantez has no prior arrests. Records available to me at the time of evaluation contain no information about the following: Quantez's level of cognitive functioning (i.e., IQ); whether there is any reason to doubt the credibility of the statement that S.N. provided to police; and whether Y.J. provided a statement/confession to police and how consistent his statement is with S.N.'s and with Quantez's version of events. Finally, I have no information to suggest that this matter has yet been adjudicated. Therefore, Quantez's guilt or innocence has yet to be established.

I reported the limits of the information available to me. That is, this is the information I wanted, but did not have, that might affect my conclusions and recommendations.

Records provided by the Division reveal that Quantez was removed from the care of his parents because of parental substance abuse. In addition, his mother perpetrated acts of physical abuse against him. He has been receiving mental health services to address traumatic sequelae secondary to this abuse.

Clinical Interview

The present evaluation was conducted over the course of two sessions. The first session was conducted at the Division's Big Urban Local Office in Big Urban. The second session was conducted at the Essex County Juvenile Detention Center in Newark, New Jersey. After his DYFS worker signed the consent form for forensic evaluation,

In a previous paragraph, I mentioned that he had been removed from the care of his parents. The Division was his legal guardian.

Quantez read the consent form and provided written assent to proceed with the evaluation. The nature and purpose of the evaluation had been explained verbally, as well, as were the limits of confidentiality. He attended to these explanations as they were provided to him.

Quantez's affect was flat on presentation and varied little throughout the evaluation. He was quite reserved and generally spoke only when spoken to. His level of personal grooming appeared to be appropriate for an adolescent his age. There was no evidence of psychotic symptoms at the time of evaluation. He appeared to be quite tired during both evaluation sessions.

His fund of knowledge and ability to express himself appeared to be within the average range for an adolescent his age. (No formal assessment of cognitive functioning was conducted.) Quantez provided an adequate description of the difference between "the truth" and "a lie" and he agreed to be truthful during his assessment.

In contrast to the youth discussed in the first sample report, this examinee has no obvious intellectual or mental health impairments.

When asked where he had lived prior to his incarceration, his response revealed a history of disrupted attachment to caretakers and of having experienced maltreatment. He listed five different placements he had been in between having lived at home and his incarceration. He said that his mother is currently in nursing school. The family became involved with the Division "because she was physically abusing us (my brother and myself), mentally abusing us, and doin' drugs." The physical abuse began when Quantez was about seven years old. His mother punched him in the face, kicked him, beat him, and occasionally left bruises on his face and arms. She had been abusing alcohol, marijuana, and "angel dust" since before Quantez was born. When asked about his relationship with his mother, Quantez said, "I didn't like her because she kept abusin' me, but I love her because she's my Mom." Over the years, teachers asked him how he had gotten his bruises. Quantez lied so that his mother would not "get in trouble." He recalled numerous incidents during which his mother displayed inappropriate and bizarre behavior. When asked about the mother–child relationship, he said, "The only time she paid attention to me was after she beat me." After having administered beatings, his mother apologized and typically bought him something.

The information in this paragraph suggests the need for trauma-focused treatment as a victim of (alleged) physical abuse.

Quantez's step-father came into his life when Quantez was five or six years old. Quantez said, "I don't like him." They have never had a good relationship and "the only reason I respect him is because of my mother." Quantez told me that his step-father has a history of perpetrating acts of domestic violence against his mother.

According to the examinee, his mother and step-father modeled interpersonal violence. Such modeling of interpersonal violence may be one factor (among many) that contributed to his (alleged) sexual offense in which violence was used.

I asked Quantez about his father. Quantez met his father when he was 10 years old. His father took him to McDonald's while he was intoxicated. Although his father promised to take Quantez for the summer, he never came. His father changed his address and phone number and Quantez has not had any contact with his father since that time. Quantez reported that he gets angry when he thinks about his father.

Quantez was asked about an assortment of symptoms that individuals sometimes experience. He acknowledged experiencing sleep-related problems since sometime in 2010. He generally gets into bed between 10 and 10:30 PM, falls asleep, then awakens in the middle of the night and is unable to get back to sleep. He reported being tired during the day as a result. He has been experiencing nightmares about his mother abusing him and spontaneously told me that that is why he has been in psychotherapy. (He reported having a positive experience in therapy.) He denied current suicidal ideation and intent, but acknowledged having had thoughts about slicing his own neck at times when he was being abused by his mother. He denied that he ever attempted to hurt or kill himself. He denied all of the following: both daytime and nighttime wetting and soiling; homicidal ideation; ever having injured or killed animals; and having experienced auditory and visual hallucinations.

> He denied having displayed an additional diagnostic indicator of Conduct Disorder (in which violence is employed "just for the fun of it," rather than to achieve an end, such as gaining compliance of his alleged victim).

Quantez denied all of the following, as well: neglect of his basic material needs; ever having been sexually abused; use of tobacco products, alcohol, use of illicit drugs, and abuse of prescription and over-the-counter medications;

> Assuming he is reporting honestly, disinhibition of (alleged) sexual aggression cannot be (partially) attributed to the effects of illicit drugs or alcohol.

and having any prior arrests.

I asked about the reason for his poor school attendance during September and October of this academic year. He said that he has been preoccupied with concerns about the possibility of his mother being unable to achieve permanency on his behalf and becoming legally free for adoption. This is quite upsetting because he would like for reunification to occur, despite the abuse his mother had previously perpetrated against him. He gets in trouble for his inattention during classes and seeks to avoid being reprimanded by not attending school. He acknowledged that at other times, he does not go to school simply because he does not want to do schoolwork.

Findings from Psychological Testing

Quantez completed the Personality Assessment Inventory—Adolescent (PAI-A). The PAI-A contains several validity scales. These scales suggest that while results are valid, the PAI-A should be interpreted with some caution. It appeared that Quantez had some problems understanding or attending to test items. There are several possible explanations for such a response pattern: reading problems; lapses in attention; and idiosyncratic interpretation of test items. Validity scales also suggest that Quantez responded in a reasonably forthright manner, in contrast to having responded in a socially desirable manner.

His clinical profile suggests that he is probably experiencing significant symptoms related to traumatic stress. He also experiences some difficulties consistent with relatively mild or transient depressive symptoms. It is probable that Quantez is worried and concerned about issues to the degree that his ability to concentrate is significantly compromised.

These hypotheses are consistent with information displayed earlier in this report.

During stressful times, Quantez is probably more self-critical and indecisive than are most adolescents.

Interpersonally, Quantez is likely to be unassuming. Despite his unassuming tendency, he is probably not shy or socially avoidant and is probably reasonably effective in his social interactions. Others likely perceive him as being a quiet adolescent who is fairly eager to please.

His responses suggest that he has a greater interest in, and motivation for, mental health treatment than is typical of adolescents. The foregoing suggests an awareness of important problems in his life requiring professional assistance to remedy.

Quantez completed the Trauma Symptom Checklist for Children (TSCC). Scores on validity scales embedded within this instrument revealed a valid test protocol. There was no indication of trauma symptoms of clinically significant severity.

This is NOT consistent with PAI-A findings and other information displayed in this report. Such inconsistencies occur for assorted reasons, including how a particular test assesses a particular construct, and psychometric quirks of instruments. Bracken (1988) provided a useful discussion of reasons why similar tests sometimes yield dissimilar results.

Inquiry About and Measures Used to Assess Quantez's Sexual History

I asked Quantez to complete Friedrich's Adolescent Sexual Behavior Inventory (ASBI) to facilitate discussion about his sexual history. When he was seven or eight years old, he awakened at 2 or 3AM and saw his mother and her boyfriend having intercourse. He recalled that both of them were "butt naked," he was on top of her, and she was moaning. He denied having experienced any sexual feelings while seeing this. When asked what impact, if any, the foregoing had on him, Quantez said that he continues to have intrusive memories of the foregoing sight, which he found unpleasant. Until the time of his incarceration, Quantez periodically saw this man on the streets in Big Urban.

He reported having seen a pornographic video twice last year while living at home. He accessed the movie through a cable TV controller. The video contained images of adult men and women engaging in consensual sexual behaviors.

Quantez does not recall having masturbated prior to puberty. He reported that he reached puberty at the age of 13. He masturbated while looking at a pornographic magazine of men and women engaged in consensual sexual behavior, ejaculated, and experienced his first orgasm at that time. He usually masturbates to orgasm two or three days per week and stops masturbating after having had one orgasm. He commonly masturbates to fantasies of engaging in vaginal intercourse with females in their early 20s. He usually, but not always, masturbates to scenarios involving consensual sex.

Although little is known about the base rate of masturbation in "normal" adolescents (Bromberg & O'Donohue, 2013, p. 21), his sexual history seems to be generally within normal limits.

He denied ever having had a nocturnal emission (i.e., "wet dream").

He reported having limited sexual experience with others (appropriate for his age). Quantez said that he has been dating a same-age female peer named "Keisha" intermittently since they met in eighth grade. Their relationship is non-sexual in nature by her choosing. Physical contact is limited to hugs and kissing on the cheek.

Quantez was asked to provide me with details about the (alleged) sexual assault on S.N. Consistent with her statement to police, he, S.N., and 14-year-old Y.J. entered the abandoned stadium. They went to the upper level of the stadium and engaged in some horseplay. Y.J. asked S.N. if she wanted to "have sex." S.N. declined to have sex that day, but agreed to have sex on Friday of that week. Y.J. said that he won't be around on Friday. Quantez then went behind S.N. and unbuttoned her pants. Y.J. pulled her pants, but not underpants, down. Y.J. said that he wanted to have sex with her first, to which Quantez agreed. Quantez said that he would not watch while they had intercourse, turned around, and played with some sticks that he found in the stadium. About 20 minutes later, Y.J. reported that S.N. would not allow him to have sex with her and that she kept closing her legs. Quantez then approached S.N., and she willingly had vaginal intercourse with him. When asked what led him to believe that the intercourse was consensual, Quantez told me that S.N. grabbed him and pulled him toward her while they were having intercourse and moaned during intercourse. Although there was no dialogue during intercourse, S.N. said to Quantez, "Let's do it (have sex) already," before intercourse began. I asked about Quantez's thoughts and feelings after he had achieved intromission. He said that he was "scared, nervous" because this was his first experience with sexual intercourse. He thought, "I can't believe I'm doin' this (having intercourse)." Quantez did not ejaculate during intercourse because the sexual activity had not gone on long enough for him to achieve orgasm. The activity stopped and all three quickly pulled their pants up when they heard other people inside the stadium. However, before the sexual activity ceased, Y.J. came over while he and S.N. were having intercourse, asked S.N. for oral sex, and put his penis near her face. S.N. refused Y.J.'s request.

On the second day of the evaluation, I told Quantez of the discrepancies between what he had told me and what S.N. reported to police. He said that he was aware of what S.N. told police and said that he had heard that S.N. reported different versions of events to law enforcement officers at different times. S.N. had denied that she was Quantez's cousin and he maintained that "she never told us to stop." When asked why she might have reported this consensual sexual behavior to be a sexual assault, Quantez said that S.N. had had sex with so many boys that "people think she nasty." S.N. told her younger sister about the foregoing "sexual" experience, and her sister told others in school. S.N. was embarrassed that her peers were laughing at her because of her sexual promiscuity. Therefore, to dispel information about her promiscuity, she claimed that the consensual sexual behavior had, in fact, been non-consensual.

Quantez completed the Adolescent Sexual Interest Cardsort and provided implausible responses. Although he acknowledged that he found several scenarios depicted to be mildly sexually arousing, he denied finding any of the scenarios depicted to be strongly arousing. Those scenarios that he acknowledged to be mildly arousing were those in which he was engaging in consensual sexual behaviors with females between 15 and 18 years of age. (There were no scenarios depicting consensual sexual behaviors with females older than 18 years of age.) He denied finding scenarios involving sexual coercion of females to be arousing, as well as scenarios involving males of any age. I told Quantez that I was surprised that he did not find any of the scenarios depicted to be greatly arousing and asked him to generate a scenario that he finds greatly arousing. He provided the following scenario: He is in a bathtub with a 20-year-old woman, there are bubbles in the tub, and they are talking about how their life together will be; they get out of the tub and move to the bed in their bedroom to have vaginal intercourse; initially, she is on top of him and they then switch positions; Quantez ejaculates in her vagina (but the woman never achieves orgasm), and they then tell each how much they love one another; the couple goes to sleep, and in the morning, Quantez awakens and makes tea for the woman.

The Adolescent Cognitions Scale—Revised was also administered to Quantez. His responses suggested that he has some cognitive distortions that sometimes accompany/enable sexual offending behaviors. He endorsed the following statements as being true: if a child or adult stares at his penis while he is showing his penis, it would mean that the individual enjoys looking at it (rather than staring because (s)he is shocked); a young child of any age can make a decision regarding having sex with Quantez; and if he had sex with a young child and the child did not disclose the sexual activity, that would mean that the child enjoyed the sex and desired further sexual contact with Quantez. He denied that having sex with his brother or sister might make him/her afraid of having sex with other people later on.

Assessment of Risk for Engaging in Sexual Offending Behaviors

At the present time, there are no empirically validated, actuarial instruments that can be used to accurately estimate the risk of adolescent sexual re-offending. However, based on the best available research data and consensus in professional clinical opinion, a number of high-risk factors have been identified in the literature. The Estimate of Risk of Adolescent Sexual Offense Recidivism (The ERASOR: Worling & Curwen, 2001) summarizes the available research and expert clinical opinion, and this instrument can be used to estimate an adolescent's risk of sexual re-offense.

Because

> **A common issue that referral sources want addressed is risk for re-offending. Because there were no judicial findings at the time of the evaluation, there is no basis for assuming that a sexual offense occurred.**

the present matter remains an allegation and has not yet been decided in a court of law, it is inappropriate to use the ERASOR at the present time. (However, if the Court determines that he is guilty of the charges he faces, I will be pleased to then generate an estimate of his risk for re-offense.)

Summary

Quantez Brown was referred for evaluation by the Division of Youth and Family Services (DYFS), Big Urban Local Office. He is a 15-year-old male who has been incarcerated at the Essex County Juvenile Detention Center (ECJDC) in Newark, New Jersey, for allegedly sexually assaulting a 16-year-old female peer. The Division requested a juvenile-sex-offender-specific evaluation to assist in determining Quantez's placement and service needs.

Information provided by the Division indicated that Quantez has no prior arrests. Records available to me at the time of evaluation contain no information about the following: Quantez's level of cognitive functioning (i.e., IQ); whether there is any reason to doubt the credibility of the statement that S.N. provided to police; and whether Y.J. provided a statement/ confession to police and how consistent his statement is with S.N.'s and with Quantez's version of events. Finally, I have no information to suggest that this matter has yet been adjudicated. Therefore, Quantez's guilt or innocence has yet to be established.

Quantez has a history of disrupted attachments to caretakers and of childhood maltreatment. He reported that he experiences symptoms of mood-related problems (i.e., anxiety and depression) including sleep-related difficulties, nightmares about the physical abuse perpetrated by his mother, and preoccupation regarding whether reunification will eventually occur. All of the foregoing is generally consistent with hypotheses generated on personality testing based upon Quantez's responses.

Quantez reported having accidentally witnessed his mother having sex with a boyfriend when Quantez was seven or eight years old. When asked about his own sexual history, he reported generally non-problematic sexual behaviors. However, he said that he usually, but not always, masturbates to scenarios involving consensual sexual behaviors with females in their early 20s. His report of masturbating two to three times weekly and never having had a nocturnal emission (i.e., "wet dream") tentatively suggests that he either underreported his frequency of masturbation or was untruthful about never having experienced a nocturnal emission. He described having a generally age-appropriate dating relationship with a female peer. The fantasy scenario that he reported finding most arousing seemed overly romantic, rather than focused on genital sex, for an adolescent male. Although it is probable that Quantez provided what he perceived to be a socially desirable response, it is also plausible that the fantasy reflects a desire to have an emotionally intimate relationship with an older female, a relationship he never had with his own mother. The foregoing hypothesis should be explored within a psychotherapeutic context.

There were some inconsistencies in his version of the instant (alleged) offense. Although he was clear that S.N. never objected to the sexual behavior in which he and Y.J. engaged her, he claimed that Y.J. reported that S.N. would not allow him to have sex with her and that she kept closing her legs. It seems implausible that an adolescent girl would have consensual sex in a public place in the presence of another male.

Quantez displayed some cognitive distortions that often accompany/enable sexual offending behavior.

Despite the assortment of concerns identified in this report, there is cause for cautious optimism. He reported having a good experience in psychotherapy. Scales embedded within one psychological test (i.e., the PAI-A) supports the view that he perceives the need for mental health treatment to address the issues with which he presents. This is cause for cautious optimism because many adolescents with a history of engaging in antisocial behaviors do not perceive any need for a change in their behaviors.

The following recommendations are offered within a reasonable degree of psychological certainty based upon the information currently available to me. If additional information becomes available that is substantially inconsistent with information currently available to me, modifications to the psychological recommendations may be warranted.

Recommendations

1. The least restrictive environment for placement that seems most appropriate is continued placement in foster care (with no other minors in the home), *if and only if* he is closely monitored by juvenile probation. Although he has no known history of substance abuse, frequent, random urine screens should be conducted because substance use would significantly increase his risk for (re)offending. Although it seems appropriate for him to continue attending a public school, he should not have any unsupervised contact with minors. Violation of any conditions of probation suggests the need for a greater level of structure and supervision (i.e., residential placement). (Residential placement may also be needed for practical reasons because it is unlikely that the Division will be successful in placing an adolescent with pending charges for Aggravated Sexual Assault in a foster home.) Repeated violation of rules in a residential placement setting should suggest the need for placement in a JJC secure care facility.
2. Quantez should participate in juvenile-sex-offender-specific treatment (if found guilty of the offenses for which he has been charged). This treatment may take place on an outpatient or inpatient basis. Unsupervised contact with minors should again be permitted upon the recommendation of his treatment provider.
3. Quantez will need continued mental health treatment to address the assortment of issues with which he presents. He should participate in individual psychotherapy with a clinician experienced in conducting trauma-focused cognitive-behavioral therapy (TF-CBT; Deblinger & Heflin, 1996) with adolescents. If the services of a practitioner with such expertise cannot be readily obtained, trauma-focused therapy should be conducted and a clinician with experience in TF-CBT might serve as a consultant to Quantez's therapist. This therapy may take place concurrently with juvenile-sex-offender-specific treatment.
4. Quantez should undergo a psychiatric evaluation to determine whether medications are needed to address his sleep problems and to control symptoms associated with anxiety and depression.

5. Quantez's academic programming should be reviewed and he should be provided with remediation in basic academic skill domains as needed. He would also benefit from job sampling, and supervision by a job coach. These recommendations are offered so as to assist Quantez in acquiring the skills necessary to becoming a productive member of society.

Daniel Bromberg, Ph.D., ABPP
Licensed Psychologist, NJ Lic. #SI004033
Board Certified in Cognitive & Behavioral Psychology
American Board of Professional Psychology

NON-COURT-ORDERED EVALUATION OF A 16-YEAR-OLD MALE DISPLAYING ASSORTED PROBLEMATIC SEXUAL BEHAVIORS

Psychosexual Evaluation

Note that I label this as a "Psychosexual Evaluation," rather than as a "Forensic Psychological Evaluation." The evaluation was sought to determine treatment needs, NOT to address any psycholegal question or to assist a judge with any sort of decision-making.

Name	Date of Birth	Dates of Evaluation	Date of Report
Marco Reyes	xx/xx/96	xx/xx/12; xx/xx/12	xx/xx/12

Reason for Referral

Marco Reyes was referred for evaluation by the Youth League of Big Urban County (YLBUC). He is a 16-year-old male who has a history of multiple placements and sexual abuse before having been adopted. He has been displaying problematic sexual behaviors and YLBUC sought an evaluation to assist in determining the services that Marco needs.

Sources of Information

Records received from adoptive parents

Individualized Education Program (IEP); Meeting date of 11/30/11

Untitled documents (that appear to be reports of pediatric neurological evaluations) that are also unsigned, from David Marks, MD, and Michele Wickstrom, RN, CPNP, of Nice Town NJ; documents are dated 11/23/11 and 08/03/11, respectively

Pages 9–13 of an untitled document (that appears to be a report from a psychiatric evaluation); signed by Jane M. Shrink, D.O.; Date stamp from FAX indicates the document was FAXed from Shrink Psychiatric on 12/11/07

Psychosocial Evaluation conducted by James Wong, LCSW, of Metropolitan Regional Child Abuse Diagnostic and Treatment Center; evaluation conducted 07/14/03

Assorted Psychological, Psychiatric, Neurological, Educational, Speech-Language, and Social History Evaluations conducted at Xxxxx Hospital in Serene Hills, NJ

Pediatric Neurodevelopmental Evaluation; conducted by Michael Watts, MD, of Children's Medical Center, Child Development Center; evaluated on 03/24/00

Child Summary Outline, Parts A & B; (Presumably generated by DYFS)

Clinical interview with Marco Reyes

Psychological testing of Marco Reyes

Collateral information provided by adoptive parents

Background & Collateral Information

I interviewed Mr. Jones and Mr. Smith to assess the scope of their concerns about Marco's behaviors. Concerns included the following: a 40-something-old woman who is a friend of the family had been with Marco and went down to the basement—she came upstairs and found Marco masturbating, with his penis in plain sight; Marco had previously "stalked" a female peer, walking her home against her will, and would not allow other boys to talk to her; when Marco was 14 or 15 years old, Mr. Smith found him naked in the basement with Mr. Smith's seven- or eight-year-old male nephew; Marco talks to others indiscriminately about his sexual history and has sent text messages to older females asking them for sex; he sometimes touches the family's female dogs inappropriately and sometimes keeps them locked in his room; he lies "compulsively"; he spends a great deal of time in the bathroom; he exposed himself to a same-age female peer at school before Christmas of 2011; and he is gullible and easily led by peers.

At the time of the collateral interview, Marco was taking Abilify and Dexedrine.

Marco's intellectual potential (i.e., IQ) was evaluated in October of 2007 by use of the WISC-IV. At that time, he earned a Full Scale IQ score of 96, and he earned Verbal Comprehension and Perceptual Reasoning Index scores of 99 and 96, respectively. He had a Working Memory Index score of 91 and a Processing Speed Index score of 100. These results suggest that his overall intellectual functioning is well-within the average range.

Marco has a long-standing history of displaying behavioral and mood-related problems. He had had multiple foster placements prior to having been adopted. He also experienced sexual abuse and sustained a chemical burn that necessitated a one month stay in a hospital burn unit.

Records reflect that Marco has been displaying problematic sexual behaviors at least since he was seven years old. Mr. Smith and Mr. Jones were then Marco's pre-adoptive parents. At that time, it was reported that Marco pulled down the bathing suit of Mr. Smith's 12-year-old nephew and attempted to touch the nephew's penis. Marco also attempted to touch Mr. Smith's genital area. It was reported that Marco was preoccupied with the genitalia of the family's dog. During a conversation with his DYFS worker about his behavior, Marco disclosed that his 11-year-old foster brother, "Rashon," pulled down Marco's pants and touched all over his body, including his genitalia. He also reported that his eight-year-old foster brother, Isaiah, touched his (Marco's) genitalia.

Clinical Interview

Marco's affect was flat on presentation but began to vary appropriately with content being discussed as the evaluation progressed. His height, weight, and level of personal grooming were generally appropriate for an adolescent his age. He displayed no evidence of psychotic thought processes at the time of evaluation. He articulated the difference between "the truth" and "a lie" and agreed to be truthful throughout his evaluation.

Prior to the start of the psychological evaluation, I spent a significant amount of time discussing the limits of confidentiality. Marco was given the opportunity to ask questions regarding (relative lack of) confidentiality. He verbally agreed to undergo the present evaluation and provided written assent, as well.

Placements and Attachment to Caretakers/Parents

Marco lives at home with his adoptive fathers, his 21-year-old biological brother, Steven, and one grandfather (that is, Mr. Smith's father). His description of each individual tentatively suggested that he has at least an adequate degree of emotional attachment to each. In response to inquiry, he identified other adults in his extended family to whom he has emotional attachments. He denied experiencing any form of child maltreatment in the care of his adoptive parents.

I asked Marco about his placement history before having been adopted. Although unable to recall the name of the foster parent, he reported having been locked in the basement and hit with a belt as a disciplinary strategy. He recalls having been "hit a lot." Before that, he was in the home of "Ms. Hamilton (he thinks)." He said, "It was the worst house ever. They put me in a diaper like a little kid. I hated it." He has no recollection of his placement prior to that time.

Mental Status Screening and Substance Use History

Marco was asked questions about his overall emotional functioning. He denied all of the following: sleep-related problems, including bad dreams and nightmares (since taking psychoactive medications—he also noted that he sometimes walks in his sleep); both daytime and nighttime wetting and soiling; somatic complaints; experiencing prolonged periods of sadness; engaging in self-injurious behaviors; suicidal ideation; thoughts of hurting animals or other people; and homicidal ideation. However, he reported having had unusual sensory experiences, apparently in the absence of sensory stimulation. On one occasion, he heard a "little girl" say "goodbye" to him, although there were no children present at the time. He also reported having had experiences with "ghosts" or the "undead" in which shadows or human figures ask him to help them "move on." These apparitions then turn into a blue mist and evaporate. He denied that these specters issue commands but told me that they have occasionally moved his books from one location to a nearby location.

It is unclear if these experiences are the result of psychosis, thoughts resulting from watching television shows or movies about supernatural phenomena, et cetera. Although these experiences should be monitored by a mental health professional, I did NOT label them as symptoms of psychosis. Readers sometimes go through reports quickly rather than carefully reading the entire report. I do not want readers to erroneously believe that I am saying this adolescent has a psychotic disorder.

Marco denied experimentation with, and use of, all of the following: alcohol; illicit drugs; prescription medications for recreational use; and tobacco use.

Sexual History

Marco recalled having first ejaculated when he was approximately 14 years old. Ejaculation occurred after having masturbated to orgasm. He identifies himself as being bisexual and said that he "embraces it (his sexual orientation)" as a part of who he is. After I informed him of the normalcy (from an actuarial perspective) of bisexual thoughts and feelings during the adolescent years, I asked if he seems to prefer males or females or if he finds himself having roughly equivalent attractions to persons of both sexes. After a few moments of thought, he said that he finds himself more attracted to females than to males. His attraction to males is limited to those males who are quite muscular.

Additional information about Marco's sexual arousal pattern was obtained by way of a written self-report inventory (i.e., Adolescent Sexual Interest Cardsort). Findings tentatively suggest[3] that he experiences the strongest degree of sexual arousal to scenarios involving consensual sex with both males and females between 14 and 18 years of age. He indicated relative disinterest in, or disgust by, scenarios involving physical coercion and to sex involving prepubescent boys and girls.

Despite the foregoing, Marco reported having had sexual experiences with prepubescent boys when younger, and denied ever having had a consensual sexual relationship with approximately same-age male or female peers since the age of 12. The first sexual contact with another person that Marco was able to recall involved his own sexual abuse. He had vague, disjointed recollections of several incidents occurring when he was six years old during which an older person fondled him and "did some other stuff." Marco was unable to recall the identity of the perpetrator. He reported that the sexual contact was unpleasant and recalled that "I just wanted it to end." When Marco was seven years old, he and another 7-year-old boy "felt each other's dicks." The incident was interrupted when "Dad walked in." He reported another incident that occurred at about the same age when he and another boy "felt each other's dicks" in a bathroom stall in an elementary school. When Marco was 12 years old, he and a 10-year-old

[3] There are several shortcomings inherent in assessing sexual interest and arousal by way of self-report measures. The most accurate method of assessing sexual interest and arousal in males is by way of physiological responses (i.e., penile plethysmography) to either auditory stimuli of assorted sexual scenarios or visual stimuli of nude males and females of different ages. However, there is an assortment of ethical and practical issues that arise regarding use of plethysmography with adolescents. Moreover, to the best of my knowledge, plethysmography is not currently used in the State of New Jersey.

boy engaged in mutual genital touching and "humped" one another with their clothes on. Marco said, "I kinda wanted it. I knew it was wrong." In response to inquiry, the experience was of a mixed valence. That is, although cognizant that he was engaging in behavior that was "wrong," he was sexually aroused during the incident. I inquired about an incident during which he and Mr. Smith's seven- or eight-year-old nephew were found naked in the basement (Marco was 14 or 15 years old at the time). Marco told me, "I wanted to try anal sex with him."

I asked Marco about a relationship that he attempted to initiate with an approximately same-age female peer. He reported that his relationship with his "girlfriend" ended in March of 2011. He enjoyed talking and "spending quality time" with this girl. The girl disliked that Marco followed her home and there was some concern, as well, after he told other boys that he would "fuck them up" if they talked to her. When their relationship ended, Marco began masturbating four times a day. I asked why he began masturbating with such frequency at that time. He said that he had been feeling "bored" and "upset" and "wanted to feel good. I didn't want to do drugs, so I did that." I wanted to be certain that I correctly understood what Marco was attempting to communicate. After having sought clarification, it was clear that Marco had been using somewhat excessive masturbation as a way of coping with negative emotional states.

I inquired about the amount of time that Marco spends in the bathroom. He denied engaging in excessive masturbation in the bathroom and informed me that he had been having stomach problems.

I inquired about the incident during which a 40-something-year-old woman who was in his home found Marco masturbating. He told me that this woman was his tutor. She came up from the basement, found him masturbating, became angry, and told him that she will never be able to erase the sight from her memory. I asked Marco why he had been masturbating in a place and at a time that he was likely to be interrupted. He said that he was "too lazy to get up" and added that this woman had not previously "caught me" when he had been masturbating. The antecedent to masturbation appears to have been that he was reading boring material. He added that he had been "jerking off" to images of "black chicks."

I also inquired about the possibility that Marco had engaged in sexual behaviors with the family's dogs. Although he acknowledged that his parents are concerned about this possibility, he flatly denied engaging in any such behavior.

Readers will recall that there was concern about Marco engaging in excessive masturbation. Approximately one week had elapsed between the first and second assessment sessions. During the second session, I asked Marco approximately how many times he had masturbated since I had last seen him. He said that he had masturbated one time.

I asked Marco for his perception of his own need for services to address psychosexual matters. He said that he would benefit from learning how to talk to others, especially same-age female peers. Further clarifying questions revealed that Marco has difficulty engaging others, particularly girls, in casual, age-appropriate conversation. This skill deficit presumably interferes with his ability to engage girls in friendships, and in emotionally intimate and physically intimate relationships. He said that he also needs "to learn how to stop masturbating so much." Inquiry revealed that he generally masturbates four times a day, five days a week (Monday through Friday). I asked why he perceives his masturbatory pattern as being problematic. He replied that masturbation is "wrong" and "dirty." I inquired why he perceives masturbation as being "wrong." He said that it is "wrong to think about somebody in that way," that is, being used for strictly sexual purposes. I provided brief psychoeducation on the normalcy of masturbation and of using fantasies during masturbation.

In addition to all of the foregoing, Marco completed Abel, Becker, & Kaplan's Adolescent Cognitions Scale (Revised) to assess for beliefs that often accompany and/or contribute to sexual behavior problems. Of the 32 items on the inventory, he endorsed three that were concerning. He endorsed as "true" two items indicating that individuals leave their shades up and/or walk around their homes naked hoping that others outside the residence will be secretly watching them. He also endorsed the notion that if he were to engage a "young child" in sexual behavior and the young child did not disclose, that would mean that the child enjoyed the sexual behavior and wanted to continue engaging in sexual behavior with him.

Tests Administered

Personality Assessment Inventory—Adolescent (PAI-A)
Trauma Symptom Checklist for Children (TSCC)

Test Results

Scores on the validity scales embedded within the PAI-A suggest that Marco responded to PAI-A items in a reasonably forthright manner.

There was no indication of significant psychopathology. However, his interest in, and motivation for, mental health treatment, appears to be high. His responses suggested an acknowledgment of important problems and a perception of the need for assistance in dealing with these problems.

Marco completed the TSCC so as to permit a more formal assessment of possible trauma-related symptoms. His scores on validity scales embedded within this instrument suggested that he responded to test items in a reasonably forthright manner. There was some indication of a preoccupation with sexual matters.

Summary

Marco Reyes was referred for evaluation by the Youth League of Big Urban County (YLBUC). He is a 16-year-old male who has a history of multiple placements and sexual abuse before having been adopted. He has been displaying problematic sexual behaviors and YLBUC sought an evaluation to assist in determining the services that Marco needs.

Review of records provided to me revealed that Marco's level of cognitive functioning (i.e., IQ) is well-within the average range.

Therefore, he should have no difficulty understanding, and being able to profit from, commonly-used psychotherapeutic techniques.

He experienced maltreatment at a young age and became legally free for adoption before the age of eight. He had experiences of unwanted sexual contact before that time.

There is a mental health issue that is of importance to note. Marco described having some unusual sensory experiences, apparently in the absence of sensory stimulation. It is noteworthy that, during a prior psychiatric evaluation, the psychiatrist noted a similar concern. Although there was no indication of psychosis during the present evaluation, Marco's parents should be alert to the possibility that psychotic symptoms might emerge, as such symptoms sometimes become apparent during the late adolescent/emerging adulthood years.

Marco provided a significant amount of information about his sexual history. He identified himself as being bisexual and stated that he is comfortable with his sexual orientation. He expressed a stronger preference for female, in contrast to male, sex partners. He reported that his attraction to males is limited to those who are quite muscular. Information obtained from the Adolescent Sexual Interest Cardsort tentatively suggests[4] that he experiences the strongest degree of sexual arousal to scenarios involving consensual sex with both males and females between 14 and 18 years of age. He indicated relative disinterest in, or disgust by, scenarios involving physical coercion and to sex involving prepubescent boys and girls. Discussion about his masturbatory fantasies yielded information consistent with a bisexual pattern of arousal. Despite the foregoing, Marco reported having had sexual experiences with prepubescent boys when younger, and denied ever having had a consensual sexual relationship with approximately same-age male or female peers since the age of 12. There is a plausible explanation for the apparent inconsistency between Marco's sexual arousal pattern and his sexual behavior. First, readers should be aware that it is normative for adolescent boys to become easily aroused by a wide range of sexual stimuli. Therefore, he may have become sexually involved with prepubescent boys simply because they were present in his environment and, given his apparent social skill deficits, much more easily engaged in sexual behaviors than same-age males or females. Furthermore, it is often difficult for adolescent boys to seek out romantic/sexual relationships with other boys because of the prejudice surrounding male homosexual behavior that is often present in high school settings. This scenario implies that therapy to address social skill deficits is warranted. Of course, given the fluidity of male sexual arousal patterns during adolescence, it is equally as plausible that there is an emerging and problematic pattern of sexual arousal to prepubescent boys. This scenario suggests the possibility that sexual reconditioning procedures may need to be implemented.

Marco has previously attempted to establish a meaningful interpersonal (not simply sexual) relationship with an approximately same-age female peer. However, he did so in a socially inept manner. He reported that excessive masturbation (approximately four times daily) began when that relationship ended and was used to cope with the unpleasant emotional states that resulted from rejection. The foregoing suggests the need

[4] There are several shortcomings inherent in assessing sexual interest and arousal by way of self-report measures. The most accurate method of assessing sexual interest and arousal in males is by way of physiological responses (i.e., penile plethysmography) to either auditory stimuli of assorted sexual scenarios or visual stimuli of nude males and females of different ages. However, there is an assortment of ethical and practical issues that arise regarding use of plethysmography with adolescents. Moreover, to the best of my knowledge, plethysmography is not currently used in the State of New Jersey.

for psychotherapeutic assistance in finding alternative strategies for managing aversive emotional states. Social skills training would be warranted, as well.

Marco is cognizant that he has problems in the psychosocial/psychosexual domains and expressed an eagerness to receive services to address these issues. This recognition and willingness to receive assistance bodes well for the successful resolution of problems identified in the present report.

Recommendations

1. The information obtained during the present evaluation suggests that Marco should receive services on an outpatient basis while living at home. As of the time of evaluation, any out-of-home placement should be viewed as being too restrictive. (Part of the rationale underlying this recommendation is Marco's early history of having disrupted attachments to caretakers.)
2. Marco should not have unsupervised contact with minors under 14 years of age. Interactions with children of family friends, younger cousins, etc., should be supervised by one or more responsible adults who engage in "line of sight" supervision of his interactions with minors under the age of 14. Clearly, Marco should not serve in any position in which he would have authority over younger minors (e.g., as a camp counselor, religious school instructor, or babysitter).
3. Marco should not be in a bathroom or the sleeping quarters of minors under the age of 14 while they are toileting, bathing, or changing clothes, even in the company of a responsible adult.
4. Marco would benefit from the following "package" of psychological services:

> Some components of this package would commonly be incorporated into juvenile-sex-offender-specific therapy. However, he was never criminally charged for his sexual behaviors, nor was he substantiated for sexual abuse by a child protective service agency (because he was not in a position of caring for/supervising other minors). Therefore, he is technically not a juvenile sex offender (JSO) and would probably be ineligible to participate in JSO treatment.

   a. Social skills training specific to instruction in initiating and maintaining interactions with peers;

b. Discussion of sexual and emotional self-management skills to address excessive masturbation as his sole strategy for coping with aversive emotional states;

c. Exploration of thoughts and feelings about the normalcy of masturbation and;

d. Exploration and correction of cognitive distortions regarding females wanting to be covertly observed while naked and the possibility of prepubescent children enjoying sexual contact with him.

e. Finally, he should be provided with information about healthy sexuality(reading and discussing portions of Ruth Bell's book Changing Bodies, Changing Lives might be useful in providing information and addressing some of the foregoing issues in a non-threatening manner).

f. Unusual sensory experiences should be monitored. If auditory/visual experiences in the absence of sensory stimuli persist, psychiatric re-evaluation is warranted.

Daniel Bromberg, Ph.D., ABPP
Licensed Psychologist, NJ Lic. #SI004033
Board Certified in Cognitive & Behavioral Psychology
American Board of Professional Psychology

NON-COURT-ORDERED EVALUATION OF A 15-YEAR-OLD MALE SEXUALLY ATTRACTED TO HIS YOUNGER SISTERS

Psychosexual Evaluation

Name	Date of Birth	Date of Evaluation	Date of Report
Jeffrey Wodrich	xx/xx/95	xx/xx/10	xx/xx/xx

Reason for Referral

Jeffrey Wodrich was referred for an evaluation by the Division of Youth and Family Services (DYFS), Affluent Suburban Local Office. On {date}, Jeffrey's father contacted State Central Screening and notified the Division that Jeffrey had been displaying an assortment of inappropriate and problematic sexual behaviors, was at the Xxxxx Xxxxxx in Xxxxx Xxxx, NJ, and that hospital planned to discharge Jeffrey and refer him for outpatient services. Family members were uncomfortable having Jeffrey return home. An evaluation of Jeffrey's treatment needs and a recommendation for appropriate placement (e.g., return home vs. out-of-home placement) was sought.

Sources of Information

Records provided by the Division of Youth and Family Services

State of New Jersey, Department of Children and Families, Screening Summary (DCF 1-1); Intake Name of Jane Wodrich; Date of Intake was {date} (Referral made by Mr. Wodrich)

State of New Jersey, Department of Children and Families, Screening Summary (DCF 1-1); Intake Name of Jane Wodrich; Date of Intake was {date} (Referral made by Xxxxx Xxxxxx staff) Xxxxx Xxxxxx Initial Assessment

Clinical interview

Psychological testing

Collateral information provided verbally by Jackson Taylor, DYFS Case Manager

Background Information

Records reflect that this family has not had any previous involvement with the Division.

There are three minors in the home other than Jeffrey. The eldest child is Michael, age 16. Jeffrey's younger sisters are Sophie, age 12, and Elizabeth, age 10.

Concerns that prompted referral to Xxxxx Xxxxxx and the Division included the following: entering the bathroom while Sophie was showering and "sexually assaulting" her; Jeffrey having attempted to covertly video-record his sisters while undressing; viewing of pornographic sites pertaining to incest; exposing himself in front of his sisters; and frequent masturbation.

> **This information suggests more than acting out sexually with a younger sibling and raises concern about a pattern of problematic sexual arousal.**

He has a pervasive developmental disorder (PDD), impulse control problems, and a mood disorder.

Clinical Interview

The present evaluation was conducted at the Xxxxx Xxxxxx's Adolescent Unit in Xxxxx Xxxx, New Jersey. His mother signed the consent form for forensic evaluation and the form was returned to me via FAX. Before the start of the psychological evaluation, I spent a significant amount of time discussing the limits of confidentiality. Jeffrey was given the opportunity to ask questions regarding (relative lack of) confidentiality. He verbally agreed to undergo the present evaluation and provided written assent, as well.

Jeffrey's affect was flat on presentation but began to vary appropriately with content being discussed as the evaluation progressed. Although his height and weight made him appear older than his actual chronological age, his level of personal grooming was generally appropriate for an adolescent his age. He displayed no evidence of psychotic thought processes at the time of evaluation. He articulated the difference between "the truth" and "a lie" and agreed to be truthful throughout his evaluation.

Relationships with Family Members

Before his hospitalization at Xxxxx Xxxxxx, Jeffrey had been living at home with his parents, 16-year-old brother, and 12- and 10-year-old sisters. His descriptions of family members suggested that he has a reasonably strong degree of attachment to his parents and siblings. The content of his statements also suggested that he acknowledges having a problematic pattern of sexual arousal and that he perceives himself as having significant impairments in functioning. For example, he said that his brother "is the opposite of me (and is) becoming more and more social.... He used to shut himself up in his room." He spoke of his father quite fondly and said, "He's a great father. He tries real hard. It's me that's the problem." When discussing 13-year-old Sophie, he said, "She's nice. I regret what I did to her. (Q: Tell me more about her.) She's going through puberty. That's what turns me on."

Mental Status Screening and Substance Use History

Jeffrey was asked questions about his overall emotional functioning. He denied all of the following: sleep-related problems, including bad dreams and nightmares; somatic complaints; experiencing prolonged periods of sadness; engaging in self-injurious behaviors; suicidal ideation; thoughts of hurting animals or other people; homicidal ideation and; experiencing both auditory and visual hallucinations. In response to inquiry, he acknowledged that he sometimes verbalizes suicidal ideation when "upset," but added, "I would never take my own life in a million years."

Jeffrey denied experimentation with, and use of, all of the following: alcohol; illicit drugs; prescription medications for recreational use; and tobacco use.

Sexual History

I asked Jeffrey about his sexual history. He began by reporting that his first memory of anything "sexual" was when he was at or about six years of age and he and his sister Sophie looked at one another while naked. He recalled experiencing curiosity, rather than sexual arousal at that time.

Although uncertain when he began masturbating, he believes that it was approximately two years ago. He recalled having rubbed against his bed covers "by accident" and ejaculating. When asked to describe that experience, Jeffrey said, "It got all over. It felt weird, then good. I got hooked on it. (Q) On pleasure." He continues to masturbate by rubbing against objects and then ejaculates either into a rug on the floor or into his hand. Although he often masturbates in his bedroom, he also masturbates in a small room off the family's living room if he believes that no one else is home. At other times, he masturbates in the basement. He usually "forgets" to close the door to the room in which he is masturbating. Jeffrey denied ever having had consensual sexual experiences with others.

Jeffrey was asked about the assortment of fantasies that he uses during masturbation. Sometimes he masturbates while having "random thoughts," sometimes to fantasies of Sophie's or Elizabeth's (clean) underwear,

This raises the possibility of a paraphilia.

and sometimes to fantasies of a woman from his imagination. Because Jeffrey acknowledged that he sometimes masturbates while thinking about Elizabeth's underwear, I asked if he thinks about engaging in sexual behavior with Elizabeth while masturbating. He said, "Not usually." However, he often masturbates to fantasies of having oral sex or vaginal intercourse with Sophie.

He acknowledged sexual arousal to a younger female sibling.

He denied having any interest in anal intercourse. When asked which of Sophie's physical features he finds most arousing, Jeffrey initially gave a "don't know" response, but after a moment's thought, said, "Maybe her breasts." Further inquiry revealed the following: Jeffrey masturbates to sexual fantasies of girls between the ages of 10 to 15 (inclusive),

He acknowledged sexual arousal to other pre- and peri-pubertal girls, as well.

but not to males of any age; sometimes, he masturbates to fantasies of underwear, or of a girl wearing underwear; and the feature he finds most arousing in girls is the onset of puberty, specifically, the start of breast development and the early stages of pubic hair growth.

I asked Jeffrey about incidents discussed in records provided by the Division. We began by discussing the incident during which he entered the bathroom while Sophie was showering. He said that he touched her breasts, back, buttocks, and the pubic hair on her vulvo-vaginal area. He said that he felt ashamed of himself for what he had done. Jeffrey told me that he had used the video feature on his camera to make video recordings of both of his sisters while undressing. His sisters discovered his attempt to video record. In response to inquiry, Jeffrey said that he would have masturbated to the captured video images.

He acknowledged a problematic pattern of sexual arousal.

When asked about the content of the flash drive discussed in the records, he told me that it contained Google images of women in their 20s and 30s. When asked if there were also images of children or teenagers, he said that some of the females "could be a little underage." Although he denied having any recollection of attempting to video-record Elizabeth's friends, Jeffrey acknowledged that he sometimes masturbates to fantasies of having sex with those friends of Elizabeth's who are both peri-pubescent and physically attractive.

More information about a problematic pattern of sexual arousal.

Other Sources of Information About Sexual Arousal Patterns and Cognitions

Additional information about Jeffrey's sexual arousal pattern was obtained by way of a written self-report inventory (i.e., Adolescent Sexual Interest

Cardsort). Findings tentatively suggest[5] that he experiences sexual arousal to scenarios involving both consensual and coerced sex with females between 8 and 18 years of age.

Further acknowledgment of a problematic pattern of sexual arousal.

He indicated relative disinterest in, or disgust by, scenarios involving sex with males of any age. Significantly, he endorsed scenarios involving sex with his sisters to be sexually arousing.

Again, more information about a problematic pattern of sexual arousal.

Jeffrey also completed Abel, Becker, & Kaplan's Adolescent Cognitions Scale (Revised) to assess for beliefs that often accompany and/or contribute to sexual behavior problems. He did not endorse any items indicative of cognitive distortions.

I asked Jeffrey for his perception of his need for services to address psychosexual matters. He is cognizant that his arousal pattern is both uncommon and problematic and that he needs professional assistance to address these issues. However, he was hopeful that he would be able to receive treatment on an outpatient basis while living at home with his sisters.

Tests Administered

Personality Assessment Inventory—Adolescent (PAI-A)
Trauma Symptom Checklist for Children (TSCC)

Test Results

Scores on the validity scales embedded within the PAI-A suggest that Jeffrey responded to PAI-A items in a reasonably forthright manner.

Although there was no indication of significant psychopathology, there was evidence of a possible depressive disorder. In addition, it appeared that

[5] There are several shortcomings inherent in assessing sexual interest and arousal by way of self-report measures. The most accurate method of assessing sexual interest and arousal in males is by way of physiological responses (i.e., penile plethysmography) to either auditory stimuli of assorted sexual scenarios or visual stimuli of nude males and females of different ages. However, there is an assortment of ethical and practical issues that arise regarding use of plethysmography with adolescents. Moreover, to the best of my knowledge, plethysmography is not currently used in the State of New Jersey.

he has a fixed, negative view of himself. He is probably self-critical and focuses on past failures. In addition, it is probable that he is more troubled by self-doubt and misgivings about his adequacy than is readily apparent to others.

Interpersonally, it is likely that Jeffrey is both withdrawn and introverted. He probably gets little enjoyment from social interactions, makes no special effort to appear friendly, and is likely to be passive and distant in those relationships he does maintain.

His interest in, and motivation for, mental health treatment, appears to be high. His responses suggested an acknowledgment of important problems and a perception of the need for assistance in dealing with these problems.

Jeffrey completed the TSCC so as to permit a norm-referenced assessment of possible trauma-related symptoms. His scores on validity scales embedded within this instrument suggested that he responded to test items in a reasonably forthright manner. There was no indication of trauma-related symptoms. However, his responses strongly suggested a preoccupation with sexual matters (T = 91) and distress regarding sexual matters (T = 67).

Summary

Jeffrey Wodrich was referred for an evaluation by the Division of Youth and Family Services (DYFS), Affluent Suburban Local Office. On {date}, Jeffrey's father contacted State Central Screening and notified the Division that Jeffrey had been displaying an assortment of inappropriate and problematic sexual behaviors, was at the Xxxxx Xxxxxx in Xxxxx Xxxx, NJ, and that Hospital planned to discharge Jeffrey and refer him for outpatient services. Family members were uncomfortable having Jeffrey return home. An evaluation of Jeffrey's treatment needs and a recommendation for appropriate placement (e.g., return home vs. out-of-home placement) was sought.

Jeffrey is a socially isolated adolescent who appeared to be reasonably forthright when discussing his masturbatory pattern, his attempts to video-record his sisters in states of undress, and his contact offense against his 13-year-old sister. The foregoing reveals a pattern of repetitive and compulsive sexual interest in pre-and peri-pubescent girls, including his biological sisters. This repetitive and compulsive pattern, in addition to his excessive masturbation in inappropriate locations (i.e., rooms with doors open and then ejaculating into carpeting) reveals an extremely problematic pattern of deviant sexual arousal and behavior. This pattern, in combination with the availability of potential victims at home, strongly suggests the need for intensive treatment in a setting in which close supervision is provided.

Recommendations

1. Jeffrey should ***not*** be permitted to return home within the foreseeable future because he poses a significant risk of harm to both of his sisters and their friends who might come to the family home to visit. Moreover, because of his pattern of problematic sexual arousal to his sisters, returning home would be expected to undermine treatment for his pattern of problematic sexual arousal (i.e., living in close proximity to, fantasizing about, and masturbating to, images of his sisters).
2. Jeffrey should be placed in a residential treatment facility that offers a very high level of structure and supervision. At a minimum, the following services would need to be available: juvenile-sex-offender-specific therapy (both individual and group); psychiatric monitoring; and counseling to address problems that might arise on a daily basis. If such services are not regularly available on-site, arrangements should be made for such services to be delivered at the earliest time possible. It is probable that juvenile-sex-offender-specific therapy will need to include sexual reconditioning procedures

Scott & Bromberg (this volume), provide a useful summary of such strategies.

   in addition to other more common treatment components.
3. Jeffrey should undergo a psychosexual re-evaluation before return to the family home is contemplated.
4. Elizabeth and Sophie should be referred for evaluations to determine if/the extent to which they might need mental health services to address exposure to/experiences with inappropriate sexual stimuli.

Daniel Bromberg, Ph.D., ABPP
Licensed Psychologist, NJ Lic. #SI004033
Board Certified in Cognitive & Behavioral Psychology
American Board of Professional Psychology

REFERENCES

American Psychological Association, (2002). Ethical principles of psychologists and code of conduct. *American Psychologist*, *57*, 1060–1073.

American Psychological Association, (2013). Specialty guidelines for forensic psychology. *American Psychologist*, *68*, 7–19.

Bracken, B. A. (1988). Ten psychometric reasons why similar tests produce dissimilar results. *Journal of School Psychology*, *26*, 155–166.

Bromberg, D. S., & O'Donohue, W. T. (2013). Research methods: Current strategies, obstacles to research, and future directions. In D. S. Bromberg & W. T. O'Donohue (Eds.), *Handbook of child and adolescent sexuality: Developmental and forensic psychology* (pp. 21–40). San Diego, CA: Elsevier.

Daly, E. J., O'Connor, M. A., Daro, P. M., Strong, W., & Sommerhalder, M. (this volume). Academic intervention. In D. S. Bromberg & W. T. O'Donohue (Eds.), *Toolkit for working with juvenile sex offenders* (pp. 361–402). San Diego, CA: Elsevier.

DeMier, R. (2010, December). Forensic report writing. Paper presented at the American Academy of Forensic Psychology Workshop Series, Philadelphia, PA.

Grisso, T. (2010). Guidance for improving forensic reports: A review of common errors. *Open Access Journal of Forensic Psychology*, *2*, 102–115.

Grisso, T. (2013). *Forensic evaluation of juveniles* (2nd ed.). Sarasota, FL: Professional Resource Press.

Heilbrun, K., Grisso, T., & Goldstein, A. M. (2009). *Foundations of forensic mental health assessment*. New York, NY: Oxford.

Heilbrun, K. (2001). *Principles of forensic mental health assessment*. New York, NY: Plenum.

Kinscherff, R., & Latham, C. (this volume). Informed consent or assent for assessment or treatment and releases of information. In D. S. Bromberg & W. T. O'Donohue (Eds.), *Toolkit for working with juvenile sex offenders* (pp. 1–28). San Diego, CA: Elsevier.

Scott, S. E., & Bromberg, D.S. (this volume). Modifying problematic sexual interests of males. In D. S. Bromberg & W. T. O'Donohue (Eds.), *Toolkit for working with juvenile sex offenders* (pp. 259–266). San Diego, CA: Elsevier.

Tillbrook, C., Mumley, D., & Grisso, T. (2003). Avoiding expert opinions on the ultimate legal question: The case for integrity. *Journal of Forensic Psychology Practice*, *3*, 77–87.

Worling, J. R., & Curwen, T. (2001). Estimate of Risk of Adolescent Sexual Offense Recidivism (Version 2.0: The "ERASOR"). In M. C. Calder (Ed.), *Juveniles and children who sexually abuse: Frameworks for assessment* (pp. 372–397). Lyme Regis, Dorset, UK: Russell House.

ADDITIONAL HELPFUL RESOURCE

Medoff, D., & Kinscherff, R. (2006). Forensic evaluation of juvenile sexual offenders. In S. N. Sparta & G. P. Koocher (Eds.), *Forensic mental health assessment of children and adolescents*. New York, NY: Oxford.

CHAPTER 6

Tools for Testifying in Court

William T. O'Donohue
Department of Psychology, University of Nevada, Reno, NV, USA

INTRODUCTION

Delivery of assessment or treatment services to juvenile sexual offenders and their victims often requires interaction with the legal system. Therefore, professionals working in this area sometimes face the prospect of testifying in court. For many professionals, this prospect can cause considerable anxiety. Some of this anxiety may be due to the fact that testifying is a somewhat novel situation for them: mental health professionals are trained and experienced in providing therapy and assessment but, generally, have much less experience as participants in the American legal system. Secondly, it can be anxiety provoking for the mental health professional because court appearances take place in the context of an adversarial legal system. The American legal system is structured so that each side can present its own best case but each side can also challenge and criticize the other's case. Then the judge or jury makes the ultimate decision or decisions. Thus, when one testifies as an expert one needs to be prepared to be challenged (some would say "attacked") by the side that does not like what you are saying because it hurts their case. These sorts of challenges can be tough, as these can be prolonged (lasting for hours) and can cover a wide range of issues (including your past testimony from many years prior, and can even criticize weaknesses in your qualifications and thus seem a bit personal). To make things worse, for many, this often occurs in a very public context in which dozens of people can be present (even reporters from the media). In nearly all cases, your testimony is transcribed by a court reporter and preserved for years.

Thus, the first piece of advice is that your anxiety should be normalized. There are good reasons for you to think this is not a "day at the beach". However, this is not to say that this anxiety should be of a magnitude that results in your avoidance of testifying. Your expertise can be invaluable. I have observed such extreme anxiety and avoidance

Toolkit for Working with Juvenile Sex Offenders.
DOI: http://dx.doi.org/10.1016/B978-0-12-405948-1.00006-2

in otherwise very competent professionals: a sort of "court-phobia". Court-phobics may not serve their clients well or may not use their expertise to the fullest advantage. The issues discussed in this chapter ought to help you have a reasonable amount of trepidation (think of arousal and performance graphs such as the Yerkes–Dodson curve) but, again, not so much that you want to avoid this activity altogether.

This chapter is meant to provide you with some basic tools in the form of information, advice, and strategies to help you both cope and perform well when you are testifying in court. To do this, several key topics will be covered: (1) defended a thesis/dissertation? Some of the same skills apply; (2) Legal system 101: understanding the basics; (3) tips for when you are on the stand.

THESES/DISSERTATIONS

Have you defended a thesis or dissertation? Some of the same skills needed for a successful oral defense apply to giving courtroom testimony. A comparison of skills needed in both domains is displayed in Table 6.1.

LEGAL SYSTEM 101

It may be useful for you to read a basic overview of the legal system so you understand something about the general legal context. Brogdon, Adams and Bahri (2004) presented a useful practical summary of the legal and court systems. However, here are some of the most important pieces of information:

1. First, gain a basic understanding of the context in which you are asked to behave. You can interact with the court in several ways. For example, you can submit a report to an attorney or to a judge. From a legal perspective, one shortcoming of a report is that a report cannot be cross-examined. Generally, parties have a right to criticize all evidence and, therefore, cross-examine the expert who wrote the report. Often, your report or notes will not be sufficient and you will also be asked to testify. There are many kinds of witnesses but, for our purposes, they fall into two broad categories – material witnesses and expert witnesses. You generally will be testifying as an expert witness. An expert witness is someone who has special skills and knowledge that are relevant to the legal question(s) at hand. A material witness is someone like an eyewitness – they have something to say due to their direct knowledge of the particulars in the case (for example, an

Table 6.1 A Comparison of Skills Needed

Thesis/Dissertation Defense	**Serving as an Expert Witness**
Dress professionally and be well groomed	Dress professionally and be well groomed. Judges and jurors will assess your credibility, in part, based on how professional you appear to be
Your professional background is probably minimal and of little importance	Your professional background should be clearly and accurately written. Background is quite relevant because it is part of determining if you qualify as an expert in a particular domain. If you qualify, your background may well influence the weight the trier(s) of fact place on your testimony
Adequate to compulsive preparation is good. Have more relevant information than you will probably need. Know which research is relevant and why	Adequate to compulsive preparation is good. Have more relevant information than you will probably need. Know which research is relevant and why
Being truthful is very important. Demonstrate what you know relevant to the subject matter. If you claim to have knowledge about something but do not, a committee member who has such knowledge may want to engage you in an intellectual discussion on the topic	Being truthful is very important. Say everything that is necessary but not one thing more. Remember, the more you say, the more material on which you may be cross-examined. If an attorney is very interested in discussing a particular topic, be careful. (S)he is not asking out of intellectual curiosity. Rather, the attorney is pursuing that line of discussion for a strategic reason
Be able to explain your methods, procedures, why you used these (rather than others), conclusions, and limitations of your approach. Purpose is to discover how a particular phenomenon works	Be able to explain your methods, procedures, why you used these, and conclusions. Do not discuss limitations of your approach. Cross-examining attorney will elicit this information. Purpose is to assist trier(s) of fact understand information not otherwise accessible
Committee members question your methods to determine if you have really thought through relevant issues and can provide a cogent rationale why/how your findings fit into the extant knowledge base	Cross-examination occurs in an attempt to demonstrate that you did not do an adequate evaluation and/or to undermine the credibility of your conclusions and/or of you as a professional

eyewitness – "I saw him enter the liquor store") but may not offer opinions or interpretations of what they saw or heard.

2. The United States legal system is an adversarial one. It is assumed that the most persuasive arguments will lead to delivery of "justice". First, you will give direct testimony. The lawyer who retained your services will ask you questions and, subsequently, the other side will cross-examine you. Don't take cross-examination personally – all witnesses experience this sort of probing and criticism. Understand that it is the lawyer's job to do this. The lawyer who retained your services can then "re-direct" and the second lawyer can "re-cross" until both have no more questions. If you are careful and thoughtful (you don't need to be perfect) you will probably do an adequate job.
3. Understand what general kind of legal proceeding you will be testifying in – is this family court (e.g., to determine custody or placement of a minor); civil court (e.g., to determine damages); or criminal court (e.g., to determine guilt or innocence)? Understand what jurisdiction applies – if this is a county criminal court (many criminal cases occur in this context); a federal court (different legal rules apply – e.g., many child pornography charges are tried as federal crimes); or even a military court (again, different rules apply). Even in criminal matters there can be different types of legal issues (e.g., testimony in front of the judge so he or she can initially rule on admissibility and if the judge rules that your testimony or parts of your testimony are admissible you will then be allowed to testify in front of the jury); testifying in the trial itself; or testifying during the sentencing phase. Ask the attorney who has retained you which of these are relevant and ask for a brief explanation of relevant legal issues your testimony must address in this type of court. Get broadly oriented to the context of your testimony.
4. Understand that the basic way of eliciting information is for lawyers (and sometimes the judge) to ask questions. You cannot just take the stand and lecture, although you might think this would be more efficient and comprehensive. There are a lot of rules for what kinds of questions the lawyer can ask (e.g., generally compound questions are not permitted) and what topics the lawyer can cover. Part of the lawyer's strategy is to ask certain types of questions and not others. For example, the lawyer may want to avoid asking questions about the person's prior arrests, and if he or she inadvertently asks this type of question or if you mention something regarding prior arrests, this can open the door, and the opposing attorney can then ask all sorts of

questions on this topic. This is one reason why your answers should be responsive to the question – answer it as succinctly as possible.

5. Not all theories, techniques or results can be presented in court. Theories, tests, and interventions are admissible only when they are based on sound science. For example, one cannot use voodoo or astrology as assessment or treatment techniques because these are not good science. The basic idea is that the judge is a gatekeeper who attempts to keep out "junk science" that would confuse, rather than elucidate, the issues. The legal system uses either the older Frye standard or the newer Daubert standards for admissibility of scientific evidence. You should be familiar with these standards and be able to argue that the theories and techniques you used meet these standards. The Frye standard basically states that techniques (such as Rorschach or polygraph) are admissible only if they are generally accepted as reliable in the relevant scientific community. The Daubert standard is more complex and requires a technique or theory to pass several tests including: having a known error rate; it must be falsifiable; it must have been subjected to peer review; and it must be generally accepted by the relevant scientific community. These are complex issues and experts may disagree on the rigor of the peer review and the extent to which a technique or theory is "generally accepted". For example, I have argued that the Child Abuse Accomodation Syndrome is junk science and does not meet these standards (O'Donohue & Benuto, 2012).
6. Know the relevant psycholegal issues. The courts are generally bound by the exact letter of the law (or their interpretation of it). For example, even if you think a custody determination ought to be influenced, by say, attachment, parental skills, and abuse history; if the law in the relevant jurisdiction states that custody is to be determined by child preferences, attachment, religious training and mental health of the parents, you are bound by the law. Don't walk into the court not knowing how the law impacts your opinions or practice.

TIPS FOR PREPARING FOR YOUR TESTIMONY

1. Get oriented to the specifics of the case. A common question you can ask the lawyer is, "On what issues would you like me to opine (give an opinion)?" Listen carefully and ask clarifying questions to make sure you and the attorney have the same understanding of key words (e.g., "risk," "profile," "probability of re-offending," "psychopathy,"

"suggestibility," "effective therapy," "personality testing," etc.). You then need to give the attorney feedback on whether you can opine on these issues. There are a variety of reasons why you may be unable to opine on a particular issue. You may state that you cannot opine for various reasons including the following: (a) you do not believe that it is within your expertise. You may believe that a different type of expert is needed. For example, you may believe that a pediatrician is better qualified to opine on what you see as a medical/developmental issue. (b) The issue may be within your expertise but you may not have not formed a clear opinion. Perhaps you have not had sufficient contact with the client, or the information you have gained thus far is ambiguous. (c) You may believe that it is inappropriate for you to give an opinion on a particular issue. Let's say the attorney is asking you to give an opinion regarding custody and you have treated a juvenile (but have not conducted a custody evaluation). You might need to say that you cannot render an opinion because your role was as a therapist, not a custody evaluator. You can negotiate what you think are reasonable issues on which you can opine. (d) You may believe that testifying is precluded by confidentiality duties. You may need a release of information before you testify and if you cannot get one, and if your are subpoenaed, you will be in a bind. (e) You may believe that it is not in your client's best interest for you to testify. If the lawyer is representing your client, you may need to explain this to him or her. (f) Logistically, it may be impossible for you to testify – you may be out of town on vacation or attending a conference that day. Sometimes the procedure can be continued to accommodate your schedule.

2. The next step is to see what information you need to form a sound opinion and to work with the attorney to get this information: Do you need certain records or materials (e.g., school records, arrest records, treatment records, etc.)?; Do you need to have clinical contact or more clinical contact with the client to test or interview – gather more clinical information relevant to the issues on which you will opine? Give a timeline for when this can be completed (ask the attorney if there are any set dates already) as well as a budget to be certain the attorney who retained your services is willing to pay for your professional time. Do you need to meet with collaterals or even the attorney to obtain more information? The heuristic I use is I want all relevant information so that if the other side poses a question such as "Doctor, if I represent that this document says x, and given

that you have testified that you have not reviewed this document, could reviewing this document potentially alter the opinion on issue y that you are giving here?" I can say "No". That is, I want to review all materials that are potentially relevant. In addition, ask the attorney if he or she wants a written report. There are advantages associated with a written report – it helps you organize your thoughts; it makes clear what your opinions are and why you have come to these; and it can be a guide for the attorney for his or her direct examination when you are on the stand. Most attorneys regard written reports as having one significant disadvantage. It allows the other side to see your opinions and have a chance to prepare to cross-examine you or call their own expert to rebut your opinion(s). The other major disadvantage is financial: it takes more of your time and thus the cost associated with hiring you will be greater.

3. Keep up with research specific to juvenile sexual offending. Also, keep up with research on "normal" sexual development and "normal" (non-sexual) development throughout the lifespan.
4. All conclusions must be made "within a reasonable degree of psychological certainty". It is unclear exactly what this means, but can be interpreted as meaning that you are not merely guessing about what you are saying – presumably, it is based on good science. So, yes, you should be able to assert that your recommendations were made "within a reasonable degree of psychological certainty".

   Make sure you understand the question to which you are responding and do not respond until you understand the question. (Attorneys sometimes use complex wording or embed some true and some untrue assertions in one question.) Ask the attorney to rephrase the question as many times as necessary until you understand what is being asked.
5. Provide your vita to the attorney who retained your services. This is important because before you can testify you will go through a process called voir dire. This means that there will be a questioning by both the attorney who retained you and the attorney on the other side to ensure you are an expert on the issue(s) about which you are being called to testify. You will be asked about your education, professional licenses, publication history, employment history, teaching history, past testimony history, attendance at workshops or special trainings, awards, grants, memberships in professional organizations, etc. to determine if you are indeed an expert on issues x, y, and z. There are actually two matters that voir dire is intended to address: (a) do you meet the legal

threshold of being an expert; (b) and by how much do you exceed this? – what weight should be given to your opinions due to the degree of your expertise. In general, it should be relatively straightforward that you meet the threshold of being an expert. Roughly, a legal expert is someone who has knowledge and skills beyond the ordinary layperson. You do not need to be the "top" expert in your field – just have specialized knowledge. However, the degree of your expertise is also relevant. An example can help explain this. Suppose each side is calling experts on the same matter. On side A, the expert has one peer-reviewed publication on the issue and has testified once before in court on the issue. However on side B, the proposed expert has 100 publications, and has testified 100 times before on the issue. Both professionals will probably be considered "experts" by the judge, but the testimony of the second might be given more weight. The only additional issue is the scope of your expertise and you and the attorney should talk about this carefully. Are you attempting to qualify as a general expert on child sexual abuse (and generally about all areas, causes, treatment of both offenders and victims, assessment, false allegations, interviewing procedures, etc.) or are you qualifying as an expert on more restricted domains, e.g., as an expert on victim reactions and treatment but not offender treatment. It is important to get this straight because if during voir dire the attorney has you qualified as an expert in say, victim treatment, but then asks you a question regarding offender treatment, you probably will not be allowed to answer this question, because you have not been qualified in this domain.

6. Remember, your role is *to educate* the trier of fact (the judge or the jury). You are not in court to advocate for one side or another. You have expertise that can help the trier of fact make certain key legal decisions. Think of your role as that of an educator. Tell the judge or jury about relevant research findings. You can describe these studies in a bit of detail so the judge and jury can see their strengths as well as their limitations. Feel free to talk about limitations to these studies or results that have been inconsistent with the general trend. Your job is to be informative and even-handed. This will serve you best in the short term as well as the long term. Good lawyers (and most lawyers are good) want fair experts, not what are called "whores". When you are giving a clinical opinion, "This person meets diagnostic criteria for Major Depressive Episode", state the reasons you came to this conclusion. For example, "The person's BDI score was 25 which is regarded as moderately depressed. In my clinical interview I found he met these specific diagnostic criteria x, y, z… I had seen that his primary care doctor also gave him this diagnosis and put him on an antidepressant. I also interviewed his spouse who confirmed the depressive symptoms, etc.". Just because you are an expert does not mean you can just throw out opinions – give the rationale underlying your opinions and demonstrate that you have been fair, comprehensive, and reasonable.

7. During the initial contact, ask the attorney what his or her "theory of the case" is. This will help you understand the context for your testimony. You might also give the attorney feedback on how your opinions help and/or do not help him or her with this theory. This may be useful for the attorney and (s)he may revise the theory of the case. On the other hand, it may become clear that the attorney may not want to call you.
8. Get all financial agreements ironed out before beginning any work on a case. Do you require a retainer? What is your hourly rate for such work – does this differ by activity – reviewing documents, report writing, clinical contact, testifying? Are there any limits to the sum that can be paid to you and can you complete your work well within any such limits? As an aside, opposing counsel will often ask you about these financial arrangements during your testimony. Often, it is suggested that your opinion is not due to the facts and evidence you reviewed, but simply due to the fact that you are being paid. Do not worry too much about this. All professionals involved in the court are being paid. You are not an exception.
9. Know that scheduling, like war, is hell. Remember that dates and times the lawyer is giving you are his or her best estimates and these rarely turn out to be accurate. Cases often get continued (legalese for rescheduled). Prior evidence and testimony takes longer or shorter than the estimate and it can be your turn to testify hours or days before or later than the estimate you were given. Sometimes the issues resolve and you will not need to testify at all. Your court appearance will be cancelled. Sometimes these issues resolve at the last minute. I have been involved in cases in which the morning before I was to board a flight, the attorney called and said that I no longer needed to come. In another case, I traveled for a day, arrived the next day at the courtroom, found that the parties were in conference and, ultimately, was informed that they had resolved the issue. Prepare for delays and unexpected schedule changes.

10. When you are actually testifying, first make sure you understand the question. It is perfectly legitimate for you to say you do not understand the question or want a key term in the question clarified. Sometimes it is the lawyer's strategy to get you to answer a vague question or use a vague term and then later use it against you. Ponder each question for a bit to make sure you understand it. This pause is also useful in that it can give the other side a chance to raise an objection to the question. Objections vary from relevancy, "ask and answered", compound, "hearsay", outside the scope of the expert's qualification, vague, etc.
11. Some lawyers and judges want you to try to give only "yes" and "no" answers. Material witnesses are generally confined to "yes" and "no" answers. Experts generally have more latitude to explain their answers. For example, an attorney may ask you the question, "Is your client cured of the mental health issues you treated him for? and want a "yes" or "no" answer. If you feel you can answer it this way, do so. However, if you feel the need to explain your answer then do so (or attempt to do so – it ultimately depends on the judge's decision). You may say, "I can't give a simple yes or no answer because it is more complex. We don't really have a good definition of "cure" in our field since there is often relapse. Furthermore, my client made differential progress toward resolving the three problems I treated him for...". Usually, the judge will let you give this sort of answer because he or she believes it best conveys the necessary information. The lawyer may not like this, as he or she thought that if the answer was to be confined to "yes" or "no," you would have to answer in the negative and it is this answer the attorney wanted before the judge or jury.
12. Give clear, substantive answers. Don't be wishy-washy or give too many "on the one hand and on the other hand answers". (Remember Harry Truman's reactions to economists giving these kind of answers – he only wanted to listen to one-handed economists). These answers are generally not very educational. If, for example, the vast majority of over 100 studies show how suggestible children are under certain conditions, say this; do not say, "well some studies show the suggestibility effect, some studies do not". While literally true, this is misleading, as the vast majority show the suggestibility effect.
13. Be organized. Know where information is in your report. Give information in a coherent manner (e.g., give your educational background chronologically).

14. A small matter – but you may ask for a break at any time. If you have been on the stand for a couple hours you may feel fatigued and that your answers are not as sharp as they initially were. Ask the judge for a break. In general, judges accommodate such requests. Don't let your answers wander. An objection is "non-responsive". For example, if you are asked, "How old are you", a responsive answer is "40". A non-responsive answer is, "Well my mother and father met in Pittsburgh and dated for over two years before becoming married and then it was another two years before my mother became pregnant with me…" Make sure each sentence you say is relevant to the question.
15. Don't be afraid to say you don't know when you don't know (although some lawyers prefer you to say "I don't recall"). Also, clearly label any estimate as an estimate. For example, if an attorney asks when you took a workshop on relapse prevention and you cannot recall the exact date (a common occurrence), your answer can simply be "I don't recall" – because you don't. Or you can answer, "I don't recall the exact date, but I estimate it was in late 2011". If you give a wrong answer, e.g., if you don't label it as an estimate and say " January, 2012" and then the opposing attorney sees on your vita that you said it was September 2011, he or she can point out this discrepancy in their next question: "But Doctor, on your vita you say it was September 2011, but here today under oath you say it was January, 2012, which was it?" The next set of questions can have the same tone, "So Doctor, which is inaccurate, your vita or your testimony?" So Doctor, you obviously make mistakes, isn't that correct…?"
16. Do not get emotional. Especially, do not get defensive. You may feel that the lawyer is attacking you (and sometimes they are), but remember that it is his or her job to do so. Testimony and legal work in general is not a love fest. You may also feel that the lawyer is being disrespectful. Lawyers are not supposed to roll their eyes at your answers, etc. If the other lawyer is good, he or she will object and point this out to the judge and the judge will admonish the attorney not to do this again. In addition, sometimes, lawyers will have certain strategies of which you should be aware. For example, an attorney may mischaracterize your prior testimony. Do not agree to an attorney's summary if it is incorrect. If an attorney says, "but Doctor, you have already testified that the client is cured, and thus why are you recommending him for continued treatment". State (if true), "I never testified that he is cured. That mischaracterizes my prior testimony. I did testify that he has improved significantly but this is different than cured…".

Probably the worst gambit I have experienced was during voir dire. The opposing side asked me a rather long series of questions about books that I read. They asked questions like, "Doctor, have your read Brown and Smith's, *Handbook of the Treatment of Sexual Abusers*?; Doctor, have you read Jones and Haley's, *Evidence Based Treatment of the Juvenile Offender*?" He asked about a dozen or so books, none of which I had read (or had heard of). Of course, to all of these questions, I said, "No, I haven't read that book." To the jury, it must have sounded like I had not read a lot of key books in the field. Because I had not heard of these books, I subsequently looked them up and found that none of these books exists! Thus, if I had answered, "Yes, I had read the book", the lawyers next question would have been something along the lines of, "Really, what if I tell you this book doesn't exist?" My credibility would have been significantly diminished. Other miscellaneous issues:

1. The opposing attorney may want to meet with you before you testify. Generally, attorneys do not like to ask questions in the courtroom unless they know how you are going to answer. Check with the attorney who is retaining you before having any such meetings. Clarify who will pay for this time well in advance of the meeting.
2. All e-mails, correspondence, etc. you have with the attorney may be subpoenaed. Be careful what you write. Some lawyers prefer telephone conversations for this reason.
3. Wear professional attire (e.g., suit and tie for men, skirt and blouse for women). Most courtrooms are formal and this shows respect for the Court.
4. As always, feel free to consult with your colleagues, especially colleagues who have a lot of forensic experience. In an unusual case, you might also need to consult your attorney on any especially complicated legal issue.
5. Bring all records that are subpoenaed. There is usually a list and respond in writing if some of these are unavailable. Conversely, do not bring any records that have not been subpoenaed. In many courts, opposing counsel has the right to review such documents and question you on any documents you have brought to court.
6. Meet all deadlines. The lawyer needs time to prepare or time to send your report to the judge or opposing side (who, in turn, needs to read it). If you do not meet a deadline, your report may not be admitted into evidence and you may be putting other people in binds.

7. Prepare to be ignored. The lawyer who is calling you may have dozens or even hundreds of other cases (public defenders often have 200–300 cases). They may call you at the last minute (never a good situation) or may get materials to you and then turn their attention to other cases only to refocus on you a few weeks or days before the legal proceeding. But, if you need to talk to the lawyer retaining you, do not hesitate to contact him or her.
8. Decide if you need any charts, visual aids or other materials. For example, some defense lawyers make charts of all the inconsistencies found in children's allegations of their abuse. It is best to avoid jargon, but if you decide to use it, explain clearly what each and every technical term means. Have empathy for the judge or jury – they are not mental health professionals. So, explain terms like DSM-V, pedophilia, relapse prevention, actuarial assessment, validity, reliability, empathy, etc. Many of these words may have a colloquial meaning, but remember, we are using them in a technical context. These meanings, if you are to be understood properly, need to be explained.

CONCLUSIONS

Being an expert and testifying in court is an important and complex task. As such, one needs to ask questions and gain information regarding several issues that were outlined above. One needs time to prepare, and much of this preparation needs to be done with the attorney retaining you. Remember that your job is to educate the trier of fact. Be able to present information in a clear and even-handed manner. Do not be too harsh on yourself – the other side will probe for weaknesses and will usually find some (if that attorney is worth his or her salt). As with anything, preparation and practice will result in improvement in one's skill in providing courtroom testimony. Consider testifying to be a challenge and not as something overwhelming and terrifying to be avoided.

REFERENCES

Brogdon, M. G., Adams, J. H., & Bahri, R. (2004). Psychology and the law. In W. O'Donohue & E. Levensky (Eds.), *Handbook of forensic psychology: Resource for mental health and legal professionals* (pp. 3–26). San Diego, CA: Elsevier.

O'Donohue, W., & Benuto, L. (2012). Problems with the child abuse accommodation syndrome. *Scientific Review of Mental Health Practice, 16*, 12–23.

ADDITIONAL RESOURCES

For a handy reference pertaining to a wide range of issues regarding child and adolescent sexuality:

Bromberg, D. S., & O'Donohue, W. T. (2013). *Handbook of child and adolescent sexuality: Developmental and forensic psychology*. New York: Elsevier.

For additional tools on testifying:

Brodsky, S. L. (2004). *Coping with cross-examination and other pathways to effective testimony*. Washington, DC: APA.

Brodsky, S. L. (1999). *The expert expert witness: More maxims and guidelines for testifying in court*. Washington, DC: APA.

Stern, P. (1997). *Preparing and presenting expert testimony in child abuse litigation: A guide for expert witnesses and attorneys*. Thousand Oaks, CA: Sage.

CHAPTER 7

Assessing and Modifying Denial in Juvenile Sexual Offenders

William T. O'Donohue
Department of Psychology, University of Nevada, Reno, NV, USA

WHAT IS DENIAL?

Some juvenile sex offenders admit that they committed their offenses. Some categorically deny that they did anything wrong at all, while others partially admit to their crimes. This complex state of affairs raises two questions: (1) what exactly does admitting or denying (regarding some sexual offense) mean?; and (2) does this denial/admission dimension matter (e.g., does denying one's involvement in a sex offense have implications for therapy or risk for future offenses)? This chapter will address these issues and provide a model for overcoming denial in juvenile sexual offenders.

IS DENIAL IMPORTANT?

Nunes and Jung (2013) found that denial correlated with the magnitude of cognitive distortions in a sample of adult sex offenders and argued that denial should not be looked at as simply another cognitive distortion, but as a separate construct. Jung and Nunes (2012) found that those offenders with higher levels of denial also had more negative views of treatment. Levenson & McGowan (2004) examined levels of denial and engagement in a sample of 61 adult offenders in group therapy and found that levels of denial were related to poorer treatment engagement and poorer treatment outcomes. However, Yates (2009), in a literature review, argued that there is not convincing evidence that denial is a risk factor for re-offending or that targeting denial leads to improved treatment outcomes. It is important to note, though, that these conclusions are mitigated by the common practice that many clients who stay in "complete" denial do not enter into therapy. Part of the reason why modifying denial is important is that many treatment programs will not allow individuals to

Toolkit for Working with Juvenile Sex Offenders.
DOI: http://dx.doi.org/10.1016/B978-0-12-405948-1.00007-4

enter therapy when they are in complete denial and this can result both in problems for the individual (failing to enter in treatment may result in probation or parole to be revoked) and negative consequences for others if they offend again.

In addition, contemporary construals of therapy caution against assuming that all clients are ready to change. Probably the foremost proponent of this has been Miller and Rollnick (2002) who has developed an intervention called Motivational Interviewing to help clients move along a proposed continuum related to their readiness to change. Juvenile sex offenders who are in complete denial of their offenses would in all likelihood share important similarities to an individual in the earliest stage of change – precontemplative. There are currently no studies of motivational interviewing with juvenile sex offenders in denial, but this approach should be studied in the future. We will turn first to an attempt to address the first issue: an attempt to define and measure denial.

ASSESSMENT OF DENIAL

Definitions

Denial as part of its meaning has something to do with not agreeing with some statement or statements that are themselves true, or at least presumed to be true. If an accurate state of affairs is that, in the past, Bob did act x, but Bob disagrees with this statement, it can be said that Bob is in denial with regard to this act. However, one of the major issues in defining denial is whether this is a categorical or linear variable. That is, is this a simple dichotomy "in denial vs not in denial" or does this category have varying degrees? That is, can denial be quantified along some quantitative scale? Another controversy concerns whether the construct of denial is one-dimensional or whether it has various components, such as:

1. complete denial of the act(s)/crime(s)
2. denial of the extent of the acts/crimes (e.g., it happened 2× vs 20×)
3. acknowledgment of the act(s), but denial of responsibility for the act(s)
4. denial of intent (e.g., the touch was "accidental")
5. denial of negative impact of the act(s)/crime(s) on the victim
6. denial of planning/grooming to commit the act(s)
7. denial of the possibility of relapse
8. denial of any problems related to the offense (from alcoholism to problematic cognitions)
9. denial of the need for treatment.

Kennedy and Grubin (1992) found in interviews with 102 men convicted of sex offenses that there were four main patterns of denial. In their first group consisting of 18 individuals, subjects admitted their offenses but denied causing any harm to their victims. Kennedy and Grubin called these individuals "rationalizers" and found that these included a large proportion of offenders against children and were the individuals with the highest rates of recidivism. Their second group consisting of 20 "externalizers" was made up mostly of offenders against young females. These offenders tended to blame the victim for the offense, as well as a third party, such as a spouse. Their third group consisted of 26 "internalizers", and included many heterosexual incest offenders and was characterized by a combination of ready admission of the offense as well as an acknowledgment of harm to the victim. The fourth group consisted of 34 "absolute deniers" most of whom were convicted of offenses against adult females. This final group included more than 75% of subjects who were from ethnic minorities. These partitions are interesting but have not been replicated and their relevance to juvenile offenders is thus unclear at this point in time.

It is important to note that the definition of denial usually has a pragmatic component in that it often assumes some prior legal decision to be definitive. The truth of the statements is assumed to be settled. That is, if the offender has been found guilty or some victim has made convincing statements, then these are considered to be decisive even in the context of the adolescent's continued protestations (e.g., that his lawyer was not good; the jury made the wrong decision; that he was set up by a vengeful person; or that the alleged victim is lying). The pragmatic assumption is that the offender has had his "day in court" and any continued protestation of the result is, at this point, moot. A major problem with this tact is that the legal system is fallible thus leading to the possibility that some of these protestations are indeed accurate. However, there are considerable advantages to this tact: (1) mental health professionals are not put in the position of determining the "facts" of the matter; and (2) admitting to committing a sexual offense can be a very difficult thing to do and this difficulty is seen to be part of the pathway to the client's denial (Marshall, 1994). Rape and child sexual abuse are some of the most stigmatized acts and admitting to committing such acts, even after being convicted of the crime, can have significant repercussions for self-concept and social acceptance. Thus, offenders can persevere in their denial because admitting to their past offenses involves serious negative psychological and social consequences for them. (3) Finally, a client usually has a few supporters, i.e., individuals who believe that the perpetrator's denial is accurate. Coming out of denial will result not only in a loss of this often important support, but these individuals may feel anger and disappointment after having been lied to for a prolonged period of time.

As we will see below, it is important to deal with these issues in any intervention targeted at changing denial. The adolescent needs to understand that it is a waste of his time to attempt to press his case for his innocence in this forum. Retrying the case or convincing the therapist(s) of the unfairness of their legal proceedings is not an acceptable topic for therapy. A client can be told that if he wants to continue to advocate for his innocence, his parent or guardian should retain the services of an attorney for an appeal. However, in therapy, it is necessary to assume that the finding of "fact" is accurate.

In addition, the therapist should be supportive of the adolescent and explicitly recognize that what he is being asked to do is difficult. It is advisable to mention possible loss of friends and the support of those who stuck by him while he was in denial. Clients should be supported as they cope with a new self-concept: part of their history is that they have hurt another person by committing a sexual offense or offenses against him or her. These are all complex issues in therapy but, as we shall see when we discuss a recommended protocol for intervention with regard to denial, there are a number of complex issues such as these that must be successfully handled to support someone coming out of denial.

SPECIFIC ASSESSMENT PROCEDURES

A clinical interview can be useful for assessing the magnitude and other key properties of denial. In the clinical interview, the therapist can ask the client whether he agrees or disagrees with the statements describing his crimes. Remember that many times there are plea bargains or legal decisions such that the charges that have brought them to therapy may not fully reflect the past acts. It is most useful to examine victim statements and see to what extent the client admits or denies these. It can also be useful to ask questions about each of the dimensions listed above (e.g., did this happen?; how many times did it happen?; did someone get hurt as a result of this?; do you admit responsibility for this?).

There are also some paper and pencil measures that have been constructed to measure denial. One of these is the Facets of Sex Offending

Denial Scale (FOSOD; Schneider & Wright, 2001) which is a 65-item self-report instrument that can be useful for measuring the key dimensions of denial described above. It should be noted that this scale does not have many data regarding its psychometric adequacy and has been designed for adults rather than adolescent perpetrators, so its use with juveniles should be undertaken with caution. Another instrument, the Comprehensive Inventory of denial – Sex Offender (Jung, 2005), suffers from similar problems. Thus, at this point in time, the clinical interview seems to be the best procedure to assess denial.

TREATMENT OF DENIAL

Importance

One of the most important reasons why denial needs to be an initial target is that there is some consensus that if a client is in complete denial, they cannot or should not be accepted into sex offender treatment. The underlying rationale is that sex offender treatment requires an admission of the offense or offenses. For example, in relapse prevention therapy (Marshall, Laws & Barbaree, 1990), an admission is needed to complete key components of therapy (e.g., generating offense and re-offense chains and understanding risk factors, as well as an examination of irrational beliefs that led to the offense). If the adolescent is not admitting that any offense occurred, one cannot complete these key components of therapy. In addition, when therapy is court ordered, the implicit or explicit directive is to do all one can to lower the likelihood of future offenses. In general, the view is that in order to do that one has to deliver therapy that requires an admission of the past offenses, perhaps again to implement key components of relapse prevention therapies. It is generally viewed that listening to the client deny all offending and listening to his complaints regarding the unfairness of the judicial system, etc., is not what the court is envisaging.

Intervention with Deniers and Outcome Research

There are too few studies that examined the outcomes of interventions with deniers and still fewer have examined the effectiveness of denial interventions with juveniles. In addition, those that have examined outcomes have not used gold standard designs, such as randomly controlled trials with follow-up assessments over a period of years. For example, O'Donohue & Letourneau (1993), in one of the first outcome studies, used a pre-post design with no control groups. Their intervention model was indirectly replicated by Ulrich (1997) in a group that did not face the adverse consequences (having probation revoked) in the original O'Donohue & Letourneau (1993) sample. In both studies, the majority of subjects came out of denial despite the mean denial length being over 2 years. In addition, in the O'Donohue & Letourneau study, subsequent therapists indicated that the subjects remained out of denial and rated them as being above average in treatment engagement. Although these were adult offenders whose denial was treated mainly in groups (the Ulrich study also had some subjects treated individually), it remains one of the best researched interventions for denial with some of the best outcome data and thus, this model will be described in more detail below. However, again, this model must be used with some caution as it has not been studied in a sample of juvenile offenders and its efficacy or effectiveness has not been studied in randomly controlled trials. Thus, because of the absence of research with juveniles, the overall rationale is to extrapolate the preliminary positive findings related to overcoming denial in juveniles.

Treatment components

In Ulrich (1997) and O'Donohue & Letourneau (1993), the major treatment components were: victim empathy; cognitive restructuring; sex education; assertiveness and social skills; education about sex offender therapy. Because in the O'Donohue and Letourneau (1994) study if clients were not accepted into sex offender treatment and because therapists refused to accept them until they came out of denial, a discussion of the possible consequences of continued denial, which included renewed incarceration, was also included. The subjects were all run in groups in the original study, while Ulrich ran both group and individual treatment. Data are unclear regarding any differential effectiveness and generally this has not been studied sufficiently. However, groups have the following advantages: (1) they are less costly per client; and (2) there can be modeling created by clients coming out of denial during the group which can serve as an impetus for other clients to come out of denial. However, it must be said the reverse can also be true: clients staying in denial can model this for other clients. However, it was our observation that clients who came out of denial early on in the group would also confront others still in denial by saying things like they could empathize with their fears about coming out of denial. They also would discuss how many of their fears of coming out of denial did not come true, e.g., their support network disintegrating. However, it may be the case that practicalities will determine whether an individual therapist decides to run deniers in a group or conduct individual therapy with them. O'Donohue and Letourneau used a group format partly because the state Department of Probation and Parole referred a sizeable number of clients in a short period of time. These clients served a number of years in prison for their crimes but maintained their denial throughout their incarceration. Part of their agenda was to avoid the costs of reincarceration by successfully placing them on parole. However, a condition of the parole was that they had to be successfully enrolled in outpatient sex offender therapy.

Empathy

Empathy may be defined as an accurate understanding of the perspective or the experience of someone else. To be empathic would mean, to some extent, seeing another's perspective (both intellectual and emotional) and having some understanding of the legitimacy of that perspective. It is important to note that, in most cases, an intellectual understanding is insufficient – to be empathic one must understand the emotional experience of that individual. It has been established that it is often the case that sex offenders have poor empathy, although this can either be a trait-like deficit, i.e., in most situations and with most people, sex offenders can only see and understand their own perspective. However, of particular concern is the notion that failing to see the victim's perspective increases the likelihood of abuse. In this group we had several subgoals regarding empathy:

1. Provide education on the meaning of empathy and the importance of empathy for positive relationships. This was accomplished by discussing the definition of empathy as well as with exercises. Examples of these include attempting to describe accurately other group members' perspectives and receiving feedback on this to having the clients describe the experience of individuals in other situations – e.g., hearing that they had been fired, going to a surprise birthday party, etc.
2. The therapist also modeled empathy expressing his or her understanding of the difficulty of coming out of denial and empathy regarding the tough situation in which group members found themselves.
3. We ran exercises in which group members had to imagine that they were the victims of a sexual offense. The objective was to learn that how each member felt would in all likelihood be similar to how their victims felt.

4. Finally, empathy exercises were oriented toward their victims. They were required to write accounts (and the group giving feedback on these – both positive and negative) regarding both their victims' experience while they were being abused and also now while they were being called a liar for their allegations.

Cognitive restructuring

Cognitive restructuring is an essential component of cognitive therapy. The underlying rationale is that clients hold irrational beliefs which are causing them harm. These beliefs need to be identified, a process of disputation needs to take place and then these irrational beliefs need to be replaced with more accurate and functional beliefs. Because this group was oriented toward decreasing denial, the typical irrational beliefs associated with sex offending were not targeted (e.g., when someone says "no" they really mean "yes"). Rather irrational beliefs associated with denial were targeted. For example, after presenting the general rationale and giving examples of how these irrational beliefs can hurt people, the following irrational beliefs were examined:

1. Continuing to deny my offenses will provide me with the best quality of life in my future
2. If I continue to deny then eventually everyone will believe I did not do it
3. Continuing to deny my offenses does not continue to hurt my victims
4. Sex offender therapy is worthless and it does not work
5. Sex offender therapy is odd and uncomfortable
6. Sex offender therapy is interminable.

We sought to dispute these beliefs and replace these beliefs with more functional and accurate alternatives such as:

1. Admitting my offenses and successfully being treated will provide me with the best quality of life in my future
2. No further people will be persuaded of my innocence and many individuals currently just see me as a liar
3. Continuing to deny my offense continues to harm my victims
4. Sex offender therapy can work
5. Sex offender therapy is rational and reasonable
6. Sex offender therapy is intensive for a year or two and then much less intensive.

Of course, we were always vigilant for unique irrational beliefs expressed by any clients in the group. We found that many clients were committed to a lot of fairly misogynistic beliefs – all women lie or all women are not to be trusted. We would identify and dispute these as they arose. Eventually, our goal was to enable each group member to identify irrational beliefs in themselves and others and to begin a process of disputation.

Sex Education

The goal of this segment was not to teach the basic of the birds and the bees as the clients were older males who presumably knew this. However, with juveniles, it might be useful to cover some of these basics. The goal in the group was to teach healthy sexuality and healthy attitudes towards sex. Topics covered were consent, intimacy, the difficulty and complexity of sex, the relationship between caring and good sex, values and sexuality and focusing on the needs and pleasures of others. In a 1.5-hour session, none of these topics could be explored in any depth. However, the overall message was that sex can be complex and confusing for all of us, but it is important to focus not only on your desires but also to use the "golden rule" and to be considerate of others. An important point emphasized was that the other person has to consent to this activity (and, of course, be of age to be able to consent). Another point stressed is that the best sex – and quality does differ – is sex that takes place in a context of mutual respect and with an equal. We often used somewhat crude analogies – both an individual driving a stolen Yugo and one driving one's own Mustang are driving cars – but one, because of their prioritizing certain features of driving, is having a lot better time and even enjoys the additional bonus of not getting into trouble in the future. Here, we stressed that coming out of denial can be the first step on the road to re-learn sexuality and eventually to have better sex than the problematic sex in which they had been engaging.

Assertiveness and social skills

Assertiveness is generally defined as standing up for your rights while not violating the rights of others. It is often distinguished from aggression in which one gets what one wants while violating the rights of others. We discussed how sexual offending meets the definition of aggression while good sex meets the definition of assertion. We thought what was particularly important to stress was the rights of others. We thought that there could be some general deficits in this area. Here we stressed that others have the right not to be called a liar when they are accurately describing how they have been victimized in the past. We described how society even has the right to make sure anyone who has committed an act such as this undergo rehabilitation, such as sex offender therapy, to decrease the probability of having future victims. We indicated that they had rights too, such as being respected as a person even though they had done some terrible crimes in the past. We used the analogy of "loving the sinner while hating the sin". We finally discussed the rights each would have in therapy (e.g., confidentiality, the right for the therapist to be their advocate, the right to the least intrusive therapy).

In the social skills section, we briefly discussed that relapse prevention therapy would help them with their interpersonal problems and emotional struggles. We discussed how dealing with people is often challenging and complex but that each of us through having a good coach, getting feedback and practicing can get better at this and sex offender therapy would help them with this if they came out of denial. We discussed how social skills deficits could be situational – e.g., they could be good at dealing with men but not women and it is rare for someone to be good at dealing with all social situations.

Education about Sex Offender Therapy

In this component, we wanted both to debunk any irrational beliefs about sex offender therapy (e.g., one has to talk about one's mother all the time) as well as allow group members to see how it can be successful. We also wanted them to see that their admitting to their offenses was not just an irrational power struggle but necessary for them actually to engage in therapy. We did an overview of the major components of relapse prevention therapy. We discussed how it would be impossible to uncover offense chains or cognitive distortions, or empathy deficits if they simply say the offense never happened. Again, the goal was for them to see therapy as reasonable, in their self-interest and the requirement to come out of denial as necessary to engage in the components of therapy and not just some sort of power struggle.

We also brought in a sex offender who came out of denial and who had been successfully engaged in relapse prevention therapy for the past 2 years. This seems particularly powerful as it was a use of a coping model. This person who was similar to them demographically in most respects often spoke in the vein of "I was in your shoes once so I get it but I am so glad I came out of denial and got into therapy because my life is so much better now". He also answered a lot of their questions which seemed to revolve around both how did people react to his coming out of denial (he said he lost only one or two "friends" but his real friends stuck by him) and what his experience of therapy was like. He also emphasized how his coming out of denial and apologizing to his victim for both the abuse and for indirectly calling her a liar when he was in denial felt really good to him and became one of his proudest moments in his life. He also emphasized that he learned a lot in therapy, that it helped him in numerous ways and that he did not feel extraordinarily uncomfortable.

Outcome expectances

We used this section (not done in Ulrich, 1997) as a final section to wrap things up and to tie all these components together. The theme was you now have a decision to make: continue in denial or come out of denial. This is an important choice point in your life. We wanted to have group members face this choice point with no illusions. We framed it in the following way. You have the choice of two paths:

1. Path 1: continue to deny. This also results in the following consequences: (a) you will return to prison; (b) you will continue to call your victim a liar; (c) you will continue to fail to improve your life by getting into therapy and changing: or
2. Path 2: you come out of denial. This results in the following consequences for you: (a) you stay out of prison; (b) you stop victimizing your victim; and (c) you can start on the road to a new improved life by going into therapy.

We discussed how choosing Path 2 could be scary as it was a new behavior and that it would take courage but it clearly was in their own interest and the interest of others for them to choose this. But, again, they were in control and the choice was theirs.

We then held a half-hour meeting in which group members were asked what elements of their past crimes they would now admit to. We kept a record of this and sent this to their parole officer. Again, the majority of clients came out of denial and successfully participated in relapse prevention therapy.

Additional considerations

There were other elements that might have contributed to a positive group outcome:

1. The group was led by both a male and female co-therapist. We believed this provided a perspective from both genders. The style of the therapists was direct without being confrontational.

2. The therapists never waivered from the message that the choice was theirs but the negative consequences of staying in denial were inevitable. There was no "negotiation" regarding this matter. The groups were run in a positive way – we strove to keep them interesting and constructive. The therapists were supportive, empathic, and very goal directed – we were explicit that we thought the best way we could help them was to help them through the process of getting out of denial.
3. Some members came out of denial at different points in the group – we overtly reinforced those for this.
4. We stayed focused on the goals of each session and did not let the group wander onto other topics.

CONCLUSIONS

Certainly, more research is needed with juvenile offenders, but we believe that many of the same principles used with these adults can be used to help juveniles come out of denial. Randomly controlled trials with denying juveniles needs to be a priority. However, juvenile offenders in denial should not be viewed as untreatable but rather as candidates for an intervention aimed at modifying that denial. Empathy should be expressed about the difficulty of admitting to these sort of highly stigmatized behaviors. Then a model of what might maintain denial and what factors might be modifiable to increase the likelihood of finding a pathway to come of our denial need to be hypothesized and implemented. Unfortunately, no intervention is a panacea; some will not come out of denial and must be then given the appropriate consequences. However, again, we must not regard that all our clients come to us in a position where they are ready to admit and change and must try to meet our clients where they are and help them to become ready to change.

REFERENCES

Jung, S. (2005). Comprehensive inventory of denial. *Dissertation Abstracts International, 65*, 6650.

Jung, S., & Nunes, K. L. (2012). Denial and its relationships with treatment perceptions in sex offenders. *Journal of Forensic Psychiatry and Psychology, 23*, 485–496.

Kennedy, H. G., & Grubin, D. (1992). Patterns of denial in sex offenders. *Psychological Medicine, 22*, 192–196.

Levenson, J., & McGowan, M. J. (2004). Engagement, denial and treatment progress among sex offenders in group therapy. *Sexual Abuse: A Journal of Research and Treatment, 16*, 49–63.

Marshall, W. L., Laws, D. R., & Barbaree, H. (1990). *Handbook of sexual assault*. New York: Springer.

Marshall, W. (1994). Treatment effects on denial and minimization incarcerated sex offenders. *Behavior Research and Therapy*, *32*, 559–564.

Miller, W. R., & Rollnick, S. (2002). *Motivational interviewing: Preparing people to change*. New York: Guilford Press.

Nunes, K. L., & Jung, S. (2013). Are cognitive distortions associated with denial and minimization among sex offenders? *Sexual Abuse: A Journal of Research and Treatment*, *25*, 166–188.

O'Donohue, W., & Letourneau, E. (1993). A brief group treatment for the modification of denial in sex offenders: Outcome and follow up. *Child Abuse and Neglect*, *17*, 299–304.

Schneider, S. L, & Wright, R. C. (2001). The FOSOD: A measurement for reconceptualizing the role of denial in child molesters. *Journal of Interpersonal Violence*, *16*, 545–564.

Ulrich, J. (1997). A case study comparison of brief group treatment and brief individual treatment in the modification of denial among child sexual abusers. *Dissertation Abstract International*, *57*, 7239.

Yates, P. (2009). Is sex offender denial related to sex offense risk and recidivism? A review and treatment implications. *Psychology, Crime & Law*, *15*, 183–199.

CHAPTER 8

Relapse Prevention as a Treatment Modality for Juvenile Sex Offenders

Charlene Steen* **and Daniel S. Bromberg****
*Private Practice (Retired), Napa, CA, USA
**Special Psychological Services, LLC, Bloomfield, NJ, USA

INTRODUCTION

Relapse prevention (RP) is a self-management treatment approach in which individuals who are trying to change their behaviors are taught how to anticipate and cope with the problem of relapse. Relapse refers to a setback in a person's attempt to change or modify any particular behavior or class of behaviors (e.g., sexual offending). RP combines behavioral skills training, cognitive interventions, and lifestyle change strategies. Because it includes both behavioral and cognitive components, it is similar to other cognitive-behavioral treatment strategies (Marlatt & Gordon, 1985, p. 3). RP treatment can be done individually and/or with groups and is the standard of care for juvenile sex offenders in the United States (Letourneau & Miner, 2005).

There are certain core assumptions and principles underlying cognitive-behavioral therapies. An exhaustive list of these assumptions and principles is beyond the scope of our discussion. However, understanding some of these assumptions and principles is important to understanding RP as a treatment approach. For our purposes, the most important of these are as follows: (1) treatment is based on an ever-evolving formulation of the client and his problems in cognitive terms; (2) therapy is based upon a sound therapeutic alliance; (3) therapy is goal oriented and problem focused; (4) although the present, rather than the past is emphasized, attention shifts to the past when work directed toward current problems produces no changes or when the therapist believes that it is important to understand how and when certain dysfunctional ideas came to be and how these ideas currently affect the client; (5) therapy is educative, aims to teach the client to be his own therapist, and emphasizes relapse prevention; (6) therapy

Toolkit for Working with Juvenile Sex Offenders.
DOI: http://dx.doi.org/10.1016/B978-0-12-405948-1.00008-6

sessions are structured; (7) therapy is intended to teach the client to identify, evaluate, and respond to his own dysfunctional thoughts and beliefs; and (8) in therapy, a variety of strategies are used to change thoughts, feelings, and behaviors (Beck, 1995). Later in this chapter, we will provide a sample case so that readers will see an application of these principles.

In the following section, we describe some of the modules that should be included in an RP model of juvenile sex offender specific therapy. These modules can be covered in group or individual format, or in a group format with supplemental individual sessions to address specific problem areas. Essentially, the material presented is a quite condensed version of *The Relapse Prevention Workbook for Youth in Treatment* (Steen, 1993).

BASIC RELAPSE PREVENTION

Because one of the main reasons the youth has been referred for treatment is to prevent re-offense, it makes sense to begin with basic relapse prevention strategies. An easy way to understand the steps toward re-offense (or any negative behavior) is to diagram the steps in the form of a huge mud hole, with each step toward re-offense deeper into the hole until the bottom – re-offense – is reached. At each step along the way, however, there is the possibility of climbing out of the hole – not re-offending. The further one is in the hole, the more difficult it is to climb out. This "mud hole" analogy is displayed visually in Figure 8.1.

There is a predictable progression of thoughts, feelings, and behaviors that lead to sexual (re)offending behavior. Steen (1993, p. 7) provided a visual display of this chain of events. The first step begins with a *seemingly unimportant decision (SUD)*. This is a decision that does not *appear* to be of importance on the surface but, if one does not recognize the decision for what it is (i.e., *seemingly* unimportant, in contrast to *actually* important), one takes the first step toward falling into the hole. An example is a youth who has molested a child in the past and agrees to babysit for a neighbor who needs to take an injured child to the hospital. By babysitting in this situation, the youth continues down the (re)offense chain to the second step – a *dangerous situation*. This is a situation in which (re)offense is possible, even if he[1] has

[1] In one major study employing nationwide data, males committed 93% of all sexual offenses committed by juveniles (Finkelhor, Ormrod, & Chaffin, 2009). Because a high percentage of known juvenile sexual offenses are committed by males, and for ease of communication, we will use masculine pronouns when referring to juvenile sex offenders. However, readers should recognize that strategies presented in this chapter are equally as useful with juvenile sex offenders who are female.

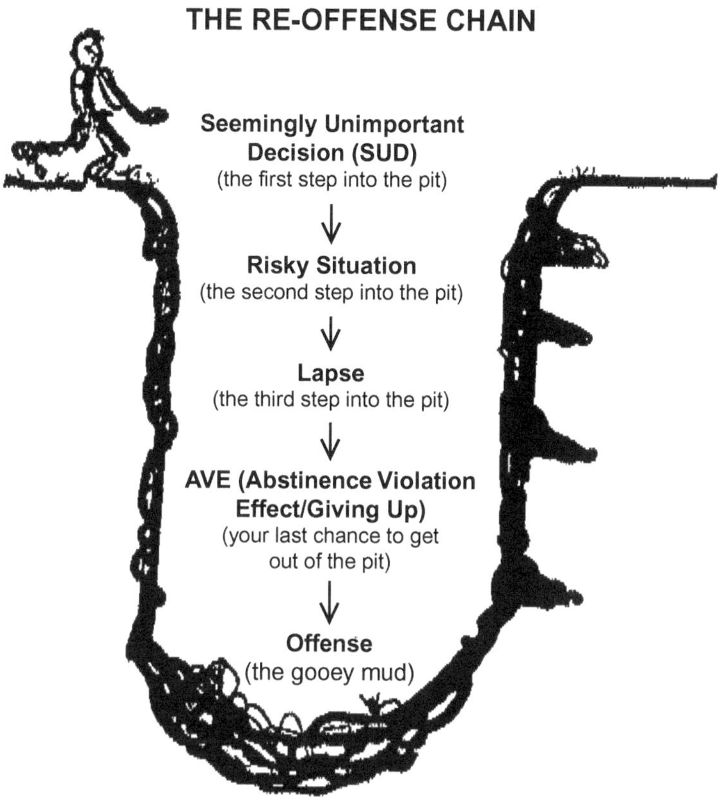

Figure 8.1 The re-offense chain. From *The Adult Relapse Prevention Workbook* (p.4), by C. Steen, 2001, Brandon, VT: Safer Society Press. Copyright 2001 by Charlene Steen. Reprinted with permission.

no intention of (re)offending at the time. Being in a dangerous situation can lead to the third step toward (re)offending – experiencing a *lapse*. A lapse is either a fantasy of offending or an action that is dangerously close to offending. Once the youth experiences a lapse, the *abstinence violation effect (AVE)* occurs. When the AVE occurs, the expectation of success (i.e., not offending) is lost. Thc youth either gets so caught up in the fantasy that he wants to live it out or feels like he has already gone too far to stop. The feeling of having gone too far to stop is sometimes called the "giving up" stage. At this point, it is an easy step down to the bottom of the hole – committing a sex offense. This progression is called the *offense chain* (Figure 8.2). By understanding and working with this chain, impulsive sexual behaviors may be decreased.

There are two main ways to stop from descending into the hole: *avoidance* and *escape*. *Avoidance* is keeping away from, or stopping oneself from,

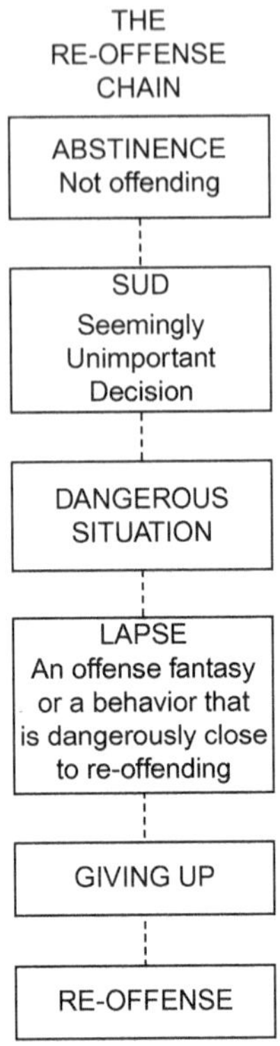

Figure 8.2 The re-offense chain. From *The Relapse Prevention Workbook for Youth in Treatment* (p. 6), by C. Steen, 1993, Brandon, VT: Safer Society Press. Copyright 1993 by Charlene Steen. Reprinted with permission.

doing something. In the example above, the youth could initially say he is unable to babysit, thereby *avoiding* a dangerous situation. *Escape* involves getting out of a situation at any point in the chain. Youths can be taught these various terms in game form. For example, they could play the letter game "Hangman" with these terms and other terms they will be learning. They can be given situational examples and asked to pair a term with the situation. For example, "Which of the words explains what Johnny did, *avoid* or *escape?* Johnny told his aunt that he was sorry, but he could not pick up his cousin at the cousin's preschool." The correct answer is that this is an example of avoidance.

These concepts can be applied to other problematic behaviors, as well. For example, if Johnny's sister has a weight problem and has difficulty restraining herself from eating cookies, she can apply the same *offense chain* and *avoidance* and *escape* strategies. She can decide to go home through the front door and directly to her room rather than going in the back door through the kitchen where there are likely to be cookies. In this way, she would be *avoiding* a dangerous situation.

Making an offense chain for one's own offense(s) will help a youth gain awareness of his own thought processes. As noted above, breaking offenses down into their component steps makes it easier to understand how a youth can change thoughts and/or behaviors either initially or at each step to prevent re-offense. Often, there may be more than one SUD, dangerous situation, or lapse. All SUDs, dangerous situations, and/or lapses can be included.

Some youthful offenders will claim that there was no progression and that the offense was spontaneous. It should be explained that committing a sexual offense impulsively is even more problematic than one in which a buildup to the offense occurred. Therefore, it is critically important to analyze their actions step-by-step. Assisting an offender to break actions down into these steps can be instructive in how successfully to avoid or escape from dangerous situations in the future.

After developing (an) offense chain(s) detailing the particular behaviors that led to the offense(s), the *thoughts* that led to those behaviors and the resultant feelings generated by the thoughts must be added in to provide a complete understanding of the process.

The next step is to identify *alternative thoughts, feelings, and behaviors* at each step of the chain, and seeing how those alternatives can change the behavioral outcomes. An exercise designed to assist youth in examining such alternatives is displayed in Steen (1993, pp. 12–13).

CHOICES AND CONSEQUENCES

The keystone of RP is *choice.* RP-based programs teach youth to recognize the likely consequences of their choices and subsequent behaviors so that they can make well-reasoned choices before acting. RP-based programs stress taking responsibility for one's own thoughts, feelings, and behaviors. The treatment provider's role is to give individuals the tools needed to make healthy choices. This is important, because youth and their families will eventually end treatment. If they have not mastered the methods to prevent re-offense, it will be much easier to regress to prior dysfunctional thoughts and behaviors.

Intelligent and informed decision making requires that one understand the nature of *choices* and *consequences. Choices* are under an individual's control. There are innumerable possibilities in every given situation, of which the youth must be aware. Unlike choices, however, *consequences* cannot be controlled. They are the likely and natural result of the choices made. These likely consequences can usually be predicted in advance. By giving a young offender exercises describing various situations and having him brainstorm the choices a person would have in a given situation, the adolescent can see that there are a myriad of choices available, some of which will produce more desirable outcomes than others. Then, a youth can attach likely consequences to each choice, so he can ascertain which choices will bring about desirable consequences and which lead to undesirable outcomes. Samples of the foregoing process are displayed in Steen (1993, pp. 45–46).

Another characteristic of *choice* is that every choice made in life has both desirable and undesirable consequences. Let us say that a juvenile offender chooses to skip a therapy session. A desirable consequence might be going out and having fun with friends instead, but undesirable consequences may include out-of-home placement, incarceration, or other punishment. Often, poor choices give short-term pleasure but have undesirable consequences over time. Even sexual offending has both desirable and undesirable consequences. At the time of the offense, there may be a release of sexual tension, a release of painful emotions, feelings of power or intimacy, etc. However, undesirable consequences will probably prevail in the long run. Such consequences may include getting caught, feelings of shame and guilt, criminal sanctions, having to be in treatment, being removed from home and family, and/or being incarcerated. Usually the long-term undesirable consequences far overshadow the initial desirable consequences. Conversely, when sexual offending behaviors are not chosen, there may be a loss of the initial pleasure or release but, in the long run, there will not be adverse outcomes.

A youth's parents should be taught these concepts, as well, so they can assist the youthful offender make better choices. Having an adolescent who makes better choices is likely to improve their own lives as well as the home environment.

CORRECTING DISTORTED THINKING (THINKING ERRORS)

Juveniles who have committed sexual offenses often do not seem to understand or care about the effects of their offenses on their victims. This is because their thinking has affected their perception of themselves and their victims. They have somehow fooled themselves into denying the harm they have done. Offenders sometimes make statements such as the following: "She deserved it"; "he came on to me"; "we were just playing"; "she liked it"; "I didn't hurt him"; and "she never said 'no' or 'stop it.'" Some useful psychotherapeutic strategies for correcting thinking errors, also known as "stinking thinking," are displayed in Steen (1993, pp. 23–30).

There are additional strategies that clinicians might wish to employ. Having guest speakers, adults who were sexually abused as youth, talk about the effect sexual offenses have had on their lives can help youth begin to connect with the pain experienced by their own victims. Speakers might explain why they did not object to inappropriate sexual behaviors foisted upon them, why they did not like what was being done to them, how they were afraid of losing someone important to them, how they did not deserve what was done, and so on. One of the reasons for cognitively distorting the painful results of sexual offenses is that most offenders want to be seen as good, caring, worthwhile people. Therefore, understanding the experiences of sexual abuse victims is sometimes a powerful motivator for them not to re-offend.

For youthful offenders who are also victims of sexual abuse, listening to adult survivors may help connect a youth to his own victimization. Victims who have not adequately processed their own feelings may be more likely to take on the role of an aggressor. Exercises that help them to connect with their emotions can include the following:

1. drawing pictures or making collages of how they are or were feeling when they were victimized;
2. writing letters to themselves from their victim's perspective followed by the reading of actual victim letters (which are usually much stronger) and a discussion of how victims are likely to feel;
3. role-playing scenarios in which a victim discloses but is not believed.

These are all ways of correcting thinking errors about victims.

Some youth lack awareness of emotions in general. Using emotion word lists to find words that describe how a youth felt in a particular situation (e.g., Steen, 1993, pp. 31–44), storytelling using emotion words, drawing, painting or using clay to express specific emotions, playing emotion charade games, writing emotions in poetry, and playing emotion guessing games are all ways of sensitizing adolescents to emotions and correcting distortions of, or disregard for, feelings. Adolescents should also be made aware of the physical manifestations of emotions to help them recognize what they, their victims, and others felt or are feeling.

Offenders' parents frequently rationalize the offenses their children committed, utilizing many of the same thinking distortions about victims, or they characterize their child as evil because of the inappropriate sexual acts. Their thoughts about victims need the same type of correcting as does the thinking of the young offender.

Parents may have a difficult time recognizing or admitting to abuse suffered by their offending child, particularly if the parent or the parent's partner committed the offense(s). Parents may also blame their child's offense on the child's own victimization. Parents should be encouraged to require their child to take responsibility for his actions, just as they must take responsibility for their own. Otherwise, what is being presented to the adolescent in treatment may be undermined by the parent(s).

SELF-UNDERSTANDING AND NEEDS SATISFACTION

This treatment component is based on the premise that those who are healthy, aware of their needs, and have appropriate coping strategies are unlikely to commit socially unacceptable acts. Some useful exercises for assisting youth to understand themselves and their emotional needs are displayed in Steen (1993, pp. 69–82).

There are other useful strategies, as well. Autobiographical assignments, including journaling, are effective methods for attaining self-understanding. (Youth who have difficulty expressing themselves in writing can use recording devices, check-off lists, drawings, or other means.)

General needs and needs the youth was satisfying by committing a sexual offense can be explored by brainstorming, followed by explanation of all the different ways these needs can be satisfied. The most promising solutions should be noted and can then be used in behavioral assignments. Planning to use these appropriate measures in lieu of offending may be a useful strategy for decreasing the likelihood of re-offense. This can also be formulated as a homework exercise. The usual needs behind sex offenses are listed, and the youth must list both the inappropriate ways he has met each need in the past and more appropriate ways of satisfying his needs (Steen, 1993, p. 55).

IDENTIFYING AND DIFFUSING RISK FACTORS FOR RE-OFFENSE

Risk factors for re-offense are usually painful emotions that interfere with normal, satisfactory functioning. The manner in which risk factors are cognitively processed can determine what behavior will follow. If one has inadequate coping strategies, the stage is set for inappropriate behaviors, such as re-offense. However, with adequate coping strategies that have been practiced, the risk factors can be ameliorated. This, in turn, decreases risk for engaging in inappropriate behaviors.

It can be helpful to break identification of risk factors into component parts. First, the *triggers* that cause the risk factor to arise should be identified. A trigger is usually something that occurs in the environment, such as a youth's mother screaming at him that he is no good and will never amount to anything. This leads to the emergence of such *risk factors* as feelings of depression, worthlessness, hopelessness and, perhaps, anger. If the youth lacks coping skills, he may believe his mother's statements, then look for something to make him feel better, more powerful or appreciated, or look for someone on whom to take out his anger. Committing another sex offense could be that something that gives feelings of power and control, appreciation and love, or could be an aggressive expression of the anger.

Each youth needs to recognize his own typical triggers and the risk factors typically elicited, then plan ahead for ways to diffuse the risk factors as a means of preventing re-offense. Adequate coping strategies, which would diffuse the likelihood of inappropriate behavior, could include reframing what his mother said, such as "she's having problems, must have had a bad day and is taking it out on me," or "she's gone crazy again – it has nothing to do with me." Alternative behavioral strategies for coping with painful feelings can also be employed, such as talking with a counselor, painting a picture, engaging in vigorous physical exercise, etc.

Table 8.1 demonstrates one way youths may identify and diffuse risk factors. Practice assignments in the community utilizing possible appropriate tactics helps prepare youth for situations they are likely to encounter in the future.

Table 8.1 One Way Youths May Identify and Diffuse Risk Factors

Trigger	Risk Factors	Possible Resultant Behaviors
Being ridiculed at school	Feelings of inadequacy, anger, depression, and helplessness	Beat someone up Hit the wall Talk to a counselor or therapist Molest someone younger Play a sport you are good at Write down what you are feeling Do something creative

Work on the steps in the cycle of offense can assist youth to recognize their prior dysfunctional patterns of behavior so that they can self-monitor and change the progression of behaviors in the future.

Family members can be helped to modify some of their own trigger behaviors, changing the ways they relate to the offending adolescent. While modifying one's responses is very difficult without a total restructuring of each individual's responses and the total family functioning (usually not possible), small inroads and increased awareness can be of help to the offending youth. Similarly, with increased awareness, the family can learn to intervene, cue, or help the offending youth effectively intervene in the cycle of offense before re-offense occurs.

IMPROVING COMMUNICATION

Communication is important to successful functioning and coping. People often only think of communication as talking – expression through words. But half of communication is listening. In addition, communication includes non-verbal expression – such as a parent's cooking being an expression of his/her love and caring, and body language – the way the posture, tension, vocal tone and production indicate the mood of the individual.

Listening skills can be taught to youths in a group setting in a variety of ways. Paired listening, in which youth take turns telling each other about some personal issue, can be an effective focused listening exercise. Afterward, the pair discusses how it felt to listen, how the content made them feel, how they felt about each other afterward, etc. Then the whole group might discuss the experience (but not the content of each dialogue).

There are numerous games that can be employed to help increase communication. Charade-type games, for example, in which individuals act out what they are feeling or wanting without words, and the others must guess what the body language is showing, are fun learning tools for non-verbal communication.

Such listening exercises can be applied to sexual situations to aid a youthful offender gain awareness of what others may be feeling. An offender will learn to attend to the body language and words of anyone with whom they might be having, or want to be having, sexual contact. It can be useful to discuss how he felt when his communication was not attended to or understood by another individual.

Youths also need to learn multiple strategies for getting someone to pay attention to them when they have something to say. Multiple strategies can be brainstormed, and pros and cons associated with each strategy can be discussed. The following are some of the ways to get another person's attention. Some are appropriate while others are inappropriate. The adolescents might be asked to determine which are which:

1. looking at, and speaking to, a person directly from a close place;
2. asking the other person to set a time to talk;
3. screaming at the person you want to talk to;
4. throwing something at the person you want to talk to;
5. writing a note to let the person know you need to communicate;
6. go through an intermediary, such as a counselor, if direct methods do not work.

Within one's family, a system can be developed wherein when one person touches another's hand, the other person agrees to stop and listen.

Assertiveness skills are important to develop. An exercise to help youths determine the differences between aggressive and assertive statements can be found in Steen (1993, pp. 115–117).

Asking assertively for what one wants, particularly when the issue is a sensitive one, may be practiced with role plays. It should be emphasized that it is important to speak up when someone says or does something that the youth does not like. Reasons for speaking up or not speaking up in these situations should be explored.

Another aspect of assertiveness training is teaching refusal skills. Adolescents need to learn how to decline firmly to engage in inappropriate behavior. It can be helpful to role play situations in which a youth wants to say "no," but has difficulty doing so because of peer pressure. It is also important for adolescents to learn if, how, and when to confront (appropriately) an adult authority figure.

Therapists should emphasize the importance of effective communication to the adolescent's family members. If an adolescent can talk about things that are bothering him, this communication becomes one possible means by which to prevent the youth from moving down the offense chain.

SEXUALITY – EDUCATION AND APPROPRIATENESS

Juveniles who have committed sexual offenses sometimes have deficits in sexual knowledge. It is sometimes helpful to have a nurse or sex educator come to the group and talk about basic sexual functioning. Obtaining knowledge regarding sexual matters, including contraception, can also be of utility in preventing unwanted pregnancies and the spread of sexually transmitted diseases. There are numerous books available that provide age-appropriate information regarding all aspects of sexuality. Ruth Bell's (1998) *Changing Bodies, Changing Lives* is one such book.

Discussion of age-appropriate sexual behavior should be conducted. Discussion of what is appropriate and what is inappropriate touch can be clarified through short vignettes illustrating different types of touches with various people. Steen (1993, pp. 135–137) provided such vignettes.

Some juvenile sex offenders display poor interpersonal boundaries. They may not differentiate between appropriate and inappropriate interpersonal behaviors. For example, a parent giving a child a wet kiss on the lips is inappropriate in our society, as is a parent talking to a child about the parent's own sexual relations with a spouse. Discussions through short vignettes can help to better define these boundaries. While what is appropriate attire or lack of appropriate attire in the home varies depending on family attitudes, once a member of the family has committed a sexual offense, more stringent rules regarding clothing should apply. The parents and all family members, including the adolescent, must understand that family members dressing modestly is for the protection of potential victims and to decrease the likelihood of inappropriate behavior by the adolescent.

Another focal area for this module is the differentiation between sex, love, and friendship. Just because someone wants to feel close and loved does not mean that sex is an appropriate way to attain that closeness, particularly if there is an age discrepancy or the persons involved are close relatives. Similarly, a person extending friendship does not mean that person wants a love, intimate, or a sexual relationship. A technique for increasing understanding of these issues is to have the adolescent generate situations in which one or another of these entities (sex, love, or friendship) are present without the others. If the adolescent cannot think of such situations, treatment providers can suggest such situations. For example, a man may love his dog, but he should not have sex with the dog. Similarly, loving a sibling should not result in sexual activity between siblings.

BUILDING RELATIONSHIPS

Adolescents sometimes jump into relationships without adequately knowing the other person. This can result in painful betrayals and rejections. For adolescents who have previously committed a sexual offense, the betrayal or rejection can also serve as a trigger for offending behavior. Teaching and encouraging adolescents to move more slowly through relationship building – both romantic and general friendships, can avoid problems.

The nature of relationships can be visualized as a target, with acquaintances as the outermost ring, moving inward as follows (Figure 8.3):

1. Acquaintances – persons you may see occasionally (but with whom you do not socialize, such as a supermarket checker, mail carrier, or restaurant server);
2. Casual friends – people with whom you engage in activities (e.g., working, bowling buddies, etc.);
3. Good friends – people with whom you do a variety of things and know beyond those activities;
4. Close friends – the people you can call on for help, with whom you have serious conversations, particularly of a self-disclosing nature, and who you are there for as well, when needed;
5. Most intimate relationships – usually only one or two people who are always there for you and with whom you share your innermost thoughts and they share theirs.

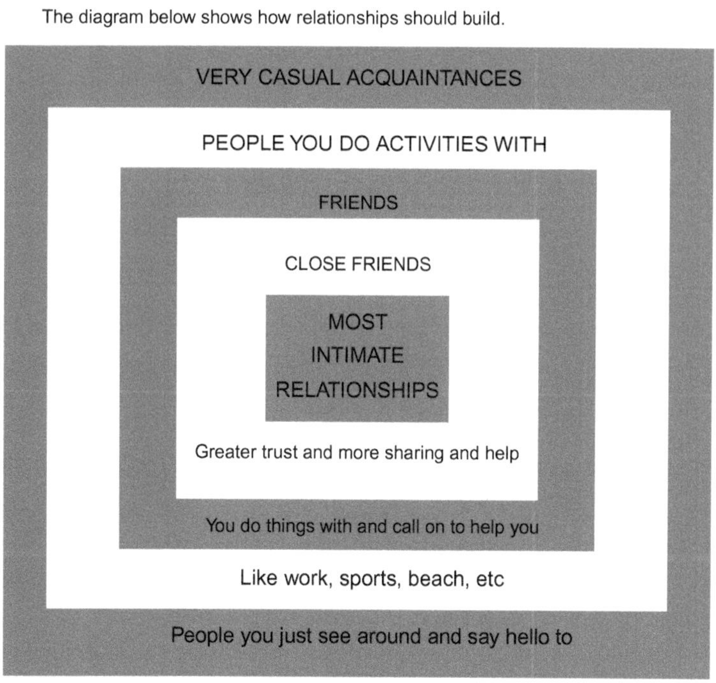

Figure 8.3 How relationships should build. From *The Relapse Prevention Workbook for Youth in Treatment* (p. 133), by C. Steen, 1993, Brandon, VT: Safer Society Press. Copyright 1993 by Charlene Steen. Reprinted with permission.

Sharing innermost thoughts with someone who the adolescent does not know well is very risky. That person may not be trustworthy and keep the confidence. The sharer has also relinquished great power to someone who could use the confidence in a hurtful manner, leaving the sharer vulnerable and helpless. Emotional states, such as vulnerability and helplessness, may serve as risk factors for re-offense. Therapeutic discussions should cover the types of communication and behaviors appropriate with each class of individual. Therapists should also teach strategies for diffusing hurt experienced when betrayed. Such strategies include reframing and depersonalizing. It is important to help an adolescent understand how he may have gone beyond the appropriate relationship level, thereby transforming a potential sexual partner into a victim.

The youthful offender should be helped to understand that although he has had longstanding relationships with his family members, all family members are not necessarily close or trustworthy. Talking about who in the family is or is not trustworthy, with whom the adolescent is or is not close, why certain relationships are strained, or how a family member has betrayed trust in the past, may be helpful. Pre-emptive protective plans can be made to encourage talking with "safe" family members and to avoid sharing important information with untrustworthy ones.

In addition, development of healthy prosocial relationships with peers should be encouraged. Therapeutic assignments might include attending a recreation department or church youth group, becoming involved in a special interest group at school, or playing as a member of an athletic team.

URGE CONTROL AND DELAYING GRATIFICATION

It is critical that juvenile sex offenders understand their fantasies and urges. They need to learn how to stop dangerous fantasies and urges, and how to employ self-manangement skills when problematic fantasies and urges are experienced.

Sometimes, adolescents do not know what a fantasy is, or say they do not have any fantasies. A fantasy is simply a daydream or mental image, which we all have. They can be about any subject. Sexual fantasies can become a problem when they involve engaging in proscribed behaviors. Such fantasises can develop into bodily urges which the person may want to fulfill.

An urge is a need that propels a person toward certain behavior unless certain constraints are present. Urges come and go in waves. Sexual urges, in particular, do not have to be satisfied, and can be waited out or can lessen with distractions. Consequently, urges that youth may have often dissipate if they wait them out or switch their thoughts to other things. Scott & Bromberg (this volume) describe some strategies for modifying fantasies of engaging in proscribed sexual behaviors to fantasies of engaging in more socially-acceptable sexual behaviors.

However, if the problematic fantasies and urges do not dissipate, adolescents should have plans to prevent themselves from acting on such fantasies. Such plans may include the following: weighing all of the likely consequences of committing another sexual offense; avoiding situations in which sexual offending is possible, such as not (further) engaging the object of their sexual desire in dialogue and not being alone with that person; reading over an urge control card (which is a technique useful for prevention of impulsively acting on sexual urges); calling or going to a friend, parent, or counselor and talking about these feelings; writing down the situations that triggered the fantasies or urges; or doing a relaxation or meditation exercise. Adolescents should select techniques that work for them, write these strategies down on a card to keep in their wallets, and practice using these strategies with other problem areas of their lives as well. (A sample of an urge control card can be found in Steen, 1993, p. 63.)

It is important for parents to know that it is not unusual for adolescents to have recurrences of problematic fantasies and/or urges. A youth should not be demeaned for having such experiences. Parents should be open to listening to what a youth is experiencing and praise the adolescent for appropriately managing problematic fantasies and urges. Parents should also encourage the adolescent to contact his treatment provider for additional assistance as needed.

SAMPLE CASE

We are including a sample case to illustrate how some of the relapse prevention strategies discussed in this chapter may be applied and documented. The vignette is one in which the adolescent offender is uncommonly forthright about his offense. However, he displays an incomplete understanding of his own motivations and behaviors when completing an offense chain, safety plan, and self-help sheet[2] early in the therapeutic process. He displays significant cognitive distortions about the impact his

[2] The safety plan and self-help sheet formats were developed by Jackson Tay Bosley, Psy.D. We thank Dr. Bosley for granting us permission to use these forms.

sexual offense had on his victim (i.e., his victim enjoyed the sexual contact). His core belief appears to be that he should not re-offend because of the consequences to *himself*, rather than to his victim and future potential victims. As a result of RP procedures employed, including psychoeducation about sexuality and trauma, he attains a more complete understanding of his own motivations and behaviors, and of the impact the sexual contact had on his victim. He displays more appropriate, less vulgar language as he progresses in his therapeutic tasks, as well. Because of all of the foregoing factors, he is able to produce a more complete and useful relapse prevention plan later in the therapeutic process.

Summary of the Offense

A 16-year-old boy met his 8-year-old victim while working in a summer day camp. He was the boy's junior counselor. He, along with a senior counselor and a counselor-in-training, was responsible for overseeing the safety and planning for the recreation of a group of 8- and 9-year old boys from approximately 9am to 4pm Monday through Friday during the camp season. The 16-year-old was shy and awkward with same-age peers and had no dating or sexual experiences with peers. Nonetheless, he had an excellent rapport with children. He felt very mature when working with children and children enjoyed the energy and physical affection (e.g., piggy back rides, roughhousing in the swimming pool, sitting on the counselor's lap) he displayed. Although the adolescent was almost always attentive to the boys in his group, he made sure to be present in the group's cabin when the boys were changing their bathing suits before and after swimming. He found himself quite sexually aroused while watching the younger boys naked and, after camp, often masturbated to fantasies of engaging in various sexual acts with the younger boys.

Camp overnights took place twice each summer. After evening activities had ended, campers slept in sleeping bags in the woods. During one such camp overnight, some of the adolescent's campers became homesick and were frightened by the shadows and animal sounds of the forest. The counselor offered to take the boys out of the woods and keep them company in their cabin. One of the boys had a stomach-ache and needed to use the toilet. The counselor accompanied the boy to the toilet, and because the boy was not feeling well, offered to wipe him and began doing so before the younger boy had the opportunity to formulate a verbal objection. As the counselor wiped the boy, the younger boy's penis became erect. The counselor began stroking the 8-year-old's penis and then performed fellatio on him. He stopped when he heard other boys coming toward the bathroom. The following afternoon, the 8-year-old told his parents about what had occurred and the parents notified law enforcement authorities. The 16-year-old was detained for questioning, arrested, and eventually convicted of one count of Aggravated Sexual Assault.

The 8-year-old's parents brought the boy for a forensic psychological evaluation. Whereas the boy had previously been well adjusted and there had been no concerns about his emotional or behavioral functioning, his functioning changed markedly after the incident with his counselor. He displayed the following: hyperactivity; hypervigilance; refusal to use the toilet and encopresis; sleep-related problems, including nightmares; and he began masturbating in front of peers and adults.

Offense Chain (Completed Early in Treatment)

Abstinence (Not committing any sexual offenses and not planning to)

- I was not engaged in sexual offending behavior and was not planning to sexually abuse anyone.

Seemingly Unimportant Decision(s) (Everyday decisions you make that seem reasonable, but are risky because they have the possibility of placing you in a situation where you might offend)

- I was really horny and took the kid to the bathroom.

Dangerous Situation(s) (Situation that's dangerous because it places you in a situation where you have the opportunity to offend)

- I took the kid to the bathroom and stayed with him while his pants were down.

Lapse (A behavior that brings you close to a sex offense or a fantasy of committing a sex offense)

- I kept thinking about all the times I jerked off thinking about being alone with him with his pants down.
- As he sat on the toilet, my dick got really hard and all I could think about was touching him.

Giving Up (You figure you have crossed the line, there is no turning back, so you may as well commit the sex offense)

- I figured I could get away with wiping him cause he's a little kid and had a stomach-ache. I knew he wouldn't tell because I'd give him such good feelings. I figured I might as well do what I really felt like doing.

Offense (Molesting a child or raping someone)

- I stuck my finger in his butt, started to jerk him off, then sucked him off.

Safety Plan
(Initial)

____
Your Name

This contract is designed to help me prevent myself from re-offending by: (a) listing the situations I might be in and thoughts and feelings I might have that indicate I am in danger of re-offending; and (b) listing the things I can do to prevent myself from acting on my impulses.

High Risk Factors

Physical Factors: (These are the situations that I must avoid)

1. Being with little boys while they're naked, like when they're changing clothes or in the bath.

Emotional Factors: (These are the feelings that indicate that I am not doing so well and might need some help)

1. Feeling shy with kids my own age.

Cognitive Factors: (These are examples of negative ways of thinking that indicate that I am at higher risk for re-offending)

1. I dunno. This shit's stupid and therapy sucks.

Alternatives to Sexual Offending

If I find these or any other risk factors in my life, I will do the following to prevent a recurrence of my sexual offending behavior:

1. Stay away from little kids.
2. Jerk off in the morning and again before I go to sleep so I don't feel so horny all the time.
3. Go talk to you or call another kid in our treatment group. I know you guys will understand and help me.
4. I dunno what else to write.

______________	______________	______________
Your Signature	Therapist's Name	Today's Date

Adolescent Sexual Offender Self-Help Sheet

Fill out this sheet honestly. If any of the words are difficult to understand, please ask your therapist to explain them.

1. I offended against: one of the boys in my camp group.
2. The specific acts involved in the offense were: sticking my finger in his butt, jerking him off, and sucking his dick.
3. I gained the victim's cooperation in these acts by: being really nice to him and helping him by wiping him.
4. I tried to maintain my victim's silence about these acts by: I didn't. I just did it. Other kids came in and I stopped. I knew he wouldn't tell cuz he liked it and got hard.

Two cognitive distortions are evident in this sentence. First, the offender erroneously believes that his victim having experienced an erection in response to sexual touch indicated that the 8-year-old boy enjoyed the sexual contact. Further, he erroneously concluded that his victim would not report the sexual abuse because he enjoyed the sexual contact.

5. I rationalized that these acts were not so bad by telling myself: I dunno. His parents and the camp thought it was bad, but he liked it. His dick got real big.

The adolescent displays cognitive distortions here, as well. Again, he erroneously assumed that the 8-year-old boy enjoyed the sexual contact because he experienced an erection in response to sexual touch. Moreover, his phrasing suggests that although the 8-year-old's parents and camp administrators viewed the sexual contact as being problematic, the adolescent himself does not perceive the contact as having been problematic.

6. The acts I performed gave me feelings of: good. I loved giving him so much pleasure.

Again, further evidence of a significant cognitive distortion. Although it is the adolescent's perception that he gave the 8-year-old boy "so much pleasure," sequelae the boy experienced after the incident suggests otherwise.

7. I fantasized that the victim felt: I dunno.

8. The following things increase my risk of re-offense: being alone with a kid and not jerking off enough.

Although probably accurate about immediate antecedents of his sexual offending, the adolescent displays no insight into the thoughts and emotions that increase his risk for reoffending.

9. The things about me that led to these offenses include: I was really horny and he was right there.
10. To prevent myself from re-offending, I will do the following: not be alone with little kids and jerk off more.

Re-Offense Chain (Completed Toward the End of Treatment)

Abstinence (Not committing any sexual offenses and not planning to)

- I was not engaged in sexual offending behavior and wasn't planning to sexually abuse anyone.

Seemingly Unimportant Decision(s) (Everyday decisions you make that seem reasonable, but are risky because they have the possibility of placing you in a situation where you might offend)

- I decided to work in a job with little kids all day and I know that little boys turn me on.

Note that the adolescent displays a much more complete understanding of the assortment of antecedents to engaging in sexual offending behaviors than he did earlier in treatment. He identifies some of his own cognitive distortions.

- I spent a lot of time with my campers, more than all the other counselors spent with their campers, and thinking about them during my free time. I thought about if their parents love them as much as I do. (They shouldn't have meant that much to me. Also, that was stinkin' thinkin to think I loved them more than their parents do.)
- I always went into the bunk with them while they were changing, watched them, and had fantasies about doing different sexual things with many of my campers. (That made me want them even more.)
- I spent a lot of time masturbating to fantasies of having sex with my campers. (The more I did it, the more I wanted to have sex with little boys.)

Dangerous Situation(s) (Situation that's dangerous because it places you in a situation where you have the opportunity to offend)

- I took the kid I molested to the bathroom and stayed with him while his pants were down.

Lapse (A behavior that brings you close to a sex offense or a fantasy of committing a sex offense)

- I kept thinking about all the times I masturbated

Note the use of appropriate (non-vulgar) language here and throughout the remaining worksheets.

thinking about being alone with him with his pants down. This was my dream coming true.

- As he sat on the toilet, I got an erection and all I could think about was touching him.

Giving Up (You figure you've crossed the line, there's no turning back, so you may as well commit the sex offense)

- I figured I could get away with wiping him because he's a little kid and had a stomach-ache. Now I know I fooled myself, because a kid that age can wipe himself.

Here, the adolescent identified plausible (distorted) thoughts that led to disinhibition of inappropriate sexual behavior.

Now I realize that he was probably gonna tell someone and that I lied to myself that he wouldn't tell. I figured I might as well do what I really felt like doing because I'm already in big trouble.

Offense (Molesting a child or raping someone)

- I didn't just wipe him. I rubbed around his anus, and stuck my finger in his anus a few times. Then I masturbated him, and did oral sex to him.

Note the more complete description of the offense sequence relative to the description provided earlier in therapy.

Adolescent Sexual Offender Self-Help Sheet
(Second Administration)

Fill out this sheet honestly. If any of the words are difficult to understand, please ask your therapist to explain them.

1. I offended against: one of the boys in my camp group.
2. The specific acts involved in the offense were: sticking my finger in his anus, masturbating him, and doing oral sex to him.

Again, the adolescent uses appropriate (non-vulgar) terminology when writing about sexual acts.

3. I gained the victim's cooperation in these acts by: being really nice to him so I could get him to do what I wanted and doing sexual stuff to him before he knew what to say to stop me.

The adolescent's report of how he gained his victim's "cooperation" is consistent with information contained in background information provided regarding this offense.

4. I tried to maintain my victim's silence about these acts by: I didn't. I just did it. Other kids came in and I stopped. Becuz of stinkin thinkin, I fooled myself into thinking he wouldn't tell cuz he liked what I was doin.

The adolescent identifed one significant cognitive distortion underlying his own sexual offense.

5. I rationalized that these acts were not so bad by telling myself: I used stinkin thinkin and I lied to myself that he liked the sexual stuff as much as I did. (Now I know it felt good to his body but he was probably confused by what I did and it felt gross in his mind. I hope he doesn't hate me 4 ever and I hope he gets better by working with his therapist.)
6. The acts I performed gave me feelings of: good feelings in my body. I got hard and would have had him do oral sex to me if the other boys didn't come in. I also felt really loved like the boy really cared about me and I really cared about him. I felt like an adult also because finally I was having sex. It made me feel really grown up and powerful.

The adolescent disclosed that his offense sequence was interrupted and that additional sexual acts would have occurred had others not interrupted the offense sequence. He also identified the non-sexual (emotional) needs he was meeting through his sexual offending behaviors.

7. I fantasized that the victim felt: like he loved the sex as much as I did and that he loved me and wanted to live with me.

The adolescent identified additional cognitive distortions underlying his sexual offense.

8. The following things increase my risk of re-offense: being alone with children, especially if I'm horny and especially if I feel lonely or not loved.

Probably an accurate list of the immediate antecedents of sexual offending, and more complete than the list generated earlier in therapy. This list includes an unpleasant emotional state antecedent to sexual offending.

9. The things about me that led to these offenses include: I was real horny I had the chance and I took it. I was lonely and I'm scared to try to hook up with kids my age. Most of all, I learned that I want to hook up with kids my age so I don't feel like a freak because now I know it's really little boys that turn me on. Since I know this, I know I gotta be careful for the rest of my life that I don't try to do sex with little boys. I gotta have a real good safety plan.

In this section, the adolescent displays significant (and painful) insights into his own sexual arousal pattern and his attempts to hide the sexual arousal pattern from himself and from peers.

10. To prevent myself from re-offending, I will do the following: not be alone with little kids. I will avoid or escape dangerous situations. I will do the exercises my therapist taught me to get more turned on by kids my age and people in their 20s and less turned on by little boys. I will pay attention to if I start using stinkin thinkin again and will call my therapist if I feel like this stuff isn't working and I might have sex with a little kid again.

The adolescent provided a reasonable summary of a RP plan.

Safety Plan
(Final)

____

Your Name

This contract is designed to help me prevent myself from re-offending by: (a) listing the situations I might be in and thoughts and feelings I might have that indicate I am in danger of re-offending; and (b) listing the things I can do to prevent myself from acting on my impulses.

High Risk Factors

Physical Factors: (These are the situations that I must avoid)

1. Being in a position of authority over little kids, especially little boys.
2. Being alone with little kids, especially boys, especially when I'm horny.
3. Being with little boys or girls while they're naked, like when they're changing clothes or in the bath.

Emotional Factors: (These are the feelings that indicate that I am not doing so well and might need some help)

1. Feeling shy with kids my own age.
2. I feel like I want to have sex with kids my age, but I'm not good enough to get a girlfriend and and I can't even do sex with guys my age because they'll laugh at me because I have a small penis. I need to remember what we learned that the size of your penis doesn't really matter and I need to work on self-esteem. By the way, I know the last sentence is really thoughts and not feelings and really belongs in the next section.

> The adolescent displays knowledge of the connection between thoughts, feelings, and behaviors.

3. Feeling really bummed out.

4. Feeling like I'm on top of the world and deserve to get whatever I want no matter what. I think that's parta why I abused the kid in my group.

The adolescent identified a narcissistic tendency underlying his offense, as well as an additional cognitive distortion underlying the offense.

I felt like I loved him so much I deserved to have sex with him. I kinda fooled myself into forgetting that he's a little kid and can't feel about me what I feel about him. I wrote this here because it's kinda an emotional thing but it's also kinda a stinkin thinkin thing that I coulda wrote below.

Cognitive Factors: (These are examples of negative ways of thinking that indicate that I am at higher risk for re-offending)

Look at what I wrote in the other section.

Alternatives to Sexual Offending

If I find these or any other risk factors in my life, I will do the following to prevent a recurrence of my sexual offending behavior:

1. Stay away from little kids, especially boys, and never be alone with a little kid.
2. Masturbate in the morning and again before I go to sleep so I don't feel so horny all day. Try to think about kids my age or older when I masturbate and not younger kids. If I do think of younger kids, switch images to someone older before I come.
3. Go talk to you (my therapist) or call another kid in our treatment group. I know you guys will understand and help me.
4. Stay away from Pastor John!!! When he says I'll burn in hell if I do it with boys or if I do it to myself, I get really pissed, I feel bad, and then I REALLY want to do it with little boys.

In this section, the adolescent displays reasonable strategies for decreasing his risk of committing future sexual offenses.

Your Signature	Therapist's Name	Today's Date

FREQUENTLY ASKED QUESTIONS

What is the evidence base supporting the efficacy of RP?

The evidence base supporting the efficacy of RP with juvenile sex offenders is mixed (Polaschek, 2003). Although many studies seem to support the efficacy of RP, other studies lead one to question the efficacy of RP.

When viewing outcome studies for RP with juvenile sex offenders, a strong caveat is in order. It is important to remember that much traditional psychotherapy outcome research employs group research designs. In such research designs, outcomes for all individuals are *averaged, thereby obscuring outcomes for individuals who comprise the group* (Barlow & Hersen, 1984). Some individuals generally improve, others seem to obtain no benefit, while the condition of others deteriorates. Paul (1967) suggested that the question "Is psychotherapy effective?" is too simplistic. We echo Paul's assertion, as well as his response that the more appropriate question for psychotherapy outcome researchers to address is the following: "*What* treatment, by *whom*, is most effective for *this* individual with *that* specific problem, and under *which* set of circumstances?" (p. 111).

When we consider this significant shortcoming of much of the outcome research, we believe the most complete and accurate response is as follows: "RP is effective for some of the adolescents some of the time. However, we do not know which adolescents are more likely to benefit from RP programs than others." Recent research (discussed below) suggests strategies/supplemental treatment approaches to enhance the efficacy of RP with a broader range of clientele.

Can RP be combined with other treatment approaches?

The RP format of treatment need not be exclusive. It can serve as a kind of umbrella concept for various treatment modalities, both as the goal of therapy and as one of the specific techniques to be used.

RP can and should include other modalities, based on the needs of the individual youth. Multisystemic therapy (MST) might be incorporated and has demonstrated utility with juvenile sex offenders (e.g., Borduin et al., 2009; Henggeler et al., 2009). Elements of MST include family participation and empowerment, collaborative efforts with community entities, and utilizing interventions designed to promote treatment generalization and long-term maintenance of therapeutic change.

In recent years, the Good Lives Model for treatment of sex offenders has received attention. Willis et al. (2012) provided a thoughtful overview of the GLM and provided suggestions for integrating the GLM into other treatment programs that address sexual offending behaviors. It is assumed that all human beings, including individuals who committed sexual offenses, value certain states of mind, personal characteristics, and experiences. These "primary human goods" are as follows: (1) life (including healthy living and functioning); (2) knowledge; (3) excellence in play; (4) excellence in work (including mastery experiences); (5) excellence in agency (i.e., autonomy and self-directedness); (6) inner peace (i.e., freedom from emotional turmoil and stress); (7) relatedness (including intimate, family, and friend relationships); (8) community; (9) spirituality (in the broad sense of finding meaning and purpose in life); (10) happiness; and (11) creativity. The GLM assumes that people organize their lives around their core values and follow some sort of good life plan, be it implicit or explicit. Sexual offending behavior relates to the pursuit of primary goods and is considered to result from problems in an individual's good life plan (GLP).

The GLM postulates four different flaws individuals may have in their good life plan. These flaws are as follows: (1) inappropriate or harmful means to obtain primary goods (e.g., seeking out relatedness by engaging in sexual behavior with a child); (2) lack of scope in a good life plan (e.g., allocating so much time to excellence in work that the goods of relatedness and happiness are ignored); (3) experiencing conflict between primary and secondary goods (e.g., securing autonomy by dominating one's partner conflicts with satisfying the good of relatedness in the same relationship); and (4) lack of internal and external capabilities to satisfy primary goods (e.g., antisocial orientation might be a barrier towards the filling the primary good of autonomy by way of frequent incarcerations.)

It is beyond the scope of this chapter to provide a complete discussion of the GLM. Despite some of the philosophically appealing elements of the GLM, it has been noted (Willis et al., 2012) that the extent to which the GLM "enhances program outcomes remains unknown." Moreover, some researchers (e.g., Andrews et al., 2011) have noted that "at the present time, there is nothing unique in GLM…".

ADDITIONAL RESOURCES

Readers are encouraged to review the books and journal articles referenced in this chapter for more information about CBT and RP. The Association for the Treatment of Sexual Abusers (ATSA) is a national organization that provides training and other resources for professionals engaged in the assessment and treatment of individuals who commit sexual offenses. ATSA training resources may be found online at http://www.atsa.com/education-and-training. In addition, *The Sex Addiction Workbook* (O'Donohue & Sbraga, 2003) contains useful information about RP strategies for use with individuals with sexual behavioral problems. Finally, Safer Society Press has an assortment of books, workbooks, and videos on relapse prevention and a variety of other topics of interest and utility to professionals who work with individuals who have committed sexual offenses.

SUMMARY

This chapter serves as an introduction to the treatment modules utilized in relapse prevention programs. Relapse prevention is a self-management treatment approach in which individuals who are trying to change their behaviors are taught how to anticipate and cope with the problem of relapse. Relapse refers to a setback in a person's attempt to change or modify any particular behavior or class of behaviors (e.g., sexual offending). RP combines behavioral skills training, cognitive interventions, and lifestyle change strategies. Because it includes both behavioral and cognitive components, it is similar to other cognitive-behavioral treatment strategies. We have included a case sample to illustrate how RP strategies may be implemented to reduce the risk of engaging in future sexual offending.

REFERENCES

Andrews, D. A., Bonta, J., & Wormith, J. S. (2011). The risk-need-responsivity (RNR) model: Does adding the Good Lives Model contribute to effective crime prevention? *Criminal Justice and Behavior, 38*, 735–755.

Barlow, D. H., & Hersen, M. (1984). *Single case experimental designs: Strategies for studying behavior change* (2nd ed). New York: Pergamon.

Beck, J. S. (1995). *Cognitive therapy: Basics and beyond*. New York: Guilford.

Bell, R. (1998). *Changing bodies, changing lives* (3rd ed). New York: Harmony.

Borduin, C. M., Schaeffer, C. M., & Heiblum, N. (2009). A randomized clinical trial of multisystemic therapy with juvenile sexual offenders: Effects on youth social ecology and criminal activity. *Journal of Consulting and Clinical Psychology*, 77, 26–37.

Finkelhor, D., Ormrod, R., & Chaffin, M. (2009). *Juveniles who commit sex offenses against minors: Juvenile justice bulletin*. Washington, DC: OJJDP.

Henggeler, S.W., Letourneau, E. J., Chapman, J. E., Borduin, C. M., Schewe, P. A., & McCart, M. R. (2009). Mediators of change for multisystemic therapy with juvenile sexual offenders. *Journal of Consulting and Clinical Psychology*, 77, 451–462.

Letourneau, E. J., & Miner, M. (2005). Juvenile sex offenders: A case against the legal and clinical status quo. *Sexual Abuse: A Journal of Research and Treatment, 17*, 293–312.
Marlatt, G. A., & Gordon, J. R. (Eds.) (1985). *Relapse prevention: Maintenance strategies in the treatment of addictive behaviors*. New York: Guilford.
O'Donohue, W. T., & Sbraga, T. P. (2003). *The sex addiction workbook: Proven strategies to help you regain control of your life*. Oakland, CA: New Harbinger.
Paul, G. L. (1967). Strategy of outcome research in psychotherapy. *Journal of Consulting Psychology, 31*, 104–118.
Polaschek, D. L. L. (2003). Relapse prevention, offense process models, and the treatment of sexual offenders. *Professional Psychology: Research and Practice, 34*, 361–367.
Steen, C. (1993). *The relapse prevention workbook for youth in treatment*. Brandon, VT: Safer Society Press.
Willis, G. M., Yates, P. M., Gannon, T. A., & Ward, T. (2012). How to integrate the Good Lives Model into treatment programs for sexual offending: An introduction and overview. *Sexual Abuse: A Journal of Research and Treatment, 25*, 123–142.

CHAPTER 9

An Outpatient Treatment Response for Youth Assessed as Low to Moderate Risk

Robert Stuyvesant*, Diane G. Mercier* and Ashley Haidle**
*Private Practice, Reno, NV, USA
**Marriage and Family Therapist Intern

INTRODUCTION

The roots of our treatment approach with adolescents who commit sexual offenses extend back to 1981. At that time, we worked for an agency that provided treatment services to youth and their families. Encountering many adolescents exhibiting sexual problems or charged with sexual offenses, we realized that neither our education nor our professional training had adequately prepared us to meet the treatment challenges with which these youth presented. These were the pre-Google days and the days of rotary telephone. We began searching for resources and training. As we began to educate ourselves, we realized that other agencies within our community were struggling with many of the same issues. Our community worked together to create a network to encourage interagency communication as well as to provide training for therapists, police and probation officers, and school personnel relevant to this problem.

Now, over three decades later, a vast landscape of resources has become available nationally and internationally and such resources are more easily accessed (Wong, 2013). Over these intervening decades, best practice standards in the treatment of adolescents who commit sexual offenses have been delineated. Interestingly enough, some of the early treatment directions that seemed just to make good sense in the early 1980s, such as a team approach, relapse prevention and the promotion of healthy social skills, today have the support of years of research. Some of the same treatment questions have persisted over time. Is group treatment the best approach? Should group treatment be co-ed? How important are techniques such as confrontation, disclosure, clarification, empathy building? How useful is the polygraph with juvenile offenders? Do we include

Toolkit for Working with Juvenile Sex Offenders.
DOI: http://dx.doi.org/10.1016/B978-0-12-405948-1.00009-8

objective assessment of sexual arousal and interest via penile plethysmograph or viewing time approaches with juveniles? Along with these treatment approach challenges, there are emerging legislative and community response issues (i.e., the Adam Walsh Act and Megan's Law, which go toward mandated registration and community notification for juveniles as young as age thirteen in some jurisdictions). The techniques, strategies, and philosophies proposed here are a result of over thirty years of experience and training in the treatment of youth with sexual behavior problems and/or who have been charged with committing sexual offenses.

THE TREATMENT PHILOSOPHY

Sexual deviance/sexual behavior problems are complicated and multidetermined. The treatment interventions proposed here are focused on assisting the clients so that they accept responsibility, increase self-awareness, institute change and manage approaches to living in healthy and productive ways. This treatment philosophy is built around the core theme of "healthy living and positive life promotion".

Treatment includes simple, practical techniques that can be applied throughout an individual's life. The core of the treatment model is healthy living and positive self-regulation, with the goal to create positive connections with self and others, thereby preventing the need for abusive sexual behaviors. This treatment philosophy incorporates various approaches while acknowledging the unique and special needs in regard to adolescent growth and development. A central idea in this philosophical approach to promoting change is that our perception of an event or situation powerfully affects our emotional, behavioral, and physiological response to that event/situation. Therefore, the emphasis is on developing the insight to recognize dysfunctional, distorted or self-defeating belief systems, challenge them and engage in active problem solving to apply healthy responses. Hopefully, this will lead to lasting cognitive, behavioral, emotional, and relationship changes that promote a healthy lifestyle. This basic philosophy is applied when working with individuals and families and is in line with the fundamental principles of cognitive-behavioral therapy (Daly, 2008). The key to a favorable outcome is education, awareness, skill-building and hard work. Developing new responses to life can be challenging, awkward and uncomfortable. This treatment approach can provide a "springboard" to change by providing encouragement, support, direction and hope.

Incorporated in this approach are the concepts of self-regulation (Ward & Hudson, 2000) and relapse prevention (Hanson, 1996) which address emotional, cognitive and behavioral self-management, supported by external supervision. This treatment helps clients to positively take control of their lives with help, support and monitoring by their therapist, probation officer, family, school and significant others. Some elements of Multisystemic Therapy (MST) (Borduin, Schaeffer, & Heiblum, 2009) and the containment model (California Sex Offender Management Board, 2012) are very useful with this population given the multitude of systems within which adolescents operate and function.

Throughout the treatment process, the treatment provider coordinates with court services, parole/probation, social services, schools, outside clinicians, parents/guardians, etc., to enhance services to this population. The community "as a team" is a critical concept, and a philosophy which is embraced in similar treatment programs throughout the country (Center for Sex Offender Management, 2007). Treatment goals are based on individual needs consistent with the risk-needs-responsivity model common in treatment programs for adult sexual offenders (Andrews & Bonta, 2010). Specific treatment responses are applied to the identified needs.

This program is designed to address the needs of those youth assessed in the low to moderate risk range for sexual re-offense or with relatively minor sexual behavior problems. The majority of youth referred are males (close to 100%). The treatment program is open to treating females. The reality is the number of females referred for treatment is very low. There may be times when a youth assessed in the moderate to high risk for sexual re-offense is accepted into the program. This only occurs if the program has an ability to respond to that client's specific needs thereby mitigating re-offense risk. In addition, there are certain factors that will preclude a client from being accepted into the program. Clients who have a history of major mental illness and present with clinical signs of psychosis are not accepted. Clients who, by virtue of severe developmental impairment, would not be amenable to cognitive-behavioral treatment are not accepted. During the course of treatment, it is possible that ancillary mental health services would need to be utilized in response to the client's behavioral and emotional challenges. Clients who deny a history of sexual offending or sexual behavior problems, yet have been mandated to treatment, require a separate response that is developed specific to that type of situation (Levenson, 2011). In some cases, youth referred for treatment may have admitted to a sexual offense charge in court, yet upon intake for treatment categorically deny the offense. There are varied reasons that a youth might admit to a charge in court, then categorically deny once in treatment, i.e., their lawyer advised that admission to the charge would create the most favorable outcome; the youth may claim they admitted to the charge in court "just to get it over with". In this type of situation where categorical denial is evident at intake, it must be made clear to the client and supervising agency (probation/parole) that treatment completion is not contingent upon the client admitting to the charge in treatment. The treatment phases remain the same, though categorical denial will restrict the interventions to educational while limiting opportunity for process. The treatment approach can be modified if the client were to admit to all or parts of the allegations leading to the charge. If this agreement cannot be met, the categorical denier will not be accepted into the treatment program. Levels of denial or minimization are anticipated during treatment, which is different than categorical denial and can be addressed during the treatment phases, especially the accountability/responsibility phase.

THE TREATMENT PROGRAM

This program is a community-based, private practice outpatient program. Referral for treatment consideration may come from various sources, including courts, schools, family members, self-referral, law enforcement, and other clinicians. To be considered for treatment, however, a comprehensive assessment that is specific to the sexual behavior problem and/or sexual offense history is preferred prior to acceptance into the treatment program. If an assessment has not been completed prior to referral, the assessment can be provided within the program. Assessments provide the basis for identification of risk factors, and the appropriate treatment response specific to the needs of each client (Worling, 2012; Worling, & Langton, 2012).

The treatment program consists of three levels. Each level is designed to address the specific risk and needs of each youth on an individualized basis. Level one is a brief, psychoeducational program in response to youth assessed as low risk with limited needs. Level two is a comprehensive response to youth assessed with higher risk and greater needs. Level three responds to the needs of those youth transitioning to the community from intensive residential and/or correctional facilities and have demonstrated completion of sex offense specific treatment. The youth placed in level three are generally in need of continued monitoring as they work to apply previous treatment gains in their transition to the community.

The program operates from the general philosophy that "one size" does not fit all. Treatment frequency and intensity is in response to the specific needs identified for each client. To elaborate further, what follows is a brief description of the types of youth treated in each of our three levels.

Level One

This level is designed to address the needs of youth who, at assessment, present as low risk with relatively few treatment needs. Assessment tools that target static and dynamic risk factors, such as the Juvenile Sexual Offense Recidivism Assessment Tool-II (J-SORAT-II; Epperson, Ralston, Fowers, DeWitt, & Gore, 2006) and the Estimate of Risk for Adolescent Sexual Offense Recidivism (ERASOR; Worling & Curwen, 2001) when utilized with these adolescents identify factors that warrant a comprehensive treatment response. Static factors are those which do not change over time, such as the offender's age at the time an offense occurred, or the gender of the victim. Dynamic factors are changeable, such as emotions, family constellation, and use of drugs or alcohol. Dynamic factors become treatment targets. Typically, these youth do not present with deviant sexual interests, attitudes or behaviors and are often younger adolescents, though this level is not determined by age. Their sexual offense history is less extensive. Their psychosocial, family and environmental functioning is primarily stable and the environment does not support opportunities for re-offense. These factors are considered in the ERASOR. This treatment level is designed to be primarily psychoeducational and short term. The treatment format is individual and family therapy. Many of the adolescents deemed appropriate for this level are sexually naïve and have minimal awareness of consequences for self and others. More often than not, the motivation is to satisfy naturally developing interests in sexual behaviors, sexual body parts, and exploration of sexual feelings. They may lack full understanding of true consent in sexual situations and the referral behaviors are often situational and opportunistic as opposed to predatory and planned. The referral behaviors might have been determined to be problematic, and concerning, but did not result in a legal charge. In some cases, there is a legal charge and typically no formal adjudication. Most of these youth are placed on deferred adjudication status through the juvenile court system. Parents are typically involved in the process on a strategic basis, to promote healthy styles of communication regarding the subject matter addressed. The estimated number of treatment sessions required is based upon information obtained through the assessment and intake. Typically, this level of intervention can occur over an 8–12-month timeframe with treatment sessions occurring two to three times per month.

The following is a brief case example of an adolescent appropriate for this level of response.

A 13-year-old male was evaluated in response to a legal charge resulting from sexual behaviors against a 9-year-old female neighbor. He was assessed as low risk for sexual re-offense and placed on deferred adjudication by the juvenile court. The referral offense involved one instance of digital penetration of the victim's vagina and having her fondle his penis over his pants. The behaviors occurred in the context of play, as they were involved in a game of "truth or dare". In this game, which took place in the residence of the victim, the offender and victim were dared by her two brothers, ages 11 and 12, to go into a closet and "make out". The offender had no history of sexual experiences with others and no history of sexual victimization. On assessment, he presented with limited knowledge of adolescent sexual growth and development, and was functioning adequately at school and in family life. The motivation for the referral offense behavior was the need for peer acceptance and to satisfy sexual curiosity.

Level Two

This level of treatment is comprehensive and longer term, typically a minimum of one year with an average length of treatment being 18 months. Level two treatment addresses the needs of youth who (in most situations) have a sexual offense charge against them, and have been recommended for this level of intervention at assessment. Treatment sessions for these youth occur on a weekly basis early on as needs are assessed during the course of treatment. Frequency of sessions can be adjusted with positive evidence of adjustment to dynamic factors associated with offense behaviors. When utilized with these adolescents, assessment tools that target static and dynamic risk factors identify significant risk factors that warrant a comprehensive treatment response. These youth may present with deviant sexual interests, attitudes or behaviors supportive of sexual offending, and sexual preoccupation. Their sexual offense history is more extensive, in that they may have more victims, more instances of offending behaviors, and display more evidence of more sophisticated offense engagement strategies such as bribes, threats, manipulation, abuse of authority or relationship with the victim. They may lack positive peer associations, present with antisocial traits, and lack emotional management skills. There is evidence of instability in family and environmental functioning, as they may be experiencing parental rejection, and lack healthy attachments to family members. These factors are identified within the six assessment domains in the ERASOR (Worling & Curwen, 2001).

The following is a brief case example of an adolescent appropriate for this level of response.

A 15-year-old male was evaluated in response to a sexual offense charge. Prior to evaluation, he admitted to multiple instances of exposing his 5-year-old sister to adult pornography. Then, over a one-year time period, he engaged her in a range of sexual behaviors including the following: digital penetration; exposing his penis to her; having her masturbate him; and instructing her not to inform others of these sexual behaviors or they would both "get into trouble". No additional victims were identified. He was detained for one month after the offense was reported. Upon his release from detention, he was placed with relatives who did not have younger children in the home. He was formally adjudicated on the sexual offense charge and placed on probation. He was assessed as moderate risk for sexual re-offense. The youth had no history of consensual sexual experiences with others and no history of sexual victimization. On assessment, he displayed some knowledge of adolescent sexual development. Academically, he was functioning in the below-average range and his parents were separated when the offending behaviors began. The client was socially isolated and spent the majority of his free time pursuing solitary interests such as playing video games, computer games, and watching pornography on the Internet. Responses to depression scales indicated a moderate degree of depressed mood. There were multiple motives for the offending behaviors. He became reliant on sexual behaviors to manage negative moods, such as anxiety and depression. His persistent and repeated viewing of Internet pornography served as a superficial social outlet by which he could get some social and sexual needs met, albeit via fantasy. This pattern helped him avoid forming healthy attachments to his peers and pursuing positive social connections.

Level Three

This level is designed to respond to the treatment needs, and associated risk, for youth who have completed treatment in a residential facility, yet require a period of monitoring and assistance as they transition back into the community. These youth may have been assessed at higher risk levels upon admission to the residential placement. Their level of risk at acceptance to the level three program may vary and some high-risk youth might be appropriate for this program. Upon intake to the level three program, frequency of sessions is based on recommendations from previous providers. The vast majority of these youth who successfully completed residential treatment participate in a minimum of 6 months of therapy, attending sessions twice per month. If they have a specific period of probation or parole, treatment length will coincide with that timeframe, though frequency of sessions will still be based on identified need. As with youth in the level two program, frequency of sessions can be modified with evidence of adjustment to dynamic factors associated with offense behaviors or evidence of increased risk.

The following is a brief case example of an adolescent appropriate for this level of treatment response.

A 17-year-old male was released from a secure sex-offense specific residential treatment program after successful completion of that program over an 18-month period of time. He returned to his community but, because of opportunities for sexual re-offense if reunified with his family, he was placed in a community-based group home. Although the group home provided supervision, it lacked a therapy component. He was referred for follow-up services while he remained on parole. Prior to being committed to the residential program, he had had negative peer associations, had committed other delinquent acts aside from sexual offending, and engaged in impulsive behaviors that generally led to negative outcomes. He was abusing marijuana, and was diagnosed with attention deficit hyperactivity disorder (ADHD). He had previously offended against a younger brother and sister. Family dysfunction was evident, in that his mother had a history of substance abuse leading to legal charges, and his father was never involved in his life. The family moved frequently and had a history of involvement with social service agencies. The adolescent had been removed from parental care by a child protective service agency three times before the age of 12.

Because the treatment content provided is essentially the same across the levels, but the intensity varies by what the clients' needs are, should information become available during the treatment process that warrants a more comprehensive approach, the program has the flexibility to accommodate such shifts. The treatment modalities utilized are individual and family therapy. Although at the outset of this program 30 years ago sex offender specific groups were a major component of the treatment approach, several considerations led to eliminating the group modality over the past few years. As a community-based private practice outpatient program, the population of youth being treated at any given time would fluctuate frequently. There were times when it became necessary to run multiple groups simultaneously, and times when the population being treated could not support a group. The open-ended group process with a fluctuating population did not seem to address adequately each youth's individual needs. Although the practical reality of "numbers" was a consideration in eventually eliminating the group modality, as our training and experience progressed over the years, we began to see the value of emphasis on the individual and family. This approach allowed us to tailor treatment to the specific needs of each youth, allowed for greater treatment flexibility, and created a more positive alliance between the therapist and the clients. Not restricting youth to a "locked in" time for group therapy created more flexibility for each youth and his family. The benefit of not having a set group time seemed greatest for those youth who were pursuing prosocial activities and interests, such as participating on sports teams, or who were active in clubs or other school-sponsored activities. Promoting opportunities for healthy peer interactions can help youth develop prosocial skills and positive relationships. These are skills that can last a lifetime. Eliminating group therapy enhanced specificity to the individual client, strengthened protection of privacy, intensified family commitment, and avoided the potential harm that can come from putting youth together in groups. Grouping delinquent youth together for treatment carries the risk of harmful side effects, such as making less delinquent youth even more delinquent (Letourneau & Borduin, 2008). This is not to say that group therapy does not provide value to youth. Because this program addresses the needs of low- to moderate-risk youth, it was determined that referral to programs providing a group-based format specific to that client's need could be considered as a viable option and adjunct to the sex offense specific programming. For example, if a youth evidenced extremely poor social skills, they could be referred to a general social skills group or to additional services available through the juvenile probation department, such as job training. These types of groups tend to be structured, and time-limited so that the client can participate during periods in which there is less likelihood of disrupting their pursuit of other age-appropriate activities.

THE TREATMENT PROCESS

Information garnered from the initial assessment is utilized to make a decision about the placement level within the program and from there, treatment commences. The first phase of the treatment process is the introductory phase which typically consists of approximately five sessions. Each youth begins this treatment phase in family therapy starting with an overview of the program specific to the level of treatment assigned. In instances where immediate family is not available to participate in treatment, other members of the youth's social system are integrated into this role, thereby utilizing the community as extended family. The format for these early sessions is family-based to encourage family investment and to set the stage for family participation throughout the course of treatment. At intake, each family is provided with a written description of the program that discusses the specific level of treatment, and program philosophy. Any necessary paperwork is provided and forms are completed, including the following: informed consent (see Appendix A); signed releases to allow for communication between the treatment provider and other identified members of the team (e.g., probation officer, judge, school counselor, etc.); information about confidentiality; and the treatment contract (see Appendix B). The family participates in the development of the treatment plan that specifies the primary challenges/problems, establishes goals in response to the problem, and delineates steps to attain goals (see Appendix C). A useful tool for identifying specific treatment needs is the Youth Level of Service/Case Management Inventory (Hoge & Andrews, 2006). In the event this tool was not administered at the time of the assessment of sexual re-offense risk, it can be administered at intake into the program.

An important part of this early process is to create an alliance between the treatment provider and the family with the overall goal of addressing the sexual behavior problem from a "team" approach. Communicating this concept to the family helps to enhance the family's commitment, builds motivation for the youth and the family to participate in treatment, and avoids polarization between the therapist and the clients. The treatment approach is discussed as a "shared" responsibility while delineating expectations and responsibilities for all the participants. Outcome measures are described as well, so that the youth and family are aware that there are concrete benchmarks throughout the treatment process that will inform stakeholders about treatment progress. General outcome measures include the following: attendance and participation in therapy; demonstration of competency based on the client's response to tests through each phase of treatment; completion of treatment tasks; compliance with probation/parole; evidence of stability in the community; positive school grades/attendance; evidence of prosocial connections; no further arrests for sexual and non-sexual offenses; and parent feedback.

Once the treatment plan has been created, each client is introduced to the program monitoring tool. This tool is utilized to enhance therapist accountability while simultaneously encouraging the client to track their progress. This tracking process creates an ongoing and readily accessible record for the client to share information about treatment progress with their family and those designated to receive information about their treatment. Such individuals may include a probation officer, social worker, and judge. The program monitoring tool is organized in a three ring binder, which has five divided sections. These sections are ongoing work, education about, and normalization of, adolescent sexual interests and behaviors, accountability/responsibility, empathy training, and healthy living/positive self-regulation (see Appendix D). These divided sections are designed to store completed and ongoing work and materials designed for each specific phase. The "ongoing" divider is used to store the client's treatment log, positive experience log, motivational worksheet, and reminder cards to enhance motivation and help the youth remain committed to the process. There are pockets in the front and back of the binder. The front pockets are used to store treatment assignments the client is currently working on or needs to review in therapy, and the back pockets are used to store extra material. An additional benefit of this tool is that it requires use of organizational techniques that the youth can apply to other settings, such as school and work.

Prior to beginning the core treatment phases, each client is provided with brief statements related to the concepts of healthy living and responsibility (see Appendix D). The client is asked to respond in writing to the following: "What are the primary reasons you are in treatment? What goals do you have as far as your treatment goes, and for the immediate future? Provide a brief summary of your family and background. Identify your top five strengths. Identify what your biggest challenges are that could get in the way of your being successful in treatment".

The rationale for providing the foregoing material is to encourage adolescent clients to develop healthy values and morals as they transition to young adult life. Teaching youth to conceptualize values and morals consistent with a healthy life early in the treatment process creates a positive and optimistic approach in response to the sexual behavior problem, and the difficult challenge of taking responsibility for the referral behaviors. During the introduction to treatment phase, each client develops a list of benefits of working hard and staying dedicated to the treatment process. This is kept in the "ongoing" section of the binder. In addition, each client is presented with a log to track positive experiences in all areas of his life, to be reviewed at the start of each treatment session (see Appendix D). This approach is aimed at promoting awareness of "when they get it right" as they work to create healthy approaches to managing their lives. A treatment log is provided in which the client tracks the content of each session, his reaction to the session, and treatment tasks assigned (see Appendix D). This log assists the client in summarizing treatment content with family and probation officers or others involved in supervising them and is kept in the "ongoing" section of the binder. Every 2 months, each client is asked to create a summary of treatment and life experiences which is combined with the therapist's report to the probation officer. Maintaining this treatment log helps in developing this report. Different from the 2-month summary report to the probation officer are two additional forms that are introduced early in treatment: a parent/guardian feedback form and a client "between session" summary report (see Appendix E). Parents and/or guardians and the client are asked to complete these forms from session to session. The primary purpose of these reports is to enhance awareness of positive experiences, life challenges and responses to those challenges, to enhance a goal-oriented approach and strengthen communication among the team. In this introduction to treatment phase, the youth and his family are introduced to the concept of lapse reporting and management (see Appendix F). The youth is provided with a form to track all lapses, regardless of severity, which is kept in the "ongoing" section of the treatment binder. Although lapse reporting is consistent with a prevention model, it also serves to promote awareness through accountability which honors the participant's commitment to moving toward a healthy life. Finally, in concluding the introduction to treatment, for some youth, an early safety plan is developed in keeping with relapse prevention concepts (see Appendix F). This plan is designed to create awareness early in treatment of situations, behaviors, beliefs and emotions that could generate increased risk for a range of negative outcomes, including sexual behavior problems and offending. In this plan, participants develop simple strategies for responding to risk factors, along with options for promoting healthy living on a consistent and regular basis. In completing the plan, each client is asked to identify people they believe to be responsible and capable of providing positive interventions for them.

Having completed the introduction to the treatment process, individual and family therapy is scheduled based on identified risk and need. To address the treatment goals, the treatment program provides four distinct phases regardless of the placement level. The phases are as follows: education about, and normalization of, adolescent sexuality; accountability and responsibility; empathy building; and healthy living/positive self-regulation, and are presented in all three program levels in varying degrees. These phases are sequentially based. The approach is process-oriented and didactic while utilizing a range of educational/support materials. The amount of time spent on each phase with an individual client is determined by need, as identified at intake. This approach allows for an individualized approach, not available in a group therapy format. Each client must demonstrate a degree of competency regarding the information addressed, which is assessed by responding to questions targeting the material covered. They must also be able to openly process with their parents the material covered. Though sequentially based, the phase concept allows for some overlap regarding content and materials provided. An individual may have progressed through a specific phase, yet some of the concepts addressed continue into the next phase as they work to apply awareness to "pull it all together". Any areas of weakness are addressed at test-taking time, and will be revisited until competency is demonstrated to the therapist's satisfaction. A brief summary of each phase is described below.

Education and Normalization of Adolescent Sexual Interests and Behaviors

The goal of this phase is to promote open communication about sexual growth and development while enhancing the client's ability to make positive and informed decisions regarding sexual interests and behaviors to prevent recurrence of further sexual offenses or problematic sexual behaviors. This phase is especially useful with adolescents who present as sexually naïve, and whose offenses were motivated by sexual curiosity and opportunity. The content addressed in this phase emphasizes the following: identification of normal, healthy adolescent sexual interests/behaviors; problematic, dangerous, risky and illegal sexual behaviors (including issues with use of social networking via the Internet); consent in sexual relationships; consequences for violating social rules/laws pertaining to management of sexual interests and behaviors; potential problems associated with persistent and repeated use of pornography; and factors associated with responsible decision making in sexual and non-sexual relationships (see Appendix G).

Accountability/Responsibility

The goal of this phase is to promote assumption of responsibility for the referral sexual behavior problem by being accountable. Accountability occurs through close examination of motivational/dynamic factors associated with the decision to engage in the referral behaviors. This is achieved by providing a simple introduction to the core principles of cognitive-behavioral therapy (CBT), with an emphasis on the relationship between thoughts, feelings and behaviors. This concept is also introduced as a life skill for assuming responsibility as the client works to develop skills to respond effectively to various life challenges. Once the general idea of CBT, or as taught to the client "how to connect the dots" (see Appendix H) is understood, the concept is broken down more specifically, allowing for the introduction of more traditional sex-offense specific treatment concepts. These concepts include "thinking errors", the problem of immediate gratification, and recognition of emotions. Essentially, this involves teaching young people how to develop responsible ways to think about their lives and challenges. The "no blame frame" is introduced as the pivotal point in assuming responsibility for what each participant thinks, feels, and does. The connection between cognitive distortions and immediately gratifying behaviors that lead to negative outcomes is presented via story-telling and vignettes with examples of when and how people blame, contrasted with examples of assumption of responsibility. These concepts are initially presented in situations that are non-sexual and can be applied to other experiences in the client's life. The youth in treatment are taught in simple terms what a thinking error is and its association to the problem of immediate gratification (see Appendix I). These are terms that have been omnipresent in the history of relapse prevention-based interventions for over 30 years. Clients are then taught to apply this skill to understanding sexual situations, followed by specific application to the referral behaviors. In order to assume responsibility for the referral behaviors, it is critical that participants spend some time examining other dynamics and challenges in their lives prior to, and at the time of, the behaviors. This examination creates opportunity to apply the newly developed skills regarding assumption of responsibility to those challenges, and supports the "no blame frame". This effort is followed by a comprehensive examination and disclosure of the referral behaviors and/or other problematic and illegal sexual behaviors in their history. The accountability and responsibility process is completed when the client can recognize the primary motivating factors for the sexual offense(s) and identify and confront thinking errors that supported the behavior. The client then must communicate this path to his family.

Empathy Training

The goal of this phase is to introduce the concept of empathy as a critical relationship skill, and barrier to behaviors that violate the rights of others. Empathy is defined, supported by process-based discussions regarding development of empathy, its usefulness on the path to healthy living, and its application to the referral offense. Clients are taught how to utilize the skill in daily life, which is supported by maintaining a restitution log that emphasizes giving back to others. The impact of violating others' rights is processed from a general perspective, then with application to victims of sexual abuse and then specifically to their sexual offense history. Empathy is distinguished from sympathy, shame, remorse, and guilt. Once the youth has a grasp of this concept, he moves to a clarification process as he assumes responsibility for his offending behaviors by being accountable to those he has harmed. This process is identified as a significant step in the path to healthy living. Each youth is evaluated at the end of this phase to assess competency regarding materials addressed.

Healthy Living/Positive Self-Regulation

The goal of this phase is to incorporate many of the core concepts addressed in the three previous phases while adding additional skills as the client prepares for treatment completion. Awareness, assumption of responsibility, and demonstration of responsible behaviors and connections are all components of this phase. The path to healthy living discussed at intake is revisited, along with the concept of responsibility, while also creating an internal compass. The internal compass consists of three character traits that, when honored, help maintain the path to a good and healthy life. These traits are empathy, honesty, and self-discipline. Three general risk factors to healthy living are revisited (i.e., emotional dysregulation, immediate gratification, and early exposures/experiences). The client identifies his specific risk factors, as the safety plan is revisited, with emphasis on skills, techniques and strategies for responding effectively. When needed, special instruction is provided on problem solving, anger management and assertiveness techniques. The prevailing theme of "assumption of responsibility" is reiterated throughout this phase. Clients are provided with simple reminder cards that specify the various skills and techniques addressed during the course of treatment. Their relationships and connections are reviewed as they are encouraged to provide evidence of positive and prosocial interests (e.g., school, social relationships, family relationships, and extra-curricular activities). These pursuits are recorded on the positive experience log maintained throughout the course of treatment. This log is highlighted in the last phase of treatment as the client is encouraged to "make his case" for release from treatment and probation. A final safety plan is developed, with adjustments based on any changes in dynamic risk factors. The client is evaluated for competency at the end of this phase regarding the information addressed. He is also asked to identify the most difficult, most useful, and least useful aspects of treatment. Each participant is also asked to provide recommendations for change to the treatment approach.

After Care/Follow Up

Progression through treatment is based on multiple factors, including: attendance; participation; demonstrating competency regarding the materials addressed; completion of treatment assignments/materials; completion of treatment phases; positive reports from school, family members, and the youth's probation/parole officer; evidence of day-to-day responsible behaviors; and no recurrence of sexual deviance or sexual and non-sexual offense behaviors. Upon completion of the comprehensive program, a follow-up period is provided. This typically covers a 3- to 6-month period. The modality remains consistent – individual and family therapy. This follow-up period is provided to monitor progress and provide ongoing support to program graduates with reduced intensity regarding treatment frequency. Upon completion of the follow-up period, a report is sent to the court or agency involved in monitoring the case, indicating that the client has completed the treatment program.

SUMMARY AND CONCLUSIONS

Although the foundation for the program described here is cognitive-behavioral therapy, aspects of other theoretical approaches are integrated, leading to a "holistic" treatment approach (Hall, 2011). The overall treatment interventions are designed to educate, promote responsibility, and develop skills for healthy living beyond responding to the referral offense. Cognitive behavioral interventions have been demonstrated to be an effective approach to addressing sexual offending behaviors in adolescents (Bankes, 2011; Worling, Josefowitz, & Maltar, 2011). The strategies described here are found in various programs addressing the problem of juvenile sexual offending. Readers should note that some of the components we have incorporated into our treatment program are emerging and have less empirical support than strict CBT approaches.

The primary strength of the approach described here is that the foundation is based in the principles of CBT while incorporating evolving approaches in treating youth with sexual behavior problems. For instance, multisystemic therapy (MST) has been established as an evidenced-based intervention for juvenile delinquency. One could postulate that application of that model would be a sensible approach to addressing juvenile sexual offending. Additional strengths of this approach include: creation of a fluid balance between traditional relapse prevention approaches and promotion of prosocial skill development for healthy living; it provides flexibility and is tailored to the specific needs of each individual; it promotes responsibility for one's problematic sexual behaviors; it invites youth and their families to consider core values consistent with a healthy life; and it encourages a "team" approach in response to the problem, thereby preventing polarization with youth and their families.

A critical component of the team approach is the coordination between local juvenile probation departments, the juvenile justice system, and treatment providers. This "systemic" response to youth who offend sexually serves to promote consistency and continuity which encourages responsibility through accountability for youth and their families. With an organized and accountable response to the problem, the treatment provider is in a better position to educate and inform the components of the team regarding the client's response to treatment and specific needs of the individual and family. This individualized approach also assists the juvenile justice system in developing responses specific to each individual, especially regarding levels of supervision. The assessment process occurring at the onset of treatment incorporates the R-N-R model. This model works to identify those youth who have greater risk-needs, and would therefore require higher levels of supervision in the community, while also identifying those youth with lower risk and fewer needs. Ongoing consultation with agencies responsible for supervising these youth allows for adjustments to levels of supervision along the way. This systemic response is akin to some components of the traditional "containment" model more commonly utilized in developing case management strategies for adults who have committed sexual offenses.

As with most treatment models, this approach has its limitations. There are challenges associated with conducting outcome studies. Providers are interested in determining not only if treatment prevents sexual re-offense, but if it promotes productive and responsible living. Most jurisdictions lack an organized system for tracking youth over extended periods to assess for sexual offense and non-sexual offense recidivism. It is even more difficult to track adjustments to prevailing dynamic factors associated with youth who offend sexually. The latter is especially important when a youth is determined to have re-offended sexually. In our community (i.e., City, State), the local juvenile probation department is attempting to gain approval to begin follow-up studies on such youth that would allow access to criminal databases. In addition, this treatment model may not be suitable in response to the needs of high-risk youth, or with youth who have significant cognitive limitations, or serious mental health problems. Other limitations might include treatment costs, transportation, and cultural and language barriers. In such a team approach, one dysfunctional faction could negatively impact treatment effectiveness. For example, a family could undermine the process by minimizing the youth's responsibility, or ostracizing the youth. That being said, the latter are typical challenges for any program responding to youth who sexually offend.

In response to research and new developments in the field, our treatment program has changed significantly over the last 30 years from a traditional relapse prevention-based model to a holistic approach and continues to evolve as we face new challenges in providing therapy for these youth. Fortunately, for practitioners new to this field, educational and training resources are abundant and research continues (see Appendix J). As therapists who treat adolescents who have committed sexual offenses, we are mindful of both the obligation to provide evidenced-based treatment to our clients as well as to consider community safety needs. The program strives for a balance between promoting a healthy life and reducing risk. Shouldering this dual challenge can be difficult. We strongly recommend that providers seek the support of professional organizations that provide various training opportunities and resources, such as The Association for The Treatment of Sexual Abusers (ATSA, 2011). ATSA also has many state chapters, and regions across the country have formed associations and organizations designed to address specifically the problem of juvenile sexual offending. The California Coalition on Sexual Offending is an example of one such organization. Accessing websites that provide information about various state sexual offender management boards can also provide critical information about standards of care and ethical considerations. Attending conferences, consulting with other professionals, and following list-serves can help the provider have a sense of the current professional developments regarding new treatment challenges. In the absence of definitive research results, remaining open and receptive to new developments keeps the provider accountable and can reinvigorate us as we learn more effective ways to address this serious public safety problem.

APPENDIX A

INFORMED CONSENT FORM

This form is intended to explain some of the risks and benefits to you in participating in assessment and/or treatment specific to sexual behavior problems. As part of the assessment process, consideration is given to the risk that your behavior presents to the community. You also understand that if you are Court ordered to participate in this assessment/treatment, your participation or non-participation will be reported to the Court. If you are referred by another social service agency, i.e., juvenile probation, parole/probation, social services, school district, etc., your participation and progress during assessment and/or treatment will be reported to the agency you have designated via the release of information form. You understand that you will be asked questions regarding your history, and particularly about your sexual behavior. You will also be asked to fill out questionnaires, computer generated and paper and pencil tests that explore your general emotional state as well as your sexual behavior. If you are under age 18, a parent or guardian will also participate in the assessment and/or treatment process.

Some of the benefits of an assessment for you include: identification of treatment needs and level of response specific to those needs. The assessment may also be the first step in addressing the problem, and can create a sense of relief, direction and hope. A major benefit of treatment is that it may help prevent you from further sexual behavior problems which can harm others and yourself. By learning skills to prevent further sexual behavior problems you could develop insights and skills that can lead to additional behavioral changes that contribute to a healthy and productive life. The results of the assessment and recommendations will be communicated to you and designated third parties and your parent(s) or guardians. Any information that is given in the course of the assessment and/or treatment will be recorded in your official record maintained by your therapist. The information will be kept completely confidential in accordance with applicable laws and regulations. This means that information regarding your assessment and/or treatment will not be given to anyone without your written consent, except under the following conditions:

1) If a court orders your records and/or orders your therapist to provide information about you.
2) If you express intent to harm yourself or others.
3) If you reveal a previously unreported case of child/elder abuse.

You are encouraged to be honest in responding to your therapist's questions during the assessment and/or treatment process. For your own protection, you may decide to withhold information regarding any history of past behaviors that could result in additional legal charges or negative consequences for you. You can also decide to provide this information but eliminate details, i.e., names, relationships, places of occurrence. In doing so you would be able to benefit from treatment specific to those behaviors.

There are potential risks involved in the assessment and/or treatment process. Some of the risks include: increased feelings of anxiety, fear, guilt, embarrassment, shame, a sense of hopelessness; restrictions from certain activities or places; interruption in current placement or living situation; and referral for placement in a more restrictive setting.

Treatment encourages you to assume responsibility for your sexual behavior problem by developing a clear understanding of thoughts, feelings and actions that contributed to your decision to engage in the behavior that brought you to treatment. Treatment generally includes phases specifically designed to address sexual behavior problems while promoting skills for healthy living. Although there are core components covered in treatment, the treatment plan will be individualized and specific to your needs. (Please read program description handout.)

You acknowledge that any questions you had regarding the assessment and/or treatment process have been answered to your satisfaction. You realize that you can ask additional questions during the course of your participation in the assessment and/or treatment. You understand that your participation is voluntary and that you may withdraw at any time. You also understand that if your participation is mandated by the court and/or other agency, your withdrawal from the assessment process or treatment or lack of satisfactory participation, may have an effect on your standing with that particular agency.

Your signature below means that you (and your parent(s)/guardian(s) if applicable), understand this assessment and treatment consent form and agree to it. (If the client is under 18, parent/guardian signature is required.)

Client Signature _______________	Date _______
Parent/Guardian Signature _______________	Date _______
Parent/Guardian Signature _______________	Date _______
Therapist Signature _______________	Date _______

APPENDIX B

TREATMENT CONTRACT

Depending on the level of treatment you have been assigned, you will participate in treatment components that may include individual, group, family therapy and follow up. The length of treatment depends on the individual. Please read and sign the treatment contract below. Make sure any questions you have regarding your treatment contract have been asked and answered.

Treatment Contract

I, _________________, hereby enter into the following agreement with ____________________________________, as a condition of acceptance into the program. I understand and agree to the following conditions:

1. I agree to be honest and assume full responsibility for my offenses and my behavior.
2. To notify my therapist in advance (24 hours) if I must miss a session. There must be strong rationale for missing any scheduled appointments. All missed appointments will be reported to my probation/parole officer.
3. To pay my assigned fee at the time of each session, or in advance unless other arrangements have been made.
4. Not to come to any session under the influence of alcohol/drugs.
5. Not to engage in verbally or physically assaultive behaviors, in treatment or in the community.

6. To make my best efforts to cooperate in the treatment process.
7. To complete all treatment related tasks, homework and assignments.
8. Not to commit any crimes.
9. Not to involve myself in any activity/situation in which I may be creating greater risk for re-offense or where I have access to the person(s) I have sexually victimized (unless approved by those in position to do so).
10. Not to disclose the identity of other participants in treatment.
11. To abide by all treatment rules.
12. To share with my treatment provider any contact I may have with a treatment participant outside of therapy.
13. I will abide by my terms of probation.
14. Consent to release of information about my treatment to my parole/probation officer.
15. Develop a treatment plan specific to my risk and needs.
16. Sign waivers of confidentiality/release of information to allow for open communication with other professionals responsible for my supervision.
17. I have the right to refuse treatment and not sign confidentiality waivers while acknowledging certain consequences may be imposed, i.e., arrest, violation of parole/probation.
18. Additional Terms:
    I understand that my probation/parole officer and/or social worker, parent or guardian (if client is a minor child) will be notified of any violation of this contract. I also understand that local law enforcement may be contacted if necessary to maintain victim or community safety. I understand and agree that any violation of the conditions of this contract may be grounds for termination from treatment. I agree that my treatment provider may terminate my treatment for any other problem behavior that may be disruptive to other participants.

______________________________	____________
Client	Date
______________________________	____________
Parent(s)/Guardian(s)	Date
______________________________	____________
Therapist	Date

APPENDIX C

TREATMENT PLAN

Date: ______________ Client: ____________________________

DOB/Age: _________ Sex/Ethnicity: _____________________

Therapist: ____

1. Presenting Problem(s) in Narrative Form
2. Brief Mental Status Checklist

   Appearance: ____

   ____

   Behavioral observations: ____________________________

   ____

   Affect/Mood: _______________________________________

   ____

   Orientation: ____

   ____

   Cognition: ____

   ____

   Thought Content: ____________________________________

   ____

3. Preliminary Diagnosis: DSM-IV

   Axis I ___________________________

   Axis II ___________________________

   Axis III ___________________________

   Axis IV ___________________________

   Axis V ___________________________

   Additional information/comments:

Problem List/Life Challenges:	Date Established	Dates Reviewed
Treatment Goals: (correspond to problem list)	Date Established	Dates Reviewed

Objectives for each goal (identify specific modalities, interventions and therapeutic approaches to be utilized with estimated frequency of treatment/anticipated length of treatment).

Identify specific outcome measures to be utilized during the course of treatment or as pre- and post-test measures.

Identify referrals made for additional services, i.e.; psychiatric consult, psychological testing, medications,etc.

______________________	______________________
TREATMENT PROVIDER	DATE
______________________	______________________
CLIENT	DATE
______________________	______________________
PARENT/GUARDIAN DATE	PARENT/GUARDIAN DATE

APPENDIX D

PROGRAM MONITORING TOOL

FRONT POCKET:

INTRODUCTION PACKET:

Program Description

Program Philosophy

ONGOING WORK:

Statement of Healthy Living: having a healthy life involves making and honoring a commitment to managing my life in positive, creative, and productive ways that promotes my personal pursuit of happiness. While managing my life in positive, creative and productive ways, I respect the rights of others and honor my community by being a valuable contributor. This path leads to growth in all areas of my life, including health, relationships, spirituality, education, and employment. It is based in longer, more lasting rewards. Though I may experience pleasure in my pursuit of happiness, this approach is not pleasure based.

Statement of Responsibility: The road to healthy living starts with: Assuming responsibility while creating Response Abilities. Keep it simple. I am responsible for everything I think, feel and do…it is like magic! Magic acts are straightforward techniques. Giving up blame and committing yourself to be responsible for how you respond to various life challenges is a very straightforward technique that can be mastered through increased awareness and practice. Picture yourself in the "no blame frame". This doesn't mean bad things won't happen…it means you are responsible for your response. This belief can generate healthy power in your life because it places you in charge.

Creating Motivation Worksheet: How will I benefit from working hard, and doing my treatment?

My weekly log of positive and productive experiences that give evidence I am taking good care of myself.

Treatment log: summarize therapy session, feelings about session and track assignments (whether completed and when).

Parent/guardian feedback form

Client between session summary report

Lapse reporting form

Safety Plan: start of treatment

TAB 1 Education and Normalization

TAB 2 Accountability/Responsibility

TAB 3 Empathy Training

TAB 4 Healthy living/Positive self-regulation

TAB 5 After care/follow up

BACK POCKET:

Work to be reviewed

Completed work

Example of ongoing treatment log summaries:

My Weekly Log of Positive and Productive Experiences That Give Evidence I am Taking Good Care of Myself

Date	Evidence of Taking Good Care of Myself

Treatment Log

Date	Brief Summary of Meeting	Your Thoughts About the Meeting	Assignment	Done?

APPENDIX E

FEEDBACK FORM

This form is designed to coordinate efforts between treatment providers and guardians/parents of youth in treatment. Each section is to be completed by a guardian/parent prior to each therapy appointment. The youth will be required to turn in the completed form at each session. Thank you for your cooperation.

Name of Youth:

Name of Parent/Guardian completing form:

Time period: ___/___/___ To ___/___/___

Please Comment on the Following Areas

Strengths of Youth Observed:

Special Concerns:

Noteworthy Changes:

Special Comments:

Client Between Session Summary Report

This form will help you prepare for your meetings with your Probation officer and therapist. Please complete before you attend those meetings.

What have my accomplishments and successes been since the last meeting? i.e., attended all my classes, did my school work on time, helped my mother bring in groceries, exercised.

What specific challenges/problems did I have, and what attempts did I make to respond to those challenges in a positive and productive way?

How did my responses to my life challenges work out for me? Did I recognize any risk factors to healthy living, including thinking errors, negative emotions, negative behaviors, or negative situations?

What plans do I have for staying on the path to a healthy life over the upcoming week(s)?

APPENDIX F

LAPSE REPORTING FORM

Reminder: *A lapse is any thought, feeling, behavior or situation that can move you off the path to healthy living, and put you at risk to engage in behaviors that are problematic, risky, dangerous or even illegal and violate the rights of others.*

Please describe specifically what happened using the definition of a lapse from above.

What makes this a lapse for you?

How far did the lapse progress on a 1–10 scale, with 10 being the most serious?

What interventions, if any, did you use to interrupt the present lapse?

What was motivating (your reasons) the lapse and what were your thoughts that kept the lapse going?

What were your emotions/feelings before, during and after the lapse?

What kept you from using interventions if you did not use them?

What interventions do you think would work to keep this lapse from progressing in the future?

What consequences might this lapse have for you and others?

How do you feel about reporting this lapse?

Safety Plan: Start of Treatment

This contract is designed to help me maintain and promote healthy approaches to managing my life, thereby preventing behaviors that are problematic and risky, dangerous or even illegal and violate the rights of others. It is my responsibility to identify the situations, thoughts, feelings, and behaviors that indicate I am at higher risk for problematic, risky, dangerous or even illegal behaviors, and to move myself in a healthy direction.

High-Risk Factors

Situations/behaviors to pay attention to

Feelings that indicate I am not doing well, and might need some help

Negative ways of thinking that maintain unhealthy behaviors

Quick Interventions

If I am involved in any of the above-mentioned risk factors, these are some things I can do to redirect immediately my behavior to avoid acting out in risky, dangerous, or illegal ways.

Healthy Living and Positive Life Promotion

The following are ideas, behaviors, situations, interests, etc., that I could involve myself in that help me feel good about myself, and promote my life in positive ways.

Below are the names of people who are aware of my commitment to healthy living, and I can count on for help along the way.

APPENDIX G

RULES TO FOLLOW TO HAVE TRUE CONSENT IN A SEXUAL RELATIONSHIP

1. Each person involved must be of legal age. Know the law for your state. When in doubt, check it out!
2. Each person involved is old enough, aware enough, and responsible enough to make a good decision about the behaviors being proposed.
3. The behaviors are occurring based on mutual agreement and understanding without force, threats, bribes, or other types of manipulation. In other words, trying to make someone do something they don't want to do does not follow true consent.
4. The sexual behaviors are occurring without someone being impaired by substances, especially when it could influence their decision making.
5. Hopefully, the behaviors are occurring with someone you know well based on the "rules for engagement", and there is a level of caring, respect and healthy communication between the people involved.

Rules for Engagement

1. Do I know the person's age? How did I confirm that? e.g., check ID; ask other people.
   Reminder: people are not always honest about their age, and can have fake IDs.
2. Have I met friends associated with the person I am interested in?
   Reminder: meeting friends only is not enough information.
3. Have I met their family, especially parents? I have provided information to the parents, so they know my age, and they are informed about what she told me about her age.
   Reminder: Don't be shy about giving information about yourself, and asking questions about the other person.
4. What information do I have about the person I am interested in beyond name, age, parents? Do I know where they work, go to school, who they spend time with?
   Reminder: the pace is slow, gather information on the way.
5. How does this person like to spend any free time they might have?
   Reminder: don't be afraid to ask questions, like what are your interests, what do you do for fun, what are your favorite events and things to do?

Write down any other points to consider that would help you make good decisions when it comes to relationships.

APPENDIX H

LEARNING TO CONNECT THE DOTS

Life is full of events, situations, or experiences that challenge or invite us to respond. Some of those events, situations and experiences are out of our control, like the weather, or how others might treat us. What is always within our control is our response to those events, situations, and experiences. The trick to healthy living is committing yourself to taking responsibility for your response, which means everything you think, feel and do. This is called the "no blame frame". Unfortunately, sometimes we want to place responsibility for what happens on the event, situation or life challenge. If we spend more time examining our thinking, and connect our thoughts to our feelings we will be in a better position to respond to events, situations and challenges in ways that keep us on the path to a healthy life.

The triangle below helps to visualize how this pattern can develop. **B** is the most critical point in the triangle because what we think about an event, situation, or challenge greatly influences how we feel in response to the event, situation or challenge. What we think and feel often motivates our behavioral responses, or what we do in response to **A. It is important to remember, emotions are not right or wrong…it is how we respond that matters!**

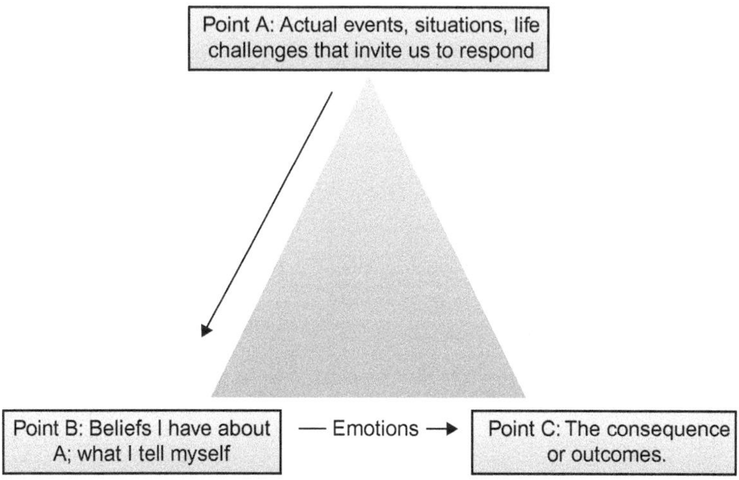

APPENDIX I

THINKING ERRORS

A thinking error is a twisted, or distorted belief that takes away from the truth, and most often allows someone to engage in a behavior that is pleasure based, irresponsible, harmful to self or others, possibly illegal, and violates others rights.

Thinking errors help someone avoid responsibility, defeat themselves, or promote self-centered actions. These types of thoughts help us stray from the path to healthy living, and get in the way of empathy.

The Problem of Immediate Gratification

Affectionately known as:

The Pig

The problem of immediate gratification is about wanting satisfaction right away, and not waiting for longer, more lasting and greater rewards.

Wanting immediately to gratify, or satisfy ourselves, to feel good, or gain relief from certain experiences, situations, challenges, events and negative emotions is a normal human response.

There are certain forms of immediate gratification that are not a problem. For instance, you just ran six miles and after you immediately grab a bottle of water and drink it. You feel your thirst being satisfied. Drinking the water immediately feels good to your body and gives you a sense of relief. This is a healthy form of immediate gratification. It is important to learn the difference between types of immediate gratification that are healthy and harmless, and those types that can be risky and dangerous.

A simple test: when confused about whether the type of gratification you seek is healthy or not, be willing to ask yourself this basic question: "Is what I am about to do helping me stay on the path to a good and healthy life?"

APPENDIX J

RESOURCES

The Association for The Treatment of Sexual Abusers: http://www.ATSA.com
NEARI Press: http://Nearipress.org
National Center on Sexual Behavior of Youth: http://NCSBY.org
National Adolescent Perpetration Network: http://www.Kempe.org
Safer Society Press: http://www.safersociety.org
Center for Sex Offender Management: http://CSOM.org
California Coalition on Sexual Offending: http://www.ccoso.org
Office of Juvenile Justice and Delinquency Prevention: http://www.ojjdp.gov
Stop It Now!: http://www.stopitnow.org

REFERENCES

Andrews, D. A., & Bonta, J. (2010). *The psychology of criminal conduct* (5th ed.). New Providence, NJ: Anderson Publishing.

Association for the Treatment of Sexual Abusers. (2011). ATSA. Retrieved from <http://www.atsa.com>.

Bankes, N. (2011). *A brief CBT programme for low risk adolescent sex offenders. Contemporary practice with young people who sexually abuse evidence-based developments*. Holyoke, MA: NEARI Press.

Borduin, C., Schaeffer, C., & Heiblum, N. (2009). A randomized clinical trial of multisystemic therapy with juvenile sexual offenders: effects on youth social ecology and criminal activity. *Journal of Consulting and Clinical Psychology*, 77, 26–37.

California Sex Offender Management Board. (2012). *Certification standards*. Retrieved from <http://www.casomb.org/certification.htm>.

Center for Sex Offender Management. (2007). *The comprehensive assessment protocol: A system-wide review of adult and juvenile sex offender management strategies*. Retrieved from <http://cepp.com/documents/Comprehensive-Assessment-Protocol.pdf>.

Daly, R. (2008). *Treatment and reentry practices for sex offenders: An overview of states*. New York: Vera Institute of Justice. <http://www.ovsom.texas.gov/docs/Reentry-and-Treatment-Practices-for-Sex-Offenders.pdf>.

Epperson, D. L., Ralston, C. A., Fowers, D., DeWitt, J., & Gore, K. S. (2006). Actuarial risk assessment with juveniles who sexually offend: Development of the Juvenile Sexual Offense Recidivism Risk Assessment Tool-II (JSORRAT-II). In D. S. Prescott (Ed.),

Risk assessment of youth who have sexually abused (pp. 118–169). Oklahoma City: Wood N' Barnes.

Hall, S. (2011). *Evidence for working holistically with young people who have sexually harmed. Contemporary practice with young people who sexually abuse: Evidence-based developments.* Holyoke: NEARI Press.

Hanson, K. R. (1996). Evaluating the contribution of relapse prevention theory to the treatment of sexual offenders. *Sexual Abuse: A Journal of Research and Treatment, 8*, 3.

Hoge, R. D., & Andrews, D. A. (2006). *YLS/CMI: Youth level of service/case management inventory*. Multi-Health Systems, Inc.

Letourneau, E. J., & Borduin, C. M. (2008). The effective treatment of juveniles who sexually offend. *Ethics and Behaviors, 18*, 286–306.

Levenson, J. S. (2011). "But I didn't do it": Ethical treatment of sex offenders in denial. *Sexual Abuse: A Journal of Research and Treatment, 23*, 346–364.

Ward, T., & Hudson, S. M. (2000). Sexual offenders' implicit planning: a conceptual model. *Sexual Abuse: A Journal of Research and Treatment, 12*, 3.

Wong, K. (2013). A prosocial collaborative model for juveniles who sexually offend. *ATSA Forum, 25*, 1. Retrieved from <http://newsmanager.commpartners.com/atsa/issues/2012-12-13/6.html>.

Worling, J. (2012). The assessment and treatment of deviant sexual arousal with adolescents who have offended sexually. *Journal of Sexual Aggression, 18*, 36–63.

Worling, J. R., & Curwen, T. (2001). Estimate of risk of adolescent sexual offense recidivism (ERASOR; Version 2.0). In M. C. Calder (Ed.), *Juveniles and children who sexually abuse: Frameworks for assessment* (pp. 372–397) [The ERASOR is also available free of charge as a pdf file from the author at < jworling@ican.net>.].

Worling, J. R., Josefowitz, N., & Maltar, M. (2011). Reducing shame and increasing guilt and responsibility with adolescents who have offended sexually: a CBT-based treatment approach. In S. Hall (Ed.), *Contemporary practice with young people who sexually abuse: Evidence-based developments*. Holyoke: NEARI Press.

Worling, J. R., & Langton, C. M. (2012). Assessment and treatment of adolescents who sexually offend: clinical issues and implications for secure settings. *Criminal Justice and Behavior, 39*, 814–841.

CHAPTER 10

Modifying Problematic Sexual Interests of Males

Stephanie E. Scott and Daniel S. Bromberg
Special Psychological Services, LLC, Bloomfield, NJ, USA

INTRODUCTION

We know that adolescent sexual arousal patterns are fluid and that one's sexual behaviors and stated orientation during adolescence do not necessarily correspond to one's sexual arousal patterns during adulthood (e.g., Diamond, 2013). So, under what circumstances is a sexual arousal pattern "problematic"? We consider a sexual interest to be problematic if acting on the sexual interest would be unlawful in the society in which the adolescent lives and/or would deviate significantly from generally accepted norms of the society in which the adolescent lives. Problematic sexual arousal patterns range from relatively high incidence patterns, such as arousal to prepubertal children, to relatively low incidence patterns, such as sexual arousal to deceased persons.

In this chapter, we discuss modification of problematic sexual interests of teenage boys only. It is probable that the strategies discussed have limited applicability to teenage girls. O'Sullivan and Ronis (2013) pointed out that there is a dearth of information about the development of "normative"[1] sexual interests in girls. Even less is known about the development of "non-normative" sexual interests and behaviors in adolescent girls.

Stuyvesant and his colleagues (this volume) presented a treatment approach for working with juvenile sex offenders. Their approach is useful with "generalist" offenders. Generalist offenders are similar in many respects to other adolescents who commit non-sexual criminal offenses. They may have antisocial personality traits, associate with delinquent peers, and engage in substance use. An implication of the generalist perspective is that the same treatment models that have been developed for use with other juvenile delinquents would be useful for work with

[1] We use the term "normative" from an actuarial perspective.

Toolkit for Working with Juvenile Sex Offenders.
DOI: http://dx.doi.org/10.1016/B978-0-12-405948-1.00010-4

adolescent sex offenders (Pullman & Seto, 2012). A substantial percentage of known adolescent sex offenders seem to be generalist offenders.

This chapter addresses treatment strategies for use with "specialist offenders." Specialist offenders are those who commit sexual offenses due to atypical sexual interests. Atypical sexual interests may have been acquired by premature exposure to adult sexuality, including having had experiences of sexual abuse (Pullman & Seto, 2012; Seto & Lalumiere, 2010).

Studies have shown that adolescent sex offenders as a group show relatively more sexual arousal to stimuli depicting prepubescent children or coercive sex than do young adult comparison groups (Robinson, Rouleau, & Madrigano, 1997; Seto, Lalumiere, & Blanchard, 2000). Furthermore, research reflects that such arousal to stimuli depicting children predicted sexual recidivism among adolescent sex offenders (Clift, Rajilic, & Gretton, 2009; Rice & Harris, 2009). Similarly, Worling and Curwen (2000) found that self-reported sexual interest in prepubescent children was associated with sexual recidivism among adolescent sex offenders. Seto, Murphy, Page, and Ennis (2003) found that sexual arousal to stimuli depicting children was correlated with child victim characteristics among adolescent sex offenders in a similar fashion to that of adult sex offenders. Clearly, it is of importance to modify problematic sexual arousal patterns.

TREATMENT STRATEGIES FOR MODIFYING PROBLEMATIC SEXUAL AROUSAL PATTERNS

Marshall, Marshall, Serran, and Fernandez (2006, pp. 65–69) provided a useful description of treatment strategies for modifying problematic sexual arousal patterns. These methods have demonstrated efficacy with adult male sexual offenders. However, these strategies have been used with male juvenile offenders as well. Slight modifications to the general procedures presented can be made as necessary for use with adolescents. Later in this chapter, we provide an example in which procedures described below have been slightly modified.

The four strategies most often employed to address problematic sexual arousal are as follows: masturbatory reconditioning (also called "thematic shift" or "directed masturbation"); verbal satiation; covert association; and olfactory aversion (Marshall et al., 2006; McAnulty & Adams, 1992). We will summarize clinical indications and procedures for these interventions.

Masturbatory Reconditioning

- Useful for increasing sexual arousal to appropriate stimuli.
- Help the adolescent identify a (real or imagined) peer-age female (or male) with whom the adolescent might have a consensual sexual relationship.

- Allow use of visual images initially, if necessary, but encourage use of fantasy material involving an appropriate partner.
- During therapy sessions, check to be sure the adolescent is using appropriate imagery of persons and behaviors. For example, use the adolescent's self-report to make sure he is not masturbating to images of prepubescent children and/or of physically coercive sex.
- The adolescent should be instructed to use this procedure *every* time he masturbates.
- Begin masturbating by using whatever images are needed to generate sexual arousal. At that point, switch to an appropriate image and continue masturbating to orgasm. If sexual arousal diminishes during masturbation while using appropriate imagery (i.e., the adolescent loses his erection), switch back to use of whatever images are needed to generate sexual arousal. When sufficiently aroused again, switch back to appropriate imagery and continue masturbating to orgasm.
- Continue to switch back and forth between problematic and appropriate imagery until orgasm. *Be certain* to switch to appropriate imagery when orgasm feels inevitable and employ that imagery until shortly after orgasm has occurred.
- If a client indicates a religious objection to masturbating, try to recruit clergy from the adolescent's religion who you already know will assure the client that masturbation is permissible for psychotherapeutic purposes.

Verbal Satiation

- Useful for decreasing sexual arousal to inappropriate stimuli.
- Performed soon after orgasm when in the refractory period. This is the period after ejaculation when the client is (relatively or absolutely) unresponsive to sexual stimuli that would otherwise be sexually arousing.
- The client, while generating vivid images, verbalizes fantasies of problematic sexual scenarios for 10 minutes after ejaculating.

Covert Association

- Least invasive form of aversive conditioning. Useful for decreasing sexual arousal to inappropriate stimuli (i.e., targets inappropriate fantasies directly linked to overt sexual deviance).
- The client is assisted in constructing several offense sequences or chains. Some of the sequences are of prior offenses while others are reconstructions of fantasies.

- The client is then helped to construct aversive consequences to engaging in each offending behavior. Offense sequences are written on one side of pocket-sized cards with the consequences being written on the other side.
- The client is instructed to read each sequence and its consequence at least three times each day between treatment sessions.
- When the procedure is begun, the client is told to read each sequence through the last behavior before reading the consequences. Over the weeks of practice, he is to move the interruption of the sequence and the reading of the consequences to progressively earlier steps in the sequence. After 4–6 weeks, he is reading the consequences at the point when he is thinking about initiating the offense or fantasy sequence.

Olfactory (Ammonia) Aversion

- Useful for decreasing frequent and intrusive problematic sexual thoughts.
- The client is instructed to carry a small vial of ammonia (salts) with him at all times, which permits him to utilize this technique as problematic sexual urges occur in his environment.
- When problematic thoughts occur, the client should open the vial of smelling salts, and sniff it.
- The client begins to associate his deviant fantasy with the unpleasant odor.
- Concerns arise regarding the clinician's ability to control the parameters of the aversive stimulus. In addition, client drop-out rate may be higher due to the unpleasant nature of the smells.

Additional Procedural Considerations

- All four intervention strategies are discussed in individual client sessions.
- Between-sessions work is practicing the combination of masturbatory reconditioning and verbal satiation on every occasion the client masturbates and rehearsing his covert association exercise daily.
- Each client keeps a daily log of the frequency and intensity of problematic, as well as appropriate, urges and fantasies.

A SAMPLE TREATMENT PLAN

Assume that a hypothetical 14-year-old boy has a 9-year-old sister and that he has been caught fondling and digitally penetrating preschool age girls. He is restrained from his home because of concern that he may pose an unacceptably high level of risk to his younger sister. He seemed reasonably forthright during his forensic psychological evaluation. He told the examiner that he masturbates to fantasies of girls his age and older, but loses his erection soon after he begins masturbating. He then shifts fantasies and thinks about preschool and elementary school age girls, regains a full erection, continues masturbating, and ejaculates while fantasizing about prepubescent girls. We will present a sample treatment plan for this adolescent. The goal is for him to return home as soon as possible *while simultaneously* minimizing the level of risk to his younger sister. The treatment plan incorporates elements discussed in other chapters in this volume.

Treatment Goal 1: Eliminate Problematic Sexual Arousal Pattern while Simultaneously Increasing Arousal to Appropriate Stimuli (i.e., women from 18 to 21 years of age)

- Establish a current baseline
  - Client keeps a log of problematic sexual thoughts and fantasies, noting the date, time of day, frequency and intensity of urges
  - Assess sexual interests by way of self-report inventory
  - Obtain results of penile plethysmography
- Phase I of Treatment
  - Generate a preliminary sexual abuse sequence/sexual assault cycle and a preliminary relapse prevention plan
  - Masturbatory reconditioning
    - Masturbate to ejaculation while using fantasies of women from 18 to 21 years of age
    - Since fantasies may be insufficient at first, provide photos
    - *No* pornography for both ethical and legal reasons
    - Consider using Sports Illustrated swimsuit issue or calendar
    - Consider selected Victoria's Secret catalog images (*not* the whole catalog because of erotic images of prepubescent and peripubescent girls)
    - If he starts to lose his erection or has other difficulty masturbating to orgasm, switch and use problematic imagery. Once he has a full erection again, go back to using appropriate imagery and masturbate until ejaculation using appropriate imagery.

  Followed by
- Verbal satiation
  - Thirty seconds to one minute after ejaculating, begin visualizing problematic fantasies and/or actual offenses committed. Visualize and verbalize these scenarios for approximately 10 minutes.

- Re-assess 3–6 months later to see if changes in arousal pattern are durable over time
  - Re-assess sexual interests by way of inventory
  - Penile plethysmography
- Accomplish goals often set in juvenile sex offender (JSO)-specific treatment
  - Learn laws pertaining to interpersonal sexual behavior in one's state of residence
  - Learn about healthy sexuality (perhaps use Bell's *Changing Bodies, Changing Lives*)
  - Refine the sexual abuse sequence/sexual assault cycle and relapse prevention/safety plan previously generated

Treatment Goal 2: Adolescent Will Return Home[2]

- Phase II of Treatment
  - Adolescent generates a tentative prevention/safety plan and his parents generate a tentative prevention/safety plan, as well. Joint adolescent–parent sessions are held to refine and generate a final safety plan. All three sign this agreement and it becomes a contract. All three get copies of the signed contract.
  - The 9-year-old sister has individual sessions with a therapist to learn about personal boundaries and appropriate and inappropriate touching. She is informed that anyone, even a trusted relative, can engage in inappropriate touching and is provided with instruction in what to do if inappropriate or confusing touching occurs. Role plays are used.
  - The adolescent returns home. He continues JSO-specific work on an outpatient basis (e.g., social skills, dating, ongoing problem solving if he becomes aroused by his sister or significantly younger minors).

CONCLUSIONS

In this chapter, we discuss modification of problematic sexual interests of teenage boys. We consider a sexual interest to be problematic if acting on the sexual interest would be unlawful in the society in which the adolescent lives and/or would deviate significantly from generally accepted norms of the society in which the adolescent lives. Problematic sexual arousal

[2]Assuming that problematic sexual arousal is significantly decreased or eliminated and that arousal to appropriate targets has been increased.

patterns range from relatively high incidence patterns, such as arousal to prepubertal children to relatively low incidence patterns, such as sexual arousal to deceased persons. We provided an example of how these basic strategies can be applied within the context of a case scenario.

Three final caveats are warranted. We have presented a general framework for implementation of strategies to modify problematic sexual arousal patterns. The efficacy of these strategies with adult male sexual offenders, as well as with male juvenile offenders, is supported by research. Should these procedures not produce sufficient results, we suggest referring the client to a psychiatrist to determine if a medication trial is warranted.

Discussion of the second caveat may be aided by an analogy of purchasing a man's suit or a woman's dress "off the rack." While the garment may be a generally good fit, it may be too tight in some places and too baggy in others, or too long. In other words, the garment will need to be tailored to fit the individual making the purchase. Similarly, the interventions we have discussed are "off the rack" and may need to be tailored to fit the specific needs of specific clients. Just as an experienced tailor would be needed to make a garment fit a purchaser, a professional with a strong background in implementing behavioral interventions is needed to customize interventions for clients. One should have a thorough understanding of classical and operant conditioning, extinction, and other behavior analytic principles to properly customize interventions to meet the needs of specific clients. Without such expertise, a clinician may prescribe an intervention that is ineffective. Worse yet, improper implementation might result in an intervention package that increases, rather than decreases, problematic sexual arousal patterns.

Finally, readers should be aware that we presented an overly simplistic scenario for reunification of a juvenile sex offender with his parents and prepubescent sister. There are multiple factors that must be taken into account when making decisions about the advisability and timing of reunification. Our example is not intended to serve as any sort of guideline for circumstances under which reunification should occur. Rather, we used this example to place modification of problematic sexual interests within some sort of context.

REFERENCES

Bromberg, D.S.(this volume). Writing dispositional evaluations of juveniles adjudicated for sexual offenses and juveniles with sexual behavioral problems. In D.S. Bromberg & W.T. O'Donohue (Eds.), *Toolkit for working with juvenile sex offenders*. San Diego, CA: Elsevier.

Clift, R. J. W., Rajilic, G., & Gretton, H. J. (2009). Discriminative and predictive validity of the penile plethysmography in adolescent offenders. *Sexual Abuse: A Journal of Research and Treatment, 21*, 335–362.

Diamond, L. M. (2013). Sexual-minority, gener-nonconforming, and transgender youths. In D. S. Bromberg & W. T. O'Donohue (Eds.), *Handbook of child and adolescent sexuality: Developmental and forensic psychology* (pp. 275–300). San Diego, CA: Elsevier.

Knight, R.A., & Sims-Knight, J.E. (this volume). Assessment of dynamic treatment targets for juveniles who sexually offend. In D.S. Bromberg & W.T. O'Donohue (Eds.), *Toolkit for working with juvenile sex offenders*. San Diego, CA: Elsevier.

Marshall, W. L., Marshall, L. E., Serran, G. A., & Fernandez, Y. M. (2006). *Treating sexual offenders: An integrated approach*. New York: Routledge.

McAnulty, R. D., & Adams, H. E. (1992). Behavior therapy with paraphilic disorders. In S. M. Turner, K. S. Calhoun, & H. E. Adams (Eds.), *Handbook of clinical behavior therapy* (pp. 175–201). Hoboken, NJ: Wiley.

O'Donohue, W.T. (this volume). Tools for testifying in court. In D.S. Bromberg & W.T. O'Donohue (Eds.), *Toolkit for working with juvenile sex offenders*. San Diego, CA: Elsevier.

O'Sullivan, L. F., & Ronis, S.T. (2013). Sexual development in girls: "Normative" development and development of paraphilias and sexual offending behaviors. In D. S. Bromberg & W. T. O'Donohue (Eds.), *Handbook of child and adolescent sexuality: Developmental and forensic psychology* (pp. 193–219). San Diego, CA: Elsevier.

Pullman, L., & Seto, M. C. (2012). Assessment and treatment of adolescent sexual offenders: Implications of recent research on generalist versus specialist explanations. *Child Abuse and Neglect, 36*, 203–209.

Rice, M. E., & Harris, G.T. (2009). *Adolescent sex offenders: Is phallometry developed for adult sex offenders valid for adolescents?* Paper presented at the annual conference of the Association for the Treatment of Sexual Abusers, Dallas, Texas.

Robinson, M. C., Rouleau, J. L., & Madrigano, G. (1997). Validation of penile plethysmography as a psychophysiological measure of the sexual interests of adolescent sex offenders. *Revue Quebecoise de Psychologie, 18*, 111–124.

Seto, M. C., & Lalumiere, M. L. (2010). What is so special about adolescent sexual offending?: A review and test of explanations through meta-analysis. *Psychological Bulletin, 136*, 526–575.

Seto, M. C., Lalumiere, M. L., & Blanchard, R. (2000). The discriminative validity of a phallometric test for pedophilic interests among adolescent sex offenders against children. *Psychological Assessment, 12*, 319–327.

Seto, M. C., Murphy, W. D., Page, J., & Ennis, L. (2003). Detecting anomalous sexual interests in juvenile sex offenders. *Journal of Sexually Coercive Behavior, 989*, 118–130.

Worling, J. R., & Curwen, T. (2000). Adolescent sexual offender recidivism. Success of specialized treatment and implications for risk prediction. *Child Abuse and Neglect, 24*, 965–982.

CHAPTER 11

Developing Healthy Sexuality

Joshua Medjuck, Olga Cirlugea and Natalie Bennett
Department of Psychology, University of Nevada, Reno, NV, USA

WHAT IS HEALTHY SEXUALITY?

Sexual health may be defined as "a state of physical, mental and social well-being in relation to sexuality. It requires a positive and respectful approach to sexuality and sexual relationships, as well as the possibility of having pleasurable and safe sexual experiences, free of coercion, discrimination and violence" (WHO, 2013a). This definition is both aspirational and vague. For example, what is a "respectful approach to sexuality?"

Sexual health is defined, in part, by the society in which an individual lives as well as by the era in which the individual lives in that particular society (Bhugra, Popelyuk, & McMullen, 2010; Bromberg & O'Donohue, 2013, p. 37). Factors such as religious beliefs (Bromberg & O'Donohue, 2013, p. 37) and one's personal code of morality also influence what is and is not considered to be healthy sexuality. An adolescent's personal code of morality is probably dependent upon an assortment of factors including, but not limited to, one's religious values, values transmitted by one's family, values transmitted by one's peers, and values depicted in the media.

For an adolescent who has committed one or more sexual offenses, it is important for the adolescent's sexual attitudes and behaviors to conform to what his or her society judges healthy sexuality to be. Otherwise, the adolescent may be subject to further legal sanctions and rejection by peers.

Adolescents are in the process of development that should lead to healthy sexuality. According to McKee et al. (2010), there are fifteen key points to understand when determining what is healthy sexual development. These points are as follows:

1. Freedom from unwanted activity – Children and adolescents should be protected from any unwanted sexual activity.
2. An understanding of consent and ethical conduct more generally – Children and adolescents must understand what sexual morality is and develop a sound ethical system to guide their behavior including concepts of duties, respect for others, and unethical behaviors.

Toolkit for Working with Juvenile Sex Offenders.
DOI: http://dx.doi.org/10.1016/B978-0-12-405948-1.00011-6

3. Education about biological aspects of sexual practice – Children and adolescents must understand how the reproductive system works. They must understand what behaviors are associated with pregnancy and the consequences of having a baby or abortion.
4. An understanding of safety – Children and adolescents should understand what safe sexual practice is, including physical safety as well as contraception and protection from sexually transmitted diseases (STDs).
5. Relationship skills – Children and adolescents should learn these skills more generally, such as communication skills and assertiveness, and then may learn to apply them to sexual relationships.
6. Agency – Children and adolescents should understand their rights and know that they are in charge of their own bodies.
7. Lifelong learning – Learning about sex occurs in various forms throughout childhood and adolescence, and also continues into adulthood.
8. Resilience – Children and adolescents should understand that bad sexual experiences can be learning opportunities rather than damaging occurrences.
9. Open communication – Children and adolescents should be able to communicate about sexual matters openly with adults, and adults should be open about such matters when communicating with children.
10. Sexual development should not be "aggressive, coercive, or joyless".
11. Self-acceptance – Children and adolescents should be taught to develop positive attitudes toward their sexual identities and self-concepts of their bodies.
12. Awareness and acceptance that sex is pleasurable – Children and adolescents should know that it is not shameful to enjoy sex when it occurs in healthy situations.
13. Understanding of parental and societal values – Children and adolescents understand that values regarding sex vary widely and must be able to make informed decisions that relate to such values.
14. Awareness of public/private boundaries – Children and adolescents should understand public and private boundaries regarding sex in their own specific cultures and thus be able to navigate through these boundaries.
15. Competence in mediated sexuality – Children and adolescents should learn how to respond appropriately to sexuality seen in the media.

COMMON SEXUAL BEHAVIORS SEEN IN ADOLESCENTS

Sexual behaviors are displayed by pre-adolescents and adolescents and are not necessarily indicators of unhealthy sexuality. Common behaviors may differ according to the age of the adolescent. According to the Sex Information and Education Council of the United States (SIECUS, 2004b), children aged 9 through 12 years may:

- Become more modest and desire privacy as they begin puberty
- Be more curious about developed male and female bodies
- Look at erotic magazines and Internet sites
- Develop romantic crushes on friends, older teens, celebrities, and other people that play a role in their life like a teacher, coach, or counselor
- Show an interest in dating
- Wonder "Am I normal?" and compare themselves to others
- Experience pressure to conform to family and societal expectations of appropriate behavior for boys and girls
- Use sexual language and explore romantic and sexual fantasies
- Masturbate until orgasm occurs.

Children aged 13–18 years may:

- Want to date
- Feel pressured by peers to engage in activities, including sexual behaviors that they might not be ready to experience, but go along with because they want to be perceived as "cool"
- Continue to masturbate
- Fantasize about romantic or sexual scenarios
- Fall in love
- Experiment with kissing and touching that may include oral sex and intercourse.

The following sections on Developing Healthy Non-Sexual Relationships, Sexual Behavior, Masturbation, and Sexual Health review key concepts and topics discussed in *Guidelines for Comprehensive Sexuality Education: Kindergarten-12th Grade* (SIECUS, 2004a).

DEVELOPING HEALTHY NON-SEXUAL RELATIONSHIPS

The adolescent should understand that a healthy sexual relationship occurs in the context of a more general healthy relationship. In a healthy relationship, both members treat each other with respect. Both people show support and value each other. As such, all decisions that affect the relationship are made together. Any disagreements between the couple are settled through honest discussion rather than aggressive arguments. Importantly, both members of the relationship have friends and interests outside of the relationship. Neither person should make fun of the other's interests, hobbies, friends, or opinions. Additionally, neither person should try to change the other to make the relationship work. Both members should maintain a sense of individuality and freedom; one person should not be checking in on the other at all times by calling or texting. Finally, there are more good times than bad in a healthy relationship (Tharp, 2013). While all these are reasonable aspirations, expectations must also be set realizing the child's developmental course and the limitations this implies.

Competency Exercises

1. What does it mean for an individual to *consent* to sexual activity?

____

____

____

2. Is it ever acceptable to be sexually aggressive or to coerce another person into sexual activity?

____

____

____

3. What are your family's values regarding sexual activity?

____

____

____

4. What are considered acceptable public and private boundaries regarding sex?

____

____

____

5. Name at least three components of a healthy non-sexual relationship.

____

____

____

6. Is it normal for adolescents to fantasize about sex and desire to engage in sexual behaviors?

____

____

____

SEXUAL BEHAVIOR

An important part of healthy sexuality is knowing how to behave in situations that involve sexual feelings. There are numerous factors to consider when determining what constitutes healthy sexual behavior. What may be considered healthy behavior for one person may be inappropriate or unacceptable to another. Before we review competency exercises for sexual behavior, there are some important factors to consider when evaluating sexual behavior in adolescents:

1. **Age** – How old is the individual? Some sexual behaviors that are deemed acceptable for an 18 year old may be considered too advanced for a 12 year old. Older adolescents are more likely to have the emotional maturity and experience to deal with certain sexual situations compared to younger adolescents. Age is also an important consideration when evaluating what is legally acceptable sexual behavior for adolescents. The clinician will have to use his/her judgment regarding this but also may need to obtain input and permission from the adolescent's parent or guardian.
2. **Religion** – Does the individual have any religious or spiritual beliefs that may be in conflict with mainstream ideas about what constitutes healthy sexual behavior? Faith plays an important role in shaping sexual behavior that is both socially acceptable and personally relevant. A major component of healthy sexuality is feeling psychologically prepared to engage in sexual behaviors that are safe and enjoyable. It is extremely difficult to feel comfortable experimenting with sexual behavior if it challenges personal beliefs about what is morally correct.
3. **Sexual Orientation** – What kind of sexual feelings does the adolescent have toward members of the opposite and/or same sex? Does he or she identify as having a particular sexual orientation? Healthy sexual behavior may look very different depending on the sexual orientation of the adolescent and the context in which the behavior is being applied. Adolescents beginning to explore a non-heterosexual orientation may require special considerations, as well. For example, non-heterosexual adolescents may experience different cultural or social challenges depending on the attitudes of those in their environment. If non-heterosexuality violates personal beliefs of family or friends, it is possible the adolescent may experience discomfort regarding his or her sexuality and sexual behaviors.

Competency Exercises

Shared Sexual Behavior

A key competency for any sexual behavior is understanding that each person has control over their own sexuality. This means that everyone has the right to choose if and when they engage in sexual behavior. Intrapersonal sexual behaviors are easier to navigate because adolescents can decide when and how to explore their own sexuality. Sexual behaviors that involve a partner are usually more challenging for adolescents because interpersonal sexual behavior requires considering the needs of another individual. Below are some questions to evaluate for competency with shared sexual behavior in adolescents:

1. What is a shared sexual behavior?

___

___

___

2. How do you know when someone wants to participate in shared sexual behavior?

___

___

___

3. How do you know if someone does not want to participate in shared sexual behavior?

___

___

___

4. What if you aren't sure if you want to participate in shared sexual behavior?

___

___

___

5. How do alcohol or other drugs affect judgment around shared sexual behavior?

___

___

___

6. Is it okay to engage in shared sexual behavior when intoxicated?

______

______

______

7. What if you are participating in a shared sexual behavior and want to stop?

______

______

______

8. Who makes the final decision about participating in shared sexual behavior?

______

______

______

9. What is the legality of the shared sexual behavior?

______

______

______

10. What is the morality of the shared sexual behavior?

______

______

______

11. What does my faith or religion say about the shared sexual behavior?

______

______

______

12. Is this something I need to discuss with my therapist, religious leader, parent or guardian to get help or input?

______

______

______

The take home point from these questions is that each person is different when it comes to sexual behavior. The only way to know if someone is ready to participate in shared sexual behavior is if they verbally communicate readiness to a partner. The partner must respect the autonomy of the individual by allowing him or her to make the decision about sexual behavior on his or her own. Uncertainty about partaking in shared sexual behavior usually indicates the individual is not ready and should not participate. Lastly, it is important that adolescents understand the effects of alcohol and/or drugs, how intoxication blurs judgment around shared sexual behavior, and what constitutes consent to engage in sexual behaviors.

Considerations

Age – Is the adolescent capable of making an informed decision about participating in shared sexual behavior? Are there legal restrictions associated with the sexual behavior based on age? Evaluate how knowledgeable the adolescent is regarding the sexual behavior and its potential consequences (physical, emotional etc.). These indices will help determine if the adolescent can make educated choices about participating in shared sexual behavior.

Religion – Is consenting to the shared sexual behavior consistent with the personal beliefs of the adolescent? How would family react to knowing about their sexual behavior? Discuss what the spiritual, religious and familial implications would be for the individual to participate in the sexual behavior. Assist the adolescent conduct a cost-benefit analysis to assist him/her them with his/her decision.

Sexual Orientation – Is consent to shared sexual behavior different depending on the sexual orientation of the adolescent? Does (s)he feel vulnerable because (s)he is experimenting with a member of the same sex? Explore what is motivating the adolescent to participate in the shared sexual behavior so (s)he can feel confident when making a final decision about the behavior.

Helpful Resources

1. Consent and Consensual Sex
   http://www.pamf.org/teen/abc/sex/consent.html
2. Making the Decision: Deciding Whether or Not to Have Sex
   http://www.iwannaknow.org/teens/relationships/decision.html
3. I Think I Might Be Bisexual/Gay/Lesbian/Transgender, Now What Do I Do?
   http://www.advocatesforyouth.org/publications-on-glbtq-issues

MASTURBATION

Masturbation is a sexual behavior in which adolescents frequently engage. It is seldom discussed openly. It can function as a sexual behavior shared with a partner or as an individual sexual event. Healthy masturbation can help adolescents explore their sexuality in a safe environment. It is important for adolescents to understand what constitutes healthy masturbation. Unhealthy masturbation includes the following: masturbating with frequency and/or intensity such that one's genitalia become raw; masturbating with such frequency that it interferes with other important life activities, such as attending school; masturbating in public; and masturbating to fantasies that, if acted upon, would be illegal.

Here are some true/false questions that can help educate adolescents about masturbation:

1.	Masturbation is a normal human behavior	T/F
2.	Masturbation in public is acceptable	T/F
3.	Masturbation is good for your health	T/F
4.	Masturbation helps to relieve stress	T/F
5.	Masturbation is only for people without a sexual partner	T/F
6.	Masturbation will disrupt parts of your life	T/F
7.	Masturbation talk in public is acceptable	T/F
8.	Masturbation is fun	T/F
9.	Masturbation might be viewed by some as immoral	T/F
10.	Masturbation should only be done in certain contexts	T/F

Answers: 1) T 2) F 3) T 4) T 5) F 6) F 7) F 8) T 9) T 10) T

Considerations

Age – There is no specific age when masturbation is developmentally appropriate because every person matures differently. A young adolescent may not understand that masturbation is a normal part of sexual development and feel guilty when experimenting with it. Older adolescents are likely to have more experience with masturbation but may need clarification about what constitutes healthy masturbation.

Religion – It is important to assess for beliefs that masturbation is unhealthy or immoral. Many religious groups view masturbation negatively and create shame in adolescents who have thought about or engaged in this type of behavior. Help the adolescent explore what (s)he thinks about masturbation in order to develop an ideological and behavioral framework from which the adolescent can operate.

Sexual Orientation – Does the adolescent's sexual orientation influence their masturbation behavior? Masturbation may be the only outlet for an adolescent to express his/her sexuality if (s)he feels uncomfortable opening up to friends or family. This may contribute to negative self-judgments or interpersonal problems. Normalize the behavior and communicate how sexual orientation and preferences can be explored through healthy masturbation practices.

Helpful Resources

1. Masturbation
   http://www.plannedparenthood.org/health-topics/sex-101/masturbation-23901.htm
2. Masturbation: 5 Things You Didn't Know
   http://men.webmd.com/guide/masturbation-5-things-you-didnt-know?page=1

SEXUAL HEALTH

It is important for the adolescent to understand what it means for his or her body to be sexually healthy. There are several key areas to discuss when considering sexual health.

Reproductive Health

Both males and females must care for their reproductive health. According to the World Health Organization (WHO, 2013b), reproductive health is defined as:

> *"the reproductive processes, functions and system at all stages of life. Reproductive health, therefore, implies that people are able to have a responsible, satisfying and safe sex life and that they have the capability to reproduce and the freedom to decide if, when and how often to do so.*

Once an adolescent reaches puberty, he or she should receive regular sexual health exams from a health care provider. It is important to note that certain factors may affect future reproductive capability, such as untreated STDs or drug use (SIECUS, 2004a).

Considerations

Age – Has the adolescent reached puberty? If so, he or she should receive regular sexual health exams.

Religion – Not applicable in this case.

Sexual Orientation – Not applicable in this case.

Contraception

The use of contraception allows people to have sexual intercourse while avoiding unintended pregnancy. Many adolescents may not realize all that is involved in having a baby and subsequently raising a child. A calculator for the financial cost of raising a child can be found at http://www.babycenter.com/cost-of-raising-child-calculator. Additionally, the hard work involved in raising a child may be underestimated by some adolescents. For more information, access http://www.babycenter.com/0_is-parenthood-for-you_7169.bc.

There are several methods of contraception that the adolescent should understand so that he or she may make an informed decision when a healthy sexual relationship arises. Religious, cultural, or parental values may influence the adolescent's decision to use contraception (SIECUS, 2004a). The adolescent may also discuss methods of contraception with a health care provider before engaging in sexual relationships. Some methods of contraception require a prescription whereas others are available over-the-counter (SIECUS, 2004a). It is important to note that not all of these methods prevent the spread of STDs.

The most effective way to prevent pregnancy is abstinence, where one chooses not to engage in a sexual relationship with a partner. However, if a person chooses to be sexually active, there are assorted methods for reducing the possibility of unwanted pregnancy from occurring. These methods vary in their effectiveness at preventing pregnancy. Certain methods, such as condoms and hormonal contraception (when used correctly), are generally more reliable whereas others, such as natural family planning and withdrawal, are generally unreliable, especially for adolescents.

"Outercourse", or sex play in which the penis does not penetrate the vagina, is one option. Some consider "outercourse" to preclude oral and anal penetration as well (Planned Parenthood, 2013). Natural family planning is another contraceptive strategy. A female using this method charts her ovulation and menstrual cycle to determine the days of a month when she is likely to get pregnant; she then abstains from sex on these days. This strategy is notoriously unreliable, especially for young adolescents.

Withdrawal is a commonly used method of contraception. In this method, the male pulls his penis out of the vagina before he ejaculates. This method is known to be less effective than other forms of contraception (SIECUS, 2004a). Furthermore, this method is not recommended for adolescents, as it requires much experience for a male to know when he is going to ejaculate (Planned Parenthood, 2013).

Spermicides are chemicals that can be applied to kill sperm. They are available in several forms including creams, gels, foams, etc. Barrier methods are another form of contraception. A barrier is an object that is placed either around the penis or inside of the vagina that keeps sperm from entering. Many barrier methods exist, including the male condom, female condom, sponge, diaphragm, and cervical cap.

Hormonal methods of contraception are used by females, but both members of a relationship should make decisions about their use together (SIECUS, 2004a). Hormonal methods regulate the woman's menstrual cycle as well as prevent the fertilization of an egg after sexual intercourse. There are many types of hormonal methods available, including the combination pill, the mini pill, the shot, the ring, the patch, and the implant. Emergency contraception, also known as the "morning after pill," is a form of hormonal contraception in which the female takes a pill within 72 hours after having unprotected sexual intercourse in order to prevent fertilization of an egg.

Additionally, an intrauterine device (IUD) is an object that is placed into a woman's uterus by a health care provider in order to prevent pregnancy. IUDs are designed for long-term use, as they can remain in a woman's body for 5–10 years (Centers for Disease Control CDC, 2013a). Permanent methods to prevent pregnancy also exist; these include both female and male sterilization. These surgeries must be performed by medical professionals and are irreversible.

Considerations

Age – In certain states, parental permission is required for a minor to use prescription contraception. Is the adolescent at an age where parental consent is required? Is the adolescent responsible enough to use reliably certain forms of birth control? Discuss the importance of using contraception reliably. Is the adolescent mature enough to make decisions about permanent methods of birth control? Make sure to discuss the implications of permanent methods of contraception.

Religion – Do the adolescent's personal beliefs affect his or her view of contraception? How would the adolescent's family react to the use of contraception? Evaluate how the adolescent's religious beliefs (or the beliefs of his or her family) play a part in the decision to use or not to use contraception and discuss the implications.

Sexual Orientation – Even if the adolescent is not worried about preventing pregnancy, certain forms of contraception (e.g., condoms) help prevent the transmission of STDs. Discuss the importance of protecting against STDs using contraception.

Helpful Resources

1. Birth Control
   http://www.plannedparenthood.org/health-topics/birth-control-4211.htm
2. Contraception
   http://www.cdc.gov/reproductivehealth/UnintendedPregnancy/Contraception.htm
3. How Much Does Birth Control Cost?
   http://money.usnews.com/money/blogs/alpha-consumer/2010/08/27/how-much-does-birth-control-cost
4. Comparing Effectiveness of Birth Control Methods
   http://www.plannedparenthood.org/health-topics/birth-control/birth-control-effectiveness-chart-22710.htm
5. An Overview of Minors' Consent Law
   http://www.guttmacher.org/statecenter/spibs/spib_OMCL.pdf

Pregnancy and Prenatal Care

Adolescents who are pregnant or considering becoming pregnant should be attentive to their reproductive health and seek prenatal care to ensure a safe and healthy pregnancy. A pregnant adolescent should see a health care provider for regular checkups throughout her pregnancy to make sure that she and the fetus are healthy. Furthermore, a pregnant adolescent should understand that different drugs, medications, and vitamins may have a negative effect on her fetus. If an adolescent suspects she is pregnant, she should avoid tobacco, alcohol, and other drugs (SIECUS, 2004a). Special prenatal vitamins may help to keep the fetus and mother healthy.

Different tests are available to help determine the health of the fetus prior to its birth. Health care providers may perform ultrasounds, multiple marker screenings, amniocentesis, or chorionic villus sampling to examine various aspects of the pregnancy and to detect any abnormalities if present (Office on Women's Health, 2010). It is important to note that even with prenatal care, a baby may still be born with medical problems. This may be due to a parent's genetic disorder or other factors. Men and women should be screened for genetic disorders prior to attempting to conceive a child (SIECUS, 2004a).

Considerations

Age – Is the adolescent at an age where a pregnancy may be especially unsafe? Be sure to address the importance of checkups with a health care professional to ensure the health of the adolescent and the fetus.

Religion – Does the adolescent's religious beliefs affect how he or she feels about pregnancy, especially outside of marriage? What about the adolescent's family's beliefs? Discuss the implications.

Sexual Orientation – Depending on the sexual orientation of the adolescent, pregnancy and prenatal care may not be relevant.

Helpful Resources

1. Prenatal Care Fact Sheet
   http://womenshealth.gov/publications/our-publications/fact-sheet/prenatal-care.cfm
2. Prenatal Care for Pregnant Teens
   http://www.pregnantteenhelp.org/help/prenatal-care-for-pregnant-teens/
3. Teen and Tween Health: Teenage Pregnancy
   http://www.mayoclinic.com/health/teen-pregnancy/MY00820/NSECTIONGROUP=2

Abortion

If an adolescent experiences an undesired pregnancy, she has several options available to her. She may choose to carry the pregnancy to term and raise the child, give the child up for adoption, or have an abortion (SIECUS, 2004a). Abortion is a procedure through which a pregnancy is terminated. This is legal in the USA for part of the pregnancy, although state laws vary on the length of pregnancy allowed for an abortion as well as a teenager's ability to get an abortion. Abortions may be done through the use of hormone medication (medical abortion) to remove the fetus and placenta from the expecting mother's uterus, or through surgery (i.e., surgical abortion), which uses a vacuum to remove the fetus and other pregnancy material (National Institutes of Health NIH, 2013). Two types of abortions can be performed: therapeutic (due to some harmful medical condition); and elective (because the woman chooses to terminate the pregnancy). In the USA, some states such as Alabama, Florida, and Texas require one or both parents to provide consent for abortion services, while other states, such as California, Nevada and New York do not (Planned Parenthood, 2009). Minors have the option of petitioning the court to excuse them from having to obtain parental consent (judicial bypass), to have a guardian provide consent in place of a parent, or to forego parental consent if she can prove she is independent from the care of her parents. In some states, a minor may also be excused from having to obtain parental consent if she can provide evidence that she was a victim of abuse or neglect.

Medical abortions can be performed within 7 weeks of the adolescent's first day of her last menstrual period and have fewer harmful side effects than surgical abortions (NIH, 2013). Surgical abortions are more intrusive and carry greater risks. These risks include damage to the cervix, scarring inside the uterus, and side effects associated with anesthesia. Reasons an adolescent may consider an abortion include the fetus having a birth defect, the pregnancy posing a health risk to the woman's health, the pregnancy resulting from rape or incest, or simply a desire no longer to be pregnant. The decision to seek an abortion to terminate pregnancy is a very personal and difficult one (SIECUS, 2004a). It may be particularly difficult if the adolescent is at an age at which she is still being supported primarily by her family (e.g., financially, as she may not be able independently to afford the cost of an abortion). Additionally, an adolescent's cognitive development may interfere with her ability to consider all factors relevant to making this difficult choice. Factors such as religion, culture, and family values all influence an adolescent's decision about having an abortion. Generally, female clients considering abortion are advised to seek support from parents or other trusted family members, mental health professionals, a religious leader, and other support figures (SIECUS, 2004a).

Considerations

Age – Is the adolescent at an age when parental consent is needed for an abortion? This generally means under 18 years of age, although the necessity of parental consent varies by state. Adolescents should contact their local Planned Parenthood center for more information. Are there legal restrictions associated with the abortion based on age of the mother or the age of the fetus? Evaluate how knowledgeable the adolescent is regarding potential consequences (physical and emotional) of abortions. These indices will help determine if the adolescent can make educated choices about whether to seek out an abortion.

Religion – Is terminating a pregnancy consistent with the personal beliefs of the adolescent? How would family react to knowing about the abortion? Discuss what the spiritual, religious and familial implications would be for the individual to terminate the pregnancy. Assist the adolescent to conduct a cost-benefit analysis to assist her with her decision.

Sexual Orientation – Not applicable in this case.

Helpful Resources

1. Thinking about Abortion
   http://www.plannedparenthood.org/health-topics/pregnancy/thinking-about-abortion-21519.htm
2. Consent Laws by State
   http://www.plannedparenthood.org/health-topics/abortion/parental-consent-notification-laws-25268.htm
3. Post-abortion Support
   https://exhaleprovoice.org/after-abortion-support

Sexually Transmitted Diseases

Sexually transmitted diseases, also referred to as sexually transmitted infections (STIs), currently affect over 20 million individuals each year, and young people ages 15 to 24 make up half of all new cases of STDs (CDC, 2013b). Two types of STDs exist: bacterial ones that can be cured with antibiotics and include chlamydia, gonorrhea, and syphilis; and viral STDs that include human papillomavirus (HPV, the most common STD), human immunodeficiency virus (HIV), hepatitis B and genital herpes (CDC, 2013b). Viral STDs cannot be cured, but advances in medicine have led to better treatments to manage STD symptoms and have improved the prognosis for individuals with viral STDs (Morquin, Le Moing, Mura et al., 2012). It is important to note that there has been a growing concern regarding antibiotic-resistant gonorrhea. Vaccines have been developed for both hepatitis B and HPV, although Gardasil, the HPV vaccine, only prevents some of the most common types of virus that have been found to cause cervical cancer and genital warts.

Common symptoms include abnormal discharge from the genitals, burning upon urination, and abdominal and pelvic pain. If left untreated, STDs can cause serious problems to the reproductive organs, including infertility. Because many STDs do not produce symptoms, it is important for teenagers who may have been exposed to someone infected to seek testing from a medical provider. Often, teenagers may obtain such testing without parental consent at public or private clinics, hospitals, and Planned Parenthood.

There are several ways in which a person may contract an STD: through unprotected sexual activity, including vaginal, oral and anal sex; through the sharing of needles (for example, in contracting HIV); and from an infected mother to child during pregnancy, birth, or breastfeeding (SIECUS, 2004a). Although condoms are very effective in preventing transmission of STDs, the most reliable way to prevent an STD is to abstain from sex with a partner. Additionally, maintaining a monogamous relationship in which the partners practice safe sex can also help prevent both partners from contracting an STD.

Considerations

Age – Is the adolescent capable of making an informed decision about utilizing methods such as condoms to prevent STDs? Evaluate how knowledgeable the adolescent is regarding STDs, especially as it pertains to methods and consequences of contracting an STD. Additionally, evaluate the adolescent's knowledge about birth control/STD prevention methods. This information will help determine if the adolescent can make educated choices about practicing safe sexual behavior. Furthermore, assess the adolescent's motivation for using methods to protect against STDs, and for possible barriers to utilization of such methods.

Religion – Is utilizing birth control consistent with the personal beliefs of the adolescent? Is abstinence from sexual behavior until marriage the only method allowed by the beliefs of the adolescent? How would family react to knowing about attempts to prevent STDs/pregnancy? Discuss what the spiritual, religious and familial implications would be for the individual to utilize birth control methods vs remaining abstinent.

Sexual Orientation – Is utilization of birth control/STD prevention methods different depending on the sexual orientation of the adolescent? Are they less likely to be monogamous or protect themselves during sexual activity if they are in a same-sex relationship? Explore what is motivating the adolescent to practice or not practice safe sex.

Helpful Resources

1. About Sexually Transmitted Diseases
   http://kidshealth.org/teen/infections/stds/std.html
2. STD Teens Support Group
   http://www.mdjunction.com/std-teens

Sexual Abuse

Sexual abuse is defined as any unwanted sexual contact, including acts such as kissing, touching, digital or penile penetration, as well as non-touch acts such as voyeurism and exposing someone to pornography (American Psychological Association, 2013). Sexual abuse is a crime that may be punished by law and sentences vary based on type and number of offenses, victim's age, etc. Most sexual abuse is perpetrated by someone known to the victim, and both men and women can be perpetrators, although most known sex crimes are committed by males. Sexual abuse can also occur in the context of a relationship, even if the partners may have engaged in consensual sexual acts in the past. Children should report any unwanted sexual contact to a trusted adult. Trusted adults may include a parent, teacher, or a counselor.

Although not every child who is abused goes on to experience distress, some common sequelae include post-traumatic stress disorder (Kingston & Raghavan, 2009), depression (Shea, 2008), and substance abuse (Kingston & Raghavan, 2009; Pirard, Sharon, Kang, Angarita, & Gastfriend, 2005). Additionally, behavioral problems, such as sexual acting out, have been observed in some children who were sexually abused (Taylor, 1998). Some perpetrators have been using the Internet as a tool to lure young victims and, as a result, children and teenagers should be careful when interacting with an unknown individual over the Internet, and should refrain from sharing personal information, photographs, etc. The decision to report sexual abuse may be a difficult one, especially if the perpetrator is someone who is close to the victim. It is important for victims to be aware of the many resources available to them including STD and pregnancy testing, counseling, the Crisis Hotline (phone number: 1-800-273-8255) and the National Sexual Assault Hotline (phone number: 1-800-656-HOPE). Although some sexual abuse cannot be prevented, tools such as "learning self-defense techniques, assessing whether a situation may be dangerous, avoiding alcohol and other drugs, and developing assertiveness skills" (SIECUS, 2004a, p. 69) may all help decrease the likelihood that an individual will be sexually assaulted.

Considerations

Age – Is the adolescent capable of consenting to participating in sexual behavior? Is (s)he capable of assessing a situation to determine if their potential partner is giving consent? Are there legal restrictions associated with the sexual behavior based on age? Evaluate how knowledgeable the adolescent is regarding what constitutes mutually desired sexual behavior versus sexual behavior elicited through coercion or threats. These indicators will help determine if the adolescent can make educated choices about participating in shared sexual behavior.

Religion – Is coercing or forcing someone into participating in unwanted sexual behavior consistent with the adolescent's beliefs? Discuss what the spiritual, religious and familial implications would be for the individual to participate in the unwanted sexual behavior or force someone else into it. Assist the adolescent in conducting a cost-benefit analysis to assist the adolescent with decision-making.

Sexual Orientation – Not applicable in this case.

Helpful Resources

1. Rape, Abuse & Incest National Network
   http://www.rainn.org/
2. Teen Sexual Assault
   http://www.weaveinc.org/post/teen-sexual-assault

CONCLUSION

'The aim of this chapter has been to provide clinicians with tools for helping juvenile sex offenders learn about healthy sexuality. Ideally, these tools, which include psychoeducation, competency exercises, and resources for teaching about shared sexual behavior, masturbation, and sexual health, will serve to provide the adolescent with appropriate behaviors to replace the problematic behaviors (e.g., sexual offending, coercive sexual behaviors, etc.) that brought him or her into treatment.

REFERENCES

American Psychological Association. (2013). *Sexual abuse*. Retrieved from <http://www.apa.org/topics/sexual-abuse/>.

Bhugra, D., Popelyuk, D., & McMullen, I. (2010). Paraphilias across cultures: Contexts and controversies. *Journal of Sex Research*, *47*, 242–256.

Bromberg, D. S., & O'Donohue, W. T. (2013). Research methods: Current strategies, obstacles to research, and future directions. In D. S. Bromberg & W. T. O'Donohue (Eds.), *Handbook of child and adolescent sexuality: developmental and forensic psychology* (pp. 21–40). New York: Elsevier.

Centers for Disease Control. (2013a). *Contraception*. Retrieved from <http://www.cdc.gov/reproductivehealth/UnintendedPregnancy/> Contraception.htm>.

Centers for Disease Control. (2013b). *Sexually transmitted diseases*. Retrieved from <http://www.cdc.gov/std/>.

Kingston, S., & Raghavan, C. (2009). The relationship of sexual abuse, early initiation of substance use, and adolescent trauma to PTSD. *Journal of Traumatic Stress*, *22*, 65–68.

McKee, A., Albury, K., Dunne, M., Grieshaber, S., Hartley, J., Lumby, C., et al. (2010). Healthy sexual development: A multidisciplinary framework for research. *International Journal of Sexual Health*, *22*(1), 14–19. doi:10.1080/19317610903393043.

Morquin, D., Le Moing, V., Mura, T., et al. (2012). Short- and long-term outcomes of HIV-infected patients admitted to the intensive care unit: impact of antiretroviral therapy and immunovirological status. *Annals of Intensive Care*, *2*, 1–11.

National Institutes of Health. (2013). *Abortion*. Retrieved from <http://www.nlm.nih.gov/medlineplus/abortion.html>.

Office on Women's Health, US Department of Health and Human Services. (2010). *Pregnancy.* Retrieved from <http://womenshealth.gov/pregnancy/you-are-pregnant/prenatal-care-tests.cfm#b>.

Pirard, S., Sharon, E., Kang, S. K., Angarita, G. A., & Gastfriend, D. R. (2005). Prevalence of physical and sexual abuse among substance abuse patients and impact on treatment outcomes. *Drug & Alcohol Dependence, 78*, 57–64.

Planned Parenthood. (2009). *Parental consent and notification laws*. Retrieved from <http://www.plannedparenthood.org/health-topics/abortion/parental-consent-notification-laws-25268.htm>.

Planned Parenthood. (2013). *Birth control*. Retrieved from <http://www.plannedparenthood.org/health-topics/birth-control-4211.htm>.

Sex Information and Education Council of the United States. (2004a). *Guidelines for comprehensive sexuality education: kindergarten–12th grade*, 3rd edn.

Sex Information and Education Council of the United States, (2004b). What is normal childhood sexual development? *Families Are Talking, 3*, 4.

Shea, D. J. (2008). Effects of sexual abuse by Catholic priests on adults victimized as children. *Sexual Addiction & Compulsivity, 15*, 250–268.

Taylor, P. E. N. (1998). *The relationship of child and adolescent sexual aabuse with symptomatology: A meta-analytic and nnarrative rreview*. USA: ProQuest Information & Learning.

Tharp, A. (2013). *Talk with your teen about healthy relationships.* Retrieved from <http://healthfinder.gov/HealthTopics/Category/parenting/healthy-communication-and-relationships/talk-with-your-teen-about-healthy-relationships#the-basics_3>.

World Health Organization. (2013a). *Reproductive health*. Retrieved from <http://www.who.int/topics/reproductive_health/en/>.

World Health Organization. (2013b). *Sexual health*. Retrieved from <http://www.who.int/topics/sexual_health/en/>.

CHAPTER 12

Trauma-Focused Cognitive Behavioral Therapy for Juvenile Victims of Sexual Abuse

Lorraine T. Benuto
Administrative Faculty Department of Psychology, University of Nevada, Reno and Northcentral University, The Graduate School, CA, USA

INTRODUCTION

Sexual abuse has been defined in different ways. (Readers will find some definitions in Gordon and Schroeder, 1995, pp. 47–48; Gorey & Leslie, 1997; O'Donohue, 1992, pp. 14–37.) One particularly useful definition is as follows:

> *Sexual exploitation involving physical contact between a child and another person. Exploitation implies an inequality of power between the child and the abuser on the basis of age, physical size, and/or the nature of the emotional relationship. Physical contact includes anal, genital, oral, or breast contact (Cohen & Mannarino, 1993, p. 347).*

Epidemiological findings shed light on the incidence of child sexual abuse. In 1999, an estimated 285 400 children were victims of sexual assault and 35 000 were victims of some other type of sexual offense (Finkelhor, Hammer, & Sedlak, 2008). Juveniles accounted for more than one-third of those known to police to have committed sexual offenses against minors (Finkelhor, Ormrod, & Chaffin, 2009). Moreover, in a recent meta-analysis examining explanations for male adolescent sexual offending (Seto & Lalumiere, 2010), it was found that having a sexual abuse history produced the second largest effect size. (Only having atypical sexual interests produced a larger effect size.)

Minors who have been sexually abused often experience an assortment of sequelae. Boney-McCoy and Finkelhor (1995) conducted a national telephone survey of youth 10–16 years of age. One thousand forty-two males and 968 females responded to questions regarding experiences of victimization. Ten and a half percent of all respondents (15.3% of the females and 5.9% of the males) acknowledged having been

Toolkit for Working with Juvenile Sex Offenders.
DOI: http://dx.doi.org/10.1016/B978-0-12-405948-1.00012-8

sexually victimized. Respondents who had been sexually abused reported higher levels of psychological symptomatology (more symptoms of post-traumatic stress disorder (PTSD), more dysphoria, and more school problems) than did non-victimized respondents. The authors concluded that sexual victimization is associated with substantial mental health morbidity in the child and adolescent population.

Kendall-Tackett, Williams, and Finkelhor (1993) reviewed 45 studies that examined effects of sexual abuse on children. These investigators found that abused children had significantly more psychological symptomatology (i.e., fears, frequent nightmares, poor self-esteem, promiscuous sexual behavior, and general conduct problems) than control children and that abuse accounted for 15–45% of the variance. Clearly, the sexual victimization of minors often results in poor psychological outcomes for the children involved.

TRAUMA-FOCUSED COGNITIVE BEHAVIORAL THERAPY

Trauma-focused cognitive behavioral therapy (TF-CBT) is an evidence-based treatment package that has demonstrated efficacy in addressing the assortment of cognitive, behavioral, and affective problems that often come to the fore after a child has been exposed to trauma and/or has experienced a traumatic loss. In one meta-analysis examining psychosocial treatments for children and adolescents exposed to traumatic events, TF-CBT was the only intervention package meeting criteria for being "well-established" (Silverman, Ortiz, & Visweszaron, 2008).

Pollio, Glickman, Behl, & Deblinger (2013) provided an excellent review of evidence-based treatments to address sequelae resulting from sexual abuse, research supporting the efficacy of trauma-focused cognitive behavioral therapy (TF-CBT), a summary of TF-CBT components, and a case example of TF-CBT implementation. Readers are encouraged to review Pollio et al. (2013) for essential information about TF-CBT. I will summarize information about implementation and provide readers with additional resources to employ.

TF-CBT uses the general principles of CBT and is a treatment package that can be implemented in its entirety in as few as 12 sessions (although additional sessions can be implemented as needed). Treatment involves the child or adolescent as well as the caregiver (e.g., parent) of the child. A review of the extant literature did not yield evidence of efficacy specific to juvenile sex offenders who have a trauma history. The focus of this chapter is on TF-CBT with a focus on how this treatment package can be employed with juvenile offenders. Included in this chapter is a treatment outline and worksheets that correspond to the various components of TF-CBT.

Where Can I Learn More About It?

There are many resources available on TF-CBT for the interested therapist including websites (e.g., http://tfcbt.musc.edu/; https://www.childwelfare.gov/pubs/trauma/) that offer general information, overviews of this treatment, and training opportunities; webinars (e.g., http://www.youtube.com/watch?v=evEL519QAks); and a plethora of books (e.g., *Trauma-focused CBT for children and adolescents: Treatment applications* [Child Welfare Information Gateway, 2012]; Treating Trauma and Traumatic Grief in Children and Adolescents [Cohen, Mannarino, & Deblinger, 2006]). As indicated above, a rendition of this treatment that is tailored to offenders is absent. Nonetheless, theoretically, this treatment can be easily tailored to meet the needs of the juvenile offender as many of the cognitive aspects of the treatment call for the therapist to work in concert with the adolescent and tailor the treatment to meet the needs of the adolescent. An overview of the steps involved in TF-CBT follows and the worksheets included in this chapter are discussed in the context of their use.

Using TF-CBT

The Child Welfare Information Gateway (http://www.childwelfare.gov) offers an overview of the features and key components of TF-CBT that is reflective of the content presented in the treatment manuals for TF-CBT and empirical literature (Child Welfare Information Gateway [CWIG], 2012). The CWIG notes that TF-CBT is short term and is typically completed in 12–18, 50–90 minute sessions and consists of eight components that together spell out the word "PRACTICE". An overview of each of these components follows.

Assessment & Rapport

It is important to note that prior to initiating treatment, some time should be spent assessing the presenting concerns by meeting with both the caregiver (often times a non-offending parent) and the adolescent to determine what reactions to trauma exist and also to establish rapport with all parties who will be involved in treatment. Worksheets 1a and 1b both offer a guide for establishing rapport with the adolescent. In terms of assessment, there are two very useful assessments that are available online for free.

SCARED

The Screen for Childhood Anxiety Related Emotional Disorders (SCARED; Birmaher et al., 1999) consists of a child/adolescent and a parent version. This measure is appropriate for use with adolescents up to the age of 18, consists of 41 items, and takes approximately 10 minutes to complete. It assesses for symptoms associated with general anxiety disorder, separation anxiety disorder, panic disorder, social phobia, and school avoidance. It is available in several languages. More information about this measure and directions on how to access the measure can be found at: http://www.cebc4cw.org/assessment-tool/screen-for-childhood-anxiety-related-emotional-disorders-scared/

CAPS-CA

The Therapist-Administered PTSD Scale for Children and Adolescents (CAPS-CA; Nader, Kriegler, Blake, Pynoos, Newman et al., 1996) is a 33-item therapist-administered PTSD scale for youths aged 8 to 18 years. It assesses the frequency and intensity of symptoms and is very useful in determining if the client meets diagnostic criteria for PTSD. It is an effective means of assessing symptoms associated with the experience of trauma (Nader, 2004; Ohan, Myers, & Collett, 2002). Information on obtaining the CAPS-CA for free can be found here: http://www.ptsd.va.gov/professional/pages/assessments/caps-ca.asp

ASEBA

The Achenbach System of Empirically Based Assessment (ASEBA; www.aseba.org) offers a comprehensive assessment approach and can be useful for identifying anxiety, depression, social problems, somatic complains, attention difficulties and behavioral problems (including rule-breaking and aggressive behavior). There are multiple forms of this measure available and, specific to adolescents, this includes the Youth Self-Report (which is completed by the adolescent), the Child Behavioral Checklist (completed by the primary caregiver), and the Teacher's Report Form (which is completed by the adolescent's teacher). These can be completed individually or in concert with each other obtain a more complete view of the adolescent's functioning. These are available for purchase at www.aseba.org

P: Psychoeducation & Parenting Skills

It can be useful for the therapist to work with the caregiver (often a non-offending parent) at the outset of treatment to obtain information about the presenting concern and to assess for behavioral problems. Often, caregivers will need assistance managing behavioral problems (this will likely be the case when working with juvenile offenders). The therapist should first provide the caregiver with information about common reactions to trauma and obtain information about the presenting concerns. Worksheet 2a, "Common Reactions to Trauma", lists several of the common reactions to trauma and can be used to solicit information from the caregiver about their observations of the adolescent client. The assessment measures described above can also be used to assist with this process.

During this phase of treatment, the caregiver can be provided with parent skills training. This should include psychoeducation regarding basic behavioral principles, providing positive attention (see Worksheet 2b for a more detailed overview and Worksheet 2c for an example of a tracking sheet), and giving effective commands (see Worksheet 2d).

Once the caregiver has increased the positive interactions he/she has with the adolescent, a behavioral contract can be established between the caregiver and the adolescent. The caregiver will first need to establish privileges and tasks in which (s)he wants their adolescent to engage. Worksheet 2e contains a behavioral contract that can be tailored to the adolescent's privileges and the tasks in which the caregiver wants the adolescent to engage. A tracking sheet is also included on the worksheet. It is important that, at this juncture, the caregiver focus on behaviors he or she wants to increase as opposed to behaviors that the caregiver does not want the adolescent to engage in.

The last phase of parenting skills training involves the use of response cost – that is penalties or fines are added to the behavioral contract and house rules are established. Worksheet 2f offers a space to list out house rules and the added contingencies of the behavioral contract. A tracking sheet is also included on the worksheet.

R: Relaxation Techniques

During this phase of treatment, the adolescent is taught relaxation and stress management skills. Worksheet 3a is designed to assist the adolescent in identifying where and how he or she physically experiences stress. Worksheet 3b offers a breathing exercise that can be used to help the adolescent combat anxiety and a guided imagery relaxation exercise can be found here: http://www.drbenuto.com/voca/Victims_of_Crime_Treatment_Center/e_Health_Options.html. Progressive muscle relaxation can also be used to teach the adolescent to relax and scripts for relaxation can be downloaded here:

http://www.cpri.ca/uploads/section000159/files/handout%20-%20session%205%20(PMR%20Script).pdf

http://www.themindfulword.org/2012/guided-imagery-scripts-children-anxiety-stress/

A: Affective Expression and Regulation

During this phase of treatment, the adolescent develops better skills for managing his or her emotional reactions to reminders of the trauma and for identifying and expressing emotions. This is accomplished by having the adolescent generate a list of feelings (it can be useful to ask the adolescent to name all of the emotions that he or she can in the span of one minute) and then to share a time when he or she experienced each feeling. Worksheet 4a offers an exercise that can be completed with the adolescent that involves drawing expressions on faces. The adolescent can then be taught skills to cope with the various emotions that he or she identifies (this skills overlap somewhat with the *Cognitive Coping & Processing* phase of treatment). This can be accomplished by asking the adolescent to identify a situation in which he or she had a strong negative emotional reaction. The therapist can then employ the following practices (see Worksheets 4b & 4c):

- Ask the adolescent to identify negative thoughts that he or she had about the incident and then together the therapist and adolescent can brainstorm alternative thoughts that are more positively valenced. This can help the adolescent increase his or her use of positive self-talk.
- Ask the adolescent to identify any problems with how he or she responded and to share any negative consequences that ensued as a result of his or her reaction. This would be a good time to discuss how the adolescent's behaviors may impact others (including the crime

that he or she perpetrated). Have the adolescent brainstorm alternative (ideally positive) reactions (this might include taking a time out, walking away from the situation, practicing relaxation, etc.) and what the consequences of those alternative reactions might be. Have the adolescent practice throughout the week more positive reactions and to document the consequences of these reactions.

- Ask the adolescent to identify how he or she knows that a negative emotion is brewing. What are the early "signs" that a negative emotional reaction is coming? Teach the adolescent how to use positive self-talk, relaxation, and problem solving as soon as he or she sees the early "signs" of a negative emotional reaction. Have the adolescent track during the week these "signs" and how she or he coped with them.

C: Cognitive Coping and Processing

During this component of treatment, the goal is to help the adolescent see the connection between thoughts, feelings, and behaviors. Worksheet 5a provides some structure for this discussion using the cognitive triad to illustrate and for soliciting helpful vs unhelpful thoughts and beliefs. This discussion can be tailored to the adolescent and, in the context of juvenile offenders, this offers a place for the therapist to discuss the offense committed and how they may relate to the adolescent's beliefs and thoughts. Some of the exercises presented above under *Affective expression and regulation* can also be used here.

T: Trauma Narrative and Processing

Prior to crafting a trauma narrative, it can be useful for the adolescent to develop a Subjective Unities of Discomfort Scale (SUDS) for rating his/her distress levels during both imaginal and in-vivo exposure exercises (the latter of which is discussed below). Worksheet 6a offers a picture of a thermometer with anchor points of 0 (no distress/perfectly relaxed); 50 (between relaxed and complete distress); and 100 (the most distressed the adolescent has ever felt). The therapist should help the adolescent develop an individualized rating scale so that distress can be tracked during the trauma narrative and also during in-vivo exposure homework exercises.

Crafting the trauma narrative can occur in a number of ways. The adolescent can close his/her eyes and recount the trauma out loud in the first person, recount the trauma eyes open in the past tense, write the trauma out, draw the trauma, or any combination of the above. Regardless of the approach, the adolescent will need to review the trauma repeatedly (over several sessions) and for a prolonged period of time (typically 20–40 minutes). During this process, the therapist should provide a warm and supportive environment and record the adolescent's SUDS scores throughout the process (approximately every 5 minutes). The therapist should identify unhelpful thoughts or beliefs and, after the trauma narrative is complete, the therapist should work with the adolescent to develop a healthier and more helpful way of thinking about the trauma. In this context, the therapist can also discuss with the adolescent the offense that he or she has perpetrated and how it may be (or may not be) related to the trauma that he or she experienced. Worksheet 6b is designed to help the therapist record the adolescent's SUDS, take notes during the narrative, etc.

I: In-Vivo Exposure

During this component of treatment, the adolescent and therapist establish an in-vivo exposure hierarchy (see Worksheet 7a) in which trauma reminders are listed and rated. The therapist can ask the adolescent about things that cause him or her anxiety that are related to the trauma. After the list is formulated, the therapist should ask the adolescent to give a SUDS rating for each thing on the list. It is important that in-vivo exposure occur in a systematic manner whereby the adolescent starts with the least-distressing item and moves up to the next item only when he or she has successfully "conquered" the first item. Worksheet 7b can be used to track the adolescent's assigned homework and also can be used to illustrate how the adolescent's SUDS decreased from the initial to the final rating.

C: Conjoint Parent/Child Sessions

During these sessions the caregiver and adolescent work together to improve communication and to give the adolescent the forum to share the trauma narrative if they wish to do so.

E: Enhancing Personal Safety and Future Growth

In the final component of treatment, the adolescent develops a safety plan and can list out the things that make him/her feel safe and unsafe as well as a plan that can be implemented if/when he/she feels unsafe (see Worksheets 8a and 8b). Finally, treatment progress is reviewed and the adolescent is asked to share what he/she has learned.

Treatment Plan/Timeline Component	Session Plan/Goals	Worksheet
Establishing rapport & conducting assessment	Establishing rapport & getting to know the client. Assessment can also be conducted at this juncture using the CAPS-CA, the SCARED, or the ASEBA	1a & 1b
Psychoeducation & parenting skills	Complete parenting skills training. Provide information about common reactions to trauma	2a, 2b, 2c, 2d, 2e, & 2f
Relaxation techniques & stress management	Assist the adolescent in establishing how she or he experiences stress and then teach the adolescent relaxations skills	3a, 3b, & 3c
Affective expression & regulation	The adolescent develops better skills for managing his or her emotional reactions and for identifying and expressing emotions in general	4a
Cognitive coping & processing	The adolescent is taught about the relationship between thoughts, feelings, and behaviors	5a
Trauma narrative & processing	A trauma narrative is crafted and the trauma memory is re-processed. Homework tracking sheet 6/7 can be used here	6a & 6b
In-Vivo exposure	The adolescent and therapist establish an in-vivo exposure hierarchy where they list and rate trauma reminders. Homework tracking sheet 6/7 can be used here	7a
Conjoint parent/child sessions	During these sessions the caregiver and adolescent work together to improve communication and to give the adolescent the forum to share their trauma narrative if they wish to	Worksheets from other sessions that the client wishes to share with the caregiver can also be included
Enhancing personal safety & future growth	A safety plan is established, treatment progress is reviewed, and future plans are discussed	8a & 8b

*It is recommended that the therapist and client complete the worksheets together as opposed to having the adolescent complete them on their own.

TREATMENT OUTLINE

Worksheet 1a

These are a few of my favorite things....

Food:

____

____

Music/song:

____

____

Movie:

____

____

TV show:

____

____

Sport:

____

____

School subject:

____

____

Worksheet 1b

Things I am good at!
Please share some things that you are good at and/or that you enjoy:

____

____

____

My Family
Who do you live with?

____

____

Who is in your family?

____

____

What types of things do you do with your family?

____

____

Worksheet 2a

Common Reactions to Trauma

Fear & anxiety: ______________________________

Feeling on edge: ______________________________

Re-experiencing the trauma: ____________________

Thinking about the trauma non-stop: _____________

Having nightmares about the trauma: _____________

Avoiding things or people or places
that remind me of the trauma: __________________

Trying not to think about the trauma: ____________

Emotional numbness: __________________________

Anger: _____________________________________

Guilt and shame: _____________________________

Feeling like you are "losing it" or
"going crazy": ______________________________

Negative thoughts about myself: ________________

Feeling hopeless: _____________________________

Worksheet 2b

Parenting Skills Training: Step 1

There are two ways that we can change behavior – we can implement consequences or we can anticipate the behavior and devise a plan

To be successful at changing your adolescent's behavior, you need to:

- Be specific
- Be immediate
- Make sure your adolescent can predict consequences
- Make consequences and rewards meaningful
- Remember that positive reinforcement is key
- Expect and plan for misbehavior
- Remember that what your adolescent sees you do can impact how she or he behaves – so act as you want your son or daughter to act!

  Step 1 →
- For 15 minutes 3–4 times a week provide positive attention to your son or daughter by engaging in an activity with them that he or she enjoys. During this time you cannot ask questions, give directions, or correct them

- 3–4 times a week when your child is engaging in an activity that she/he enjoys take a minute to provide positive attention in a relaxed and casual way; make a positive comment about what he or she is doing, how well she is accomplishing it, or how quiet and well-behaved he is; don't ask questions that imply disapproval or criticism – your goal is to show your adolescent that you are interested in what he or she is doing
- Praise your adolescent when he or she is doing well – the first step in behavior modification is to provide POSITIVE attention – during this first phase (at least a week) no NEGATIVE attention is allowed!

Worksheet 2c

How many times did you practice positive attention with your adolescent?

Activity	Monday	Tuesday	Wednesday	Thursday	Friday	Saturday	Sunday
During an activity your adolescent enjoys							
During good behavior							
When you were busy							
When your adolescent helped you with something							
Thanked your adolescent for complying							

Worksheet 2d

Parenting Skills Training: Step 2 → Give Effective Commands

- Make sure you mean it! → only ask your adolescent to do things you want them to do and that you are willing to ensure that they do

- Do not present the command as a question or favor – Don't say: Can you please clean your room? Instead say: Clean your room. Give commands one at a time → instead of asking your adolescent to pick up the living room, do the dishes, and take out the trash ask them to do each one individually and don't add a task until the first one is complete
- Be specific → for some kids asking them to clean their room is good – for others you may have to be more specific → Pick up your dirty clothes and put them in the laundry basket; make your bed etc.
- Don't compete with the TV, iPhone etc. When you give a command make sure there are no distractions
- Use a timer or stopwatch if you need to get your adolescent to complete a task in a predetermined amount of time

Track your progress throughout the week below – tally and make notes daily

Requests	Mon	Tues	Wed	Thurs	Fri	Sat	Sun
Make sure you mean it!							
Do not present the command as a question or favor							
Give commands one at a time							
Tell your child what to do as opposed to what not to do							
Avoid competing distractions when giving commands							

Worksheet 2e

Parenting Skills Training: Step 3 → Establishing a Behavioral Contract

At this point you are focused on getting your adolescent to do things – don't focus on the things you want them to stop doing. It is much easier to increase a behavior than to decrease a behavior.

Establish "Privileges"

____________________ ____________________

____________________ ____________________

____________________ ____________________

What specific task do you want your child to do?

____________________ ____________________

____________________ ____________________

____________________ ____________________

For the first behavioral contract, parents should choose a request of relatively low difficulty and a privilege of moderate value to the teen

I, name__________________, agree that I will task_____________. If I, task_____________I can privilege______________. If I do not task_____________, I cannot privilege__________________

Behavior	Mon	Tues	Wed	Thurs	Fri	Sat	Sun
Did your adolescent do what you asked?							
Did your adolescent receive the "privilege"?							

Worksheet 2f

Parenting Skills Training: Step 4 → Using Response Cost

Goal – introduce the use of fines or penalties into home-based contingency management as punishment for non-compliance and unacceptable social conduct

Review – how the behavioral contract went
Add – a consequence to the behavioral contract
Establish – House Rules

House Rules

1) ____________________ 2) ____________________

3) ____________________ 4) ____________________

5) ____________________ 6) ____________________

7) ____________________ 8) ____________________

9) ____________________ 10) ____________________

I, name__________________, agree that I will task_____________. If I, task_____________I can privilege______________. If I do not task_____________, I cannot privilege__________________and instead will consequence__________________

Behavior	Mon	Tues	Wed	Thurs	Fri	Sat	Sun
Did your adolescent do what you asked?							
Did your adolescent receive the "privilege"?							
Did your adolescent receive the "consequence"?							

Worksheet 3a

People often report that they "feel" stress in their body. This could be internal feelings (like your heart pounding or your shoulders tensed up) or external sensations (like your palms sweating). Circle the various places where you "feel" stress.

Where do you feel stress?

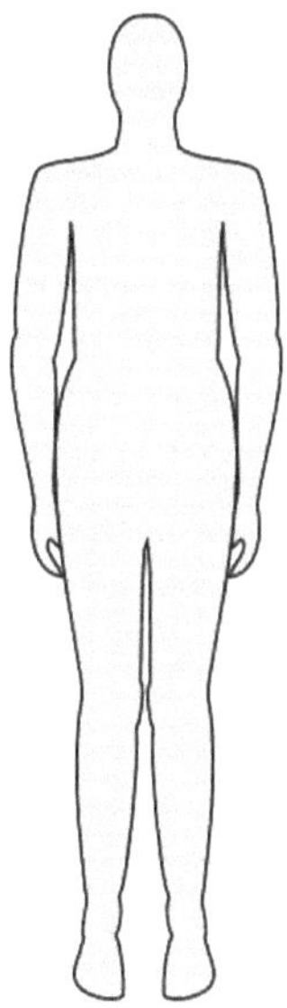

Worksheet 3b

Using Breathing to Combat Anxiety

Can you share some times when you feel nervous?

What can you (or do you) do in those situations to help yourself feel less nervous?

Often times we are told to just take a deep breath and this will help us to calm down. It is actually not deep breathing, but SLOW breathing that can help us feel more relaxed and calm. Let's practice slow breathing together.

What is a color or word that you associate with relaxation?

Let's take a normal breath in and then let's take a long slow exhale… and then another normal breath in and another long, slow exhale. Let's continue to breath this way – normal breath in followed by a long slow exhale. As we exhale we will use your relaxation word to help us relax even more. On exhale I will say your relaxation word slowly and you can focus on just relaxing!

Now that you have learned about using breathing to help you relax, what types of situations can you practice this in the upcoming week?

____

____

____

Can you commit to practicing breathing this way everyday at a set time – maybe before bed or right when you wake up in the morning?

Worksheet 4a

Reading Faces

Have you ever heard the expression, "She wears her heart on her sleeve"? This expression is used to describe people who "show" their emotion. Often times we can "read" people's emotions by looking at their faces. Below are several faces. Below each face write in an emotion and then draw the corresponding "expression".

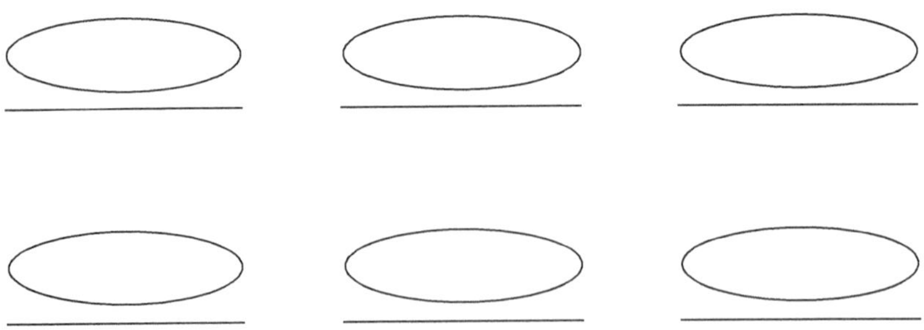

Worksheet 4b

Managing Emotions

Name all the feelings you can think of (therapist times 1 minute):	Share a time when you felt this way	How did you react?	Positive & negative consequence of your reaction	Alternative ways you could have reacted

Worksheet 4c

Share a time when you had a strong emotional reaction: ______________

____

How might you have acted differently? If you could go back what would you change about how you responded?______________________

What are some signs that you are going to have a strong, negative emotional reaction?

	Strong emotional reaction	Alternative emotional reaction
What behaviors did you engage in?		
What thoughts did you have?		
What were the problems or negative consequences associated with your response?		
What were the positive consequences associated with your response?		

Worksheet 5a

Why is thinking positive important?

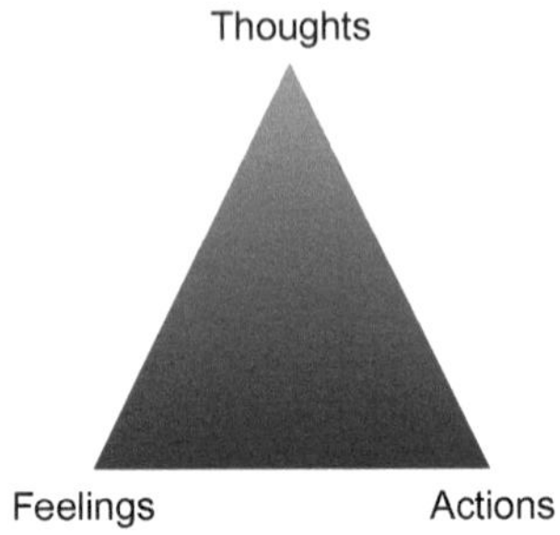

Unhelpful thoughts & beliefs	Helpful thoughts & beliefs
____________________	____________________
____________________	____________________
____________________	____________________

Worksheet 6a

Your Rating Scale

We are going to create your own personal rating scale! We will use this scale to track how anxious/nervous/distressed you are feeling.

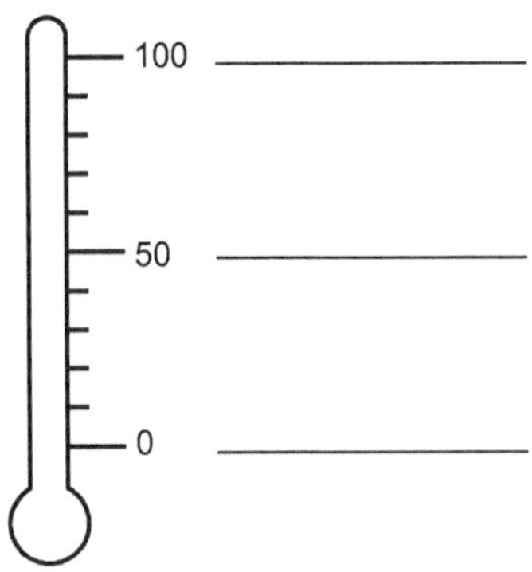

Worksheet 6b

Trauma Narrative

So far, we have learned about how trauma can impact us and also how treatment can help common reactions to trauma. Even though it can be hard to talk about things that happened to us that are scary or make us sad, it is important for us to do so that we can move on with our lives and get back to the things we used to enjoy. Sometimes it can seem like trying to forget about what happened to us is the best thing to do – but a lot of the time the harder we try not to think about something the more that something invades our mind! Today I am going to ask you to tell me about your trauma. I am going to write down everything you tell me. I don't want you to worry about how it sounds, I just want you to tell me everything you can remember.

Time	SUDS	Trauma narrative/therapist notes
____	____	______________________________
____	____	______________________________
____	____	______________________________
____	____	______________________________
____	____	______________________________
____	____	______________________________
____	____	______________________________
____	____	______________________________
____	____	______________________________
____	____	______________________________

Date:__________Therapist Notes:____________________

____

Worksheet 7a

In-vivo Exposure Hierarchy

Initial rating	Item	Final rating
____	1. ______________________	____
____	2. ______________________	____
____	3. ______________________	____
____	4. ______________________	____
____	5. ______________________	____
____	6. ______________________	____
____	7. ______________________	____
____	8. ______________________	____
____	9. ______________________	____
____	10. ______________________	____

Therapist Notes: ____

____

____

____

____

Worksheet 6/7

Homework Log

Homework Assignment __________

Date	Time	Rating before	Rating after	Highest rating	Notes/thoughts

Homework Assignment __________

Date	Time	Rating before	Rating after	Highest rating	Notes/thoughts

Worksheet 8a

Safety

Things that make me feel safe:

____

____

____

What can I do if I don't feel safe?

____

____

____

Things that make me feel unsafe:

____

____

____

TREATMENT WRAP-UP

What did I learn in treatment?

____

____

What did I gain from treatment?

____

____

What did I like (or not like!) about treatment?

____

____

Where do I go from here?

____

____

REFERENCES

Birmaher, B., Brent, D. A., Chiappetta, L., Bridge, J., Monga, S., & Baugher, M. (1999). Psychometric properties of the Screen for Child Anxiety Related Emotional Disorders (SCARED): a replication study. *Journal of the American Academy of Child and Adolescent Psychiatry*, *38*, 1230–1236.

Boney-McCoy, S., & Finkelhor, D. (1995). Psychosocial sequelae of violent victimization in a national youth sample. *Journal of Consulting and Clinical Psychology*, *63*, 726–736.

Child Welfare Information Gateway (CWIG). (2012). *Trauma-focused cognitive behavioral therapy for children affected by sexual abuse or trauma*. Retrieved from: <https://www.childwelfare.gov/pubs/trauma/>.
Cohen, J. A., & Mannarino, A. P. (1993). Sexual abuse. In R. T. Ammerman, C. G. Last, & M. Hersen (Eds.), *Handbook of prescriptive treatments for children and adolescents* (pp. 347–366). Boston: Allyn & Bacon.
Cohen, J. A., Mannarino, A. P., & Deblinger, E. (2006). *Treating trauma and traumatic grief in children and adolescents*. New York: Guilford.
Finkelhor, D., Hammer, H., & Sedlak, A. J. (2008). Sexually assaulted children: National estimates and characteristics: *National incidence studies of missing, abducted, runaway, and thrownaway children (NISMART)*. Washington, DC: OJJDP.
Finkelhor, D., Ormrod, R., & Chaffin, M. (2009). Juveniles who commit sex offenses against minors: *Juvenile justice bulletin*. Washington, DC: OJJDP.
Gordon, B. N., & Schroeder, C. S. (1995). *Sexuality: A developmental approach to problems*. New York: Plenum.
Gorey, K. M., & Leslie, D. R. (1997). The prevalence of child sexual abuse: Integrative review adjustment for potential response and measurement biases. *Child Abuse & Neglect*, *21*, 391–398.
Kendall-Tackett, K. A., Williams, L., & Finkelhor, D. (1993). Impact of sexual abuse on children: A review and synthesis of recent empirical studies. *Psychological Bulletin*, *113*, 164–180.
Nader, K., Kriegler, J. A., Blake, D. D., Pynoos, R. S., Newman, E., & Weathers, F. W. (1996). *Clinician administered PTSD scale, child and adolescent version*. White River Junction: National Center for PTSD.
Nader, K. O. (2004). Assessing traumatic experiences in children and adolescents: Self-reports of DSM PTSD Criteria B-D symptoms. In J. Wilson & T. Keane (Eds.), *Assessing psychological trauma and PTSD* (pp. 513–537) (2nd ed.). New York: Guilford.
O'Donohue, W. (1992). Definitional and ethical issues in child sexual abuse. In W. O'Donohue & J. H. Geer (Eds.), *The sexual abuse of children: Theory and research* (Vol. 1, pp. 14–37). New Jersey: Lawrence Erlbaum.
Ohan, J. L., Myers, K., & Collett, B. R. (2002). Ten-year review of rating scales. IV: Scales assessing trauma and its effects. *Journal of the American Academy of Child and Adolescent Psychiatry*, *41*, 1401–1422.
Pollio, E., Glickman, A., Behl, L., & Deblinger, E. (2013). Treating children and adolescents in the aftermath of sexual abuse. In D. S. Bromberg & W. T. O'Donohue (Eds.), *Handbook of child and adolescent sexuality: developmental and forensic psychology* (pp. 371–400). New York: Elsevier.
Seto, M. C., & Lalumiere, M. L. (2010). What is so special about adolescent sexual offending?: A review and test of explanations through meta-analysis. *Psychological Bulletin*, *136*, 526–575.
Silverman, W. K., Ortiz, C. D., Visweszaron, C., et al. (2008). Evidence-based psychosocial treatments for children and adolescents exposed to traumatic events. *Journal of Clinical Child & Adolescent Psychology*, *37*, 156–183.

CHAPTER 13

Assessment and Intervention with Young People who Sexually Offend

Gary O'Reilly
School of Psychology, University College Dublin, Republic of Ireland

INTRODUCTION

Assessing young people who sexually abuse is a complicated process that is best undertaken in a planned, supported, and systematic manner informed by the available research literature. This chapter outlines how practitioners might approach assessment and intervention with a young person who sexually abuses including available members of the young person's family. In keeping with the aims of this volume, a focus on "what to do" is offered but the link to "why we do it" is kept in view for follow up for those who would like to do so.

THINKING CRITICALLY ABOUT RESEARCH AND THEORY IN THIS AREA IS VITAL

Sexual offending is understandably a very emotive topic. Consequently, it is vitally important we exercise critical thinking in relation to research and practice in this area. There are many gaps in our theoretical knowledge and research evidence concerning sexual offending by young people and adults. Studies that explore the characteristics of young people who sexually offend are retrospectively based only on those whose behavior is detected and there are no randomized control trials regarding the effectiveness of intervention outcome. Conducting high quality scientific studies in any area of human functioning is difficult but this area is constrained by many additional factors that make our knowledge less reliable, such as the hidden nature of sexual offending behavior and the many potential costs to a person who acknowledges engaging in it. Despite these limitations, some useful sources of information are available to us, particularly

Toolkit for Working with Juvenile Sex Offenders.
DOI: http://dx.doi.org/10.1016/B978-0-12-405948-1.00013-X

those that use high quality research designs or attempt a combination of evidence rather than offering a perspective based on a single study.

Seto and Lalumiere (2010), for example, ask the question: are young people who sexually abuse different or similar compared to other young people who engage in non-sexual criminal behavior? Through a systematic review of the literature they integrated and compared studies that contrasted varying sized samples of young people who engage in non-sexual criminality with those young people whose offending is sexual but not more broadly criminal. Table 13.1 outlines the areas of similarity and difference identified in Seto and Lalumiere's review. A Venn diagram-like relationship emerges. There is evidence of similarity between these two groups in their age of first criminal contact, conduct problems, exposure to familial and non-familial physical violence, family dysfunction and criminality, social skill deficits, psychopathology and general cognitive ability. Young people who sexually abuse differ in lower levels of previous criminal history and antisocial association, more exposure to sexual abuse, family sexual violence and areas of lower overt antisocial behaviors and associations, greater history of sexual, physical and emotional abuse, less well developed heterosocial skills, greater withdrawal and isolation, more atypical sexual interests and exposure to pornography, increased social and other anxiety, and more specific learning difficulties. In reality, practitioners encounter young people who engage in sexual offending on its own, and young people whose offending is part of broader criminal behavior. Each group has nuanced differences in their development and presentation as well as overlap. Good assessment and intervention follow the same broad principles with both groups while allowing for the nuanced differences in their presentation. The approach to assessment and intervention described below allows for this.

ADOPT A STRUCTURED CLINICAL TOOL TO ASSIST YOUR ASSESSMENT

In the field of adult sexual offending, there is progress in the development of actuarial approaches that inform us of an individual's risk of re-offending (Hanson & Morton-Bourgon, 2009). Progress in the risk assessment of young people is not as advanced. Hempel, Buck, Cima, & van Marle, (2013) review the six most commonly used structured risk assessment instruments for young people. These are:

Table 13.1 Similarities and Differences Between Young People Who Engage in Broad Criminal but Non-Sexual Offending and those Whose Offending is Sexual

Similar	Different	Effect Size for Difference
Antisocial Tendencies	**Antisocial Tendencies**	
Age of first court contact	Less previous criminal history	Medium
Conduct problems	Less general antisocial attitudes	Medium
Antisocial personality traits	Less antisocial association	Medium
Antisocial sexual attitudes	Less substance abuse	Small
Exposure to Abuse	**Exposure to Abuse**	
Exposure to family physical violence	Sexual abuse 5 times more likely	Medium
Exposure to non-family physical violence	More exposure to family sexual violence	Small
	Physical abuse 1.6 times more likely	Small
	More emotional abuse or neglect	Small
Family Functioning	**Family Functioning**	
Family relationship problems	–	
Separation from a parent		
Family substance abuse		
Family criminality		
Interpersonal Functioning	**Interpersonal Functioning**	
Social skills deficits	Heterosocial skills deficits	Small
General social problems	Poorer social relations, withdrawal, isolation	Small
Sexuality	**Sexuality**	
Sexual experience	More atypical sexual interests	Medium
	Greater exposure to sex or pornography	Small
Psychopathology	**Psychopathology**	
General psychopathology	Anxiety	Small
Depression	Social anxiety	Small
Neuroticism	Lower self-esteem	Small
Psychoticism		
Suicidal tendencies		

(*Continued*)

Table 13.1 (Continued)

Similar	**Different**	**Effect Size for Difference**
Cognitive Abilities	**Cognitive Abilities**	
General intelligence levels	Specific learning difficulties	Small
Verbal intelligence levels	Academic problems	Small
Performance intelligence levels		
Neurological anomalies		

Identified through meta-analysis by Seto and Lalumiere (2010).

1. Juvenile Sex Offender Assessment Protocol-II (J-SOAP-II; Prentky & Righthand, 2003)
2. Juvenile Sexual Offence Recidivism Risk Assessment Tool-II (J-SORRAT-II; Epperson, Ralston, Fowers, & DeWitt, 2005)
3. Estimate of Risk of Adolescent Sexual Offence Recidivism (ERASOR; Worling & Curwen, 2000)
4. Juvenile Risk Assessment Scale (JRAS; New Jersey Attorney General's Office, 2006)
5. Structured Assessment of Violent Risk in Youth (SAVRY; Borum, Bartel, & Forth, 2003)
6. Psychopathy Checklist-Youth Version (PCL:YV; Forth, Kosson, & Hare, 2003).

Hempel et al. identified 19 empirical studies that used one of these measures at assessment and reported the relationship between scores on the assessment instrument and rate of recidivism or re-adjudication at follow-up periods ranging from 1 to 16 years depending on the study. The results were mixed. Eleven studies reported data on the *J-SOAP-II*. Of these, seven indicated the relationship between Total *J-SOAP-II* scores and sexual recidivism. Three found a fair to good relationship while four did not. Two of three studies with the *J-SORRAT-II* found a poor to fair relationship between assessment scores and sexual re-offending. Four of six found a fair to good relationship for the *ERASOR*, one poor relationship of two studies for the *JRAS*, none of two for the *SAVRY*, and one strong relationship of three studies for the *PCL-YV*. Many factors contribute to this mixed outcome. These include the as yet not well understood heterogeneity in the various samples of young people involved in these studies, the incompleteness of the items used in these instruments as identified through previous research, and the fluidly developmental nature of adolescence itself. As such, there is no risk assessment instrument that predicts sexual, violent or general recidivism that is sufficiently reliable for us to use it universally with all young people who sexually offend and its unclear with whom these instruments are currently at their most reliable.

Nevertheless, assessing and offering intervention to any group of people who engage in some form of offending is best offered when it incorporates a guided or structured approach. This allows us to anchor our assessment to instruments that are reflective of functioning identified in young people who sexually offend even if they are not necessarily reliably predictive of recidivism.

One such approach is the AIM-2 (Assessment, Intervention and Moving-on 2; Griffin, Beech, Print, Bradshaw, & Quayle, 2008; Print, Griffin, Beech, 2007). It is an attempt to gather the research literature in order to guide assessment for therapeutic intervention. It comprises 75 items which assessors can judge to be present or absent from their assessment with a young person and his family. It is intended for use with males aged 12–18 years in the normal range of intellectual functioning who acknowledge their abusive behavior. Each item falls into one of three sources:

1. Evidence-based items where there are at least two credible research studies that link it with recidivism
2. Evidence-supported items which have a small research base or are linked with adult recidivism or non-sexual recidivism in juveniles
3. Theoretically supported items where a research base is absent but theoretical support is found in the literature linking it to juvenile sexual offending recidivism.

Information to guide the scoring of the 75 items is elicited through gathering as much information as available concerning the young person from reports or other professionals coupled with the completion of a comprehensive assessment of a young person and his caregivers. Each item in the AIM-2 framework can be thought of as either static, i.e., something that is historic and unchanging about a young person (e.g., previous sexually abusive behavior), or dynamic, i.e., a current aspect of functioning that may or may not change in the future (e.g., mood). There are four domains covered by the AIM-2 framework: developmental; family; environment;

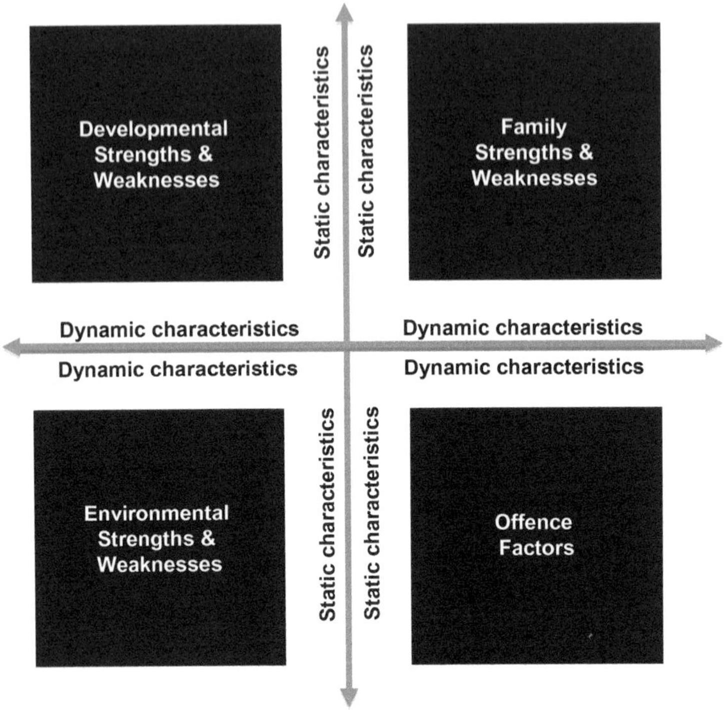

Figure 13.1 The AIM-2 conceptual framework.

and offense, with some items reflecting concerns while some reflect strengths (Figure 13.1).

Despite its identification of items from the literature, the AIM-2 framework also lacks an empirically well-driven system of recidivism prediction. However, it does provide practitioners with clear and holistic guidance on topics of importance in understanding a young person and available members of his family/care system that leads to a picture of his strengths and weaknesses that can contribute to the formulation of an individually tailored intervention plan. In time, assessment of young people will need to incorporate both recidivism and therapeutic intervention requirements into their approaches. The AIM-2 system is the beginning of a reasonable compromise between assessment that is concerned purely with identifying risk factors and the more traditional formulation of an individual's psychological needs used in clinical interventions with young people that includes their risk factors. However, practitioners need to keep sight of the serious limitations of this instrument's practically unknown predictive value.

CONDUCTING A CLINICAL ASSESSMENT

Plan and execute an assessment that evolves over a number of sessions and incorporates information from a number of sources. Gathering as much background information as possible about the young person and his offending behavior is a key component to completing a good quality assessment. Any referral information and available reports from other professionals who may have previous contact with the young person is an important part of the preparation. So, too, is access to reliable information on the details of the young person's offending or alleged offending behavior. O' Reilly and Carr (2004) recommend a four appointment assessment process with a young person and his family that takes place over the course of a number of sessions working with the young person and important parts of his family or care network in combination and individually. Such a process allows professionals to gather the information required to complete a structured risk assessment as outlined above, and to engage a young person and his family into an intervention service while formulating their recidivism related and broader intervention needs.

Session one begins by inviting the young person and his parent(s) or carer(s) to a joint meeting. This allows the purpose and nature of the assessment to be explained and agreed. It can be very helpful at this meeting to provide clarity on the purpose of the assessment – is it for a court report, or for assessment for suitability for intervention, or both? Who will have access to information from the assessment and what are the limits to confidentiality? How long will the assessment take and what are the potential outcomes? This initial assessment appointment is also an opportunity to engage a young person and his family or carers. Towards this end, it is helpful to adopt a therapeutic style that is accepting of the young person and the situation he is in, conveys an understanding of how difficult a process it can be for him and his family to attend an assessment and offers appropriate hope for the future. Most young people and their families are under considerable pressure when they attend a service for an assessment. It is not uncommon for young people and members of their family or care system to be at different points of acceptance, minimization and denial about the sexually abusive behavior. Great shame and anxiety are not uncommon emotions about what happened. Fear of being imprisoned, taken into care or retribution from members of the community are also likely to feature highly. Tables 13.2–13.5 outline the content that might be covered during the assessment.

Table 13.2 Suggested Topics for Assessment Session One
Main Areas Covered in a Developmental Interview During Assessment Session One

Development During Infancy and Early Childhood
• Mother and child's health status during pregnancy • Any complications during delivery • Mother and child's health after delivery • Any disruptions to parental bonding after delivery due to health difficulties or other factors • Child's temperament as an infant • Child's pattern of sleeping as an infant • Child's pattern of feeding as an infant • Child's accomplishment of main motor milestones including ages for sitting up, crawling, standing, walking with assistance and walking independently • Any unusual features of motor development, such as delay in motor development or not crawling, unusual gait or attendance with an occupational therapist for assessment and intervention • The child's level of activity as reflected in their accomplishment of different stages of motor development – (inactive, normal, overactive) • Child's accomplishment of main speech and language milestones including ages for babbling, first words, two-word combinations, and use of sentences • Any unusual features of speech and language, such as delayed speech, articulation difficulties or attendance with a speech and language therapist for assessment and intervention • Accomplishment of toilet training and any difficulties with toileting, such as encopresis or enuresis • Any significant separations from primary caregivers during infancy and early childhood • Opportunities for the development of social skills in early childhood through contact with siblings, members of the extended family, peers and family friends • Any unusual features of social skills development • Any general behavior difficulties • Any sexualized behavior difficulties • Any difficulties in learning rules of social behavior • Any difficulties in the regulation of affect, such as temper tantrums • Any significant emotional difficulties • Any significant family events or difficulties during early childhood • Attendance at preschool including the child's reaction to separation from primary caregivers, relationships formed with teachers, relationships formed with peers, and response to preschool rules and tasks • Any additional strengths from infancy and early childhood not previously identified • Any other important information from infancy and early childhood

(*Continued*)

Table 13.2 (Continued)
Main Areas Covered in a Developmental Interview During Assessment Session One

Development During Middle and Late Childhood
• Attendance at primary school including the child's reaction to separation from primary caregivers, relationships formed with teachers, relationships formed with peers, and response to primary school rules and tasks • Any significant behavioral problems in primary school • General academic performance in comparison to peers in primary school • Any significant general or specific learning difficulties in primary school • Any additional educational resources made available during primary school • Any change in class or school • Relationships developed with peers outside of primary school • Relationships with siblings and adult family members • The general development and expression of social skills in middle and late childhood • Any significant family events or difficulties during middle or late childhood • Any significant life events influencing development during middle or late childhood • Any significant general behavior problems including any disruptive or emerging delinquent behavior, or use of alcohol or drugs • Any sexualized behavior difficulties or exposure to pornography • Any significant emotional problems • Any additional strengths from middle and late childhood not previously identified • Any other important information from middle and late childhood
Development During Adolescence
• Attendance at secondary school including the child's reaction to separation from primary caregivers, relationships formed with teachers, relationships formed with peers, and response to secondary school rules and tasks • Any significant behavioral problems in secondary school • General academic performance in comparison to peers in secondary school • Any significant general or specific learning difficulties in secondary school • Any additional educational resources made available during secondary school • Any change in class or school • Relationships developed with peers outside of secondary school including any engagement with delinquent peer group • Relationships with siblings and adult family members • The general development and expression of social skills in adolescence • Development of interest in age appropriate relationships that have a sexual dimension • Any significant family events or difficulties during adolescence • Any significant life events influencing development during adolescence • Any significant general behavior problems • Any sexualized behavior problems • Any significant emotional problems

(*Continued*)

Table 13.2 (Continued)

Main Areas Covered in a Developmental Interview During Assessment Session One

- Use of alcohol or drugs
- Use of pornography
- Any additional strengths from adolescence not previously identified
- Any other important information from adolescence

Medical History

- Any current medical conditions
- Any current medication
- Any significant past medical conditions
- Any past hospitalization
- Any significant past head injuries
- Any past genital injuries
- Any allergies
- Any significant family medical history

Table 13.3 Suggested Topics for Assessment Session Two

Main Areas Covered in Assessment Session Two with the Young Person and his Primary Caregivers

- Obtaining a detailed genogram of members of the young person's immediate and extended family and other important people who are not family members. A detailed guide for constructing genograms can be found in Carr (2012)
- Areas of strength and family coping skills
- Personal strengths of the young person referred with sexually abusive behavior problems
- Difficult problems that have been faced by the family and effective and non-effective coping skills that have been utilized to manage these
- Any additional current difficulties that are being faced by the family
- Close, positive relationships within the family system
- Negative and conflictual relationships within the family system
- The caregiver's reaction to the young person's sexually abusive behavior, particularly responses of anger, shame, fear, self-judgment, sense of pressure or trauma
- The caregiver's understanding of the young person's account of his sexually abusive behavior
- The level of acceptance by the primary caregivers of the young person's responsibility for his sexually abusive behavior
- The caregiver's availability and capacity for supervision of the young person
- The caregiver's attitude towards the provision of assessment and intervention for the young person

(Continued)

Table 13.3 (Continued)
Main Areas Covered in Assessment Session Two with the Young Person and his Primary Caregivers

- The caregiver's opinion on the level of readiness of the young person for assessment and intervention
- The level of awareness of the young person's sexually abusive behavior within the extended family system and within the broader community and any related threats to family member's well-being from this
- The primary caregiver's attitude towards participation in carer's work as part of the young person's intervention program
- In the case of intrafamilial abuse – the impact on victim and other family members, family relationships and the extent to which those affected are in receipt of services
- Any immediate or extended family history of substance abuse, mental health difficulties, sexual victimization, physical violence, sexually abusive behavior difficulties, criminality and the quality of the family's social environment
- Positive goals for the future

Table 13.4 Suggested Topics for Assessment Session Three
Main Areas Covered in Assessment Session Three

General Areas Covered in Interview 3

- The young person's interests, hobbies, likes, and dislikes
- Important friendships in the young person's life
- Activities engaged in by the young person with friends and peers
- Any socialization difficulties reported by the young person
- Any conduct disorder type behavior engaged in by the young person individually or with peers
- Any difficulties with low mood experienced by the young person and approaches used to manage them
- Any difficulties with strong angry feelings experienced by the young person and approaches used to manage them
- Any difficulties with conflict and aggression experienced by the young person and approaches used to manage them
- Any difficulties with attention and concentration experienced by the young person and approaches used to manage them
- Use of alcohol and drugs
- The young person's positive and negative engagement with technology (gaming, social media, pornography, information seeking/sharing, cyber-bullying, messaging)
- Use of pornography

(Continued)

Table 13.4 (Continued)
Main Areas Covered in Assessment Session Three

Comprehensive Sexual History

- What age was the young person the first time they had a "crush" on someone? Who was that person and what were the circumstances?
- What age was the young person the first time they kissed someone? Who was that person and what were the circumstances?
- What age was the young person the first time they saw a male naked? Who was that person and what were the circumstances?
- What age was the young person the first time they saw a female naked? Who was that person and what were the circumstances?
- What age was the young person the first time they touched someone in a sexual way? Who was that person and what were the circumstances?
- What age was the young person the first time someone touched them in a sexual way? Who was that person and what were the circumstances?
- Any atypical sexual interests or experiences
- The young person is invited to provide information on each person with whom they have had any form of sexual contact. Information sought should clarify who each person was, what age they were, the level of activity engaged in and whether the activity was wanted or unwanted by either party. If it becomes apparent that the young person has been the victim of sexually abusive behavior, then the appropriate child protection guidelines should be fully followed in relation to this

Table 13.5 Suggested Topics for Assessment Session Four
Main Areas Covered in Assessment Session Four

Antecedents to the Sexually Abusive Behavior

- Where was the young person before the offense took place? Who else was around or nearby?
- What was the young person doing before the offense?
- What was the young person thinking before the offense?
- How was the young person feeling before the offense?
- When did the young person start to think about offending (including pre-offense fantasy)?
- How did the young person set up the offense situation?
- How did the young person select the person whom they assaulted?
- What steps did the young person take to avoid detection?

Abusive Behavior

- Where did the offense take place? Who else was around or nearby?
- What behaviors did the young person engage in during the offense?
- How did the young person feel during the offense?

(*Continued*)

Table 13.5 (Continued)
Main Areas Covered in Assessment Session Four

- What thoughts were going through the young person's mind during the offense?
- What did the young person notice about the reaction of the person who was assaulted during the offense?
- What methods of coercion were used by the young person during the assault?

Consequences

- What did the young person do after the offense?
- How did the young person feel immediately after the offense?
- What thoughts were going through the young person's mind immediately after the offense?
- What did the young person notice about the reaction of the person who was assaulted after the offense?
- What did the young person say or do to the person who was assaulted in an effort to prevent detection of their abusive behavior?
- What other steps did the young person take to avoid detection?
- What thoughts went through the young person's mind as he took steps to avoid detection or after a period of time had passed?
- How did the young person feel as he took steps to avoid detection or after a period of time had passed?
- How was the young person's offense discovered?
- How did the young person feel about and respond to the discovery of his abusive behavior?
- The young person's understanding of the harmfulness and illegality of his abusive behavior.
- How did others respond to the discovery of the young person's abusive behavior?
- How does the young person feel about his abusive behavior now?
- What does the young person recognize as risky thoughts, feelings, behaviors and situations now? How does he manage these?
- What does the young person think and feel about his participation in assessment? Has there been any change in his attitude since his first attendance?
- What does the young person think and feel about participating in intervention?
- What does the young person think and feel about his caregiver's participation in intervention in support of him?

Concluding Questions

- How does the young person feel about the future with and without intervention?
- What positive wishes does the young person have for his future?

In session one, the young person and his caregivers are welcomed and engaged in the assessment process. The young person's sexual offending behavior is *not* the primary focus of the first appointment. Instead, the first session is an attempt to provide clarity on the aims and nature of the work that will be completed with the assessment service. It allows the assessor to get to know the young person and to take a developmental history. In session two, the focus is again with the young person and his primary carers. The main aim is to establish as much information as possible about his family life including any disruptions or experiences of living in care. In session three, the young person is seen individually. Again, the aim is to continue to engage him, using the emerging therapeutic alliance better to understand his current world, his peers, his school/work life, challenges he faces, his drug and alcohol use, his sexual history, and his strengths. Finally, in assessment session four, the focus turns to the young person's sexually abusive behavior. It can be helpful to explain to the young person that the purpose of this session is not to embarrass him or put him under pressure. Instead, the aim is to understand how he came to a point in his life where he engaged in sexually abusive behavior and to use this understanding to help him build a safer healthier life for the future.

FORMULATING AND REPORTING ASSESSMENT FINDINGS

Once the assessment is complete, the next session is to develop a formulation of the young person and compile a report making recommendations that logically extend from the assessment. A case example is presented here for "Douglas Murray", a 14-year-old boy who sexually abused his 7-year-old cousin Sally. The report is based on the approach to assessment described above and also illustrates the utility of including psychological testing in an assessment. Figure 13.2 presents a formulation of Douglas based on the approach to formulation in clinical psychology developed by Carr (2006). At the conclusion of the assessment process, it is good practice to sit down and read through the report and its recommendations with a young person and his carers. In doing so, you can check the accuracy of what is reported and discuss and agree your recommendations with the young person and those involved in his care. From the report, the reasons for the recommendations should be evident and so are more likely to be agreed.

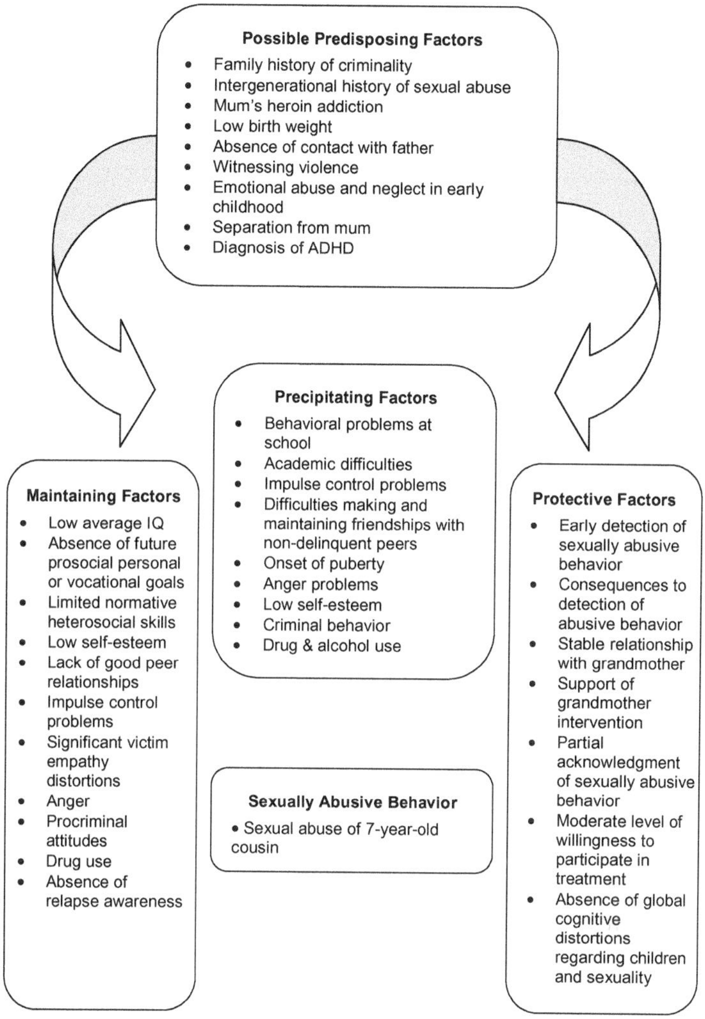

Figure 13.2 Formulation diagram for "Douglas Murray".

ASSESSMENT REPORT

Name: Dougie Murray.
DOB: 10/11/1999. **CA:** 14 years.
Date of Report: 17/02/2014.
Family Composition:
Douglas (Dougie) Murray – referred client, 14 years
Michelle Murray – mother, 31 years
Emma Murray – Grandmother, 49 years

The Purpose of This Report

This purpose of this report is to outline the findings from a comprehensive therapeutic assessment with Douglas (known as Dougie) Murray (14 years), and his grandmother Mrs Emma Murray following confirmed allegations that he sexually abused his cousin Sally (6 years). The information in this report is drawn from the following sources. The letter of referral from Steve Swan (Social Worker) incorporating relevant information from the assessment reports from the Community Care Social Work Team who completed the sexual assault validation assessment with Sally and her family, individual and joint assessment appointments with Dougie Murray, and Mrs Emma Murray, and psychological testing with Dougie Murray.

Reason for Referral

Dougie Murray was referred for assessment with our intervention service by Steve Swan, Community Social Worker. In his letter of referral, Mr Swan provided the following information: in October 2013 Dougie (aged 14) was minding his cousin Sally (aged 6) and her younger brother John (aged 5) at the home of his aunt Nicole Murray. The following morning Sally was out of sorts and was upset and tearful and told her mum that Dougie did "bold things" the previous evening. In discussing this with her daughter, Nicole understood this to mean that Dougie had touched her inappropriately and also that he got Sally to touch him inappropriately. She took her daughter to Accident and Emergency where she was assessed, a referral was made to the child sexual abuse assessment and treatment unit and a notification made to the local child protection services and to the police. Sally's allegation was confirmed by the child sexual abuse assessment team and she was referred for counseling. The assessment team confirmed that while he was acting as baby-sitter Dougie touched Sally on her vagina with his hand and got her to touch his penis. He told her it was a game and a way people show each other that they like each other and that if she didn't do it she would be saying she did not like him. He told her afterwards that she would be in more trouble than he would if she told anyone what happened. Mr Swan was the allocated social worker who visited Dougie who lives with his maternal grandmother Mrs Emma Murray. Dougie initially denied the allegation but, at a second meeting, with Mr Swan said that something did happen but he was "just curious" to see a girl's private parts and did not think it would do any harm.

Developmental History

Dougie and his family are previously known to the Social Services Department. Dougie lives with his maternal grandmother. His mother Ms Michelle Murray has a heroin addiction that she has struggled with since she was 16 years of age. Michelle was 18 years of age when she became pregnant. Dougie was born at full term but had a low birth weight. Dougie lived with Michelle following his birth and he has never had any contact with his father. Dougie and his mum had supported accomodation at first but then they moved to rented accommodation. Michelle was drug free for a brief period of time following his birth, however, she later relapsed. Little is known about the first few years of Dougie's development as Ms Murray was unavailable to take part in this assessment. It is understood that Dougie experienced extensive neglect while his mother struggled with her addiction and he witnessed domestic violence perpetrated on Michelle by her partner at that time. Following a report to Social Services, Dougie was taken into voluntary care and, at 4 years of age, went to live with his grandmother Ms Emma Murray.

While attending his local primary school, Dougie displayed a number of difficulties in class and with peers. As he progressed through the school system, they became more pronounced. He found structured schoolwork challenging. He was restless and found it hard to stay in his seat. He had limited concentration and would lose interest in most school-based activities quickly. Other children did not want to sit beside him. He found the completion of school work and homework difficult. His reading and writing skills were slower to develop compared to his peers and he had failing grades in many subjects. He would frequently shout out in class. He found it difficult to make friends and would frequently get into fights with other children. At home, he expressed much unhappiness about the school reporting that other children called him "Dougie the druggie" because it was widely known that his mum had an addiciton. He found this very upsetting and it would make him uncontrollably angry. At 6 years, he was referred to his local Child and Adolescent Mental Health Services (CAMHS) team for an assessment of his behavioral poblems and with a query that he may have attention deficit hyperactivity disorder (ADHD). There was a 7-month waiting list so he was 7 years of age when he was seen. The local CAMHS team diagnosed ADHD and oppositional defiant disorder. He was prescribed methylphenidate and his grandmother was offered a parenting intervention that she found somewhat helpful. Nevertheless, he continued to struggle in school and with peers throughout his time in primary school.

Dougie enrolled at his local secondary school at 12 years of age. He continues to struggle with his behavior, social and academic development. He was suspended from school last year for figthing with another pupil. He has made some friends in his locality but his contact with them is discouraged by his grandmother as she feels they are a bad influence on him and she suspects they are involved in alcohol and drug use. This has been a source of much conflict between Dougie and his grandmother. Dougie was arrested and cautioned by the local police last year when he was caught stealing from a local convenience store. Since moving to his grandmother's, Dougie has had limited contact with his mum. At times, when she has been managing her addiction she has had supervised access visits. However, she has not been able to keep in reliable contact with him and is often not in touch. His grandmother reports a lot of guilt at how things have turned out for her daughter and wishes there was more that she could have done to help her. She tries to cope with these feelings by making things as "normal" as she can for Dougie, especially at times when Michelle "lets him down", such as his birthday. Mrs Emma Murray says she believes that Dougie is very upset by the absence of contact with his mum and is particularly hurt at times such as his birthday. However she describes him as "very deep" and that he does not show his hurt and will fight with anyone who expresses a negative view of his mother.

Family History

As noted previously, Ms Michelle Murray is understood to have significant problems with drug addiction since she was 16 years of age. At that time, she dropped out of school and left home. At the same time, her younger sister Nicole disclosed in school that she was being sexually abused by her uncle (her father's brother) who was a frequent visitor to their home including two times he stayed with them while homeless post-release from prison. Over time, it emerged that this man had abused Nicole and Michelle on and off for a number of years. He was arrested and subsequently went to prison. This was an extremely stressful time for their family. Mrs Emma Murray reports that she was horrified at her daughter's disclosure and felt that people blamed her for what happened. There was much conflict within the family, her health deteriorated and she and her husband split up. Although she and Nicole remain in close contact, she feels there is an underlying tension in their relationship since that time. The disclosure of Dougie's sexual abuse of Nicole's daughter Sally has brought a lot of this tension to the surface and Nicole has accused her of "sheltering a pervert" because she allows Dougie to remain living with her. Mrs Murray reports that she finds herself in an impossible position as she feels guiltly and responsible for how things have turned out for Michelle and, despite her anger at him, she recognizes that Dougie has no one else in his life who will care for him, and she fears the continuing damage the current situation does to her relationship with Nicole and her two other grandchildren.

Dougie's Participation in the Assessment

Dougie was quiet during his first assessment appointment. He said he did not need to attend as he was "sorry" and "wouldn't do it again". Over time, he became more engaged in the assessment. He reported that he does not remember much from when he lived with his mother. He reported that he hates school and cannot wait to leave. He has a number of friends his own age in his local area. He describes where he lives as a "hard" neighborhood. He acknowledges that some of his friends get into trouble with the police but this is because they are being picked on. All of his friends drink and some smoke hash which he too has tried "a few times". He loves motor bikes and would like one of his own. He was unable to express positive future goals for his personal or vocational life.

Dougie reports that he finds it hard to speak to girls his own age. He has not had a girlfirend but there was a girl whom he liked until recently but he has not seen her around for some time. He had his "first crush" when he was 11 years of age. This was on a girl in his class who was the same age. He is attracted to girls and stated that "queers are weird". Dougie reported no sexual experience that made him feel uncomfortable or which he regards as abusive. He reports his friends have shown him pornography on their phones. He states he does not look at pornography himself without his friends. Mrs Murray reports no sexualized behavior by Dougie as a child.

Dougie's Account of his Sexually Abusive Behavior

During the course of this assessment, Dougie acknowledged that he sexually abused his cousin Sally. He reported on the evening this occurred he was annoyed at having to babysit and wanted to be out with his friends instead. Sally and her brother were dressed for bed when he arrived. They were allowed to watch TV for a short while and then he was expected to send them to bed. John was tired and went to bed without difficulty but Sally asked him to read her a story. Dougie did not want to do this as his reading is delayed and he gets embarrassed by this. He decided to play a board-game she had in her room instead. It was during this game that he thought about abusing her. He acknowledged that he asked to see her private parts and that he "rubbed" his hand against them. He denied making her touch his penis. He said afterwards he was scared so told her not to tell anyone but denied telling Sally she would be in trouble if she did tell or that he told Sally touching each other was what people do to show they like each other. Dougie said he knows what he did was wrong but was unable to elaborate on why it was wrong. He reported he is sorry and swears he will not do it again. He was unable to offer an understanding of thoughts and emotions that led up to his behavior or what might be helpful in avoiding its repetition again in the future. He is unsure if he needs to attend an intervention program but would think about it. He is afraid he will be sent to prison.

Psychometric Assessment

As part of this assessment, Dougie and Mrs Murray completed a number of psychological tests. These are briefly reported here. They are also consistent with our clinical opinion of Dougie based on his assessment.

- On a standardized brief intelligence test (The Weschler Abbreviated Scale of Intelligence), Dougie demonstrated a current level of cognitive functioning in the "Low Average" range of ability. His Verbal Comprehension Index is currently functioning in the "Borderline" range of ability and his Perceptual Reasoning Index is in the "Low Average" range.
- On a standardized measure of carer's ratings of a young person's behavioral and emotional difficulties (the Child Behavior Checklist), Mrs Murray rated Dougie in the Clincial Range for Total Problems, Externalizing Problems, Aggressive Behavior, Rule-Breaking Behavior, and Attention Problems.
- On the young person's eqivalent standardized measure of behavioral and emotional difficulties (the Youth Self-Report), Dougie rated himself in the Clincial range for Externalizing Problems, Aggressive Behavior, Rule-Breaking Behavior, Attention Problems, and Anxious/Depressed problems.
- On a standardized test of self-concept (The Beck Self-Concept Inventory for Youth), Dougie's responses rated his self-concept in "Lower than Average" range.

- On the Trauma Symptom Checklist for Children, Dougie had a valid profile. He had significantly elevated scores on the Anger, Post-traumatic Stress and Sexual Concerns subscales.
- On a measure of victim empathy (unpublished Victim Empathy Scale from the Adolescent Sexual Offender Assessment Pack – Richard Beckett), Dougie reported lower levels of understanding of the impact of his behavior on Sally when compared with the average levels of victim empathy based on data from young people who have completed an intervention program for sexual offending.
- On the AIM-2 assessment protocol, Dougie's profile was scored as presenting with "medium concerns" and "low strengths". This places him in the "medium level of supervision" required category which recommends community-based intervention that offers a combination of individual, group and family/carer therapeutic input.

Formulation and Recommendations

Dougie Murray is a 14-year-old boy who partially admits to sexually abusing his 6-year-old cousin Sally on one occasion. Predisposing factors to Dougie's sexually abusive behavior identified during this assessment are there is history of criminality in his extended family who have intergenerational experiences of sexual abuse. His mum Michelle has struggled throughout her adult life with a heroin addiction. Dougie at birth had a low birth weight. His early childhood care was detrimentally affected by his mother's drug addiction. He experienced neglect and witnessed domestic violence. He had no contact with his father. At four, he was seperated from his mother. He has a diagnosis of ADHD. Predisposing factors to his sexually abusive behavior identified during this assessment include Dougie's extended history of behavioral, impulse control, and academic problems at school. Throughout childhood he has struggled to make and maintain friendships with non-delinquent peers. With the onset of puberty, Dougie has continued to struggle with feelings of anger and low self-esteem. He has increasingly become involved with a delinquent peer group, engaging in criminal behavior, alcohol and drug use. Factors identified in this assessment that could potentially maintain his sexually abusive behavior include his current cognitive functioning is in the low average range, his difficulties managing school life and absence of positive future goals, he has limited normative social and heterosocial skills, his low self-esteem, absence of positive peer relationships, his continued impulse control problems, his currently limited insight into the thoughts, feelings and behaviors that precipitated his sexually abusive behavior, his pro-criminal attitudes, alcohol and drug use and absence of relapse awareness and skills. Protective factors identified during this assessment are the early detection of Dougie's sexually abusive behavior, his stable relationship with his grandmother who supports his attendance at intervention, his partial acknowledgment of sexually abusive behavior, and moderate level of willingness to participate in intervention.

It is recommended that Dougie, supported by his grandmother, should attend a community-based intervention to address his sexually abusive behavior. This intervention should combine group-based work with individual work, and carer-support work.

Specific goals that Dougie should address within this program are:

- Stabilizing his current behavior, particularly his alcohol and drug use and his involvement with peers who engage in delinquent behavior
- Improving Dougie's moderate degree of motivation to acknowledge and change his abusive behavior
- The development of healthy relationship and sexuality skills
- Developing an understanding of the thoughts, feelings and behaviors that led up to Dougie's sexually abusive behavior and the impact of sexually abusive behavior on Sally, her family, and others affected
- Life story work, and the development of healthy emotional expression and coping skills
- The development of a healthy life plan with positive prosocial personal and vocational goals and relapse prevention skills.

Specific goals for Mrs Emma Murray as she supports Dougie through the intervention program are:

- Assisting her to adjust to the discovery that Dougie has sexually abused his cousin and the impact this has on her and her relationship with him and her extended family
- Supporting her in the monitoring of Dougie to ensure he is not in situations where he may have the opportunity to engage in sexually abusive behavior
- Supporting her in the continued provision of care for Dougie as he develops more postivie behaviors and plans for his future
- Ensuring that she understands the various aspects of Dougie's intervention and his progress through regular review meetings with him and his intervention team.

The contents of this report have been read through with Dougie and his grandmother. They have decided to accept a place with our service to work on these goals.

Dr Gary O' Reilly
Clinical Psychologist

INTERVENTION

As indicated above, the program of intervention recommended for a young person and his available carers should be a logical outcome of the assessment process. Some key principles that assist engagement in intervention are: (1) making a distinction between the individual as a person and their sexual offending behavior; (2) encouraging the young person to take on responsibility rather than shame for their behavior; (3) adopting a combination of intervention formats utilizing group work, individual work, and family/systemic work; (4) the young person is provided with a clear understanding of program rules, expectations and limits to confidentiality; (5) the young person understands the timescale involved; (6) a modular group program is followed such as that described below; (7) progress is regularly reviewed with the young person, his carers and those providing the intervention; (8) a positive encouraging non-collusive therapeutic style is adopted by staff; (9) staff are supported and have supervisory space to process issues and therapeutic dilemmas that will arise; (10) if possible, a carer's/parents program is available that complements the young person's intervention; (11) a rolling group format is used. There are many advantages to a rolling group. Young people joining the group see a model of where you would like them to progress to from group members who have been in the program for a while. Those who have been in the group for a period of time can be invited to take a prosocial role encouraging the engagement of new members into the program. This also allows them to reflect on the progress they have made to date in the program and the distance still to travel. It is a very effective feature of a program if a peer appropriately challenges a new member to engage in intervention or let go of aspects of denial or minimization.

Hackett, Masson, & Phillips, (2006) surveyed services offering intervention to young people who sexually abuse. They found 80–100% reported that their program included work with the young person on the following topics: (1) the development of emotional competence skills, including the management of anger and distress; (2) changing cognitive distortions about sexuality and relationships; (3) the development of prosocial emotional, cognitive, and behavioral skills; (4) the young person gaining an understanding of their offense cycle and/or pathways into sexually abusive behavior; (5) sexuality education; (6) life-story work; (7) developing relapse prevention skills; (8) family work; (9) understanding the consequences of further abusive behavior; and (10) the development of empathy.

A different approach is described through an illustrative case study by Wylie and Griffin (2012). Building on the *Good Lives Model* advocated by Ward and Gannon (2006) they argue, while not dispensing with the notion of risk, an individual's future safe functioning will be best assisted by working with them to achieve in a more prosocial manner the goals that their criminal behavior accomplishes in a maladaptive manner. They simplify the ten "Primary Goods" (or Good Life aims) of the Ward model into five "Primary Needs" for young people as follows:

1. Having people in my life (incorporating personal, family, peer, community relationships)
2. Being healthy (physical, emotional, sexually, and psychologically)
3. Having fun and achieving (play, excitement, knowledge, creativity, status and competence)
4. Being my own person (self-directedness, independence, autonomy and empowerment)
5. Having a purpose that makes a difference (generosity, charitable acts, and spirituality).

Wylie and Griffin describe in their case study how this approach has been developed and used as the primary lens through which assessment and intervention are planned on a case-by-case basis at G-MAP, which is the intervention service in the UK who also developed the AIM-2 assessment.

DOES INTERVENTION WORK?

This is arguably the most important question we can ask and finding the answer is fraught with difficulty. In short, there over 100 published studies that compare groups of adults or adolescents who have sexually offended who have received intervention with those who have not received any. Almost without exception these studies are scientifically very poor in their design – sexual re-offending is a hidden behavior and services are reluctant to randomly assign offenders to no intervention to see if they re-offend at the same or different rates compared to those in intervention. The most recent attempt to give an integrated view of the available research evidence initially identified 129 studies (Hanson, Bourgon, Helmus, & Hodgson, 2009). These were then judged in terms of the quality of their study design. One-hundred and four studies were rejected based on poor study design (such as inappropriate control group), two studies were rejected for other design issues (for example, one study concerned children with sexual impulse control problems rather than offending behavior), 19 studies were found to have weak but acceptable designs, four were categorized as having good design, and no studies had a strong design. This leaves us with a clear indication that we need to adopt a strongly skeptical perspective when reading the "what works" literature with regard to the effectiveness of intervention in reducing sexual offence recidivism. Based on the combined data from the 23 studies retained in the Hanson et al. review (19 weak, 4 good, 0 strong), those who received intervention had a sexual re-offence rate of 10.9% compared to 19.2% in the no-intervention group reflecting a 57% reduction in sexual offending. There was no reduction evident in rates of non-sexual violent offending, but there was a reduction in general offending. The strongest evidence comes from studies in the weakly designed category. There was variability of evidence from the good design studies. This is problematic as weakly designed studies raise the possibility that factors other than intervention may explain differences between those with and without intervention. The principles of Risk-Need-Responsivity explained the variability in study findings. That is, programs that reduce offending are those that target higher risk individuals, formulate a plan to provide an intervention reflective of the person's needs, and are responsive to acute fluctuating aspects of an individual's functioning. In short, we cannot presume theoretically and research informed, well-designed interventions simply work. In conclusion, we need to ask for the evidence that all approaches to assessment and intervention as described in this chapter, volume, and elsewhere work-based on studies that apply the highest standards of research design. Currently, that evidence is largely absent.

REFERENCES

Borum, R., Bartel, P., & Forth, A. (2003). *Manual for the structured assessment of violence risk in youth, version 1.1.* Tampa: University of South Florida.

Carr, A. (2006). *Handbook of child and adolescent clinical psychology: a contextual approach* (2nd ed.). London: Brunner Routledge.

Carr, A. (2012). *Family therapy: concepts, process and practice* (3rd ed.). Chichester: Wiley.

Epperson, D. L., Ralston, C. A., Fowers, D., & DeWitt, J. (2005). *Development of a sexual offense recidivism risk assessment tool-II (J-SORRAT-II)*. Ames: University of Iowa. Unpublished Manuscript.

Forth, A. E., Kosson, D. S., & Hare, R. D. (2003). *The psychopathy checklist: youth version*. Toronto: Multi-Health Systems.

Griffin, H. L., Beech, A., Print, B., Bradshaw, H., & Quayle, J. (2008). The development and initial testing of the AIM2 framework to assess risk and strengths in young people who sexually offend. *Journal of Sexual Aggression*, *14*, 211–225.

Hackett, S., Masson, H., & Phillips, S. (2006). Exploring consensus in practice with youth who are sexually abusive: Findings from a Delphi study of practitioner views in the United Kingdom and the Republic of Ireland. *Child Maltreatment*, *11*, 146–156.

Hanson, R. K., & Morton-Bourgon, K. E. (2009). The accuracy of recidivism risk assessments for sexual offenders: a meta-analysis of 118 prediction studies. *Psychological Assessment*, *21*, 1–21.

Hanson, R. K., Bourgon, G., Helmus, L., & Hodgson, S. (2009). The principles of effective correctional treatment also apply to sexual offenders: a meta-analysis. *Criminal Justice & Behavior*, *36*, 865–891.

Hempel, I, Buck, N., Cima, M., & van Marle, H. (2013). Review of risk assessment instruments for juvenile sex offenders: What is next? *International Journal of Offender Therapy and Comparative Criminology*, *57*, 208–228.

New Jersey Attorney General's Office. (2006). *Juvenile risk assessment scale manual*. Retrieved from <http://www.state.nj.us/lps/dcj/megan/jras-manual-scale-606.pdf>.

O' Reilly, G., & Carr, S. (2004). The clinical assessment of young people who sexually abuse others. In G. O' Reilly, W. Marshall, L. Beckett & A. Carr (Eds.), *The handbook of clinical intervention with young people who sexually offend*. London: Brunner-Routledge.

Prentky, R. A., & Righthand, S. (2003). *Juvenile sex offender assessment protocol (J-SOAP-II): Manual*. Bridgewater, MA: Justice Research Institute.

Print, B., Griffin, H., Beech, A., et al. (2007). *AIM-2 an initial assessment model for young people who display sexually harmful behaviour*. Manchester: G-MAP.

Seto, M. C., & Lalumiere, M. (2010). What is so special about male adolescent sexual offending? A review and test of explanations through meta-analysis. *Psychological Bulletin*, *136*, 526–575.

Ward, T., & Gannon, T. A. (2006). Rehabilitation, etiology and self-regulation: The comprehensive good lives model of treatment for sexual offenders. *Aggression and Violent Behaviour: A Review Journal*, *11*, 77–94.

Worling, J. R., & Curwen, T. (2000). *The ERASOR: estimate of risk of adolescent sexual offence recidivism*. Toronto: SAFE-T Program, Thistletown Regional Centre.

Wylie, L. A., & Griffin, H. L. (2012). G-map's application of the Good Lives Model to adolescent males who sexually harm: A case study. *Journal of Sexual Aggression*, *1*, 1–12.

CHAPTER 14

Social Skills, Substance Abuse, and Sexual Behavior Problems in the Adolescent

Jennifer G. Wheeler*, Kirk A. B. Newring and Ken D. Schafer*****

*Pacific Evaluation, Consultation, & Treatment Services, PLLC, Seattle, Washington, WA, USA
**Forensic Behavioral Health, Papillion Nebraska and Nebraska Wesleyan University, Lincoln, Nebraska, NE, USA
***Griffin Home Friends of Youth, Renton, and Private Practice, Burien, Washington, WA, and Department of Educational Psychology, University of Nebraska-Lincoln, Lincoln, NE, USA

INTRODUCTION

This chapter is intended to provide the clinician with a resource for working with individuals and groups in which the identified concerns are substance abuse together with sexual behavior problems. The chapter presumes that the youth have already been evaluated with a thorough psychological and psychosexual assessment, as well as assessment specific to substance abuse. This module is also intended for youths who exhibit deficits in their social functioning, such as at school, at work, with their peers or family members, or in the context of their dating relationships (or lack thereof). Specifically, this chapter provides an evidence-based skill-building program, which was designed to help increase youths' interpersonal effectiveness across a broad range of social situations.[1] This program was developed as a psychoeducational, group-based treatment tool, although these group modules can easily be adapted for individual use. We note that there are several other workbooks and resources available for the clinician (i.e., this text, Pathways: A guided workbook for youth beginning treatment, 4th edition, Safer Society Press). We have used the materials in this chapter as a way to supplement and enhance "treatment as usual" for youth with sexual behavior and substance abuse problems.

The most popular risk assessment approaches for youth with sexual offense behaviors include risk factors that overlap with aspects of social skills and substance abuse. The Estimate of Risk of Adolescent Sexual

[1] This curriculum was inspired by the Interpersonal Effectiveness Skills module, in the *Skills Training Manual for Treating Dialectical Behavior Therapy* (Linehan, 1993).

Toolkit for Working with Juvenile Sex Offenders.
DOI: http://dx.doi.org/10.1016/B978-0-12-405948-1.00014-1

Offense Recidivism, 2nd edition (ERASOR 2.0) includes: antisocial interpersonal orientation, lack of intimate peer relationships/social isolation, negative peer associations and influences, interpersonal aggression, recent escalation in anger or negative affect, impulsivity, and problematic parent–offender relationships/parental rejection. Each of these risks includes a social component, with social isolation the clearest example of social skills deficits being linked to adolescent recidivism. The Juvenile Sex Offender Assessment Protocol, 2nd edition (J-SOAP-II) includes risk factors: pervasive anger, school behavior problems, and quality of peer relationships. Youth with sexual offense behaviors and social skills deficits are at a relatively higher risk of re-offense in comparison to peers without such social skills deficits.

The rationale for developing this module was to create a developmentally appropriate version of the "interpersonal effectiveness" (IE) skills module in Dialectical Behavior Therapy (DBT). One of the first studies to demonstrate the utility of DBT was with adjudicated youth (Trupin, Stewart, Beach, & Boesky, 2002). In the decade following that publication, aspects of DBT (typically the skills modules) have been widely adapted in a variety of community, correctional and confinement settings, with a variety of client populations. The authors of the current chapter recognized that many behavior problems exhibited by adolescents, including substance use and sexual behavior problems, actually reflected maladaptive efforts to meet otherwise adaptive needs. Fortunately, DBT skills specifically focus on training individuals to pursue reasonable wants and needs, but in a manner that does not violate the rights and needs of others, and that will not create more problems for the individual in the long run. Unfortunately, the IE module was developed for adult clients, whose wants and needs (and barriers to those wants and needs) are not the same as those of adolescents. Accordingly, this module was developed to integrate developmentally specific language, goals, and activities, into an extant evidence-based skills module.

One of the first steps in treatment is identification of the roles of substance abuse and sexual misbehavior for the youth. From a cognitive-behavioral perspective, we look to identify the functional aspects of the antecedents, problem behaviors, and consequences (Newring & Wheeler, 2012). The principles of behavior therapy apply here: behaviors are maintained by the variables of which they are a function. For many youth, substance use and sexual behavior are explained by a combination of what the youth gains or accesses through these behaviors, as well as what the youth can avoid or escape via substance abuse or sexual behavior.

When conducting a functional analysis of a youth's behavior, it is important to remember the rewards inherent in the activity. Specifically, it cannot be ignored that sex (usually) feels good, and/or that some drugs lead to feelings of euphoria or other pleasant affect (e.g., stimulants, cocaine). Similarly, other drugs (e.g., alcohol, marijuana) may lead to temporary feelings of escape from unpleasant affect). It is also important to consider that substance abuse and sexual behavior problems are often multidetermined, with each having both an approach-aspect and an avoidance-aspect.

Assessment of the function of the substance abuse and sexual behaviors can be conducted in a variety of ways. The behavior chain common to "relapse prevention" is a treatment stalwart (Newring, Loverich, Harris, & Wheeler, 2009). We have developed another way in which to gather behavior chain information, which we call the "BDA" for "Before, During, After" (instead of using more complex terms like antecedents and consequences). The BDA form is included at the end of this chapter.

We also recommend that the form be presented with the following rationale: the form is designed to help us understand what has worked, and what has not worked for you. Much like in a sports game when the coach uses videotape or a DVD to review plays, we are going to use this form to help find out how things have worked for you. (Based on your interactions with the youth, pick the analogy that works best.) The BDA can be used to help find out what the youth did that set him up to be successful (e.g., identification of controlling variables for success, both antecedents and consequences) and also to see what made it hard for the youth to be successful.

It is helpful first to use the BDA form on an innocuous event, such as eating breakfast earlier that day. It is presumed that the youth will have eaten breakfast, and have easy access to those memories. From a teaching perspective, it is much easier to teach the concept first, before delving into substance use and sexual abuse. After the youth demonstrates understanding the concept of the BDA, we then get into more of the "work" in using the BDA to develop behavior chains. For example, consider using the following progression to help the youth learn how to use the BDA:

1. A BDA (or two, or three, etc.) on a success within the past week
2. A BDA on a success from the past year
3. A BDA on a success from their lifetime
4. A BDA on a positive/healthy sexual event
5. A BDA related to substance use

6. A BDA on a harmful/inappropriate (but still legal) sexual event (e.g., unhealthy fantasy/masturbation)
7. A BDA on their offense/offenses
8. A BDA on an event that involved both substance use/abuse and sexual behavior.

When it comes to youth substance abuse, the following social–emotional variables are often identified as relevant precursors:

- Peer pressure (feeling awkward when pressured, drugs make the awkward feeling go away)
- Social anxiety or other negative emotional state (drugs make feelings of anxiety/sadness go away; and/or may increase sense of social affiliation/acceptance)
- Attention (feeling important/special/admired by others)
- Stimulation-seeking/risk-taking (feeling excited, and/or alleviating boredom, and/or satiating cravings)
- Poor supervision/rule defiance/risk-taking (having few or no rules/structure/supervision, and/or feeling like the rules do not apply to them).

When using the BDA, we suggest starting with the behavior/action that is the focus, and then working out the form from there. Some clinicians or youth may prefer to proceed chronologically, while others might go by content area (thoughts, emotions, etc.), and others still may be comfortable going back and forth, adding more, and revising. Until the youth is expert at using the form, the bottom row (regarding functions, intended functions, and outcomes) will require assistance from the therapist.

We have also included a pros and cons worksheet. As with the BDA, our preference has been to teach the concept of "pros and cons" with an innocuous decision (e.g., watching a movie versus playing a board game; spending time with a friend versus finishing a homework assignment). The adolescent brain is vulnerable to over-focusing on reward while underestimating associated risk (Newring, Parker, & Newring, 2010). For some youths, this presents as "adventure-seeking", without fully or accurately assessing the risks and rewards in any given situation. The pros and cons worksheet is intended to assist the youth in identifying likely outcomes of all available choices (including both short-term and long-term consequences). Having the youth present the worksheet and solicit feedback in a group can be a helpful activity, as well as assisting the youth in the solicitation and integration of feedback.

It may be worthwhile to have the youth complete a few retrospective pros and cons (much like the BDA), though the goal is to highlight the youth's current thinking and decision-making process. A clinical challenge will be to validate the youth's motivation for the misbehavior (e.g., it made sense at the time that youth would not want to feel sad/jealous, etc; it made sense that the youth would want to feel good, and that sexual behavior/drugs was one way of feeling good) without condoning the action. Instead, this is used as an opportunity to identify the "normal" aspects of the youth's motivation, and then find more effective yet still reinforcing alternatives to getting those needs met. By completing some retrospective pros and cons worksheets, the youth may identify some of the variables controlling their behavior, or some of the more common "links" in the chain (e.g., feelings of loneliness often led to use of marijuana; feelings of abandonment led to compulsive masturbation).

In the social skills group modules, we include several examples for role-play scenario. Of course, clinicians and group members can add their own ideas to these scenarios as needed. The idea is to practice the skills, and generalize the concepts to the "real world" (and maybe even have some fun in the process!).

SUMMARY

Risk assessment for youth with sexual offense behavior emphasizes the role of social skill deficits as a contributor to elevated risk. It follows that treatment that addresses known areas of risk should assist in the mitigation of risk for youth with sexual offense behaviors. For youth with co-occurring substance abuse problems, social skills deficits appear linked to substance use and abuse, as well as sexual offense behaviors. By addressing these social skills deficits in treatment, practitioners can assist the youth in identifying the function of their substance abuse, and in the development of healthy and prosocial interpersonal skills, in service of the youth living a healthy, offense free, and vibrant life in the community.

GROUP SCHEDULE

Group 1: Introduction to social skills group
Group 2: Social skills: basics & necessities
Group 3: Daily interactions: being polite & appropriate
Group 4: BEFORE you have a social interaction: things to consider
Group 5: DURING a social interaction: be aware of yourself
Group 6: DURING a social interaction: be aware of the other person

Group 7: AFTER you have a social interaction: responding & consequences
Group 8: Putting it all together: using your social skills before, during, and after an interaction
Group 9: Dating 1
Group 10: Dating 2
Group 11: Handling peer pressure
Group 12: ULTIMATE SOCIAL SKILLS

GROUP 1 INTRODUCTION TO SOCIAL SKILLS

Introduce Group

- Group norms & expectations
- What are social skills?
- Why do we need social skills?
- Use of social skills in group

Group Norms & Expectations

- Review standard group norms/rules & expectations
- Consider "special" group rules for social skills (e.g., use of role plays)

What are Social Skills?

- Verbal
- Non-verbal

Why do We Need Social Skills?

- Being effective at getting what you want
- Meeting your goals without victimizing others
- Secret to being successful in whatever you do
- Getting people to like you and want to be around you

How Your Behavior Affects Other People

- How you speak and act affects the people you are interacting with
- This affects the response you get
- This affects whether or not you get your goals met effectively

How this Affects YOU

1. Your goal → Skilled interaction → **Positive effect on others** → Your goals are met
2. Your goal → Unskilled interaction → **Negative effect on others** → Unmet goals (OR your goals are met ineffectively)

Social Skills & Sexual Offending

- How do you think that social skills (or NOT HAVING social skills) is related to substance abuse and sexual offending?
- Were your goals met? At what cost to you? At what cost to others? How could you have met your goals more effectively?
- What other strengths do you have that you could have drawn upon to avoid abusing substances/sexually offending?

GROUP 2 SOCIAL SKILLS: BASICS & NECESSITIES

Review

Why are social skills important?

1. Your goal → Skilled interaction → **Positive effect on others** → Your goals are met
2. Your goal → Unskilled interaction → **Negative effect on others** → Unmet goals (OR your goals are met ineffectively)

First Impressions

- Hygiene
  - Brushing your teeth
  - Showering & shaving
  - Combing your hair
  - Deodorant
  - Cleaning and trimming your fingernails
  - Laundry/dressing
  - Room care
- Posture/body language
  - Standing
  - Sitting
  - Movements & mannerisms
- Personal space/physical boundaries
  - Being too close
  - Being too far
  - Orienting yourself to the other person/away from the other person
  - Touching (versus grooming)
- Eye contact
  - Too much (staring, glaring, leering)
  - Too little (nervous, guilty, shy, evasive)

- Facial expressions
  - Matching your words to your expression (happy, sad, angry)
  - Giving non-verbal feedback with expressions (smiling, rolling eyes, sneering)
- Voice tone/volume
  - Too quiet
  - Too loud
  - Matching tone to what you are saying (happy, angry, sad)

GROUP 3 DAILY INTERACTIONS: BEING POLITE & APPROPRIATE

Review Last Week's Group

- Basics & Necessities
- First impressions
- Feedback about issues addressed last week
- Boundaries
  - Physical
  - Verbal
  - Emotional

    Your own emotional boundaries

    Emotions of others: clowning
- Listening to Others
  - Signs to let others know you are listening
  - Verbal
  - Non-verbal
- Manners
  - Please
  - Thank you
  - You're welcome
- Compliments & Recognitions
  - Giving a compliment
  - Receiving a compliment
  - Why give compliments or make recognitions?
- Being Appropriate with Peers vs Adults & Authority Figures
  - How would these interactions be similar to each other?
  - How would these interactions be different from each other?
  - What are the things you need to consider when interacting with adults & authority figures?

GROUP 4 BEFORE YOU HAVE A SOCIAL INTERACTION: THINGS TO CONSIDER

Review Last Week's Group

- Being Polite & Appropriate
- Feedback about issues addressed last week
- What are your *goals*?
  - Think about your hopes, needs, wants
  - What are you trying to "get" out of an interaction?
    A change in your environment?
    An effect on your relationship?
    Improve your feelings about yourself?
- Consider both short-term and long-term goals
  - Be careful not to get one at the expense of the other
  - Problem of Immediate Gratification (PIG)
  - Example: Clowning
- Considering the *consequences* BEFORE you act:
  - Immediate consequences for you
  - Immediate consequences for the other person
  - Long-term consequences for you
  - Long-term consequences for the other person
  - ALWAYS consider the benefits of NOT acting:
  - *If you can delay the PIG, you might benefit even more*
- What is the most *effective* way to get what you want?
  Effective = Getting your goals met WITHOUT:
  - Victimizing or exploiting others
  - Damaging your relationship with the other person
  - Losing self-respect

  ALSO – to be effective, your behavior has to be:
  - Socially appropriate
  - Legal

  The Pros and Cons worksheet is often used extensively in this module.

GROUP 5 DURING A SOCIAL INTERACTION: BE AWARE OF YOURSELF

Review Last Week's Group

- BEFORE an Interaction: Things to Consider
- Feedback about issues addressed last week
- What are your *goals*?

- Considering the *consequences* BEFORE you act
- What is the most *effective* way to get what you want?

"The basics" + Being Yourself + Being Aware of the Other Person = Effective Interaction

Step 1: Be aware of *YOURSELF* during the Interaction

- The Basics
  - Hygiene
  - Posture/body language
  - Personal space/physical boundaries
  - Eye contact
  - Facial expressions
  - Voice tone/volume
- Being Yourself
  - You're not trying to put on a show
  - Have confidence in your own personality (what makes you *you*)
  - Know your limitations – you can't control the whole situation
  - Be flexible – allow other people to be themselves, too
  - Use humor (without victimizing); be able to laugh at yourself

GROUP 6 DURING A SOCIAL INTERACTION: BE AWARE OF THE OTHER PERSON

Review Last Week's Group

- DURING a Social Interaction: The Basics + Being Yourself
- Feedback about issues addressed last week

REMEMBER:

- What are your *goals*?
- Considering the *consequences* BEFORE you act
- What is the most *effective* way to get what you want?

"The basics" + Being Yourself + Being Aware of the Other Person = Effective Interaction

Step 2: Be Aware of the *Other Person* in the interaction!!

- Reading other People's Responses
  - Use what you know about the basics, but in "reverse"
  - What does their *tone of voice* sound like? *(Nervous? Angry? Happy?)*
  - What is their *facial expression* like? *(Smiling? Annoyed? Scared?)*
  - What is their *body language* and use of *personal space* telling you? *(Are they moving away from you? Towards you? Hands in front? Clenched fists? "Recoiling?")*
  - What is their *eye contact* like? *(Looking away? Staring? Glaring?)*

- Listen to What the Other Person is Saying:
  - Don't just start thinking about the next thing you want to say
  - Don't just turn the conversation back to yourself
  - Try asking the other person *questions*
  - Try to *reflect* back to the person something they've just said
  - *Be validating* to the other person – validating means that you accept and respect the feelings or responses they have, and let them know that what they are saying and/or feeling is worthwhile & important to you.
  - *Don't be judgmental* – remember that not everyone is exactly like you, or thinks exactly like you. Accept the ways that people are different from you, and different from each other

GROUP 7 AFTER YOU HAVE A SOCIAL INTERACTION: RESPONDING & CONSEQUENCES

Review Last Week's Group

- DURING a Social Interaction: Be Aware of the Other Person in the Interaction
- Feedback about issues addressed last week
- Deal with Not Always Getting What You Want:
  - Even the most effective social skills won't *always* work
  - *Don't push* your wants/needs on the other person
  - Don't resort to inappropriate/illegal behavior just to get what you want
  - Don't forget the "basics" just because you don't get what you want
  - Learn to *compromise* – meeting "half-way" with the other person
  - You don't always have to be "right" – be open to the idea that *you do not know everything*
  - It's OK to be wrong, to "give in," or to say "I don't know"
  - If the person doesn't want to meet halfway, *accept their right* to disagree and move on
- Repairing & Apologizing
  - Based on what you observe from the other person's response, be prepared to "*repair*" the situation
  - Maybe you need to *clarify* or explain yourself better
  - Maybe you were offensive, and you need to say *you're sorry*
  - You might just have to *accept* the consequences if the person is mad/upset
  - If you didn't "repair" at the time, try to do it later (better late than never)

GROUP 8 PUTTING IT ALL TOGETHER: USING YOUR SOCIAL SKILLS BEFORE, DURING, AND AFTER AN INTERACTION

Review Last Week's Group

- AFTER a Social Interaction: Responding & Consequences
- Feedback about issues addressed last week
- The "Big Picture" of Social Skills
  - Every "small" skill put together is what makes *you* "socially skilled"
- "BEFORE" Skills:
  - What are your *goals*?
  - Consider the *consequences* BEFORE you act
  - What is the most *effective* way to get what you want?
- "DURING" Skills
  - "The Basics" + Being Yourself = Effective Interaction
  - Read other People's Responses
  - Listen to What the Other Person is Saying
- "AFTER" Skills
  - Deal with Not Always Getting What You Want
  - Repair & Apologize

GROUP 9 DATING 1: INTERACTING WITH SOMEONE YOU ARE ATTRACTED TO OR SOMEONE YOU WANT TO ASK OUT

Review Last Week's Group

- Using Your Social Skills Before, During, and After an Interaction
- Feedback about issues addressed last week

The Social Skills you use when it comes to dating are similar to the skills you use during any other kind of social interaction. But there are also some ways that "dating skills" are a little more challenging than any other kind of interaction.

We're going to spend the next two groups specifically addressing the challenges that are specific to interacting with someone you are attracted to, want to ask out, or are going out with already.

- BEFORE the Interaction
  - What are your motivations for asking this person out?
    What is it that you are attracted to about the person?
  - What are your goals in talking to the person?
    Getting to know them better? Trying to figure out if they like you?

  - How do you feel when you think about talking to them? Excited? Anxious? Nervous? Worried? Insecure?
  - How are you going to handle these feelings?
- Things to try
  - Use your skilled peers as *role models* for how you'd like to be
  - Use positive "*self-talk*" before the interaction
  - *Plan out* what you want to say beforehand
  - *Practice* what you want to say
  - *Get feedback* from your skilled friends
  - *Drop the drama*: think about the person as a friend, not about what the interaction is "supposed" to mean
  - Think about their possible reactions in advance, and *prepare yourself* for the possible positive and negative outcomes
- Things you must *not* do:
  - *Objectify* the person (in your own mind, to your friends)
  - *Victimize* the person (in deviant fantasies, clowning behind her/his back)
- DURING the Interaction
  - Try to implement everything we've talked about so far
  - Things to do:
    - Be aware of yourself
    - Be aware of the other person
  - Things you must *not* do:
  - DON'T Objectify the person
    - By making them into a goal, something to "get" or win
    - By talking about their body parts
    - By assuming you know what they want or need
  - DON'T Victimize the person
    - By making inappropriate comments/gestures/contact
    - By giving them inappropriate letters/notes
    - By clowning on them or insulting them
  - DON'T Make demands on the person
    - They don't owe you anything
    - They are not there to meet your needs
    - They have needs too, and these might not include you
    - Sometimes you have to be patient – you might not meet your goals right away
- AFTER the Interaction
  - If the person indicates that they are not interested, for whatever reason
    - Accept and respect what they want
    - DO NOT try to pressure them or change their mind

- If they give you any other kind of cue (*like "I have to go, I can't talk to you right now"*)
  - Accept and respect their request
  - DO NOT try to pressure them into responding to you right then
- If you can't tell how they feel about you:
  - *It can't hurt to ask* (unless they've given you a cue otherwise, then you need to accept and respect this)
  - *DO NOT assume* you know how they feel or what they are thinking if they haven't told you
- If they give you an "in-between" response (like "I don't know," "I'm not sure," "Maybe," "I have to think about it")
  - Accept and respect their ambivalence.
  - DO NOT use this as an opportunity to pressure them or influence their thoughts and feelings
  - Give them the space they need and asked for

GROUP 10 DATING 2: INTERACTING WITH SOMEONE YOU ARE GOING OUT WITH: BEING SOMEONE'S "BOYFRIEND"

Review Last Week's Group

- Interacting with Someone You Are Attracted to or Want to Ask Out
- Feedback about issues addressed last week
  - What is "dating," "going out," or being a "boyfriend"?
  - Make sure you and your partner are talking about the same thing!!
  - What do "*boyfriend*" and "*girlfriend*" mean to you?
  - What do "*boyfriend*" and "*girlfriend*" mean to your partner?
  - *Talk about this* – and make sure you are talking about the same thing!
- "Dating" interactions
  - Phone calls
  - Letters
  - Dates: *What is a date?*
    What activities can you do that you both would enjoy?
    Why is that important?
    Who pays for the date?
    What can you expect from your date?
- Mutual Consent
  - What is mutual consent?
    How do you give consent?
    How do you know if you have been given consent?
    Why is consent important?

    - How do you initiate sexual activity appropriately?
    - The same social skills you've already learned apply here

    Don't just think about yourself in the situation – think about the other person
- Disclosing past history (when applicable)
    - When should you disclose your offense to your partner?
    - Why is this important?
- Breaking Up
    - When is it time to break up?
    - What makes a break up "effective"?
    - What should you NOT do when breaking up?
    - What should you NOT do when someone breaks up with you?
    - Balancing *your* needs with *being respectful* to the other person

GROUP 11 HANDLING PEER PRESSURE

Review Last Week's Group

- "Being Someone's Boyfriend"
- Feedback about issues addressed last week
- What is Peer Pressure?
    - Why would peers pressure you into doing something?
    - What types of things are peers likely to try to pressure you in to doing?
    - How do they try to pressure you? (What do they say? What do they do?)
- How to respond to peer pressure?
    - Know yourself:
        1. *What are your morals and beliefs*: What kinds of things do you NEVER want to see yourself doing? Why not?
        2. *Think about the consequences*: Even if you don't think it's "a big deal," you need to think about the negative consequences you will face.
        3. *What are your vulnerabilities*: What are the "weaknesses" or vulnerabilities you have that might make you give in to peer pressure?
        4. *What is your relationship with the person who is trying to pressure you?* This may influence how you want to respond to them.
    - Skills you can try to use:
        1. *Use a "scapegoat"*: Come up with an excuse that will safely keep you out of the situation, and that your friends will accept.
        2. *Use humor*: Try to lighten up the situation, or distract them, by using humor and sarcasm. You can also use humor to point out the fact that it is a bad idea in the first place.

3. *Challenging the idea*: Is it REALLY going to be all that fun? Is it REALLY going to be all that cool? Why not point out what a lame idea it is.
4. *Come up with something else to do instead*: Distract them from an unsafe, illegal, or victimizing activity by suggesting something else to do instead.

- Examples of times you have given in to peer pressure
  What made you give in?
- Examples of times you have resisted peer pressure
  What kept you from giving in?

GROUP 12 ULTIMATE SOCIAL SKILLS

Role Plays and In Vitro Practice (Field Trip!)

- Sample role plays
  - Set clear limits and guidelines about role plays!
  - Cut out each of the scenarios and put them in a hat
  - Cut out each of the kids' names and put them in a hat
  - Draw names of kids for each scenario
  - Have one of them draw the scenario
  - Have them consider their goals *before* the interaction
  - After role play, debrief what worked, what was ineffective
- In-vitro practice
  - Set clear limits and guidelines about the field trip!
  - Have them consider their goals *before* the event
  - After event, de-brief what worked, what was ineffective

Teacher & Student

STUDENT: You got a B on a paper and you think you deserved an A. Talk to your teacher about it.

✂ -

Teacher & Student

STUDENT: You have an assignment due today that you left at home. This is the second time you've done this. Go to your teacher to explain.

✂ -

Principle & Student

STUDENT: You have been sent to the principle's office for being late to class 3 times in one week. Interact with your principle about this.

Police Officer & You

YOU: You get approached by a police officer on the street, because he wants to know what you are doing out so late. Interact with him.

Employer & Employee

EMPLOYEE: You want a raise. Talk to your boss about it.

Parent & Kid

KID: There is a party this weekend that you really want to go to, but you don't know if your parents will let you. Talk to your parent about it.

Girl & Guy

GUY: Talk to a girl in your class that you have never talked to before.

Girl & Guy

GUY: Ask a girl you like if she wants to go out with you sometime.

Girl & Guy

GUY: Find out if the girl you like is already dating someone else.

Girl & Guy
GUY: Tell the girl you are dating that you don't want to go out with her anymore.

✂ ---

Girl & Guy
GUY: Talk to the girl you are dating about going "steady" (not dating other people).

✂ ---

Girl & Guy
GUY: You are on a date with your girlfriend at the movies. You are sitting in the movie theater, and the movie isn't going to start for a few more minutes. Make conversation with her.

✂ ---

Girl & Guy
GUY: You are at a social, dancing with a girl. She asks you if you want to dance another dance. You think she's alright, but the next song you'd like to ask someone else to dance.

✂ ---

Girl & Guy
GUY: You have plans to go out with your girlfriend this weekend, but you've been grounded by your parents. Call your girlfriend to break your plans.

✂ ---

Girl & Guy
GUY: Talk to your girlfriend and try to determine whether or not you have mutual consent to have sex with her.

✂ ---

Guy 1 & Guy 2

GUY 1: Talk to a new guy in your class who you don't know, but who you think seems kind of cool.

✂ -

Guy 1 & Guy 2

GUY 1: Ask a new guy in your class if he wants to get together to shoot hoops this weekend.

✂ -

Guy 1 & Guy 2

GUY 1: You heard that a guy in your class was spreading rumors about you to other kids. Confront him about this.

✂ -

Guy 1 & Guy 2

GUY 1: You just started dating a really pretty girl in your class. A friend of yours asks you for details about your relationship. Interact with him.

✂ -

Guy 1 & Guy 2

GUY 1: Your friend asks you if you think he should ask this girl out. You like her too, and were thinking about asking her out. Interact with him about this.

✂ -

Guy 1 & Guy 2

GUY 1: Your friend asks you if you think he should ask this girl out. You don't like her, and you don't think your friend should go out with her. Interact with him about this.

✂ -

Guy 1 & Guy 2

GUY 1: You want to ask a guy you work with if he'll switch shifts with you on Saturday night, so that you can go out.

✂ -

Guy & Restaurant

GUY: Make reservations at a restaurant.

✂ -

Guy & Job

GUY: Call someplace that put a "Help Wanted" ad in the newspaper to find out more about the job.

✂ -

Guy & Store Clerk

GUY: You are trying on pants in a store and can't find your size. Get help from the sales clerk.

✂ -

Guy & Shoe Store Clerk

GUY: You bought a pair of shoes, and when you got home you decided you don't want them anymore. Go to the shoe store clerk and return them at the store.

✂ -

Guy & Your Girlfriend's Mom

GUY: You call your girlfriend's house to talk to her. She's not home, so her mom answer's the phone. You need to leave a message for your girlfriend to call you at 7 p.m. at your friend's house.

✂ -

Guy & ?

GUY: The phone rings in your house, and there is no one else at home. You answer the phone, but the call is not for you.

✂ -

Guy & Waiter

GUY: You are at a restaurant, ordering food. You want fried chicken – which is supposed to come with mashed potatoes, but you want French Fries instead, and the menu says "no substitutions, please". Order your meal.

✂ -

Guy & Girl

GUY: A 12-year-old neighbor girl has a crush on you, and asks you if you will kiss her. What do you do?

✂ -

Guy & Girl

GUY: You're at the mall. A very pretty young girl that you've never seen before walks up to you and starts chatting. After a while, she asks you if you want to go out sometime. What do you do?

✂ -

Guy & a Neighbor

GUY: You sometimes do odd jobs for your neighbor, like mowing his lawn and sweeping his driveway. One day he asks you if you want to come over that night and watch a movie with him. How do you handle this?

✂ -

Guy & Girl

GUY: There is a girl you like from school. Call her on the phone and ask her out.

✂ -

Guy & a Friend

GUY: You have a fight with your mom. You text a friend and he invites you to come over and play video games. You know he likes to smoke pot when he plays video games. How do you handle this?

✂ -

Guy & an Uncle

GUY: You are at a family holiday gathering. Your uncle says he has something fun to show you. He pulls up some porn on his phone and shows them to you. What do you do?

✂---

Guy & a Friend

GUY: You're home watching football on Saturday and a friend drops by to hang out. After watching television for a while, he says he has to go to the bathroom. A few minutes later, you hear bottles clinking, and see that he's poured a couple glasses from your dad's whiskey. How do you handle this situation?

✂---

Guy & Girl

GUY: You're over at your aunt and uncle's house, when your cousin comes home from the mall. She's a little older than you are, and you always thought she was cute. She says she's going to take a shower, and you notice that she left the door open. What do you do?

✂---

Guy at a Party

GUY: You are at a party, and a girl you like is talking with you. She says she took some of her mom's pain pills, because they help her relax. She's a little bit giggly, and asks you if you want to have one of the pills too. What do you tell her?

✂---

Guy & Therapist

GUY: Your therapist just said you didn't do a good job on an assignment. Ask him for extra help.

✂---

Guy & a Friend

GUY: You are having a really bad day. You want to call a friend, just to blow off some steam. Ask a friend to just listen.

✂---

Before-During-After (BDA) Form

	Before		*During*	*After*	
	Long term ***Vulnerabilities***	**Short term** ***Right before***		**Short term** ***Right away***	**Long term** ***Weeks, months, years***
Thoughts *What you were thinking?*					
Feelings & emotions *What you were feeling?*					
Behavior *What you were doing?*					
Physical body *What your body was like?*					
Need being addressed:		Intended function (how you wanted this to work):		Actual function (how it actually worked):	

Form may work best on landscape 11 × 14 paper.

PROS AND CONS WORKSHEET

Name

Date

I am thinking about doing

Be sure to include thoughts, feelings, emotions, and other people when doing the pros and cons.

	Pros ***Good Stuff***		**Cons** ***Bad Stuff***	
	Short-term **Immediate**	**Long-term** **Down the road**	**Short-term** **Immediate**	**Long-term** **Days, weeks, year**
Do It!				
Don't Do It				

I decided to ____
____.

REFERENCES

Kahn T. J. (2011). *Pathways: A guided workbook for youth beginning treatment* (4th ed.). Brandon, VT: Safer Society Press.

Linehan, M. L. (1993). *Skills Training Manual for Treating Borderline Personality Disorder*. New York: Guilford.

Newring, K. A. B., Loverich, T. M., Harris, C. D., & Wheeler, J. G. (2009). Relapse prevention. In W. O'Donohue & J. Fisher (Eds.), *General principles and empirically supported techniques of cognitive behavior therapy*. Hoboken J: John Wiley & Sons.

Newring, K. A. B., & Wheeler, J. G. (2012). Functional analytic psychotherapy (FAP) with juveniles with sexual offense behaviors. *International Journal of Behavioral and Cognitive Therapy*, 7, 102–110.

Newring, R. W., Parker, C, & Newring, K. A. B. (2010). Functional analytic psychotherapy and adolescents. In J. W. Kanter, M. Tsai, & R. J. Kohlenberg (Eds.), *The practice of functional analytic psychotherapy*. New York: Spring Publishing Company.

Trupin, E. W., Stewart, D. G., Beach, B., & Boesky, L. (2002). Effectiveness of dialectical behavior therapy program for incarcerated female juvenile offenders. *Child and Adolescent Mental Health*, 7, 121–127.

Worling, J. R., & Curwen, T. (2001). Estimate of risk of adolescent sexual offense recidivism (ERASOR; Version 2.0). In M. C. Calder (Ed.), *Juveniles and children who sexually abuse: Frameworks for assessment* (pp. 372–397) [The ERASOR is also available free of charge as a pdf file from the author at <jworling@ican.net>].

CHAPTER 15

Academic Intervention

Edward J. Daly III, Maureen A. O'Connor, Polly M. Daro, Whitney Strong and Mackenzie Sommerhalder
Department of Educational Psychology, University of Nebraska-Lincoln, NE, USA

INTRODUCTION

Juvenile sex offenders (JSOs) typically experience concurrent difficulties in family, peer, and school relationships – all the major systems of their young lives (Ronis & Borduin, 2007). The relationships are bidirectional: JSOs are influenced by and influence each social context, all too often in maladaptive ways. Effective treatment plans, therefore, will require multi-component, multicontextual intervention packages that reverse negative interaction patterns and establish healthy and adaptive functioning across family, peer, and school contexts. With respect to educational concerns, Veneziano and Veneziano (2002) recommend "facilitation of positive school attachments" (p. 255) as a part of multisystemic therapy treatment plans. Treatment planning to improve school functioning is critical because JSOs, like non-sex juvenile offenders, have lower grades on average than non-delinquent peers and display significant deficits in all the basic skill areas, including reading, math, oral language, and writing (Foley, 2001; Leone, Krezmien, Mason, & Meisel, 2005), which often leaves them one or more years behind their non-delinquent peers (Ronis & Borduin, 2007). Getting caught by the authorities for offending sets in motion a protracted series of events that will be very disruptive to their education: arrest, legal proceedings, and probable incarceration, all of which often leaves them further behind than they were before the offense(s) occurred. This lack of continuity in educational services poses major challenges for narrowing the gap academically between JSOs and their peers. Furthermore, two natural characteristics of high school – increasing personal responsibility for work and increasing difficulty in academic content over time – probably do little to help the JSO feel that the school is reaching out to facilitate a positive attachment to it.

Although JSOs have a host of difficulties across all the major systems in their lives (Ronis & Borduin, 2007; van Wijk, Vermeiren, Loeber,

Toolkit for Working with Juvenile Sex Offenders.
DOI: http://dx.doi.org/10.1016/B978-0-12-405948-1.00015-3

Hart-Kerkhoffs, & Doreleijers, 2006; Veneziano & Veneziano, 2002), the point of departure for this chapter is that the poor academic achievement that is common in this population should be viewed as a quantitative and not a qualitative difference with their higher achieving peers. Therefore, the interventions to be described in this chapter are drawn from studies in which participants display poor achievement (rather than a diagnostic condition that is presumed to interact in some way with treatment outcomes) and are appropriate for any low-skilled student. There are two reasons for this starting assumption. First, efforts to identify effective academic interventions based on psychodiagnostic status are fraught with problems and have failed to receive empirical support (Fletcher, Coulter, Reschly, & Vaughn, 2004; Kavale, 1990; Macmann & Barnett, 1999). Meaningful differences between students – even for psychoeducational diagnoses – have consistently been shown to be based on quantitative and not qualitative differences between students (Vellutino, Fletcher, Snowling, & Scanlon, 2004). The second reason is more pragmatic. There is a dearth of literature on academic interventions for JSOs. The extant research suggests that they do not differ from non-sex offenders (Ronis & Borduin, 2007). Therefore, until research proves otherwise, it seems best to design academic interventions for JSOs on the basis of a low skill level and not on the basis of presumed population characteristics. Because this chapter deals with JSOs' academic needs in some type of an educational context (school or correctional remedial program), they will be referred to as students from this point forward.

Yet, when one considers the bigger picture, there is a significant pattern that is probably typical of most students' school trajectories, one that should influence the approach to be taken with academic intervention. It appears that the window of opportunity to do academic intervention with these students may be open only briefly. Incarceration interrupts a student's school experience, the effects of which are compounded by the fact that the student's peers are progressing to more complex skills in the curriculum as academic requirements are getting progressively harder over time. Less than half the youth released from correctional facilities return to school (even if they did participate in correctional remedial education programs) and, of those who do, only a small percentage stay in school for more than 5 months (Foley, 2001). Therefore, to be effective, academic intervention should produce relatively rapid effects and it should help the student's adjustment back to school be a positive experience. To this end, the interventions presented in this chapter are designed to quickly produce reinforcing consequences that strengthen academic skills while also giving sufficient support to make school work less aversive and provide instruction that is adapted to the student's skill level. The model and methods of this chapter represent an extension of functional assessment to academic dysfunction (Daly, Witt, Martens, & Dool, 1997; Daly, Martens, Barnett, Witt, & Olson, 2007). Functional assessment seeks to enrich the natural environment with instructional strategies and reinforcement contingencies that foster adaptive behavior (academic performance in this case) while diminishing reinforcement for maladaptive behavior (e.g., classroom disruption; Cooper et al., 2007).

A FUNCTIONAL APPROACH TO ACADEMIC INTERVENTION

When it comes to improving academic achievement, there is no way to "make" a student achieve. The only thing a teacher can directly influence is the number of responses given by the student to relevant curricular tasks (Heward, 1994). In a classic series of longitudinal studies at the Juniper Garden's Children's Center, Greenwood and colleagues demonstrated that academic engagement (i.e., responding to curricular tasks) during instructional time had a significant effect on reading achievement (Greenwood, 1991; Greenwood, Terry, Arreaga-Mayer, & Finney, 1992; Greenwood, Hart, Walker, & Risley, 1994). They also showed that engagement differences between students over time affected academic achievement: students with lower cumulative engagement rates achieved well below same-grade peers with higher cumulative engagement rates. Further statistical analyses of their findings revealed that student engagement mediated the effects of instruction on academic achievement (Greenwood, 1996; Greenwood, Terry, Utley, Montagna, & Walker, 1993). In other words, instruction was more or less effective according to the level of academic engagement it promoted. Therefore, the primary focus of academic intervention should be to increase students' responding to instructional tasks (Skinner, Fletcher, & Henington, 1996); the more instruction promotes active responding, the better the results (Heward, 1994). So, instruction and intervention should be designed to maximize accurate student responding; that's the best you can do.

Academic intervention, however, involves far more than just assigning more work to low-skilled students to increase their responding. The effective teacher strategically controls what happens before, during, and after student responding to maximize responding during instructional time in the most relevant instructional activities. There are, however, two problems that an academic intervention must address. First, for low-skilled students, the routine instructional tasks administered to a classroom of students are often just too difficult. They do not know how to respond correctly; they have a *behavior deficit* – too little academic behavior in this case. Giving them more work to increase their response opportunities alone will not improve their skills. Instruction must be adapted to their instructional level. Second, the other problem in dealing with the academic needs of low-skilled students is all the appealing alternative activities available to them that are much more reinforcing than doing their schoolwork. When the student is faced with the choice between doing difficult instructional assignments and engaging in pleasure-producing activities, doing school work loses out. In other words, engaging in undesired behavior (e.g., drug use, truancy) has a competitive edge and wins out over doing their work. In this case, *behavior excesses* are impeding the student's engagement with instructional tasks, exacerbating the behavior deficit as their peers move forward in the curriculum. The key to academic intervention is creating an instructional context in which the student *chooses* to do his or her work instead of doing something else.

Before proceeding to the instructional and motivational strategies that should make up an academic intervention, let's do a behavioral analysis of why these behavior deficits and competing behavior excesses are creating problems for the student and broadly define how intervention should proceed. In the case of a behavior deficit (i.e., insufficient academic responding), the student is often unable to respond to the instructional task and even the most powerful reinforcement contingencies will fail to evoke a correct response. The teacher has to arrange instruction such that responding *can* occur so that it can then be reinforced. The details of how this is done are described in a later section of this chapter. The strategies largely boil down to use of prompting methods, error correction, and frequent opportunities to respond. Strategic use of instructional strategies is essential to effective intervention and, therefore, we will describe when the strategies are most appropriate as we explain what they are. However, the picture would be incomplete without an analysis of the consequences of responding. One of four relevant consequences can occur when a person behaves: behavior (1) produces stimulation that increases behavior in the future (a positive reinforcement effect); (2) eliminates (or avoids) an aversive form of stimulation that also results in an increase in behavior in the future (a negative reinforcement effect); (3) produces an aversive form of

Table 15.1 Examples of Reinforcement and Punishment Effects for Academic Responding

	May Increase Behavior (reinforcement effect)	May Decrease Behavior (punishment effect)
Addition of a stimulus (positive)	Giving a student fast-food vouchers for completing homework, increasing future homework completion	Giving harder work once the student finishes easier work, decreasing future work completion
Removal of a stimulus (negative)	Allowing a student to skip a homework assignment based on good test performance, increasing future good test performance	Removing access to preferred activities (e.g., band, theater) based on poor test performance, decreasing future poor test performance

stimulation that decreases behavior in the future (a positive punishment effect); or (4) eliminates a reinforcing form of stimulation that decreases behavior in the future (a negative punishment effect). These types of consequences are relevant because they influence the future probability of behavior – academic responding in this case. The principles of reinforcement and punishment apply to both adaptive and maladaptive behavior patterns. Simple examples of each as they relate to academic performance appear in Table 15.1. For students who engage in unhealthy behavior excesses, peer attention and pleasurable states that result from illegal and illicit activities strengthen problem behavior through positive reinforcement. Also, they can develop elaborate behavioral repertoires that allow them to escape or avoid aversive tasks. For instance, disruptive behavior in the classroom may lead to removal from the classroom and hence removal of instructional demands, thereby negatively reinforcing the behavior in spite of the teacher's intention to punish the disruptive behavior. As such, the teacher may actually witness an increase in disruptive behavior because he or she is negatively reinforcing the student. The threat of a bad grade is hardly menacing when disruptive behavior results in such a powerful effect – escaping school work. Furthermore, anything that takes on aversive properties (e.g., hard and boring school work) can quickly become a punishing stimulus that is then actively avoided by the students in the future. Punishing consequences often eventually lead to escape-motivated behavior. Keep in mind that punishment does not necessarily need to be intentional on the part of the teacher. Contingent application of an aversive stimulus or contingent removal of a desirable stimulus, regardless of what they are, will have punishment effects (if behavior decreases), which then may lead to escape-motivated behavior, as the student tries to avoid the consequences in the future. Therefore, to assure that an academic intervention is appropriate for a particular student, the plan should be based on an analysis of sources of both desirable and undesirable consequences (from the student's and not necessarily the teacher's perspective) that influence his or her behavior.

The challenges to developing an effective academic intervention for a student are significant when one considers the implications of this behavioral analysis. The academic intervention must simultaneously account for both a possible skill deficit as well as competing reinforcing *and* punishing contingencies that may be drawing the student's attention elsewhere when he or she should be doing school work. The behavioral excesses that occur when school work should be occurring are being maintained by (usually strong) positive and/or negative reinforcement contingencies that have developed over time, whereas the behavior deficit (academic responding) is not currently under sufficiently strong reinforcement contingencies to help it compete effectively. Put more simply, the contingencies favor undesirable behavior over desirable behavior.

O'Neill, Horner, Albin, Sprague, and Storey (1997) described three things that an intervention plan should accomplish when selecting consequences for behavior: (1) it should make problem behavior *irrelevant* due to newly available reinforcement for appropriate behavior; (2) it should make problem behavior *inefficient* by making it easier to obtain reinforcement for appropriate behavior than for inappropriate behavior; and (3) it should make problem behavior *ineffective* by eliminating reinforcement for problem behavior. The first two are more realistic targets for school-based interventions for adolescents because they have considerable autonomy and control over their access to reinforcement. Adolescents typically have more control over their environment than younger children or populations who depend on others for care and maintenance (e.g., those with developmental disabilities), which makes it harder totally to eliminate reinforcers over which teachers and/or parents do not have direct control in the first place (the third strategy). Therefore, the emphasis in this chapter will be on the first two approaches – making problem behavior inefficient and ineffective.

Realistically, an intervention should at least attempt to make problem behavior irrelevant and inefficient by making it easier for the student to access reinforcement for engaging in school work. Changing the reinforcement contingencies is as vital to academic intervention as selecting instructional material and presenting it effectively. Therefore, given the pressing need to deliver a strong treatment with students, the academic intervention should be designed to accomplish three things: (1) provide the necessary instructional support to make academic responding occur so that it can then be reinforced (positively and/or negatively); (2) design reinforcing consequences for work completion and skill improvement that compete effectively with available reinforcement for undesirable behavior; and (3) address aversive properties of students' academic work in a manner that increases academic responding. The intervention strategies described below address all three components. These strategies are based on well validated principles and practices of functional assessment. We recommend that you incorporate as many as possible into a comprehensive intervention package.

PREPARING FOR ACADEMIC INTERVENTION

Keeping in mind that efficient intervention is vital with this population, we recommend that you follow a 6-step process for academic intervention. The intervention steps are outlined in Table 15.2. Each step is discussed in turn.

Step 1: Establish a Baseline

Before deciding what you should do as an intervention, you must decide what you should change (the behavior targeted for intervention) and choose or design a measure of it. Bushell and Baer (1994) describe "*close, continual contact with relevant outcome data*" as a hallmark of effective teaching (p. 7). Frequent assessment of instructionally relevant outcomes establishes a feedback loop for gaging the effectiveness of instruction. Systematic formative evaluation of student progress has been shown significantly to increase student achievement (Fuchs & Fuchs, 1986). Formative evaluation is characterized by repeated assessments of academic skills using brief and efficient measures that are sensitive to instructional effects. Collecting data and plotting the results on a graph over time facilitates decision making. A case-study evaluation design is the best method for organizing your data for meaningful interpretation. In a case-study design (illustrated in the upcoming examples), a baseline is first established, followed by an intervention phase. Collecting data repeatedly throughout each phase will allow you to determine the current level of responding and whether there are significant trends in the data. The function of the baseline is to give an indication of the current level of behavior prior to intervention. It will serve as a point of comparison for intervention results if you continue to

Table 15.2 Steps for Designing and Conducting an Academic Intervention

Preparing for academic intervention
1. Establish a baseline for (a) work production, (b) basic skill fluency, and/or (c) academic engagement 2. Conduct a preference assessment to identify potential rewards 3. Conduct a performance-deficit analysis to determine whether there is a skill or a performance deficit
Selecting and delivering an academic intervention
4. Strengthen current instruction as needed to address any skill deficits through: a. Prompting correct responses b. Guided practice c. Error correction d. Fluency building e. Generalization training 5. Enrich the instructional context through positive reinforcement by: a. Establishing criteria for performance improvements b. Motivating the student to perform by (i) communicating a criterion for reinforcement, (ii) offering access to highly preferred items or activities for meeting the criterion before work starts, and (iii) giving performance feedback when work is finished c. Allowing contingent access to highly preferred reinforcers if the criterion is met 6. Address escape-motivated behavior by: a. Allowing escape contingent on work completion b. Identifying and altering aversive features of demands, and/or c. Using choice to improve motivation

collect data during intervention. The goal of academic intervention is to see the data points that are currently near the bottom of the page reach the top of the page. Ideally, one would see a stable baseline followed by an increasing trend during the intervention phase – the steeper the trend the better. Therefore, before you select an intervention, we advise you to establish a baseline and plan to measure performance repeatedly once you initiate the intervention. There are three targets for intervention that are particularly appropriate and for which measures are readily available or easily designed: students' work products, basic skill fluency (measured with curriculum-based measurement), and academic engagement (measured through direct observation). We recommend that you select one or more of these areas as a target for intervention and measure it repeatedly over the course of intervention.

Work Products

Work products – things like classroom exercises, homework, quizzes, and tests – are not behavior per se. They are the *result* of behavior. Yet, they are a direct reflection of learning and therefore tell us a lot about a student's progress. They are easy to gather and score (if certain conditions are met; see discussion below), and constitute an excellent data source for making decisions about just how much the student has learned (Cooper, Heron, & Heward, 2007). Whenever possible, we strongly recommend that you measure completion and accuracy of work products as an indicator of learning.

The first thing you must do is to determine how suitable they are for assessing the student in question. Their suitability hinges on two issues: whether they appropriately reflect the problem and whether assessments will yield interpretable data. Chances are good that the students referred for academic intervention are not getting their work done. As you discuss the student's problems with the person making the referral, ask to look at work samples, particularly examples that are typical of their current work. If work completion and accuracy are poor, work products may be the best indicator of the problem. We recommend that you prioritize a subject matter (e.g., English, social studies, math) as your starting point for intervention. Pick the subject in which the student is displaying the poorest performance.

The next thing to determine is whether the work products will give you interpretable data. If the time devoted to completing work and/or the type of work varies vary considerably on a day-to-day basis, then work products will not be feasible. For example, if students are given writing assignments that are very different from one day to the next (e.g., creative writing one day, vocabulary the next, and grammar on another day), using work products will not work out very well. The following questions can be used to investigate whether work products will be appropriate. First, does the teacher devote a consistent amount of time to the instructional activity that produces a written product? For example, math worksheets and problems completed would be appropriate if the student has a regularly scheduled amount of time (e.g., 30 minutes) for completion. Conversely, if a teacher assigns work (e.g., social studies exercises) only infrequently, measuring work products will not produce many data and therefore may not be an appropriate target for intervention. Second, is the teacher willing to standardize the devoted time for measurement purposes? In other words, is the teacher willing to keep the time consistent from instructional session to instructional session? Measuring work products will not be useful if the results vary from session to session as a function of the length of instructional sessions. It is critical to keep this time consistent. Finally, are the instructional items (e.g., math problems, comprehension questions) largely consistent from one day to the next, or do they vary from day to day? Difficulty level and/or problem type can have a large effect on the outcomes, independent of the intervention. Therefore, work product measurement will only work if the instructional items are similar to one another. If the answers to all the questions are "yes", then you can use permanent products as part of your data collection procedures to determine how much the student has learned. Again, we strongly recommend that you inspect previous work products and discuss them with the teacher with these questions in view. This process will tell you whether work products will be a good target for intervention.

If you decide to target work products for intervention, you can measure two things: completion and accuracy. Both can be calculated as a percentage. Work completion is calculated by dividing the number of problems assigned by the number of problems actually completed by the student. Accuracy is calculated by dividing the number of problems completed accurately by the number of problems attempted. Both are simple and easy to calculate. We suggest that you always calculate both. An example appears in Figure 15.1. In the example, Ryan's teacher gave him 30 minutes to complete math worksheets in class on a daily basis. The top graph is a baseline for work completion, the middle graph is a baseline for accuracy, and the bottom graph is a baseline for homework completion and accuracy. You can see that Ryan's work completion is quite variable (top graph). On average, he completes 58% of his daily assignments, clearly well below his teacher's expectation of finishing all the problems. His accuracy, although somewhat variable too, is much higher (middle graph). He's completing 92% of the problems correctly, on average. Therefore, it looks as if the work is not too difficult – or at least the problems that he is completing; it's just that he is not doing the work consistently. Ryan's teacher was also concerned about his homework completion and accuracy. The bottom graph in Figure 15.1 displays baselines for both completion and accuracy. Both are much more variable than expected and well below the teacher's expectations. Work products are an excellent source of data because they reflect exactly what the teacher expects the student to do and, when the conditions are appropriate for measurement, yield an excellent target for intervention.

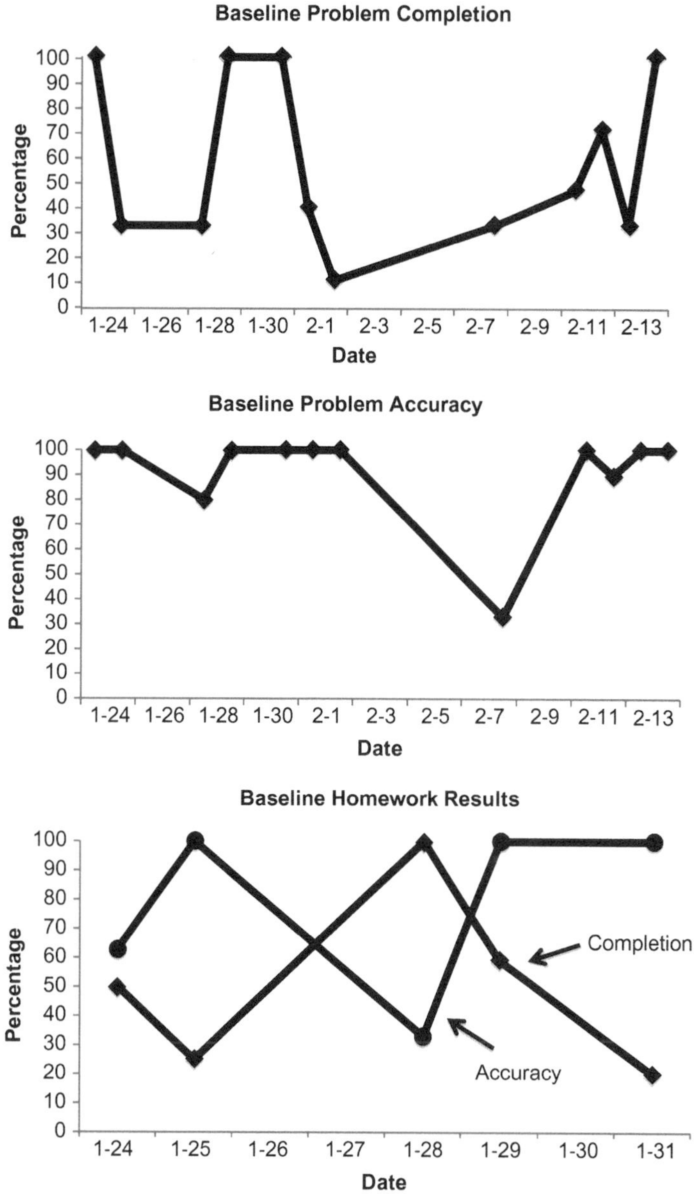

Figure 15.1 Baselines for Ryan's work Products.

Basic Skills Fluency

It has been our experience that most students referred for academic intervention – even older students – suffer from deficits in basic skills – oral reading fluency, math computation skills, and/or writing skills. Students have often been passed on in the curriculum despite the fact that they have not mastered basic skills. A basic skills problem is easily diagnosed using curriculum-based measures (CBM; Shinn, 1989, 1998). In fact, Foley (2001) recommends their use in correctional educational programs for incarcerated youth. They only take a few minutes to administer and score and have solid reliability and validity data supporting their use (Shinn, 1989, 1998). Basic skill fluency is a critical factor in learning harder skills (Binder, 1996; Howell & Nolet, 2000; Johnson & Layng, 1992). All too often, school personnel fail to assess the prerequisite skills that are necessary for mastering higher-order skills. We strongly recommend that you assess this area. Due to space limitations, we can describe them only briefly. However, you can find more information (including materials, training, norms, and technical adequacy data) at either Aimsweb (www.aimsweb.com) or DIBELS (https://dibels.uoregon.edu/).

For oral reading fluency, three randomly chosen passages (from a single grade level in passages obtained either through Aimsweb or DIBELS) are administered to the student for 1 minute each. The student is instructed to read each passage aloud. The examiner calculates the number of correctly read words and errors per minute for each passage. Student performance is estimated as the median correctly read words per minute and median errors per minute. An example baseline for oral reading fluency is displayed in Figure 15.2. Math computation fluency is assessed by having the student complete math problems on single-skill or multiple-skill worksheets for 2 minutes. Results are calculated as correct *digits* (and not problems) per 2 minutes. Calculating digits per 2 minutes gives a more fine-grained measure of performance that is more sensitive to change. Materials and instructions can be obtained at http://www.interventioncentral.org/. For written expression, the student is given an age-appropriate story starter, 1 minute to think about what they will write, and 3 minutes to write. Story starters can be found on the Internet. For example, see the Writing Probe Generator at http://www.interventioncentral.org/. Results can be scored as total number of words written, number of correctly spelled words, and/or number of correct writing sequences.

Direct Observation of Academic Engagement

If work products and/or CBM are not suitable targets for intervention, we recommend that you conduct behavioral observations of academic engagement (AE) to generate intervention data. Academic engagement is a critical indicator of how much responding is occurring during instructional

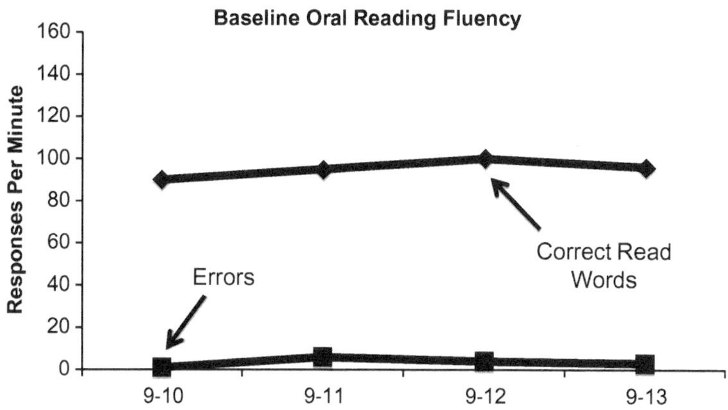

Figure 15.2 Baseline oral reading fluency data.

time (Greenwood, 1991, 1996). The downside is that direct observations are more labor intensive because someone must be actively attending to the student during the problematic instructional time. However, if you can improve the student's academic engagement, you significantly increase the chances of improving his or her academic skills, as noted earlier.

An observation form appears in Appendix A. To prepare for establishing a baseline, academic engagement must be defined in observable terms. A definition for academic engagement (based on the work of Greenwood and his colleagues in their longitudinal research) appears on the observation form. Note that the definition focuses on directly observable forms of academic responding. Again, this is important for evaluating a student's response opportunities. Next, the observer must determine when and how long to observe the student. Observations should be conducted during times when the student is having the most difficulty (e.g., during science class), and the length of the observation should be long enough to establish a clear pattern in the behavior.

The observation form is set up for *momentary time-sampling*. With this method, the behavior is observed and recorded *at* a particular interval (e.g., 30 seconds, 5 minutes) and not in between. It is as if you are taking samples of ongoing behavior from a stream of continuous behavior. Although it does not measure all occurrences of academic engagement, it is a practical and generally reliable method of observation. During the observation period, the observer records with a marking of some type (e.g., "+") whether academic engagement is occurring at the pre-specified interval (e.g., 5 minutes, 10 minutes, 15 minutes, etc.). If academic engagement is not occurring, we suggest that you make an alternate mark on the form for that interval (e.g., "0"); doing so will help you avoid losing your place as you record from interval to interval. The length of intervals should be determined based on feasibility for the person doing the recording and how reliably he or she will be able to observe the student at each interval. For example, if someone like a school psychologist is present only to collect data and has no other responsibilities, shorter intervals (e.g., 30 seconds) may be used. If the observer is someone who has other responsibilities during the observation period like a classroom teacher, longer intervals (e.g., 5 minutes) will be more feasible. If you look closely at the form, you will see that every sixth interval is reserved for recording a peer's behavior. Note that the blank cells for recording are in the rows below the rows for recording AE for the target student. This convention will make it easier to calculate the results separately. Concurrently observing a peer will give you normative information about other students in the class. This way, you can compare the target student to peer behavior.

By dividing the number of intervals containing academic engagement by the total number of observation intervals at the end of the observation, you can determine the percentage of academic engagement during instructional time. For instance, if a student was academically engaged for 3 out of 15 total intervals, the result would be a score of 20% academically engagement (3 engaged intervals/15 total intervals = 20%). This means that the student was engaged for 20% of the observation intervals. The same formula is used to compute the percentage of engagement of a peer in the classroom for comparison to the target student. Because the observation form contains data for both the target student and the peer, adjustments need to be made to separate the results as you make calculations. The formulas at the bottom of the observation form will help you to do that and calculate the results for both the target and peer. An example of a scored observation form appears in Appendix A. An example of a baseline graph for academic engagement appears in Figure 15.3. The results revealed that the target student's academic engagement is considerably lower than that of his peers. The target student was academically engaged 34% of the time, on average, and the peer was engaged 85% of the time, on average. Again, these results establish a baseline for monitoring progress over the course of the entire intervention process. Therefore, assessments should continue once the intervention has begun. The baseline will serve as a point of comparison that will allow you to determine if the student is improving following intervention.

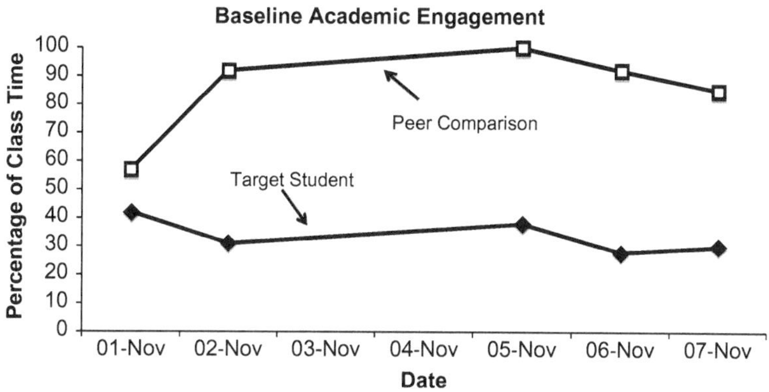

Figure 15.3 Baseline results for academic engagement.

Step 2: Conduct a Preference Assessment

The second step is an assessment as well. This assessment also prepares you for intervention. Identifying potentially effective reinforcers early on in the intervention process can be helpful for at least two reasons. First, competing with already established reinforcers (e.g., social attention of negative peer influences, illegal substances, physical pleasure) for behaviors that are incompatible with academic responding (e.g., truancy, illegal sexual activities) is a tall order. As such, a valid method for selecting reinforcing consequences is needed. Second, in some cases, a simple reinforcement program may be sufficient to improve academic responding. A performance-deficit analysis (described below) will tell you whether this is the case or not. The multiple-stimulus without replacement (MSWO) procedure (DeLeon & Iwata, 1996) is appropriate for use in school settings (Daly, Wells, Swanger-Gagné, Carr, & Kunz, 2009; Resetar & Noell, 2008). In three short sessions (i.e., less than 10 minutes each), high-, medium-, and low-preference items or activities can be identified, which can then be used as a part of a contingency-management program.

A protocol for administering the sessions appears in Appendix B. Before sessions are conducted, however, you should consult with the teacher or person who will be managing the academic intervention to identify eight activities or items for which the student appears to show a preference and which the teacher would be willing to use following intervention sessions. Actual food and tangible items (e.g., pens, markers, etc.), as well as activities (e.g., access to the gym to play basketball) can be used for the assessment. For activities or items that are not readily accessible, their names, a picture, or both the name and picture should be placed on index cards. A survey of items that may be appropriate for this population appears in Appendix C. Note that the survey contains a column for items currently used by the teacher and a column for items that are not currently being used by the teacher, but which he or she would be willing to use. This step of the preference-assessment process is very important. First, the teacher often knows the student well and can provide useful information about likes and dislikes. Also, you should not use items that the teacher would not be willing to use in the classroom. There's no better way to sabotage an intervention than to promise something that will not be delivered. Therefore, the person responsible for managing potential rewards should give their input prior to the assessment.

At the beginning of each session, place all eight items (index cards, edibles, or tangibles) directly in front of the student in random order in a linear array on the table so that he or she can easily see and reach each item. Students should be given brief exposure to each item if possible to ensure familiarity. The student is then instructed to select the item for which they would be willing to do work. When a selection is made, the card containing the preferred item is removed. Items are recorded as "1" to "8" in the order in which they are selected. A score sheet appears in Appendix D. Following the next selection, fill the gap and reposition the items according to the directions on the protocol (Appendix B). These procedures are followed until all items are selected and recorded. When this is done, the session is terminated. This assessment should be repeated two more times, preferably on separate days. Because students' preferences tend to vary from day to day, doing these separate assessments will increase the reliability of the results by reducing the effects of outliers on the results.

When all trials have been completed, results are scored to identify high-, medium-, and low-preference activities/items/edibles. Directions appear on the protocol (Appendix B). Briefly, each item will have three selection scores, one for each day of assessment. These scores need to be combined into a single score for each item and, for the purpose of graphing the results, high-preference items have to be converted into larger scores and lower preference items need to be converted into lower scores. This is done through a reverse-scoring process that is outlined on the protocol. An example of a scored data sheet appears at the bottom of Appendix D, and an example of typical results is displayed as a bar graph in Figure 15.4. In Figure 15.4, items are plotted from highest preference to lowest preference. Scores of 7 or 8 are plotted as high-preference

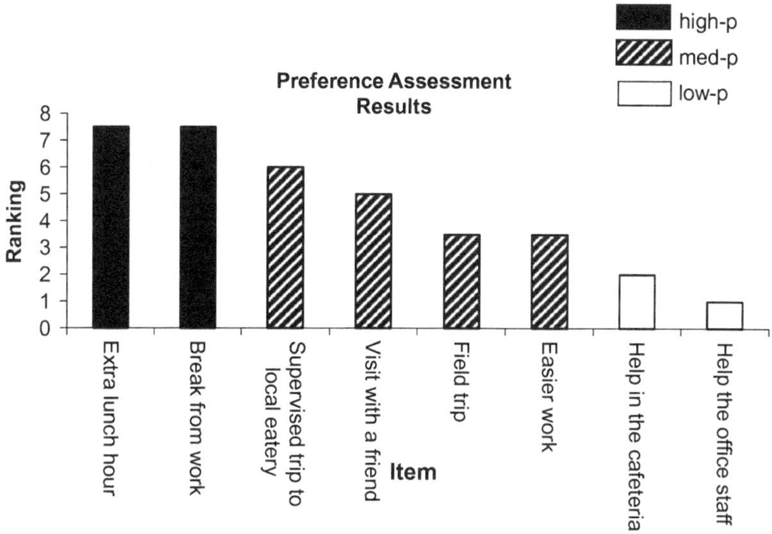

Figure 15.4 An example of a bar graph displaying the results of a preference assessment.

items, scores of 3–6 are plotted as medium-preference items, and scores of 1–2 are plotted as low-preference items. The results can be used to plan reinforcing consequences for completing work, improving scores, and/or improving academic engagement. In our experience, both high- and medium-preference items can generally serve as effective rewards for improving academic performance. So, the results give you a number of items that can be used as incentives to improve performance.

Step 3: Conduct a Performance-Deficit Analysis

Steps one and two established the level of behavior and potential items for a reinforcement program, both necessary prerequisites to effective intervention. The third step – conducting a performance-deficit analysis – examines whether the student is *able* to do assigned work without additional instruction. This information tells you just how elaborate the intervention should be. Lentz (1988) popularized the idea of distinguishing between performance and skill deficits. A student with a performance deficit has the skills necessary to do the work. The problem is that the reinforcement contingencies are not powerful enough to promote academic responding. A student with a skill deficit is probably unable to do the work even with the most powerful of rewards available. For the former student, a simple contingency management plan is sufficient. For the latter student, instructional strategies are also necessary. Doing a performance-deficit analysis will tell you what kind of problem you have and give you strong clues as to what should be included in the intervention.

A protocol for doing a performance-deficit analysis appears in Appendix E. Two assignments which the student has previously failed or on which they scored well below expectations should be used for the analysis. These can be gathered from the teacher. During the assessment, the student is presented the first assignment and told that if the performance goal (see the protocol) is met or exceeded, a reward will be given upon completion. Preference-assessment results are particularly helpful in this regard: select from the highest-ranking items from the assessment. You should present several options. Allowing them to choose from among multiple items (high- and medium-preference items from the preference assessment) will naturally adjust for possible satiation or other factors affecting their motivational level at the time the session is being conducted. If the student is able to meet or exceed the performance goal when a reward is available, a reinforcement plan should be developed. If, however, the student's performance does not improve under the reward condition, instructional strategies will be necessary as a part of the intervention plan. (Instructional strategies are described in the next section.) To facilitate decision making, results should be plotted on a bar graph. An example appears in Figure 15.5. The graph at the top of the figure illustrates typical results for a performance deficit. The student's scores increased considerably when offered high-preference rewards on previously failed assignments. The graph at the bottom of the figure illustrates typical results for a student whose performance did not improve with the offer of a reward. In this case, instructional strategies are probably needed as a part of the intervention package. Although, it is possible that the rewards were just not effective. Their demeanor and reaction to the rewards will usually tell you if this is the case.

SELECTING AND DELIVERING AN ACADEMIC INTERVENTION

Step 4: Strengthen Current Instruction to Address any Skill Deficits

The baseline and performance-deficit analysis results will reveal whether the student needs instructional modifications or not. As mentioned earlier, instruction should be tailored to produce the most correct responses

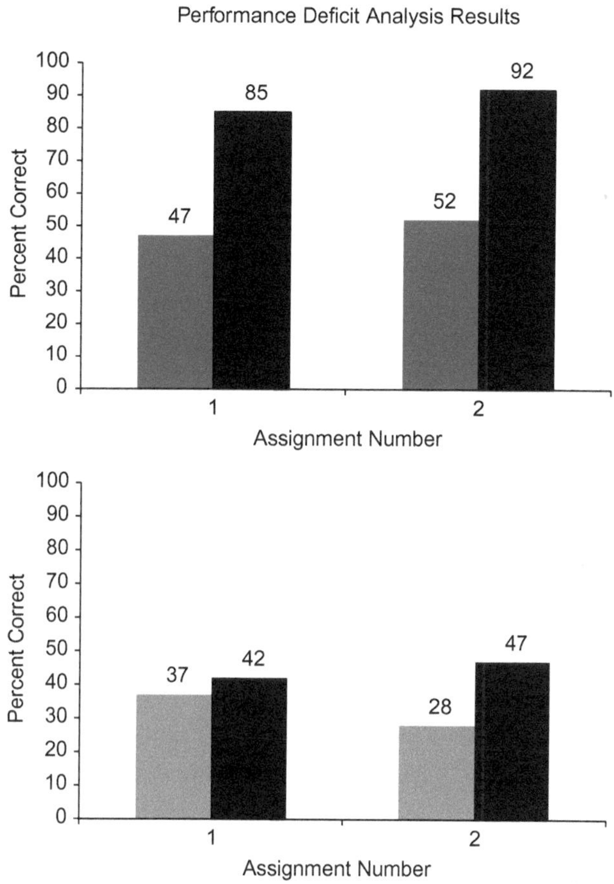

Figure 15.5 An example of results of a performance-deficit analysis. The results at the top illustrate a performance-deficit problem. The results at the bottom illustrate a skill-deficit problem.

during the available time. Heward (1994) and Skinner et al. (1996) present convincing evidence that the best way to increase correct responding is through the use of complete learning trials. A learning trial consists of an instructional antecedent (e.g., presenting a flashcard with a vocabulary term), prompting a student response, and giving feedback (praise or error correction). Although other instructional models may use different terms, the learning trial is at the core of all learning and is a simple yet powerful way to conceptualize how the teacher should be delivering instruction. Instruction can be thought of as a basic sequence of presenting instructional content, prompting frequent responses, and providing consistent feedback. However, instructional strategies should also be differentiated according to how proficient the student is with the task. This means that this basic instructional sequence should be modified as the student is progressively learning the content. Haring and Eaton (1978) articulated a useful heuristic model – the Instructional Hierarchy (IH) – for describing how instruction should change as a function of student progress. Haring and Eaton pointed out that for a behavior deficit, effective instruction first promotes accurate responding (i.e., the student goes from no responding to giving correct responses with few errors), then improves fluency (slow, accurate responding becomes more rapid), and then leads to generalization (i.e., the student now uses the skill consistently, uses it for novel problems, and uses it with other skills for harder tasks).

According to the IH, teachers should use modeling, prompting, and error correction to build accuracy. At this point, it is important that the teacher address all of the student's responses so that he or she does not practice errors. When accuracy improves and error rate is low, the teacher should give lots of practice. Feedback at this point will be for a collection of responses (e.g., completing an entire worksheet). The teacher can speed up fluency by reinforcing students for improving their rate of responding (discussed in Step 5 below). Although generalization emerges later in the learning process, the teacher should be teaching the student to generalize from the very moment instruction begins. Students learn to generalize more readily when teachers teach to high fluency levels (e.g., becoming fluent in math computation makes learning harder math skills easier), when teachers give rules for when to use the skill with clear examples (e.g., teaching grammar rules and showing examples of when they apply and when they do not apply), when they teach generalizable skills (e.g., learning to decode through phonics instruction helps students to read words they have never encountered before), when they teach skills in natural contexts (e.g., teaching money skills in the context of shopping for items), and when they reinforce generalized use of the skill (e.g., when a student uses a recently instructed vocabulary term correctly in a new context; Alessi, 1987; Binder, 1996; Daly et al., 1997; Daly et al., 2007; Stokes & Baer, 1977). The IH is a vintage heuristic that has proven itself to be very useful for understanding how to design academic interventions for over 30 years (Ardoin & Daly, 2007; Daly, Lentz, & Boyer, 1996). It can be used in intervention design to plan for how to adjust learning trials as the student is learning a skill.

The temptation with academic interventions is to scour the research or the Internet for *a* specific intervention that works as broadly as possible.

The problem is that, even for effective interventions, claims are often over-exaggerated or over generalized. From a functional perspective, the critical question to ask is, which instructional components are needed at this time, given the student's current level of proficiency with the task? Therefore, we do not present a list of intervention strategies. Instead, we will explain how to supplement or revise current instruction with the types of instructional components a student will need at different points across the learning continuum (i.e., from accuracy to fluency to generalization). To this end, we suggest that academic intervention strategies should be embedded in a sequence of *preparation, presenting, prompting, performing*, and *praising* (or correction) during instructional time (Daly et al., 1997; Daly et al., 2007; Howell & Nolet, 2000; Lentz, Allen, & Ehrhardt, 1996; Lentz & Shapiro, 1986). Specific strategies for each part of the sequence appear in Table 15.3. For preparation, tasks that are neither too hard nor too easy should be

Table 15.3 Instructional Components

Instructional Sequence	Strategies
Preparation	Tasks of appropriate difficulty level Clear instructions for (a) how to do the task and (b) what will happen as a result of finishing the task Teach any rules that may help the student discriminate when and when not to use the skill Teach use of the skill in the natural context if possible
Presenting	Use a rapid pace Present initial items singly and provide feedback for every response Present multiple practice opportunities when building fluency
Prompting	Model correct responding when building accuracy Progressively delay modeling prompts as accuracy is improving
Performing	Supervise skill use (responding) as accuracy is being established Practice to fluent levels of performance when accuracy is established
Praising (or correction)	Praise and corrective feedback: For every response on initial trials (see Presenting) Summarized as percentage correct and rate for all responses after practice trials Actively look for generalized use of the skill and praise the student

selected. Careful sequencing of instructional task will make practice more productive (Daly et al., 2007; Lentz & Shapiro, 1986). Instructions to the student should make both the task (i.e., what needs to be done) and the consequences for completing the task (addressing what will happen as a result of finishing the task) crystal clear for the student (Howell & Nolet, 2000).

When it comes to presenting, instruction should move at a relatively rapid pace so the student does not have time to think about or engage in other activities. While presenting instruction, the teacher should use prompting to provide just enough assistance to the student to help him or her get the right answer, but doing so in such a way that the student becomes progressively less reliant on the assistance. For instance, when students are learning something new (e.g., reading a complicated chemistry term), the teacher should initially *model* the response by saying it for them and then having them repeat it back. A teacher might prompt students about what to look for before applying a newly learned response. After initial teaching trials, a teacher might begin delaying prompts for a few seconds to give the student a chance to respond without assistance. If the student makes frequent errors with the prompt delay, the instructor should go back to modeling.

Instruction should also demand performance. In other words, there should be a lot of practice opportunities. Moving on too quickly in the curriculum without sufficient practice actually reduces students' chances of generalizing newly learned skills to harder tasks, resulting in a growing cumulative skill deficit and increasingly harder work for the low-skilled student (Binder, 1996). Teachers will have greater success if they set high standards for both accurate and fluent (i.e., rapid) responding before moving on in the curriculum (Binder, 1996; Daly et al., 2007). Finally, effective instruction provides heavy doses of praising and corrective feedback for skills that are being newly acquired and fades that feedback as student responding becomes more reliable (Daly et al., 1997). This sequence can be used to diagnose current instruction: which pieces are missing from the student's current instruction? Adding those components which are currently missing will assure that you are maximizing responding during the instructional time and adapting it to the student's current proficiency level.

Step 5: Enrich the Instructional Context Through Positive Reinforcement

For reasons described earlier, we strongly recommend that academic interventions include explicit, programmed rewards for work completion and performance improvements. Too often, when students finish one task in the classroom, the only thing they get to do is more work! What's more, the work is often harder! Thus, in the interest of keeping students motivated and engaged, use the preference-assessment results to establish a positive reinforcement plan for work completion. To do so requires: (1) selecting a criterion for academic performance; (2) communicating something about that criterion to the student (there are various ways to do this); (3) selecting a reinforcer; (4) giving performance feedback; and (5) allowing access to reinforcement if the criterion is met. Reinforcing academic responding is a differential reinforcement procedure – specifically, differential reinforcement of alternative behavior (Cooper et al., 2007). Academic responding serves as the alternative to what the student would otherwise be doing. Effective use of differential reinforcement leads to increases in the desired behavior and decreases in undesired behavior, the goal of academic intervention.

The first task is to select a criterion for reinforcement. Academic skills improve incrementally over time. The criterion should represent a clear increase in behavior (relative to prior performance), but it should also be achievable and not too lofty. This is a tricky part of the intervention process, and there is no easy formula for doing it. The criterion needs to be high enough that the promise of a reinforcer motivates the student to improve relative to past performance, yet at a level at which the student will actually experience some reinforcement, at least periodically. If it is set too high, the student will never receive reinforcement, and performance will drop back down to baseline levels (or worse – below baseline levels out of sheer frustration). This is where your assessment data become very useful in the intervention process. Their highest performance in baseline can serve as a starting point for selecting a criterion. The reinforcement criterion can be set just above the highest level of responding to date. Using this method will adjust the criterion upwardly as the student's performance improves over time. Once the student's performance reaches the desired level of responding, the criterion can be fixed at that level, and reinforcement faded over time.

Before instruction begins, you should do everything in your power to motivate the student to do his or her best. The way you communicate the criterion for reinforcement, the reinforcers offered prior to work, and the type of performance feedback you give after the task will affect just how motivating the instructional exercise is. There are a couple of simple ways to communicate the criterion for reinforcement, each achieving different ends in terms of motivating the student. One way to do so is to challenge the student to beat his or her highest score to date. In this case, the criterion for performance is made very explicit. If he or she responds well, then the criterion progressively increases as the student becomes more proficient, as noted above. With this strategy, you should communicate what their highest score to date is and tell them that they will earn reinforcement for improving on it. Sometimes, however, setting an explicit criterion may produce an undesirable limit on just how much work the student does. If, for example, a criterion is set for the number of words to be written in an essay, the student may write precisely enough words to meet the criterion and then stop writing. This would be especially troubling if the student stopped in the middle of the story or even in the middle of a sentence!

A way to deal with this potential problem is to vary the criterion from day to day and reveal the criterion only *after* they have finished the academic task. For example, values that vary around the highest performance to date (such that some are slightly higher than the highest performance and some are slightly lower than the highest performance) can be randomly selected, written on flash cards, and placed in envelopes that are then sealed. At the beginning of the instructional session, the teacher informs the student that he or she will be rewarded for meeting a goal, allows the student to select the reinforcer (discussed below), and explains that the goal is written in one of the sealed envelopes that the student will be able to choose at the end of the session. If the reinforcer is powerful enough for the student, concealing the goal may lead the student to maximize his or her performance. Having both higher and lower criteria that vary from day to day increases the likelihood of the student being reinforced from time to time. Over sessions, students will learn to pace themselves, yet be encouraged to give their best performance.

To maximize motivation, you should offer the biggest and juiciest reinforcers available. The results of your preference assessment will tell you which activities or items are most highly desired by the student. We have found that both high- and medium-preference reinforcers can increase academic performance (Daly et al., 2009). To avoid satiation, we strongly recommend that you offer a choice of reinforcers for each instructional session. Allowing students to choose for themselves allows them to adjust for fluctuating motivation levels (Fisher, Thompson, Piazza, Crosland, & Gotjen, 1997). If they are tired of an activity, they can select something else.

Performance feedback – specific information about some aspect of a student's performance (Ysseldyke & Elliott, 1999) – should be delivered at the end of the instructional session. Feedback may be given about accuracy (e.g., scoring 95% correct on an assignment), fluency (e.g., reading 150 words correctly in 1 minute), duration (e.g., working on problems for 23 minutes straight), or latency (e.g., taking 17 minutes to finish an assignment). This is another part of the intervention process in which the assessment results are particularly useful. Performance feedback can be tied directly to the assessment results. Performance feedback has been shown to improve math (e.g., Codding, Lewandowski, & Eckert, 2005), reading (e.g., Eckert, Dunn, & Ardoin, 2006; Van Houten & Van Houten, 1977), spelling (Bourque, Dupuis, & Van Houten, 1986), and writing (Scriven & Glynn, 1983). Performance feedback can be provided orally and/or visually through a graph of the student's performance (Codding et al., 2005; Lingo, Jolivette, & Barton-Arwood, 2009). We suggest you do both. You should verbally describe the results of the student's performance (e.g., how many correctly read words per min he or she read), present a graph of the results, compare it to the criterion (stating whether they failed to meet, met, or exceeded it), and praise them if they met it or encourage them to keep working toward the goal if they did not meet or exceed the criterion (Lingo et al., 2009). Performance feedback should be provided immediately following the completion of the academic task. It should also be coupled with delivery of the reinforcer, if the student met the criterion. It is usually best (although not always feasible) if the reinforcer can be delivered immediately. Students may be willing, however, to delay access to reinforcement if a larger and more appealing reinforcer is available at a later point in time (e.g., getting 30 minutes at the end of the day to spend in the gym to play basketball). It is absolutely essential that reinforcement be delivered as promised. Failure to follow through is the kiss of death for an academic intervention. Therefore, reinforcers must be chosen wisely. Be sure you have access to them and that they are acceptable to all the important stakeholders. For example, food reinforcers may not be acceptable to parents who are concerned about their child's health, and they may express concern if word gets back to them that their child is eating food they consider unhealthy or unacceptable.

Step 6: Address Escape-Motivated Behavior

Escaping an aversive task is often as motivating as, or may be even more motivating than, positive reinforcement. We send our tax forms and money to the Internal Revenue Service to avoid penalties rather than recruit their praise and admiration for our civic diligence. In schools, students will sometimes go to great lengths to avoid school work. Forfeiting a good grade is a trivial matter to a student who finds school aversive, but getting sent to the Principal's office for disruptive behavior may be a significant incentive if it means that the teacher will stop "hounding" the student to get his or her work done. So, the student may disrupt the classroom because a contingency has developed between his or her behavior and the teacher's behavior. Alternately, a student may avoid school tasks altogether through truancy. These short-sighted actions on the part of the student are still functional – they allow them to escape or avoid things they do not like, even if they are not healthy or in their best interest.

A strong academic intervention should address *both* positively and negatively reinforcing contingencies. Positive reinforcement has already been examined. Negative reinforcement is addressed by taking steps to reduce the aversiveness of assigned school work. Does that mean we are recommending that you make work easier or less demanding for the student? Not necessarily, but maybe under some circumstances. Three general strategies are presented in Table 15.2. These strategies are a proactive means of anticipating and alleviating aversive properties of school work with the purpose of increasing work completion. Keep in mind that the student is probably not getting much work done in the first place. Look at your baseline data. If they are currently getting little done, the first step should be to get them to do *something more* than they are currently doing. Over time, with aggressive intervention you may be able progressively to increase their productivity to a level commensurate with that of their peers. But, we suggest that you start with small successes. School has probably been aversive for a long time. It is going to take a while to eliminate those negative properties in the eyes of the student. These strategies will help you do just that.

Allowing Escape Contingent on Work Completion

One strategy is to allow the student to escape work by doing work. Yes, you read that correctly. We are recommending that you allow students to get a break for doing some work. Although it may sound counterintuitive, the basic idea is to (negatively) reinforce the student for doing work by allowing them to get out of work for a while, rather than allowing him or her to get out of work for doing something inappropriate. This intervention is referred to as differential negative reinforcement of alternative behavior (DNRA; Geiger, Carr, & LeBlanc, 2010). In other words, the student is allowed to have a break (i.e., escape) from an instructional task contingent on a desired response (e.g., work completion) but not allowed to escape for problem behavior. In this way, DNRA provides continued access to the functional reinforcer (i.e., escape), "disconnecting" it from the problem behavior (by no longer reinforcing it), and substituting it for more appropriate behavior (work completion). The key to making DNRA effective is to configure it such that the inappropriate, escape-motivated behaviors are irrelevant, inefficient, and ineffective. This means first of all that it should be easier to get out of doing work by doing some work rather than by disrupting the classroom. Begin by examining just how much work they are doing during baseline. Use the results as a starting point for establishing a contingency plan that requires initially just a little more work than their current level of productivity. For example, if a student is completing between 0 and 2 problems correct during independent seatwork time in math, provide him or her with a brief break for finishing 3 or 4 problems. When the break is over, prompt him or her to complete another 3 or 4 problems and remind them that they can take a break when those are done. If you use this method, you will need to decide and communicate to the student what activities are appropriate during the break time. Again, if you make it easier for them to complete some work than it is for them to engage in disruptive behavior *and* they learn that they can get a break sooner than if they go through elaborate escape routines, the strategy can be highly effective. Over time, you can increase the number of problems that need to be completed in order to earn a break.

Identifying and Altering Aversive Features of Demands

Another approach is to identify and alter the aversive features of the school work, which renders escape-motivated behavior irrelevant (Butler & Luiselli, 2007; Geiger et al., 2010). Previous research has demonstrated that some instructional and curricular factors like difficult tasks, non-preferred tasks, and novel tasks might establish escape from academic instruction/work as negatively reinforcing (e.g., Dunlap, Kern-Dunlap, Clarke, & Robbins, 1991; Munk & Repp, 1994; Smith, Iwata, Goh, & Shore, 1995). By identifying those factors, alterations can be made to alleviate them. For example, Dunlap et al. (1991) found that long-duration tasks were associated with high rates of problem behavior and low rates of on-task behavior for a female student with multiple disabilities and an extensive history of disruptive behavior. Once they began shortening tasks and offering more interesting content and activities relating to the student's daily living routines, the student's problem behavior was eliminated and on-task behavior increased.

Other ways in which on-task and work productivity have been improved include reducing the amount of time spent in instruction, decreasing the difficulty level of tasks to match better students' skill level, embedding novel tasks into routine or repetitive tasks, and increasing the rate of positive reinforcement (Butler & Luiselli, 2007; Dunlap et al., 1991; Ferro, Foster-Johnson, & Dunlap, 1996). Decreasing task difficulty is a strategy that deserves further comment. Some may object to making work easier on the grounds that students should do the same work as everyone else. While this is a laudable goal for the student, the reality often is that the student is more low skilled than his or her peers. Repeatedly giving students difficult work that they do not know how to do is going to make school quite aversive, if it is not already. Furthermore, and perhaps more importantly, if the student lacks the prerequisite skills, he or she is not likely to make much progress in the first place (Daly et al., 2007; Howell & Nolet, 2000). Stepping back in the curriculum to a more appropriate instructional level will often improve learning and motivation (Wolery, Bailey, & Sugai, 1988).

Using Choice to Improve Motivation

A considerable research base has demonstrated that offering choices can have a dramatic effect on behavior, both decreasing problem behavior (e.g., off-task behavior, non-compliance) and increasing desired behavior (e.g., work completion, accuracy, on-task behavior; Bambara, Ager, & Koger, 1994; Dyer, Dunlap, & Winterling, 1990; Kern, Vorndran, Hilt, Ringdahl, & Adelman, 1998; Parsons, Reid, Reynolds, & Bumgarner, 1990). Offering choice is the simplest of strategies and has wide application. Students can be offered choices of instructional tasks and consequences for work completion. For example, students can be permitted to select a math worksheet from a pool of worksheets or to determine the order in which they complete the assignments (Ramsey, Jolivette, Patterson, & Kennedy, 2010; Romaniuk, Miltenberger, Conyers, Jenner, & Jurgens, 2002). Students can also be allowed to choose the reinforcer they receive for meeting a predetermined performance criterion (Tiger, Hanley, & Hernandez, 2006). Choice appears to be effective at reducing escape-motivated behavior because the act of choosing allows an individual to avoid or delay engagement in more aversive tasks which, in turn, makes the escape-motivated behaviors irrelevant (e.g., Dunlap et al., 1991; Romaniuk et al., 2002; Seybert, Dunlap, & Ferro, 1996). For example, Umbreit and Blair (1996) compared a teacher-selected tasks condition to a condition that offered two low-preference academic tasks and found that the choice condition produced more appropriate behavior and less problem behavior. Through choice, the person has the option of selecting a more preferred activity or consequence, and the relative contrast between options (even when they are both low-preference tasks) appears to create strong motivating conditions (Bambara et al., 1994; Dunlap et al., 1991; Fisher et al., 1997; Umbreit & Blair, 1996;Vaughn & Horner, 1997).

CONCLUSION

Improving the academic skills of a JSO is no easy task, especially because these youths generally have a long history of academic failure and are often embroiled in outside distractions that compete for their time, attention, and priorities. So, we do not wish to oversimplify the issues. However, a clear, simple, and educationally valid model seems to be the best approach to helping interested readers sort through all the things they need to include as they design academic interventions. It starts with the skills that are targeted for intervention. Basic academic skills are emphasized in this chapter because they are necessary for obtaining employment, which may help adolescents to lead a law-abiding lifestyle. We strongly believe that a principled approach is much better than providing a menu of interventions of dubious applicability to your situation. A principled approach will guide you in the steps you need to follow while outlining the key decisions to be made and giving guidance in next steps. To this end, we recommend that you focus primarily on increasing academic responding. This focus will force you to observe student performance carefully. We also recommend that you conceptualize intervention in terms of the antecedents and consequences that need to be delivered to increase academic responding. Addressing both antecedents and consequences is essential. For planning instructional modifications, it is best to start with the current instruction and look for "holes" relative to the strategies described in this chapter. The framework presented in this chapter will guide you in how to adjust instructional sessions. For planning motivational conditions, it is best to look for incentives that are motivating to the student and that are readily deliverable in the educational context. Also, it is worthwhile looking for ways to alleviate aversive conditions that may be causing the student to avoid school work. Finally, and perhaps most importantly, we recommend that you carefully measure student performance. There is never a guarantee that an intervention will work. Repeatedly measuring the student's performance over time, however, will give you the necessary feedback needed to adjust the intervention to maximize its outcomes. For those readers seeking more in-depth treatment of these topics, a list of resources can be found in Appendix F.

APPENDIX A

CLASSROOM OBSERVATION FORM

Student: Date: Instructor/Tutor: Time of Day:

Length of Lesson:____________ Length of Interval:____________

Academic Engagement (AE): Record student behavior at regular intervals using momentary time sampling; AE includes reading aloud, answering an academic question, asking an academic question, writing in response to teacher request, and silent reading (eye movements indicate student is scanning text). At regular intervals, observe the behavior of a peer.

	Target'AE	Target'AE	Target'AE	Target'AE	Target'AE	Peer'AE	Total'for'Row Target'AE	Peer'AE
Interval	1	2	3	4	5	6		
Target								
Peer'								
Interval	7	8	9	10	11	12		
Target								
Peer'								
Interval	13	14	15	16	17	18		
Target								
Peer'								
Interval	19	20	21	22	23	24		
Target								
Peer'								
Interval	25	26	27	28	29	30		
Target								
Peer'								
Interval	31	32	33	34	35	36		
Target								
Peer'								
Interval	37	38	39	40	41	42		
Target								
Peer'								
						Sum'of'each'"total'"column		

Target Student:

Total # of Observation Intervals = ______

# of Peer Intervals = − ______ (subtract from above)

# of Observation Intervals for Target = ______

Sum of AE Column = ______

(Sum of AE Column)______/(# of Observation intervals)____ = ____ % **AE**

Peer:
Total # of Observation Intervals = ______
# of Target Intervals = –______ (subtract from above)
# of Observation Intervals for Target = ______
Sum of AE Column = ______
(Sum of AE Column)______/(# of Observation intervals)____= ____ % **AE**

Classroom Observation Form Example

Student: Sam Date: 11/9/13 Instructor/Tutor: Mr Smith Time of Day: 9:20 Length of Lesson: 90 min

Student: Sam Date: 11/9/13 Instructor/Tutor: Mr Smith Time of Day: 9:20 Length of Lesson: 90 minutes Length of Interval:____5 minutes____________

Academic Engagement (AE): Record student behavior at regular intervals using momentary time sampling; AE includes reading aloud, answering an academic question, asking an academic question, writing in response to teacher request, and silent reading (eye movements indicate student is scanning text). At regular intervals, observe the behavior of a peer.

							Total'for'Row	
	Target'AE	Target'AE	Target'AE	Target'AE	Target'AE	Peer'AE	Target'AE	Peer'AE
Interval	1	2	3	4	5	6		
Target	o	o	o	o	o		0	
Peer'						x		1
Interval	7	8	9	10	11	12		
Target	o	x	o	o	x		2	
Peer'						o		0
Interval	13	14	15	16	17	18		
Target	x	o	o	o	o		1	
Peer'						x		1
Interval	19	20	21	22	23	24		
Target								
Peer'								
Interval	25	26	27	28	29	30		
Target								
Peer'								
Interval	31	32	33	34	35	36		
Target								
Peer'								
Interval	37	38	39	40	41	42		
Target								
Peer'								
Sum'of'each'"total'"column							3	2

Target student:

Total # of Observation intervals = ____18____

# of Peer intervals = −____3____(subtract from above)

# of Observation intervals for target = ____15____

Sum of AE column = _____3____

(Sum of AE column)____**3**____/(# of Observation intervals)____**15**____= ____20 % **AE**Peer:

Total # of Observation intervals = ___18_____
# of Target intervals = –___15_____(subtract from above)
# of Observation intervals for target = ____3_____
Sum of AE column = ____2_____
(Sum of AE column)___**2**_____/(# of Observation intervals)____**3**____
= __**66% AE**

APPENDIX B

PREFERENCE-ASSESSMENT PROTOCOL

Steps for preference assessment

1. Select 8 teacher-approved items/activities and write each one on an index card
2. Place the cards in front of the student in a row, assuring visibility and easy access to all items
3. Explain to the student that (a) you want to find out what kinds of rewards he or she would be willing to do work for, and (b) that each of the cards represents an item or activity that could be used as a reward for completing work
4. Read each item to the student and then have the student read each item back to you to ensure he or she understands what each card represents
5. Ask the student to pick one thing he or she would be willing to do work for. Once the student has selected the first stimulus item, remove the card from the array and reposition the items to fill the gap and recenter the items:
   a. Shift all items to the right of the gap one place to the left, filling the gap
   b. Shift the item furthermost to your left to the place furthermost to your right
   c. Continue this process until all 8 items have been selected
6. Record items selected as 1 (first selected) to 8 (last item) rankings with each student choice on the recording form
7. Repeat steps 1–6 on two separate days
8. Final scoring:
   a. After step 7 is completed, circle the median score for each item on the stimulus recording sheet
   b. Convert the median score to rank orderings by reverse scoring:
      i. The lowest median score (e.g., 1 for the first selected item) receives the highest rank-order score of 8. Then, the next lowest receives a rank-order score of 7, and so on until the highest median score receives a rank-order score of 8
      ii. In the case of a tie (e.g., top two items receive median scores of 2), give the mean of the two proximal rankings (e.g., the mean of 8 and 7 is 7.5) and do not assign a whole number score for the two must proximal scores
   c. Plot the rank orderings on a bar graph

APPENDIX C

PREFERENCE-ASSESSMENT SURVEY

Please check off any items you currently use as incentives for classroom behavior. Also, please check off any items you would be willing to use as rewards if you are not currently using them. Indicate only items that are developmentally appropriate for the student.

Activity/privilege	Currently use with students	Willing to use in my classroom
1. Fast food coupon		
2. $1 app for a cell phone		
3. Soft drinks		
4. Edibles like candy, chips, popcorn, pretzels		
5. Early release (5–10 min) from class		
6. Homework pass		
7. Homework due date extended		
8. Computer time		
9. Leisure reading		
10. Select a friend to study/work with on an in-class assignment		
11. Listen to music (Ipod) while working individually		
12. Help the school secretary, custodian, other		
13. "Adopt" a younger student and become a mentor		
14. Free entrance to a school event (dance, football game, talent show)		
15. Earn a free pass to a community activity (zoo, movie theater, museum)		
16. Make announcements over the PA		
17. Have lunch with a friend in the principal's office		
18. Eat lunch with a preferred adult (teacher, principal)		
19. Off-campus supervised lunch		
20. Assist a coach for any sport		
21. Special parking for a day (get to park in teacher's parking lot or principal's parking space)		
22. Assist with the scoreboard at a school athletic event		
23. Sit in the teacher's chair		

Activity/privilege	Currently use with students	Willing to use in my classroom
24. Teach the class a lesson or game		
25. Wear a special item for the day (hat, slippers)		
26. Reserved seating (score box, front row) at a school event (play, talent show, sporting event) for the student and 3–5 friends		

Do you have other suggestions?

APPENDIX D

SCORE SHEET FOR THE PREFERENCE ASSESSMENT

Multiple-Stimulus Preference Assessment (Without Replacement)

	Item								
Date:___	1								
Date:___	2								
Date:___	3								

Median Rank Order:									
Reverse Score Median Rank Order:									

Scored example:

Multiple-Stimulus Preference Assessment (Without Replacement)									
	Item:	Visit with a friend	Field trip	Break from work	Easier work	Extra lunch hour	Supervised trip to local eatery	Help the office staff	Help in the cafeteria
Date: ___	1	④	⑤	1	6	②	③	⑧	⑦
Date: ___	2	6	4	②	⑤	3	1	8	7
Date: ___	3	4	6	2	5	1	3	7	8

Median Rank Order:		4	5	2	5	2	3	8	7
Reverse Score Median Rank Order:		5	3.5	7.5	3.5	7.5	6	1	2

APPENDIX E

PERFORMANCE-DEFICIT ANALYSIS

Preparation

1. Obtain from the teacher two previously failed assignments (or assignments on which the student performed well below expectations).
2. Make fresh copies of the assignments with no markings or answers provided.
3. Identify high-preference, teacher approved rewards.
4. Calculate the criterion by determining how many items must be correct to get a score of at least 80%. Write the criterion number of items correct (80%) in the two blanks in step 5.

Conducting Sessions

5. Present the first previously failed assignment to the student and say, "If you are able to get ________ (80%) number of items correct, then you can select from one of these (show list of rewards) and get it right after you complete the assignment. If you get fewer than ________ (80%) correct, then you will not get to select anything today".
6. Have the student select the reinforcing item or activity and set it in a prominent spot so that it is visible to the student.
7. Allow the student to do the assignment and score it immediately upon completion.
8. If the student achieved the goal of 80% correct or markedly improved his or her performance, allow access to the reinforcer. If the student does not reach the goal, tell him or her that the goal was not reached and that the reinforcer will not be available this time.
9. If the student achieved the goal of 80% correct or markedly improved his or her performance, administer the second previously failed assignment in the same manner to validate the results.

Analyzing Results

10. After sessions have been completed, compare the results from the classroom administration (failed version) to the reward condition.
    - If the student failed to improve substantially under the reward condition, one should consider a skill deficit
    - If the student substantially improved under the reward condition, one should consider a performance deficit.

APPENDIX F

ADDITIONAL RESOURCES

Cooper, J.O., Heron, T.E., & Heward, W.L. (2007). *Applied Behavior Analysis*, 2nd edn. New York: Macmillan.

Gardner R., III, Sainato, D.M., Cooper, J.O., et al. (eds.), *Behavior Analysis in Education: Focus on Measurably Superior Instruction*. Pacific Grove: Brooks/Cole Publishing Co.

Gimpel, G.A., Ervin, R., Daly, E.J., III, & Merrell, K.W. (eds). (2010). *The Practical Handbook of School Psychology: Effective Practices for the 21st Century*. New York: Guilford Publications.

Howell, K.W., & Nolet, V. (2000). *Curriculum-based Evaluation: Teaching and Decision Making*, 3rd edn. Belmont: Wadsworth.

Lentz, F.E., Allen, S.J., & Ehrhardt, K.E. (1996). The conceptual elements of strong interventions in school settings. *School Psychology Quarterly*, 11, 118–136.

Lentz, F.E., & Shapiro, E.S. (1986). Functional assessment of the academic environment. *School Psychology Review*, 15, 346–357.

Miltenberger, R.G. (2012). *Behavior Modification: Principles and Procedures*, 5th edn. Belmont: Wadsworth, Cengage Learning.

REFERENCES

Alessi, G. (1987). Generative strategies and teaching for generalization. *The Analysis of Verbal Behavior, 5*, 15–27.

Ardoin, S. P., & Daly, E. J., III (2007). Introduction to the special series: Close encounters of the instructional kind – how the instructional hierarchy is shaping instructional research 30 years later. *Journal of Behavioral Education, 16*, 1–6.

Bambara, L. M., Ager, C., & Koger, F. (1994). The effects of choice and task preference on the work performance of adults with severe disabilities. *Journal of Applied Behavior Analysis, 27*, 555–556.

Binder, C. (1996). Behavioral fluency: Evolution of a new paradigm. *The Behavior Analyst, 19*, 163–197.

Bourque, P., Dupuis, N., & Van Houten, R. (1986). Public posting in the classroom: Comparison of posting names and coded numbers of individual students. *Psychological Reports, 59*, 295–298.

Bushell, D., & Baer, D. M. (1994). Measurably superior instruction means close, continual contact with the relevant outcome data. Revolutionary!. In R. Gardner, III, D. M. Sainato, & J. O. Cooper (Eds.), *Behavior analysis in education: focus on measurably superior instruction*. Pacific Grove: Brooks/Cole Publishing Company.

Butler, L. R., & Luiselli, J. K. (2007). Escape-maintained problem behavior in a child with autism: Antecedent functional analysis and intervention evaluation of noncontingent escape and instructional fading. *Journal of Positive Behavior Interventions, 9*, 195–202.

Codding, R. S., Lewandowski, L., & Eckert, T. (2005). Examining the efficacy of performance feedback and goal-setting interventions in children with ADHD: A comparison of two methods. *Journal of Evidence-Based Practices for Schools, 6*, 42–58.

Cooper, J. O., Heron, T. E., & Heward, W. L. (2007). *Applied behavior analysis* (2nd ed.). Upper Saddle River: Pearson: Prentice Hall.

Daly, E. J., III, Lentz, F. E., & Boyer, J. (1996). The instructional hierarchy: A conceptual model for understanding the effective components of reading interventions. *School Psychology Quarterly, 11*, 369–386.

Daly, E. J., III, Witt, J. C., Martens, B. K., & Dool, E. J. (1997). A model for conducting a functional analysis of academic performance problems. *School Psychology Review, 26*, 554–574.

Daly, E. J., III, Martens, B. K., Barnett, D., Witt, J. C., & Olson, S. C. (2007). Varying intervention delivery in response-to-intervention: Confronting and resolving challenges with measurement, instruction, and intensity. *School Psychology Review, 36*, 562–581.
Daly, E. J., III, Wells, N. J., Swanger-Gagné, M. S., Carr, J. E., Kunz, G. M., & Taylor, A. M. (2009). Evaluation of the multiple-stimulus without replacement preference assessment method using activities as stimuli. *Journal of Applied Behavior Analysis, 42*, 563–574.
DeLeon, I. G., & Iwata, B. A. (1996). Evaluation of a multiple-stimulus presentation format for assessing reinforce preferences. *Journal of Applied Behavior Analysis, 29*, 519–533.
Dunlap, G., Kern-Dunlap, L., Clarke, S., & Robbins, F. R. (1991). Functional assessment, curricular revision, and severe behavior problems. *Journal of Applied Behavior Analysis, 24*, 387–397.
Dyer, K., Dunlap, G., & Winterling, V. (1990). Effects of choice making on the serious problem behaviors of students with severe handicaps. *Journal of Applied Behavior Analysis, 23*, 515–524.
Eckert, T. L., Dunn, E. K., & Ardoin, S. P. (2006). The effects of alternate forms of performance feedback on elementary-aged students' oral reading fluency. *Journal of Behavioral Education, 15*, 149–162.
Ferro, J., Foster-Johnson, L., & Dunlap, G. (1996). Relation between curricular activities and problem behaviors of students with mental retardation. *American Journal of Mental Retardation, 101*, 184–194.
Fisher, W. W., Thompson, R. H., Piazza, C. C., Crosland, K., & Gotjen, D. (1997). On the relative reinforcing effects of choice and differential consequences. *Journal of Applied Behavior Analysis, 30*, 423–438. 3.
Fletcher, J. M., Coulter, W. A., Reschly, D. J., & Vaughn, S. (2004). Alternative approaches to the definition and identification of learning disabilities: Some questions and answers. *Annals of Dyslexia, 54*, 304–331.
Foley, R. M. (2001). Academic characteristics of incarcerated youth and correctional educational programs: A literature review. *Journal of Emotional and Behavioral Disorders, 9*, 248–259.
Fuchs, L. S., & Fuchs, D. (1986). Effects of systematic formative evaluation: A meta-analysis. *Exceptional Children, 53*, 199–208.
Geiger, K. B., Carr, J. E., & LeBlanc, L. A. (2010). Function-based treatments for escape-maintained problem behavior: A treatment-selection model for practicing behavior analysts. *Behavior Analysis in Practice, 3*, 22–32.
Greenwood, C. R. (1991). A longitudinal analysis of time, engagement, and achievement in at-risk versus non-risk students. *Exceptional Children, 57*, 521–535.
Greenwood, C. R. (1996). The case for performance-based instructional models. *School Psychology Quarterly, 11*, 283–296.
Greenwood, C. R., Terry, B., Arreaga-Mayer, C, & Finney, R. (1992). The classwide peer tutoring program: Implementation factors moderating students' achievement. *Journal of Applied Behavior Analysis, 25*, 101–116.
Greenwood, C. R., Terry, B., Utley, C. A., Montagna, D., & Walker, D. (1993). Achievement, placement, and services: Middle school benefits of classwide peer tutoring used at the elementary level. *School Psychology Review, 22*, 497–516.
Greenwood, C. R., Hart, B., Walker, D., & Risley, T. (1994). The opportunity to respond and academic performance revisited: A behavioral theory of developmental retardation and its prevention. In R. Gardner, III, D. M. Sainato, & J. O. Cooper (Eds.), *Behavior analysis in education: focus on measurably superior instruction* (pp. 213–224). Pacific Grove: Brooks/Cole.
Haring, N. G., & Eaton, M. D. (1978). Systematic instructional procedures: An instructional hierarchy. In N. G. Haring, T. C. Lovitt, M. D Eaton, & C. L. Hansen (Eds.), *The fourth R: Research in the classroom* (pp. 23–40). Columbus: Merrill.

Heward, W. L. (1994). Three "low-tech' strategies for increasing the frequency of active student response during group instruction. In R. GardnerIII, D. M. Sainato, & J. O. Cooper (Eds.), *Behavior analysis in education: focus on measurably superior instruction* (pp. 283–320). Pacific Grove: Brooks/Cole.

Howell, K. W., & Nolet, V. (2000). *Curriculum-based evaluation: teaching and decision making* (3rd ed.). Belmont: Wadsworth.

Johnson, K. R., & Layng, T. V. J. (1992). Breaking the structuralist barrier: Literacy and numeracy with fluency. *American Psychologist, 47*, 1475–1490.

Kavale, K. (1990). Effectiveness of special education. In T. B. Gutkin & C. R. Reynolds (Eds.), *Handbook of school psychology* (pp. 868–898) (2nd ed.). New York: John Wiley.

Kern, L., Vorndran, C. M., Hilt, A., Ringdahl, J. E., Adelman, B. E., & Dunlap, G. (1998). Choice as an intervention to improve behavior: A review of the literature. *Journal of Behavioral Education, 8*, 151–169.

Lentz, F. E., Jr. (1988). Effective reading interventions in the regular classroom. In J. L. Graden, J. Zins, & M. J. Curtis (Eds.), *Alternative educational delivery systems: enhancing instructional options for all students* (pp. 351–370). Washington, DC: The National Association of School Psychologists.

Lentz, F. E., Jr, & Shapiro, E. S. (1986). Functional assessment of the academic environment. *School Psychology Review, 15*, 346–357.

Lentz, F. E., Jr, Allen, S. J., & Ehrhardt, K. E. (1996). The conceptual elements of strong interventions in school settings. *School Psychology Quarterly, 11*, 118–136.

Leone, P. E., Krezmien, M., Mason, L., & Meisel, S. M. (2005). Organizing and delivering empirically based literacy instruction to incarcerated youth. *Exceptionality, 13*, 89–102.

Lingo, A. S., Jolivette, K., & Barton-Arwood, S. M. (2009). Visual and oral feedback to promote appropriate social behavior for a student with emotional and behavioral disorders. *Preventing School Failure, 54*, 24–29.

Macmann, G. M., & Barnett, D. W. (1999). Diagnostic decision making in school psychology: Understanding and coping with uncertainty. In C. R. Reynolds & T. Gutkin (Eds.), *The handbook of school psychology* (pp. 519–548) (3rd ed.). New York: John Wiley & Sons.

Munk, D. D., & Repp, A. C. (1994). The relationship between instructional variables and problem behavior: A review. *Exceptional Children, 60*, 390–402.

O'Neill, R. E., Horner, R. H., Albin, R. W., Sprague, J. R., Storey, K., & Newton, J. S. (1997). *Functional assessment and program development for problem behavior: a practical handbook* (2nd ed.). Pacific Grove: Brookes/Cole.

Parsons, M. B., Reid, D. H., Reynolds, J., & Bumgarner, M. (1990). Effects of choice versus assigned jobs on the work performance of persons with severe handicaps. *Journal of Applied Behavior Analysis, 23*, 253–258.

Ramsey, M. L., Jolivette, K., Patterson, D. P., & Kennedy, C. (2010). Using choice to increase time on-task, task-completion, and accuracy for students with emotional/behavior disorders in a residential facility. *Education and Treatment of Children, 33*, 1–21.

Resetar, J. L., & Noell, G. H. (2008). Evaluating preference assessments for use in the general education population. *Journal of Applied Behavior Analysis, 41*, 447–451.

Romaniuk, C., Miltenberger, R., Conyers, C., Jenner, N., Jurgens, M., & Ringenberg, C. (2002). The influence of activity choice on problem behaviors maintained by escape versus attention. *Journal of Applied Behavior Analysis, 35*, 349–362.

Ronis, S. T., & Borduin, C. M. (2007). Individual, family, peer, and academic characteristics of male juvenile sexual offenders. *Journal of Abnormal Child Psychology, 35*, 153–163.

Scriven, J., & Glynn, T. (1983). Performance feedback on written tasks for low-achieving secondary students. *New Zealand Journal of Educational Studies, 18*, 134–145.

Seybert, S., Dunlap, G., & Ferro, J. (1996). The effects of choice-making on the problem behaviors of high-school students with intellectual disabilities. *Journal of Behavioral Education, 6*, 49–65.

Shinn, M. R. (1989). *Curriculum-based Measurement: Assessing special children*. New York: Guilford Press.
Shinn, M. R. (Ed.). (1998). *Advanced applications of curriculum-based measurement*. New York: Guilford Press.
Skinner, C. H., Fletcher, P.A., & Henington, C. (1996). Increasing learning rates by increasing student response rates: A summary of research. *School Psychology Quarterly, 11*, 313–325.
Smith, R. G., Iwata, B. A., Goh, H. L., & Shore, B. A. (1995). Analysis of establishing operations in self-injury maintained by escape. *Journal of Applied Behavior Analysis, 28*, 515–535.
Stokes, T. F., & Baer, D. M. (1977). An implicit technology of generalization. *Journal of Applied Behavior Analysis, 10*, 349–367.
Tiger, J. H., Hanley., G. P., & Hernandez, E. (2006). An evaluation of the value of choice with preschool children. *Journal of Applied Behavior Analysis, 39*, 1–16.
Umbreit, J., & Blair, K. -S. (1996). The effects of preference, choice, and attention on problem behavior at school. *Education & Training in Mental Retardation & Developmental Disabilities, 31*, 151–161.
Van Houten, R., & Van Houten, J. (1977). The performance feedback system in the special education classroom: An analysis of public posting and peer comments. *Behavior Therapy, 8*, 366–376.
Vaughn, B. J., & Horner, R. H. (1997). Identifying instructional tasks that occasion problem behaviors and assessing the effects of student versus teacher choice among these tasks. *Journal of Applied Behavior Analysis, 30*, 299–312.
Vellutino, F. R., Fletcher, J. M., Snowling, M. J., & Scanlon, D. M. (2004). Specific reading disability (dyslexia): What have we learned in the past four decades? *Journal of Child Psychology and Psychiatry, 45*, 2–40.
Veneziano, C., & Veneziano, L. (2002). Adolescent sex offenders: A review of the literature. *Trauma, Violence, & Abuse, 3*, 247–260.
van Wijk, A., Vermeiren, R., Loeber, R., Hart-Kerkhoffs, L. T., Doreleijers, T., & Bullens, R (2006). Juvenile sex offenders compared to non-sex offenders. *Trauma, Violence, & Abuse, 7*, 227–243.
Wolery, M., Bailey, D. B., Jr, & Sugai, G. M. (1988). *Effective teaching: principles and procedures of applied behavior analysis with exceptional children*. Boston: Allyn & Bacon, Inc.
Ysseldyke, J. E., & Elliott, J. (1999). Effective instructional practices: Implications for assessing educational environments. In C. Reynolds & T. Gutkin (Eds.), *The handbook of school psychology* (pp. 497–518). New York: John Wiley & Sons, Inc.

CHAPTER 16

Integrating the Good Lives Model with Relapse Prevention: Working with Juvenile Sex Offenders

Clare-Ann Fortune[*], Tony Ward[*] and Bobbie Print[**]
[*]School of Psychology, Victoria University of Wellington, New Zealand
[**]G-MAP Services Limited, Sale, Cheshire, UK

INTRODUCTION

The problem of young people who have engaged in sexually abusive behaviors has attracted increasing interest over the last 30 years or so because of the realization that they are responsible for a substantial proportion of reported sexual offences (Worling & Langton, 2012). During this time, there has been a marked growth in the number of specialized programs that address adolescents' sexually abusive behaviors (Worling, Litteljohn, & Bookalam, 2010). Offender rehabilitation, including that for young people who have engaged in sexually abusive behaviors, is primarily focused on reducing further offending. The core idea underpinning the approach is that the best way to reduce re-offending rates is by focusing treatment resources on eliminating or managing an individual's cluster of dynamic risk factors. Historically, the risk management perspective has dominated the field of offender rehabilitation in both the sexual and general offending domains. The pre-eminent risk management model is that proposed by Andrews, Bonta and their colleagues (the Risk, Need and Responsivity – RNR; Andrews & Bonta, 2010; Andrews, Bonta, & Hoge, 1990). This influential intervention model primarily concentrates on the detection and modification of dynamic risk factors or what have been termed criminogenic needs.

While the application of the RNR to sexual deviancy has been empirically well supported, there are significant practice and ethical problems associated with this approach as well (Laws & Ward, 2011). Prescott (2002) has previously warned that purely risk oriented approaches to treatment and a lack of cohesion within a treatment team (e.g., between staff) can inhibit treatment progress for young people in specialized sexual offender

Toolkit for Working with Juvenile Sex Offenders.
DOI: http://dx.doi.org/10.1016/B978-0-12-405948-1.00016-5

programs. In line with these concerns, there has been a surge of interest over recent years in formulating alternative approaches to offender rehabilitation which allow for the inclusion of strengths-based perspectives and that encourage the development of an offender's knowledge, skills, opportunities (i.e., internal and external capabilities), and resources that also reduce the risk of further offending (Laws & Ward, 2011; Ward & Maruna, 2007). Assessments and interventions based on a strength-based framework aim to identify an individual's aspirations and fundamental values, as well as areas of strength. The hope is that by doing so, treatment will help offenders to acquire the necessary psychological and social resources to achieve goals that are personally meaningful and which will also reduce their risk of further offending. A key component of more positive treatment approaches has been a focus on process variables, such as the nature of the therapeutic relationship. For example, research reveals that the quality of the therapeutic alliance is associated with better therapeutic outcomes (e.g., see Horvath, & Luborsky, 1993; Shirk & Karver, 2003); strength-based approaches have been shown to improve this aspect of treatment (Mann, Webster, Schofield, & Marshall, 2004).

RELAPSE PREVENTION

Relapse prevention, as it has been historically conceptualized in substance abuse treatment, is an intervention framework designed to enhance the effectiveness of the maintenance stage of treatment for those with substance use related difficulties (Marlatt, 1985; Rich, 2011; Thakker, Ward, & Tidmarsh, 2006). Relapse prevention (RP) emerged from the realization that therapeutic gains made during cognitive behavioral therapy for those with substance difficulties were often not maintained post-treatment. In essence, in RP, cognitive-behavioral techniques are employed at different points of the relapse process in order to avoid or escape from high-risk situations and, if a lapse does occur, lessen the chances of a return to problematic substance use (e.g., drugs, alcohol, smoking etc.). Since about the mid-1980s, RP has been integrated into sexual offender treatment either as an overarching intervention framework or as a separate module at the end of a treatment program (Thakker et al., 2006; Ward & Mann, 2004). There are other models of the relapse and offence process such as the self-regulation model (e.g., see Ward, Bickley, Webster, Fisher, Beech, & Eldridge, 2004; Ward & Hudson, 1998, 2000), which will not be reviewed here.

As stated above, in traditional RP approaches, individuals are prepared to cope with the likelihood of lapses and/or relapses occurring. This preparation includes learning how to identify and manage high-risk situations, cope with feelings, thoughts and behaviors facilitating lapses, and planning in advance how to manage each internal or external risk factor (Mann et al., 2004; Rich, 2011). The focus is primarily on avoidance of risk factors or situations by recognizing possible triggers for relapse and developing the necessary skills to escape from high-risk situations and thus prevent relapses (i.e., re-offending) occurring (Rich, 2011).

Traditionally, RP has focused on the formulation of what have been termed avoidance treatment goals. That is, risk–need relapse prevention in the area of sexual offending is primarily (negatively) focused on the individual avoiding the possibility of further sexual offending (Thakker et al., 2006). Rich (2011) has described an RP plan as representing "a problem recognition and avoidance plan" (p. 343). Thus, the primary goal is to assist individuals to control their problematic thoughts, feelings, and behaviors so they do not go on to re-offend. There are a number of other sub-goals associated with RP, including providing offenders with effective strategies to self-monitor, helping them identify potential risky thoughts, feelings, people or situations, providing them with the appropriate skills to prevent a lapse/relapse occurring, such as developing a plan to cope with high-risk situations, people or interactions, and assisting individuals to identify appropriate people or other resources to support them with their relapse prevention plan (Rich, 2011).

However, there are limitations associated with this approach that have been inherited from its theoretical alignment with the RNR. Although it is necessary to consider risk variables in treatment, an emphasis on this factor alone is unlikely to be sufficient to promote successfully enduring therapeutic change. Therefore, it is important to utilize approaches that are more likely directly to motivate individuals to shift from an offending to a prosocial lifestyle (Thakker et al., 2006; Ward & Hudson, 1998). Additionally, it has been suggested that relapse prevention is too narrow in its scope and assumes a single pathway to sexual offending rather than recognizing the heterogeneity of individuals and their different paths to sexual offending (Worling & Langton, 2012). Furthermore, relapse prevention planning with young sexual offenders should take into account developmental aspects, such as family and community contextual factors (Thakker et al., 2006), as well as situations, thoughts, feelings and behaviors that are associated with the onset of abusive behaviors (Worling & Langton, 2012).

The move to include family and other relevant individuals in treatment acknowledges the fact that adolescence is a period of change and transition for young people as they move from childhood towards adulthood; while also ensuring appropriate supports are put in place to increase their chances of success in desisting from further offending.

Strength-based intervention frameworks make use of approach as well as avoidance goals. The inclusion of goals that they want to achieve makes it clearer to the young person what needs to occur in order to live "better lives"; by "better lives" we mean those that are prosocial, personally meaningful, and hopefully more fulfilling. These goals should be consistent with the ultimate goal of reducing recidivism (Mann et al., 2004). We will discuss the relationship between good lives plans and the reduction or elimination of criminogenic needs later in this chapter. But, in brief, the idea is that building capabilities in certain ways can directly or indirectly result in reduced risk of re-offending. There is evidence to suggest that the use of approach goals by sexual offenders is associated with more positive treatment engagement compared with those who use traditional avoidance goals (Mann et al., 2004).

The Good Lives Model (GLM – see below) has been proposed as an alternative approach to the risk-based approaches, such as the RNR. It is an approach that incorporates the major RNR principles yet extends the scope of rehabilitative efforts to include individual personal priorities as well. The GLM is a strengths-based approach to offender rehabilitation first proposed by Ward and Stewart in 2003, and which has been subsequently further developed by Ward and his colleagues (e.g., see Laws & Ward, 2011; Ward & Gannon, 2006; Ward & Marshall, 2004; Ward & Maruna, 2007; Yates, Prescott, & Ward, 2010). As stated above, the RNR and GLM are not necessarily mutually exclusive models. Ward (2010) has suggested the GLM has the capacity to integrate components of treatment which may not be adequately addressed by the RNR model, such as the development of the therapeutic alliance, increased agency (e.g., self-direction), and motivation to commit to treatment, and desistance from further offending.

GOOD LIVES MODEL

The Good Lives Model (GLM) is an example of a strength-based approach, which is garnering growing interest and is increasingly being adopted and integrated into offender rehabilitation, including with juveniles who have engaged in sexually abusive behaviors. It offers an alternative to more traditional risk–need–responsivity rehabilitation approaches as it seeks to reduce risk while also explicitly supporting offenders to develop more personally meaningful and fulfilling lives (Fortune, Ward, & Willis, 2012). The GLM focuses on approach goals and is designed to be directly responsive to individual offenders' interests, abilities, and aspirations. This rehabilitation model advocates for a positive, community-oriented approach to rehabilitation and encourages the development of intervention plans which will assist offenders in ensuring they have the capacities (e.g., skills, knowledge, opportunities) and can access the external resources they require in order for them to accomplish their life goals, while also taking into account the issues of public safety and risk reduction (Purvis, Ward, & Willis, 2011). The GLM allows for different levels of scaffolding as offenders may require varying degrees of support in order to develop the requisite skills and resources required to implement their life plans in post-release environments (Ward, 2010).

Underlying the GLM is the assumption that, to some extent, all individuals have similar basic needs and aspirations that they strive to meet and realize in their lives. From the GLM perspective, offenders are viewed as seeking to achieve their personal priorities or values through whatever means are available to them, just like the rest of us. The difficulty is that their approaches are often counter-productive, ineffective, and/or socially unacceptable. Within the GLM framework, sexually abusive behaviors are conceptualized as reflecting the individual's maladaptive or inappropriate strategies, often associated with inadequate internal and external resources, to obtain their desired "primary human goods" (Ward & Stewart, 2003). Primary goods are outcomes, states of affairs, or experiences that individuals seek for their own sake and that are likely to result in higher levels of well-being. According to the GLM, the level of primary goods obtainment should not fall below a particular threshold if individuals are to achieve an acceptable level of well-being. However, due to individual differences in the weighting of values, abilities, and life experiences, there is variability in what matters most to offenders. Thus, practitioners need to ensure they identify individual's personal motivations and ascertain how each person prioritizes the 11 primary goods (Ward, 2010; see below for further discussion of the primary goods). Once this assessment task has been completed a Good Lives Plan (GLP) is constructed that revolves around the most heavily weighted primary goods. The basic idea is that interventions should provide alternative ways of achieving these primary goods that are responsive to individuals' abilities, environments, and agency resources.

There are two ways risk reduction can occur during intervention. First, the establishment of the internal and external capacities needed to achieve a primary good (or, more broadly, implement a good lives plan) in socially acceptable and personally fulfilling ways, can directly alter criminogenic needs. For example, learning the skills necessary to become a carpenter could make it easier for an offender to develop concentration and emotional regulation skills, thereby reducing impulsivity, a criminogenic need. Second, the reduction of risk can occur indirectly when an offender is strongly motivated to work hard in treatment because of his involvement in projects that personally engage him. For example, an individual might work hard at overcoming his substance abuse problems because he is keen to attend a mechanics training course. In actual practice, offender good lives plans both directly and indirectly impact on dynamic risk factors.

Within the GLM framework, interventions are "wrapped around" an offender's central values and "practical identities" (e.g., that of student, son, friend, sportsman, mechanic) to assist them in obtaining primary goods, in socially acceptable ways, while simultaneously addressing criminogenic needs/risk factors. The GLM, therefore, addresses dynamic risk factors directly and indirectly (see above) through the application of cognitive behavioral techniques and social interventions, which are used to assist offenders in acquiring the necessary competencies to achieve their plan. The focus is on increasing agency, individual psychological well-being, and maximizing opportunities that will assist offenders in living a more prosocial life (Ward & Gannon, 2006).

The GLM was developed for use in the treatment of adult sexual offenders and the preliminary evidence suggests that, when its principles are incorporated, the therapeutic alliance is enhanced, and treatment is effective (e.g., see Gannon, King, Miles, Lockerbie, & Willis, 2011; Lindsay, Ward, Morgan, & Wilson, 2007; Ware & Bright, 2008; Whitehead, Ward, & Collie, 2007). The GLM has also been found to be helpful with other populations, such as forensic mental health clients (Barnao et al., 2010). Research has not yet looked at the GLM's effectiveness when applied to juvenile offender rehabilitation. However, as juvenile offender programs utilizing the GLM framework are established, research will ensue.

One of the issues frequently identified by researchers and clinicians working in the area of treatment of young sexual offenders is that adult models and approaches are commonly applied with little or no attempts to take into account developmental and other contextual factors (e.g., the systems they are part of, such as family, school and community) of the young people concerned (Jones, 2003; Thakker et al., 2006). The remainder of this chapter will help address this issue by providing an overview of how the GLM can be adapted to work effectively with juvenile sexual offenders, particularly with reference to the area of relapse prevention, using the case example provided by the work of G-MAP in the UK.

THE GLM AND JUVENILE SEXUAL OFFENDERS

As mentioned above, one of the difficulties associated with applying adult models to young people is that their developmental level may not be adequately taken into consideration. For example, a key difficulty for those working with young people is that the terminology and concepts may prove too complex for them. Organizations, such as G-MAP (an organization based in North West England which provides specialized treatment services for young people who have engaged in sexually abusive behaviors along with their families and caregivers and other relevant professionals – Print, in press), are developing programs which adapt the GLM for juveniles in consultation with the young people, their family/caregivers and other professionals.

One of the adaptations G-MAP has made is to translate the GLM using terminology and concepts that are more meaningful to juvenile offenders, referring to it as the GLM-A (Print, in press). For example, they make reference to "My needs" rather than "primary goods", secondary goods are referred to as "How I meet my needs" and overarching need is referred to as "My most important need". Further examples to illustrate this are provided in Table 16.1.

Table 16.1 GLM and Adapted Terminology for Juvenile Offenders

Original GLM Terminology	Adapted Language
Primary goods	My needs
Secondary goods	How I meet my needs
Overarching need	My most important need
Internal conditions (capabilities)	The strengths and skills I have to help me meet my needs
External conditions (capabilities)	How others can help me meet my needs
Internal obstacles	The things about me that get in the way of meeting my needs
External obstacles	The things around me that get in the way of meeting my needs
Conflict	Which of my needs fight against each other
Scope	What needs do I neglect

In the GLM, 11 classes of primary goods have been identified: (1) life (including healthy living and functioning); (2) knowledge; (3) excellence in work (including mastery experiences); (4) excellence in play (including mastery experiences); (5) excellence in agency (i.e., autonomy and self-directedness); (6) inner peace (i.e., freedom from emotional turmoil and stress); (7) friendship or relatedness (including intimate, romantic, and family relationships); (8) community; (9) spirituality (in the broad sense of finding meaning and purpose in life); (10) pleasure; and (11) creativity (Ward & Gannon, 2006, p. 79). G-MAP have reduced the 11 primary goods from the GLM into eight key needs in the GLM-A using more accessible terminology for young people: (1) sexual health and physical health; (2) achieving; (3) having fun; (4) being my own person; (5) emotional health; (6) having people in my life; (7) having purpose; and (8) making a difference (see Table 16.2 for how these relate to the terminology used in the GLM for primary goods).

Each of these needs (primary human goods) is defined in ways that young people and their family/caregivers will understand. For example, "Achieving" is discussed with reference to a need that "relates to the human desire to attain a sense of mastery and accomplishment. It involves

Table 16.2 Primary Goods – Terminology

GLM	**Adapted for Juvenile Program (based on G-MAP)**
Life (including healthy living & functioning)	Sexual health Physical health
Knowledge	Achieving
Excellence in work (including mastery experiences)	Achieving
Excellence in play (including mastery experiences)	Achieving
Excellence in agency (i.e., autonomy and self-directedness)	Being my own person
Inner peace (i.e., freedom from emotional turmoil & stress)	Emotional health
Friendship (including intimate, romantic, & family relationships)	Having people in my life
Community	Having people in my life
Spirituality (in the broad sense of finding meaning & purpose in life)	Having purpose and making a difference
Pleasure	Having fun
Creativity	Achieving

any activity or pursuit through which the young person gains a sense of achievement. It includes knowledge, learning, talents, fulfillment, competence and status" and maps onto the GLM primary goods of excellence in play and work.

The GLM also notes that there is a difference between primary and secondary needs. Secondary or instrumental needs represent how the young peoples' important personal goals and basic needs are met (i.e., how they achieve their primary goods or needs); for example, undertaking a car mechanics course may assist a young person in realizing the need to attain the primary good of mastery at work. As with other offenders, for young people, the problem does not reside in their commitment to more abstract, primary goods, but rather with the inappropriate strategies employed to secure them (Ward, 2010).

The GLM-A allows clinicians to explore with juvenile sexual offenders what their conception of a good life looks like (i.e., what are the things they value and want to have in their lives) and develop their individual "good lives plan" (intervention plans). It allows for an exploration of any personal or environmental factors (internal or external obstacles) that may be getting in the way of living a desired "good" life.

The GLM-A recognizes four main types of difficulties evident in offenders' (implicit) good lives plans that adversely affect their ability to achieve personal goals. Concerning a direct route to offending, a common difficulty is use of inappropriate secondary means to achieve primary needs. For young people who have committed sexual offences, an obvious example is the use of sexually abusive behaviors (a secondary need) as a maladaptive attempt to be emotionally connected to another person (the equivalent to the primary good of friendship or relatedness). Second, another common difficulty is a lack of scope (the G-MAP program refers to this as needs the young person has "neglected") resulting in an imbalance in their lives whereby some needs are absent or underdeveloped. Third, in some instances, conflict (the G-MAP program refers to "needs that fight against each other") can occur between the needs being pursued contributing to the individual experiencing acute psychological stress and/or unhappiness. This conflict often arises when there is a lack of coherence in the way in which needs are sought or when the individual attempts to achieve their needs in an uncoordinated manner resulting in frustration and possibly a lack of purpose or meaning (Ward & Stewart, 2003). The GLM-A also takes horizontal and vertical coherence into consideration. Horizontal coherence refers to the extent to which the young person's needs are related to each other in a logical or mutually facilitative way. Vertical coherence refers to the extent to which the young person's more abstract needs are translated into concrete and practical actions or ways of living that make it more likely they will achieve them. Fourth, a young person may fail to obtain their desired needs in a prosocial manner, within their current environment, due to a lack of appropriate internal (e.g., skills or knowledge) and external (e.g., supports, resources, employment opportunities) capacities to implement or adapt their good life plan to changing circumstances. GLM-A refers to the internal capabilities as "strengths and skills" the young person has to "meet [their] needs" while, in contrast, internal obstacles are "things about [the young person] that get in the way of meeting [their] needs". The GLM-A defines external capabilities as "How others can help [the young person] meet [their] needs", while external obstacles are "things around [the young person] that get in the way of meeting [their] needs". Therefore, risk factors are still incorporated within the GLM-A in the sense that they highlight possible difficulties (i.e., internal or external obstacles) in ways individuals go about achieving desired needs in a personally meaningful and prosocial manner, and how come there are difficulties with conflict between needs or in the prioritizing of primary needs (Willis, Yates, Gannon, & Ward, 2013). Identifying and addressing these issues will increase the chances of young people achieving their personal life goals.

A detailed assessment is an integral part of the above process as the quality and breadth of the assessment will directly impact on the value of the case formulation and adequacy of the identification of treatment needs (Wylie & Griffin, in press). The inclusion of the young person as part of the assessment (along with a range of other sources of information, such as parents/caregivers, school, file reviews, etc.) is important as it allows an understanding of his interpretation of events to be obtained and fits in with the GLM's endorsement of personal agency. During assessment, a thorough understanding of the contexts in which the sexually abusive behavior occurred should be acquired as well as a detailed understanding of their present situation. This includes primary and secondary needs, internal and external obstacles as well as internal and external capabilities.

For clinicians, G-MAP has developed the Good Lives Assessment Tool (GLAT; G-MAP, 2012) to provide a detailed assessment of young offenders' needs, vulnerabilities, and relevant environmental variables. The GLAT was designed to be utilized with young people aged 12–18 years of age and can be employed at the time of referral, during the early treatment phase, end of treatment (within the last 4 weeks of treatment), and post-treatment follow-up (about 6 months after the end of treatment). The GLAT has been developed to gather information related to dynamic risk as well as strength factors. It allows for a review of the needs that sexual offending has been used to meet (inappropriately) by the young person. In essence, it brings together all the available information; it goes through the individuals key "needs" (primary goods) in some detail, describing how appropriately (or not) the young person is meeting the need; and highlights external (e.g., environmental or situational factors) and internal (personal skills, knowledge, capabilities, characteristics) barriers that impede its achievement and external and internal resources that assist in its achievement. As mentioned above the GLM encourages a review of scope, coherence and conflicts of needs and this aspect of assessment also occurs with young people. The GLAT provides a means to gather and record information on the range of needs that a young person exhibits in his offending and general lifestyle: whether the range of need is restricted or not and whether or not they are in conflict. We have included an example from the GLAT (Figure 16.1) to demonstrate how information in relation to the need of "Having people in my life" is recorded (G-MAP, 2012). Similar information is collected for each of the other seven needs, identified above, in the GLAT. This information is used to prioritize the extent to which the various needs are a focus of treatment. Ongoing reviews allow for monitoring of progress on needs, ensuring the appropriate internal and external resources, supports, etc. are being put in place to assist the young person in achieving their GLP, and making any necessary adjustments to the (treatment) GLP. It also allows for monitoring of the level to which needs are being met through inappropriate means (see below for further discussion).

Juvenile offenders are not expected to undertake this process alone. Clinicians working with juvenile sexual offenders rarely view them in isolation but rather take a systems perspective that includes the young person, their family, caregivers and other relevant professionals in the process. In the development of a GLP, community, family, caregivers and other relevant supports (e.g., schools, social workers, mental health professionals, etc.) are specifically identified so that they can support the young person to achieve their personally meaningful goals. G-MAP has developed an assessment protocol and a range of documents which takes these important considerations into account. They have developed the Good Lives Approach Questionnaires which are completed by the young person and also by parents/caregivers in order to collect information on the

Good Lives Assessment Tool

4. **Having People in My Life**

'Having People in My Life' might be defined as having a number of relationships with other people. These might range from intimate relationships to relationships with friends. It refers to close relationships, where the young person spends time with these people and can feel supported by them, rather than superficial relationships.

1.1 To what extent does the young person appropriately meet the need 'Having People in My Life'?
Never or Rarely ☐ **Occasionally** ☐ **Often** ☐ **Most of the time** ☐

1.2 Is this need being met through inappropriate means?
No ☐ **Partially** ☐ **Yes** ☐
If yes or partially, how?

1.3 Young person has opportunities and support (external resources) in the area of 'Having People in My Life':
Never or Rarely ☐ **Occasionally** ☐ **Often** ☐ **Most of the time** ☐

1.4 There are things in the young person's environment (external barriers) that prevents them from 'Having People in My Life':
Never or Rarely ☐ **Occasionally** ☐ **Often** ☐ **Most of the time** ☐

1.5 Evidence of opportunities/support and external barriers

1.6 There are things about the young person themselves (internal resources) that help them in the area of 'Having People in My Life':
Never or Rarely ☐ **Occasionally** ☐ **Often** ☐ **Most of the time** ☐

1.7 There are things about the young person themselves (internal barriers) that prevents them from 'Having People in My Life':
Never or Rarely ☐ **Occasionally** ☐ **Often** ☐ **Most of the time** ☐

1.8 Evidence of skills and internal barriers

1.9 Overall importance of this need to the young person: **Low** ☐ **Moderate** ☐ **High** ☐

1.10 Does this young person focus on this need to the detriment of other needs (scope)?
No ☐ **Yes** ☐

If yes please detail:

1.11 Is this need in conflict with other primary needs?
No ☐ **Yes** ☐

If yes please detail:

[redacted]
1.12 Has this need been assessed as relevant to the young person's sexual offending (is a risk factor)? **No** ☐ **Yes** ☐

1.13 How much of a priority is this in treatment? **Low** ☐ **Moderate** ☐ **High** ☐

Why has it been given this level of priority?

Figure 16.1 Example from the Good Lives Assessment Tool (G-MAP, 2013) of information recorded during an assessment.

offenders' personal needs (primary goods). The use of these instruments is also intended to encourage both groups to reflect on their perception of how well the young person is currently meeting their needs, identifies any obstacles to achieving these, and helps them reflect on how important each of these is to the young person. The questionnaires can be used at multiple points of time through treatment from the assessment phase through to follow-up post-treatment.

The GLAT records details from Good Lives meetings including noting those who are present and actively reports the views of the young person, and their therapists and supporters and what tasks they all agree to undertake during the Good Lives meeting. These people are referred to as the young person's Good Lives Team in the GLM-A program. Thus, the G-MAP approach ensures that the relevant network of individual's are included in the young person's plan and that they are kept well informed about the areas of concern and the plan that is being put in place to assist the young person in moving towards a more prosocial life – including managing any risk issues. This ensures the appropriate people have the relevant knowledge, are engaged in the process, and can actively support the therapeutic work and plan.

MAINTAINING AND DEALING WITH THREATS TO GOOD LIVES PLANS (RELAPSE PREVENTION)

Relapse prevention can be conceptualized within a GLM framework, informing both the treatment component and the individualized GLP (Thakker et al., 2006). Use of avoidance goals (i.e., not offending) can be difficult for adolescents to embrace and seeing a life before them that involves the avoidance of certain situations, feelings, behaviors could be overwhelming and leave them with a sense of hopelessness or resignation to their current life path. The GLM approaches relapse prevention through the use of approach goals which are aimed at motivating offenders to engage in treatment as well as also to motivate them to maintain changes after treatment by the development of a well thought through GLP.

When working with young people using the GLM-A approach it can be explicitly stated that their sexualized behavior was inappropriate (i.e., the way they went about achieving their need/s were harmful to others) but that this does not fully define them as individuals. Use of approach goals should aid them in seeing what their life could look like in the future and how they can go about achieving their personal goals in a way that does not involve further offending, contact with the justice system or treatment. Thus, strength-oriented approaches that use approach goals and good lives plans are likely to be more motivating and engaging for individuals undergoing treatment (Mann et al., 2004).

A GLP is directly driven by the values, goals, and identities of the young person concerned. The GLM-A assists young people and clinicians to work through the process of identifying their individual needs and to note what psychological and social resources are required in order for these to be realized in the future. It is important that therapists working with the young person help them to formulate their personally meaningful short-, medium-, and long-term goals/needs, and working collaboratively ensures that the GLP is balanced, realistic, and that ways of meeting identified needs do not conflict with each other. A practically useful GLP should therefore describe in a detailed, systematic manner the various stages and transitions necessary to acquire the capabilities and resources to be successfully implemented. The GLP should also be comprehensive and cover the young person's most important identified needs (i.e., prioritized needs) and the various aspects of their current and future environment that impacts on them. Needs that may be related to their offending are identified along with other needs they would like to achieve, thus ensuring balance in their lives and in their life goals. By constructing a GLP in this kind of collaborative way, young offenders should ideally feel that they can move on to live satisfying and offending free lifestyles. The clinician should also consider other relevant and important considerations, such as the ethical entitlements of victims and the safety of the wider community.

The process of change should be monitored on an ongoing basis to ensure that young sex offenders are on track to achieve their goals, reduce their risk of further offending and build the capacity required to successfully implement their GLPs. The GLAT developed by G-MAP includes sections for ongoing review (see Figure 16.2 for an example, taken from the Good Lives Assessment Tool, G-MAP, 2012) which can assist in this process by tracking progress and dealing with any threats to the implementation and maintenance (i.e., risk of possible relapse) of the young person's GLP.

As can be seen in Figure 16.2, the review document records information on the eight needs and notes how well the young person has progressed in achieving each of these in a prosocial manner and the extent to which change has occurred in the replacement of appropriate for inappropriate means. Other items in the GLAT allow a record to be made of any changes to the opportunities and supports assisting the young person in meeting their needs while others record any internal or external obstacles or barriers that have changed (items C–H). At each review meeting such a document allows all those present to review each of the eight primary needs and examine whether they are meeting each need appropriately while also noting those that are not being met through appropriate means. It also provides a mechanism for ongoing monitoring of change including the capacities and obstacles (both internal and external) that might have changed since the last meeting or where insufficient change has occurred.

Good Lives Assessment Tool

Six Monthly Good Lives Review (1): **Date Completing Review:** ____________

Name of Young Person:	**Young person's Date of Birth:**
Name of Practitioner(s):	**Organisation:**

(NB: If you are only rating needs that have changed over the last 6 months, you may need to refer back to your previous completion of the GLAT, otherwise rate all the needs, and the researcher will do comparisons to assess change from 6 months ago)

A) **Has the extent the young person appropriately meets the following needs changed over the last 6 months?** (Indicate below)

Need	NO (not changed)	YES has changed. Currently they meet this need (please circle):			
1. Having Fun		Never/Rarely	Occasionally	Often	Most of the Time
2. Achieving		Never/Rarely	Occasionally	Often	Most of the Time
3. Being My Own Person		Never/Rarely	Occasionally	Often	Most of the Time
4. Having People In My Life		Never/Rarely	Occasionally	Often	Most of the Time
5. Having a Purpose/Making a Difference		Never/Rarely	Occasionally	Often	Most of the Time
6. Emotional Health		Never/Rarely	Occasionally	Often	Most of the Time
7. Sexual Health		Never/Rarely	Occasionally	Often	Most of the Time
8. Physical Health		Never/Rarely	Occasionally	Often	Most of the Time

B) **Over the last six months, has the extent the need is being met through inappropriate means changed?** (Indicate below).

Need	NO (not changed)	YES has changed. Currently, is this need met through inappropriate means? (please circle)			If 'Yes' it has changed, please briefly outline how this has changed) (please use additional paper for responses if necessary)
1. Having Fun		No	Partially	Yes	
2. Achieving		No	Partially	Yes	
3. Being My Own Person		No	Partially	Yes	
4. Having People In My Life		No	Partially	Yes	
5. Having a Purpose/Making a Difference		No	Partially	Yes	
6. Emotional Health		No	Partially	Yes	
7. Sexual Health		No	Partially	Yes	
8. Physical Health		No	Partially	Yes	

C) **Over the last 6 months, have opportunities and support to help the young person meet their needs changed?** (indicate below

Need	NO not changed	Yes, this has changed. Currently they have access to opportunities and Support: (please circle)			
1. Having Fun		Never/Rarely	Occasionally	Often	Most of the Time
2. Achieving		Never/Rarely	Occasionally	Often	Most of the Time
3. Being My Own Person		Never/Rarely	Occasionally	Often	Most of the Time
4. Having People In My Life		Never/Rarely	Occasionally	Often	Most of the Time
5. Having a Purpose/Making a Difference		Never/Rarely	Occasionally	Often	Most of the Time
6. Emotional Health		Never/Rarely	Occasionally	Often	Most of the Time
7. Sexual Health		Never/Rarely	Occasionally	Often	Most of the Time
8. Physical Health		Never/Rarely	Occasionally	Often	Most of the Time

D) **Over the last 6 months, have external barriers that prevent the young person meets their needs changed?** (indicate below).

Need	NO not changed	Yes, this has changed. Currently they are prevented from meeting need(s) due to External Barriers: (please circle)			
1. Having Fun		Never/Rarely	Occasionally	Often	Most of the Time
2. Achieving		Never/Rarely	Occasionally	Often	Most of the Time
3. Being My Own Person		Never/Rarely	Occasionally	Often	Most of the Time
4. Having People In My Life		Never/Rarely	Occasionally	Often	Most of the Time
5. Having a Purpose/Making a Difference		Never/Rarely	Occasionally	Often	Most of the Time
6. Emotional Health		Never/Rarely	Occasionally	Often	Most of the Time
7. Sexual Health		Never/Rarely	Occasionally	Often	Most of the Time
8. Physical Health		Never/Rarely	Occasionally	Often	Most of the Time

Figure 16.2 Example taken from the Good Lives Assessment Tool (GLAT) of the information discussed and recorded at the 6-monthly Good Lives Review. *(From the Good Lives Assessment Tool – GLAT with permission, G-MAP, 2012)*

Further items also permit a review of the prioritizing, scope, conflict and coherence of needs. Together the Good Lives team can make any required changes to the plan (e.g., addressing a resource or capacity deficit or poor balance) in order to ensure that the young person is on track to successfully implementing his GLP. Being approach focused also allows the young

Good Lives Assessment Tool

E) **If access to opportunities and support or external barriers have changed for any of these needs, please briefly outline how they have changed, and which needs these changes affect:** (please use additional paper for responses if necessary)

____

____

____

F) **Over the last six months, have the young person's skills changed for, affecting how they meet their needs? (please indicate below). If so how would you currently rate these?**

Need	NO not changed	Yes, this has changed. Currently they have skills for meeting the needs: (please circle)			
1. Having Fun		Never/Rarely	Occasionally	Often	Most of the Time
2. Achieving		Never/Rarely	Occasionally	Often	Most of the Time
3. Being My Own Person		Never/Rarely	Occasionally	Often	Most of the Time
4. Having People In My Life		Never/Rarely	Occasionally	Often	Most of the Time
5. Having a Purpose/Making a Difference		Never/Rarely	Occasionally	Often	Most of the Time
6. Emotional Health		Never/Rarely	Occasionally	Often	Most of the Time
7. Sexual Health		Never/Rarely	Occasionally	Often	Most of the Time
8. Physical Health		Never/Rarely	Occasionally	Often	Most of the Time

G) **Over the last six months, have Internal Barriers changed for the young person, affecting how they meet their needs? (please indicate below). If so how would you currently rate these?**

Need	NO not changed	Yes, this has changed. Currently they are prevented from meeting need(s) due to Internal Barriers: (please circle)			
1. Having Fun		Never/Rarely	Occasionally	Often	Most of the Time
2. Achieving		Never/Rarely	Occasionally	Often	Most of the Time
3. Being My Own Person		Never/Rarely	Occasionally	Often	Most of the Time
4. Having People In My Life		Never/Rarely	Occasionally	Often	Most of the Time
5. Having a Purpose/Making a Difference		Never/Rarely	Occasionally	Often	Most of the Time
6. Emotional Health		Never/Rarely	Occasionally	Often	Most of the Time
7. Sexual Health		Never/Rarely	Occasionally	Often	Most of the Time
8. Physical Health		Never/Rarely	Occasionally	Often	Most of the Time

H) **If the young person's skills or internal barriers have changed for any of these needs, please briefly outline how they have changed, and which needs these changes affect:** (please use additional paper for responses if necessary)

____

____

____

I) **Over the last six months, has the overall importance of the needs to the young person changed?**

Need	NO not changed	Yes, this has changed. Currently the overall importance of the need to the young person is (please circle):		
1. Having Fun		Low	Moderate	High
2. Achieving		Low	Moderate	High
3. Being My Own Person		Low	Moderate	High
4. Having People In My Life		Low	Moderate	High
5. Having a Purpose/Making a Difference		Low	Moderate	High
6. Emotional Health		Low	Moderate	High
7. Sexual Health		Low	Moderate	High
8. Physical Health		Low	Moderate	High

Ji) **Does the young person focus on any Primary Needs to the detriment of other Needs (scope)?** (please tick) No☐ Yes☐

If yes which needs are focused on and which are neglected: ____________________

Jii) **Are any Primary Needs in conflict with other Needs?** (please tick) No☐ Yes ☐

If yes which needs are in conflict: ____________________

Jiii) **Where relevant, briefly outline how conflict/scope have changed, and which needs these changes affect:**

____

____

Figure 16.2 (Continued)

person and their Good Lives team to reflect on the positive aspects of the young person's achievements and the strengths, supports, resources, etc., that are helping to attain personally meaningful goals.

CASE EXAMPLE

This case is a fictional one drawn from characteristics of a number of juvenile sexual offenders we have worked with clinically. The case study of Nico has been included to provide an example to help illustrate the

GLM-A's use in clinical practice, including its use during assessment, treatment, and through the review process, highlighting aspects that contribute to maintaining and dealing with threats to the GLP (i.e., relapse prevention).

Initial Assessment Information and Formulation

Nico is a 14-year-old male. He was referred by his social worker to a specialist community-based sex offender treatment program due to his sexual abuse of his 6-year-old half-sister and 9-year-old male neighbor. The abuse included several incidents of touching of the victims' genitals and digit penetration on one occasion for each victim. Nico demonstrated poor understanding of issues related to sexual health and normal aspects of sexual development and intimate relationships. He reported there was no one he felt able to talk to about these issues. Nico also reported a history of stealing.

Nico's parents separated when he was 3 years old and he has had limited contact with his father until recently. Throughout his life, Nico's mother experienced periods of depression during which time she struggled to be available to care for or support her children in a consistent manner. This meant that both his parents had been emotionally unavailable to Nico for much of his childhood. Up until his sexually abusive behavior became known, Nico lived with his mother and stepfather (which he described as a "mixed" relationship). He reported enjoying working on car engines with his stepfather but also frequently commented on the fact that they were not biologically alike. Once his abuse was revealed, Nico moved to live with his paternal grandparents who had maintained a good relationship with him throughout his life and regularly had him to stay during school holidays. He described them as strict but "pretty cool" for grandparents as he got to go hunting and fishing with his grandfather and his grandmother provided a regular supply of baking. He had a history of being physically abused by an adult male (his mother's ex-partner) over a 4-year period and also witnessed domestic violence towards his mother by the same ex-partner.

Nico was a talented cricket player but was not a part of a team due to his change in address at the time of the assessment. He had a limited range of other interests, reporting he only enjoyed playing computer games. He had a few friends but did not spend much time with them outside school resulting in a limited social network. He had also experienced bullying at school over the previous year which had made him withdraw further from interacting with his peers and impacted adversely on his self-esteem. Although he was still attending school at the time of the assessment there were increasing reports of truancy and a decline in his academic achievement.

Initial Therapeutic Plan

During the initial assessment, it became evident that Nico's sexually abusive behavior served the purpose of meeting a number of primary needs; primarily those of (1) emotional health; (2) having people in my life; (3) sexual health; and (4) achieving. The assessment also highlighted that he had a lack of scope evident in the primary needs that were being met. For example, his need of "having fun" was not being adequately met. It was agreed that therapy would focus on the following key issues:

- Assisting Nico to develop his capacity for emotion regulation and distress tolerance
- Trauma focused work
- Assisting Nico to understand and manage his sexually abusive behavior
- Enhancing Nico's problem-solving skills
- Active engagement with Nico's family and wider systems (e.g., school).

It was anticipated that implementing Nico's GLP would directly reduce his criminogenic (i.e., dynamic risk factors) needs by providing him with the internal and external capacities to engage in more rewarding and meaningful interactions with peers through activities, such as football, and helping him to manage emotional responses that made this more difficult. Additionally, the GLP was expected indirectly to reduce his risk for further offending by motivating Nico to address his sexually abusive actions because of the positive features of his GLP, such as access to football, cricket, computers, etc.

First 6-Monthly Good Lives Review

Nico had been in the program for 6 months when his first review meeting occurred. Present at the review were his Good Lives Team including his therapists, social worker, mother, father, stepfather, paternal grandparents and school counselor. They reviewed progress using the Good Lives Review document (see Figure 16.2). Overall, the review showed that Nico was making good progress in areas connected to the primary need of "sexual health" as he had increased his knowledge about normal sexual development. Progress was also noted in the areas connected to the primary needs of "emotional health", with some progress made in the area of "having people in my life". However, there were internal and external barriers noted to exist in relation to the needs of "having people in my life" and "having fun". While Nico had increased his network of friends at school, he continued to have little contact with peers outside school. The Good Lives Team agreed that he would receive support around this at school through his school counselor, and that social skills training would be included as part of individual therapy. Additionally, his grandparents and parents would be encouraged to support Nico more actively to engage with peers outside of school. For example, by assisting him to arrange and attend a movie or paintball with some friends. Nico also had a limited range of leisure activities he engaged in, the primary one being playing computer games alone. Nico had previously enjoyed playing cricket for club and school teams but was concerned about re-joining the teams due to possible repercussions if his sexual offending became known. It was agreed this would be actively pursued through contacting the club and finding out if he could re-join the team.

Second 6-Monthly Good Lives Review

Nico had been attending the program for approximately 12 months when his second review meeting occurred. His Good Lives Team involved the same members as attended the initial review meeting, with the addition of his coach from the cricket club. Since the previous review, Nico had re-joined the cricket club who had been supportive of this occurring once they had been fully informed of the plan and supports that were in place. Nico was reported to be a positive team member who was punctual and participated well in training. He had increased in his confidence in social situations and thus was viewed to have shown marked change in the areas of "having people in my life" and "having fun". Positive change was also continuing in the areas of "emotional health" and "sexual health". Nico continued to reside with his grandparents but was spending increasing amounts of time with his father as their relationship continued to develop. However, continued difficulties were noted in Nico's relationship with his mother so a plan was developed to address this in the subsequent 6-month period by the way of family therapy.

Comments

By the end of treatment there were no known incidents of further sexually abusive behaviors by Nico. During treatment the aim was explicitly to identify and develop the developmentally appropriate internal skills, knowledge, supports and resources (e.g., coping and problem-solving skills, social skills, stress management techniques, learning to challenge dysfunctional thoughts, etc.) and external resources and supports to assist Nico in achieving his GLP during treatment and into the future. The GLP was sufficiently detailed and practical to be put into practice. During treatment, this process was formalized in the GLAT and thus it provided a framework that could be used in the regular review meetings, and future. Nico, therefore, not only gained the necessary skills to implement his current GLP but was also provided with the skills to monitor and adjust his plans in the future (i.e., to "avoid" relapse). He also had acquired the necessary internal and external capabilities to continue to achieve his personally meaningful goals.

CONCLUSIONS

In this chapter, we have provided an overview of a strength-based model of offender rehabilitation, the Good Lives Model, and described how this model can be applied to relapse prevention with young people who have engaged in sexually abusive behavior. The GLM is a rehabilitative framework rather than a treatment program. Thus, it provides a structure that can inform the rehabilitative process including assessment, treatment, and relapse prevention. Specific, empirically supported treatment techniques for juvenile sex offenders, such as those used to develop empathy skills, social skills, or emotional regulation are "wrapped around" a GLM-derived good lives plan to build capabilities and reduce dynamic risk factors (criminogenic needs). From a therapeutic perspective, it makes sense to work with treatment and case management plans that revolve around what a person wants and can achieve, rather than simply listing situations they should avoid.

As mentioned previously, research has been undertaken, and continues, exploring the application of the GLM to adult offenders, including sexual offenders and other populations. There is, however, a scarcity of research exploring the application of the GLM to juvenile offender rehabilitation as the implementation of the theory to this younger offending population is in its infancy. However, we believe the GLM can make a positive contribution to the area of juvenile offender rehabilitation and that the GLM framework offers exciting opportunities for future rehabilitation and research efforts.

ACKNOWLEDGMENTS

We would like to thank G-MAP Services Limited for being so willing and generous in sharing their program resources.

ADDITIONAL RESOURCES

Print, B. (in press) (Ed.), Applying the Good Lives Model to adolescents who sexually harm. Brandon: The Safer Society Press.

Yates, P. M., Prescott, D., & Ward, T. (2010). *Applying the good lives and self-regulation models to sex offender treatment: A practical guide for clinicians*. Brandon: The Safer Society Press.

www.goodlivesmodel.com This website includes information on relevant publications and research as well as contact details for individuals available for additional consultation in relation to the GLM and its implementation.

REFERENCES

Andrews, D. A., & Bonta, J. (2010). *The psychology of criminal conduct* (5th ed.). New Providence: Matthew Bender & Company Inc.

Andrews, D. A., Bonta, J., & Hoge, R. D. (1990). Classification for effective rehabilitation: Rediscovering psychology. *Criminal Justice and Behavior, 17*, 19–52.

Barnao, M., Robertson, P., & Ward, T. (2010). The Good Lives Model applied to a forensic population. *Psychiatry, Psychology, & Law, 17*, 202–217.

Fortune, C. -A., Ward, T., & Willis, G. M. (2012). The rehabilitation of offenders: Reducing risk and promoting better lives. *Psychiatry, Psychology and Law, 19*, 646–661.

Gannon, T. A., King, T., Miles, H., Lockerbie, L., & Willis, G. M. (2011). Good lives sexual offender treatment for mentally disordered offenders. *British Journal of Forensic Practice, 13*, 153–168.

G-MAP. (2012). *Good lives assessment tool (GLAT)*. Cheshire: G-MAP Services Ltd.

Horvath, A., & Luborsky, L. (1993). The role of the therapeutic alliance in psychotherapy. *Journal of Consulting and Clinical Psychology, 63*, 561–573.

Jones, R. (2003). Research and practice with adolescent offenders: Dilemmas and directions. In T. Ward, D. R. Laws, & S. M. Hudson (Eds.), *Sexual deviance: Issues and controversies* (pp. 190–206). Thousand Oaks: Sage.

Laws, D. R., & Ward, T. (2011). *Desistance and sexual offending: Alternatives to throwing away the keys*. New York: Guilford Press.

Lindsay, W. R., Ward, T., Morgan, T., & Wilson, I. (2007). Self-regulation of sex offending, future pathways and the Good Lives Model: Applications and problems. *Journal of Sexual Aggression, 13*, 37–50.

Mann, R. E., Webster, S. D., Schofield, C., & Marshall, W. L. (2004). Approach versus avoidance goals in relapse prevention with sexual offenders. *Sexual Abuse: A Journal of Research and Treatment, 16*, 65–75.

Marlatt, G. A. (1985). Relapse prevention: Theoretical rationale and overview of the model. In G. A. Marlatt & J. R. Gordon (Eds.), *Relapse prevention: Maintenance strategies in the treatment of addictive behaviors* (pp. 3–70). New York: Guilford Press.

Prescott, D. S. (2002). Collaborative treatment for sexual behavior problems in an adolescent residential center. *Journal of Psychology & Human Sexuality, 13*, 43–58.

Print, B. (in press) (Ed.), *Applying the Good Lives Model to adolescents who sexually harm*. Brandon: Safer Society Press.

Purvis, M., Ward, T., & Willis, G. M. (2011). The Good Lives Model in practice: Offence pathways and case management. *European Journal of Probation, 3*, 4–28.

Rich, P. (2011). Understanding: *Assessing, and rehabilitating juvenile sexual offenders* (2nd ed.). New Jersey: John Wiley & Sons.

Shirk, S. R., & Karver, M. (2003). Prediction of treatment outcome from relationship variables in child and adolescent therapy: A meta-analytic review. *Journal of Consulting and Clinical Psychology*, *71*, 452–464.

Thakker, J., Ward, T., & Tidmarsh, P. (2006). A reevaluation of relapse prevention with adolescents who sexually offend: A Good-Lives Model. In H. E. Barbaree & W. L. Marshall (Eds.), *The juvenile sex offender* (pp. 313–335) (2nd ed.). New York: Guildford Press.

Ward, T. (2010). The Good Lives Model of offender rehabilitation: Basic assumptions, aetiological commitments, and practice implications. In F. McNeill, P. Raynor, & C. Trotter (Eds.), *Offender supervision: New directions in theory, Research and practice oxford* (pp. 41–64). Willan Publishing.

Ward, T., Bickley, J., Webster, S. D., Fisher, D., Beech, A., & Eldridge, H. (2004). *The self-regulation model of the offence and relapse process, volume I: Assessment*. Victoria: Pacific Psychological Assessment Corporation.

Ward, T., & Gannon, T. A. (2006). Rehabilitation, etiology, and self-regulation: The comprehensive Good Lives Model of treatment for sexual offenders. *Aggression and Violent Behavior*, *11*, 77–94.

Ward, T., & Hudson, S. M. (1998). A model of the relapse process in sexual offenders. *Journal of Interpersonal Violence*, *13*, 700–725.

Ward, T., & Hudson, S. M. (2000). A self-regulation model of relapse prevention. In D. R. Laws, S. M. Hudson, & T. Ward (Eds.), *Remaking relapse prevention with sex offenders: A sourcebook* (pp. 79–101). New York: Sage.

Ward, T., & Mann, R. E. (2004). Good lives and the rehabilitation of sex offenders: A positive approach to treatment. In A. Linley & J. Stephen (Eds.), *Positive practice in psychology* (pp. 598–617). Chichester: Wiley.

Ward, T., & Marshall, W. L. (2004). Good lives, aetiology and the rehabilitation of sex offenders: A bridging theory. *Journal of Sexual Aggression, Special Issue: Treatment & Treatability*, *10*, 153–169.

Ward, T., & Maruna, S. (2007). *Rehabilitation: Beyond the risk assessment paradigm*. London: Routledge.

Ward, T., & Stewart, C. A. (2003). The treatment of sex offenders: Risk management and good lives. *Professional Psychology: Research and Practice*, *34*, 353–360.

Ware, J., & Bright, D. A. (2008). Evolution of a treatment programme for sex offenders: Changes to the NSW Custody-Based Intensive Treatment (CUBIT). *Psychiatry, Psychology and Law*, *15*, 340–349.

Whitehead, P. R., Ward, T., & Collie, R. M (2007). Time for a change: Applying the Good Lives Model of rehabilitation to a high-risk violent offender. *International Journal of Offender Therapy and Comparative Criminology*, *51*, 578–598.

Willis, G. M., Yates, P. M., Gannon, T. A., & Ward, T. (2013). How to integrate the Good Lives Model into treatment programs for sexual offending: An introduction and overview. *Sexual Abuse: A Journal of Research and Treatment*, *25*, 123–142.

Worling, J. R., & Langton, C. M. (2012). Assessment and treatment of adolescents who sexually offend: Clinical issues and implications for secure settings. *Criminal Justice and Behavior*, *39*, 814–841.

Worling, J. R., Litteljohn, A., & Bookalam, D. (2010). 20-Year prospective follow-up study of specialized treatment for adolescents who offended sexually. *Behavioral Sciences and the Law*, *28*, 46–57.

Wylie, L., & Griffin, H. (in press). Assessment. In B. Print (Ed.), The Good Lives Model and the treatment of young people who sexually offend. Brandon: Safer Society Press.

Yates, P. M., Prescott, D., & Ward, T. (2010). *Applying the good lives and self-regulation models to sex offender treatment: A practical guide for clinicians*. Brandon: The Safer Society Press.

CHAPTER 17

Increasing Self-Control

Danielle C. Shumack*, James M. Ogilvie*, Stephen Smallbone and Eleanor L. Woodford***
*Griffith Youth Forensic Service, Griffith University, Mt Gravatt, Queensland, Australia
**School of Criminology and Criminal Justice, Australian Research Council, and Griffith Youth Forensic Service, Griffith University, Mt Gravatt, Queensland, Australia

INTRODUCTION

Self-control refers to the ability to control one's impulses, emotions, and behavior to obtain reward and/or avoid punishment. It has long been theorized that low self-control is a major individual-level characteristic associated with engagement in criminal and delinquent acts (Gottfredson & Hirschi, 1990). Individuals with low self-control are said to have little tolerance of frustration and limited capacity to solve problems through verbal rather than physical means; lack diligence, tenacity and persistence; find it difficult to delay gratification; lack interest in and preparation for long-term pursuits; tend to be self-centered; are indifferent or insensitive to the experiences and needs of others; and tend to be adventuresome, active and physical (Cauffman et al., 2005). There exists a large research literature examining links between self-control and a wide range of antisocial activities, including risk taking, substance use, juvenile delinquency, violent offending, and sexual offending.

The focus of this chapter is on therapeutic strategies to improve self-control for juvenile sexual offenders. First, to provide a context for the chapter, we present a summary of conceptual issues related to self-control. Next, we briefly review research examining the links between self-control and juvenile sexual offending. We then provide an overview of self-control assessment measures and resources. Finally, we summarize therapeutic strategies for improving self-control, and provide some tools that may be used to facilitate this process.

WHAT IS SELF-CONTROL?

The construct of self-control is multifaceted and definitions vary widely across scientific disciplines and practice approaches. Self-control may also be referred to as self-regulation, self-discipline, willpower, effortful control,

Toolkit for Working with Juvenile Sex Offenders.
DOI: http://dx.doi.org/10.1016/B978-0-12-405948-1.00017-7

ego strength, or inhibitory control. Given the wide use of the construct in explaining human behavior, there are significant challenges in establishing an overarching method for defining and measuring self-control, and its converse, impulsivity or impulsiveness. Duckworth and Kern (2011, p. 260) argue that the shared conceptual thread underpinning varied definitions of self-control is the idea of "voluntary self-governance in the service of personally valued goals and standards". From a psychological perspective, self-control may best be understood as involving "top-down" and effortful psychological processes (e.g., higher-level cognition, such as executive function) that inhibit or counter impulses generated by other "bottom-up" or more automatic psychological processes (e.g., impulses or emotions). Based on this definition, improving top-down cognitive processes becomes the primary target for individual-level interventions to improve self-control.

SELF-CONTROL AND JUVENILE SEXUAL OFFENDING

It has been argued that some sexual offending may be associated with self-regulatory failure; that is, some individuals may fail to inhibit appropriate sexual impulses and engage in sexually abusive behavior. In their integrated theory, Smallbone, Marshall, and Wortley (2008; see also Smallbone & Cale, in press) framed sexual offending essentially as a failure of individual and/or social controls for inhibiting biologically-based and situationally-precipitated motivations for sexual violence and abuse. At an individual level, problems may arise in both the capacity and commitment to exercise self-restraint in the face of particular opportunities, cues, social pressures, temptations, and so on. At an ecological level, problems may arise because of breakdowns in the usual formal (e.g., policing, child protection systems) or informal social controls (e.g., guardianship, social attachments). While the focus of the present chapter is on individual-level problems associated with self-control, the reader is urged to bear in mind that treatment may require ecological as well as individual interventions.

Ward et al. (1998) outlined a self-regulatory model of sexual offending identifying a number of pathways through which sexual offending may occur from a self-control perspective: (1) underregulation (failure to control sexually deviant intentions/impulses); (2) misregulation (attempts to manage sexually deviant thoughts, fantasies or affective states that may result in a loss of control); and (3) effective regulation (intact self-regulation skills used for inappropriate or harmful goals). Depending on the pathway associated with sexual offending, interventions will target different components of self-control. However, it is important to note that not all sexual offending is associated with self-control, and this highlights the importance of reliable and valid assessment to determine whether self-control problems are an appropriate target for intervention (i.e., identifying criminogenic needs).

ASSESSMENT OF SELF-CONTROL

Researchers have noted the challenges involved in attempting to define and measure self-control, given the diversity in definition, particularly across disciplines. Critiques have been made in the literature in relation to whether or not researchers are indeed measuring the same underlying construct. Ongoing contention surrounds the measurement of the concept of self-control, including unresolved debates surrounding the efficacy of behavioral and attitudinal measurements, including factor structure, group invariance, survey response, conceptual overlap between self-control and other personal factors, and social desirability (for additional information see Piquero, 2008). Although both behavioral and attitudinal measures yield similar results, measurement problems are associated with both approaches.

A recent meta-analysis by Duckworth and Kern (2011) on the convergent validity of self-control measures included measures of executive function, delayed gratification, and self- and informant-report questionnaire measures of self-control. Results suggested that self-control is a coherent but multidimensional construct best assessed using multiple methods. A combination of both behavioral and attitudinal measures may therefore be most appropriate.

With behavioral measures, a history of behavioral concerns (behaviors which lead to longer-term negative consequences) may indicate that a youth presents with limited self-control. Behavioral measures of self-control can be obtained through multiple sources of information including through direct behavioral observation, assessment interviews with the young person, parents, or caregivers, as well as from collateral information including juvenile justice and educational records.

Reviews of the self-control literature suggest four approaches to the measurement of the construct, including cognitive measurement (cognitive tests, e.g., executive function and delay gratification tasks), comprehensive assessment measures (e.g., as subscales of personality and psychopathology measures), unidimensional screening tools and measures, and those specific to self-control. Available measures associated with these approaches are summarized in Table 17.1. Test reliability and validity

Table 17.1 Available Measures for Measurement of Self-Control

Measure	Name	Author(s)	Constructs Measured
Tests of cognition	Go/no-go task	Rosvold, Mirsky, Sarason, Bransome, and Beck (1956); Van der Meere, Stemerdink, and Gunning (1995)	Response inhibition
	Stroop task	Stroop (1935)	Response inhibition, cognitive flexibility, processing speed
	Set switching task (Wisconsin card sorting task)	Heaton and Pendleton (1981)	Impulse responding, cognitive flexibility, abstract thinking
	Iowa Gambling Task	Bechara, Damasio, Damasio, and Anderson (1994)	Behavioral activation and inhibition, decision making, risk-taking behavior
	Risk task (balloon analogue risk task)	Lejuez, Read, and Kahler (2002). BART-Y: Lejuez et al., (2007)	Assesses risk-taking behavior, impulsivity and behavioral inhibition (within the same behavior option, as opposed to choosing different response options, e.g., Iowa Gambling Task)
Comprehensive Assessment Measures	Achenbach system of empirically based assessment ASEBA:	Achenbach and Rescorla (2001)	Competence, adaptive functioning, problem and DSM oriented
	Youth Self-Report Form (YSR) ASEBA Child Behavior Checklist (CBCL) ASEBA Teacher Report Form (TRF)		Competence, adaptive functioning, problem and DSM oriented Academic, adaptive, syndromes and DSM oriented
	Millon Adolescent Clinical Inventory (MACI)	Millon (1993) Millon et al. (2006)	The MACI™ consists of 31 scales: 12 Personality patterns scales (Axis II), 8 Expressed concerns scales, 7 clinical syndrome scales, 3 modifying indices, and a validity scale
	Minnesota multiphasic personality inventory – adolescent (MMPI-A)	Butcher et al. (1992) Graham et al. (2006)	An empirically based measure of adolescent psychopathology. Provides information to aid in problem identification, diagnosis, and treatment planning for adolescents.
	Personality inventory for children, second edition (PIC-2);	Lachar and Gruber (2001)	Assesses emotional, behavioral, social, and cognitive adjustment
	Personality inventory for youth (PIY);	Lachar and Gruber (1995)	Assesses emotional and behavioral adjustment, family interaction, and neurocognitive and attention-related academic functioning.

Scales/Subscales	Format	Age Group	Time to Administer	Published	Contact
Continuous performance task	Computerized	6 yrs +	3–5 min (per block of 200 trials)	Yes	(No cost) http://pi.psyc.virginia.edu/implicit
Continuous performance task	Individually administered: Paper or computerized	5–14 15 +	5–10 min	Yes	(Online distributor) www.ecom.mhs.com; http://www.stoeltingco.com
Continuous performance task	Individually administered	6.5–89	20–30 min	Yes	(Online distributor) https://shop.psych.acer.edu.au/acer-shop/group/QBQ
Continuous performance task	Computerized	18–79	15–20 min	Yes	(Online distributor) http://www4.parinc.com/Products/Product.aspx?ProductID=IGT
Continuous performance task	Computerized	Adult: BART Youth: BART-Y	10–15 min	Yes (both BART and BART-Y)	No cost (Department of Psychology, University of Maryland): http://www.addiction.umd.edu/CAPERWebSite/downloads.html
e.g., Attention problems; rule breaking and aggressive behavior subscales across	Self-report	11–18	15–20 min	Yes	Online distributor: http://www.aseba.org/
As above	Parents/carers	6–18	15–20 min	Yes	Online distributor: http://www.aseba.org/
As above	Educational personnel	6–18	15 min	Yes	Online distributor: http://www.aseba.org/
e.g., Unruly personality pattern; impulsive propensity clinical syndromes subscale	Self-report	13–19	20–25 min	Yes	Online distributor: http://pearsonassessments.com/pai/
Psychopathic deviate; disconstraint subscales	Self-report	14–18	60–90 min	Yes	Online distributor: http://pearsonassessments.com/pai/
Impulsivity/distractibility subscales including dyscontrol	PIC-2 Parent report;	5–19	Full scale: 40 min	Yes	Online distributor: http://portal.wpspublish.com/
Impulsivity/distractibility subscales; delinquency subscales	PIY Self-report	9–19	Behavioral summary: 15 min	Yes	Online distributor: http://portal.wpspublish.com/

(*Continued*)

Table 17.1 (Continued)

Measure	Name	Author(s)	Constructs Measured
	Student behaviour survey (SBS)	Lachar et al. (2000)	Provides teacher's perspective on student's emotional and behavioral adjustment, academic resources, and social functioning
	Early adolescent temperament questionnaire – revised (EATQ-R)	Capaldi and Rothbart (1992); Ellis & Rothbart (2001)	Assesses aspects of temperament and behavior related to self-regulation in adolescents
Unidimensional screening tool	ADHD rating scale-IV	DuPaul, Power, Anastopoulos, and Reid (1998)	Assesses parent and teacher ratings of the symptomatic frequency of each ADHD symptoms as based on DSM-IV criteria
	Attention deficit disorders evaluation scale – second edition (ADDES-2)	McCarney (1995a,b)	Assesses parent and teacher ratings of symptomatic frequency of ADHD
	Connors rating scales third edition (CRS-R)	Conners (2008)	Assess attention deficit/hyperactivity disorder (ADHD)
Measures of self-control	Grasmick scale	Grasmick, Tittle, Bursik, and Arneklev (1993)	Assesses six characteristics of low self-control
	Consideration of future consequences scale	Strathman, Gleicher, Boninger, and Edwards (1994)	Assesses the extent to which individuals consider, and are influenced by, the distant outcomes of current behavior
	Weinberger adjustment inventory	Weinberger and Schwartz (1990)	Assesses self-restraint xand socioemotional adjustment within the context of external constraints
	Barratt impulsiveness scale – version 11	Barratt (1985); Patton, Stanford, and Barratt (1995)	Assesses impulsive personality traits, including. Factors include attentional, motor and non-planning
	Self-regulation questionnaire (SRQ)	Brown, Miller, and Lawendowski (1999)	Assesses ability to develop, implement and flexibly maintain planned behavior in order to achieve one's goals

Scales/Subscales	Format	Age Group	Time to Administer	Published	Contact
Adjustment problems and disruptive behavior subscales	SBS Teacher report	5–18	Full scale, 45 min; Screener composed of first 80 items, 15 min	Yes	Online distributor: http://portal.wpspublish.com/
Inhibitory control, activation control	Self- and parent report	9–15	15 min (65 items) 20–30 min	Yes	Contact author: lellis@westminstercollege.edu
Subscales include inattention, hyperactivity-impulsivity	Parent and teacher report	5–17	5–10 min	Yes	Online distributors (www.guildford.com)
Subscales include inattention and hyperactivity-impulsivity symptoms	Parent and teacher report	4–19	15–20 min	Yes	Online distributors (Hawthorne Educational Services www.hes-inc.com)
Hyperactivity/impulsivity, conduct disorder, oppositional disorder	Parent and teacher report; Self-report	6–18 8–18	Full length: 20 min; Short: 10 min	Yes	Online distributor: http://pearsonassessments.com/pai/
Impulsivity, simple tasks, risk taking, physical activities, self-centered and temper subscales	Self-report	Adolescents & adults	15 min	Yes	Available in original journal article.
Two subscales: immediate consequences and future consequences	Self-report	10 +	5 min	Yes	Available online: http://web.missouri.edu/~strathmana/CFC%20%20English.pdf
Subscales: impulse control, suppression of aggression, consideration of others, and temperance	Self-report	10–17	15 min	Yes	Scale is copyrighted, available online: http://www.cdc.gov/ncipc/pub-res/pdf/YV/CDC_YV_SecII.pdf Contact Daniel A. Weinberger dweinbergerphd@aol.com
30 Item inventory, includes self-control subscale	Self-report	Adolescents	15 min	Yes	No Cost http://www.impulsivity.org/pdf/BIS11English.pdf
Searching for options, evaluating information, triggering change, formulating a plan, assessing plan's effectiveness	Self-report	Adolescents	15–20 min	Yes	No Cost http://casaa.unm.edu/inst/SelfRegulation%20Questionnaire%20%28SRQ%29.pdf

(Continued)

Table 17.1 (Continued)

Measure	Name	Author(s)	Constructs Measured
	Self-control questionnaire	Brandon, Oescher, and Loftin (1990)	16-Item instrument that assesses self-control of health behaviors, with 25% of items specifically examining eating patterns. Gender bias also highlighted in literature
	Self-control schedule	Rosenbaum (1980)	Clinical tool that assesses the usage of strategies, such as the self-distraction and cognitive reframing to solve particular behavioral problems
	Self-control scale (Full version: 36 items; brief version: 13 items)	Tangney, Baumeister, and Boone (2004)	Assesses behaviors that have been found to be predictive of criminal activity, such as controlling of thoughts, emotions, impulses, regulating behavior/performance and habit breaking (e.g., "I do certain things that are bad for me if they are fun")

are not provided here, but practitioners are advised to be mindful of the methodological (as well as conceptual) strengths and limitations of chosen tests. The list in Table 17.1 is intended to assist the practitioner to review the measurement tools they may already use in their practice, and as an aid to considering other measures that may further inform whether a young person may benefit from interventions targeted at increasing self-control.

THERAPEUTIC ENGAGEMENT WITH LOW SELF-CONTROL YOUTH

Disengagement from treatment, whether manifested as non-attendance, non-completion of treatment goals, or poor engagement with therapists, is a common problem in general clinical settings, and particularly for children and adolescents with conduct and externalizing problems (Dadds, 1997). High treatment dropout rates have been reported specifically with juvenile sex offenders (Hunter & Figueredo, 1999; Kraemer, Salisbury & Spielman 1998; Seabloom, Seabloom, Seabloom, Barron & Hendrickson 2003), with studies showing impulsivity and general antisocial behavior problems

Scales/Subscales	Format	Age Group	Time to Administer	Published	Contact
Five factors (derived from factor analysis): weight control, time management, emotional control, financial planning, social behavior	Self-report	Adolescents and adults	5–10 min	Yes	Available in original journal article
Subscales (derived from factor analysis): delay of immediate gratification, planful behavior, control of unwanted thoughts, impulse control, mood control, and pain control	Self-report	Adults	10–15 min	Yes	Available in original journal article
Subscales: self-control in the domains of work ethic, self-discipline, non-impulsivity, health habits, and reliability	Self-report	Adolescents and adults	5–10 min	Yes (Both full and brief versions) (Validated for offender population)	Contact author: jtangney@gmu.edu

to be associated with higher dropout rates in this population (Edwards, Beech, Bishopp, Erikson, Friendship, et al., 2005; Kraemer et al., 1998). If low self-control has been properly assessed and identified as a treatment goal, practitioners should consider the implications of this for engaging and maintaining their therapeutic involvement with the young client.

Smallbone, Crissman, and Rayment-McHugh (2009) reported increased therapeutic engagement (TE) for high-antisocial/impulsive juvenile sex offenders after modifying their program to shift the responsibility for TE away from the youth offender and on to the practitioners themselves. Essentially, this involved placing additional emphasis on assessing potential barriers to TE and on improving the problem-solving efforts by practitioners to address these barriers. Examples include: (1) framing TE as a primary treatment goal; (2) scheduling appointments for locations and times most convenient to the client; (3) instructing clinicians to spend time building and enhancing TE on an ongoing basis; and (4) recruiting collaborative partners identified by the young person (e.g., family members, teachers, responsible friends) to assist with TE and with some treatment components.

THERAPEUTIC STRATEGIES FOR INCREASING SELF-CONTROL

Numerous interventions for juvenile sexual offenders, general offenders, and at-risk groups are described in the research literature. These include family treatments, parent training programs, behavioral intervention programs, school-based and community interventions, and individual and group-based programs. As an outcome of evidence-based practice initiatives, much of the research and evaluation has focused specifically on brand name "model" programs. Evaluations of individual programs are informative in their own right, but they generally do not focus on those factors found consistently across programs to increase program effectiveness.

Meta-analyses have identified a number of factors or principles that characterize the most effective interventions (e.g., Andrews, Zinger, Hoge, Bonta, Gendreau, 1990; Lipsey, 2009; Lipsey & Wilson, 1998). These have indicated that re-offending rates are most likely to be reduced by multimodal, behavioral, skills-focused treatment programs. Izzo and Ross's (1990) meta-analysis of rehabilitation programs focused on reducing recidivism found that programs are more effective when theoretical principles are made explicit and when fidelity with program-as-intended is maintained. Lipsey's (2009) findings suggested that in comparing variable generic programs with "model" programs, the former can be quite effective if implemented well and targeted on high risk offenders, suggesting "it does not take a magic bullet program to impact recidivism, only one that is well made and well-aimed" (p. 145).

Numerous programs exist that include components targeted at increasing youth's capacity for self-control. Cognitive behavior therapy (CBT) programs have emerged as an efficacious treatment modality for reducing recidivism with both adult and adolescent offending populations (Landenberger & Lipsey, 2005; Lipsey, Chapman & Landenberger, 2001; Pearson, Lipton, Cleland & Yee, 2002; Wilson, Bouffard & MacKenzie, 2005). Meta-analyses of programs designed for adult offenders have shown cognitive behavioral programs to be effective in reducing recidivism rates (Little, 2005; Lipsey et al., 2001; Pearson et al., 2002; Walker, McGovern, Poey & Otis, 2004; Wilson et al., 2005). The most widely used approaches to treatment in criminal justice today are variations of CBT (Little, 2005). A meta-analysis by Landenberger and Lipsey (2005) examined whether certain components of CBT programs used with adult and juvenile offenders were associated with greater effect sizes with respect to reducing recidivism. They concluded that programs with better implementation quality and fidelity, and that targeted higher-risk offender populations, were associated with greater effect sizes. Programs incorporating anger control and interpersonal problem-solving components enhanced effectiveness, while those incorporating victim impact and behavior modification components diminished effectiveness. Meta-analyses have consistently indicated that CBT, on average, has significant positive effects on recidivism and it can be adapted to a range of juvenile and adult offenders and delivered in a variety of settings as part of a multifaceted program or as a stand-alone intervention.

Multicomponent programs have been developed that include components targeted at increasing self-control for use with youth who are at risk of non-sexual and sexual re-offending. Single component CBT treatment programs have included social, communication and problem-solving skills training, anger management and control, and moral reasoning interventions. Two multicomponent programs are briefly reviewed below: Aggression Replacement Training (ART®; Goldstein, Glick, Reiner, Zimmerman & Coultry, 1986; Goldstein, Glick, & Gibbs, 1998), and Mindfields *A Self-Regulatory Intervention to Empower Young People At-Risk to Change Their Lives* (Carroll, Ahsman, Hemingway, Bower & Houghton, 2012). In addition, a single component intervention will be discussed.

ART® is a cognitive behavioral intervention program to help children and adolescents improve social skill competence and moral reasoning, better manage anger, and reduce aggressive behavior. The program was first developed for aggressive and violent adolescents aged 12–17 who were incarcerated in juvenile institutions, and specifically targets chronically aggressive children and adolescents. ART® has been implemented in schools and juvenile delinquency programs internationally. ART® has been adapted for children in schools and mental health settings and for adults. The ART® program is a multimodal intervention consisting of three components: social skills training, anger control training, and training in moral reasoning. Lessons in this program are intended to address the behavioral, affective, and cognitive components of aggressive and violent behavior. The program consists of 10 weeks (30 sessions) of intervention training. Incremental learning, reinforcement techniques, and guided group discussions enhance skill acquisition and reinforce the lessons in the curriculum.

The ART® program is associated with skills improvements including significant increases in constructive social behaviors and moral reasoning, and decreases in impulsivity, as compared to no treatment (Goldstein & Glick, 1994). Follow-up studies have indicated decreases in problem behaviors (Gundersen & Frode, 2006) and re-arrest rates at 18 months follow-up (Barnoski, 2004; Washington State Institute for Public Policy, 2004). Another study demonstrated no differences other than in social skills development between youth who received ART® as compared to a control group (Coleman, Pfeiffer & Oakland, 1992). There is, at this stage, little evidence for generalization of skills over longer-term follow-up, and further research and evaluation are required.

Mindfields (Carroll et al., 2012) is a self-regulatory intervention designed to enhance the development of life skills and self-set goals among school-aged adolescent offenders. Mindfields uses an interactive multimedia format presentation, is founded on a social cognitive perspective of self-regulation, and is based on an empirical and theoretical understanding of at-risk youth. Its treatment components are based on cognitive-behavioral principles (Carroll et al., 2012).

Mindfields provides a coherent framework, commencing with a thorough screening and evaluative process, and teaches young people a number of self-regulation strategies with supported guidance while providing weekly opportunities to fulfill a self-set goal. This is achieved in a range of modes to provide variety while minimizing the need for literacy skills that are often not well developed among young people at risk. Preliminary findings provide evidence for the effectiveness of this new self-regulatory intervention for school-aged adolescents (Carroll et al., 2012). Mindfields has yet to be subjected to rigorous evaluation, however, a preliminary evaluation of the program conducted by its authors (Carroll et al., 2012) has indicated reductions in prodelinquency and improvements in self-satisfaction among school-aged adolescent offenders as compared to a control group. Preliminary findings are promising, although further evaluation is required.

Single component interventions may include the following treatment elements: education about stages of change; goal setting (short and long term); consequential thinking; change planning; social skills development; communication skills training including conflict resolution; identification of triggers to negative affective states; mediational and behavioral self-control strategies; arousal control strategies; cognitive restructuring; problem-solving strategies; relapse prevention planning; and maintenance plans. The following worksheets focus on four specific targets:

1. Identification of triggers that may increase motivation to engage in dysregulated behavior (internal and external) (e.g., relational stress, negative affective states, substance abuse etc.)

2. Consequential thinking, brainstorming the ways in which poor self-control has negatively impacted on their daily life (e.g., harm to self and others, engagement with legal systems, delays in meeting short-term and longer-term goals). Identification of the negative consequences of poor self-control for themselves and others (e.g., participation in antisocial behavior, engagement with antisocial peers). Identification of the positive consequences of managing impulses
3. Mediational and self-control strategies (e.g., self-talk strategies such as stop, listen, think and act; count to ten; walk away; time out; thoughts stopping; distraction; relaxation strategies) tailored to the individual to assist in delaying gratification and inhibit impulses to achieve meaningful short-term goals
4. Effective problem solving skills (identification of the problem, brainstorming possible solutions, selecting implementing and evaluating the chosen course of action).

IDENTIFICATION OF TRIGGERS (VOLCANO)

Lots of things can cause pressure to build within our lives and make it more difficult for you to resist the temptation to "lose control". Similar to a volcano which erupts as the result of pressure building from within the core of the earth, can you identify the pressures in your life that contribute to you "losing it" or doing things without thought for the consequences? Some of the triggers often experienced by young people may include: relationship problems with friends; relationship problems with parents/carers; trauma; stress; substance abuse; depression/hopelessness; lack of support; lack of housing/food/money; anxiety; poor self-esteem.

Can you think about the pressures within your life that often serve as a trigger for "losing it" and doing what you want without thinking of the consequences and write or draw these in the box below.

CONSEQUENTIAL THINKING

Similar to a volcanic eruption the consequences of "losing it" can be disastrous and harmful. Can you think of the consequences for both you and for others of "losing it", write or draw these in the box below.

Can you consider what will happen if you are better able to manage the pressures in your life and manage these so you can stay in control? Write or draw these in the box below. Compare these two boxes, which would you prefer?

MEDIATIONAL AND SELF-CONTROL STRATEGIES

What strategies do you currently have that assist you in staying calm and in control, managing the pressures in your life that can place you at risk of losing it? Write or draw these in the box below.

Some strategies assist us in controlling our impulses and behavior. Some of these can include things that we can do, and others include different ways in which we can think about problems that help us keep our cool, or Chillax. Some Chillax plans can include: self-talk strategies such as stop, listen, think and act, count to ten, walk away, time out, thought stopping, distraction, relaxation strategies.

Each of these Chillax Plans can assist you in helping you stay in control. Your counselor can assist you in learning these plans.

PROBLEM SOLVING

Often we feel overwhelmed by the pressures in our life and find it difficult to think of solutions to the pressures that are confronting us, we feel trapped within them and often out of control. In order to make sure that you can stay in control alongside Chillax Plans finding solutions to problems is another way to reduce the pressures in our lives. In order to attempt to fix a problem, similar to a motor mechanic, we first need to be able to recognize what the problem is. Try to identify what is maintaining the problems, not just what caused it and be specific (what you observe) rather that using feelings to describe the problem. Can you identify and write in the box below the pressures in your life that you find difficult to manage or solve?

Often it is useful to brainstorm with you counselor or group ways in which you might be able to manage or solve this problem, asking for assistance from others and getting their perspective often allows us ideas that we may have been too pressured to think about for ourselves. Brainstorm possible solutions and write these in the box below.

Out of the possible solutions chosen, now consider the possible consequences of each. In the table below, draw or write the potential positive and negative consequences for each potential solution. After you have completed the table, consider each solution and decide which has the best outcomes.

Solution	Advantages	Disadvantages	Which would be best?

Now decide on one or two solutions that have the best outcomes and develop an action plan to implement the solution.

Action steps	Who may I need to include in this step	When will I carry out this step?

The next step is to implement the solution and evaluate whether the solution was effective, if not return to this worksheet and develop a new action plan.

For clients who may be especially resistant, or who may find the completion of worksheets challenging, the use of a case study can be implemented initially within worksheets in order to decrease resistance and increase comprehension. After they are familiar with the application of the case study to the worksheets, the young offender client may be more able and willing to discuss and reflect upon their own circumstances within worksheet completion. An example of such a case study is provided in Box 17.1.

Box 17.1 Case Study: Larry

Larry is a 15-year-old male youth living in residential care for children removed from their families. Larry lives with two other male youth around the same age, with a rotating roster of youth workers living in the residence to care for and supervise the boys. Larry is enrolled in high school, but usually only attends school two to three times a week, preferring to skip school and spend time with friends at the local skate-park.

Before coming into residential care, Larry lived with his family that included his mother, stepfather and two younger sisters. While growing up, Larry's stepfather would drink beer heavily and would often be very drunk at home. His stepfather would usually become angry when drunk and become abusive toward his mother, Larry himself, and his sisters. Larry would say that almost every day he would see his stepfather yell at and hit his mother, and that his stepfather would also yell at and hit him and his sisters for minor issues (e.g., being too loud, not cleaning their rooms or doing chores). Larry committed sexual offences against his 12-year-old sister while still living in the family home. One night, Larry was asked to look after his sister, who was feeling sick, while his mother, stepfather and other sister went out to see a movie. Larry had recently broken up with his girlfriend from school, and was still feeling sad and lonely about this. After his parents and other sister left the house, Larry went to his room to go on the Internet, while his sister stayed in the lounge room watching television. While on the Internet, Larry came across a pornographic website, and started watching videos of men and women having sex. After watching these videos for a while, Larry decided he would show one to his sister in the lounge room. She was disgusted by these videos, and asked Larry to turn it off. Larry did turn the video off, but then asked his sister to touch his penis to copy what he had seen on the video. Even though his sister refused to do this, Larry started touching his sister's vagina without her permission and forced her to touch his penis. At this point, Larry's parents returned home, and he quickly ran back to his room. Larry's sister immediately told her mother what had happened.

Since being in residential care, Larry has been experiencing some problems with his carers. Larry has been refusing to go to school and to do his chores around the house more often recently. Because of this, Larry has been getting into regular arguments with his carers. On one occasion, Larry was asked by one of his carers to clean his room, and Larry refused to do this because he was busy chatting to friends on the phone. Larry's carer continued to ask him to get off the phone and clean his room, and Larry started to get frustrated, thinking that the carer was nagging him. Larry became so angry at the carer's continued nagging that he threw his phone and hit them in the head, causing the carer to fall over and break their arm.

Larry has also been in trouble at school recently. Larry has been stealing other student's belongings. He has been teased by older kids at school, who have been calling him names and making fun of him in front of girls. One time, Larry has become so angry at one of these kids, that he has lost his temper and started punching them and screaming until a teacher came and pulled them apart.

CONCLUSIONS

Low self-control is one of the most widely recognized individual-level factors associated with delinquency and crime. Definitions vary, but most center on the idea of "voluntary self-governance in the service of personally valued goals and standards". For any client, including juvenile sex offenders, careful assessment is needed to establish whether improving self-control is required as a treatment target. A range of behavioral and attitudinal measures are available for use in such assessments. If low self-control is identified as a problem, practitioners should think through the implications for engaging the youth client and take steps to maximize therapeutic engagement. A range of proven or promising multimodal and single-component intervention strategies is available for improving self-control. Practitioners should be mindful that, particularly for juvenile offenders, treatment may require attention to family-, peer-, and school-level, as well as individual-level, interventions.

REFERENCES

Achenbach, T. M., & Rescorla, L. A. (2001). *Manual for the ASEBA adult forms and profiles*. Burlington: University of Vermont, Research Center for Children, Youth, and Families.

Andrews, D. A., Zinger, I., Hoge, R. D., Bonta, J., Gendreau, P., & Cullen, F. T. (1990). Does correctional treatment work? A clinically relevant and psychologically informed meta-analysis. *Criminology, 28*, 369–404.

Barnoski, R. (2004). *Outcome evaluation of washington state's research-based programs for juveniles*. Olympia: Washington State Institute for Public Policy.

Barratt, E. S. (1985). Impulsiveness substraits: Arousal and information processing. In J. T. Spence & C. E. Izard (Eds.), *Motivation, emotion, and personality* (pp. 137–146). North Holland: Elsevier Science.

Bechara, A., Damasio, A. R., Damasio, H., & Anderson, S. W. (1994). Insensitivity to future consequences following damage to human prefrontal cortex. *Cognition, 50*, 7–15.

Brandon, J. E., Oescher, J., & Loftin, J. M. (1990). The self-control questionnaire: An assessment. *Health Values, 14*, 3–9.

Brown, J. M., Miller, W. R., & Lawendowski, L. A. (1999). The self-regulation questionnaire. In L. VandeCreek & T. L. Jackson (Eds.), *Innovations in clinical practice: A source book* (Vol. 17, pp. 281–289). Sarasota: Professional Resource Press.

Butcher, J. N., Williams, C. L., Graham, J. R., et al. (1992). *Minnesota multiphasic personality inventory – adolescent (MMPI-A): Manual for administration, scoring, and interpretation*. Minneapolis: University of Minnesota Press.

Capaldi, D. M., & Rothbart, M. K. (1992). Development and validation of an early adolescent temperament measure. *Journal of Early Adolescence, 12*, 153–173.

Carroll, A., Ahsman, A., Hemingway, F., Bower, J., & Houghton, S. (2012). A preliminary evaluation of mindfields: A self-regulatory cognitive behavioural program for school-aged adolescent offenders. *Australian Educational and Developmental Psychologist, 29*, 81–94.

Cauffman, E., Steinberg, L., & Piquero, A. R. (2005). Psychological, neuropsychological and physiological correlates of serious antisocial behavior in adolescence: The role of self-control. *Criminology, 43*(1), 133–176.

Coleman, M, Pfeiffer, S., & Oakland, T. (1992). Aggression Replacement Training with behaviorally disordered adolescents. *Behavioral Disorders*, *18*, 54–66.

Conners, C. K. (2008). *Conners rating scales: manual* (3rd ed.). North Tonawanda: Multi-Health Systems. (Conners 3).

Dadds, M. R. (1997). Conduct disorder. In R. T. Ammerman & M. Hersen (Eds.), *Handbook of prevention and treatment with children and adolescents*. New York: Wiley.

Duckworth, A. L., & Kern, M. L. (2011). A meta-analysis of the convergent validity of self-control measures. *Journal of Research in Personality*, *35*, 259–268.

DuPaul, G. J., Power, T. J., Anastopoulos, A. D., & Reid, R. (1998). *ADHD rating scale-IV: Checklist, norms, and clinical interpretation*. New York: Guildford Press.

Edwards, R., Beech, A., Bishopp, D., Erikson, M., Friendship, C., & Charlesworth, L. (2005). Predicting dropout from a residential programme for adolescent sexual abusers using pre-treatment variables and implications for recidivism. *Journal of Sexual Aggression*, *11*, 139–155.

Ellis, L. K., & Rothbart, M. K. (2001). *Revision of the early adolescent temperament questionnaire*. Minneapolis: Minnesota: Poster presented at the biennial meeting for the Society for Research in Child Development.

Goldstein, A. P., & Glick, B. (1994). Aggression replacement training: curriculum and evaluation. *Simulation & Gaming*, *25*, 9–26.

Goldstein, A. P., Glick, B., & Gibbs, J. C. (1998). *Aggression replacement training: A comprehensive intervention for aggressive youth*. Champaign: Research Press. (Rev. ed.).

Goldstein, A. P., Glick, B., Reiner, S., Zimmerman, D., & Coultry, T. (1986). *Aggression replacement training: A comprehensive intervention for aggressive youth*. Champaign: Research Press.

Gottfredson, M. R., & Hirschi, T. (1990). *A general theory of crime*. Stanford, California: Stanford University Press.

Graham, J. R., Archer, R. P., Tellegen, A., Ben-Porath, Y. S., & Kaemmer, B. (2006). *Minnesota multiphasic personality inventory – adolescent (MMPI-A): Manual supplement for administration, scoring, and interpretation*. Minneapolis: University of Minnesota Press.

Grasmick, H. G., Tittle, C. R., Bursik, R. J., & Arneklev, B. J. (1993). Testing the core empirical implications of Gottfredson and Hirchi's general theory of crime. *Journal of Research on Crime and Delinquency*, *30*, 5–29.

Gundersen, K. K., & Frode, S. (2006). Aggression replacement training in Norway: Outcome evaluation of 11 Norwegian student projects. *Scandinavian Journal of Education Research*, *50*, 63–81.

Heaton, R. K., & Pendleton, M. G. (1981). Use of neuropsychological tests to predict adult patients' everyday functioning. *Journal of Consulting and Clinical Psychology*, *49*, 807–821.

Hunter, J. A., & Figueredo, A. J. (1999). Factors associated with treatment compliance in a population of juvenile sexual offenders. *Sexual Abuse: A Journal of Research and Treatment*, *11*, 49–67.

Izzo, R. L., & Ross, R. R. (1990). Meta-analysis of rehabilitation programs for juvenile delinquents. *Criminal Justice and Behaviour*, *17*, 134–142.

Kraemer, B. D., Salisbury, S. B., & Spielman, C. (1998). Pretreatment variables associated with treatment failure in a residential juvenile sex-offender program. *Criminal Justice and Behavior*, *25*, 190–202.

Lachar, D., & Gruber, C. P. (1995). *Personality inventory for youth (PIY): Manual; Administration and interpretation guide; technical guide*. Los Angeles: Western Psychological Services.

Lachar, D., & Gruber, C. P. (2001). *Personality inventory for children, 2nd edn (PIC-2): Standard form and behavioral summary manual*. Los Angeles: Western Psychological Services.

Lachar, D., Wingenfeld, S. A., Kline, R. B., & Gruber, C. P. (2000). *Student behavior survey: manual*. Los Angeles: Western Psychological Services.

Landenberger, N. A., & Lipsey, M. W. (2005). The positive effects of cognitive-behavioral programs for offenders: a meta-analysis of factors associated with effective treatment. *Journal of Experimental Criminology*, *1*(4), 51–76.

Lejuez, C. W., Aklin, W., Daughters, S., Zvolensky, M., Kahler, C., & Gwadz, M. (2007). Reliability and validity of the youth version of the Balloon Analogue Risk Task (BART-Y) in the assessment of risk-taking behavior among inner-city adolescents. *Journal of Clinical Child and Adolescent Psychology*, *36*, 106–111.

Lejuez, C. W., Read, J. P., Kahler, C. W., et al. (2002). Evaluation of behavioral measure of risk taking: The Balloon Analogue Risk Task (BART). *Journal of Experimental Psychology: Applied*, *8*, 75–84.

Lipsey, M. W. (2009). The primary factors that characterize effective interventions with juvenile offenders: A meta-analytic overview. *Victims and Offenders*, *4*, 124–147.

Lipsey, M. W., Chapman, G., & Landenberger, N. A. (2001). Cognitive-behavioral programs for offenders. *Annals of the American Academy of Political and Social Science*, *578*, 144–157.

Lipsey, M. W., & Wilson, D. B. (1998). Effective intervention for serious juvenile offenders: A synthesis of research. In R. Loeber & D. P. Farrington (Eds.), *Serious and violent juvenile offenders: Risk factors and successful interventions* (pp. 313–345). Thousand Oaks: Sage.

Little, G. L. (2005). Meta-analysis of moral reconation therapy(r): recidivism results from probation and parole implementations. *Cognitive-Behavioral Treatment Review*, *14*, 14–16.

McCarney, S. B. (1995a). *The attention deficit disorders evaluation scale – home version: technical manual* (2nd ed.). Columbia: Hawthorne Educational Service.

Millon, T. (1993). *Millon adolescent clinical inventory*. Minneapolis: National Computer Systems.

Millon, T., Millon, C., Davis, R., & Grossman, S. (2006). *Millon clinical multiaxial inventory –III (MCMI-III) manual* (3rd ed.). Minneapolis: NCS Pearson.

Patton, J. H., Stanford, M. S., & Barratt, E. S. (1995). Factor structure of the Barratt impulsiveness scale. *Journal of Clinical Psychology*, *51*, 768–774.

Pearson, F. S., Lipton, D. S., Cleland, C. M., & Yee, D. S. (2002). The effects of behavioral/cognitive-behavioral programs on recidivism. *Crime and Delinquency*, *48*, 476–496.

Piquero, A. R. (2008). Measuring self-control. In E. Goode (Ed.), *Out of control: assessing the general theory of crime* (pp. 26–37). Stanford: Stanford Social Sciences.

Rosenbaum, M. (1980). A schedule for assessing self-control behaviors: Preliminary findings. *Behvaior Therapy*, *11*, 109–121.

Rosvold, H. E., Mirsky, A. F., Sarason, I., Bransome, E. D., Jr, & Beck, L. H. (1956). A continuous performance test of brain damage. *Journal of Consulting Psychology*, *20*, 343–350.

Seabloom, W., Seabloom, M. E., Seabloom, E., Barron, R., & Hendrickson, S. (2003). A 14- to 24-year longitudinal study of a comprehensive sexual health model treatment program for adolescent sex offenders: Predictors of successful completion and subsequent criminal recidivism. *International Journal of Offender Therapy and Comparative Criminology*, *47*, 468–481.

Smallbone, S., & Cale, J. (in press). An integrated life course developmental theory of sexual offending. In A. Blockland & P. Lussier (Eds), Sex offenders: a criminal careers approach. New York: Wiley.

Smallbone, S., Crissman, B., & Rayment-McHugh, S. (2009). Improving therapeutic engagement with adolescent sexual offenders. *Behavioral Sciences and the Law*, *27*, 862–877.

Strathman, A., Gleicher, F., Boninger, D. S., & Edwards, C. S. (1994). The consideration of future consequences: Weighing immediate and distant outcomes of behavior. *Journal of Personality and Social Psychology*, *66*, 742–752.

Stroop, J. R. (1935). Studies of interference in serial verbal reactions. *Journal of Experimental Psychology*, *18*, 643–662.

Tangney, J. P., Baumeister, R. F., & Boone, A. L. (2004). High self-control predicts good adjustment, less pathology, better grades, and interpersonal success. *Journal of Personality*, *72*, 271–322.

Van der Meere, J., Stemerdink, N., & Gunning, B. (1995). Effects of presentation rate of stimuli on response inhibition in ADHD children with and without tics. *Perceptual and Motor Skills*, *81*, 259–262.

Walker, D. F., McGovern, S. K., Poey, E. L., & Otis, K. E. (2004). Treatment effectiveness for male adolescent sexual offenders: a meta-analysis and review. *Journal of Child Sexual Abuse, 13*, 281–293.

Ward, T., Hudson, S. M., & Keenan, T. (1998). A self-regulation model of the sexual offense process. *Sexual Abuse: A Journal of Research and Treatment, 10*, 141–157.

Washington State Institute for Public Policy, (2004). *Outcome evaluation of washington state's research-based programs for juvenile offenders*. Olympia: Washington State Institute for Public Policy.

Weinberger, D. A., & Schwartz, G. E. (1990). Distress and restraint as superordinate dimensions of self-reported adjustment: A typological perspective. *Journal of Personality, 58*, 381–417.

Wilson, D. B., Bouffard, L. A., & MacKenzie, D. L. (2005). A quantitative review of structured, group oriented, cognitive-behavioral programs for offenders. *Journal of Criminal Justice and Behavior, 32*, 172–204.

CHAPTER 18

Documenting Treatment for Sexually Abusive Youth

Jackson Tay Bosley* **and Sean Hiscox****
*University Behavioral Health Care, Rutgers University Piscataway, NJ, USA
**Associates in Psychological Services, Somerville, NJ, USA

INTRODUCTION

Sex-offense-specific treatment programs for sexually abusive youth are faced with the inevitable tension between the administrative convenience of delivering a standardized treatment package and individually tailoring their services to the specialized needs of each youth. This tension is increased by programs that are often short-staffed and operate on limited budgets, creating a premium for efficiency and the careful allocation of resources.

For example, some youth may benefit from individual treatment prior to attending group therapy, yet are placed directly into group therapy exclusively. As our knowledge base regarding sexually abusive youth has increased, programs that offered a standardized approach to all offenders (known as the "cookie cutter approach") have given way to programs that incorporate more flexibility in the types of treatment and in the intensity of the interventions.

As this shift in treatment programming occurs, more programs are recognizing and subscribing to the Risk/Need/Responsivity model (RNR) (Andrews & Bonta, 2006; Andrews, Bonta & Hoge, 1990) to structure their programs. The RNR model involves matching interventions to the level of risk the youth poses (i.e., risk), targeting areas in treatment related to their criminal behavior (i.e., need), and applying treatment strategies that coincide with the optimal learning abilities of the offender (i.e., responsivity). For example, treatment of a youth who commits an isolated act of illegal sexual behavior that is not part of either a broader pattern of sexual deviance or an antisocial interpersonal orientation is usually appropriate for short-term, community-based therapy focused on psychoeducation. It would be counterproductive and potentially harmful to place

Toolkit for Working with Juvenile Sex Offenders.
DOI: http://dx.doi.org/10.1016/B978-0-12-405948-1.00018-9

such a low-risk youth in a residential setting with therapy groups that include highly delinquent youth.

This chapter incorporates a contemporary understanding of documentation requirements and the effective and ethical communication required to deliver state-of-the-art treatment for sexually abusive youth. We will address the documentation needs of services available in varied settings and incorporate the level of flexibility required to offer services based on the individualized needs of each youth as established through a comprehensive assessment using the RNR model.

In preparation for writing this chapter, a wide range of program development tools in the field of sex-offense-specific treatment was reviewed in order to obtain a thorough grounding from professional sources. Surprisingly, we found few articles or book chapters that provided concrete examples of the kinds of documentation that were used in treatment programs, although many sources included suggested content.

One of the best sources for this kind of information is the somewhat dated, yet excellent, *Treating Adolescent Sexual Offenders in the Community*, by Steen and Monnette (1989). Although the present chapter extends beyond treatment provided in the community to include treatment in secure-correctional or hospital settings, Steen and Monnette's appendices are quite helpful.

DOCUMENTING SEXUAL OFFENSE-SPECIFIC TREATMENT

The purpose of this chapter is to offer program developers, evaluators, and therapists examples of the types of documentation that are appropriate to create and maintain in programs for sexually abusive youth. Appended to this chapter are examples of documentation, some of which were requested by funding sources for a program developed by one of the authors in a secure (correctional) setting for juveniles adjudicated for sexual offenses in New Jersey.

Recognizing that program documentation is greatly affected by contextual issues relating to the location of the program, source of treatment participants, and numerous other factors, we can provide only a basic framework for common types of documentation. We will address such areas as intake and biographical information, assessment information, treatment participation and progress information, and treatment termination information with recommendations.

Many states/locations have developed standards for programs in their jurisdiction. For example, the requirements in Colorado (Colorado Sex Offender Management Board, 2002) and Minnesota (Listiak, 2003) are representative of the kinds of mandates included in legislation or departmental policy of funding agencies. Such mandates often include the type of treatment that is required (e.g., group and/or individual) and topics that must be addressed (e.g., empathy, denial, deviant arousal, etc.). Program developers are encouraged to conduct a thorough review of the unique requirements for their particular jurisdiction prior to developing program documentation forms.

INTAKE/BIOGRAPHICAL INFORMATION

Every client will need identification information noted in the clinical record. This biographical information can be as limited as name, date of birth, and identification number of some sort, or as complete as can be obtained through interviews of parental informants and school sources. In addition to the information needed to identify the client, ancillary information is helpful to get a more complete picture of the context from which the client emerges.

MEDICAL INFORMATION

Some youth have long histories with medical providers, while others have had little medical attention. An initial assessment should inquire into the youth's physical health and prior interactions with medical professionals. For example, it is possible that the youth has been prescribed medications for attention deficit hyperactivity disorder or other psychological disorders; if no inquiry is made, the youth might not think it important enough to mention. It is also important to obtain information that might indicate neurological problems, since these sorts of issues often require that treatment be tailored on an individual basis. A sample intake form incorporating biographical and medical information is displayed in Appendix A.

FAMILY/BACKGROUND INFORMATION

Some youth come with a complicated lineage. Parents are often unmarried and use different last names. Or, the youth could have been raised in an official or unofficial foster home setting. Youth are sometimes sent to live with an aunt, grandmother, or other family member when their birth parent(s) cannot care for them due to a variety of reasons, such as disability, substance abuse, incarceration, or through court intervention after being deemed unfit. Such information is important for a treating clinician and/or supervisor to know so that optimal treatment can be provided, particularly in terms of understanding the context in which the sexually abusive behavior occurred and to start considering discharge planning, even at the beginning of the treatment process.

Although generating a genogram might involve considerable effort for an intake interview, it can add important information useful for assessment and treatment. It can quickly provide the assigned clinician a snapshot of the youth's history and family relationships. Over the course of treatment, particularly if in a program for an extended period of time, the youth may work with several therapists. In these types of situations, the genogram offers an excellent cursory overview of the client's upbringing.

At a minimum, treating clinicians should know the parental situation/involvement, the nature of the family constellation (including the family's history of criminality and psychological problems), and anything else that might highlight this influential aspect of a youth's environment. A significant proportion of sexually abusive youth emerge from disadvantaged and/or chaotic environments which often leads to dysfunctional attachment styles. These dysfunctional attachment styles are a relevant treatment concern and affect the client's responsivity to treatment interventions (Smallbone, 2006). One way to address this during an intake session is to ask about the client's current placement and work backward chronologically exploring attachment to caretakers, siblings, peers and inquiring about any maltreatment that might have occurred in each setting.

In the process of gathering this information, it is important to gather the objective data and the youth's impression of, and reaction to, these circumstances. For example, in a situation where a youth's parents have had their parental rights terminated or he/she was given up by his/her parents to live with a grandparent or relative, this information is relevant in and of itself, but the youth's perspective and the consequences such actions have had on his/her life are critically important for successful treatment to occur. For example, one youth might perceive this as abandonment, while another might view it as his parents caring for him by making sure he had adequate parenting (from a different source). Again, these issues are not only important at the beginning of the assessment/treatment process, but these sorts of family-related dynamics need to be considered early on for discharge planning, such as whether the youth can be reunited with his or her family.

Many clients emerge from severely dysfunctional environments and have no appropriate adult role models. Often, the adults in their lives have engaged in criminal activity and/or domestic violence, both of which can leave the youth with traumatic sequelae that contribute to adjustment problems and a world view that normalizes criminal behavior. These sorts of problems are also sometimes replicated within the therapeutic relationship and with peers in group therapy. There are multiple pathways that lead our clients to commit sexually abusive behaviors, and a close examination of the youth's upbringing usually offers clues that are helpful in understanding the pathway that is specific to each client. A sample form for collecting information about a youth's family background appears in Appendix B.

EDUCATIONAL INFORMATION

A youth's experience in school often influences how he/she feels about him/herself. An adolescent who gets good grades, is liked by his teachers, and has peer-aged friends is more likely to feel stable and secure. Many of the criminogenic issues that contribute to sexually abusive behavior are reflected in problems that emerge in a school setting. Special education classifications, academic/learning difficulties and disabilities, and social problems are common among youth who engage in sexually abusive behaviors. Thus, gathering information about school adjustment and intellectual functioning is helpful in determining specific issues that might need to be addressed in treatment (social awkwardness/isolation) or how treatment might need to be delivered, such as in cases where a learning disability makes completing written treatment assignments difficult.

Again, it is also important to gather subjective information to determine how the youth feels about his/her school experience and whether, for example, a youth's difficulty in school reflects a defeatist attitude. Such an attitude can affect the child's willingness or ability to engage in treatment efforts, particularly if those efforts involve written work (treatment worksheets or homework assignments).

A sample form for collecting information about educational background is presented in Appendix C.

LEGAL AND OFFENSE-RELATED INFORMATION

Although the term "sexual offender" connotes that an individual has broken a municipal, state, or federal law, the nature of the behaviors that result in this label vary widely. Obtaining adequate information to understand the nature of the offense usually requires access to the information used in the legal process that resulted in the charges and adjudication, which is usually referred to as "discovery". In some cases, adolescents are mandated into treatment without a legal adjudication (or in lieu of a legal adjudication) and, in those cases, it is important to obtain as much information as possible about the sexually abusive behavior from sources other than the youth. The self-report of offenders (or anyone else) about their misdeeds is often colored by self-interest and justification. Listening to the rationalizations and justifications that our clients use to excuse their behavior is helpful in understanding the types of thinking errors and underlying cognitive schemas that will need to be addressed in treatment; however, it usually does not give us accurate information about what actually occurred in the commission of the offense(s). Although it is common for youth to provide incomplete and, at times, misleading information when initially assessed, it is important to keep in mind that it is not done maliciously to con the therapist, but rather, it is due to shame and embarrassment about their behavior.

In addition, it is important to gather information about other issues relating to legal status. Does the adolescent have other sexual offenses? Other non-sexual offenses? Has the adolescent been under legal supervision, such as probation or parole? If so, what was his or her adjustment to these conditions and did the youth comply? All of these important questions need to be answered in order to use the RNR model.

The legal and offense-related information will provide some understanding of the reasons the client is being referred for treatment. This can be found in police reports, charge sheets, judgments of conviction, and victim statements. Some clients, particularly those with conduct disorders, develop an extensive relationship with local criminal justice authorities due to the persistent nature of their criminal behavior. It is important to know the legal status of the youth since local laws differ in how these crimes are managed. A sample form for collection of these data is displayed in Appendix D.

INITIAL ASSESSMENT INFORMATION/DEVELOPING TREATMENT GOALS

Prior to engaging a youth in treatment, it is important to determine the issues that warrant treatment intervention. Although this truism seems self-evident, many programs developed in the 1980s and 1990s (including those developed by one of the authors of this chapter and carried out by the other) were created based on widely-accepted notions of the most common kinds of problems that lead to sexually abusive behavior. This clinical lore (Chaffin, 2009) guided the development of many structured treatment programs for adults and juveniles with illegal and hurtful sexual behaviors. With our research base expanding, this scattershot method has been replaced by a more modern understanding of the nuanced causes and contributors to sexual offenses and the development of programs tailored to each individual client's presenting problems.

Considering this, a thorough assessment of the strengths and problem behaviors of any client is necessary prior to the assignment of a treatment regimen (Leversee, 2010). This is accomplished by first reviewing all of the documentation and then interviewing the client and, if possible, other collateral sources. It is not unusual for outside administrators or supervisors to suggest just "putting him into a group" without any kind of intake assessment. As mentioned earlier, however, it is not good practice for a number of reasons. The youth might not be appropriate for the treatment setting, or the style of treatment offered might not be appropriate for that particular youth.

There are several good sources for suggested interview content in this area: Leversee's chapter in Ryan, Leversee and Lane (2010) *Juvenile Sexual Offending: Causes, Consequences, and Correction*; Rich's (2003) excellent *Understanding Assessing and Rehabilitating Juvenile Sexual Offenders*; and the O'Reilly and Carr chapter in Barbaree and Marshall's (2006), *The Juvenile Sex Offender*.

A recommended way to obtain initial assessment information and develop treatment goals is to complete one of the common risk assessment instruments as a part of the process. Often, a risk assessment was done during the legal process and, if so, it should include treatment and management recommendations, which can then be used to guide the clinician in treatment planning. If this was not done, we strongly recommend that the clinician score the youth on one of the commonly used risk assessment instruments, such as the J-SOAP-II (Prentky & Righthand, 2003). Conducting an assessment and/or intake interview while being guided by this instrument, or comparable instrument, such as the ERASOR (Worling, 2004) or the J-RAT (Rich, 2009), provides a structured way to obtain data necessary for both risk assessment and treatment planning. The manual for the J-SOAP-II notes that the instrument was intended as an "aid in the systematic review of risk factors that have been identified in the professional literature as being associated with sexual and criminal offending" (Prentky & Righthand, 2003, p. 1).

Some of the most researched items in risk assessment instruments are static in nature in that they are data points locked in time (e.g., number and gender of victims, age at initiation of sexually abusive behavior, history of own sexual victimization) and cannot change. Although they are usually easier to code on the scoring sheet, they cannot be changed through therapeutic interaction. Many of the items contained in the J-SOAP-II, ERASOR, and similar instruments examine common dynamic risk factors. Dynamic risk factors are those risk factors that can change with treatment intervention, such as poor coping skills, distorted views of acceptable relationships and deviant sexual arousal. As a result, we recommend that treatment programs regularly assess dynamic risk factors, such as the intervention and community stability/adjustment scale from the J-SOAP-II.

The JSORRAT-II (Epperson, Ralston, Fowers, DeWitt & Gore, 2006) has preliminary data to support its use in risk assessment, but most of the items are static in nature and of little help in the development of treatment goals. Still, its actuarial nature and ongoing research provides more scientific support for its use as a risk assessment tool, but for treatment planning purposes, we recommend using either the J-SOAP-II, ERASOR, or J-RAT protocols. In addition to using these instruments for treatment planning, it is also important to ascertain what strengths and assets (protective factors) the youth brings to therapy. These strengths contribute to the youth's resilience and ability to live a crime-free lifestyle (Bremer, 2001), and directly answer the responsivity aspect of the RNR model.

Many risk factors have been identified in the literature as contributing to sexually abusive behaviors. Rich (2009, p. 118) lists 101 factors grouped into six categories in his book, *Juvenile Sex Offenders: A Comprehensive Guide To Risk Evaluations*. These factors reflect the wide variety of problems that are encountered in the ongoing assessment of adolescents (and adults) who are referred for sexually abusive behavior. Some of these problems are common while others are rare. Our clinical task for this process is to identify the problems that led the youth to commit the sexual offense(s) and to create a treatment strategy that will teach our clients to achieve their needs though prosocial behaviors and actions.

There are multiple pathways by which clients commit harmful sexual behaviors. As such, it is necessary to examine a variety of possible contributors to the offending behaviors, with more attention directed toward the problem areas that are both evidence-based and present in the clients we are assessing. In addition, given the complexity and diversity of these pathways, the clinician and program should remain flexible while trying to understand the causes. On occasion, information is disclosed during the treatment process that can radically change our understanding of the major issues of concern.

The form in Appendix E-1 offers guidelines to assist the clinician in the process of obtaining basic information during an assessment interview. Clinicians will need to investigate other avenues of discussion that emerge in the context of the discussion to discover the underlying motives for dysfunctional behavior and potential new skills the client needs to learn to live a law-abiding and stable lifestyle. Obtaining adequately informed consent and having clients and parents sign release forms is absolutely necessary. Readers are referred to Kinscherff & Latham (see Chapter 1) for an excellent discussion of informed consent and assent.

The form in Appendix E-2 offers an example of a basic treatment plan that is very quick to complete and individualized to address the needs of the client. Printed off as a whole, the reader sees a sample treatment plan with an initial section with header, biographical data and strengths and needs listed. Each problem is a separate file picked from a larger list of possible problems and inserted into the treatment plan as indicated by the needs of the specific case. The ending section, like the first section are boiler-plate and include a place where the clinician includes a small amount of case-specific information about issues that are relevant to the case, but will not be addressed in the context of the treatment program. In the example, the client is noted as having five problems that will be addressed in the context of the program, and progress in addressing these issues is noted in the ongoing treatment documentation (monthly or weekly progress notes addressed in the next section).

TREATMENT PARTICIPATION AND GOAL ATTAINMENT

Almost all program-funding agencies expect regular reports that document client participation and progress in meeting treatment goals. The nature of this documentation varies considerably depending on the context of the treatment and the source(s) of funding. At one time, many funding sources simply wanted the most basic of documentation resembling an audit of services offered with few references to treatment content or effectiveness (e.g., the program conducted eight intake assessments,

22 individual sessions and eight weekly group sessions.). Such treatment information might be sufficient to maintain funding, but says little or nothing about the effectiveness of the services offered.

Currently, it is incumbent on program developers and managers to ensure that services offered are effective and contribute to a safer society. Although the most obvious marker of treatment effectiveness is a reduction in sexual offense recidivism, such data are difficult to obtain and often not mandated by funding sources. As a proxy for treatment efficacy, there are any number of intermediary indicators that demonstrate that clients are on their way toward meeting established treatment goals. Intermediary objectives should be those factors that have been empirically linked to re-offending, be addressed in the context of the treatment, and should be measurable. Minnesota mandates that such a process be implemented in any program that receives state funding (Listiak, 2003).

In the current adult sex offender program developed by one of the authors (JB), the monthly individual Treatment Progress Report form consists mostly of issues borrowed from the Stable and Acute 2007 (Hanson, Harris, Scott & Helmus, 2007). Integrating this instrument into the ongoing treatment progress report focuses the attention of clinicians on the research-supported issues of relevance and eliminates cursory statements such as "client attended and participated". We recommend doing something similar, such as using the dynamic risk factors in the J-SOAP-II to structure clinicians' thinking and record keeping of progress in treatment.

Another critical recommendation is to create documentation that is precise and easy to complete. The more time-consuming and complicated the paperwork, the greater the struggle it is for managers to get clinicians to maintain adequate documentation. For example, in a previous program, creating a treatment plan was relatively simple, but involved a time-consuming written project that took about half an hour. Clinicians required cajoling to complete the plans in a timely manner. In order to reduce the need for intervention by program administrators, a treatment planning system was created that allowed an individualized treatment plan to be created for each client in less than 5 minutes using the power of the modern word processor.

Important information relevant to the youth's attainment of specific treatment objectives, participation in treatment activities (group and individual), and investment in the process should be included in treatment progress reports. The report should also include mention of any treatment-interfering behaviors that are exhibited by the client, such as disruptiveness in the group setting or failure actively to participate. If the program is housed in a residential or correctional setting, it is also important that some documentation be included that addresses the client's adjustment on the housing unit.

If done correctly, treatment progress documentation will identify the issues that warranted treatment intervention, the efforts of therapists to address these issues, and the client's progress toward attaining mastery over these problem areas. Appendix F includes examples of this type of documentation. Sample F-1 is being used by an adult program and is based on items from the Stable and Acute 2007. A similar form could be created using the J-SOAP-II or any one of the instruments that incorporate dynamic risk factors that are amenable to change through structured therapeutic activity.

In 2006, one of the writers of this chapter (JTB) was approached to develop a state-wide program for 1000 high-risk adult offenders under lifetime supervision. Major problems with prior services included lack of standardization in treatment and lack of adequate documentation. The legal supervisors of the clients (parole officers of the Sex Offender Management Unit) complained repeatedly that local private treatment providers simply did not provide adequate or timely documentation of their services, and the parole officers could not tell where the clients were in their treatment process and what issues were being addressed.

The resulting program documentation was developed to include an Individual Progress Report sent monthly to each parole officer for every client in treatment under that officer's supervision. To make this work, a form was developed that documented weekly group attendance, progress in addressing identified problems and overall status in treatment (Appendix F-1). This form constitutes documentation for both distribution to the parole officers as well as documentation for our clinical files. The form for each client takes a minimal amount of time for clinicians to complete.

Sample F-2 was used in a secure facility for juveniles in response to administration complaints that the narrative treatment progress notes were incomprehensible and meaningless and a request that letter grades be assigned indicating treatment progress. Although letter grades offer an imprecise measure of treatment progress, the numerical scoring system offers many avenues for graphing progress toward attaining established treatment goals.

DISPOSITIONAL RECOMMENDATIONS

Dispositional recommendations are an important part of documenting treatment for sexually abusive youth. As a client leaves our services, we want future clinicians and/or supervisors to know what occurred in our treatment setting and what kinds of issues remain unaddressed. This is particularly true for issues that affect risk to the community.

Treatment can be discontinued in a specific setting for a number of reasons: the youth might have completed his course of treatment and is ready to be reintegrated into the wider community without treatment supports; the youth has completed his mandated sentence in a juvenile correctional facility and is being released to the community with the understanding that treatment will continue as he/she is reintegrated into the community; or youth whose treatment needs require more intensive intervention could be transferred to a more secure or therapeutic location. Dispositional considerations are particularly important to consider when youth are assigned to situations that are likely to be short term.

It is expected that clinicians who have provided services to the youth will have a good idea of the strengths and needs of the client. In many cases, change of the youth's disposition is a direct result of the clinician's recommendations, as in the case of treatment completion or transfer to a more intensive treatment setting. Even in the case of a youth's release from incarceration (where the clinician has no input into the timing of the release decision), carefully considered dispositional recommendations should be included in the treatment documentation. For example, a youth in a secure-care or residential treatment center who will be returning home will need his or her parent(s) or caretaker(s) to be involved in the treatment process prior to release.

Such dispositional recommendations should include a complete record of what kinds of services the youth has received, the specific objectives addressed in treatment to date, the progress that the youth has demonstrated toward attainment of goals, and remaining targets for treatment, if any. It is most important that this includes the remaining risk issues and factors dictating safeguards that should be in place for a risk management plan to maintain the youth safely in the community. This should include the youth's risks and needs, and recommendations about how to address these issues, such as whether he will need to be supervised around children. Appendix G includes examples of the types of information to be included in dispositional recommendations.

Documenting program services is an integral part of providing the services. It is also complicated because it involves meeting the standards of several different organizations with competing agendas. State licensing boards, certifying organizations, private agencies and legal entities can all have an impact on what kinds of records are created and kept. These influences may be totally separate from the clinical needs of our assessment and treatment services. In the Apendices of this chapter, we provide sample forms for review.

APPENDIX A

TREATMENT SERVICES INTAKE

Client Name: Last ______________________ First: ________________________

AKAs: ____

DOB: __________ County: ________________ State ID#: ________________

Parents/Last Home Address: Street ____________________________________

City/Township: ___________________________ Zip: ____________________

Parents Phone: Home ________________________ Cell __________________

Probation Officer: ________________________ Phone: ____________________

Therapist: _______________________________ Phone: ____________________

(If client was adjudicated while in treatment)

Legal Status:

Current Charge: ____

Adjudicated: __ Pled Guilty: __ Found Guilty: __ Pre-Trial Intervention: __

Judge: ___________________________

Medical Information:

Last time client had a physical: _________________

Provided by or in what setting? ______________________________________

Any medical complaint by client or by history? _________________________

____

Psychiatric history: ____

Does the youth report any head injuries? ___ What other issues are relevant?

____

____ (append as necessary)

APPENDIX B

FAMILY BACKGROUND

Born and lived where? ______________________________

Parents?

Mother: ______________________________

Father: ______________________________

Siblings?

Brothers: ______________________________

Sisters: ______________________________

(note birth order).

Approximate SES? ______________

Who lives/lived in the home? Who is the youth living with or expects to live with once he/she leaves the program?

____

Who does the youth feel closest to in the home?

____

Who is the youth closest to outside the home?

____

Who else is important in the youth's life and why?

____

____

How will this offense/charge affect the youth's living environment?

____

____

Criminal history in family? ______________________________

Mental illness/psychological problems in family? ______________

____

Child Protective Services history?

____

APPENDIX C

EDUCATIONAL/VOCATIONAL BACKGROUND

Last/current school attended? ____

Last/current grade in school? ____

Special Education Classification? ___ If yes, what kind? ________________

If youth has a Special Education Classification, please review the Individual Educational Plan and note problems below.

____

Are any IQ tests available?___ If yes, what type of test? When administered? Results?

____

What kind of grades did the youth obtain in school?

Youth's report? ____________ From school sources? ________________

How does the youth feel he/she did in school?

____

History of suspensions/expulsions/in-school suspensions?

____

____

Favorite subject in school? _______________________________________

Involvement in extra-curricular activities (sports/music/etc.) what kind and how did it go? ____

____

Does the youth feel he/she was "popular" in the school? ______________

____

How does the youth anticipate that this charge will affect being in school?

____

____

Has youth worked in the past? ___ If yes, where/doing what? ___________

____

APPENDIX D

LEGAL/OFFENSE OR PROBLEM BEHAVIOR INFORMATION

Final legal charge: ______________________________

Original charges: ______________________________

Date adjudicated: ______________________________

Any prior allegations of sexual offenses? ___ If yes, describe: ______________
____

Any prior non-sexual offenses? ___ If yes, describe: ______________
____

Are there any indications of gang membership? ___ If yes, what gang:
____

Has youth been under legal supervision? ___ If yes, describe response: _____
____

Probation violations? ___ If yes, describe: ______________
____

Has youth ever run away from home? ___ If yes, describe circumstances:
____
____

Has the school reported behavior problems necessitating suspension or expulsion? ___ If yes, describe: ______________

Note any evidence of antisocial behavior not mentioned above: _________
____

Is there evidence that the youth responds to adult guidance/counseling? ___ If yes, detail: ______________
____

APPENDIX E

1 INITIAL ASSESSMENT/DEVELOPING A TREATMENT PLAN

Youth's understanding of the reasons for his referral: ____________________

____

Youth's level of admission to the instant offense: ____________________

____

Youth's recognition of a need for treatment: ____________________

Does youth express a willingness to cooperate with assessment/treatment:

____

____

Youth's biggest fear (about offense or treatment): ____________________

____

Youth's description of offense: ____________________

_

____

Youth's description of reasons for offense (if there is an admission): ______

____

Specific Risk and Needs Assessment: (append when necessary)

Living circumstances: ____________________

_

Caregiver consistency: ____________________

Attachment to family/others: ____________________

Family characteristics, note: hyper-religiosity, homophobia, mental illness, criminality: ____________________

____

____

Evidence of psychological problems: ____________________

____

Evidence of impulse control problems: ______________________________

____

Evidence of emotional self-regulation problems: ______________________

____

Does youth express a sense of entitlement? __________________________

____

History of traumatic experiences:

Physical abuse: ____

Sexual abuse: ____

Witness DV: ____

Note youth's reactions to traumatic events: ___________________________

____

Social interactions:

Youth's self-perception of relationships: ___________________________

____

Youth's social/interactional skills with adults: ______________________

____

Adeptness at handling current situation: ____________________________

____

Anger management issues: _______________________________________

Criminal attitudes: ____

Hostile attitude: ____

History of physical altercations with peers: __________________________

____

Other antisocial behavior/involvement with antisocial peers: ___________

____

____

Sexuality:

Client self-identification of sexual orientation: ______________________

Consensual peer-aged partners: ______________________________________

____

Masturbatory behavior: ____

____

Favorite fantasy: ____

____

What went "wrong" that resulted in the current offense: _______________

____

Any signs of deviant sexual interest? ___ If yes, describe: _______________

____

Youth's perception of what s/he needs to learn to avoid a reoccurrence:

____

____

Gender of victim: _________ Age of victim(s): _________ Evidence of planning: ____

Evidence of sexual preoccupation: ___________________________________

Does youth use sex to manage problem emotions? ____________________

____

Threats/coercion in the commission of the offense: ___________________

____

Protective factors and positive leisure activities:

Positive relationships with parents/adults: __________________________

____

Prosocial involvement: ____

____

Youth's response to intervention (to this point): ______________________

____

Does youth demonstrate empathic concern or remorse (and how)? ______________________________

____

Leisure activities: ______________________________

____

Substance Abuse Problems: ______________________________

____

Treatment Plan/Treatment Goals – Issues that will be addressed in the context of treatment:

(List here the specific goals that will be addressed in structured treatment, the indicators that signal resolution of the issue, the method whereby the treatment will be delivered and the anticipated timeframe for resolution.)

2 ADOLESCENT TREATMENT SERVICES: INDIVIDUALIZED TREATMENT PLAN

Name: **DOB:** **SBI#:** **Date:**

Clinician:

Conditions for Discharge	Client will complete sexual offense-specific therapy and address the following issues that resulted in prior sexually offensive behavior.
Strengths:	(List assets here)
Needs:	(List deficits here)
Problem:	**Goals/Interventions:**
No Motivation for Treatment	Client will recognize their sexual offending behavior as a problem. Client will express a desire to change that behavior. Client will begin to use therapy as an opportunity to address problems.

	Intervention: Therapist will provide feedback to increase the desire to directly address the causes and consequences of sexually abusive behavior. This will occur in group or individual therapy.
Difficulty Managing Anger	Client will attend an anger and aggression management training module. Client will demonstrate the ability to handle anger in a role-play situation. Client will demonstrate the ability to appropriately handle potentially volatile situations in their day-to-day life. **Intervention:** Therapist will provide an anger and aggression management training module.
Criminal Attitudes	Client will explore their value system and identify attitudes that condone or accept criminal behavior. Client will express a need to live a pro-social lifestyle. Client will express empathic concern and respect for the rights of others. **Intervention:** Therapist will provide group treatment that addresses uncaring and/or criminal attitudes.
Disruptiveness	Client will recognize that disruptive behavior in the group setting is unacceptable. Client will refrain from distracting/oppositional behavior. Client will listen and participate actively in the treatment process. **Intervention:** Therapist will provide behavioral direction to counter

(*Continued*)

	interference with group functioning. If the behavior becomes too disruptive, the client will be asked to leave the group and the client's Parole Officer will be informed.
Social Skills Deficits	Client will attend basic social skills classes. Client will demonstrate these social skills in the class setting. Client will demonstrate the ability to use social skills in day-to-day situations. **Intervention:** Therapist will provide social skills training using role-play exercises in a group therapy setting.

The previous problems are all identified with this client, and will be addressed in the context of offense-specific sex offender group therapy. Progress in meeting these goals will be documented in the Group and Individual Treatment Progress Note forms. Monthly reports to the supervising officer will note these accomplishments and other impressions that will assist in the supervision process.

The following problems are also noted, but will not be dealt with in the context of our specialized treatment. Appropriate referrals will be made for issues that are amenable to intervention in this setting, i.e., need of medication referral, educational and vocational training, or referral to DDD authorities.

Special considerations:

APPENDIX F

Client Name: Group Phase/Day/Time:
Month/Year: Number of Groups Attended: of (Logo Here)
Probation/Parole Officer: Clinician:

Phase 1 Tasks___ (check when parolee has completed all tasks)

___ Learned the sexual offense laws of the state of New Jersey.
___ Learned the general and speciific conditons of parole supervision.
___ Accepts responsibility for the charged offense
___ Indicates willingness to participate in sexual offense-specific treatment.

Phase 2 Tasks___ (check when parolee has completed both major tasks).

___ Completed a Safety Plan based on Relapse Prevention principles
___ Completed the Sexual Assault Cycle/Event Chain tool indicating an understanding of the events and circumstances that led to the charged offense.

Specific problems addressed by the parolee this month: (these dynamic factors have the strongest ties to recidivism)

___ Intimacy Deficits: (capacity for relationship stability, ability to interact honestly, and showing caring for others).
___ Sexual Self-Regulation: (using sexuality as a way to cope, understanding healthy sexuality in intimate relationships, and being free of deviant sexual arousal).
___ Attitudes Supportive of Sexually Abusive Behavior: (a sense of sexual entitlement, attitudes that are tolerant of forced sex, or sexual abuse of children).
___ Cooperation with Supervision: (willingness to live with external controls, avoiding illegal activities, and maintaining a good relationship with Parole authorities).
___ General Self-Regulation: (avoiding impulsive acts, angry hostile attitudes and behaviors and learning socially appropriate problem-solving skills).

Particular High Risk Issues of Concern:

___ Deviant Sexual Desire/Arousal
___ Emotional Identification with Children
___ Negative Emotionality (angry at everything)
___ Unwillingness to Cooperate with Treatment/Supervision

Date:	General Group Topic:	Personal Group Involvement (level of participation, willingness to participate in and investment in the treatment process – learn new things, and willingness to lead a crime-free lifestyle).
		This form, designed for an adult program shows how ongoing clinical documentation can be combined with an individualized Monthly Progress Report given to Parole Officers. It combines the research-supported elements of the Stable and Acute-2007 with the "legacy" elements required by the funding agency.

2 GROUP NOTE FORM

Client: ___________________ Date of Service: ________________________

Parole Officer: ________________________ Group Phase: ______________

Treatment Topic: ____

Positive	(scale)	Negative
Group Participation Style:		
Attentive to others	5 4 3 2 1 0	Only interested in self
Adds to group discussion	5 4 3 2 1 0	Takes discussion "off track"
Cooperative/compliant	10 8 6 4 2 0	Oppositional
Interested in topic	5 4 3 2 1 0	Disinterested
Open to feedback	10 8 6 4 2 0	Resistant/defensive
Discloses own issues	5 4 3 2 1 0	Withdrawn/evasive or quiet
Positive leadership	5 4 3 2 1 0	Negative leadership
Criminogenic Needs/Attitudes:		
Prosocial attitudes	10 8 6 4 2 0	Antisocial attitudes
Concern for others	5 4 3 2 1 0	Low victim empathy
Reality-based thinking	5 4 3 2 1 0	Cognitive distortions
Understands risk factors	5 4 3 2 1 0	Denies potential risk factors
Open and honest with ideas/concerns	5 4 3 2 1 0	Manipulative or deceitful
Level of denial:		
Admits to facts of offense	5 4 3 2 1 0	Denies occurrence of offense
Accepts responsibility	5 4 3 2 1 0	Blames victim or others
Recognizes preplanning/precursors	5 4 3 2 1 0	Claims spontaneity
Acknowledges need to avoid high risk situations	10 8 6 4 2 0	Denies potential of future offending

Total Points __________ (out of 100 possible)

Comments:

____

____

____

____

____

____

____

Facilitator: ____________________________________

Facilitator: ____________________________________

APPENDIX G

DISPOSITIONAL RECOMMENDATIONS

Current Date: ________________ Client Intake date: ________________

Client involvement in treatment activities:
Number of group therapy sessions attended: ____________
Number of individual sessions attended: ____________

Has client created a Safety Plan? _______________

Can client be considered to have completed sexual offender treatment?
____

Is further treatment recommended? __________ If so, specify recommendations: ____

Main issues addressed in treatment activities: ________________________

____

____

What problems were sufficiently resolved through treatment (sexual and non-sexual)? ____

____

What problems remain unresolved (sexual and non-sexual)? __________

____

____

Primary safety issues remaining: _____________________________

____

Suggested ways to maintain safety in the community (risk management plan):

____

____

What other clinical recommendations are made for this youth? ________

____

REFERENCES

Andrews, D. A., & Bonta, J. (2006). *The psychology of criminal conduct* (4th ed.). Newark: LexisNexis.

Andrews, D. A., Bonta, J., & Hoge, R. D. (1990). Classification for effective rehabilitation: Rediscovering psychology. *Criminal Justice and Behavior, 17*, 19–52.

Barbaree, H. E., & Marshall, W. L. (Eds.). (2006). *The juvenile sex offender* (2nd ed.). New York: Guilford Press.

Bremer, J. F. (2001). *Protective factors scale: Determining the level of intervention for youth with harming sexual behavior*. St Paul: Project Pathfinder.

Chaffin, M. (2009). Can we develop evidenced-based practice with adolescent sex offenders?. In R. E. Longo & D. S. Prescott (Eds.), *Current perspectives with sexually aggressive youth and youth with sexual behavior problems*. Holyoke: NEARI Press.

Colorado Sex Offender Management Board (2002). *Standards and guidelines for the evaluation, assessment, treatment and supervision of juveniles who have committed sexual offenses*. Denver: Colorado Department of Public Safety, Division of Criminal Justice, Office of Domestic Violence and Sex Offender Management.

Epperson, D. L., Ralston, C. A., Fowers, D., DeWitt, J., & Gore, K. S. (2006). Actuarial risk assessment with juveniles who offend sexually: Development of the Juvenile Sexual Offense Recidivism Risk Assessment Tool – II (JSORRAT-II). In D. Prescott (Ed.), *Risk assessment of youth who have sexually abused: Theory, controversy, and emerging strategies*. Oklahoma City: Wood N Barnes.

Hanson, R. K., Harris, A. J. R., Scott, T. L. & Helmus, L. (2007). *Assessing the risk of sexual offenders on community supervision: The dynamic supervision project*. User Report, Corrections Research. Ottawa: Public Safety Canada. Available at <www.ps-sp.gc.ca/res/cor/rep>.

Leversee, T. (2010). Comprehensive and individualized evaluation and ongoing assessment. In G. Ryan, T. Leversee, & S. Lane (Eds.), *Juvenile sexual offending: Causes, consequences, and correction*. New York: John Wiley & Sons.

Listiak, A. (2003). Minnesota Rules, Chapter 2955: *Residential treatment of juvenile sex offenders: Guidelines and resources for the basic treatment protocol, therapeutic milieu, and quality assurance/program improvement plan*. St Paul: Minnesota Department of Corrections.

Prentky, R. A., & Righthand, S. (2003). *Juvenile sex offender assessment protocol-II: Manual*. Washington, DC: Office of Juvenile Justice and Delinquency Prevention.

Rich, P. (2003). *Understanding, assessing, and rehabilitating juvenile sex offenders*. Hoboken: John Wiley & Sons.

Rich, P. (2009). *Juvenile sex offenders: A comprehensive guide to risk evaluation*. Hoboken: John Wiley & Sons.

Ryan, G., Leversee, T., & Lane, S. (Eds.), (2010). *Juvenile sexual offending: Causes, consequences, and correction*. New York: John Wiley & Sons.

Smallbone, S. W. (2006). An attachment-theoretical revision of Marshall and Barbaree's integrated theory of the etiology of sexual offending. In W. Marshall, Y. Fernandez, L. Marshall, & G. Serran (Eds.), *Sexual offender treatment: Controversial issues*. New York: Wiley.

Steen, C., & Monnette, B. (1989). *Treating adolescent sex offenders in the community*. Springfield: Charles C Thomas.

Worling, J. R. (2004). The Estimate of Risk of Adolescent Sexual Offender Recidivism (ERASOR): Preliminary psychometric data. *Sexual Abuse: A Journal of Research and Treatment, 16*, 235–254.

CHAPTER 19

Practical Strategies for Working with Youth with Intellectual Disabilities who have Sexual Behavior Problems

Gerry D. Blasingame
Training, Program Development, and Consultation, Redding, CA, USA

INTRODUCTION

Youth with intellectual disabilities or autism spectrum disorders who have sexual behavior problems or who have offended sexually are a diverse group of young people (Blasingame, 2005, 2011). Youth with various disabilities are overrepresented in the juvenile justice system and are challenged by a number of issues including prior victimization and neglect, emotional disturbances, and disproportionally high levels of mental disorders (Gagnon & Richards, 2008; Quinn, Rutherford, Osher, & Poirier, 2005). As such, we clinicians need to appreciate the uniqueness of each youth and adapt accordingly when engaging in the treatment process.

This chapter begins with a review of the effects of impairments in cognitive functioning on the individual. Next, we introduce several evidence-based principles for guiding intervention, treatment, and case management. Strategies for engaging, educating, and empowering parents are then suggested. Finally, we offer a variety of practical checklists of ideas and forms to assist clinicians in organizing clinical information to best formulate individualized intervention plans.

EFFECTS OF IMPAIRMENTS IN COGNITIVE FUNCTIONING

For youth with intellectual disabilities, autism spectrum disorders, or other learning disabilities, their levels of cognitive functioning and comprehension have wide reaching effects on their choices and actions. These also have a significant effect on how interventions can be adapted for the individual. The most accessible information about cognitive functioning is

Toolkit for Working with Juvenile Sex Offenders.
DOI: http://dx.doi.org/10.1016/B978-0-12-405948-1.00019-0

often found in the youth's individual education plan (IEP) and psychological testing from their school. Reviewing the index and individual scale scores from intellectual quotient (IQ) testing can be much more informative than a simple look at a full-scale intellectual quotient (FSIQ) score. The following information – based primarily on the structure of the Wechsler Intelligence Scale for Children, fourth edition (WISC-IV; Wechsler, 2003) – summarizes what each index is intended to measure.

Verbal Comprehension Index

This group of scales captures capacities in the individual's ability to reason abstractly, volume of acquired information, social and practical knowledge and judgment, understanding reasons for social rules or concepts, and basic word knowledge and fluency. Impairment in this domain affects the person's abilities in understanding verbal information, social comprehension, dealing with questions and answers, thinking with words, and expressing thoughts in words.

Perceptual Reasoning Index

This group of scales captures capacities in the individual's abilities with abstract visual analysis and problem solving, attention to detail, abstract categorical reasoning, and general, fluid intelligence. Some of the simpler test items are solved by using concrete representations, such as color or shape. More complex test items require greater reasoning and use of more abstract representations, such as the function of an object. Impairments in this domain affect the person's abilities in solving non-verbal problems, using eye–hand coordination, and working quickly and efficiently with visual information.

Working Memory Index

This group of scales captures capacities in the individual's ability to pay attention to information while performing a task or manipulating the information, visual–spatial imaging, auditory memory, short-term auditory memory, and concentration. Weakness in working memory and concentration makes processing complex information more time consuming and requires more mental energy compared to others one's own age for the same task. This can lead to more errors on a variety of tasks. Impairments in this domain affect the person's abilities in maintaining attention, concentration, and ability to use short-term auditory memory.

Processing Speed Index

This group of scales captures capacities in the individual's visual–motor coordination, speed of information processing and concentration, short-term memory, accuracy with a copying task, and visual discrimination. These tests measure an individual's ability to perform cognitive tasks fluently and automatically, particularly when under pressure to maintain focus and concentration. Good processing speed enables access to the content being held in the working memory; poor processing speed would make it difficult to access that information which may be available only temporarily. Impairments in this domain affect the person's abilities with mental processing speed, visual attention, visual motor coordination, cognitive flexibility, attention and motivation.

Full-Scale Intellectual Quotient

The full-scale intellectual quotient (FSIQ) is one way to summarize an individual's overall thinking and reasoning skills. There are times, however, when the FSIQ is not a valid score and should be ignored (American Psychiatric Association, 2013). When there is an abnormal discrepancy between the index scores or within the subtests, the FSIQ may not accurately reflect a solitary construct. In such cases, it is best to focus on the individual indices, such as verbal comprehension and perceptual reasoning scales to estimate current cognitive functioning.

One could simply say that all or nearly all index scores are low when working with a youth who has been diagnosed with an intellectual disability. But that can miss the point. A low score on any individual subtest or index can be informative regarding the clinical interactions with each individual.

Appreciating the specific affects of impairment measured on these index scales can give clinicians a more empathic understanding of the unique learning challenges faced by each youth with intellectual disability. This increased empathy and understanding can empower clinicians when tailoring interventions for the individual rather than just adopting a one-size-fits-all strategy. While some intervention strategies may be relatively universal, such as use of plain language or treating all people with dignity and respect, there are individual adjustments that need to be considered depending on each youth's strengths and weaknesses. Clinicians making these adjustments are likely more effective in engaging the youth – and their parents – in the therapeutic process.

Take Jon for example. His FSIQ was reported to be in the mild intellectual disability range. Although his verbal comprehension index score was estimated at 72, his processing speed index was at 57 and his working memory index was estimated at 60. While these discrepancies between scores are modest, the differences do suggest that Jon will need his clinician to adjust:

- the vocabulary that is used in speech and in writing
- how much information is presented at any given time
- how often information may be repeated or reviewed, and
- how much time is allowed to process that information.

A clinician who is used to working with neurotypical youth whose memory and processing are in the normal range might fail to break the information into smaller units or allow more time mentally to process that information. Similarly, a clinician who is used to working with youth with typical functioning might assume that *since Jon says* he understands what he is being told that he actually does understand it – when, in reality, he does not but wants to appear as if he did. The verbal comprehension index score in the borderline intellectual functioning range might be misleading particularly when Jon gives a socially desirable response, e.g., he says *yes, I understand* or shakes his head in the affirmative. Or Jon may understand at a very superficial level but he has not sufficient understanding of the concept or the context in which the concept applies; he knows the vocabulary word so he tells the clinician he understands. It would be helpful to have Jon elaborate on what he has heard or reports that he understands. Seeking Jon's feedback moves the communication to a more meaningful level.

Or we could consider Bob and Frank. They both have a FSIQ of 67. While at first blush this might make one think they learn the same way, they do not. They also came to the FSIQ of 67 differently. Bob is really good with puzzles and has a high processing speed index score but is very low on the other indices; his FSIQ averages to 67 despite a large spread between index scores. On the other hand, Frank's scores on all four indices are in the same range, suggesting his verbal comprehension may be stronger than Bob's since his average, the FSIQ, is comprised of four index scores that are all similar. Bob and Frank will respond differently to clinician communications despite having the same FSIQ score.

GUIDING PRINCIPLES FOR EVIDENCE-BASED CASE PLANNING

Many overarching evidence-based strategies that apply to neurotypical youth who have offended apply similarly with youth with intellectual disabilities. The human service principles of *risk, need, and responsivity* (RNR), as well as use of evidence-based treatment and fidelity to the RNR model, are well supported in the youth criminal justice literature (Andrews & Bonta, 2003; Hoge & Andrews, 2011; Land, Ralph, Rasmussen, Miccio-Fonseca, & Blasingame, 2013; Latessa, 2006). Simply stated, these principles can help guide the overall assessment and intervention planning process. When adhered to faithfully, following the RNR principles helps facilitate a reduction of delinquency and crime.

The risk principle instructs us to apply supervision and intervention strategies based on the level of risk for re-offense the focus person is estimated to present (Hoge & Andrews, 2011). For example, a youth who is determined to be a low risk for re-offense can effectively be intervened with and managed using a much lower intensity than a youth determined to be a high risk. High-risk youth need a much greater degree of supervision, monitoring, treatment, and accountability than does a youth who presents as a low risk.

Mixing the low- and high-risk youth in a group may run the risk of increasing the actual risk of the low-risk youth while being ineffective in addressing the greater needs of the high-risk youth. Contamination in this context is a significant clinical concern. The dosage, intensity, and duration of treatment and supervision should match the level of risk presented by the individual youth. Rather than one-size-fits-all programming that is simply based on the type of offense the youth committed, e.g., offending sexually, applying the risk principle allows us to develop differential levels of treatment and supervision.

The need principle instructs us to focus our interventions on the life issues that matter in the specific case before us (Andrews & Bonta, 2003). There are common needs identified for the general population of delinquent juveniles that apply with youth who have intellectual disabilities. These include the youth's history of criminal misconduct, educational needs, familial and relational needs, alcohol or drug use, and antisocial or undersocialized thinking patterns (Hoge & Andrews, 2011).

Additional needs for youth who have exhibited sexual behavior problems or who have offended sexually must also be addressed. These include their own trauma history, types and levels of sexually maladaptive behaviors, socio-sexual knowledge and skills, maintaining healthy boundaries, and difficulties with sexual self-regulation (Blasingame, 2005, 2010).

The responsivity principle instructs us to adapt how we intervene with the individual before us (Andrews & Bonta, 2003; Hoge & Andrews, 2011). There are a number of elements that contribute to the individual's responsivity, including level of motivation, cognitive functioning, ethnicity and cultural issues, and the settings in which interventions will occur.

Youth with intellectual disabilities present with varying levels of motivation to engage in treatment or the change process. These youth and their families may have presuppositions or fears about what treatment will be or should be like. These expectations may be positive or negative but effect the initial interactions with clinicians nonetheless. Parents may fear their son will not be treated fairly or with consideration of the effects of having a developmental disability. Adhering to the responsivity principle, clinicians need to prioritize identifying the best way to engage and motivate the youth and his parents in order to maximize the benefits of interventions.

The treatment principle instructs us to use evidence-based strategies in our intervention and supervision efforts (Andrews & Bonta, 2003). Most often these are described as cognitive-behavioral strategies. Fortunately, these strategies have long been utilized with individuals with intellectual disabilities and have strong support in the literature (see Blasingame, 2005, 2011). Treatment is discussed in greater detail below.

The fidelity principle (Andrews & Bonta, 2003) instructs us that if we adhere to the RNR principles outlined above, there is a greater likelihood of achieving our goal of less delinquency or criminal conduct. Modifying interventions based on an individual's level of risk and his specific treatment needs, and delivering services in ways that connect and fit well for the youth and his family makes for a win–win situation, i.e., the youth avoids further problems and has a better life, his parents are assisted and empowered, and the community benefits as well.

Clinical application of the RNR principles instructs us that having every youth complete every assignment on a long checklist of therapy tasks is not clinically appropriate. Rather, thoughtfully selecting the specific areas of need for the individual youth will help formulate an intervention plan that fits well for the individual and his family.

For example, 13-year-old Lamar was asking his 8-year-old female cousin (who happens to be at his developmental age level) how to masturbate on one occasion. He has no prior sexual misconduct or delinquency, has done well with peers and in his academic programming, has involved and supportive parents, has no history of verbal or physical aggression, and has no alcohol or drug history.

In Lamar's case, it would not make clinical sense to require him to complete treatment modules on anger management or drug education. It would be more appropriate to work with Lamar on sexual boundaries, with whom it is okay to talk with about sexual matters, the rights and wrongs of sexual behavior, and the rules about private parts. He does not need intervention on anger or drug use. It would also not be appropriate to enroll Lamar in a 2-year treatment group with 16- and 17-year-old boys who committed contact offenses of child sexual abuse, indecent exposure, or sexual assault and who have anger problems. Lamar could easily be negatively influenced by these "peers". More appropriately, Lamar is likely to benefit most from time-limited individual and family counseling. Bringing his parents into the mix helps engage their support of his therapy, helps them better understand how to approach Lamar's sexual education needs, and empowers them to be the effective parents they want to be.

Henry, on the other hand, is a different case. Henry was diagnosed with mild intellectual disability at age 5 and attention deficit hyperactivity disorder when he was 6. Henry was 13 the first time he was reported to have fondled and penetrated three grade school-aged girls in his neighborhood. Although it was reported, he was not adjudicated because of his diagnosis of mild intellectual disability. He did not receive therapy but was told "don't be nasty anymore" by his parents. He did it one more time when he was 14 before the other family moved away. When Henry was 16, new children moved into the neighborhood and the apartment complex down the street. Henry was prone to roam around and his parents often did not know where he was. He told them he was just out playing games with his friends. As it turned out, some of his friends were drinking alcohol, smoking marijuana, and looking at pornography on the Internet. These friends were sometimes nice to him but joked about him being dumber than them. He would sometimes fight with them when he was mad. Twice Henry was caught stealing beer from a local mini-market. He said it was okay to do because he wanted to drink like his dad. Henry also had other friends who were not as old as he; they were in grade school. They were never rude or mean to him. He felt more comfortable with these younger friends. Sometimes when he was aroused from looking at pornography, without his older friends, he would go play with the younger friends. That play took on a lot of sexual comments and eventually led to Henry engaging in fondling, digitally penetrating, and coaxing the younger girls and boys to orally copulate him. He stopped looking at the pornography because he thought the kids were "more sexy". He told the kids not to tell about their fun as he did not want *them* to get into trouble for being nasty. This went on for about 6 months. One of the boys asked his uncle if he wanted him to do the same behavior; the uncle was appropriately alarmed and facilitated a report to local law enforcement. During the investigation, it was learned that Henry had been physically abused by his father on many occasions. Henry was adjudicated and eventually placed in a group home with other youth with intellectual disabilities who have offended sexually.

Based on the RNR principles discussed above, Henry needs a very different intervention plan than Lamar. Henry's case reveals a significantly higher number of risk factors and areas of clinical concern. Henry's level of risk appears to be high and his therapeutic needs are many and complex. Henry is a good candidate for a more traditional treatment plan with a much more comprehensive list of therapy tasks. While family therapy is also indicated, it is not likely to take on prominence in Henry's treatment due to being in placement 6 hours away from where his parents live. The group home treatment program will need not only to address Henry's identified needs but also help him prepare for the transition to adulthood and the possibility of independent living once he reaches age 18.

While these two case examples may be at the extremes of a continuum, they serve the purpose of underscoring the value of considering the risk, need, and responsivity principles when developing a case plan. Individualizing the case plan for each youth allows us to tailor treatment interventions in effort to not over- or under-pathologize the problematic sexual behavior; adjusting treatment, dosage, intensity, and duration is aided by application of these guiding principles.

EVIDENCE-BASED INTERVENTION STRATEGIES

People with developmental disabilities were historically subjected to disrespectful, humiliating and sometimes painful or abusive conditions (Blasingame, 2010; Dykens, 2006) in the name of "effective treatment". There is, however, a growing body of research demonstrating how challenging behaviors can be improved with positive, non-aversive behavioral interventions and supports (Reid, Parsons, Rotholz, Braswell, & Morris, 2004). Therapeutic intervention and supports with youth with intellectual disabilities have a growing base of evidence-based and promising practices which practitioners now can utilize. Some of these are described briefly below.

Positive Behavioral Support

Positive behavioral support (PBS) is a set of evidence-based strategies used to increase quality of life and decrease problem behavior by teaching new skills to replace problem behaviors and by making changes in a person's environment (Association for Positive Behavior Support, 2008). However, PBS is *not* a specific practice or curriculum, rather PBS is a general approach to preventing or changing problem behaviors. The PBS schema assumes that:

- behavior is learned
- problem behavior is linked to and reinforced by environmental factors
- behavior change occurs through manipulation of environmental factors as well as intervention with the focus person directly.

PBS involves interventions and supports that are multidimensional and include:

- implementing antecedent and setting event prevention strategies (i.e., preventing precursors that create the environment in which the acting out occurs)
- teaching replacement skills (i.e., teaching prosocial ways to get one's needs met)
- using non-aversive consequence or response strategies
- using positive reinforcement and extinction (Moskowitz, Carr, & Durand, 2011).

PBS emphasizes intervention strategies that:

- fit for the individual and the context where they are implemented
- prioritize the focus person's needs, goals and values
- consider the goals, values, skills, and resources of the family or other care givers (Carr, Dunlap, & Horner, 2002; Moskowitz et al., 2011).

In PBS, the term *support* refers to the use of procedures and strategies to enhance personal competencies (such as developing social and self-calming skills) and systemic changes to create healthier environments in which those competencies can be used to promote a good quality of life (Carr, 2007; Gagnon & Richards, 2008). Interventions need not only to facilitate behavior change but also sustain those changes by ensuring the support efforts will continue once professional interventions are withdrawn. With youth with intellectual disabilities, the system changes usually need to occur in family, peer, and school contexts (Gagnon & Richards, 2008). It is critical to empower parents and families in their efforts to support behavior change and maintenance.

Self-determination

Self-determination has been defined as having "a combination of skills, knowledge, and beliefs that enable a person to engage in goal-directed, self-regulated, autonomous behavior" (Jones, 2012, p. 32). The success of self-determination depends on the individual's capacity for self-determination *and* on the environment's support for the individual to make choices and exert control over his or her own life (Jones, 2012). Self-determination increases intrinsic motivation (Ryan & Deci, 2000) and encourages engagement in the treatment and change process.

Competence with several skill sets is needed to establish high levels of self-determination (Wehmeyer & Schwartz, 1997). These include skills in the following areas:

- choice making
- decision making
- problem solving
- goal setting and attainment
- self-observation
- self-evaluation
- self-reinforcement
- internal locus of control
- positive attributions of efficacy and outcome expectancy
- self-awareness.
- self-knowledge.

Helping youth with intellectual disabilities acquire these skill sets enables them to have increased socio-sexual competence in their peer relationships.

Cognitive-Behavioral Treatment

Cognitive-behavioral treatment (CBT) strategies involve changing how a person thinks, what the person thinks about, and how the person acts. CBT has a significant body of research demonstrating its effectiveness for use with adolescent offenders (Latessa, 2006) and with persons who have intellectual disabilities when modified appropriately (Blasingame, 2005, 2014). CBT practitioners use cognitive strategies to correct the individual's pro-criminal thinking or attitudes supportive of misconduct through a process known as cognitive restructuring. Self-correction of one's thinking errors or *wrong way thinking* (Blasingame, 2005) enables the individual to modify the beliefs, thoughts or values that previously supported criminal or abusive conduct. CBT practitioners also use behavioral strategies to teach a variety of skills in an effort to develop prosocial skills, such as those listed above in the self-determination section, that enable the individual to get their needs met in prosocial ways. CBT strategies such as these show the greatest impact on recidivism. These include:

- cognitive restructuring
- specific skill trainings
- use of role play and experiential learning
- liberally using positive reinforcement, and
- interventions that can be rehearsed and generalized outside the treatment setting.

The *Developmentally Disabled Sexual Offender Rehabilitative Treatment* program (DD-SORT; Blasingame, 2005) is one example of the application of CBT principles in the treatment of individuals who have offended sexually. The DD-SORT treatment materials are based on CBT principles, including relapse prevention, and offer modified program assignments using plain language addressing a number of treatment areas relevant to youth with intellectual disabilities or autism spectrum disorders. The cognitive interventions include *Stop That!* (thought stopping), identifying *Danger Zones* (high-risk factors or situations), the *Ladder to Trouble* (cycle of negative behavior), *Wrong Way Thinking* (cognitive distortions or thinking errors), and *Smart Plans* (relapse prevention plans). Behavioral interventions include role play and exercises to teach a variety of social skills, self-regulation, and problem solving.

Positive Youth Development

Positive youth development (PYD) is a newer movement in the field of working with youth in the juvenile justice system (Butts, Mayer, & Ruth, 2005). Although there is yet to be published literature on the efficacy of this approach specifically with youth with intellectual disabilities, PYD approaches focus on developing positive, prosocial capacities by using the resources available within the focus person's home and community. Building on concepts such as the *40 Developmental Assets* (Theokas, Almerigi, & Lerner, 2005) and self-determination (Jones, 2012; Wehmeyer & Schwartz, 1997), PYD strategies reach far beyond the therapy room, enabling much more holistic interventions by capitalizing on resources in the youth's community. These help move the youth towards his maximum level of autonomy, self-direction, healthy social interaction, and positive contribution to society.

ENCOURAGING PARENTAL PARTICIPATION

Being strategic to engage, educate, and empower parents can be very helpful in the course of helping youth with intellectual disabilities overcome a variety of behavioral problems, including sexual problems. Below are some suggestions for how to approach parents in ways that invite connection and support.

Engaging the youth's parents is a critical aspect of initiating community-based intervention. The following ideas are offered to encourage consideration of how clinicians can reflect on their own attitudes, how these might affect clients, and how they might attempt to engage with parents:

- Acceptance: how does my attitude towards resistant, reluctant, or resentful parents come through?
- Alignment: does my attitude reflect an interest in joining with their family to achieve their goals?
- Aspiration: do I reflect a hope and intentionality that invites the parents to join with my efforts to join them?
- Emphasize optimism about people's ability to change and grow
- Emphasize the desire to work collaboratively
- Emphasize the positive outcomes we are working towards for their son and them
- To engage parents and family members
  - Find strengths to start with; start on a positive footing
  - Avoid an overt deficit focus as this is alienating and humiliating
  - Inquire about their interests and the positive elements of life they would like their son or daughter to have
  - Inquire about their own lives and how can we work together to help them achieve better lives.

Educating the youth's parents is another important element of the youth's treatment and interventions. It is beneficial for parents to become armed with accurate information and stronger skills as they are called upon to be partners in their child's treatment.

- Develop goals *with* the parents and the youth
- Identify how to achieve those goals
- Identify more helpful skills for their child to develop in order to replace the behaviors that have not been as helpful
- Teach the parents the skills and involve them in teaching their child
- Implement personalized goal-attainment strategies
- Support the belief that they can achieve these goals

- Tactfully and discretely address the parents' own learning disabilities, trauma histories, thinking errors, or minimizations if present
- Be careful to not mistakenly imply the parent is to blame
- Teach parents about issues so that they can teach their child about the issues.

Empowering the youth's parents is also desired as well as engaging and educating them. Empowered parents are better able to intervene, and are excellent allies in the collaborative process of intervention and supervision.

- Help parents identify positive alternative ways to get one's needs met. They can then model and assist in teaching the youth about these pro-social skills. This process creates competing behaviors that reduce need for maladaptive behavior
- Help parents promote approach goals and skill acquisition while also avoiding risky situations that might undermine self-regulation
- Help parents provide positive reinforcement to their child for even the smallest efforts towards the approach goals
- Use empowering vocabulary, such as:
  - Self-management instead of relapse prevention as if it is inevitable to re-offend sexually
  - Self-regulation instead of compliance with demands
  - Sexual and social health instead of presuming deviant motives
  - Self-control with the new skills learned in therapy
  - Collaboration instead of conformity or control.

Developing treatment goals and case plans can be a complicated process. Given the nuances of the youth's intellectual disabilities, his individual risk level, underlying needs that drive his maladaptive sexual behavior, and familial and contextual variables, it can take some real effort to create an individualized case plan. It may be helpful to use the *Youth's Strengths and Family Resources Inventory* located below to assist the clinician at the beginning of the plan development process.

Sometimes case plans are developed that have the right goals but the wrong expectations. For example, supporting and improving self-determination is an excellent goal. It may, however, be misguided if the youth has yet to establish self-control of his sexual urges and desires. Better would be to prioritize self-control before self-determination. Thinking through the sequence of interventions and basic skill sets that need to be acquired before other skills trainings are attempted can prevent frustrations for the youth, the family, and the clinician. Parent input can help tremendously in this regard; they likely have many stories to tell that could elucidate the best "first steps".

Some youth and their families are involved with a number of service providers. These might include behavior specialists, special education teachers, individual aid staff persons, other relatives, independent living skills instructors, mentors, or transportation personnel. And, of course, each of these providers has their own service plan that places expectations on the youth and his parents. It can be overwhelming to parents to have more demands placed on their time, energy and resources by clinicians who are intent on change the youth's sexual behavior repertoire. Also, it can be very frustrating for parents to have their goals and values disregarded by these many services providers, including the clinicians, who may not share the parents' values. This makes it even more critical to engage and discuss the treatment goals and expectations with parents to ensure their support and increase the likelihood of their follow through with the home-based elements of intervention.

An area that exemplifies this potential values conflict is sexual expression. Because of the focus on addressing problematic sexual behavior, there can be conflicts of values. Some parents' values are expressed more overtly than others. Some parents are disinclined to discuss sexuality with their child while some are perhaps too open about adult sexuality. Likewise, some parents maintain relatively low levels of supervision while others have been described as "helicopter parents" who hover too closely for the youth to have the opportunity to experiment socially in those areas that are unlikely to be done in front of parents, i.e., exploring and expressing sexual behaviors such as masturbation, learning about "making out", or appropriate sexual involvement with an age typical peer. Discussing proposed interventions and strategies with parents in advance can be helpful in adjusting the sequence of interventions, allow for changes in plans as treatment unfolds, and creates the greatest level of normalization experiences for the youth.

Drawing from the concepts discussed in the chapter above, here is a suggested series of steps for developing realistic treatment goals and expectations in concert with the youth and his parents.

1. Gather thorough information from all the stakeholders, including the youth, his parents, and others who will be involved in the intervention(s).
2. Formulate a hypothesis of the youth's level of cognitive capacities, risk level, and the needs that underlie or drive his maladaptive

sexual behaviors. Use the *Stop & Go! Intervention Plan* format (discussed below) to organize tentatively the case plan information.

3. Consider youth- and parent-specific idiosyncrasies, strengths, and communication styles in order to establish an effective therapeutic relationship. Adjust therapist style and engagement strategies accordingly.
4. Discuss the tentative contents of the *Stop & Go! Intervention Plan* with the parents and youth. Consider, with the parents or other care providers, if the proposed interventions and strategies will fit or match with the parents' goals and parenting style.
5. Adjust and implement the treatment plan based on parent and youth feedback:
   a. Establish priorities and sequence of interventions
   b. Accept that some non-sexual behavior problems may need to be addressed prior to addressing sexual behavior problems
   c. Modify delivery strategies to fit the familial context
   d. Adapt materials to accommodate the youth's cognitive needs
   e. Integrate parents within the intervention plan.
6. Re-evaluate progress on the *Stop & Go! Intervention Plan* every few months, and adapt accordingly.

PRACTICAL CHECKLISTS AND FORMS

The following tools are intended to help clinicians be thoughtful about intervention strategies and collaborative relationships as well as to organize the assessment and intervention planning process.

Clinical Adjustments Quicknotes

As discussed above, there are a number of challenging areas for clinicians who have limited experience working with youth who have intellectual disabilities. The great majority of youth with mild intellectual disability interact with others without obvious impairments; they need less social or communicative supports than youth who are more affected (American Psychiatric Association, 2013). Keeping these characteristics in mind will help when making adjustments in working with these youth.

The *Clinical Adjustments Quicknotes* are intended to provide clinicians with an easy reminder list for adjusting how they intervene with these youth. Several of the problem areas are drawn from the *Diagnostic and Statistical Manual of Mental Disorders, fifth edition* (American Psychiatric Association, 2013).

Clinical Adjustments Quicknotes

Problem area	Suggested clinical adjustments
Limited vocabulary: cognitive functioning in the mild ID range implies the youth's vocabulary will be limited to that of about the fifth grade level	Adjusting all verbal and written communication to the early grade level will increase comprehension and retention. Also, asking the youth to define or give an example of something may provide the clinician with insight into the youth's actual comprehension rather than simply the recognition or feigned recognition of vocabulary words. Creating a mutually understood vocabulary of treatment concepts will also be helpful
Concrete thinking: concrete thinking and limited comprehension of social communication can contribute to a lack of insight, empathy, and abstract thinking	Adjusting for this will require clinicians to be highly pragmatic with more black and white illustrations or examples in communication so as to not place an unrealistic expectation on the youth's cognitive capacities. Beginning with rote memorization, using linear and non-abstract examples in teaching, and clearly labeling behavior as okay or not okay are examples of helpful adaptations
Impaired executive functioning: executive functioning refers to a number of cognitive and emotional tasks that are impaired for those who have intellectual disabilities or autism spectrum disorders. Executive functioning includes planning, decision making, problem solving, updating memory, and shifting attention from one task to another	Impairments in executive functioning decrease thoughtful, planned, and organized behavior. Some researchers have identified that youth with intellectual disability function more closely with younger persons yet who are the same developmental age (Danielsson, Henry, Ronnberg, & Nissson, 2010). Particularly helpful adjustments include minimizing distractions while the youth is encoding new information, using simple concepts or bytes of information, providing reminders and prompts to help recall of prior learned information, and assisting the youth to establish his own structure or sequence for problem solving. Most youth are benefited by providing visual aides, role plays, and gestures within experiential exercises that help rehearse use of the learned information
Socially immature: having a condition that isolates socially, many youth with intellectual disability are marginalized by peers and sometimes by their own family members. This in addition to their learning challenges undermines acquisition of age-typical social skills and competencies	Experiential training of the skills topics discussed above regarding self-determination will go a long way towards improving the youth's social competencies. Adjusting one's approach when communicating can be accomplished by revising one's expectations based on the youth's developmental age rather than chronological age. As the clinician models age-appropriate social interaction the youth is exposed to opportunities to socialize towards a higher level of maturity. Making referrals to community resources which include normalizing social opportunities is another way to incorporate positive youth development strategies and expand the youth's exposure to prosocial influences

Problem area	Suggested clinical adjustments
Emotional dysregulation: problems with overall cognitive functioning and problem solving may leave many of these youth with inadequate strategies to cope with their emotions	Since many will react to rather than regulate their emotions, it may be helpful to teach self-calming and self-control skills before delving into emotionally provocative discussions. Rehearsing deep breathing and coping skills in different venues, including at his home and during different emotional states, will help the youth be able to implement the skill outside the therapy session. Teaching these skills to parents or care providers will help with generalization
Difficulty with social cues: social and non-verbal cues are important aspects of human communication. Individuals who have cognitive impairments or autism spectrum disorders often have difficulty in reading social cues	It can be helpful specifically to teach the youth about various facial cues by using one of the commonly available charts of faces with different expressions, rehearse those expressions, and use the expressions to communicate without the use of words. Using role plays to focus on various verbal and non-verbal elements of communication can be fun and informative
Co-morbid neurodevelopmental or mental health issues: many youth with intellectual or other developmental disabilities also have co-morbid diagnosis	It may be necessary in some cases to treat these other conditions before engaging the youth in treatment for the sexual misconduct. For example, a youth with attention deficit hyperactivity disorder may need to begin treatment with medication before he can focus sufficiently to benefit from sexuality focused interventions. Or a youth with an autism spectrum disorder may first need additional adjustments in treatment approaches, such as use of Pivotal Response Training or Parent–Child Interaction Therapy to address the core issues of the autism spectrum condition (Blasingame, 2011)
Unable to perform academic functions independently:most youth with intellectual disabilities are unlikely to be able to complete traditional treatment homework	The cumulative effect of the impairments caused by intellectual disabilities diminishes the person's capacities for independent functioning. Clinicians should be cautious when assigning treatment homework. Adjusting the assigned material to the youth's level of cognitive functioning and enlisting the assistance of his parent or care provider is a good starting point. Apart from losing assignments or forgetting to do them, many youth are just not sufficiently organized to sit down and complete an emotionally challenging task unless provided therapeutic support; it may be necessary for the clinician to use sessions to do assignments rather than sending them home with the youth. These issues underscore how critical it is to involve the youth's parents or other care providers in effort to help the youth generalize treatment concepts outside the clinical setting

Documents Needed Checklist

It is not at all uncommon for youth with intellectual disabilities to have been involved with a number of different agencies and evaluators. These include developmental disability agencies, schools, speech and language therapists, psychologists, etc. Documentation from these resources often includes nuances about the youth that may not be easily solicited from parents unless one knows to inquire in a particular area. In some cases, file information may be contradictory or have large information gaps. With all due respect, juvenile probation reports are often incomplete or inattentive to characteristics associated with intellectual disabilities. Gathering as much background information about the youth, what agencies are involved in the youth's life, and a record of past interventions that did or did not work are helpful.

The *Documents Needed Checklist* is intended to assist clinicians performing intake assessment and case planning by reminding them of these various information resources.

Documents Needed Checklist

This checklist is for ______________________________ Date ______________

Check here when applicable	Document needed	Date requested	Date received	Check here when referral needed
	Developmental history			
	Social history			
	Prior psychological evaluations			
	Developmental disability agency report			
	Neuropsychological assessment			
	Cognitive assessments including subscale findings			
	Adaptive skills assessments			
	Individual educational plan records			
	Medical records			
	Medication list			
	Police reports			
	Child protection agency reports			
	Behavioral incident reports			
	Court reports			
	Probation and pre-sentencing reports			
	Foster home reports			
	Group home reports			
	Psychiatric hospital records			
	Recreation assessment			
	Audiology assessment			
	Wrap-around Assessment			

Potential Stakeholders Roster

Similar to the comments above regarding these youth having a variety of records from being involved with multiple agencies, it is likely that a youth with intellectual disabilities who is referred for treatment related to sexual behavior problems will have a number of professionals or stakeholders participating in their lives (Blasingame, 2014).

The *Potential Stakeholders Roster* is intended to remind clinicians of all the possible resource people in the youth's life. These include family members, professionals, and other people in the community who may be resources. Applying the Positive Youth Development concepts to case planning requires us to expand the intervention plan beyond simply focusing on the problematic sexual behavior. Rather, we need to call upon additional community resource people who can offer supports that will enrich the youth's life beyond correction of a sexual problem.

Potential Stakeholders Roster

This list of stakeholders is for ______________________________ date __________

Name	Phone number	Role	Date contacted
		Parent: mother	
		Parent: father	
		Step-parent:	
		Step-parent:	
		Guardian or conservator	
		Involved relative:	
		Involved relative:	
		Developmental Disability Agency case manager	
		Probation officer	
		Group home administrator	
		School teacher or administrator	
		School psychologist	
		Behavior specialist	
		Psychiatrist	
		Medical doctor	
		Attorney	
		Clergy	
		Tutor	
		Recreation program	
		Treatment program mentor	
		Community mentor	
		Sports team coach	

Youth's Strengths & Family Resource Inventory

Youth with intellectual disabilities, and all youth for that matter, need a number of resources in their lives in order to have optimal social, psychological and behavioral health. There is an extensive literature regarding indicators of positive outcomes in youth's lives.

The *Youth's Strengths & Family Resource Inventory* is not intended to be completed by the youth's parents; it should be completed by the clinician. This is a checklist that assists the treating clinician or case manager to identify individual, familial, and other resources that are known to be positive indicators of overall psychosocial health and stability. Identifying areas of strength or weakness can be helpful in case planning.

Youth's Strengths & Family Resource Inventory

Strength and resource area		Yes	No
1	Father completed college		
2	Father completed high school		
3	Mother completed college		
4	Mother completed high school		
5	Both parents are emotionally available for youth		
6	Both parents live in home with youth		
7	Mother's extended family provides emotional support to youth		
8	Father's extended family provides emotional support to youth		
9	Parents have active involvement in community (church, sports, organized social activities) or engage in volunteer activities		
10	Both parents are employed full time		
11	One parent is employed full time		
12	Parent(s) are able to support family without State aid		
13	Family has meals together at least three days a week		
14	Family has health insurance and easy access to healthcare		
15	Parents speak positively of youth's teachers		
16	Parents communicate with youth's teachers regularly		
17	Parents model effective and caring communication		
18	Parents model violence-free relationships		
19	Parents model drug-free lifestyle		
20	Parents do not drink alcohol to intoxication		
21	Parents model high value on education		
22	Father has no crime record		
23	Mother has no crime record		
24	Family friends model prosocial lifestyle		
25	Youth has caring and warm relationship with father		
26	Youth has caring and warm relationship with mother		
27	Youth has caring and warm relationship with sibling(s)		
28	Youth has no prior crime history		
29	Youth has no alcohol use history		
30	Youth has no drug abuse history		
31	Youth has positive relationship with teacher		
32	Youth has friendship with peers away from school setting		
33	Youth has prosocial peers who are a good influence		
34	Youth has not been sexually abused		
35	Youth has not been neglected		
36	Youth has not been physically abused		
37	Youth has not been bullied or harassed by peers		
38	Youth has prosocial mentors and role models apart from parents		
39	Youth is involved in social activities (sports, church, organized activities)		
40	Youth is involved in volunteer activities		

Stop & Go! Intervention Plan

Traditional treatment using relapse prevention strategies tend to focus on avoidance goals. Avoidance goals are important, particularly those involving not putting one's self in an environment in which the risk of re-offending sexually is increased. For some youth these might include being alone with young children, looking at pornography, or using sexualized thinking or behavior as a way to cope with frustrations or loneliness.

Approach goals are all about acquiring life skills and competencies that enable a better life. These include learning how to make and keep age-appropriate friends, developing self-calming skills, learning about healthy sexual expression, learning effective problem-solving skills, etc.

People are more intrinsically motivated when they are acquiring something rather than just stopping a behavior. Simply avoiding certain situations or experiences does not replace the faulty behavior. Consistent with the positive behavioral supports and self-determination strategies discussed earlier, it is important to focus also on approach goals and replacement skills to enable the youth also to have a better quality of life. Combining the avoidance and approach strategies is important. The two sets of goals can be pursued and achieved simultaneously.

The *Stop & Go! Intervention Plan* is intended to individualize case planning with the participation of the youth, his parents or care providers and the treating clinician or case manager. Stop items are the avoidance goals; Go items are the approach goals. Here is a sample *Stop & Go! Intervention Plan* and a blank form to use.

Stop & Go! Intervention Plan

This Stop & Go! Plan is to help ________________________ Date _____________

Stop	Go!	How it will help me!	Who is helping?
Being alone with kids younger than me	Learn to make friends my own age	I will have my own friends to spend time with and have fun	Me; my counselor; my parents; my mentor; my teacher at school
	Learn about my sexual feelings and how to be a normal teenager	I can feel good about having normal sexual feelings and behavior	Me; my counselor
Hitting people	Learn to handle my feelings without getting mad or hurting others	I will feel better about getting along with people and will be able to keep friends	Me; my counselor; my parents; my mentor; my teacher at school
Spending all my time looking at nasty pictures	Learn ways to handle my feelings and calm myself down	I will do better about actually handling my problems	Me; my counselor; my parents

Stop & Go! Intervention Plan

This Stop & Go! Plan is to help ________________________ Date _____________

Stop	Go!	How it will help me!	Who is helping?

SUMMARY

Youth with intellectual disabilities, autism spectrum disorders, or other learning disabilities are overrepresented in the juvenile justice system (Quinn et al., 2005). While experiencing a number of challenges, these youth are responsive to treatment and interventions that are adapted appropriately to their developmental age and level of cognitive functioning.

There are a number of cognitive and social challenges these youth face. Clinicians can deepen their understanding of each youth by reviewing the intellectual testing in greater detail. More specifically, the index scale scores from IQ testing can be very informative about how the youth is functioning in different domains, with implications for how the clinician can adjust interventions to be of greatest benefit to the individual client.

Using the risk, needs, and responsivity schema as an overarching set of strategies for case planning and intervention allows clinicians to tailor the treatment, dosage, intensity, and duration of services based on each individual client. Since these youth are each unique and have different strengths and challenges it is important to avoid one-size-fits-all thinking and programming. The RNR schema is well supported in the literature and is useful with youth involved with the juvenile justice system.

Likewise, use of evidence-based treatment strategies and methodologies is well supported in the literature. Positive behavioral supports, applied self-determination theory, cognitive-behavioral therapeutic interventions, fully embracing parents as partners in intervention, and use of positive youth development strategies are all highly applicable for our work with youth with intellectual disabilities who have sexual behavior problems.

In this chapter, we have reviewed these areas and offered insights into adjustments to be made by treating clinicians and case managers to best engage these youth and their parents in the therapeutic process. Hopefully, readers are not only more informed but also more empathic and understanding as they endeavor to assist these youth in achieving their best quality of life.

REFERENCES

American Psychiatric Association. (2013). *Diagnostic and statistical manual of mental disorders* (5th ed.). Arlington: American Psychiatric Association.

Andrews, D., & Bonta, J. (2003). *Psychology of criminal conduct* (3rd ed.). Cincinnati: Anderson Publishing Co.

Association for Positive Behavior Support. (2008). *What is positive behavioral support?*. Bloomsburg: Association for Positive Behavior Support. Available: <www.apbs.org>.

Blasingame, G. (2005). *Developmentally disabled persons with sexual behavior problems* (2nd ed.). Brandon: Safer Society Press.

Blasingame, G. (2010). Prevention of sexual violence involving persons with developmental disabilities. In K. Kaufman (Ed.), *The prevention of sexual violence: A practitioners sourcebook*. Holyoke: NEARI Press.

Blasingame, G. (2011). *An introduction to autism spectrum disorders, sexual behaviors, and therapeutic intervention*. Holyoke: NEARI Press.

Blasingame, G. (2014). Assessment, diagnosis, and risk management of sexual offenders with intellectual disabilities. In A. Phenix & H. Hoberman (Eds.), *Sexual offenders: Predisposing conditions, risk assessment and management*. Springer (in press).

Butts, J., Mayer, S., & Ruth, G. (2005). *Focusing juvenile justice on positive youth development*. Chicago: University of Chicago, Chapin Hall Center for Children. Issue Brief #105.

Carr, E. (2007). The expanding vision of positive behavioral support: Research perspectives on happiness, helpfulness, hopefulness. *Journal of Positive Behavior Interventions*, *9*(1), 3–14.

Carr, E., Dunlap, G., Horner, R., et al. (2002). Positive behavior support: Evolution of an applied science. *Journal of Positive Behavior Interventions*, *4*, 4–16.

Danielsson, H., Henry, L., Ronnberg, J., & Nissson, L.-G. (2010). Executive functions in individuals with intellectual disability. *Journal of Research in Developmental Disabilities*, *31*(6), 1299–1304.

Dykens, E. (2006). Toward a positive psychology of mental retardation. *American Journal of Orthopsychiatry*, *76*, 185–193.

Gagnon, J. C., & Richards, C. (2008). *Making the right turn: A guide about improving transition outcomes of youth involved in the juvenile corrections system*. Washington, DC: National Collaborative on Workforce and Disability for Youth, Institute for Educational Leadership.

Hoge, R. D., & Andrews, D. (2011). *Youth level of service/case management inventory 2.0 (YLS/CMI). Users' manual*. North Tonawanda: Multi-Health Systems.

Jones, J. L. (2012). Factors associated with self-concept: Adolescents with intellectual and developmental disabilities share their perspectives. *Intellectual and Developmental Disabilities*, *50*, 31–40.

Land, R., Ralph, N., Rasmussen, L., Miccio-Fonseca, L. C., & Blasingame, G. (2013). *Guidelines for the assessment and treatment of sexually abusive juveniles*. California Coalition on Sexual Offending. Available: <www.ccoso.org>.

Latessa, E. (2006). Effectiveness of cognitive behavioral interventions for youthful offenders-review of the research. In B. Glick (Ed.), *Cognitive behavioral interventions for at-risk youth*. Kingston: Civic Research Institute.

Moskowitz, L., Carr, E., & Durand, M. (2011). Behavioral intervention for problem behavior in children with Fragile X syndrome. *American Journal on Intellectual and Developmental Disabilities*, *116*, 457–478.

Quinn, M. M., Rutherford, R., Osher, D., & Poirier, J. (2005). Youth with disabilities in juvenile corrections: A national survey. *Exceptional Children*, *71*, 339–345.

Reid, D., Parsons, M., Rotholz, D., Braswell, B., & Morris, L. (2004). *Positive behavior support training curriculum: Supervisory trainees' resource guide*. Washington, DC: American Association on Mental Retardation.

Ryan, R., & Deci, E. (2000). Self-determination theory and the facilitation of intrinsic motivation, social development, and well-being. *American Psychologist*, *55*, 68–78.

Theokas, C., Almerigi, J., Lerner, R., et al. (2005). Conceptualizing and modeling individual and ecological asset components of thriving in early adolescence. *Journal of Early Adolescence*, *25*, 113–143.

Wechsler, D. (2003). *Wechsler intelligence scale for children* (4th ed.). San Antonio: The Psychological Corporation.

Wehmeyer, M. L., & Schwartz, M. (1997). Self-determination and positive adult outcomes: A follow-up study of youth with mental retardation or learning disabilities. *Exceptional Children*, *63*, 245–255.

CHAPTER 20

Integrating Families into Treatment for Adolescents with Illegal Sexual Behavior

Susan R. Schmidt
Center on Child Abuse and Neglect, University of Oklahoma Health Sciences Center, Oklahoma City, OK, USA

INTRODUCTION

Adolescents with illegal sexual behavior (AISB) represent a highly diverse population with regard to individual characteristics and functioning (Chaffin, Letourneau & Silovsky, 2002). Likewise, the families of AISB differ, spanning a broad range from intact and well-functioning to highly chaotic and abusive (Finkelhor, Ormrod & Chaffin, 2009). Historically, AISB were treated using a one-size-fits-all relapse prevention approach originally designed for and implemented with limited success in adult sex offender treatment. This approach took into account little regarding the relationship of family and social ecology to youth sexual delinquency. Additionally, it failed to account for the fact that sexual behavior and sexual offense recidivism are not the sole problems for many of these youth. Across numerous AISB treatment outcome studies, non-sexual delinquent behavior was vastly more prevalent than sexual recidivism (Alexander, 1999; Caldwell, 2002; Reitzel & Carbonell, 2007). Also, many AISB present with multiple problems in addition to their sexual behavior, including learning disabilities, social isolation, attention deficit hyperactivity disorder (ADHD), drug or alcohol problems, family instability or conflict, school or academic problems, delinquent peer affiliations, limited social or courtship skills, or general difficulties with judgment and self-control (Bonner, 2008).

Fortunately, as our knowledge of AISB has grown, so has our understanding of this population's diverse intervention needs and the relevance of family and social ecology to successful treatment and long-term delinquency risk reduction. Current best practices in AISB treatment include cognitive-behavioral (Becker & Kaplan, 1993; Kahn & LaFond, 1988)

Toolkit for Working with Juvenile Sex Offenders.
DOI: http://dx.doi.org/10.1016/B978-0-12-405948-1.00020-7

and ecological multisystemic approaches (Swenson, Schoenwald, Randall, Henggeler & Kaufman, 1998).

COGNITIVE-BEHAVIORAL APPROACHES

Cognitive-behavioral approaches to AISB treatment focus on changing attitudes and belief systems contributing to illegal sexual behavior. Interventions target increasing social skills, improving anger management, and teaching self-control techniques (McGrath, Cumming & Burchard, 2003). Cognitive-behavioral treatment is often carried out in a peer group environment (i.e., outpatient therapy, group homes, specialized residential units) with varying degrees of parental involvement across programs (Reitzel & Carbonell, 2007). Some programs focus solely on youth treatment with limited parental participation, while others actively integrate parents or other caregivers into the treatment curriculum.

Although a number of cognitive-behavioral treatment programs have published outcome data showing low sexual and non-sexual recidivism rates for youth who completed their programs, no study has been conducted to compare the outcomes for AISB randomly assigned to cognitive-behavioral treatment versus AISB who complete no treatment. This next level of research is needed within the field specifically to evaluate the effectiveness of the cognitive-behavioral approach in reducing AISB recidivism. There is evidence that AISB who complete treatment fare better than youth who do not, who drop out of treatment, or who are expelled from treatment. In their study of a cognitive-behaviorally based community-based AISB treatment program, Worling and Curwen (2000) compared recidivism rates for 58 youth who completed treatment to 90 adolescents who received an assessment only, refused treatment or dropped out of treatment. They found that youth who completed treatment had significantly lower sexual (5.17% vs 17.8%), violent non-sexual (18.9% vs 32.2%) and non-violent (20.7% vs 50%) recidivism rates than youth who failed to complete treatment.

Additionally, active parental participation in treatment appears to be critical to AISB treatment success and future non-delinquency. A 10-year review of 220 AISB participants from one outpatient cognitive-behavioral treatment program found that the strongest single predictor of successful treatment completion was caregiver involvement (Chaffin, Bonner & Swisher, 2005). Caregiver program participation also significantly predicted future rates of delinquency – the higher the rate of caregiver attendance, the greater the chance that the youth successfully completed treatment and the lower the youth's risk of future sexual and non-sexual recidivism.

MULTISYSTEMIC APPROACHES

Several evidence-based delinquency interventions have been developed and disseminated over the past decade (Muller & Mihalic, 1999). Multisystemic therapy (MST; Henggeler & Borduin, 1990; Henggeler, Schoenwald, Borduin, Rowland & Cunningham, 1998), a broad ecologically focused delinquency intervention, was one of the first to demonstrate efficacy in a series of randomized trials. A key distinction in this approach is a therapeutic focus on the youth's family and social environment (e.g., parental supervision, school engagement, peer group affiliations, parent–child communication). MST targets the improvement of caregiver supervision and parenting skills through the provision of therapeutic services in the family's natural environment, such as the home, neighborhood, or school setting.

A growing body of research suggests that MST is effective with AISB (Henggeler, Letourneau, Chapman, Borduin & Schewe et al., 2009; Letourneau, Henggeler & Borduin, 2009). An effectiveness trial by Letourneau and her colleagues (2009) compared an adapted version of MST to community-based cognitive-behavioral group interventions. Youth in the community group program (n = 60) participated in weekly 60-minute outpatient group sessions with a treatment duration average of 14.6 months. Group topics included deviant arousal, victim empathy, cognitive distortions, relapse prevention, and family counseling. Youth receiving MST (n = 67) were in treatment for an average of 7.1 months. MST is a home-based treatment model that individualizes interventions for each family. Sessions may take place in the youth's home and in community (e.g., school) settings and will vary in frequency based on treatment needs. MST teams take on individual caseloads of four to six families per therapist, with team members being available for 24-hour crisis response. The MST treatment model is detailed in a treatment manual developed by Henggeler et al. (1998). Treatment focuses on empowering parents through skill building and increasing access to resources and empowering youth to cope with familial and extrafamilial problems. Treatment strategies are derived from family therapies, behavioral parent training, and cognitive-behavioral therapy. Common treatment areas include problem solving, parental discipline and monitoring, reducing family conflict, avoiding negative peer influences, and school performance improvement. The AISB adaptation for this study included addressing youth and caregiver denial about the sexual offense, safety planning to minimize the youth's access to potential victims, and the promotion of age-appropriate and normative social experiences with peers. Compared to youth in the community group program, youth participating in MST demonstrated statistically significant reductions in sexual behavior problems, delinquency, substance use, externalizing symptoms and out-of-home placements. Approaches such as MST appear to be especially promising for AISB who have multiple problems including general delinquency. For further information about the MST model and training program, visit the website: www.mstservices.com.

INITIATING TREATMENT WITH FAMILIES OF AISB

Assessment of family functioning should be conducted early in AISB treatment and re-evaluated periodically, as needs may vary significantly across families and can change over time (Bonner, 2008). Some families entering AISB treatment may be relatively healthy and strong and will require limited intervention. Higher levels of therapeutic support may be required for families who have suffered significant consequences as a result of the adolescent's illegal sexual behavior, such as the loss of relationships with friends or family, major financial hardships, or the adolescent's victimization of a younger child in their family. Caregivers in these families may struggle with resentment, distrust, shame or fear for their teen's future. This may lead to emotional distancing from their teen and less commitment to parental supervision, treatment participation or placement stability. Other families may enter AISB treatment with a history of chronic dysfunction due to such factors as mental illness, substance abuse, family violence, or abuse. For these families, AISB treatment providers may need to enlist additional community services to support family recovery and stability. In some circumstances, the level of family dysfunction may be severe enough to warrant alternate AISB community placement in order to ensure adequate shelter, safety and supervision for the AISB or other family members.

Initial interactions with families in AISB treatment are important to the establishment of positive therapeutic working relationships. This can be particularly challenging, however, due to factors beyond the treatment provider's control, such as parent attitudes/beliefs, parent functioning, or family systems involvement. Understandably, parents may approach AISB treatment with trepidation and frustration. The legal process that most families of AISB endure prior to the start of therapy is long and arduous. They may feel as though their interactions with the police, the court system and child protective services are adversarial and non-supportive. Parents who struggle with the question of their teen's guilt may face professionals who perceive them negatively or may even accuse them of being complicit in their teen's illegal sexual behavior. Of course, there are cases in which parental behaviors have contributed to adolescent illegal sexual behavior, such as lack of appropriate supervision or allowing youth exposure to highly sexualized materials. Regardless of the family's history related to the illegal sexual behavior, treatment providers have the ability to distinguish their role with the family from the roles played by others in the judicial process.

Therapists can most effectively approach AISB treatment with caregivers from a position of educator and supporter. It is not the therapist's place to enforce probation requirements or behavioral rules. Rather, the therapist works to support caregivers in learning how to do so most effectively and facilitates a bridge between the parents and probation officers that encourages collaboration for the benefit of the youth. Likewise, it is not the therapist's function to determine a youth's guilt or innocence. This determination is left to the Court. The therapist supports families in meeting court requirements and reducing the adolescent's risk of future illegal sexual and non-sexual deviancy. It is beneficial for the therapist to communicate understanding and commitment to assisting the family in returning to normalcy. Below is an example of how this may be communicated to caregivers.

> *Mr and Mrs Jones, it's clear from what you've shared with me today that you love your son very much and want the best for him. No parent expects to have to face something like this with their child and you and your family have gone through so much as a result. I know it hasn't been easy, but you've stood by his side throughout this process and are here to support him through treatment as well. Your son is fortunate to have you as his parents. In our work with teens in your son's position, we've found that it's the teens whose parents are right beside them throughout treatment who do better in the long term. They are more likely successfully to complete treatment and are less likely to commit future illegal behavior. Also, many parents share that going through treatment with their teens brings them closer. We know you want to get back to normal daily life as soon as possible and that's what we want for you and your son as well. Our goal is to help your family move beyond this experience and become even stronger as a result.*

For parents who initially deny, minimize or are unclear about their teen's responsibility for the illegal sexual behavior, it is beneficial for the therapist to approach the issue from a position of neutrality. Attempts to convince parents of the youth's guilt can make the therapist appear biased and initiate an adversarial relationship between the therapist and parents. In such circumstances, parents may become further entrenched in their stance on their adolescent's innocence. Therapists can avoid this dynamic by refraining from voicing an explicit opinion on the youth's role in the illegal sexual behavior. For example:

> *You've shared that you don't fully understand what illegal sexual behavior your son did or if he actually did it. We've worked with many parents who have felt the same way coming into this program. Unfortunately, I can't tell you definitively what happened. What I can do is review with you the information we received about your son's charge. Also, throughout treatment your son will be asked to share details about what happened. We give teens an opportunity to share this with their caregivers, so this may also help you better understand what took place. Ultimately, though, parents sometimes have to face the ambiguity of never fully knowing. Most importantly, our goal in this program is help your son understand and safely manage his sexual impulses and learn to make healthy decisions in all areas of his life. These skills are important for all teens to learn regardless of their history. Also, since we know that parents are the most important people in a teen's life, it's also our job to support you in helping your son and family move beyond this difficulty.*

An additional educational point for parents who question their adolescent's guilt is how common it is for teens initially to deny or minimize their inappropriate or illegal behavior in an attempt to avoid consequences or to avoid disappointing parents and other loved ones. The *Common Experiences of Parents and Caregivers* handout in Figure 20.1 may be useful in addressing this topic with parents. This handout identifies feelings and reactions common to parents of AISB and offers supportive and educational points related to each.

AISB FAMILY TREATMENT ELEMENTS

For each of the current best practice AISB intervention models, the incorporation of parents and family into treatment enhances adolescent outcomes. Commonalities in family elements incorporated into AISB treatment include the areas of parental supervision, behavior management, parent–teen relationship enhancement and reunification.

COMMON EXPERIENCES OF PARENTS AND CAREGIVERS		
Adolescent illegal sexual behavior is something no parent expects or is prepared to face. Below are common reactions and experiences shared by parents and caregivers who have found themselves in this challenging situation.		
COMMON PARENT FEELINGS	COMMON PARENT REACTIONS	CONSIDERATIONS FOR PARENTS

Confusion or Disbelief	"There must be a mistake."
	"My teen wouldn't do that."
	"Stories I'm hearing about what happened are so different that I don't know who to believe."
	"Maybe someone else isn't being truthful about what my teen did in this situation."
		• It's normal for parents to question whether their teen engaged in an illegal sexual behavior. No parent expects their teen to do something like this.
		• Although it can happen, it's very rare for teens to be falsely accused of illegal sexual behavior. If you believe that your teen has been falsely accused, discuss this with your teen's lawyer. No professional wants a teen to admit to something they didn't do.
		• Many teens initially deny or don't tell everything about their illegal sexual behavior for different reasons including:
		  ◦ Trying to avoid consequences
		  ◦ Not wanting to disappoint parents or others they care about
		  ◦ Shame and embarrassment about what they did
		• To more clearly understand what happened, some parents may find it helpful to review with a therapist available police reports or interviews. The pros and cons of this should first be weighed with a therapist, as this information may be distressing to read or hear.
		• When a teen appears hesitant to be truthful, it's helpful for parents to reassure the youth of their love and commitment regardless of the teen's behavior.
		• Parents may emphasize to their teen the importance of truthfulness and responsibility for one's behaviors.

Anger	• Anger toward teen for committing the illegal sexual behavior • Anger toward the victim or victim's family • Anger toward the police, courts, or other involved agencies	• Know that it's okay to be angry. Many parents feel this way at the start of their teen's treatment. Give yourself time to forgive and recover from this experience. • Most parents involved in their teen's treatment share that their anger decreases as they see positive changes in their teen like better decision-making, increased maturity and responsibility. Don't give up. Treatment progress is rarely a steady, straight line. • Parents should limit conversations with or in front of their teen about personal anger towards the victim, victim's parents or the system. This may inadvertently send the wrong message to the teen about the importance of taking responsibility for their illegal behavior. • The goal of therapy is to help your family get through treatment and to normal daily life as quickly as possible. We want your teen to grow beyond this experience and live a safe, healthy and productive life.
Fear	"Is something wrong with my teen?" "What is the chance that my teen will do another illegal sexual behavior?" "How is this going to affect my teen's future?"	• There is no one type of teen who engages in illegal sexual behavior. Most often there are many factors that lead to this behavior. Each teen is different and each family is different. What's important now is for you and your teen to work with your treatment provider to understand which factors are most relevant for your teen and how to overcome them. • The majority of teens with illegal sexual behavior do not go on to become adult sex offenders. With treatment and good parental supervision and support, most teens will never engage in another illegal sexual behavior. Research shows that the sexual re-offense rate for teens who receive treatment is low, from 3 to 14 percent. • Teens who complete treatment and court requirements can lead happy and successful lives. An important factor in this process is parental support and guidance. • When their case is closed, teens in some states may have the ability to get their juvenile court documents sealed or expunged, which can provide an additional layer of protection.
Guilt/ Embarrassment	"Could I have done something to keep this from happening?" "I should have known…." "What will others think if they find out about what my teen did?"	• Parents often look back and wonder if they could have done something to prevent their teen's illegal sexual behavior. Only in rare cases do parents have an idea that their teen might sexually abuse another person. Teens hide their sexual behavior from adults, and especially from their parents. In most cases, parents have no way of knowing to intervene. • Unfortunately, there is a strong stigma attached to illegal sexual behavior that can lead to severe social and academic consequences for teens. It will be important to carefully think through who needs to know about your teen's illegal sexual behavior. • When you determine that it is necessary to disclose this information to someone, consider how much you need to share. In most cases, a detailed account is not necessary. It may be helpful to talk through these decisions with your treatment provider.

Figure 20.1 Common experiences of parents and caregivers handout. *Copyright © 2012 OUHSC Treatment Manual for Adolescents with Illegal Sexual Behaviors. Mark Chaffin, PhD, Barbara L. Bonner, PhD, Keri Pierce, LCSW, MPH, Lisa Swisher, PhD, Susan Schmidt, PhD. Handouts can be photocopied only for individual use in practice.*

The following sections will present ideas and tools to assist in addressing each of these elements within AISB treatment. These resources are borrowed and adapted with permission from an outpatient AISB treatment curriculum (Chaffin, Bonner, Swisher, Pierce & Schmidt, 2012). This 12-module cognitive-behavioral, ecologically-focused group curriculum includes active parental participation. Which adults participate may vary depending on the youth's current and long-term placement status, and may include birth parents, grandparents, other adult family members, foster or adoptive parents or others who are providing daily care for the adolescent. There may be multiple caregivers involved in cases of out-of-home placement or parental separation. Adolescents and caregivers attend weekly group sessions and families participate in additional services outside of group as needed (e.g., family therapy, reunification sessions, sibling victim trauma-focused therapy, etc.). During weekly group sessions, caregivers attend parent education/support groups while adolescents participate in youth groups. Each session ends with a conjoint parent–teen group session to review treatment topics and complete combined activities.

The handouts shared in the following sections have been adapted from a small selection of materials within the AISB group curriculum. Treatment providers may find these tools useful to incorporate into a larger treatment plan that is tailored to individual adolescent and family needs. For further information on this AISB group treatment program and other resources to support the treatment of youth with problematic sexual behavior, visit the *National Center on the Sexual Behavior of Youth*: www.ncsby.org

Supervision

Initial outpatient contacts with parents or caregivers of AISB should emphasize the establishment and reinforcement of supervision standards within the home, community and school (Bonner, 2008). Questions to consider:

- What is the teen's weekly schedule and who provides supervision throughout the week?
- In each setting, what are the potential risks for illegal sexual and non-sexual behavior?
- What current supervisory practices are in place in each setting?
- What do other caregivers need to know about the teen's illegal sexual behavior to assist them in deciding how best to supervise the teen? How should this be shared with them?

DO'S AND DON'TS FOR PARENTS OF ADOLESCENTS WITH ILLEGAL SEXUAL BEHAVIOR

DO:

1. Spend quality time with your teen. Make sure to create regular opportunities to give your teen your individual attention.

2. Communicate with your teen. Encourage your teen to talk with you about problems or concerns. Serve as a good role model by talking with your teen when you are bothered by something the teen is doing. Communicate your love, affection, and concern for your teen. Also talk about matters regarding sexuality and sexual behavior. Make sure you clearly convey your values in this area, while listening to your teen's views.

3. Provide effective supervision of your teen's behavior and set appropriate limits, such as establishing an age-appropriate curfew and identifying consequences for curfew violations.

4. Encourage responsibility in your teen, such as doing chores around the house, getting a part-time job, and doing well in school.

5. As treatment progresses and your teen demonstrates increasingly good decision-making at home, school and the community, encourage age-appropriate behavior, such as developing friendships, dating and taking part in extracurricular activities in church, school, and community.

DON'T:

1. Permit your teen to have unsupervised contact with others who may be vulnerable, especially children. This means that jobs such as babysitting, camp counseling, nursing home attendant, etc., should not be allowed through the duration of treatment.
2. Allow your teen to drive a car without a license.
3. Allow your teen to miss school except when medically necessary.
4. Allow your teen to use alcohol or drugs.
5. Allow your teen to associate with peers who are engaged in illegal or harmful activities, such as gang activities, shoplifting, alcohol or drug use.

Figure 20.2 Do's and don'ts for parents of adolescents with illegal sexual behavior handout. *Copyright © 2012 OUHSC Treatment Manual for Adolescents with Illegal Sexual Behaviors. Mark Chaffin, PhD, Barbara L. Bonner, PhD, Keri Pierce, LCSW, MPH, Lisa Swisher, PhD, Susan Schmidt, PhD. Handouts can be photocopied only for individual use in practice.*

The handout in Figure 20.2, *Do's and Don'ts for Parents of Adolescents with Illegal Sexual Behavior*, may assist in an introductory conversation with parents regarding the establishment of safe boundaries for AISB during treatment. Supervisory areas highlighted in this list include setting a curfew, determining allowable social and community activities, limits to contact with children, and restrictions on activities that may involve illegal activity or associations with peers who engage in illegal activity.

PARENT WEEKLY REPORT						
Date						
Teen's Name						
Person Completing Form						
Relationship to Teen						
Please rate your teen's progress since your last session.						
Area	A	B	C	D	F	Comments
School Behavior and Grades						
Behavior and Attitude at Home						
Behavior in the Community						
Problematic Sexual Behavior						
Accomplishments and Things You Appreciate						
Problems, Concerns or Things to Work On						

Figure 20.3 Parent weekly report. *Copyright © 2012 OUHSC Treatment Manual for Adolescents with Illegal Sexual Behaviors. Mark Chaffin, PhD, Barbara L. Bonner, PhD, Keri Pierce, LCSW, MPH, Lisa Swisher, PhD, Susan Schmidt, PhD. Handouts can be photocopied only for individual use in practice.*

The *Parent Weekly Report* shown in Figure 20.3 is designed to support regular communication between caregivers and treatment providers about adolescent progress between treatment sessions. This form asks caregivers to grade their teens on behavior at school, home and in the community.

Additionally, it asks about adolescent sexual behavior known to the caregiver. Caregivers are invited to share details about progress seen in the adolescent and any additional areas for improvement.

For parents who tend to be overly negativistic about their adolescent's progress, the form encourages the habit of praising positive teen behavior and aids in normalizing common teen problems like negative attitudes, not doing chores, etc. This form can be completed by parents at the start of each treatment session and reviewed in session to determine whether current supervisory practices are sufficient or in need of alteration. Treatment providers can also use this form as a mechanism for supporting open, active communication between parents and teens. Prior to reviewing the form with the teen and parent, the teen may be asked to complete a self-rating of each area and communicate to the therapist or youth group any specific problems or successes that occurred in the past week. This aids in identifying the adolescent's willingness to take responsibility for misbehavior, assesses the adolescent's accuracy in determining treatment progress, and provides opportunities for positive reinforcement of accomplishments.

As adolescents learn through treatment to manage sexual impulses, parents should provide an additional level of safety that reduces their teen's exposure to sexual situations. The *Monitoring Sexual Situations* handout in Figure 20.4 and *Monitoring Sexual Situations Exercise* in Figure 20.5 are designed to educate caregivers about potential AISB sexual risks and prioritize supervisory needs related to several common risky sexual situations.

These handouts help caregivers establish limits on which potentially sexual situations they would view as acceptable or risky, and increase caregiver acceptance of the need to supervise their adolescent in situations that pose some risk. The *Monitoring Sexual Situations* handout identifies three common risks caregivers should consider when judging a situation. The first is the risk for another sex offense. Most parents of AISB will accept that certain situations pose some risk for all youth, but they may underestimate the enhanced risks for their adolescent. Therapists can point out that even a small risk carries potentially severe consequences for an AISB, suggesting the importance of greater than average levels of adult supervision. Parents who chronically tend to minimize their adolescent's risk of further illegal sexual behavior may be more convinced of the need for enhanced supervision through a review of the second two potential

MONITORING SEXUAL SITUATIONS

Because your teen has been in trouble for illegal sexual behavior, it is critical that you monitor certain types of situations to reduce your teen's sexual safety risk. Certain situations should be considered risky automatically. For example, babysitting is considered a highly risky situation for any teenager who has been in trouble for illegal sexual behavior. Parental monitoring of risky sexual situations reduces the risk of:

1. **Another Illegal Sexual Behavior.** This is rare, but there is always some chance that there could be another sex offense. It is not completely possible to predict which teenagers will have a future illegal sexual behavior and which will not. Most will not, and we expect that your teen will not. But if it did happen, the consequences could be severe—to your teen, to the victim, and to your family.

2. **Suspicion from Others.** People may know about your teen's illegal sexual behavior, or may find out about it later. If your teen is in risky situations unmonitored or unsupervised, others may become suspicious. For example, if a teenager with past illegal sexual behavior is seen playing with young children, people will naturally become suspicious, even if the teen does nothing wrong. This sort of suspicion and stigma can have negative consequences.

3. **A False Allegation.** False allegations are rare, but can happen. For example, if someone became suspicious seeing your teen in unsupervised interactions with young children, they might question the children in a leading way that possibly extracts untrue allegations. Given your teen's past illegal behavior, authorities or others may make assumptions about your teen's current behavior, leading to potentially severe consequences.

Recommendations for Monitoring and Supervising Sexual Situations

1. **If the situation has a high risk for any of the three areas above, don't allow your teen to be in it.** For example, teens who have committed illegal sexual behaviors should never babysit. Make sure that your teen clearly understands this rule and knows how to respond if asked by an adult to babysit. Practice this conversation with your teen so that they feel comfortable saying "no."

2. **If the situation is allowed or is unavoidable, ensure that supervision is provided by a responsible informed adult.** In times when another adult has to supervise, decide how much you need to share about your teen's history. You may not need to tell everything, but you should tell enough so that the adult can understand how to effectively monitor your teen.

3. **Set rules about sexual situations.** For example, teens who have had problems with sexual behavior should not look at pornography. If this has been a problem, set clear rules about it with your teen. Or, you may set a rule that your teen is to sleep alone, with the door closed and not allow younger siblings to share the bed.

4. **Monitoring does not mean "Never let your teen out of your direct eyesight."** Sometimes monitoring needs to be strict, and sometimes it can be loose. Think about the risky situations your teen may face and create a supervision plan that fits each level of risk.

5. **Ask questions if you feel suspicious.** If you see something that doesn't feel right to you, ask your teen about it. When in doubt, talk with your treatment provider about the situation.

Figure 20.4 Monitoring sexual situations handout. *Copyright © 2012 OUHSC Treatment Manual for Adolescents with Illegal Sexual Behaviors. Mark Chaffin, PhD, Barbara L. Bonner, PhD, Keri Pierce, LCSW, MPH, Lisa Swisher, PhD, Susan Schmidt, PhD. Handouts can be photocopied only for individual use in practice.*

risks – suspicion from others and false allegations. Both of these risks can have significant consequences, and cannot be managed except by avoiding the risky situation or ensuring adequate adult supervision. Some situations listed on the Figure 20.5 handout, like babysitting, are so risky that the AISB program or treatment provider should establish a clear rule against participation during treatment.

MONITORNG SEXUAL SITUATIONS					
Below are common situations where supervision might be considered. Rate whether each situation should be allowed or forbidden for your teen, given your teen's age, maturity level and past behavior. If you would allow the situation, how closely would it need to be supervised? Add situations specific to your teen at the end.					
Situation	Allow this at all?	If allowed, how closely should it be supervised?			
		None	Loose	Moderate	Strict
Interactions with Children					
1) Babysitting	Y / N				
2) Being in a bedroom with a brother or sister with the door open	Y / N				
3) Being in a bedroom with a brother or sister with the door closed	Y / N				
4) Being in a bedroom with a child who is not a brother or sister	Y / N				
5) Sharing a bedroom with another child	Y / N				
6) Sharing a bed with another child	Y / N				
7) Being in a bathroom with another child	Y / N				
8) Taking a shower with another child	Y / N				
9) "Horseplay," tickling or wrestling with another child	Y / N				
10) Being undressed or in underwear in public areas of the house when there are children around	Y / N				
11) Playing with younger children in the neighborhood	Y / N				
12) Attending a family gathering where there are children around	Y / N				
Interactions with Peers					
13) Being in a public place, like a shopping center with a group of friends	Y / N				
14) Being in the teen's bedroom with a teen of the same sex	Y / N				
15) Being in the teen's bedroom with a teen of the opposite sex	Y / N				
16) Talking on the phone with a teen of the opposite sex	Y / N				
17) Sleeping over at a friend's house	Y / N				
18) Joining extracurricular activities like sports, music, academic or social groups	Y / N				
19) Going on a group date	Y / N				
20) Going on a solo date	Y / N				
21) Going on an overnight school trip	Y / N				
Exposure to Sexual Content					
22) Watching an R-rated movie	Y / N				
23) Listening to sexually explicit music	Y / N				
24) Listening to a conversation that includes sexual comments or jokes	Y / N				
25) Looking at internet pornography	Y / N				
26) Being on the internet, in general	Y / N				
Community Activities					
27) Working at a fast food restaurant	Y / N				
28) Volunteering at a ____________	Y / N				
29) Going to a community activity like a sporting event, concert, city festival	Y / N				
30) Attending religious services	Y / N				
Other					
31)					
32)					

Figure 20.5 Monitoring sexual situations exercise. *Copyright © 2012 OUHSC Treatment Manual for Adolescents with Illegal Sexual Behaviors. Mark Chaffin, PhD, Barbara L. Bonner, PhD, Keri Pierce, LCSW, MPH, Lisa Swisher, PhD, Susan Schmidt, PhD. Handouts can be photocopied only for individual use in practice.*

Behavior Management

As AISB are at a higher risk of engaging in future non-sexual delinquency (such as stealing and drug-related offenses) than future sexual delinquency, it is critical that effective treatment with caregivers addresses comprehensive behavior management strategies in conjunction with sex-specific supervision as described in the previous section. Teaching parents or caregivers structured behavior management skills is considered the single best-supported intervention element for youth behavior problems (Chaffin, 2008). Common behavioral parenting strategies incorporated into treatment for delinquent adolescents include (Association for the Treatment of Sexual Abusers, 2006; Barkley, 2008; Bonner, 2009; Chaffin, 2008; Patterson, Reid & Dishion, 1992):

- Establishing and enforcing developmentally appropriate rules
- Attending to and rewarding positive behavior
- Logical and natural consequences
- Monitoring peer relationships
- Monitoring school behavior and progress
- Parental consistency
- Parental warmth and sensitivity
- Effective parent–teen communication.

Numerous resources are available to assist in teaching behavioral parenting techniques, including the widely used book, *Your Defiant Teen* by Russell Barkley (2008). Additionally, the California Evidence-Based Clearinghouse for Child Welfare rates several programs designed to teach parent training and treat disruptive behavior in youth (www.cebc4cw.org).

The handouts selected for this chapter section specifically address parental peer group monitoring as this is a common concern for parents of AISB. The exercise in Figure 20.6, *Monitoring Peer Groups*, is designed to teach parents how to evaluate the quality of their adolescent's peer relationships.

For each of the adolescent's significant friendships, the parent can utilize this form to evaluate information known about the friend and to identify what additional information may be needed to determine the type of influence this friend is on the teen. Treatment providers should ask caregivers what they know about the friend's parents, as it is common for parents of delinquent youth to have limited or no information about their teen's friend's home environment and level of adult supervision. This

MONITORING PEER GROUPS				
The power of peer influence is very strong. An important part of raising a teenager is supervising and monitoring their friendships. This involves encouraging positive peer relationships and discouraging negative peer associations. Evaluate the quality of your teen's friendships using the table below. Use additional copies as needed to rate your teen's closest friends.				
Friend's Name	Rating			
	A lot	Some	Little or None	Don't Know
1) Is this friend much older or much younger than your teen?	3	2	1	DK
2) How much contact do you have with this friend?	1	2	3	DK
3) How much contact do you have with this friend's parents?	1	2	3	DK
4) How much supervision does this friend's parents provide?	1	2	3	DK
5) How polite and respectful is this friend around you?	1	2	3	DK
6) Does this friend make average grades or better?	3	2	1	DK
7) Does this friend have a good reputation?	1	2	3	DK
8) Has this friend been in trouble with the law?	1	2	3	DK
9) Does this friend look or act gang affiliated?	1	2	3	DK
10) Does this friend smoke cigarettes?	1	2	3	DK
11) Does this friend use drugs or alcohol?	1	2	3	DK
12) Does this friend get in fights and confrontations?	1	2	3	DK
13) Does the friend get suspended from school or skip school?	1	2	3	DK
14) Is this friend sexually active?	1	2	3	DK
15) Does this friend engage in inappropriate sexual talk or behavior?	1	2	3	DK
16) Do you trust this friend?	1	2	3	DK
17) Do you get a bad feeling about this friend?	3	2	1	DK
18) Do you approve of this friend?	1	2	3	DK
19) Do you approve of the friend's parents and family?	1	2	3	DK
Score each column				# of DKs:

Based on your answers, which statements below best describe your teen's friend?				
5 or more DKs	DK or 3s on #s 3, 4	19–30	31–40	41–57
I could benefit from learning more about this friend.	I could benefit from learning more about this friend's parents.	This friend may be a mostly positive influence.	This friend may be both a positive and negative influence.	This friend may be a mostly negative influence.

Figure 20.6 Monitoring peer groups exercise. *Copyright © 2012 OUHSC Treatment Manual for Adolescents with Illegal Sexual Behaviors. Mark Chaffin, PhD, Barbara L. Bonner, PhD, Keri Pierce, LCSW, MPH, Lisa Swisher, PhD, Susan Schmidt, PhD. Handouts can be photocopied only for individual use in practice.*

can be particularly problematic for AISB given their enhanced supervisory needs and common restrictions on contact with younger children. After completion of this exercise, the handouts provided in Figures 20.7 and 20.8 can be reviewed as needed to address specifically any peer group problems identified by the caregiver.

Supporting Positive Peer Relationships in Your Teen

1. **My teen doesn't have friends.** This is not an uncommon circumstance for teens who have engaged in illegal sexual behaviors. Some teens have problems fitting in with their peers due to traits like immaturity or shyness. As a result, they may feel more comfortable around younger children, which is problematic. For these youth, parents can:
   a. Encourage your teen to get involved in age-appropriate extracurricular or social activities. Look for activities that your teen might find interesting and will support feelings of competence and success. Encourage activities that develop friendships, like inviting friends for outings, allowing time on the phone, etc.
   b. Help your teen develop social skills (hygiene, appearance, talking to others). Encourage mature ways of talking and acting around peers. Give your teen feedback on social behaviors when needed.
   c. Give your teen lots of support and encouragement, especially if the teen experiences poor self-confidence or experiences rejection.
2. **My teen has a number of positive friends and I know them pretty well**. You are in the best peer group situation. Your teen's peer group is an asset. You can supervise your teen's interactions with friends from a bit of a distance. Keep up the good work on knowing about your teen's friends and their parents.
3. **My teen has friends, but I don't know much about them.** Find ways to get more involved with your teen's friends and learn more about their parents. Be curious. Create opportunities to have conversations with your teen about their friends' characteristics. Ask your teen to invite friends over to your home for a meal or visit. Chaperone them during outings. Invite your teen's friends' parents to join you during an outing or invite them for a visit to your home. Parents may also find it beneficial to regularly review their teen's social network sites for appropriate content and peer communications.
4. **My teen has friends who are both positive and negative influences.** Encourage your teen's participation in activities that increase contact with friends who are positive influences. Closely supervise interactions and limit contact with peers who negatively influence your teen. Consider steps to reduce contact with those negative peers. As a parent, you have the right and responsibility to restrict your teen's negative peer associations. However, be sure as you do this to find opportunities for your teen to participate in positive peer activities.
5. **My teen's peer group is mostly negative**. If this is your situation, it is time to take immediate steps to change your teen's peer interactions. See the "10 Tips" handout.

Figure 20.7 Supporting positive peer relationships in your teen handout. *Copyright © 2012 OUHSC Treatment Manual for Adolescents with Illegal Sexual Behaviors. Mark Chaffin, PhD, Barbara L. Bonner, PhD, Keri Pierce, LCSW, MPH, Lisa Swisher, PhD, Susan Schmidt, PhD. Handouts can be photocopied only for individual use in practice.*

Included on the handout, *10 Tips for Moving Teens Away from Negative Peers*, are six questions parents should regularly ask teens about peer activities:

1. *Who* will be there? Do I know them? Where do you know them from? How old are they?
2. *What* will you be doing?

10 TIPS FOR MOVING TEENS AWAY FROM NEGATIVE PEERS HANDOUT

1. **Don't Despair.** You can have an impact. You can get some degree of control over your teen's peer group.
2. **Enlist Support.** Moving teens away from negative peers can be a real challenge, and you want all the support you can get. Get other adults involved—family members, clergy, or family friends can help reinforce your efforts. Neighbors can give you reports about contact. You can ask coaches and teachers about your teen's peer contacts. Collaborate with your treatment provider and other professionals working with your family to support your efforts. If your teen has a probation officer, they may be able to assign a "mentor" who is another adult to serve as a positive influence on your teen.
3. **Eliminate Situations Where Your Teen Interacts With Negative Peers**. For example, if you teen interacts with negative peers after school, arrange for the teen to come directly home to adult supervision or enroll the teen in a supervised after school activity. If the teen meets negative peers at a particular place, remove the privilege of going to that place. If communication with negative peers occurs over the phone or internet, consider restricting privileges or taking away cell phones. Sometimes, radical steps might be needed—such as transferring to a different school or moving to a different neighborhood—but try other steps first.
4. **Watch Like a Hawk. Supervise your teen's interactions and activities.** Have a structure and know where your teen is, who your teen is with, and what your teen is doing. Check up on your teen. If your teen has friends you consider "borderline," (somewhere between positive and negative), consider allowing contact only under your watchful eye.
5. **Point Out The Risks. Point out the risks you see that go with negative peers**. Point out that you are focused on your teen's welfare and future. Tell your teen that you are restricting contact with negative peers because you care. Your teen may say that the risks won't happen. You can always tell your teen, "I don't want to take that chance when it comes to you." Keep reminding your teenager that you are taking these steps because you care. Get other adults, like family members, family friends, clergy, treatment providers, and others to reinforce this message with your teen.
6. **Avoid Belittling or Condemning Your Teen's Negative Friends**. Don't put down your teen's friends. You don't want to make your teen feel the need to defend their friends. Acknowledge that your teen has positive feelings about these friends or this peer group. Focus your concerns on the lifestyle of the negative peer group, rather than putting down any individuals. Keep encouraging your teen to think about the risks and the negative consequences of this lifestyle.
7. **Be Prepared to Do Battle If Necessary.** You should be prepared to set firm rules and restrictions, including forbidding any contact with peers that you think are having a seriously negative influence on your teen's behavior. Be prepared to back this up with significant consequences. For example, if a teenager sneaks out of the house to join up with a delinquent peer group, and comes home late at night, be prepared to deliver a significant consequence. Be prepared for the teen to react negatively to your restrictions and consequences. Stay calm—but remain firm and focused.
8. **At the Same Time You Discourage Contact with Negative Peers, Encourage Involvement with Positive Peers and Positive Activities**. Work to get your teen more involved with "growth privilege" activities—work with coaches, mentors, family members, employers, teachers and others to help your teen find and stick with these types of activities. Remember, for this type of problem you want to encourage more involvement in positive peer activities and should not take them away as a consequence. Make it clear that you want your teen to "have a life," and that you are not restricting everything—only the things and peers that you think pose a risk.
9. **Surround Your Teen With Positive Role Models**. Encourage activities with positive adult role models. Ask family members, family friends, clergy, older siblings, or others to get involved and spend time with your teen.
10. **If Necessary, Consider Changing Routines**. If there are major blocks of the day where your teen is unsupervised, work to change your routine, rearranging your work schedule if possible, or arranging for other adults to step in when you can't be there to supervise. For example, you might have other adults come over to the house to supervise when you aren't there, or you might have your teen go to their house until you are home.

SIX ROUTINE QUESTIONS TO ASK YOUR TEEN ABOUT PEER ACTIVITIES

1. **Who** will be there? Do I know them? Where do you know them from? How old are they?
2. **What** will you be doing?
3. **When** will you be back?
4. **Where** will you be?
5. **How** will I be able to reach you?
6. Will there be **adults** supervising? Who? How many adults will be there? How can I get in touch with them?

Figure 20.8 Ten tips for moving teens away from negative peers handout. *Copyright © 2012 OUHSC Treatment Manual for Adolescents with Illegal Sexual Behaviors. Mark Chaffin, PhD, Barbara L. Bonner, PhD, Keri Pierce, LCSW, MPH, Lisa Swisher, PhD, Susan Schmidt, PhD. Handouts can be photocopied only for individual use in practice.*

3. *When* will you be back?
4. *Where* will you be?
5. *How* will I be able to reach you?
6. Will there be *adults* supervising? Who? How many adults will be there? How can I get in touch with them?

Parent–Teen Relationship

The parent–teen relationship is critical to AISB treatment success and sexual and non-sexual recidivism (Chaffin et al., 2005). An important first step in addressing the parent–teen relationship is the normalization and acceptance of common feelings and reactions of parents of AISB. This can be effectively addressed in an AISB parent education/support group by inviting parents of youth farther along in treatment to share thoughts and feelings they experienced as they entered AISB treatment and how this has changed as therapy has progressed. If a parents' group is unavailable, the *Common Experiences of Parents and Caregivers* (see Figure 20.1) handout previously described may be useful in conveying this information. Providing a safe, confidential environment for caregivers to share their thoughts and feelings about their adolescent is important as there may be no other place for them to talk freely about the situation. Many parents refrain from telling friends or family about their adolescent's illegal sexual behavior in order to protect their adolescent from others' negative responses. When parents have a supportive outlet like group or individual therapy for communicating their thoughts and feelings about their teen, they are less likely to carry resentment into parental interactions.

Activities that foster the development of general parent–teen communication skills are important to parental engagement in treatment, supervision and behavior management. Patterson (1982) identified a coercive parent–teen interaction cycle that commonly occurs in families of youth who engage in antisocial behaviors. The cycle begins with parental overreaction to adolescent misbehavior. This triggers behavioral escalation in the teen which, over time, can lead the parent to withdraw from further attempts to manage the youth's behavior. As this interactional pattern repeats, the teen becomes less responsive to parental attempts at behavior management, resulting in further parental disconnect. As parental supervision and behavior management decreases, youth may increase their negative peer associations and take greater behavioral risks including engaging in harmful or illegal activities (Patterson, 1992). Within AISB treatment, a focus on parent–teen communication enhancement may support the prevention or interruption of coercive cycles when combined with an emphasis on effective parent behavior management and supervision.

Dr. Barbara Bonner authored a booklet for parents and caregivers of AISB, titled *Taking Action: Support for Families of Adolescents with Illegal Sexual Behavior* (2009). This booklet addresses several topics of interest to parents of AISB including understanding adolescent illegal sexual behavior, understanding the legal system and child protective services, understanding treatment, reunification, and empowering parents to enhance parent–teen communication. In the booklet, she reviews several tips to help parents strengthen their communication skills with adolescents:

- Attending to what the adolescent is saying in a conversation rather than formulating your next sentence or allowing yourself to get distracted
- Periodically restating or summarizing what your teen has said to ensure that you understand
- Asking occasional questions, which shows your interest
- Listening non-judgmentally
- Communicating in specifics, particularly when discussing rules and expectations
- Being understanding, even when you disagree with what your teen is saying
- Using "door openers" like "Tell me what happened" rather than "door closers" like "I told you so" or "I don't want to hear it" in communicating
- Learning when to stop a discussion before it escalates
- Being ready to communicate openly when you least expect it
- Showing your adolescent affection and letting them know that you support them.

Within AISB treatment, these effective communication principles can be taught to caregivers and reinforced through role playing with treatment providers. Adolescents may also be taught principles of healthy parent–teen negotiation and brought together with caregivers to practice these skills in example scenarios. The goal of these activities is to reduce the adversarial nature of interactions between adolescents and their parents and foster a sense of collaboration and mutual respect, thus reducing the potential for coercive interaction patterns to develop or worsen.

An additional communication goal for parents and teens in AISB treatment is the reduction of discomfort in discussing issues related to sex and sexuality. Understandably, this can be a challenging topic even in the healthiest of parent–teen relationships. However, it is imperative that parents learn to communicate their sexual values to their teen and are able to provide accurate information about sexual issues to their teen when needed. Parents should work toward establishing themselves as safe and trusted individuals for their teen to approach with sexual issues, including if the teen is experiencing an urge to commit an inappropriate or illegal sexual behavior. Examples of treatment activities that can support parent–teen communication about sex include state sex laws reviews, education on sexual health and development, discussing principles of healthy sexual behavior, and discussion about characteristics of the teen's illegal sexual behavior (e.g., the teen's reasons for engaging in the illegal sexual behavior, ways the teen can avoid similar risky sexual situations, etc.).

Forgiveness is an issue that commonly impedes effective communication between parents and adolescents in AISB treatment. Parents may find it difficult to forgive their teen for the harm caused by their illegal sexual behavior. Parents may question their teen's regret for having committed their illegal sexual behavior. Parental fear of their adolescent's insincerity may be further reinforced when the youth continues to engage in problematic behaviors and breaks promises to follow established rules throughout the treatment process. Teenagers in treatment may also struggle with overwhelming guilt and shame about their illegal sexual behavior. Some teens fear that they will be unable to gain their parents' forgiveness.

A method for facilitating the process of forgiveness is the incorporation of letters of restitution and apology into treatment. In this activity, the adolescent writes letters of apology to: (1) the victim and victim's family, and (2) the teen's own parents. In circumstances where the teen is burdened with overwhelming guilt, it also may be therapeutically beneficial for the teen to write a letter to him/herself. This exercise is not meant to foster guilt or shame, but focuses on providing the teen with an opportunity to take positive steps to apologize and make amends for their behavior. The apology letter written to the victim and victim's parent(s) will not necessarily be sent or read to the victim, although this may be appropriate in some cases, such as sibling victimization. Decisions to share a victim letter should be made in collaboration with the youth's parents, victim's parents, and other treating professionals. In most circumstances, letters generated through this activity are not shared outside of treatment.

Youth restitution letters should reflect some understanding or estimation of how the illegal behavior affected the victim and others. They may also include an acknowledgment of personal responsibility and explanation of what the youth is doing to ensure that no further illegal sexual behavior occurs. If the youth is in group treatment, the letters may be read to peers for feedback and revision. Once the letters are finalized, the youth is invited to read both letters to the parent(s). Parents then have the opportunity to respond to the letters. In this activity, parents are also asked to write a letter to share with their teen after the teen has shared his/her letters. The expected tone of the parent-to-teen letter is also expected to be positive and recognize the teen's progress. Parents may elect to share briefly the difficulties they have experienced as a result of the teen's illegal sexual behavior. However, the goal is to communicate support, love and instill hope for the future. If the parents are part of an AISB parents' group, it may be beneficial for them to read the letter in the group to get feedback prior to sharing it with their teen.

Reunification

For adolescents who were removed from their family homes as a result of their illegal sexual behavior, successful treatment progress may initiate plans for family reunification. This point in treatment can bring with it a number of reactions within the family. Excitement about the teen's return may be paired with hesitation and anxiety. There may be concern about the adolescent's ability to maintain appropriate sexual boundaries with family members. Additionally, the task of regaining family trust can feel daunting for some teens as they learn through treatment about how their illegal behaviors negatively impacted parents and siblings. Significant thought and preparation should be undertaken when approaching reunification. As is the case throughout AISB treatment, reunification plans should be tailored to individual family needs. The issue of reunification is best addressed while the youth remains in treatment and on probation so that professionals working with the family can provide guidance and support throughout this process (Swisher, Silovsky, Stuart & Pierce, 2008).

Several factors should be considered when determining the appropriateness of family reunification for adolescents in treatment for illegal sexual behavior (Bonner, 2009; Swisher et. al, 2008):

Parental Factors

- Are the caregivers clear about who was responsible for the abusive behavior?
- Are they supportive of both the adolescent and the sibling(s)?
- Do they know the details about the illegal sexual behavior? If it happened in their home, do they understand the conditions surrounding where and when it happened?
- Are they aware of what warning signs or behaviors to look for and how to respond?

- Have they development a safety plan for the youth, siblings and family members?
- Are they able to discuss the illegal sexual behavior with the therapist, teen and siblings?
- Do they know and are able to enforce the supervision rules in the home and community?

Adolescent Factors

- Does the adolescent understand the harm caused to the family, the child and to self?
- Is the teen making consistent progress in treatment with no major sexual or non-sexual problems at home, at school, or in the community?
- Has the teen admitted to and taken responsibility for the illegal sexual behavior?
- Does the adolescent know and agree to follow the rules for family visitation?

Sibling Victim Factors

- Is there no family pressure being placed on the sibling to agree to allow the adolescent to return home?
- Is the sibling ready for and interested in contact with the adolescent?
- Is the sibling's description of the sexual behavior similar to what the adolescent said happened?
- Has the sibling been assessed for effects related to the victimization and received evidence-based trauma treatment, if necessary?

If there are satisfactory answers to the above questions and the family is ready to begin reunification, a team meeting is recommended to establish a reunification plan. This planning meeting should involve therapists working with the family, the probation officer, the child protective services worker (if one is involved), the parents/caregivers, and the adolescent. Additionally, arrangements should be made with the parents to ensure that the sibling victim is consulted for input on the reunification plan. If the sibling is in therapy, incorporation of the sibling's treatment provider into this process is beneficial.

Effective reunification plans include steps that can be implemented in a timeframe that allows for evaluation of progress throughout the process. To ensure the comfort and safety of all family members involved, reunification steps should be graduated. Typical plans can range from several weeks to several months, depending on successful completion of each step

(Bonner, 2009). Below are example steps in a family reunification plan that gradually increases parent-supervised adolescent–sibling contact:

1. Adolescent writes letters of apology to parents and sibling(s)
2. Treatment providers assess the readiness of the adolescent, sibling(s) and parents
3. Family members work with treatment provider(s) to develop a family safety plan
4. Parent or therapist monitors phone calls between the adolescent and sibling(s)
5. Family therapy session(s) to review safety plan and review progress (as needed)
6. Family outings with the adolescent and sibling(s) to public setting (e.g., park, restaurant)
7. Parent supervised visits in the home for two to four hours
8. Supervised all-day visits in the home
9. Supervised overnight visits in the home
10. Supervised weekend overnight visits in the home
11. Supervised extended visits during holidays or vacations
12. Adolescent returns home.

Figure 20.9 includes a template for a family safety plan that may be created during the reunification planning process. This plan can be adapted to meet family needs and should be approved by each family member. Age-appropriate siblings may elect to add or modify rules depending on their comfort level.

During safety plan development, parents should review consequences for rule violations. The treatment provider should also discuss with the parents and siblings what family members can do if they feel unsafe or if someone attempts to break a safety rule with them. It can be helpful to have parents and children role play this conversation so that children learn words they can use effectively to convey their concerns to their parent. Some children feel comforted by establishing a code word that they can say to their parents when feeling unsafe. It may also be useful for the adolescent to establish a code word and role play talking with a parent if tempted to break a safety rule or engage in an illegal behavior.

Periodic review of the family safety plan is recommended throughout the reunification process and revisions can be made as needed. If during the reunification process it appears that the adolescent is incapable of consistently following established safety rules and maintaining healthy boundaries with family members, a review of the reunification plan steps and

Family Safety Plan

Each family may customize this plan to fit their needs. There are clear rules against some activities (for example, babysitting or looking at pornography). The plan will require closer than usual parental supervision, but usually will not prohibit most normal teenage activities that parents might normally approve (for example, spending time with appropriate peers, having a part-time job, engaging in school activities, playing sports, dating, etc.

Things (name) WILL NOT do

1. (name) will never babysit for any amount of time.
2. (name) will never go into a younger brother's or sister's bedroom and will say "no" if invited.
3. (name) will not have a younger sister or brother come into (name)'s own bedroom, unless a parent is notified and around to keep an eye on things and the door is left open.
4. (name) will not be in the bathroom if a sister or brother is in there.
5. (name) will keep the bathroom door locked when in there.
6. (name) will not engage in any "horseplay" or tickling with any younger sister or brother or any other young children.
7. (name) agrees not to watch any movie, TV show, or internet material or listen to music that is not parent approved.
8. (name) agrees not to talk about sexual things or make any sexual comments or sexual jokes around a sister or brother or other children.

Some things (name) WILL do

1. (name) will respect the authority of (name)'s parents and follow their house rules.
2. If (name) is doing something with a younger sister or brother, and they say, "No" or "Stop," (name) will do so.
3. (name) will be appropriately dressed when in public areas of the house.
4. If (name)'s younger brother or sister, or any other children bring up questions or ask about sexual things, (name) will tell them to go ask their parent.
5. If (name) feels temptations to engage in illegal sexual behavior, (name) will talk about it with a parent.

Some things (name)'s parents will do

1. Supervise interactions between (name) and young children and not ask (name) to babysit.
2. If parents are not around to supervise interactions between (name) and young children, they will make sure that an informed, responsible adult is there to take on this responsibility.
3. Supervise TV shows, music, videos, and internet material.
4. Monitor (name)'s activities, such as school work, homework, type of friends, whereabouts, curfew hours, and so forth, and help (name) make good choices.
5. Help (name) follow rules by reminding (name) when needed.
6. Make sure that all family members are clothed unless they are in their own room with the door closed, in the bathroom with the door closed, or in bed.
7. Be open and accepting about talking with (name) about any sexual questions or temptations.

Other rules the family may wish to add

1.
2.
3.
4.

Signed:

____________________ ____________________ ____________________

(Teen) (Parent) (Parent)

Date:____________________

Figure 20.9 Family safety plan. *Copyright © 2012 OUHSC Treatment Manual for Adolescents with Illegal Sexual Behaviors. Mark Chaffin, PhD, Barbara L. Bonner, PhD, Keri Pierce, LCSW, MPH, Lisa Swisher, PhD, Susan Schmidt, PhD. Handouts can be photocopied only for individual use in practice.*

timeframe may be in order to determine whether an adjustment to the plan is required or if the teen's return to the home is appropriate. Similarly, parental inconsistency in enforcing the agreed upon safety plan is also a red flag suggesting the need for further education and support to assist them in their supervisory role, or that a reconsideration of the reunification goal is warranted. In some cases, the level of individual (youth or caregiver) or family dysfunction may be too high to support a safe and stable environment needed for AISB reunification. For these families, treatment may need to focus on establishing a viable permanency plan for the adolescent and assisting the family in managing this relational transition.

SUMMARY

The growing field of AISB research increasingly points to the benefits of an ecological approach to treatment that incorporates active family involvement. Evolving models of AISB treatment include greater treatment participation by parents, alternate caregivers and siblings; less focus on the sexual offense; increased focus on general behavior and decision-making; and on developing specific social, behavioral, and interpersonal competencies. Parents and other caregivers can be supported in their roles through education on effective methods for AISB supervision and behavioral parenting techniques. Additionally, treatment activities can be designed to enhance and strengthen the parent–adolescent relationship. For families who have been separated due to the adolescent's illegal sexual behavior, thoughtful planning and intervention is necessary to evaluate the family's readiness for reunification and facilitate the youth's successful return to the family home. Resources to support the treatment of adolescents with illegal sexual behaviors and their families are available on the *National Center on the Sexual Behavior of Youth* website (www.ncsby.org). Additionally, the NCSBY website provides information regarding formal training in the OUHSC AISB group treatment curriculum described in this chapter. With effective treatment, the risk for AISB sexual and non-sexual recidivism is low, paving the way for safe and healthy family functioning.

REFERENCES

Alexander, M. A. A. (1999). Sexual offender treatment efficacy revisited. *Sex Abuse, 11*, 101–116.

Association for the Treatment of Sexual Abusers. (2006). *Report of the task force on children with sexual behavior problems*. <www.atsa.com/atsa-csb-task-force-report>.

Barkley, R. (2008). *Your defiant teen: 10 steps to resolve conflict*. New York: Guilford Press.

Becker, J. V., & Kaplan, M. S. (1993). Cognitive behavioral treatment of the juvenile sex offender. In H. E. Barbaree (Ed.), *The juvenile sex offender* (pp. 289–319). New York: Guilford Press.

Bonner, B. L. (2008). Adolescents with illegal sexual behavior: Current knowledge. *APSAC Advisor, 20*, 5–8.

Bonner, B. L. (2009). *Taking action: Support for families of adolescents with illegal sexual behavior.* Safer Society Press. Brandon:VT.

Caldwell, M. (2002). What we do not know about juvenile sexual re-offense risk. *Child Maltreatment, 7*, 291–302.

Chaffin, M. (2008). Our minds are made up. Don't confuse us with the facts: Commentary on policies concerning children with sexual behavior problems and juvenile sex offenders. *Child Maltreatment, 13*, 110–121.

Chaffin, M., Bonner, B. L., Swisher, L., BigFoot, D., & Pierce, K. (2005). *Ten-year Recidivism among Youth Treated in the OUHSC Adolescent Sex Offender Program.* Paper presented at the Annual Conference of the Center on Child Abuse and Neglect, Oklahoma City, OK.

Chaffin, M., Bonner, B. L., Swisher, L., Pierce, K., & Schmidt, S. (2012). *Group treatment curriculum for adolescents with illegal sexual behavior.* Oklahoma City: University of Oklahoma Health Sciences Center.

Chaffin, M., Letourneau, E., & Silovsky, J. F. (2002). Adults, adolescents, and children who sexually abuse children: A developmental perspective. In J. E. B. Myers, L. Berliner, J. Briere, C. T. Hendrix, C. Jenny, & T. A. Reid (Eds.), *The APSAC handbook on child maltreatment* (pp. 205–232) (2nd ed.). Thousand Oaks: Sage.

Finkelhor, D., Ormrod, R., & Chaffin, M. (2009). Juveniles who commit sex offenses against minors. *Juvenile Justice Bulletin* www.ojp.usdoj.gov/ojjdp.

Henggeler, S. W., & Borduin, C. M. (1990). *Family therapy and beyond: A multisystemic approach to treating the behavior problems of children and adolescents.* Pacific Grove: Brooks/Cole.

Henggeler, S. W., Letourneau, E. J., Chapman, J. E., Borduin, C. M., Schewe, P. A., & McCart, M. R. (2009). Mediators of change for multisystemic therapy with juvenile sexual offenders. *Journal of Consulting and Clinical Psychology, 77(3)*, 451–462.

Henggeler, S. W., Schoenwald, S. K., Borduin, C. M., Rowland, M. D., & Cunningham, P. B. (1998). *Multisystemic treatment of antisocial behavior in children and adolescents.* New York: Guilford Press.

Kahn, T. J., & LaFond, M. A. (1988). Treatment of the adolescent sexual offender. *Child & Adolescent Social Work, 5*, 135–148.

McGrath, R. J., Cumming, G. F., & Burchard, B. L. (2003). *Current practices and trends in sexual abuse management.* Brandon: Safer Society.

Muller, J., & Mihalic, S. (1999). *Blueprints: A violence pprevention initiative (OJJDP Fact Sheet #110).* Washington DC: US Department of Justice, Office of Justice Programs, Office of Juvenile Justice and Delinquency Prevention.

Patterson, G. R. (1982). *A social learning approach: III. Coercive family process.* Eugene: Castalia.

Patterson, G. R., Reid, J. B., & Dishion, T. J. (1992). *A social learning approach: IV. Antisocial boys.* Eugene: Castalia.

Reitzel, L. R., & Carbonell, J. L. (2007). The effectiveness of a sexual offender treatment for juveniles as measured by recidivism: A meta-analysis. *Sexual Abuse: A Journal of Research and Treatment, 18*, 13–30.

Swenson, C. C., Schoenwald, S. K., Randall, J., Henggeler, S. W., & Kaufman, K. L. (1998). Changing the social ecologies of adolescent sexual offenders: Implications of the success of multisystemic therapy in treating serious antisocial behavior in adolescents. *Child Maltreatment, 3*, 330–338.

Swisher, L. M., Silovsky, J. F., Stuart, R. H., & Pierce, K. (2008). Children with sexual behavior problems. *Juvenile and Family Court Journal, 59*, 49–69.

Worling, J. R., & Curwen, T. (2000). Adolescent sexual offender recidivism: Success of specialized treatment and implications for risk prediction. *Child Abuse & Neglect, 24*, 965–982.

CHAPTER 21

Tools for Quality Improvement

Alexandros Maragakis and William T. O'Donohue
University of Nevada, Reno, NV, USA

INTRODUCTION

Assessing and treating juvenile sexual offenders can be an extremely delicate and complex matter. In some cases, the initial assessment or the report of initial treatment progress from a mental health provider can have bearing on the decision for an individual to be imprisoned rather than having an alternative disposition, such as probation (Kalmbach & Lyons, 2006). In addition, the quality of these assessments and treatments can have an enormous impact on the safety of others – errors in prediction of recidivism or treatment failures can result in others being abused. Given the importance of a mental health professional's potential role in determining an individual's freedom and the public's safety regarding sexual offenders, it is imperative that reports and treatments of sexual offenders are as accurate and efficient as possible.

In their current state, both evaluations and treatments of sexual offenders are not always reliable or effective (Hanson, Broom, & Stephenson, 2004). Given that a type I error may lead to an innocent individual being imprisoned and a type II error might lead to an individual dangerous to society being released, the unreliability of reports and the ineffectiveness of treatments can have dire implications. The empirically supported treatment (EST) movement is an attempt to minimize these sorts of error. The basic idea is that the profession should deliver only those assessments and treatments that have been tested and shown to be safe, accurate and effective (Chambless & Hollon, 1998). However, there are three major problems with this ideal: (1) it is clear that although this movement is decades old, many therapies delivered and assessments given still do not meet this ideal (Arkowitz & Lilienfeld, 2006); (2) there are controversies concerning the demarcation regarding what is empirically supported (e.g., how many randomly controlled trials (RCTs) are required, with what sort of effect sizes, across how many independent labs); and (3) with a particular

Toolkit for Working with Juvenile Sex Offenders.
DOI: http://dx.doi.org/10.1016/B978-0-12-405948-1.00021-9

population, such as juvenile sex offenders, are there any well-supported assessments or treatments; and if not, what is the field to do?

This chapter will focus on the use of quality improvement (QI) as an essential adjunct to empirically supported assessments and treatment. The problem with the construct of EST is that it is static: a therapy either meets a predetermined criterion or it does not. While it is certainly the case that satisfying this criterion is superior to not satisfying it, there are still quality questions remaining, e.g., is this particular therapist administering the assessment device or therapy in a sufficiently faithful manner? How does one adapt the therapy to the particular circumstances of the client, for example, teletherapy, or how does one adapt the therapy for co-morbidity, say, a client with attention deficit hyperactivity disorder (ADHD) or developmental delay? Through the use of QI, mental health professionals can collect data in a useful and efficient way to make changes in assessments and treatments as needed. Also, through the use of QI, important statistics (e.g., benchmarks) can be used to ensure that individuals who are engaging in the assessment and treatment of sexual offenders are performing at or above an acceptable standard of care.

Unfortunately, we know the field of juvenile sexual offending has quality problems, although there is much missing information about these problems. The quality problems can be categorized as follows:

1. Some practice is not evidence-based
2. Some diagnoses are incorrect (i.e., diagnoses are missed and or incorrectly used)
3. Some therapy is not effective and some is not delivered as it is intended to be delivered. That is, it is delivered with low treatment integrity (Gresham, 1989; Gresham, Gansle, & Noell, 1993)
4. Some individuals are not given the therapy that they need. There are important issues of misdiagnosis, poor case conceptualization, access and equity in juvenile sexual offending
5. Some individuals are given therapeutic components that they do not need
6. Some assessments are inaccurate (e.g., these predict no recidivism when recidivism subsequently occurs)
7. Some interventions are harmful and stigmatizing.

We need to do some research to develop benchmarks regarding all of the above. We need some accurate understanding of what we are doing in terms of quality. In addition, it would be useful to attempt to identify both exceptionally good and bad evaluations and treatments. This would allow us to use the data from exceptionally good evaluations and treatments as centers of excellence in therapy and the exceptionally bad as priorities for reform. This can then be used to help other therapists learn possible ways to do their jobs better. In addition, we do not know what our customers want/expect from our services. First, it is important to point out that we have multiple customers – the adolescents we treat, their families, referring agencies, third party payers, institutions like probation and parole, judges, etc. Do all these want/expect 100% accuracy from our assessments and 100% "cures"? If so, how do we manage these expectations with information about error rates and recidivism rates? We do not want to over promise and under deliver, even if this is done implicitly. It seems to be the case that we need more research regarding the expectations of our customers and stakeholders. This research would also be relevant in obtaining information for what services can and cannot be effectively and efficiently delivered to those seeking services.

Given that QI is a relatively new process in the mental health field, this chapter will provide a brief overview of the overall strategies involved in QI. This will be followed by an overview of the theory of QI that will assist in making decisions regarding what quality data to collect, how to collect it, and how to implement resulting innovations. The last section of this chapter will include specific QI tools that are useful for those involved in assessing or treating sexual offenders.

WHAT IS QUALITY IMPROVEMENT?

Quality improvement is a phrase that has gained significant attention in many industries, including the automotive industries, retail sales, the service industries and, more recently, in the healthcare field (see for example, Berwick, 2008). Through its enormous success, particularly in the retail and manufacturing sectors, various industries have also begun to integrate QI measures to increase the value of the products that they distribute (Chassin & O'Kane, 2010). QI is a system that identifies measurable and important outcomes, develops measures for these processes and outcomes, attempts to understand the processes that influence these outcomes, and subsequently performs learning trials to attempt to improve these outcomes (Bobbitt, Cate, Beardsley, Azocar, & McCulloch, 2012). Through this QI process, barriers to improved outcomes are identified, reduced, and eventually eliminated in order to optimize the quality of the end product. Through QI, a system is not only analyzed regarding how its process functions internally, but goes a step further by analyzing how its product and system function with regard to stakeholders' interests and expectations in the product or services. Therefore, implementing QI measures may help change or retool systems that operate smoothly internally (e.g., meet daily quotas for production), in order better to meet needs of the consumer that were not fully realized in the initial design of the product or service.

Laypersons sometimes associate quality with "expensive" products or services. However, if done correctly, QI can actually reduce overall costs by eliminating waste or more efficiently satisfying consumer wants and thereby reduces the expense of the service or product. For example, through QI processes, Intermountain Health, an internationally recognized non-profit system of hospitals known for their high quality care and affordable costs, started an elective labor induction protocol that was estimated to reduce healthcare costs in Utah by $50 million dollars, increase the quality of obstetric care (e.g., lower cesarean section rates, decreased length of time women spent in labor, lower admission rate to newborn intensive care units (James & Savitz, 2011)).

While part of a total quality package, QI is not to be confused with quality management. Quality management is the process of ensuring that the product given in location X is the same as the product given in location Y. Notice how the EST movement is much more of a quality management strategy. Quality improvement on the other hand, is the process of creating and measuring standards to create continually incremental changes that exceed agreed-upon benchmarks (Bobbitt et al., 2012). While quality management is important to ensure that the variability of a product is low, which is an essential requirement of any good product, QI is the process that continually improves the overall value of a product.

APPLYING THEORY TO QUALITY IMPROVEMENT

Throughout the practice of QI, the goal has always been to increase the value of the product or service. However, pioneers of QI have had different theoretical approaches to accomplish this goal. For example, one of the most important quality improvement theorists, W. Edwards Deming defined quality as a relative term that will change in meaning depending on the consumer's needs (Suarez, 1992). To address the ever changing needs of the consumer, Deming focused on a construct he called "profound knowledge" and Plan-Do-Study-Act cycles. While this section will go into details of different theories of QI, it is important to keep in mind that these theories set a foundation of how to use a QI system. That is to say that QI is actually theoretically based, and that it is not simply collecting data to collect data or to create a façade that one is interested in quality.

The first theory we will discuss is that of W. Edwards Deming. Deming believed that fully to understand a system was the key to improving the quality of a product, and fully to understand a system one must have "profound knowledge". Profound knowledge has four key components: theory of systems; theory of variation; theory of knowledge; theory of psychology. Deming viewed the system as having multiple components (management, customers, and employees) that are interrelated (Suarez, 1992). A failure to understand these interrelations leads to fragmentation, and an inability to identify processes that will affect quality. These multiple components can also be found in treating and assessing sexual offenders. One must understand how all parties involved (e.g., the individual receiving treatment, the therapist, the probation officer, the family) interact with each other fully to capture relevant components to improve quality.

Variation is perhaps the key concept in quality improvement. Variation is simply the dispersion around some measure of a feature of product or services. For example, wait time for first session will show variation – some will get an appointment the same day, some will take 24 hours, and some longer. Deming believed that variation was caused by two types of sources, common and special. Common causes of variation, which are the most important to QI efforts, were found due to processes in the system (e.g., lack of safety protocols), while special causes were due to unique individual factors (e.g., an employee coming to work intoxicated). Identifying the sources of variation was important in order to help prevent management from identifying potential trends that do not actually exist, or blame (or give credit) to processes that are not actually contributing to variation in the system (Kelly, Paul Johnson, & Sollectio, 2013). Deming's view on the sources of variation can be particularly useful for addressing quality problems in assessment and treatment. Focusing on common causes of variation (e.g., the time it takes for therapy to be initiated or the outcomes of therapy) would produce better outcomes and improve quality faster rather than trying to tailor therapy to account for the special sources of variation.

Deming viewed knowledge as a slow on-going cumulative process, with the occasional "breakthrough" during which rapid advancements were made (Suarez, 1992). He believed that management must take a scientific approach, where hypotheses are formulated, experiments are conducted, and theories are constructed to understand the system and its sources of variation. This is important to keep in mind when implementing a QI system in one's practice, because it makes clear that knowledge takes time and persistence. When implementing QI, the benefits may be incremental until a "breakthrough" occurs.

Deming also stressed that before implementing someone else's solution to a problem, the theoretical implications must be fully understood to ensure it will meet your needs (Suarez, 1992). This is especially important for providers in general. What may have been helpful or useful for another provider may not be as useful or may even be counterproductive. Taking the time to ensure that a measure or a plan used by another practitioner would provide useful information for improving a practice is important, because other practitioners may focus on other factors that may be irrelevant to one's own situation.

Another important pioneer in QI, Joseph M. Juran, addressed QI using other methods. Juran defined quality as "fitness for use", where there is a balance between product or service features and products and services free from deficiencies (Suarez, 1992). To accomplish this balance, Juran used what is now called the "Juran Trilogy" and the Patero Principle.

Juran's trilogy focuses on quality planning, quality control, and quality improvement. The quality-planning phase focuses on developing products to meet the consumers' needs. The quality planning also includes establishing quality goals, and ways to achieve those goals. The quality-control phase involves monitoring operations, and analyzing the difference between actual production and goals. If differences arise, an individual or management must act to rectify those differences. The quality-improvement phase involves establishing an infrastructure to secure improvement, identify needs for improvement, and provide the resources and training needed to achieve improvement (Suarez, 1992).

Juran also focused on the Patero Principle that stated that the majority of poor quality can be found in a small number of causes (Suarez, 1992). Juran called these small causes the "vital few". To improve quality in a fast and efficient way, the vital few must be identified and rectified first. However, a common error in management is that there is a focus on the "trivial many" causes that can lead to massive resource expenditure with few changes.

While these two pioneers emphasized different approaches, they were both effective at achieving similar goals of QI. Both pioneers focused on the use of data to ensure that goals and quality were met and that theory and rationale were key components in determining what processes merited focus. Both made QI a scientific endeavor rather than a "professionally-based" skill.

BASIC TOOLS OF QUALITY IMPROVEMENT

This section will review the basic tools that are used in QI. It is important to note that these tools may be used in conjunction with one another, and that some tools may be more useful to a specific practice than others. To help determine which of these tools would be more useful for your practice, it is important first to take a theoretical approach, like the theories previously discussed, to ensure that the most relevant information is captured in the least obtrusive way.

It is also important to note that collecting data and identifying weaknesses is worthwhile. Many avoid collecting data due to the fact that the initial data may be "suboptimal". However, it is through these "suboptimal" outcomes that one can begin to formulate a plan in order to improve the quality of the services delivered.

Survey Questionnaires

The most basic and powerful tool in QI are questionnaires that are created to address specific processes or outcomes in a system. If properly created, the data from these questionnaires can help you determine whether what you are doing is having its intended effect on your system. When determining what you should measure, it is important that you ask, "What is important to my consumers?" and "What is important to me as a provider?" Table 21.1 provides a brief description of multiple types of questionnaires that could be useful in assessing a system. Appendix A also provides an example of a brief questionnaire. Thus, an important first step is to understand better the stakeholders in your services – what are they seeking; how can one resolve conflicts in these, how can one educate them regarding their expectations; and how can one construct and implement a system to better meet these expectations?

Whichever specific type of questionnaire you decide to use, they all should be relatively short and non-obtrusive. Ideally, these questionnaires involve a few Likert-scale questions along with one or two open-ended questions. For example, these measures could assess lawyer satisfaction with your report after your court date, or client's satisfaction with therapy.

Table 21.1 Types of Measures

Questionnaire Type	Overview	Examples of Outcomes
Proportions/ percentages	Proportions are the most commonly used measures in QI systems. They are short, to the point, and are easily readable. They also reflect the real numbers of people seen in an office (unlike ratios, which we will get to in a minute). However, these data fail to capture any variation among individuals that might provide for a more complete picture (presenting problem, severity of problems, financial reasons)	Number of clients that dropout/number of clients seen
Ratios	Not as popular as proportions or percentages, ratios use a proxy as a denominator. This proxy is usually based on epidemiological data for a given area. It should be made clear if a ratio should be high or low. (In the example given above the lower the better, but this is not always the case). A major drawback of using a ratio measure is that the denominator may be a poor proxy for the true at risk population	Number of clients that re-offend per 10 000 clients
Means and medians	Few measures are constructed as mean or median. Again, the direction of the measure should be clearly indicated (example above would be better if it was lower, but a measure that looks at the mean amount of time clear of any symptoms of depression would be better it was higher). These measures, when used appropriately, capture the subtleties of care. However, the weakness of these measures is that they may be more difficult to analyze, and are not applicable in many cases of QI	Average time between initial contact with client and start of therapy
Adverse counts	These measures are usually used for events that are very rare. The occurrence of these events usually warrants some kind of investigation. The sole reason to share these data with the public is to promote transparency. These measures are not used to compare performance across providers	Number of clients that re-offend

Benchmarks

Benchmarks are another very important construct in QI. Benchmarks can be a baseline value that provides a goal to maintain or exceed, or an industry standard that one tries to maintain or exceed. It is through benchmarks that realistic goals on how one should be performing can be made – what the "standards" are. For example, after collecting baseline data it is discovered that the dropout rate of therapy is 20%. This benchmark, 20% dropout, can then be used as a benchmark to both help manage expectations – it is simply unrealistic (currently at least) to expect 0% dropout, as well as to help examine whether the changes made to a system to improve this undesirable outcome – how can we make changes to reduce this to say 15%, and the next year, 12% etc.

Process Maps

Process maps are important in planning who does what, and what a process should accomplish. These maps are used to determine how the system "should" be operating from a theoretical standpoint. The main goals of the process map are clearly to dictate who is responsible for what process, and to establish a connection between certain processes and outcomes. Through the use of process maps, one can target which processes affect the outcomes of interest. In some cases, after data have been collected, it may be that the original process map needs to be changed, and that other processes affected certain outcomes.

It is important to remember that process maps should be easy to read. They should highlight more important processes in order to make clear what to focus on. Also, these maps should be linked to outcomes and the measurements of these outcomes (Webb, 2010). The main purpose of these maps is to improve outcomes. Finally, as mentioned earlier in the chapter, it is important to create one's own process map. A process map created by someone else could include processes or factors that are irrelevant to one's own practice. Appendix B provides an example of a simple process map.

Plan-Do-Study-Act

To help address all of these issues, as previously mentioned, Deming created the Plan-Do-Study-Act (PDSA). The PDSA is an empirical approach used to analyze whether or not an implemented process change has the hypothesized effects on quality. The "Plan" phase is where an individual or management formulate hypotheses how changing a process in the system will affect measures of interest. During the "Plan" phase is where the amount of time allotted for the test and how data will be collected are determined. The "Do" phase is where a small-scale project from the "Plan" phase is run. During the "Do" phase, it is important to document any problems or barriers that present during the trial. The "Study" phase is where all of the data are analyzed. All data including changes to variables of interest as well as barriers that presented themselves are analyzed. The "Act" phase is where an individual or management determines if the changes to the system had the hypothesized benefit, how it would need to be adapted given unexpected barriers that were encountered, and whether or not to disseminate the change throughout the entire system.

The PDSA is an important tool in tying together all of the previous tools mentioned. By effectively using the PDSA, it can help control costs of potentially expensive changes before implementing them throughout the entire system. It could be especially important in the realm of therapy to ensure that changes made to therapy are actually beneficial, and that clients are not subjected to extra material from which they would not substantially benefit. It can be useful for each clinician to have at least one PDSA cycle operating at any time – to show the constancy of purpose regarding quality improvement.

Identifying Consumers

While not a specific tool, it is important to identify properly all the consumers that a given service is intended to serve. Tailoring a QI system to target only one consumer may lead to dissatisfaction for another consumer. For example, only examining satisfaction and wants of the lawyer regarding an assessment may lead to high rating from lawyers and may lead to consistent job opportunities. However, neglecting examinee satisfaction may lead to tailoring assessment in a way that leaves examinees extremely dissatisfied with the process. Therefore, it is extremely important to ensure that all individuals that are being served are being assessed to ensure that no important aspects are being left out.

CONCLUSIONS

Assessment and treatment of sex offenders serves an important social function, in that the process is intended to rehabilitate individuals and prevent recidivism of sexual crimes. However, given its current state, it is important that continual improvements are created to ensure that the intent of the services matches the final outcome. While there are many ways that one could go about improving services, this chapter provides an avenue of improvement through QI.

The objective of this chapter is to not make an individual an expert in QI, but instead give a brief overview of what QI may look like. As mentioned throughout the chapter, the exact tools and processes one uses for a practice requires thought and preparation. In that spirit, the tools presented in the appendices of this chapter are only to be used as examples. While useful tools may match those provided, it is important that careful consideration is given to what information and data would be meaningful in a given system.

Quality improvement has been extremely effective and efficient in helping other industries improve the quality of their products, and increasing the value proposition to the general public. Through its recent success in the healthcare field, the shift to using QI in behavioral health is appropriate. Through the use of QI, the assessments and treatments of sexual offenders may have more useful information to help the field as a whole move to creating more effective and efficient ways of meeting the needs of everyone involved in the process.

APPENDIX A

REFERRAL SATISFACTION SCALE

Your referral is very important to us. Please take the time to fill out the following survey to help up improve our services.

Questions	Rating (1 – not satisfied at all to 5 – very satisfied)					
The amount of time between initial contact with the provider and intake for the client	N/A	1	2	3	4	5
The quality of the reports received from the provider	N/A	1	2	3	4	5
The timeliness of the reports received from the provider	N/A	1	2	3	4	5
The ease in which I can get a hold of the provider	N/A	1	2	3	4	5
The quality of care my client receives	N/A	1	2	3	4	5

Please provide any feedback regarding the provider. Please describe the extent to which this person is meeting your expectations and ways this service could be improved. Thank you.

APPENDIX B

PROCESS MAP OF CLIENTS SCHEDULING AN INTAKE

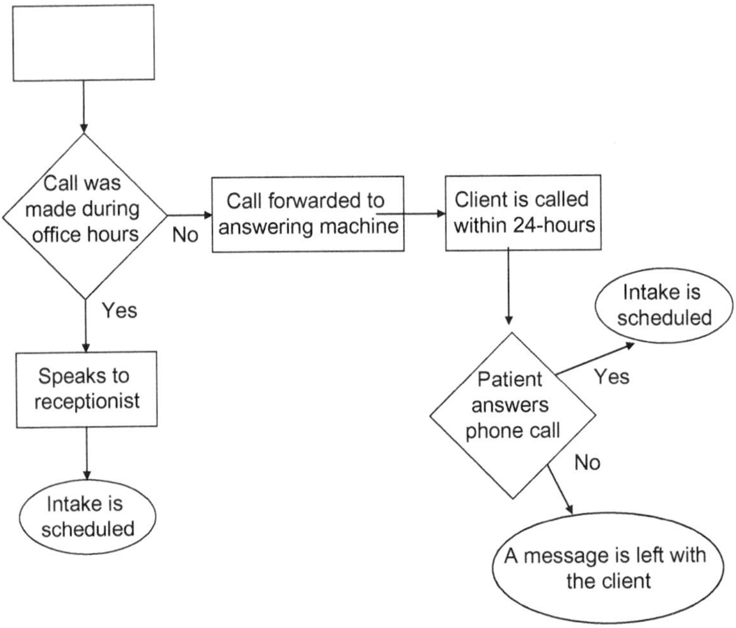

RECOMMENDED READINGS

Bobbitt, B. L., Cate, R. A., Beardsley, S. D., Azocar, F., & McCulloch, J. (2012). Quality improvement and outcomes in the future of professional psychology: Opportunities and challenges. *Professional Psychology: Research and Practice*, *43*, 551–559.

George, M. L., Rowlands, D., & Kastle, B. (2003). *What is lean six sigma*. New York: McGraw-Hill.

O'Donohue, W.T. (2013). (Ed). *Case studies in sexual deviance: toward evidence based practice*. New York: Routlege.

Walton, M. (1986). *The deming management method*. New York: Berkley Publishing Group.

REFERENCES

Arkowitz, H., & Lilienfeld, S. O. (2006). Psychotherapy on trial. *Scientific American Mind*, *2*, 42–49.

Berwick, D. M. (2008). The science of improvement. *Journal of the American Medical Association*, *299*, 1182–1184.

Bobbitt, B. L., Cate, R. A., Beardsley, S. D., Azocar, F., & McCulloch, J. (2012). Quality improvement and outcomes in the future of professional psychology: Opportunities and challenges. *Professional Psychology: Research and Practice*, *43*, 551–559.

Chambless, D. L., & Hollon, S. D. (1998). Defining empirically supported therapies. *Journal of Consulting and Clinical Psychology*, *66*, 7–18.

Chassin, M. R., & O'Kane, M. E. (2010). History of the quality improvement movement. In S. Berns (Ed.), *Toward improving the outcome of pregnancy III* (pp. 1–8). White Plains: March of Dimes Foundation.

Gresham, F. M. (1989). Assessment of treatment integrity in school consultation and prereferral intervention. *School Psychology Review*, *18*, 37–50.

Gresham, F. M., Gansle, K. A., & Noell, G. H. (1993). Treatment integrity in applied behavior analysis with children. *Journal of Applied Behavior Analysis*, *26*, 257–263.

Hanson, R. K., Broom, I., & Stephenson, M. (2004). Evaluating community sex offender treatment programs: A 12-year follow-up of 724 offenders. *Canadian Journal of Behavioural Science*, *36*, 87–96.

James, B. C., & Savitz, L. A. (2011). How Intermountain trimmed health care costs through robust quality improvement efforts. *Health Affairs*, *30*, 1185–1191.

Kalmbach, K. C., & Lyons, P. M. (2006). Unqiue nature of forensic mental health practice. *Applied Psychology in Criminal Justice*, *2*, 261–290.

Kelly, D. L., Paul Johnson, S., & Sollectio, W. A. (2013). Measurement, variation, and CQI tools. In W. A. Sollecito & J. K. Johnson (Eds.), *McLaughlin and Kaluzny's continuous quality improvement in health care* (pp. 77–116). Burlington: Jones & Bartlett Learning.

Suarez, J. G. (1992). In P. B. Crosby, W. Edwards Deming, & J. M. Juran (Eds.), *Three experts on quality management*. Arlington: Total Quality Leadership Office.

Webb, M. J. (2010, February 26). *Avoid the four most common mistakes of sales process mapping*. Retrieved from iSixSigma http://www.isixsigma.com/tools-templates/process-mapping/avoid-four-most-common-mistakes-sales-process-mapping.

CHAPTER 22

Developing a Practice Around Juvenile Sexual Offending

Daniel S. Bromberg
Special Psychological Services, LLC, Bloomfield, NJ, USA

INTRODUCTION

There are many reference materials that are commercially available about beginning and managing a forensic psychology practice (e.g., Mart & Stout, 2006; Reid, 2013). A few such resources are listed at the end of this chapter. However, developing a practice around working with juvenile sex offenders is a "niche" or "boutique" type of practice. In recent years, the term "extreme sport" has been used to describe athletic events requiring: (1) highly specialized training, and/or (2) special equipment and/or (3) daring above and beyond that which is required of "typical" sports. Similarly, a practice developed around juvenile sexual offending may be considered an "extreme" type of behavioral health practice. Practice in this domain can provide a clinician with a good living while working toward the social good. However, this type of "extreme" practice is not for the meek or poorly trained. The purpose of this chapter is to outline the various personal characteristics, professional training, and business basics necessary to starting and maintaining a successful practice working with juvenile sex offenders.

DO YOU HAVE WHAT IT TAKES TO WORK WITH THIS POPULATION?

There are certain personal characteristics that effective forensic evaluators and juvenile sex offender specific therapists need to have in their repertoire. As in every other area of human endeavor, such professionals are made, not born. If you are considering this sort of practice, you should first ask yourself if you have the personal characteristics needed to work with this population and/or if you have the motivation and ability to develop these characteristics.

Toolkit for Working with Juvenile Sex Offenders.
DOI: http://dx.doi.org/10.1016/B978-0-12-405948-1.00022-0

Do You Genuinely Enjoy Working with Adolescents and Do You Genuinely Enjoy Working with Adults in the Adolescent's Life?

Although I am unaware of any research demonstrating a causal relationship between enjoyment of one's work and efficacy in one's professional capacity, it has been my experience that clinicians who enjoy working with adolescents and their families are significantly better at engaging their clients in a therapeutic alliance than are clinicians who do not genuinely enjoy working with this population. Again, I lack research to support my claim, but I have found that adolescents and their parents are often quite adept at picking up subtleties, such as a clinician's body posture, tone of voice, and facial expressions. Similarly, adolescents and their families seem to notice and appreciate discussion of other systemic participants in their lives (e.g., their child protective service worker, probation officer, etc.).

Are You Able to Establish a Therapeutic Alliance with Adolescents, Patient Enough to Address Denial and Minimization, Able to Confront Them About Their Lies, Yet Able to Talk in a Straightforward Manner About Their Offense(s) as Well as Healthy Sexuality?

Juveniles who commit sexual offenses often come to therapy involuntarily. That is, they participate in psychotherapy because they have been court ordered to do so and risk further legal sanctions if they fail to attend treatment sessions. Although physically present for sessions, adolescents may display an assortment of behaviors that slow their own therapeutic progress as well as the progress of others (if treatment is provided in a group format). Adolescent clients may be inattentive or display disruptive behaviors.

Displaying a sense of humor is helpful in establishing and maintaining a therapeutic alliance throughout a very difficult psychotherapeutic process. For the adolescent client, much of the work is embarrassing. Moreover, it is common for treatment to last one to two years.

I have found that adopting a problem-solving stance with adolescents and their families is the best way to engage them in the (often very long, painful) therapeutic process. I often tell adolescents and their parents that I view my job as that of a problem solver who is committed to working with them to achieve their goals. I then provide a brief summary of my understanding of why the adolescent was referred to me and ask what goal(s) the adolescent and his family hope to achieve. Sometimes, agreement upon treatment goals is relatively easy and straightforward, while it can be quite convoluted and difficult in other cases. For example, a teenage boy might admit that he masturbated himself until he ejaculated while digitally penetrating his prepubescent sister. We might quickly agree that the major treatment goals are to help him understand why he sexually abused his sister, provide him with the tools he needs not to sexually abuse his sister (or anyone else) again, and for him to (lawfully) return home.

Treatment goals may be more difficult to establish if that same adolescent were to tell me that his sister is "a lyin' little bitch" and that he pled guilty on the advice of his public defender, despite the fact that he committed no sexual offense. In the latter case, I might inform the adolescent that the standards of my profession require that if a court finds a defendant guilty, I must assume that the defendant is guilty. If he pled guilty when he is, in fact, innocent, I would refer him back to his attorney or provide him and his parents with other low-cost resources to obtain legal representation to correct the miscarriage of justice. (For example, law schools often have "law clinics" in which law students, under the supervision of faculty, provide legal services.) However, unless/until the court finding is changed, I must proceed under the assumption that he is guilty of the offense(s) to which he admitted and of which he was convicted. In this way, I am showing sensitivity, a willingness to work collaboratively with the youth and his family, and behaving in an ethical manner (in case the youth really did plead guilty to an offense he did not commit). However, at the same time, I am standing firm regarding the assumptions under which therapy will proceed.

(I also review victim statements that were provided to law enforcement and statements provided by victims during forensic psychological and medical evaluations. If, for example, the adolescent's 9-year-old sister says that the adolescent's penis "stood up and got really, really big. My brother went 'uh, uh, uh', then white stuff came out of his pee-pee and went all over," I might ask the adolescent what it sounds like is being described and how a 9-year-old would know about erections and ejaculation without direct experience.) Even if the adolescent continues to deny having sexually abused his sister, perhaps we can agree that, at the very least, she witnessed him masturbating and should not have been exposed to him masturbating. This may form the basis for further discussions about his sexual habits and experiences, healthy sexuality, and may be useful for discussions about the offense later in the therapeutic process. For example, during subsequent sessions, I might make an empathic statement such as,

"It's really, *really* difficult and embarrassing to admit that we did something sexual with a little sister. I've worked with a lot of boys where it took them over a year to say what they really did." Of course, early on in the therapeutic process, I might leave the statement vague, rather than saying, "I bet it's really, really difficult for *you* to say what *you* did to *your* younger sister." The general intent is to make a youth feel safe (that is, not like a pervert) acknowledging his inappropriate sexual acts and engaging in a collaborative, problem-solving process to reduce the likelihood of engaging in future sexual misbehavior.

Are You Aware of the Impact of Your Appearance and Demeanor on Others?

As most of us learned in our graduate training, the therapist's stimulus characteristics probably have a substantial impact on the therapeutic alliance and may affect client outcomes, as well. For example, a male therapist who often wears pink shirts and jewelry may elicit comments or questions from group members about his sexual orientation. Female therapists who wear low-cut blouses and tight clothing may be perceived as seductive. Of course, how our clients perceive us and what those perceptions mean for each client's progress cannot be accurately anticipated in advance. However, practitioners are well advised to give some forethought to their manner of dress and interpersonal interactions with clients. Anticipate comments and questions about your particular stimulus characteristics so that your responses can be used to therapeutic advantage.

Although I am unaware of any research to support my opinion, I have found that it is generally best to dress in neat, clean, comfortable clothing that does not draw undue attention to the therapist's physical attributes (i.e., clothing should thoroughly cover and not accentuate the crotch or buttocks of male or female clinicians or the chest region of female clinicians). Similarly, I have found it best to avoid wearing colognes and perfumes and conspicuous jewelry. Adolescent clients, in particular, seem apt to be distracted by a clinician's stimulus characteristics rather than attending to the therapeutic tasks to be accomplished.

Are You Able to Work Well Within a Multidisciplinary Context?

Work with juvenile sex offenders takes place within a multidisciplinary context. Although the disciplines involved in each case may differ, it is common for the following stakeholders to be involved directly in the treatment process or to need relatively frequent written reports on the adolescent's therapeutic progress: the victim's and/or parents' psychotherapist(s); a case manager from a state child protective service (CPS) agency; a juvenile probation officer; and a family court judge. The importance of being able to engage adolescents in the therapeutic process has previously been discussed. However, the importance of being able to manage relationships and effectively communicate with these other stakeholders cannot be overemphasized. One must effectively engage parents to be sure that they understand why their child committed the offense(s) and what their role is in reducing the likelihood of their teenager re-offending. Effective communication with mental health service providers working with other family members is essential so that joint teenager–parent sessions and perpetrator–victim sessions can be clinically coordinated. Generally, perpetrator–victim sessions cannot be held unless and until a judge modifies a "no contact order" to permit perpetrator–victim contact for therapeutic purposes only (in cases of intra-familial sexual abuse).

When all clinicians involved in the case agree that reunification should occur (i.e., that the perpetrator should be allowed to return home), reunification cannot happen unless/until a judge orders that perpetrator and victim may live together (probably with a set of conditions to ensure the victim's safety). CPS personnel and juvenile probation officers will need to know that therapy is in progress and what risks, if any, the adolescent continues to pose to others. Their opinions will be presented to the judge hearing the case, as well. It is important for clinicians to remember that they are working as part of a larger team involving family members and professionals from other disciplines (e.g., social work, law enforcement, the judiciary).

Working as part of a team involves *carefully listening* to the experiences and opinions of other team members. Although you may disagree with other team members, it is most fruitful to do so *respectfully*. Being haughty and/or closed-minded reflects poorly on you as a clinician and will probably work to the detriment of your client. (Unbenownst to your client, he is likely to remain in an out-of-home placement longer than necessary while the professionals involved in the case work at cross purposes and leave a judge with no choice but to keep the adolescent out of his home or out of a community setting.)

Although some mental health professionals act, well, unprofessionally (e.g., "talking down" to other team members), I have seen many situations in which the mental health professional fails to accept the role of educator/leader when an opportunity to fill such a role arises. It is often the case that "the system" does not know the level of risk an adolescent poses to family members or the community, or does not know what services the adolescent and his family need. These are domains in which the mental health professional is (or should be) the expert. Other team members are often grateful when the mental health professional can offer insight into these important issues.

Are You a Good Writer and are You Willing to Write a Lot? Can You Produce High-Quality Reports in a Timely Manner?

Working in a forensic realm, whether you are a psychologist or other mental health professional, involves constant report writing. If you are serving in the role of an evaluator, expect to produce a constant flow of evaluation reports. Readers are referred to Bromberg (this volume) for samples of the sort of reports one can expect to write on a consistent basis. When you serve as a treatment provider, you can expect to write therapy progress reports. Therefore, a mental health professional doing forensic work, including evaluations and/or treatment of juvenile sex offenders, needs to be able to communicate clearly in writing. Moreover, you must be able to produce a reasonably high volume of reports *within expected timeframes*. A beautifully-written, well-conceived report is useless if it is submitted so close to a court date that nobody has time to read it or, worse, if it is submitted after a court hearing. Therefore, if your writing skills are poor, you obsess about every word you commit to writing, or have poor time-management and/or organizational skills (given the volumes of documents you will need to read and track), this area of specialization may not be for you.

Are You Willing to Develop the Skills Needed to Give Effective Courtroom Testimony?

Although you will probably have to testify with less frequency than you will have to write reports, you will inevitably need to give testimony in court. You will need to learn the legal standards that apply *in your jurisdiction* to issues about which you will be testifying. Moreover, you will need to learn how testifying in different types of court settings (e.g., family versus criminal court) differs within your jurisdiction. O'Donohue (this volume) provides a useful overview of issues pertaining to courtroom testimony. Knowledge and skills needed to give courtroom testimony can be learned. However, if you get unnerved at the prospect of public speaking or are easily rattled when your opinions are challenged, this area of practice may not be for you.

Can You Tolerate Adverse Clinical Outcomes?

Most physicians choose to practice medicine because they enjoy working with live patients and want to keep their patients that way (i.e., alive. Forensic pathologists are probably otherwise motivated). Nonetheless, during medical training, students learn that the condition of some patients will not improve, other patients will get worse, and still others will die. That is the reality of practice in many branches of medicine. Students who cannot learn to accept this reality may opt to practice a branch of medicine in which mortality is generally low (e.g., general pediatrics, sports medicine) or they may decide that a career as a practicing physician is not for them.

You will find that clinical work with juvenile sex offenders is analogous to the practice of medicine in one respect. You will have great successes with some clients, others will not benefit much from treatment despite your best efforts, and other adolescents' life situations will deteriorate markedly while they are in your care. Although recidivism is generally low among juvenile sex offender populations, a juvenile may commit a non-sexual offense and be arrested and incarcerated for that offense. Some may develop or continue to have substance abuse-related problems. One might become a "successful suicide" due to ongoing mental health problems. Perhaps after successful treatment with reunification just around the corner, the adolescent's parent(s) or caretaker(s) is/are incarcerated or killed in an accident.

My experience is that there are relatively few "success" stories and many cases with not-so-good outcomes. One relatively common outcome is that the adolescent cannot return home. The foregoing situation is probably attributable to the constellation of social ills from which known cases of sexual offending often arise (e.g., family dysfunction, insufficient privacy and living quarters due to poverty). Unlike some other types of mental health practice, clinicians who choose to work with juvenile sex offenders need to know that although they may work hard and nobly, their best efforts will not be good enough to bring about desired outcomes in a reasonable percentage of cases.

THE BASICS OF ESTABLISHING A PRACTICE SPECIALIZING IN WORK WITH JUVENILE SEX OFFENDERS

Get the Best Training You Can

Getting high-quality training in this specialty area is difficult because of the dearth of university faculty members with expertise in this domain. Ideally, a clinician would receive education and supervised clinical training in assessing and treating this population within an accredited graduate program. A reasonable alternative is to get a good mentor and/or peer consultant, read relevant books and journal articles independently, and attend high quality in-service training such as that offered through the American Psychological Association, American Academy of Forensic Psychology, and Association for Treatment of Sexual Abusers (ATSA). In addition to the technical skills needed to conduct assessment and treatment, you will need to be thoroughly familiar with the ethical code of your profession and with any statutes and laws in your jurisdiction pertaining to addressing sexual matters with minors.

Consult with an Attorney, an Accountant, and Your Professional Licensing Board Before Starting Your Practice

Although practitioners sometimes try to avoid incurring "extra" expenses because of a tight budget, I believe that taking time to do research on setting up an appropriate business structure (e.g., a limited liability company, or LLC, or limited liability partnership, or LLP), working out a plan for financing your practice, knowing best practices and regulations for keeping of both professional and financial records, and having appropriate credentialing in your jurisdiction, will probably save you much money and many headaches in the long run.

What justification is there for an initial outlay of money to consult with an attorney and an accountant? Let's say you do not establish any formal business structure (to save a few dollars), encounter a significant cash flow problem that precludes you from paying your monthly expenses, and did not realize that your failure to obtain particular experience or a particular credential in your jurisdiction invalidates your malpractice insurance policy. You're then sued. You can lose your entire practice and, in many jurisdictions, creditors and successful litigants can seize your personal assets (e.g., your home, car, bank accounts), as well. Your oversight can cost you what you've spent a lifetime working hard to achieve. Oops!

Office Space

There are several considerations when choosing office space. These considerations are displayed below:

- You need an office, but don't expect business to walk through your door. Be prepared to go to secure care facilities, child protective services offices, as well as working from your own office. Generally, the more flexible you are about locations in which you will see clients, the more business you will get. Nonetheless, the environment in which services are delivered should convey a professional, rather than a personal, relationship and there should be very clear interpersonal boundaries. Therefore, there are two caveats – *do not* agree to deliver services in a youth's home. Family members may overhear very private conversations and, due to space limitations, you may have to hold sessions in a location in which interpersonal boundaries are ambiguous. For example, you do not want to be discussing sexual exploration with others while sprawled out on your client's bed. Similarly, *do not* see clients in an office that is inside your personal residence.

- Do *not* get office space near schools, day-care centers, or other agencies that work with children. Your clientele may be court-ordered to avoid coming within a certain distance of other minors or within a certain distance of agencies that serve other minors. You do not want your examinees or clients to have to violate a court order to get to your office. Similarly, you do not want to provide a juvenile with a pool of potential victims.
- Signs should be small and discrete. (This is the opposite of what is desirable in most other businesses.) Juveniles will feel uncomfortable coming to your office if they believe a passersby will know that this is the office in which sex offenders are seen. Similarly, other business owners and nearby residents will not want to be near an office which is (correctly or incorrectly) perceived as pulling dangerous teenagers into their neighborhood.
- Security is important given the population with which you work and the sensitivity of the documents you will have in your office. Files should be kept in a locked cabinet or locked room when not in use and computers should be password protected. Your office should have doors that are solid, and doors and windows should have strong locks. The perimeter of your office and the parking area should be well lit. An alarm system with motion detectors and smoke detectors is advised, as well.

Decide on the Scope of Your Practice

Are you willing and able to provide services to any juvenile sex offender referred to you or will you set limits on the type of referrals you will accept? Can you accommodate adolescents with limited English proficiency? Are you prepared to work with clients of any cultural group? What about adolescents with a substance abuse problem or co-morbid psychiatric condition? Are you prepared to work with adolescents with developmental disabilities?

CULTIVATING REFERRALS

Referrals are cultivated by meeting people who need the unique services you offer. There is no right way to do this. It will vary considerably based on the jurisdiction in which you practice. One way to start is to work as an employee in an agency that specializes in addressing issues of child maltreatment. The multidisciplinary nature of the work virtually guarantees that you will meet CPS and law enforcement personnel, as well as other potential referral sources. Reports you generate will be read by numerous attorneys, judges, other mental health personnel, and pediatricians with fellowship-level training in child maltreatment. Strive to develop a reputation for doing quality evaluations in an ethical manner and deliver reports on time. Word will get around. (Conversely, word will also get around if you do poor quality work, behave unethically, or are chronically behind in report writing. These are excellent ways to chase away potential referral sources.)

Advertising in professional publications (e.g., a journal published several times a year by a state bar association) and having an Internet website describing your services can bring in business, as well. I suggest listing a post office box, rather than your physical address, in advertising. As mentioned previously in this chapter, you do not want to wave a red flag for local businesses and families that you are trying to attract potentially dangerous individuals to their neighborhood.

Some state child protective service agencies offer contracts to licensed mental health service providers. Providers are needed to perform the entire spectrum of child maltreatment-related assessment and treatment services, including assessment and treatment of juvenile sex offenders. Information about contract opportunities can be found on state websites.

FINANCES

If you are fortunate enough to have a contractual arrangement with one or more agencies, you will have a built-in source of relatively steady referrals. Some agencies have set fees that they pay for particular services provided. Other agencies will contact you when they need your services, ask you to tell them how much you will charge for the service to be delivered, then let you know whether or not they accept your proposal to provide services.

Private pay, fee-for-service clients and attorneys can provide a higher paying income source. However, I have found these income sources to be unstable over time. That is, a law firm might pay a large sum of money to have you perform a forensic evaluation, but once the evaluation is completed, the firm might not need your services again for weeks, months, or even years. Similarly, private pay, fee-for-service clients will need your services (and/or be able to pay for your services) for a discrete period of time.

Understand and Manage Cash Flow

Cash flow is "the difference between the cash flowing into and out of a business over the course of an accounting period" (McGuinness, 2000, p. 8). Understanding this basic concept *and managing cash flow effectively* can make the difference between running a successful practice and having to close up shop. McGuinness (2000, p. 6) pointed out that it is possible and even common for profitable businesses to be cash-flow disasters. Here is a very simple illustration of why this is the case. Assume that you have billed a state agency $9500 for all services you delivered during the past month and that your monthly expenses plus the salary you pay yourself totals only $5500 per month. That's great! You've made a profit! You need the money to pay yourself and pay bills *now*, but clerks throughout the state in which you have billed are overwhelmed with work and you get your $9500 in dribs and drabs over the course of the next three months. You receive only $1300 *this month*. Uh-oh. Although you've technically made a profit, you do not have enough money to cover your expenses. A similar situation is likely to occur each month. This is one reason why having a meeting with your accountant before starting your practice can be so important. Possible solutions to a cash-flow problem include the following: foregoing a salary and living off savings until your practice is cash-flow positive; borrowing funds from family members or a bank until your practice is cash-flow positive; or establishing a line of credit at a bank. Of course, there are other possible solutions, as well (e.g., taking on one or more partners). A frank discussion with your accountant is one of the best ways of generating a solution to a cash flow problem that is right for you.

SUPPLIES

Although no two practices are identical, there are some supplies that all practitioners who work with juvenile sex offenders are likely to need. Even in this high-tech era, business cards remain an important device by which people can remember you and your contact information. Because of the quantity of reports you will need to produce and the assortment of potential referral sources who will read your reports, it makes sense to invest in professional-quality letterhead. This is particularly important if you intend to do business with law firms. Attorneys expect a professional report to look professional.

It is difficult to imagine running any sort of practice without a computer, a printer, and a FAX machine or FAX server. Many of the test instruments you will need to administer can be scored by way of computer scoring programs. Readers are referred to Knight and Knight (this volume) and Bromberg (this volume) for ideas regarding the assortment of psychological instruments you may need to administer and score.

It is well worth the money to purchase a voice dictation program for your computer(s). Voice dictation can dramatically reduce the amount of time it takes to generate reports. Significant portions of this chapter were dictated using the Dragon Dictation program. This program is available for both Macintosh and PC users.

You will need access to an on-line database to keep abreast of journal articles and scholarly texts specific to the sort of work you do. You will also need to have a supply of books written for use by your adolescent clients. The number and type of books is virtually limitless. However, I find myself using the *Relapse Prevention Workbook for Youth in Treatment* (Steen, 1993) and *Changing Bodies, Changing Lives* (Bell, 1998) with great frequency. The latter book provides excellent coverage of healthy sexuality. Safer Society Press produces an assortment of books that are useful when working with adolescent (as well as adult) sex offenders.

CONCLUSION

A practice focusing on the assessment and treatment of juvenile sex offenders can provide a professionally challenging and rewarding career path. Clinicians with the training and personal characteristics necessary for practice in this specialty area have the potential to earn a good living while working to address a significant social problem.

REFERENCES

Bell, R. (1998). *Changing bodies, changing lives* (3rd ed.). New York: Three Rivers Press.

Bromberg, D. S. (this volume). Writing dispositional evaluations of juveniles adjudicated for sexual offenses and juveniles with sexual behavioral problems. In D.S. Bromberg &

W.T. O'Donohue (Eds.), *Toolkit for working with juvenile sex offenders*. San Diego, CA: Elsevier.

Knight, R.A., & Sims-Knight, J.E. (this volume). Assessment of dynamic treatment targets for juveniles who sexually offend. In D.S. Bromberg & W.T. O'Donohue (Eds.), *Toolkit for working with juvenile sex offenders*. San Diego, CA: Elsevier.

Mart, E. G., & Stout, C. E. (2006). *Getting started in forensic psychology practice: How to create a forensic specialty in your mental health practice*. Hoboken, NJ: Wiley.

McGuinness, B. (2000). *Cash rules: Learn and manage the 7 cash-flow drivers for your company's success*. Washington, DC: Kiplinger Washington Editors, Inc.

O'Donohue, W.T. (this volume). Tools for testifying in court. In D.S. Bromberg & W.T. O'Donohue (Eds.), *Toolkit for working with juvenile sex offenders*. San Diego, CA: Elsevier.

Reid, W. H. (2013). *Developing a forensic practice: Operations and ethics for experts*. New York: Routledge.

Steen, C. (1993). *The relapse prevention workbook for youth in treatment*. Brandon, VT: Safer Society.

ADDITIONAL RESOURCES

American Psychological Association, (2008). *Financial planning for early career psychologists: From repaying student loans to successful retirement*. Washington, DC: American Psychological Association.

DeBaise, C. (2009). *The Wall Street Journal complete small business guidebook*. New York: Three Rivers Press.

Kolt, L. (1999). *How to build a thriving fee-for-service practice: Integrating the healing side with the business side of psychotherapy*. San Diego, CA: Academic Press. <www.safersociety.org>.

INDEX

Note: Page numbers followed by *"f", "t" and "b"* refer to figures, tables and boxes, respectively.

H

I

L

M

N

O

P

Q

FSC
www.fsc.org
MIX
Papier | Fördert gute Waldnutzung
FSC® C083411

Kolibri 360 GmbH
Ferdinand-Jühlke-Straße 7
99095 Erfurt, Deutschland
produktsicherheit@kolibri360.de